Au-A-III-11

URBANIZATION OF THE EARTH
URBANISIERUNG DER ERDE   6

Urbanization of the Earth
Urbanisierung der Erde

6

Edited by Dr. Wolf Tietze, Helmstedt

Burkhard Hofmeister

Australia and its Urban Centres

GEBRÜDER BORNTRAEGER · BERLIN · STUTTGART · 1988

Australia and its Urban Centres

by

Prof. Dr. Burkhard Hofmeister

With 120 figures and 61 tables in the text

GEBRÜDER BORNTRAEGER · BERLIN · STUTTGART · 1988

Author's address:
Prof. Dr. Burkhard Hofmeister
Hagenstr. 25a
D-1000 Berlin 33

ISBN 3-443-37008-X

All rights reserved, included those of translation or to reproduce parts of this book in any form.
© 1988 by Gebrüder Borntraeger, D-1000 Berlin – D-7000 Stuttgart
Design of the cover by Wolfgang Karrasch
Printed in Germany

Preface

The author wishes to thank both the editor and the publisher for their endeavours to present this book for the Bicentennial of the Commonwealth of Australia. He should like to express special thanks to his friend and colleague Professor Thomas H. Elkins, Oxford, who took great pains in making critical comments on the original draft and in smoothing the text in a way that it has become palatable to English-speaking readers.

The contents of this book are based on two extensive journeys through all parts of the Australian nation continent. The author is grateful to the Deutsche Forschungsgemeinschaft for providing generous travel grants. During his journeys he was accompanied by his wife, Diplomgeograph Ruth Hofmeister, who was of great assistance in carrying out the field work and in preparing the first draft.

The author is also grateful to a great number of Australian geographers and other professionals for offering guided tours, unpublished material and opportunities for discussion. It is impossible to mention all of them; however, the author should like to make special reference to Mr. Harris and Mr. Beale in the Department of Housing and Construction of the Federal Government, to Drs. P. Harrison, H. Kendig, C. Paris, P. Spearritt and P.N. Troy in the Urban Research Unit and Professor C.A. Price in the Department of Demography of ANU in Canberra, Mr. J. Campbell, Chief planner of NCDC in Canberra, Professors I.H. Burnley, M.T. Daly, A.J. Rose and P. Tilley in Sydney, Mr. H. Wardlaw of the Lands Commission of N.S.W. and Mr. J. Fielder of the Water Resources Commission of N.S.W., Professors J.G. Hajdu, J. McKay, T.M. Perry, J.R.V. Prescott and J. Whitelaw in Melbourne, Mr. K.H. Burr, Director of Planning of the Melbourne and Metropolitan Board of Works, Professors C.A. Forster, R.L. Heathcote and R.J. Stimson in Adelaide, Dr. D. Scrafton, Director-General of Transport in Adelaide, Professor J. Holmes in Brisbane, Professors I.C. Alexander and D.S. Houghton in Perth, Dr. D. Carr of the Metropolitan Region Planning Authority in Perth, Professor P. Scott in the University of Tasmania, Hobart and Mr. P. Liebeknecht in the Department of Housing in Hobart, Dr. W. Mollah in the North Australia Research Unit of ANU and Mr. J. Pinney of the N.T. Department of Lands in Darwin, Mr. R.H. Hannaford of the Goldsworthy Mining Ltd., Mr. Girdlestone and Mrs. J. Hirte of the Hamersley Iron Pty. Ltd., Mr. J.G. Botting and Mrs. M. Stacey of the Mt. Newman Mining Co. Pty. Ltd. in the Pilbara mining and port towns.

Greatful acknowledgement is made for writing the final draft of the typescript to my daughter Mrs. H. Hofmeister-Bullick and to Mrs. Ch. Sanyal and for preparing the maps to Mrs. G. v. Frankenberg, Mr. H.J. Nitschke, Mrs. A. Eggert, Mr. O. Hoffmann and Mr. O. Lange, cartographers.

The material has been arranged in a way as to fit the frame set by the series 'Urbanization of the Earth'. The text thus starts with the physical, demographic, economic and political framework for settlement in Australia and continues with the history of urban development, the characteristics of the urban system, the capital cities and other important places and finally the major traits of the cities of this culture realm. At the same time the attempt was made to do justice to the peculiarities of the Australian situation. The author is confident that this compromise will be acceptable to the reader.

It was only during the author's first stay in Australia in 1981/82 that he became aware of the multitude of recent publications by Australian scholars related to urban research. Despite all this material the author trusts that he has been able to incorporate all important sources and his own observations and enquiries into a useful overview of the main features of the Australian city and the Australian urban system.

Berlin, January 1988　　B. HOFMEISTER

Contents

Preface V

1 Introduction 1
1.1 Approaching the topic: urbanization in Australia 1
1.2 Main sources of information 4

2 Historical development of the urban system in Australia 7
2.1 The elements of urban development 7
    2.1.1 Physical-geographical opportunities and constraints 7
    2.1.2 The demographic and economic framework 13
    2.1.3 Urban development policies of the three tiers of government 21
    2.1.3.1 Policies at local, state and federal levels 21
    2.1.3.2 The State Housing Authorities 25
    2.1.3.3 Decentralization and growth-pole policy 28
2.2 Stages of urban development 32
    2.2.1 Convict settlements along the coastlines 32
    2.2.2 The Macquarie towns in New South Wales 35
    2.2.3 The old mining towns and Murray River towns in the Southeast 38
    2.2.4 The parkland towns on South Australia's frontier 45
    2.2.5 The ports of Queensland 50
    2.2.6 The sawmill towns of Western Australia's southwest 52
    2.2.7 Urban development since federation in 1901 54
    2.2.8 Growing consciousness of the national heritage and the advent of urban conservation 58
2.3 The uniqueness of the Australian urban system 63
    2.3.1 The phenomenon of the primate city 63
    2.3.2 Is there a true hierarchy of central places? 68
    2.3.3 Constant changes of rank within the urban system 74
    2.3.4 Inter-urban relations in the Australian context 77

3 Towns, cities and metropolitan areas 80
3.1 The capital cities 80
    3.1.1 The metropolitan area of Sydney, New South Wales 80
    3.1.2 The metropolitan area of Melbourne, Victoria 91
    3.1.3 The metropolitan area of Adelaide, South Australia 100
    3.1.4 The metropolitan area of Brisbane, Queensland 109
    3.1.5 The metropolitan area of Perth, Western Australia 115
    3.1.6 The metropolitan area of Hobart, Tasmania 123
    3.1.7 The state capitals: a comparative perspective 128
    3.1.8 Darwin, capital of the Northern Territory 136
    3.1.9 Canberra and the Australian National Territory 142
3.2 The City of the Gold Coast in Queensland 151
3.3 Seaports other than the capital cities; important inland towns 154
    3.3.1 Port and industrial cities 154
    3.3.2 Mining towns of the interior 156
    3.3.3 Inland service and communication centres 157
3.4 New towns across Australia 160
    3.4.1 New towns in the Murrumbidgee Irrigation Areas 160
    3.4.2 Satellite cities in connection with deep-sea harbours and heavy industries 165
    3.4.3 Company towns and open towns in newly developed mining areas 169

4	**The Australian city as a distinct cultural-genetic type**	181
4.1	Aspects of urban form and structure	181
	4.1.1 Building materials	181
	4.1.2 Home ownership	185
	4.1.3 Property prices, public housing, residential densities	189
	4.1.4 Construction, ownership and use of buildings in the CBD	193
	4.1.5 The inner suburbs: renewal, rehabilitation and gentrification in the face of site-value taxation, resident actions and green bans	196
	4.1.6 Layout: the grid, irregular street patterns, urban freeways	199
	4.1.7 The suburbanization of people, jobs and retail trade	202
	4.1.8 Metropolitan planning: district centres, urban corridors, industrial zones	206
	4.1.9 Mobility and equity: The central city versus suburbia	208
4.2	Overseas immigrants and their residential patterns	211
	4.2.1 Initial ethnic concentrations	211
	4.2.2 Time of arrival and period of residence in Australia	216
	4.2.3 Demand and search for accommodation	220
	4.2.4 The immigrants' skills and the labour market	221
	4.2.5 Group cohesion and in-marriage rates	223
	4.2.6 Ethnic group services	226
	4.2.7 Peculiarities of ethnic urban distribution patterns	227
4.3	The structure of the Australian city	234
References		238
Index		252

List of tables

Table 1:	Population by settlement zones, 1976 and 1981	12
Table 2:	Employment by sectors of the economy in Victoria, 1841–91	14
Table 3:	Components of population increase in the southeastern colonies, 1861–1900	15
Table 4:	Growth rates of capital cities, 1911–47	17
Table 5:	Immigration targets and intakes, 1948–61	17
Table 6:	Annual growth rates of population, 1947–53	18
Table 7:	Components of metropolitan population growth, 1947–66	19
Table 8:	Distribution of employment by sectors, 1933–76	19
Table 9:	Increases of households and population, 1971–2001	21
Table 10:	Residential land prices in the capital cities, 1968–74	26
Table 11:	Lot production, house commencements and stock movements, County of Cumberland, 1976–80	29
Table 12:	Direct Commonwealth funding of selected growth centres, 1973–78	31
Table 13:	Population in Victorian gold mining towns	39
Table 14:	Parklands in South Australian government townships	48
Table 15:	First six trading ports of Queensland, 1860–1939	52
Table 16:	Railway mileage in operation in Australia, 1861–1981	56
Table 17:	Distribution of population in settlement categories, 1921–81	56
Table 18:	Growth rates and changes of employment in settlement zones, 1976–81	57
Table 19:	Rank orders of cities in Australia and some European countries 1970–71	63
Table 20:	Primacy indices of Australian state capitals, 1981	64
Table 21:	Population changes in states and capitals, 1911–81	64
Table 22:	Percentage of populations in capital cities, 1861–1981	64
Table 23:	Hierarchy of central places in Tasmania	69
Table 24:	Australian internal airlines, passenger embarkations, 1950–80	77
Table 25:	Length of railway tracks and railway operations, 1902–80	78
Table 26:	Rates of primacy of capital cities, 1976 and 1981	78
Table 27:	Population growth of Melbourne and Sydney, 1861–1933	96
Table 28:	District centres and free-standing shopping centres in metropolitan Melbourne, 1954–83	100
Table 29:	Occupied private dwellings: Type of structure and tenure, 1976	131
Table 30:	Growth factors in the capital cities, 1911–47 and 1947–61	131
Table 31:	Overseas and coastal cargo movements of Australian ports, 1982–83	133
Table 32:	Manufacturing production of capital cities, 1981/82 or 1982/83	133
Table 33:	Office space in the capital cities, 1985–86	134
Table 34:	State capitals population, 1851–1981	136
Table 35:	Land ownership in the Mirrool Area, 1985	160
Table 36:	Indicators of the population of five mining towns in the Pilbara region, 1981	179
Table 37:	Major building materials of outer walls of houses in the capital cities, 1976	181
Table 38:	Major construction materials in the central area of Perth, 1980	185
Table 39:	Dwelling types in the mainland state capitals, 1976, and home ownership rates, 1911–76	187
Table 40:	Home ownership rates and rank order of per capita Gross National Income, 1971	188
Table 41:	Sources of first mortgage, 1976	190
Table 42:	Distribution of residential densities of capital cities, 1981	192
Table 43:	Development applications approved by the City of Sydney, 1969–73	194
Table 44:	Land ownership in Melbourne's CBD between Collins and Bourke Streets, 1977	194
Table 45:	Distribution of urban freeways, 1981	201
Table 46:	Population change in the central cities and metropolitan areas of state capitals, 1971–76	202
Table 47:	Distribution of jobs in three metropolitan areas, 1966–76	204
Table 48:	Retail sales, changes 1968/69–1973/74	205
Table 49:	Examples of chain migration to Sydney	215
Table 50:	Immigrants by countries of origin, 1948–55	216
Table 51:	Emigration of East Europeans to Australia, 1945–72	216
Table 52:	Origins of overseas-born population in capital cities, 1976	217
Table 53:	Urbanization rates of immigrant groups, 1981	218
Table 54:	Proportion of overseas-born population in metropolitan areas, 1966–81	218
Table 55:	Distribution of four ethnic groups in Sydney and Melbourne, 1966	218

Table 56:	Index of segregation for Greeks and Italians in Melbourne, 1966–76	220
Table 57:	Lebanese residents in Sydney LGAs, 1981	224
Table 58:	In-marriage rates for selected ethnic groups, 1947–60 to 1974–80	225
Table 59:	Blue-collar workers of Ford Broadmeadows Assembly Plant by birthplaces	228
Table 60:	Proportions of overseas born in the various zones of metropolitan areas, 1976	228
Table 61:	LGAs in Sydney, Melbourne and Adelaide with over 20% non-British immigrants, 1976	229

List of figures

Figure 1:	Australian commercial television coverage areas reflecting urban distribution	2
Figure 2:	Australia's position relative to the latitudes of North Africa and Southern Europe	8
Figure 3:	Areas suitable for dryland agriculture taking into account climatic, terrain and soil constraints	9
Figure 4:	Distances in Australia	10
Figure 5:	Settlement zones in Australia	12
Figure 6:	Types of settlement by 1836	14
Figure 7:	Components of population increase 1946–47 to 1980–81	20
Figure 8:	The capitals' proportions of overseas immigrants, 1982	20
Figure 9:	Changes of Local Government boundaries of the City of Sydney, 1842–1979	23
Figure 10:	Road funding in Australia	25
Figure 11:	Flexilot system of public housing in a section of Gagebrook, Tasmania	27
Figure 12:	Worrington Downs, Sydney metropolitan area, N.S.W. Commission housing under construction	28
Figure 13:	The location of growth poles and new towns	30
Figure 14:	Buildings in the former Port Arthur penal settlement, Tasmania	34
Figure 15:	Port Arthur, Tasmania. Ruins of penitentiary in the conservation area of the old penal settlement	34
Figure 16:	Wilberforce, N.S.W. Sign identifying the town as one of the Macquarie towns	35
Figure 17:	The Macquarie towns in the Hawkesbury River valley, N.S.W.	36
Figure 18:	The Victorian goldfields and gold mining towns	38
Figure 19:	Main settlements served by paddle-steamers in the Murray-Darling network	40
Figure 20:	Business district and historical buildings in Bendigo, Victoria	41
Figure 21:	Land uses in the commercial and administrative centre of Beechworth, Victoria	42
Figure 22:	Beechworth, Victoria. Chinese burial towers and several hundred graves of Chinese on Beechworth cemetery	43
Figure 23:	Land uses in the commercial and administrative centre of Swan Hill, Victoria	44
Figure 24:	Historic district of Echuca, Victoria	45
Figure 25:	The distribution of parkland, partial parkland and non-parkland towns in South Australia	47
Figure 26:	Land uses in Maitland, S.A., 1985	48
Figure 27:	The location of urban settlements in Queensland	51
Figure 28:	Townsville, Qld. Waterfront with the modern Townsville International Hotel, the so-called 'sugar shaker'	53
Figure 29:	Forests, railways and sawmill towns in the southwest of Western Australia	54
Figure 30:	Classified historical buildings in Beechworth, Victoria	59
Figure 31:	Bendigo, Victoria. Central district with buildings registered by the National Trust (Victoria)	60
Figure 32:	Historical buildings in The Rocks, Sydney	61
Figure 33:	Sydney, N.S.W. Partial view of historic core called The Rocks with old warehouses converted to other uses	62
Figure 34:	The capital cities' proportion of total state population, 1911	65
Figure 35:	The capital cities' proportion of total state population, 1976	66
Figure 36:	The capital cities' proportion of total state population, 1982	67

Figure 37: Australia's and Canada's skeletal network of major cities 70
Figure 38: Operational bases of the Royal Flying Doctor Service 72
Figure 39: Location of the 50 largest cities in 1981 73
Figure 40: Changes of rank of the 50 largest cities, 1961–81 75
Figure 41: Sydney, N.S.W. View from Australia Building in the CBD over Port Jackson
 with Sydney Harbour Bridge and Opera House 82
Figure 42: Major land-use areas in the City of Sydney 83
Figure 43: Kings Cross, Sydney, N.S.W. Three-storey terrace houses 84
Figure 44: Harbourfield, Sydney metropolitan area, N.S.W. Federation-style house, ca. 1900 84
Figure 45: The N.S.W. Housing Commission's Wooloomooloo Project 85
Figure 46: Wooloomooloo, Sydney, N.S.W. New residences designed as to fit in this old inner residential
 suburb of two-storey terrace houses 86
Figure 47: Glebe, Sydney, N.S.W. Terrace houses after rehabilitation. Outhouses were preserved
 inspite of connecting the area to the urban sewerage system 86
Figure 48: Ethnicity and socio-economic status in Sydney 88
Figure 49: The development of corridors and district centres in Sydney according to the
 City Region Outline Plan 89
Figure 50: Value added by industry sub-divisions in Sydney, 1982/83 90
Figure 51: Value added by industry sub-divisions in Melbourne, 1981/82 92
Figure 52: The first five land sales in Melbourne 1837–39 93
Figure 53: State Government and other public land in central Melbourne, 1984 94
Figure 54: Melbourne, Victoria. Flinders Street Station on southern margin of CBD with trams
 still in operation 95
Figure 55: Overseas immigrants in Melbourne's LGAs, changes 1971–76 98
Figure 56: The development of corridors and district centres in Melbourne 99
Figure 57: Adelaide, S.A. Oblique aerial photograph taken from North Adelaide looking southeast
 toward South Adelaide and the surrounding parklands. The Mt. Lofty Range in
 the background 101
Figure 58: The alienation of parklands in Adelaide 103
Figure 59: Value added by industry sub-divisions in Adelaide, 1982/83 105
Figure 60: The growth of Adelaide's built-up area since 1880 107
Figure 61: Major land uses and zoning in the City of Adelaide 108
Figure 62: Brisbane, Qld. Oblique aerial photograph of North Brisbane and South Brisbane with site
 of Culture Centre and Expo '88 110
Figure 63: Brisbane, Qld. Partial view of northern suburbs demonstrating the ridge and valley character
 of terrain 112
Figure 64: Brisbane's growth 113
Figure 65: Value added by industry sub-divisions in Brisbane, 1981/82 114
Figure 66: Brisbane, Qld. Expanding CBD encroaching inner suburbs on north side 115
Figure 67: Perth, W.A. View of the CBD and Mitchell Freeway interchange from Kings Park Overlook 116
Figure 68: Major land uses in Perth's city centre 118
Figure 69: Perth's growth 1838–1917 119
Figure 70: Value added by industry sub-divisions in Perth, 1982/83 120
Figure 71: Statistical districts of Perth with above average Italian and Greek immigrants 121
Figure 72: The Perth Corridor Plan 122
Figure 73: Hobart, Tasmania. View from Mt. Nelson northward over Battery Point and part of
 the CBD with the casino-convention complex at Wrest Point in the foreground 125
Figure 74: Battery Point, Hobart, Tasmania. Southern inner suburb with restoration work of old
 building stock 126
Figure 75: Value added by industry sub-divisions in Hobart, 1982/83 127
Figure 76: Cargo movements at Australian ports, 1982/83 132
Figure 77: Office space development in Australia's metropolitan areas, 1984–86 135
Figure 78: Constraints on urban development in Darwin 138
Figure 79: Path of Cyclone Tracy and house damages in Darwin 139
Figure 80: Darwin N.T. Reconstruction after disaster caused by Cyclone Tracy of CBD office building
 with ruin of former Commonwealth Bank building being integrated in modern structure 141
Figure 81: Howard Springs, Darwin, N.T. Temporary Police Office in caravan during first phase of
 construction 141
Figure 82: Canberra, A.C.T. View from Black Mountain over Lake Burley Griffin with
 Captain Cook Fountain 143

Figure 83:	The design of major axes in central Washington D.C. and in Canberra A.C.T.	144
Figure 84:	Years of first settlement of Canberra's suburbs	147
Figure 85:	Canberra's suburban development according to the Y-Plan	148
Figure 86:	City of the Gold Coast, Qld. Aerial view of residential development of canal estates along the Nerang River between Surfers Paradise and Broadbeach	152
Figure 87:	Alice Springs	159
Figure 88:	Original plan of Griffith, N.S.W., by Walter Burley Griffin	161
Figure 89:	Griffith, N.S.W. Oblique aerial photograph of central part showing the great circle and CBD development along Banna Avenue	162
Figure 90:	Griffith, N.S.W. Aerial photograph of city and irrigated fields of the environs	163
Figure 91:	Leeton, N.S.W. Oblique aerial photograph of central part	164
Figure 92:	Design of the new town of Elizabeth, S.A.	166
Figure 93:	Design of Kwinana New Town, W.A.	168
Figure 94:	Old and new ports, mining towns and service centres in the Pilbara Region of Western Australia	170
Figure 95:	Shay Gap, W.A. Oblique aerial photograph showing the natural setting of the town	171
Figure 96:	Shay Gap, W.A. Houses of one precinct with surrounding hills in the background	172
Figure 97:	Cottage industries in Paraburdoo, W.A.	173
Figure 98:	Newman, W.A. Aerial photograph of town and the Mt. Whaleback mine	174
Figure 99:	Port Hedland's population growth, 1961–85	175
Figure 100:	Port Hedland, W.A. Oblique aerial photograph of 1964 showing the small port town and future site of the Mt. Newman Company's ore shipping facilities at Nelson Point	176
Figure 101:	Port Hedland, W.A. Oblique aerial photograph of 1980 showing the Mt. Newman Company's ore shipping facilities at Nelson Point	177
Figure 102:	Urban development of the Port Hedland area	178
Figure 103:	Port Hedland, W.A. Cyclone-proof houses for single men employed by the Mt. Newman Company	180
Figure 104:	Proportion of dominant building materials of outer walls of the housing stock of capital cities, 1976	182
Figure 105:	Transport of a weatherboard house on Stuart Highway	184
Figure 106:	Townsville, Qld. Hotel Buchanan, ca. 1890	185
Figure 107:	Proportion of home ownership in capital cities, 1976	186
Figure 108:	Melbourne's CBD and its extensions	195
Figure 109:	The low level of urban freeway development in the Sydney metropolitan area	201
Figure 110:	Sydney, N.S.W. Aerial view of southern outer suburbs	203
Figure 111:	Distribution of households with Chinese surnames in Rockhampton, Qld., 1981	212
Figure 112:	Distribution of households with Chinese surnames in Mackay, Qld., 1981	213
Figure 113:	Distribution of households with Chinese surnames in Cairns, Qld., 1981	214
Figure 114:	Development of second concentrations of Italian immigrants in Melbourne, 1971–76	219
Figure 115:	Spearwood, Perth, W.A. Market gardeners of predominantly South European origin growing Mediterranean crops	222
Figure 116:	Local concentrations of Lebanese Christians and Muslims in Sydney, 1981	224
Figure 117:	Italian concentration in Leichhardt, Sydney	231
Figure 118:	Shops and services run by overseas immigrants in Hindley Street, Adelaide	232
Figure 119:	Shops and services run by overseas immigrants in William Street, Perth	233
Figure 120:	Model of the urban structure of the large Australian city	236

1 Introduction

1.1 Approaching the topic: urbanization in Australia

One of the most appropriate descriptions of the conditions for urbanization in Australia was given by the American geographer A. Pred in his statement: 'Australia is different, if not unique, in the vastness of its area, its variegated mineral resource endowment, the uneven distribution of its population, and its comparatively recent superimposition of a pronounced federal political structure upon a set of colonial relationships' (Pred in: Cities Commission 1975, 32). With these background conditions in mind, it is possible to make an initial attempt to outline the characteristics of Australia's urbanization processes and urban places.

In the first place, Australia combines an extremely low population density with a rate of urbanization of 85.7% (1981), *one of the highest* in the entire world after Iceland and a few special cases such as Hong Kong, Kuwait and some small island states. This high degree of urbanization also emerged remarkably early; a rate of 66% was reached as early as 1890, 30 years earlier than in the United States and 60 years earlier than in Canada.

Australia's population is also marked by a distinct *coastal and metropolitan trend*. 'Perhaps no modern industrial society enjoys a greater territorial imbalance in population and economic opportunity than Australia' (Lonsdale 1972, 321). Approximately 70% of the total population live in coastal cities. 60% live in the metropolitan areas of the state capitals which are themselves coastal and 10% live in the other port cities and focal points of heavy industries.

There is a saying 'Australia is where most Australians don't live' which means that the true Australia is considered to be the almost empty outback. In the United States the family farm was considered the backbone of the nation and the city was looked upon as something anti-American, so that in many states a new small town was chosen as state capital rather than one of the existing larger cities.

In a somewhat parallel development of opinion in Australia, the existence of huge cities was, for a long time, simply ignored. As urban historian G. Davison put it: 'Strangely enough, local historians were slower than foreign statisticians to recognize the shape of Australian civilization. That a vast primary-producing country should also be a land of great cities was a fact that they, along with many other Australians, found hard to swallow' (1979b, 100). The unique pattern of Australia's urbanized population is best reflected in a map depicting the TV coverage of the continent (fig. 1).

Despite this early emergence of an unusually high share of urban population in the total population, the rate of increase of urbanization throughout the second half of the nineteenth century was (with the exception of the 1880s) lower than in the United States. Moreover, during the gold rushes of the 1850s and 1860s in New South Wales and Victoria, metropolitan growth was slower than urban growth in general. In explaining this apparent contradiction it is necessary to keep in mind the initially higher urban population subset in Australia.

The part of the overseas immigrants in the urbanization process will be given due consideration below. The 92.4% urbanization rate of the overseas-born exceeds even that of the Australian-born.

The special congruence of the major administrative and commercial functions of the colonies in the port-capitals brought about *early metropolitan dominance*, which 'favoured extensive settlement rather than the growth of more independent self-contained communities. In this sense, Australia was in the unusual position of urbanisation developing in advance of rural settlement' (Stilwell 1974b, 63; also Glynn 1970). In contrast to the United States, there was hardly any small-scale farm settlement in the Australian colonies. In the early decades of white settlement much of the food supply was imported; from the beginning farmers raised sheep and cattle and grew crops for the market.

Most immigrants came from urban environments and had already been alienated from rural life before their arrival in Australia. Thus there has always been a high proportion of urban dwellers and a high proportion of the workforce in tertiary occupations.

It seems appropriate, therefore, for Australia to have a *lower statistical benchmark* for urban places than is the case in most other countries. An 'urban centre' or 'urban place' as defined by the Australian Bureau of Statistics (ABS) is any clustered or nucleated settlement having a minimum population of one thousand persons. In recogni-

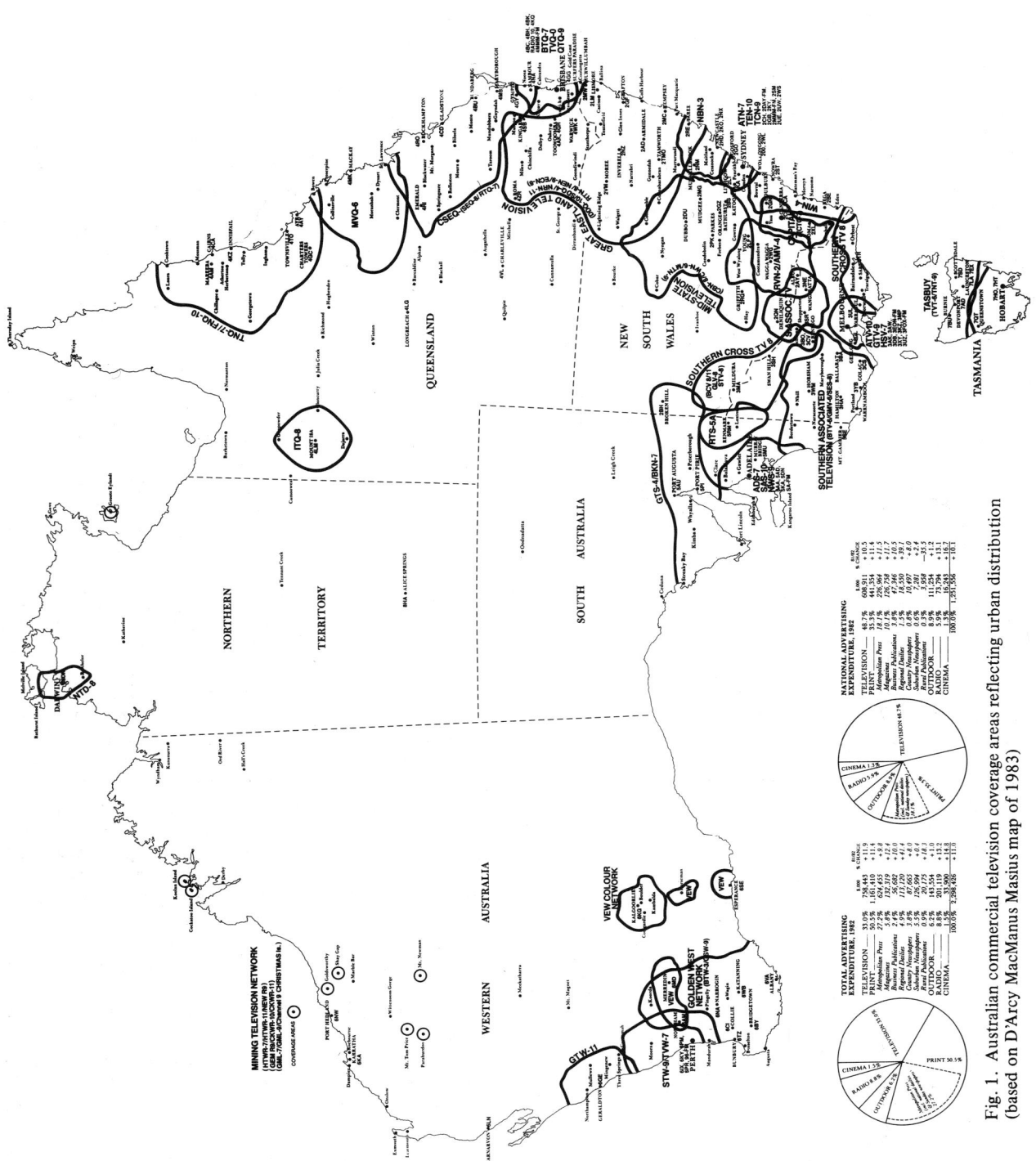

Fig. 1. Australian commercial television coverage areas reflecting urban distribution (based on D'Arcy MacManus Masius map of 1983)

tion of more recent developments, however, holiday resorts are also considered urban centres even when containing as few as 250 dwellings, of which a minimum of 100 are permanently occupied. According to the 1976 Census, there are 507 urban places in Australia, 353 of which are in the lowest category of between 4,999 and 1,000 persons. Further distinction is made between 'major urban places' and other urban places, the former being cities of more than 100,000 residents, thus corresponding with the German statistical definition of a 'Großstadt'.

It has been noted, that agriculture and rural settlement played but a minor part in Australian urbanization; the same is also true of manufacturing. In contrast to Western Europe and the United States *urbanization stimulated industrialization* rather than the reverse.

Private capital including transfers from Great Britain and other overseas sources, was at first mainly invested in mining, in the production of agricultural staples such as wool and in commerce. Initial manufacturing locations were in the already existing port-capitals where secondary industry became the third most important function following administration and overseas trade. Towards the turn of the century a few mining and industrial towns developed on the coast, such as Newcastle and Wollongong in New South Wales and Geelong in Victoria.

Australian urban settlements are extremely young even by American standards. McCarty called them '"pure" products of the nineteenth century expansion of capitalism' (1970, 110). Industrialization had already begun in England before colonization started in Australia. There was *no pre-industrial city* of the type characteristic of Western Europe. Nevertheless, Australian urban settlements did not emerge as industrial cities but rather convict settlements like Sydney, Brisbane, Hobart and Launceston and/or commercial cities like Melbourne, Adelaide and Perth. Their inhabitants had but little knowledge of the possibilities of economic development and their respective hinterlands (McCarty 1970).

Very little use was made of steam prior to 1870 due to the trade policies of the British and colonial governments, the scarcity of machinery and the small size of the local markets. Of the 25 millers listed in Sydney in 1855 only three operated steam-mills. Until the 1860s Sydney remained a city of pedestrians and horses with an appreciable number of boot and shoemakers and of craftsmen in the horse and carriage trade (Aplin 1982).

From the circumstances explained in the foregoing paragraphs Holmes drew the conclusion that "the Australian urban system is notable for its low level of functional differentiation, indicated by a relative lack of specialized or single-function towns; for its emphasis on consumer-oriented service activities both public and private, ... for recent indicators that functional spezialization is beginning some momentum' (Holmes in: Jeans 1977, 416).

The vast majority of country towns many of which had developed under government supervision are service centres with *similar functions and similar appearance*. Of course, there are the mining towns. Holmes considers them to be an exception. One would also have to add the inland river ports and the Western Australian saw-mill or timber towns. But still they are few as compared with the relatively larger number of non-specialized service centres.

The great Australian cities all date from the first wave of urban foundations. There was *no advancing urban frontier* comparable with the emergence of such metropolises as Cincinnati, Chicago, St. Louis, Seattle or Los Angeles as Wade (1964) described it for the United States. The initial urban nodes commanding the strategically and economically important portions of the Australian coastline have remained dominant from their establishment to the present. Major changes of rank have been restricted to the level below the five largest capital cities.

No truly hierarchical system of central places in terms of Christaller's theory developed in Australia. This can be attributed to the historical development of a small number of independent nodes, from which settlement eventually spread to their respective hinterlands. It also relates to the sequence, from the coastline to the interior, of very differently populated regions. In consequence, *several sub-systems* or partial networks of urban places have evolved each of them being, until recently, highly self-contained and oriented toward one multi-functional primate city. Only a few large cities such as Sydney and Melbourne and, of course, Canberra as the national capital, assumed nationwide significance.

Within each sub-system there have been *many rapid changes of rank* mainly due to the changing resource base; for example, thriving mining towns have declined while new mining and port towns have mushroomed. Adjustments also reflect changing traffic conditions and transportation networks, but also relate to the early overestimation of the carrying capacity of the land and potential population growth in some regions. On the South Australian wheat frontier several hundred service centres had been envisaged, of which only few were to reach urban status. The extent and frequency of those changes of rank have been unmatched anywhere in the world with the possible exception of Canada.

Australian cities are *less densely populated* than the cities in other advanced countries. Before the inner zone, comprising the central city and the old-established suburbs, could become built up to the point that no more land would be available for further construction, the Australian city had begun to expand and change from 'walking' to 'public transport' city (McCarty 1970). Australia's cities became at an earlier date and to a greater extent suburbanized than the cities in other countries. This is why Australia has been called 'the first sub-urban nation' in the world (Davison 1979b, 100).

In the capital cities densities range from 20 residents per hectare to 12 per hectare in Brisbane and Perth (Rose 1975).

Another source gives densities ranging from 32 per hectare in Sydney to 17 per hectare in Perth (Division of Nat. Mapping & ABS 1984). But even these figures are extremely low. The processes of suburbanization have, however, been somewhat different from those in the United States. While the oldest shopping centres in the United States date back to before World War II the first modern suburban shopping centre in an Australian metropolis was only established in 1957. Secondary industries became comparatively highly suburbanized or decentralized during the first two post-war decades. On the urban peripheries new towns such as Elizabeth on the far north side of Adelaide and Kwinana New Town to the south of Perth were established in the same period.

On the other hand, offices have to date remained highly centralized, the first true suburban office park in Australia having been commenced as late as 1980 on the northern periphery of the Sydney metropolitan area. This may at least partly be due to the rather belated construction of urban freeways except at Perth. In the United States the most favourable locations of office or business parks are provided by the access points of expressways or even the intersection of a beltway and an expressway.

1.2 Main sources of information

A book of general reference to Australiana containing material related to our topic is the *Australian bibliography* by D.H. Borchardt (1976). R. Freestone in an article for the January 1981 issue of the *Journal of Geography* gave a brief guide to bibliographies and review articles on Australian geography.

Volume 62 (1967) of the German annual publication *Geographisches Jahrbuch* was a compilation by E. Reiner of Australian and New Zealand geographical literature covering the period 1938–63. It was the continuation of an earlier bibliographical report on these countries by R. Geisler in the Jahrbuch of 1938.

Overviews of more recent geographical literature on Australia are to be found in the bibliographical reports by O.H.K. Spate and J.N. Jennings 'Australian geography 1951–1971' and by D.N. Jeans and J.L. Davies 'Australian geography 1972–1982' in the journal *Australian Geographical Studies*, volumes 9 (1972) and 22 (1984) respectively as well as in R.W. Cannon's M.S. Thesis 'Twenty years of Australian geography: A matrical classification, bibliography and review of the literature of Australian geography, 1950–1969' (University of Sydney, 1972). Mention should be made of Jean's contribution to the 1983 issue of *Progress in Human Geography* 'Experiments of fruit and experiments of light: Human geography in Australia and New Zealand' (pp. 313–43).

There has been, since 1950, a remarkable expansion of university geography in Australia. According to Jeans and Davies (1984) there were in 1951 only two geography departments in Australian universities employing eight members of staff. Within two decades university geography had grown to 17 departments with 140 staff members. The membership in the Institute of Australian Geographers grew from 54 in 1959, the year of its inauguration, to 344 in 1982. There was a parallel increase in the numbers of students, in the numbers of degrees awarded and in graduate theses. For information on the subjects of theses, reference can be made to B.S. Marsden and E.E. Tugbe *Bibliography of Australian geography theses, 1933–1971* and D.A. Wadley and E.E. Tugbe *Australasian theses in geography 1972–1982* compiled in the Department of Geography of the University of Queensland in St. Lucia (Brisbane) in 1981 and 1982 respectively.

Aside from the renowned professional journals such as the *Australian Geographer* (since 1928) and *Australian Geographical Studies* (since 1963) and a few others not equally well-known outside Australia, occasional papers or proceedings have been published in recent years by various geography departments, including *Geowest* by the University of Western Australia or *Monash Publications in Geography* by Monash University in Melbourne. There have been various publications by branches of the Australian Geographical Society.

With special regard to urban studies, the *Council of Planning Librarians Exchange Bibliography no. 89/90* 'Urban Australia and New Zealand' compiled by G. Breese is a documentation of the most important literature on all aspects of the urbanization and urban places in Australia up to 1966. In 1969 the Australian Institute of Urban Studies (AIUS) started to publish its *Bibliography of urban studies in Australia*, prepared by G. Walkley. A very brief account of Australian publications related to urban problems was given by Berry in the journal *Geographical Review* 1975. The review article by M. Williams in the *Australian Geographer* 1970 on the field of historical geography in Australia contains a number of historic-geographical contributions to urban geography. Apart from these bibliographies and review articles the reader will be forced to draw from a variety of sources, the most important of which will be mentioned below.

An overview of Australian urban history was given by G. Davison in *Urban History Yearbook 1979*. An account and bibliography of urban planning in Australia with main emphasis on the six decades from 1888 to 1948 was given by R. Freestone 'The development of urban planning in Australia 1888–1948: A bibliography and review' in the *Urban Studies Yearbook 1* (1983) edited by P. Williams.

In his review article on Australian urban research *Australia's cities: In or out of print*, Spearritt (1983) made the statement that not much of importance had appeared prior to 1970. The present writer should like to explicitly mention J.A. Rose's book *Patterns of cities* (1967). Spearritt pointed out that Stretton could not find a publisher for his *Ideas for Australian cities* (1970), but that once publication was finally achieved, the book's success made successive reprints necessary. Much inspiration in this early period of urban research came from Britain with Glynn's *Urbanisation in Australian history 1788–1900* (1970) and the special issue on the 'Australian capital cities in the nineteenth century' of the *Australian Economic History Review* by McCarty (1970).

The next three important books on Australian cities, Parker and Troy's *The politics of urban growth* (1972), Jones' *Housing and poverty* (1972) and Sandercock's *Cities for sale* (1975) were published by university presses. It was not before the end of the 1970s that a growing number of urban studies were published by commercial printers.

From the mid-1970s to date a great number of important books on various aspects of Australian urbanization have appeared, notably those by Neutze (1977, 1978), Troy (1978), Kilmartin & Thorns (1978), Burnley (1980), Stilwell (1980), Logan et al. (1981), Stimson (1982), Burnley (1982a), Maher (1982), Daly (1982). There have also been many important contributions to urban history, such as Hirst on Adelaide (1973), Lawson on Brisbane (1973), Davison on Melbourne (1979a), Spearritt on Sydney (1978), Stannage on Perth (1979), and many others on smaller cities such as those by Cusack on Bendigo (1973) or by Bate on Ballarat (1978).

Some of the books mentioned above appeared in one of the recently established series, the most relevant for urban questions being the following:

Urban Studies Yearbook, edited by P. Williams, annually since 1983: No. 1 'The social process and the city' (1983), no. 2 'Conflicts and development' (1984);

Urban Australia Series, edited by J.G. Hajdu, comprising six volumes: *The Australian urban network* by W.S. Logan and A.D. May (1979), *Why country towns?* by D.N.M. Christie (1979), *Mining communities* by J.S. Humphreys (1979), *A question of size* by W.S. Logan (1979), *Planning our communities* by J.G. Hajdu (1976) and *Our older cities* by W.S. Logan and D.J. Eccles (1977);

Australian Studies, containing among others: *The Australian urban system* by I.H. Burnley (1980), *Beyond the city* by M. Bowman (1981), *An issue of people* by Birrell and Birrell (1981), *The Australian city: A welfare geography* by R.J. Stimson (1982) and *Australian urban politics* edited by J. Halligan and C. Paris (1984);

Studies in Australian Society, edited by M.I. Logan, containing among others: M.I. Logan, J.S. Whitelaw & J. McKay *Urbanization: The Australian experience* (1981), T. Logan *Urban and regional planning in Victoria* (1981), I.H. Burnley *Population, society and environment* (1982) and C.A. Maher *Australian cities in transition* (1982);

The Making of Australia Series, containing among others: D. Latta *Early Australian architecture* (1984) and R. Gurnani-Smith *The growth of Australian cities* (1984);

Studies in Society, edited by C. Bell, containing among others: J.I. Martin *The migrant presence: Australian responses 1947–1977* (1978), L. Kilmartin & D.C. Thorns *Cities unlimited* (1978) and R. Wild *Social stratification in Australia* (1981);

Studies in Society and Culture, edited by J. Beckett and G. Haman, containing among others: G. Bottomley *After the odyssey: A study of Greek Australians* (1979), I.H. Burnley, R.J. Pryor & D.T. Rowland (eds.) *Mobility and community change in Australia* (1980);

The Australian Experience, edited by H. Radi, containing among others G. Sherington *Australia's immigrants* (1980) and R. White *Inventing Australia: Images and identity 1788–1980* (1981);

Immigrants in Australia, sponsored by the Academy of Social Sciences in Australia, containing among others A. Richardson *British immigrants in Australia* (1974).

A vast amount of information on population and settlements is contained in the many atlases that have been issued in Australia in recent years. Among the most important atlases are the following:

Division of National Mapping (ed.): *Atlas of Australian Resources*. A number of maps with commentaries is now available in the third edition;

Readers Digest Atlas of Australia (1977);

The Macquarie Illustrated World Atlas (1984);

Bicentennial Historical Atlas of Australia (to be published in the Jubilee year 1988);

Davies, J.L. (ed.): *Atlas of Tasmania*. Land and Surveys Department, Hobart 1965;

Duncan, J.S. (ed.): *Atlas of Victoria*. Victoria Government Printing Office, Melbourne 1982;

Jarvis, N.T. (ed.): *Western Australia: An atlas of human endeavour, 1829–1979*. University of Western Australia Press, Nedlands 1979;

Cochrane, D. (ed.): *Queensland Resources Atlas*. A Queensland Government Publication. State Public Relations Bureau, Brisbane 1980;

McCaskill, M. (ed.): *Atlas of South Australia*. Adelaide 1986;

Courtenay, P.P.: *Northern Australia – Patterns and problems of tropical development in an advanced country*. Sydney 1980.

In addition to these national and state atlases, atlas studies on four capital cities were commissioned on the basis of the 1971 Census and repeated on the basis of the 1976 census. The Division of National Mapping (NATMAP) in co-operation with the Australian Bureau of Statistics (ABS) produced two series of atlases on population and housing based on the 1976 and 1981 censuses. A list of the four series of urban atlases is given below:

First series:

Davis, J.R. & Spearritt, P.: *Sydney at the Census 1971*. Canberra 1974.

Australian Cities Commission & Davis, J.R.: *Melbourne at the Census 1971*. Canberra 1975.

Australian Cities Commission & McDonald, G.T.: *Brisbane at the Census 1971*. Canberra 1976.

Stimson, R.J. & Cleland, E.A.: *A socio-economic atlas of Adelaide. An analysis of the 1971 Census*. Adelaide 1975.

Second series:

Poulson, M. & Spearritt, P.: *Sydney: A social and political atlas 1976*. Sydney 1981.

McDonald, G.T. & Guilfoyle, M.J. (eds.): *Urban social atlas of Brisbane – 1976.* Brisbane 1981.
Houghton, D.S.: *Perth at the 1976 Census.* Nedlands 1979.
Lee, T.R.: *A social atlas of Hobart (1976).* Hobart 1981.

Third series:
NATMAP/ABS (eds.): *Atlas of Population and Housing, 1976 Census.* Canberra 1979–81. Vol. 1 *Perth* (1979), vol. 2 *Adelaide* (1979), vol. 3 *Brisbane and Gold Coast* (1980), vol. 4 *Newcastle and Wollongong* (1980), vol. 5 *Canberra and Hobart* (1980), vol. 6 *Sydney* (1980), vol. 7 *Melbourne and Geelong* (1981).

Fourth series:
NATMAP/ABS in association with the Institute of Australian Geographers (eds.): *Atlas of Population and Housing, 1981 Census.* Canberra 1983–84. Vol. 1 *Canberra.* Commentaries by C. Adrian (1983), vol. 2 *Sydney.* Commentaries by R.J. Horvath and D.B. Tait (1984), vol. 3 *Melbourne.* Commentaries by C.A. Maher (1984), vol. 4 *Brisbane.* Commentaries by P.C. Sharma (1984), vol. 5 *Adelaide.* Commentaries by C.A. Forster (1984), vol. 6 *Perth.* Commentaries by D.S. Houghton (1984), vol. 7 *Hobart.* Commentaries by T.R. Lee (1984).

It is evident that a great amount of information in the form of maps and commentaries for the decade 1971–81 has been made available to the urban geographer.

The state and national jubilees have given great incentives to geographical and historical research, much of which is of necessity related to urban questions.

The historians have been engaged in a bicentennial project to provide a cross-section for each of the years 1838, 1888 and 1938. Various teams started some years ago to issue bulletins containing contributions relevant to the respective epochs, including valuable material on the development of Australian cities. The final goals of these endeavours will be the commemorative series *Australia 1788–1988: A Bicentennial History* edited by F.J. McQuilton and a large *Bicentennial Historical Atlas of Australia* both to be published in 1988. Mention must be made of the new *Encyclopedia of the Australian People* edited by V.J. Jupp (Canberra 1987).

Then there are the various state jubilees. In 1979 the State of Western Australia celebrated its 150th anniversary. An Education Committee had been set up and, in co-operation with the University of Western Australia, put out a ten volume Sesquicentenary Celebration Series and a regional atlas entitled *Western Australia: An atlas of human endeavour, 1829–1979.* With regard to the sesquicentenary series special mention should be made of the three volumes *Western landscapes* edited by J. Gentilli, *Western towns and buildings* edited by J. White and *Immigrants in Western Australia* edited by R. Johnston.

Next was the sesquicentennial of the State of Victoria in 1984. On this occasion a three volume series entitled *The Victorians: An Anniversary History* was put out. All of them contain a lot of information on Victorian towns and cities throughout the history of the colony and the state. The Victorian Government Printing Office issued volume 3 of its Foundation Series edited by M. Cannon *The early development of Melbourne 1836–1839.* Already in 1982 the very informative atlas by J.S. Duncan *Atlas of Victoria* had been published.

In 1986 it was South Australia's turn to celebrate its sesquicentennial. On this occasion the *Atlas of South Australia* edited by M. McCaskill was published.

There are numerous government agencies, university institutions and other official bodies publishing source materials relevant to the urban geographer. Reference may be made, among others, to the publications of the Australian Bureau of Statistics; the Australian Council on Population and Ethnic Affairs; the Australian Institute of Urban Studies; the Cities Commission (with its predecessor the National Urban and Regional Development Authority); the Department of Environment, Housing and Community Development; the Division of National Mapping; the Indicative Planning Council for the Housing Industry; the Land Offices of the various states and the Urban Research Unit of the Australian National University.

A characteristic of Australian urban research in recent years has been the emphasis put on the problem of social equity in the city and, viewed against the background of the recession of the late 1970s, unemployment in the urban regions of Australia. Two early investigations of these problems were Jeffrey's article 'Spatial imbalance in the Australian regional economic system: Structural unemployment 1955–1970' in the *Australian Geographer* 1975 and Manning's article 'The geographical distribution of poverty in Australia' in *Australian Geographical Studies* 1976. The book *Equity in the city* edited by P. Troy (1981), is a fine collection of articles on various topics under the general heading of urban equity. This is also the major theme of Stimson's book *The Australian city: A welfare geography* (1982) while its author could refer to earlier research work, for example a paper entitled 'The provision and use of general practitioner services in Adelaide, Australia: Application of tools of locational analysis and theories of provider and user spatial behaviour' in the journal *Social Science and Medicine*, 1981. Recent examples of unemployment studies are Stilwell's paper 'The current economic depression and its impact on Australian cities' (1979), his book *Economic crisis, cities and regions* (1980) or Forster's paper 'Australian profile: Unemployment in the cities' in the journal *Geographical Education* (1983).

2 Historical development of the urban system in Australia

2.1 The elements of urban development

2.1.1 Physical-geographical opportunities and constraints

Extreme natural conditions render great portions of the Australian continent virtually uninhabitable and economically useless, resulting in an extremely uneven distribution of economic activities and human settlement. The notion of this vast negative area, just like the notion of the Great American Desert in the United States, was formerly regarded with disfavour in political circles and even considered an offense to the Australian public (Perry 1966). To be sure, this statement does not imply that the vast interior of the continent is completely barren. Most parts, apart from the extreme desert environment, are covered by rough hard grasses, Mulga shrub and salt bush. This vegetation cover, however sparse it may be, owes its existence to the fact that very heavy rainfall sporadically occurs and that because of the high daily temperature range dew is precipitated.

Australia is located in subtropical and tropical latitudes, comparable to the location of the Sahara desert in the northern hemisphere (fig. 2), with tropical monsoonal summer rains on its northern margin and subtropical winter rains on its southwestern and southeastern margins. The average annual rainfall for the continent as a whole is a mere 420 mm of which, due to high temperatures and evaporation rates, only 45 mm or 13% of the whole are available for run-off. These are the *lowest rates for any continent.*

During the 1860s Surveyor-General Goyder of South Australia drew a line beyond which he considered that agricultural development was not to be recommended because of the complete unreliability of precipitation. Goyder's Line was later found to coincide with the 300 mm isohyet. However, later optimistic views of the Australian environment and settlement possibilities made Australians forget this line and its implications.

Speaking in very general terms, the northern division of the continent is affected by monsoonal rainfalls during the summer months November to April, reflecting the seasonal shift of the vast subtropical high pressure cell. The southern division is influenced by the rain-bearing westerlies in winter, during the period May to October. However, since in some years the seasonal shift may be weak or not take place at all, there is a very high variability of rainfall from year to year. Vast areas of the continent must face the prospect of severe droughts and, associated with hot spells and extremely dry conditions, fire hazards and the frequent occurrence of *bushfires.* Such fires may endanger suburban residential areas of the metropolises, as they did when the fires swept over the Mt. Lofty Range in February 1983, reaching almost to the eastern suburbs of Adelaide (Bardsley et al. 1983) or when in a very dry and hot summer bushfires spread across the eastern flank of Mt. Wellington and destroyed some 400 houses in Hobart's 'mountain' suburbs of Ferntree and Ridgeway (Solomon 1976).

On the other hand heavy rainfall may occur sporadically, as it sometimes does in the Red Heart of the continent. Here people say that they suffer more from excess of water and floods than from drought. In the Western Australian region of winter rains, heavy rainfalls may occur during summer; for example, in February 1982, the Perth region, which has an average rainfall of 8 mm for the month, experienced two days of continuous precipitation amounting to 250 mm so that vast areas were flooded and roads had to be closed.

The only major river system on the mainland with predominantly perennial flow is the River Murray, with its principal tributaries the Darling and the Murrumbidgee. Other rivers like the Brisbane River on the east coast or the Swan River on the west coast (the latter emptying into the Indian Ocean at Fremantle), are relatively short coastal streams. Tasmania, due to its location in the cool mid-latitudes, is well endowed with both rivers and lakes, the two major rivers being the River Derwent in the south with Hobart near its mouth and the Tamar River in the north on which Launceston is situated somewhat further inland.

The availability of water for human consumption is one factor in determining the maximum possible Australian population. Various investigations of this question discussed by Burnley (1982) have produced differing findings, although they agree on the one point that the maximum must inevitably be rather low. Estimates range, however, from 37 million to 280 million inhabitants or from two and one-half times to 19 times the present population,

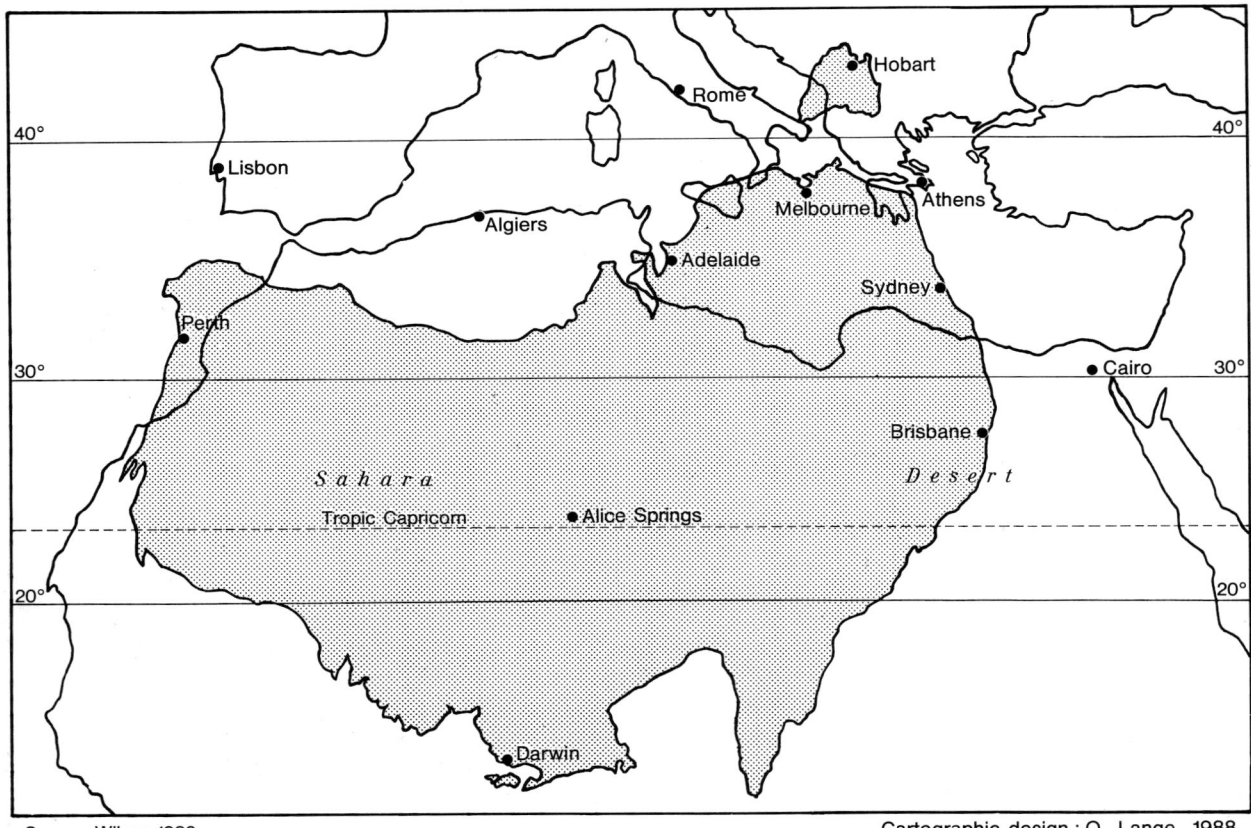

Fig. 2. Australia's position relative to the latitudes of North Africa and Southern Europe

depending upon the assessment of the proportion of the total discharge really available for human consumption. The higher estimate is based on the assumption that the amount of run-off is the only limiting factor, whereas the lower estimates take into consideration present population distribution and the present consumption of water in the more densely settled areas.

Such investigations have also touched upon the point whether the Australian metropolitan areas are threatened by *water shortages*. Such danger seems unlikely for Melbourne, Brisbane and Hobart. Sydney has to stock in reservoirs more than twice the normal summer consumption of its population and manufacturing industries, because of the variability of rainfall in its catchments; approximately one year in four is in effect a dry year. Adelaide appears to be in danger due to the fact that the semi-arid zone begins within 50 km from the city and most of its water supply is dependent on the Murray River. In Adelaide and Perth restrictions on water usage may very well have to be imposed (Burnley 1982). Possible restrictions to garden water use in Victorian cities was discussed by McMahon and Weeks (1973).

In terms of land-use capability, 531 million hectares out of a total land area of 768 million or approximately 70% of the total area are classified as arid. Nearly half of this forms Australia's 'dead heart'. This central desert is surrounded by a zone sparsely covered with numerous kinds of eucalypts and wattle trees and a variety of palatable grasses that can be used for extensive sheep grazing in the cooler parts and for cattle grazing in the hotter northern parts.

As long ago as 1926 Taylor, in his paper on the frontiers of settlement in Australia, pointed to the fact that purely on climatic grounds reasonable conditions for temperate farming exist in about 21% of the land area, but it is this portion of the continent that contains almost all the rugged mountain areas. It is accordingly necessary to subtract from the remaining 237 million hectares, 105 million because of terrain constraints and another 55 million because of poor soil conditions, so that only some 77 million hectares or approximately 10% of the total land area remain for more intensive agricultural uses. If we now subtract the 52 million hectares already farmed or in other uses there remains an area of 25 million hectares or about *one third of the present agricultural area* potentially available for the extension of farming. For further details on the problem of biophysical constraints the reader is referred to the calculations by Gifford et al. (1975; fig. 3).

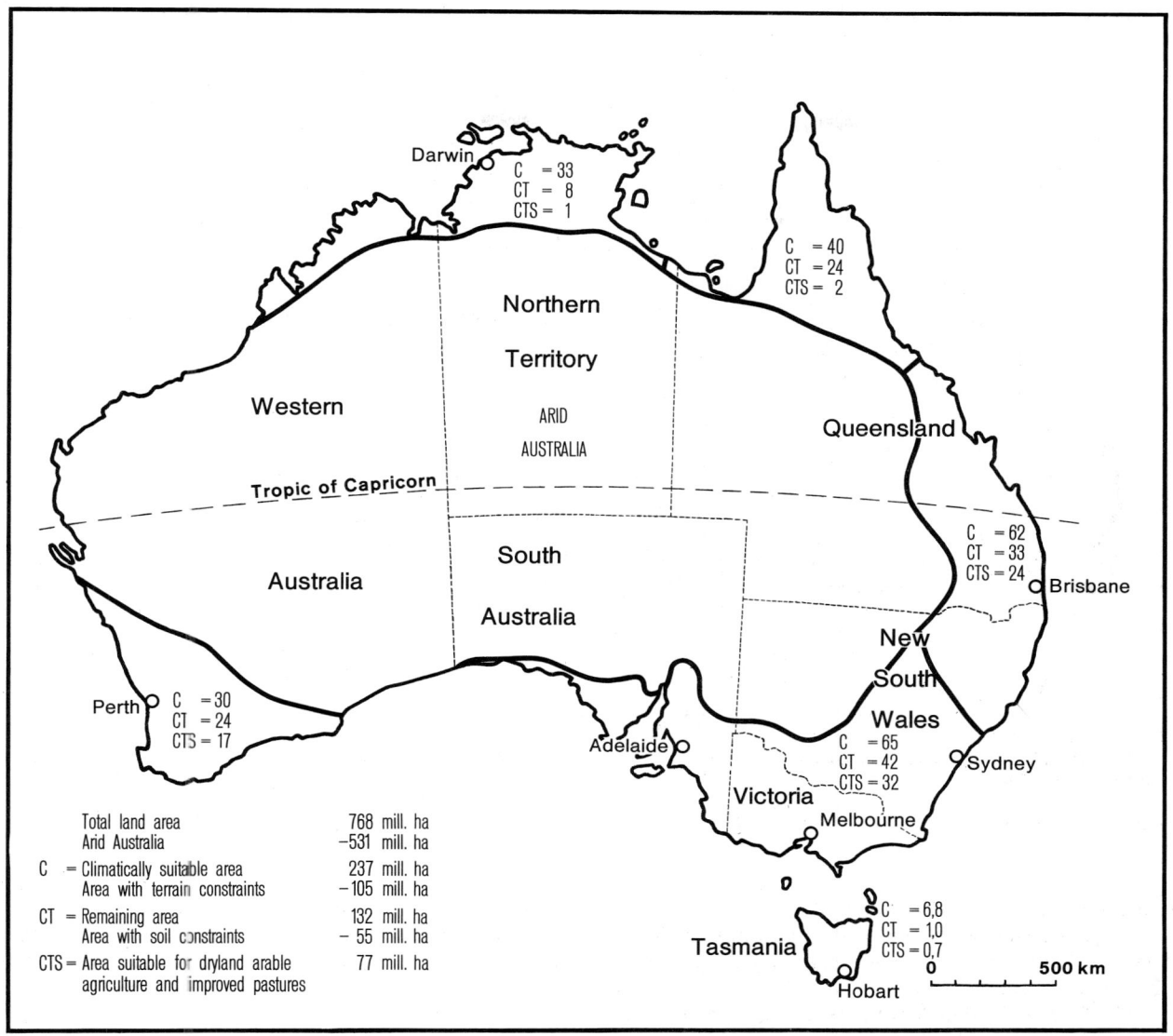

Fig. 3. Areas suitable for dryland agriculture taking into account climatic, terrain and soil constraints (after Nix 1974, Gifford et al. 1975 and Wilson 1980)

It is customary to divide Australia along the line of the twenty-sixth parallel into a tropical north and a non-tropical south, each of approximately equal size (tropical Australia 400 million hectares, non-tropical Australia 368 million). The *tropical division* comprises 130 million hectares of completely unused land and 260 million hectares used as range lands for extensive cattle and sheep grazing. Only 1.34 million hectares are used for more intensive forms of agriculture, the whole region supporting a population of less than one million persons. The agricultural capacity of this huge tropical division has been estimated to be three million persons at the utmost or just about three times the present population (Jaschke 1979). Extensive agricultural use is confined to certain coastal areas including parts of the Kimberleys, Arnhem Land and Cape York Peninsula.

Compared with the tropical division the situation of the *non-tropical division* differs only by degree. From the 368 million hectares must be subtracted the arid lands partly consisting of endoreic areas having interior drainage and extensive alkali flats such as the Lake Eyre Basin. Only 125 million hectares are climatically suitable for agricultural use. Taking into account terrain and soil constraints only some 70 million hectares remain, these being concentrated, as in the tropical division, in a coastal strip up to 500 km wide, but mostly narrower than that. Considerably less than the whole of this is in intensive agricultural use, for the coastal strip thus defined also comprises areas like the densely forested southwest of Western Australia.

We thus come to the conclusion that in both tropical and non-tropical divisions only the coastal margins carry

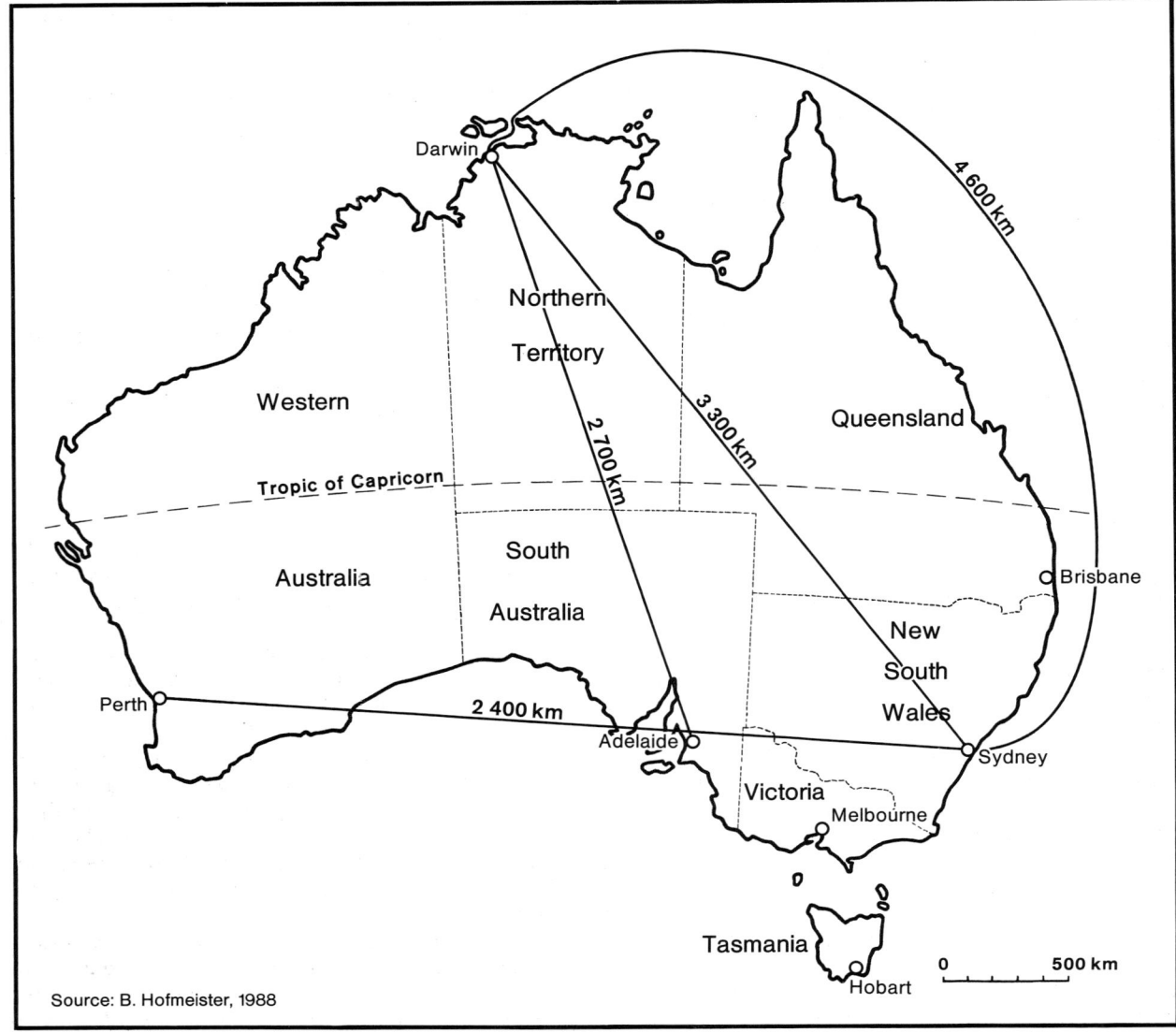

Fig. 4. Distances in Australia

a reasonable density of population, the vast interior of the continent being almost empty. There the sparse population is distributed over a number of widely scattered sheep and cattle stations and mainly confined to the relatively small tracts of arable land. There are also a few isolated points where mineral resources are exploited plus some transportation and communications nodes. An example of this category is Alice Springs, which came into being as a checkpoint along Australia's overland telegraph line.

It is often overlooked that very long stretches of the coast are uninhabitable, for example in the north, where the Great Sandy Desert adjoins the Timor Sea, and in the south, where the Nullarbor Desert adjoins the Great Australian Bight. Of more than 19,000 km of Australia's coastline, not much mor than *two-fifths make up the settled seaboard* while approximately three-fifths remain more or less uninhabited just like the vast interior of the continent. Apart from Tasmania the settled areas are confined to the eastern states, from Port Lincoln on the southern tip of the Eyre Peninsula to Cairns on the north Queensland coast (this portion of the coastline referred to by Rose 1972 as the Cairns-Whyalla arc), and to Western Australia's coast from Esperance in the south to Geraldton in the north. Thus the general statement often heard that Australia's population shows a distinct coastal trend is acceptable only with reservations. A major portion of the coast has remained unsettled to the present day.

The overwhelming part of the continent is thus characterized by warm to hot climates which are rather unfavourable to human settlement; the area of cool climates comprises Tasmania, Southern Victoria and the New South Wales Tablelands. Most of this cool zone is subject to occasional hot spells, although these are rare in the New

England Tableland. Some inland portions of the southeast, however, within drainage basins of streams, provide possibilities for urban development, such as the Ballarat region and Latrobe Valley in Victoria, southern Monaro and east New England in New South Wales (Arnot 1973a).

In general terms, the areas of dense settlement are few and rather far apart from one another. It is against this background that we must evaluate the many statements made about the importance of distance in the human geography of Australia and that we come to appreciate Blainey's choice of the title for his famous book *The tyranny of distance* (1966) (fig. 4).

Although climate has no doubt been the principal factor limiting permanent settlement in Australia, *terrain constraints* have played some part in the distribution of economic activities and human settlements. This factor accounts for the negative character of approximately 20% of the land area.

The Australian continent may be subdivided into three large regions of contrasting morphogenesis. The Australian Shield, one of the oldest land masses on earth, occupies approximately two-thirds of the continent. It is a vast peneplane rising gently from a peripheral escarpment to reach up to 350 m in the interior; it is interrupted by a number of inselbergs and isolated masses. The Shield is rich in deposits of gold, silver, lead, zinc, bauxite and uranium. Iron ores form the ranges of the Pilbara region, while other iron-ore bodies are found at Yampi Sound in Western Australia and at Spencer Gulf in South Australia. In recent years great amounts of off-shore natural gas and oil have been discovered at Learmouth and in the Bass Strait.

The second physiographic province is the Lowland Zone, the central eastern division, with its vast sedimentary deposits and the depression of Lake Eyre in its lowest part. The region is endowed with relatively good soils; its great underground water resources are tapped by artesian wells.

The third province, the eastern Highland Zone, includes numerous mountain ridges and tablelands and also the coastal plains fringed by the Pacific Ocean. It is the only physiographic province to offer considerable water resources. There are vast resources of coal mainly in Queensland's Bowen Valley and in the Illawara region of New South Wales. Brown coal (lignite) occurs in Victoria's Latrobe Valley.

Terrain constraints have been an important limiting factor in Tasmania, rendering six-sevenths of the island's area unsuitable for permanent economic use and settlement. Apart from a few isolated mining and harbour towns along the east and west coasts, population is very much confined to the lower Derwent Valley in the southeast and to the north coast.

On the mainland early toehold settlements were rather isolated from the vast interior by mountain ranges, for example Sydney by the Blue Mountains, Adelaide by the Mt. Lofty Range and Perth by the Darling Range. It took great efforts to traverse those mountain ranges. There was an interval of 27 years after the landing of the First Fleet in 1788 before Governor Macquarie founded Bathurst in 1815 on the plains beyond the Blue Mountains. The pioneers had first to find out that the steep valleys to the east were inaccessible and that the path into the interior ran along the tops of the ridges. The same ridges served as a guide line for the old road used by the bullock drays, for the railway line to Broken Hill and finally for the Great Western Highway.

Without going into details with regard to soil constraints, it is safe to say that even in areas of sufficient rainfall a *lack of soil fertility* may occur. This is due to the fact that great stretches of the land surface are very old in geological terms and that soils have in consequence been exposed to weathering for long periods of time. They are often relics of past geological ages rather than products of recent processes of soil formation. In large parts of the continent they do not show well-developed profiles (Heathcote 1975).

It must not be overlooked that the European population, particularly during the last hundred years, has had a great impact on the Australian environment and has to a high degree contributed to the *destabilization of Australian ecosystems*. To give just a few examples, such disruption has been caused by the introduction of numerous plants and animals such as the prickly pear or the rabbit. These have spread so widely that they have become plagues. Attempts to fight these and other pests have involved not only chemical means but the introduction of still more plants and animals. Environmental damage has also resulted from the overstocking in areas of thin plant covers of range land prone to soil erosion, as well as by the introduction of irrigation agriculture into areas prone to salinization of the soils.

The reason why Australian ecosystems are so vulnerable and so easily disturbed by man's activities lies in their uniqueness. This in turn is due to the isolated development of a very specific flora and fauna during long geological times after the Australian continent had been separated from other land masses (Löffler 1985). In consequence of such disturbances, agricultural uses in large areas had to be discontinued or changed. This in turn has had an impact on the small country towns servicing their agricultural hinterlands.

In conclusion we may say that the frame set by natural conditions on the Australian continent is characterized by the vast, dry and infertile interior and the large area of land subject to highly unreliable precipitation; the mountainous nature of Tasmania, and the proximity of mountain ranges to the coasts of the mainland, limiting agricultural activities in the more humid and temperate tracts; the absence of long navigable rivers, with the River Murray and some of its tributaries offering the sole exception; the long distances separating the few more habitable regions which are mainly confined to the well-endowed parts of the seaboard; the vulnerability of the Australian ecosystems, as already revealed by human interference.

Table 1. Population by settlement zones, 1976 and 1981

	Settlement zones					
	IA	IB1*	IB2**	II	III	Australia
Area as percentage of Australia total	0.9	1.9	0.5	15.3	81.4	100.0
1981 population '000	10395.1	1082.5	468.0	408.5	572.7	14926.8
1981 persons/sq.km	149.9	7.6	11.2	2.0	0.1	1.9
Total population 1981, %	69.6	7.3	3.2	16.1	3.8	100.0
Total population 1976, %	70.1	6.6	3.2	16.4	3.7	100.0
Average annual change 1976–81, %	1.1	3.3	1.0	0.9	1.8	1.2
Proportion of change due to net migration, %	39.7	74.2	23.1	-7.6	13.8	38.8
Proportion of change due to natural increase, %	60.3	25.8	76.9	107.6	86.2	61.2

* IB1 is the Queensland, New South Wales and Western Australia portion.
** IB2 is the Victoria, Tasmania and South Australia portion.
Source: Australian Council on Population and Ethnic Affairs 1983, Table 4 (modified)

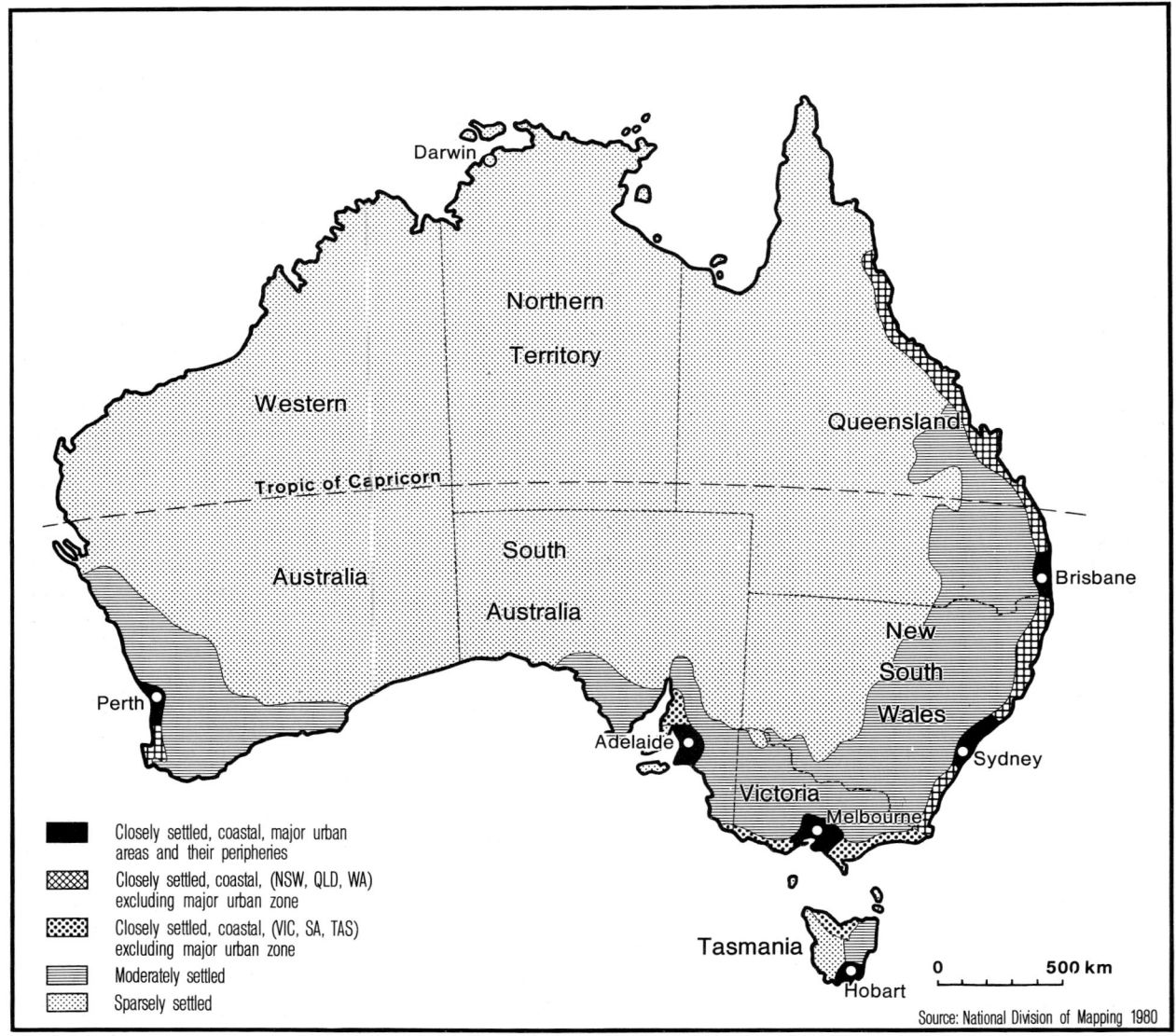

Fig. 5. Settlement zones in Australia

The resulting settlement patterns have been taken into account by the Australian Council on Population and Ethnic Affairs in its attempt to distinguish four settlement zones. Zone IA is identified as the closely settled coastal zone comprising the ten major urban areas, that is the cities of more than 100,000 residents, together with their peripheries. Canberra, although located farther inland, is also included. Zone IB is the remainder of the closely settled coastal zone outside the major urban areas. Zone IA and IB together occupy only 3% of the land area while supporting approximately 80% of the Australian population and employment. Zone II is the moderately settled zone while Zone III is the great sparsely settled zone (Australian Council 1982). Some of the population data relevant to the four settlement zones is given in table 1 (fig. 5).

2.1.2 The demographic and economic framework

Throughout two hundred years of white man's history, Australia has had only a very sparse population which has also been marked by an extremely uneven distribution. Australia's present population does not even amount to the combined numbers of residents of the two U.S. metropolitan areas of New York and Chicago. This means that, despite the high degree of local concentration of the Australian population in a limited number of large cities, these cities are not really comparable with the American metropolises.

Although there was a constant flow of convicts and free settlers during the first six decades after the landing of the First Fleet in 1788, population figures remained extremely low until the middle of the nineteenth century. The contribution of the system of transportation must not be overestimated. The total number of convicts brought to Australia before transportation was discontinued in 1853 in the eastern colonies was slightly less than 150,000. For further details on the convict settlements see chapter 2.2.1. However, Glynn (1970) has suggested that it was inherent in the fact that the early settlements were convict settlements that they should show a tendency toward development as *widespread and isolated small nodes*.

From the very beginning of white colonization in Australia there was a clear *dominance of the British*. This reflects in the first place the country of origin of the transported convicts mentioned above. Moreover, most of the early free settlers were English 'capitalists' who by purchasing land from the Crown acquired the right to select migrants for assisted migration (the bounty system). Naturally they mainly selected English labourers. The Emigration Board in London was also reluctant to accept immigrants originating from other countries, including Ireland, and tried to check their numbers so that, reflecting this restrictive policy, the South Australian Company maintained 13 emigration offices in England as compared with four in Scotland and only one in Ireland (Nance 1978).

Irish assisted immigration only took off after 1850. In the period 1840–62, 24% of assisted immigration to South Australia was from Ireland as compared with 62% from England and Wales. Of the total Irish settlers, 30% went to Victoria and 40% to Western Australia (Nance 1978).

With regard to food supply there had been difficulties from the beginning, when the First Fleet in 1788 brought ashore 780 convicts and 450 sailors and soldiers. These first white settlers in Australia found that part of the seed stocks carried in their ships had lost their viability because of the long journey. In any event a few of the sailors and soldiers and few of the convicts (the majority of whom had been sentenced in the large cities like London, Birmingham, Manchester or Dublin) were unfamiliar with agriculture. To make matters worse, the sandy soils of the Cumberland Plain proved rather unfertile. The search for better agricultural land became a major incentive for journeys of explorations to the Hawkesbury Valley to the north and across the Blue Mountains to the west into the interior plains, where Bathurst was founded in 1815 as the service centre of an early grain-growing region.

The colony of New South Wales was close to starvation before new food supplies arrived from England in 1790. The same was true of the Norfolk Island settlement during the years 1791–92 before the inhabitants succeeded in growing enough maize and wheat, and the Derwent River settlement when after the partial abandonment of Norfolk Island more than 500 of its inhabitants were transferred in 1807–08 to Van Diemen's Land and more than doubled the population, which had to be kept alive on government food supplies.

As Linge (1979) has shown, out of a total of approximately 4,200 persons in New South Wales in 1810 40% were still victualled by the government, which relied to a substantial degree on *food imports* from overseas. The majority of people in agriculture turned to *wool as a staple* after a British naval officer had, in 1797, illegally[1] brought the first merino sheep from the Cape of Good Hope to the new colony (Lighton 1958). The great advantage of wool production was that it provided an imperishable product that could easily endure long distance transport by bullock drays over rough roads and a long sea voyage before being profitably sold to overseas consumers.

During the first half of the nineteenth century the wool clip was brought once a year by wagon to the coast, from where station provisions and supplies were carried back inland. Later both the wool clip and the supplies were sent by rail. The major inputs into the productive process were vast areas of land, sheep and some station labour. This meant a rather sparse population, directly linked by the system of production to the port cities of the coast,

---

1 Illegally because as a member of the Royal Navy he was not allowed to do any private enterprise like importing and raising sheep.

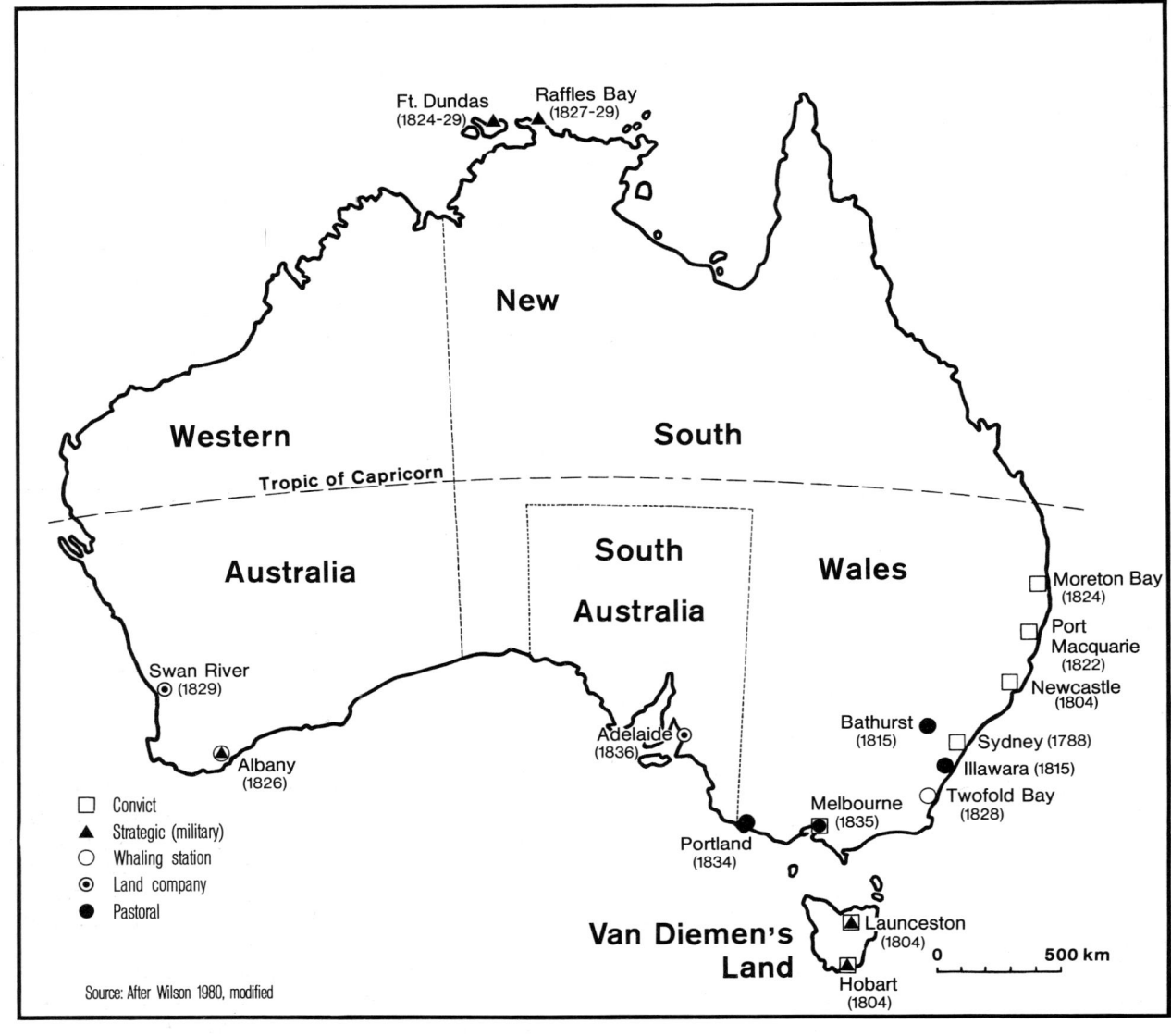

Fig. 6. Types of settlement by 1836

and not offering great incentives for the development of inland service centres. Only in grain-growing areas did a few service centres such as Bathurst come into existence, with flour-mills, bakeries and some services geared to the demand of the agricultural population of the region.

The port cities remained the focal points of the colonial economy, trade and administration being the major occupations for the urban population. A few of the coastal urban places served also as whaling stations and, due to the presence of convicts in most of them, they also functioned as military outposts (fig. 6). Cloher (1979) pointed to the early dominance of tertiary activities, which is reflected in the following data on employment in Victoria (table 2):

Table 2. Employment by sectors of the economy in Victoria 1841–1891 (%)

Sector	1841	1851	1861	1871	1881	1891
Primary	53.0	36.4	47.6	38.1	41.9	27.9
Secondary	8.5	10.7	17.1	21.5	22.1	32.7
Tertiary	38.5	53.0	35.3	40.4	36.0	39.4

Source: Statistical registers of Victoria, Census of Victoria, quoted in Cloher 1979

The *gold-rushes* in Victoria and, with a certain time lag, in Queensland and Western Australia, made for the first great population influx in each of these colonies. Victoria's population increased from 234,000 to 539,000 between 1851 and 1861; that of Queensland doubled from 61,000 to 120,000 between 1864 and 1871, and that of Western Australia increased from 50,000 to 239,000 between 1891 and 1911. Total Australian population grew from 405,400 to 1,145,000 during the 1850s.

Mining towns mushroomed in the goldfields at distances of between 110 km and 280 km from Melbourne, some attaining a population of 20,000 or even 30,000 within a decade. It is estimated that at about 1860 there were some 125,000 persons living in such towns or elsewhere in the goldfields, so that Melbourne's proportion of the total population of Victoria fell to 25% (see ch. 2.2.3).

Between 1851 and 1871 the proportion of the population born in the colony increased in Victoria from 27% to 49% and in South Australia from 13% to 55% (Nance 1978). Only during the 1860s or perhaps even as late as the 1870s did the Australian-born begin to exceed the numbers of British-born immigrants.

It may be concluded that the four decades 1850–90 witnessed considerable population increases in the southeastern colonies, as demonstrated by the following growth rates:

Table 3. Components of population increase in the southeastern colonies, 1861–1900 (%)

Period	Annual population increase (five-year averages)	Annual increase from natural increase	immigration
1861–65	4.0	2.5	1.5
1866–70	3.5	2.3	1.2
1871–75	2.9	2.1	0.8
1876–80	3.3	2.0	1.3
1881–85	3.8	1.9	1.9
1886–90	3.2	2.0	1.2
1891–95	2.1	1.9	0.2
1896–1900	1.5	1.5	0.0

Source: Demography Bulletins (quoted in Jackson 1977, 33)

It is apparent from the above data that the average annual growth rate dropped from 4% in the period 1861–65 to 1.5% toward the end of the century, although the fall was interrupted by a secondary maximum in the period 1881–85. A second conclusion is that, in spite of a considerable immigration, at least prior to 1890, natural increase has always exceeded the increase caused by immigration. The only exception was the period 1881–85 when the contribution from each source was approximately equal. As the end of the century approached, the increase due to immigration dropped to about nil and the total population growth, although reduced to 1.5% was due to *natural increase*. During the depression of the 1890s there were even years such as 1892 and 1899, when Australia experienced a net loss of settlers.

While death rates at the middle of the nineteenth century stood at about 22 per thousand, birth rates were still extremely high. In fact they were about twice the death rate, resulting in a considerable growth rate. The great difference between the two rates has been partly attributed to the age-selective immigration of young people. It has also been suggested that those with the energy and determination to emigrate were likely to be healthier individuals than the population left behind, and so more likely to produce surviving children (Burnley 1982).

The decline of death rates, after a preliminary rise between 1870 and 1885, has been particularly attributed to better housing conditions in this already highly urbanized country, rather than to improved medical provision (Burnley 1982). There were early cases of slum clearing in Australia, for example the outbreak of the plague in Sydney in 1900 gave rise to the demolition of many houses, as well as to vermin-eradication campaigns (see ch. 2.2.8).

Birth rates started to decline after 1890. They levelled off at a little below 30 per thousand between 1900 and 1920 and then fell rapidly to 13 per thousand at the end of the depression. The *demographic transition* ended in Australia in the mid-1930s with death rates standing at about 7 per thousand and birth rates at about 13 per thousand.

Early migration to Australia owed much to the theories and endeavours of *Edward Gibson Wakefield* (1796–1862), an educationist and an authority on agriculture who developed ideas on colonization. The very essence of his ideas was that the Crown should sell land for agricultural purposes at a 'sufficient price' or else reserve land for later sales by provisionally leasing it to pastoralists. The land sales would induce "capitalists" to migrate to the colonies and become land owners. They would be sure to find sufficient labourers since there would be a considerable number of migrants who would have to work for the land owners before they could in turn save enough money to buy land and become owners themselves. The money earned by means of the land sales would be spent on supporting the fares of immigrants.

By 1842, land sales had realized some £950,000, paying the fares of more than 50,000 migrants to New South Wales and the Port Phillip District. The second colonization experiment was the founding of the new colony of South Australia in 1836. Even though some land speculation and mismanagement caused difficulties in the early years of the colony, these were soon overcome and the colony grew on the basis of Wakefieldian principles.

Wakefieldian theory was very important in overcoming the unpopularity of emigration, originally so widespread in the British Isles. Assisted migration solved the problem of the high fare for the voyage, while the adverse image of Australia as a place of convict transportation was overcome by the decision that South Australia should be a colony of free settlers. Thus the success of Wakefieldian ideas was commented as opening a 'golden bridge' to Australia. For further details on Wakefield's theory and its impact on Australian colonization the reader is referred to Roberts (1968, 83–160).

At the turn of the century, out of a total of 860,000 overseas-born persons in Australia 680,000 were of British origin. Of all other ethnic groups only three were of some importance. Germans (38,150), Chinese (29,900), and New Zealanders (25,800). Since the latter may for practical purposes be added to the British, there were only two non-British groups of any size in the country.

Many of the *Germans* settled in South Australia, where a number of them promoted vegetable and fruit growing in the Adelaide Hills to the east of Adelaide and wine growing in the Barossa Valley northeast of the same city, just as they did on the western slopes of the Dividing Range in New South Wales around Mudgee. The *Chinese* originally worked in the goldfields, where their number increased during the 1850s from 20,000 to 40,000, or as cane cutters in Queensland's sugar industry. In the 1880s the Chinese made up over 50% of the total population in the goldfields of New South Wales, Victoria, Queensland and the Northern Territory. Their strong presence in the goldfields was the main reason for the restrictions imposed on further Chinese immigration. Another reason was increasing unemployment as the industry passed from the stage where it could be conducted by individuals to one which depended on machinery brought in by mining companies. This resulted in a total ban on immigration in the colony of New South Wales during the period 1867–73 (Daly 1982).

When the gold-rush was over, many people tried their fortunes in agriculture or turned to the coastal towns. Some of the gold mining towns were completely deserted and became ghost towns, others lost large portions of their populations and have been struggling for survival ever since. Some of those who left the goldfields turned to agriculture, crossing the River Murray into New South Wales and moving northward into the Riverina, there meeting another current of settlers that originated from the eastern parts of New South Wales. After 1910 the Murrumbidgee Irrigation Areas Scheme was carried out with the new towns of Griffith and Leeton becoming the district's administrative centres (see ch. 3.4.1).

Some of the Chinese from the Queensland goldfields and the cane regions partly migrated to Queensland's coastal towns such as Rockhampton, Mackay, Townsville and Cairns where their off-spring can still be traced in certain residential areas (ch. 4.2.1). Those in the south mainly migrated to Sydney, where they formed early residential clusters near the docks and the vegetable market (chs. 3.3.1 and 4.2.1). In the far north they also congregated in Darwin in the Northern Territory where in 1871 some 5,000 of them lived side by side with 400 Europeans! Other groups of minor importance were diggers from France, Poland and Hungary, also Americans from California and Nevada, in the goldfields. Pacific Islanders, Italians and Maltese worked as cane cutters in Queensland and Japanese worked mainly in the sugar refineries.

Just after the turn of the century, in the year of federation 1901, Australia's population totalled 3,774 million of whom 22.8% were overseas-born immigrants. According to the 1901 census *52% were urban*. Although population statistics in many other countries at that time were not always accurate and not completely compatible, it is safe to say 'that no other region of recent settlement was nearly so heavily urbanised as Australia at the end of the nineteenth century' (Jackson 1977, 94).

The first half of the twentieth century was a period of slow growth. Between federation in 1901 and the first post-war census in 1947, Australia's population just about doubled from 3,774 to 7,579 million. Immigration figures were down to 20,000 annually for the four decades 1900–40, this being at least partly due to the *Immigration Restriction Act of 1901* that made immigrants take a dictation test, thus in practice enforcing a White Australia policy. Intakes were somewhat higher during the 1920s when the United States imposed its immigration quota system and considerable numbers of Southern Europeans turned to Australia. However, the vast majority of migrants were assisted British immigrants under the *Empire Settlement Scheme*. Thus the 1947 census revealed that no more than 9.8% of the total population were overseas-born immigrants. Out of the 744,187 immigrants 72.7% had come from the British Isles and another 5.9% from New Zealand.

Since the end of World War I the rural areas no longer absorbed the surplus population originating from their relatively high birth rates. Their population remained stable, due to the fact that the whole of the surplus was absorbed by urban places. All growth of employment took place in the cities and towns. Thus the urban places grew primarily from their own natural increase, from the absorption of the rural population overflow in the second place, and very little from gains through immigration.

The growth of the state capitals was throughout the whole intercensal period 1911–47 well above the national average. The two exceptions were Adelaide where the growth rate in 1921–33 only managed to achieve the national average figures, and Hobart, which was consistently below it, as shown in the following table (table 4).

After World War II the situation changed completely. For a number of reasons the Australian Government started a very *active immigration policy* that became known by the slogan 'perish or populate':

1 the danger of enemy invasion had become apparent to many Australians during World War II;

2 the country's small population was insufficient for a full development of its natural resources;
3 a stronger industrial development was considered desirable but was hampered by shortage of labour;
4 because of the low birth rates of the depression years relatively small age-groups were graduating from school and entering the workforce, but were to be followed by comparatively large age-groups due to high post-war birth rates; a rectification of this imbalance was considered desirable;
5 Australia, being confronted with the legacy of World War II and increasing birth rates everywhere, was looking for some justification before the crowding world for its exclusive possession of apparently under-used resources.

Table 4. Growth rates of capital cities, 1911–47

City	Population 1911	Annual growth rate (%) 1911–21	1921–33	1933–47	Population 1947
Sydney	648,000	3.9	3.0	1.3	1,484,000*
Melbourne	593,000	2.9	2.4	1.5	1,226,400*
Adelaide	169,000	5.1	1.8	1.4	382,500
Brisbane	117,000	7.9	3.6	2.3	402,000
Perth	107,000	4.5	2.8	2.1	272,500
Hobart	40,000	3.1	1.2	1.9	76,500

* Differs from census figure due to adjustments made for boundary changes.
Source: Census figures, quoted in Burnley 1980, 68

Kmenta's (1964) analysis of the data for Australian immigration during the period 1948–61 is presented in the following table:

Table 5. Immigration targets and intakes, 1948–61

Year	Immigration target	Arrivals assisted	non-assisted	total
Calendar year				
1948	70,000	28,943	36,796	65,739
1949	110,000	118,840	48,887	167,727
1950	200,000	119,109	55,431	174,540
1951		66,674	65,868	132,542
1952	150,000	60,531	67,293	127,824
1953	80,000	27,310	47,605	74,915
1954	107,500	54,038	49,976	104,014
Financial year				
1954–55	115,000	64,226	59,954	124,180
1955–56	125,000	64,144	68,484	132,628
1956–57	115,000	60,534	60,058	120,601
1957–58	115,000	54,659	53,319	107,978
1958–59	115,000	58,020	58,677	116,697
1959–60	125,000	69,317	64,367	133,684
1960–61	125,000	66,996	71,485	138,481

Source: Kmenta 1964, 41

The considerably varying targets during the period 1948–54 are evidence of the continuous discussions on immigration and the frequent and short-term changes resulting from these debates. The figures for the subsequent 1954–61 period reveal a more consistent order of magnitude, with targets ranging between 115,000 and 125,000 per annum. An examination of the figures shows that during the period 1954–61 the actual intake was, with one exception, always slightly above the targets set by the government. It is also evident that during the years 1949–51, when the majority of displaced persons admitted to Australia arrived in the country, the assisted arrivals outnumbered the non-assisted arrivals. The proportion of assisted arrivals remained high throughout the whole period because the Australian Government signed agreements including assisted passage with Malta in 1948, Italy and the Netherlands in 1951 and the Federal Republic of Germany in 1952.

As a consequence of this immigration policy a net immigration of some *three million persons* took place between 1947 and 1981, representing a gain of approximately 100,000 migrants per annum over a period of more than 30 years!

The second important change as compared with pre-war times was the different origin of overseas immigrants. Despite the United Kingdom – Australia Assisted Passage Migration Agreement of 1947 to the effect that the ratio of British : non-British immigrants should be 10 : 1, the composition of immigration flows became quite different. Out of a total net migration of 2,917 million migrants over the period 1 July 1947 to 30 June 1980, only 41.8% were British, including 5.3% migrants from New Zealand, whereas the majority of *58.2% were of non-British origins*.

Details on the origins of post-war immigrants will be given in chapter 4.2.2, but it may be briefly noted at this point that during the period 1947–53 a total number of 612,375 immigrants were admitted to Australia, 427,603 of whom were assisted arrivals. Of the latter, 36.1% were *displaced persons* mainly from Poland, Hungary, Yugoslavia and the Soviet Union (including Ukrainians and people from the former Baltic states).

The idea of admitting refugees on humanitarian grounds dates back to the last pre-war years. There had been negotiations in 1938–39 as to whether northwestern Australia might become the place for a Jewish settlement. No decisions were made at that time, but some 11,000 Jews fleeing from persecution in Germany or escaping the German occupation of Austria and other countries arrived in Australia, and so did a ship carrying some 2,300 German, Austrian and Italian internees from Great Britain after the outbreak of World War II (Wilton & Blosworth 1984).

During the war an Association of Refugees was established in Australia, its name being changed to Association of New Citizens in 1945. In 1954 this organization ceased to exist, its concerns being further persued by the Good Neighbour Movement established in 1949. While most displaced persons arrived prior to 1953, some large groups came in later years, notably some 14,000 Hungarians after the uprising of 1956, some 5,500 Czechoslovaks after the end of the Prague spring in 1968, and some 4,000 Greeks from Cyprus in consequence of the Greek-Turkish war on the island (Wilton & Blosworth 1984).

The period 1953–71 was characterized by a strong *Southern European immigration* from Italy, Greece, Yugoslavia and Malta. In relation to its small population the former British possession of Malta ranked high in numbers of arrivals. While most Italians came in the 1950s and many Greeks in the early 1960s, Yugoslavs assumed the first rank after 1966. Over 10% of immigrants were Dutch, this influx reflecting the political change in Indonesia.

Since 1971 *Asian people* have dominated Australian immigration, this change in countries of origin being mainly due to two factors. On the one hand freedom of movement within the countries of the European Economic Community and the search by the European industrial countries for guest workers from Southern Europe caused a decline of these sources for emigration to Australia. On the other hand the restrictive immigration policy towards persons of non-European origin was relaxed in 1966 and the admission of people from these countries was more easily approved as long as general migration requirements were met by the applicants.

In the early 1970s most immigrants came from the Middle East and South Asia, that is from countries such as Turkey, Lebanon, Syria, India, Pakistan and Sri Lanka. After 1976 Southeast Asia became dominant, with many immigrants arriving from Malaysia, Singapore, Indonesia and Vietnam.

The British element, though usually below 50% of total immigration, has nevertheless held up remarkably. There was a resurgence of interest in migration to Australia in the United Kingdom, a country which had not experienced a post-war economic recovery comparable with that of other Western European countries. There was also a systematic effort to recruit manufacturing workers in the United Kingdom for newly established industrial plants, such as the automobile factories in Elizabeth north of Adelaide or Dandenong to the southeast of Melbourne. The migration from New Zealand also increased, this migration reflecting the economic gradient between the two Commonwealth countries and the role of the New Zealanders in the Australian workforce. They are admitted under the Trans-Tasman Travel Arrangement, which places no restriction on the numbers and types of New Zealand migrants.

Apart from such special arrangements, immigration has been directed since 1979 by the Numerical Migration Assessment System (NUMAS). There are four categories under which immigrants may be admitted. Family reunion and refugees need no further comment. General eligibility is a category under which applicants are admitted with regard to their skills and their ability 'to contribute to the social and economic development of Australia'. Under the category of special eligibility come persons like the New Zealanders under the special arrangement mentioned above. In 1981 NUMAS was slightly modified. In 1980–81 the four categories were represented as follows: 40.6% general eligibility, 19.6% refugees, 22.1% special eligibility, 17.6% family reunion (Austral. Council 1982, 3).

Immigration had a considerable impact on total population growth in Australia, on the growth of the capital cities in particular, and on employment growth.

The impact on total population growth rates is shown in the following table:

Table 6. Annual growth rates of population, 1947–53 (%)

Year	Natural* increase	Net migration*	Total rate of growth*	Total rate of growth at the end of the year
1947	1.44	0.14	1.58	1.60
1949	1.34	1.90	3.24	3.25
1951	1.32	1.32	2.64	2.65
1953	1.38	0.49	1.87	1.87

* refers to mean population of the current year
Source: Demography 1956 and 1960, quoted in Kmenta 1964, 44

It is apparent from the above data that during the period 1947–53 the contributions of natural increase and net migration to total population growth varied considerably. Net migration was still an almost negligable factor in 1947, but in 1949 contributed almost three-fifths of total growth. In 1951 both factors were equal. In 1953 a new period commenced when natural increase, despite a comparatively high and constant immigration influx, played the dominant part in the total population growth.

This was due to two factors: the *post-war marriage and baby boom* on the one hand and decreasing numbers of migrants since the end of the 1960s on the other. The proportion of married women increased considerably between 1947 and 1954 and the median age of women at marriage fell from 23.7 years to 21 years in 1972. Both these factors made for an increase of the proportion of young married couples in the population; the fertility of the young married couples also rose during the 1950s. In consequence of these trends natural increase prior to 1965 rose to between 1.3% and 1.4%. After 1971 fertility fell sharply, bringing the Net Reproduction Rate down to unity by 1978, as it had been in 1933. Immigration also decreased after 1970, the average annual intake for the period 1979–85 being approximately 83,000. The growth rate of 0.83 at the end of the 1970s had still remained rather high because of the high percentage of women in the reproductive age range 15 to 34 years.

Internal migration as a factor of regional population growth was studied for the period 1966–71, among others, by McKay and Whitelaw (1978). The assumption that the major streams of internal migration consisted of flows between the capital cities could not be varified. No more than 34% of Tasmania's interstate migrants, for example, had Hobart as their origin and one of the other capital cities as their destination. The respective percentages for Queensland are 37%, for New South Wales 38%, for Victoria 45%, for South Australia 49% and for Western Australia 56%.

During the period 1947–76 Sydney, Melbourne, Adelaide and Perth each owed more than 55% of their population growth to overseas immigration, as compared with 42% for the total population of Australia. Wollongong and Geelong also gained considerably through immigrations whereas Brisbane, Hobart and, prior to 1965, Newcastle, had but little gains. The components of metropolitan growth are shown in table 7 (figs. 7, 8).

Table 7. Components of metropolitan population growth, 1947–66 (%)

Capital	Average annual increase 1947–66 from		
	natural increase	net migration of foreign-born	net migration of Australian-born
Sydney	45.0	55.0	0.0
Melbourne	41.1	58.7	0.2
Adelaide	28.9	56.5	14.6
Brisbane	38.6	34.0	27.4
Perth	40.6	44.8	14.6
Hobart	50.4	32.1	17.5

Source: Census of Commonwealth of Australia, quoted in Stilwell 1974b, 29

Since immigration is age-selective in favour of the younger age groups, overseas immigration contributed more to the growth of the labour force than to the growth of total population. At the 1976 census immigrants made up approximately 30% of the labour force whereas their proportion in the total population was approximately 20%. Of the increase of the male labour force during the period 1947–66, 59% was through immigration.

There has been a considerable change in the distribution of employment over time (table 8). It is apparent that, because of the government's systematic industrialization policy during the first post-war decade, employment in the secondary sector continued to grow until the mid-1950s; the 1961 census was the first to show a decline in secondary employment. Employment in the tertiary sector had, as mentioned above, always been high and at the 1976 census exceeded two-thirds of total employment.

Table 8. Distribution of employment by sectors, 1933–81 (%)

Year	Total employment	Sectors of the economy		
		primary	secondary	tertiary
1933	2,892,557	22.8	18.7	58.5
1947	3,196,431	17.3	26.0	56.7
1954	3,702,022	15.2	28.0	56.8
1961	4,225,006	12.2	27.0	60.8
1976	5,972,400	7.8	22.0	70.2
1981	6,490,500	7.7	17.7	74.6

Sources: for 1933–76 Burnley 1980, 124; for 1981 Yearbook Australia 1985

Southern European immigrants are over-represented in the secondary sector. At the 1976 census 29.3% of the Australian-born workforce were in manufacturing and construction, but the figure rose to 64.7% for the Yugoslavs, 54.1% for the Maltese, 52.5% for the Italians (with 20.8% in construction alone!) and 50.2% for the Greek. Ironically the jobs in manufacturing and construction are, in contrast to so-called traditional occupations of immigrants like the Italian tailors of café owners, sometimes referred to as 'Australian occupations' in the literature.

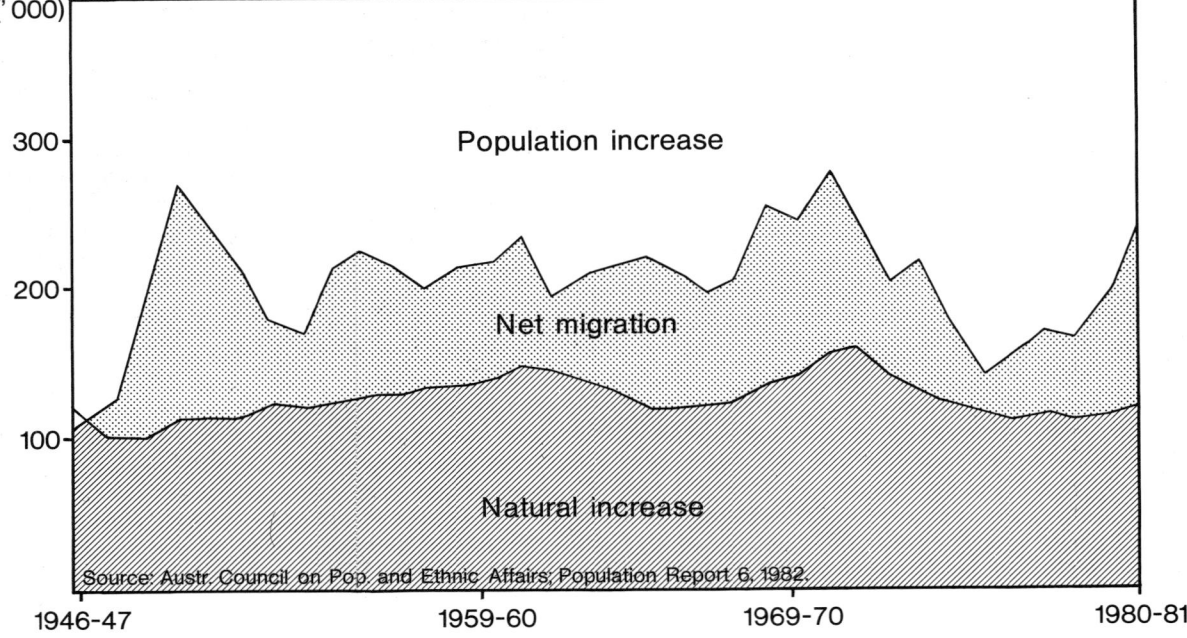

Fig. 7. Components of population increase 1946–47 to 1980–81

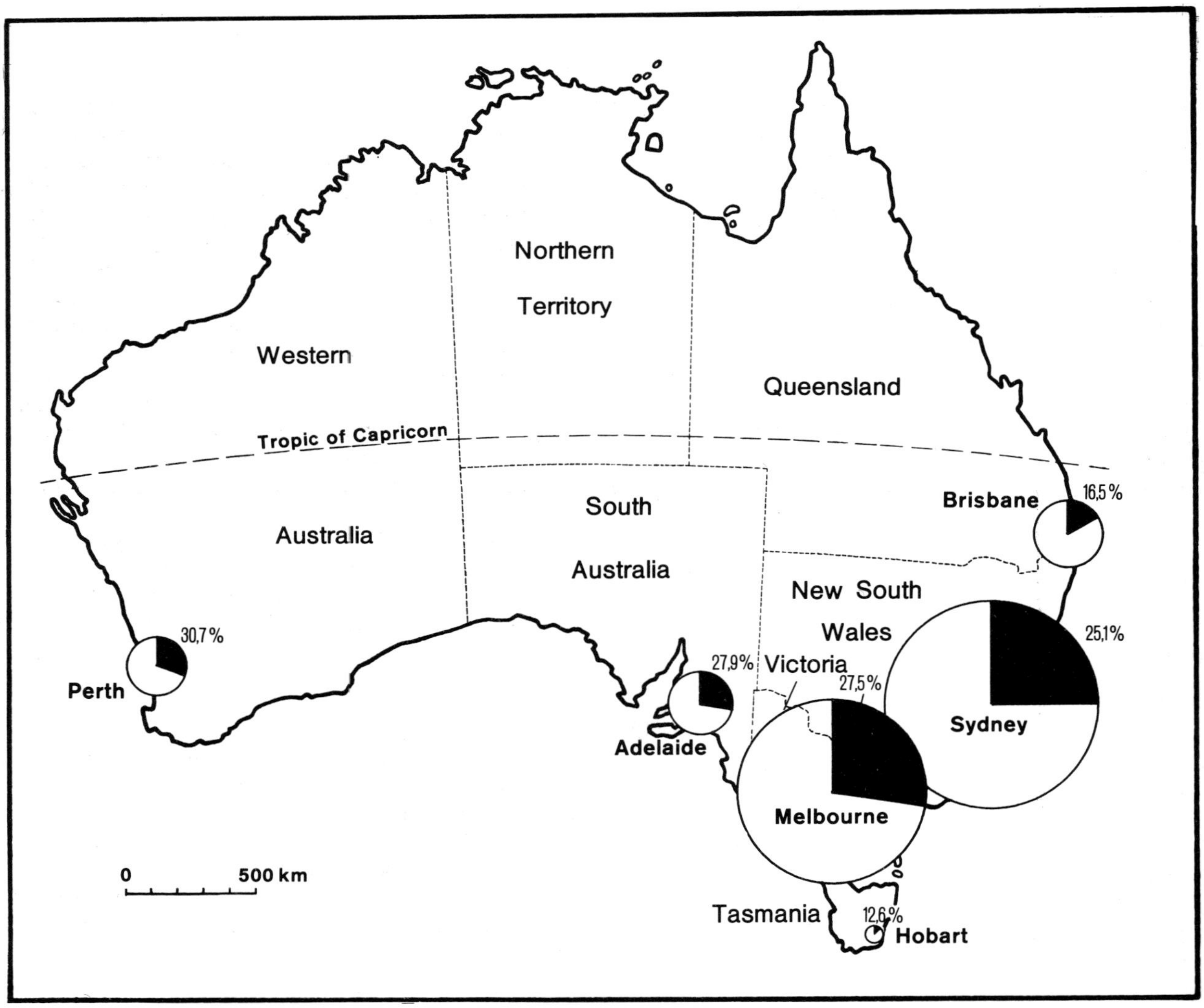

Fig. 8. The capitals' proportions of overseas immigrants, 1982

The 1980s have been characterized by slower population growth, an immigration intake usually below 100,000 per annum, growing rates of unemployment and slightly decreasing rates of home ownership (see ch. 4.1.2).

With regard to the urban building fabric it is important, however, to realize that the *number of households* has been increasing at a faster rate than total population, leading to a constant demand for new dwellings. The comparatively rapid growth of numbers of households is in part a reflection of the arrival at maturity of the post-war baby bulge, and in part reflects the post-war immigration boom prior to 1971. Together these developments have resulted in a high rate of household formation. Other contributing factors include a growing tendency for young people to leave their parents' home at a younger age, a decline in the average age of marriage, an increase in non-family or communal living situations, a rise in the number of single-parent families, and an increase in the number of elderly people living alone. Finally, a considerably increased ratio of unoccupied to occupied private dwellings (four times as high at the 1976 census as compared with 1947) indicates increasing numbers of second homes. The additional occupied dwellings required have been estimated as to the order of 900,000 for the period 1981–91 and 800,000 for the period 1991–2001. Projections of numbers of households on the assumption of a net annual immigration of 50,000 are given in table 9.

Table 9. Increases of households and population, 1971–2001

Year	Households	Financial years	Average annual growth rate (%)		
			population	persons aged 15+	households
1971	3,671,000	1966–71	2.09	2.27	3.29
1991	5,483,000	1986–91	1.09	1.26	1.78
2001	6,283,000	1996–2001	0.89	1.02	1.29

Source: National Population Inquiry 1978, quoted in Hugo 1979, 24

2.1.3 Urban development policies of the three tiers of government

2.1.3.1 Policies at local, state and federal levels

In Australia as in other countries under a federal political system three tiers of government, local, state and federal, share responsibilities for urban services, urban policy and urban development. Though it may not be essential from a geographer's point of view to go very much into the details of this political structure it is undoubtedly helpful to acquire a certain knowledge and appreciation of the functioning of the different governmental authorities. For further information of this aspect the reader is referred to the writings by Halligan & Paris (1984), Mathews (1978), Neutze (1978), Parkin (1982), Parkin et al. (1980), Rich (1982), Ryan (1978), Scott (1978) and Troy (1978, 1981).

It took considerable time before this three-tier hierarchy came into being. For several decades after the landing of the First Fleet the *Governor* had almost total legislative, administrative and judicial powers. He was appointed by, and responsible to, the Colonial Office in London. As London was some 19,000 km away and the exchange of dispatches could take anything up to a year, the governor was in fact highly independent in his decisions.

The observance of laws and regulations was very much a matter of the governor's personality as well as a matter of how he got along with the military officers and the free settlers. This also holds true for the regulations concerning the layout of settlements and the construction of houses; for example, although the first governor of New South Wales had ordered blocks in Sydney to be 60 feet by 150 feet, such regulations were often ignored so that early settlements often made a somewhat dull impression. This changed after Governor Macquarie had taken office in 1810.

In 1823 New South Wales received its first Legislative Council whose members were, however, appointed by the governor. It was not until 1842 that the Legislative Council was made up of elected representatives, although there was still a rather tight property qualification for candidates as well as for voters. In 1850 property qualifications were reduced, and between 1855 (New South Wales, Victoria) and 1890 (Western Australia) all the colonies were granted responsible government, while votes for men became universal between 1856 and 1859 in the various colonies and votes for women between 1894 and 1908 in the colonies or states respectively.

Local government in Australia is, according to Parkin (in Halligan & Paris 1984), characterized by its prime concern with physical property services ('roads, rates and rubbish'), by the small size of local-government areas (so that the local government of larger cities became extremely fragmented) and by a restricted autonomy; local-government functions are usually limited by the existence of a number of non-elected special-purpose statutory authorities; on occasion local-government bodies have been dismissed altogether and replaced by state-appointed administrators. Under the Whitlam Government the Grants Commission Act of 1973 provided for funds to Local Government in order to enable it to function at standards equal to those of other governing bodies (Thomson 1979).

'Political development in England and Europe saw central and regional government evolve from a tradition of strong, effective local government; in Australia the reverse has happened. First came the State administrations, followed much later by tentative and often abortive exercises in local government' (Colman 1971, 43).

State governments are the *principal urban governments* in Australia, a manifestation of which 'has been the prominence of central bureaucratic organisations in the delivery of urban services' (Parkin in Halligan & Paris 1984, 23). There are at least two major reasons for this. The colonial governments had been responsible for all government functions, and it is from this legacy that state governments have remained the most important authorities in Australian urban affairs to date. 'Local governments had been established mainly because the colonial governments wanted to avoid some of the detailed local administration, and especially to tap local sources for tax revenue and to finance local works such as roads and bridges' (Stimson 1982, 11). And Robinson (1962a, 74) pointed to the fact that the existing separatism in Australia was of a kind 'more suited to the federal than to the unificationist machinery'. This is why in Australia, in contrast to British traditions expenditure on housing and education is mainly the responsibility of state governments.

Since the 1940s, with the activities of the Department of Postwar Reconstruction, federal intervention into urban affairs has been remarkable but has varied a great deal, depending on the political party in power. Labor governments, and the Whitlam Government (1972–75) in particular, customarily show greater concern for urban problems than other parties and governments.

The crucial point of urban government seems to be the *small size of municipalities* and the resulting political fragmentation of larger urban places. The Municipal Act of 1854 in Victoria allowed municipal districts to be established and local councils to be elected on a petition of only 150 householders while a subsequent act of 1869 allowed these municipalities to be called cities. This system has been carried over into modern times so that, for example, contemporary Melbourne with an area of 3,100 hectares (approximately half the size of pre-World War I Berlin) but only some 63,000 residents must share its influence in the development of the metropolitan area with further 53 separate municipalities. For all practical purposes contemporary Melbourne ought to be considered as being composed of the City of Melbourne and the old-established suburbs of the nineteenth century, while the younger outer suburbs of the twentieth century constitute the metropolitan ring (see Linge 1965).

There have been attempts to reform municipal government patterns. In metropolitan Sydney 62 individual municipalities were reduced to 38 in 1949; at the same time the formerly separate municipalities of Alexandria, Darlington, Erskinville, Glebe, Newton, Paddington, Redfern, St. Peters and Waterloo were added to the city (fig. 9).

Despite such progress the major urban areas remained highly fragmented. The limited jurisdiction of local councils prevented local government from undertaking functions requiring larger areas and populations. There has often been among municipalities a lack of political will as well as a lack of resources necessary for any agreement on co-operation. Sir William Manning, Chancellor of Sydney University in 1895, was arguing the case for a Greater Sydney County Council along the lines of the recently founded London County Council. 'He discovered that it was impossible, however, to convince either the cluster of municipal councils or the ratepayers who elected them that co-ordination and strong local government were desirable objects' (Briggs 1963, 293).

In consequence of this fragmentation many functions of local government have become the responsibility of *non-elected statutory authorities*. An increasing environmental concern has led to the creation of new statutory bodies such as the Land Conservation Council, the Environment Protection Agency or the Historic Buildings Preservation Council, all of them being involved in certain aspects of planning. Their arrival on the urban scene has produced a danger of an increasing lack of co-ordination and an increasing competition for resources.

The *degree of state jurisdiction* varies from state to state. In New South Wales and Queensland there has been a stronger tendency than in other states toward the transference of municipal functions to statutory authorities, this tendency dating back well into the nineteenth century. 'In nineteenth century Australia there was a strong tendency to government intervention in most enterprises, a characteristic that derived much of its effectiveness from the government's role as principal agent of capital formation and employer of labor' (Cloher 1978, 15). Each of the colonial governments played, within its jurisdiction, a decisive part as a promoter of immigration, a major employer in government-sponsored projects, an investor in infrastructure such as telegraph lines and railways; examples of this activity include the development of the centralized railway networks in Victoria and New South Wales or the opening up by new railway lines of the Western Australian wheat belt; finally as a supervisor of land surveys and land sales like the systematic establishment of townships within each Hundred surveyed in South Australia after 1869 (ch. 2.2.4).

Each state passed a *Local Government Act* prescribing the framework for the functioning of local government. The state usually assumes responsibility for public education, hospitals and other health services, welfare services, road construction and maintenance, energy and water supply, sewerage and drainage, police services, the regulation of industrial production and labour, and for public housing. In New South Wales the Local Government Act has provided for planning on the regional scale and thus provided the basis for the Cumberland County Council and other regional councils.

Public corporations set up by the state governments have in recent years gained ever more importance with the 'progressive shift from locality-based general-purpose authorities to single-purpose technocratic authorities' (Halligan & Paris 1984, 60). Examples such as the Lands Conservation Council have been mentioned above. There has been a long discussion on the advantages and disadvantages of such a system. Parkin argued that decisions made and ser-

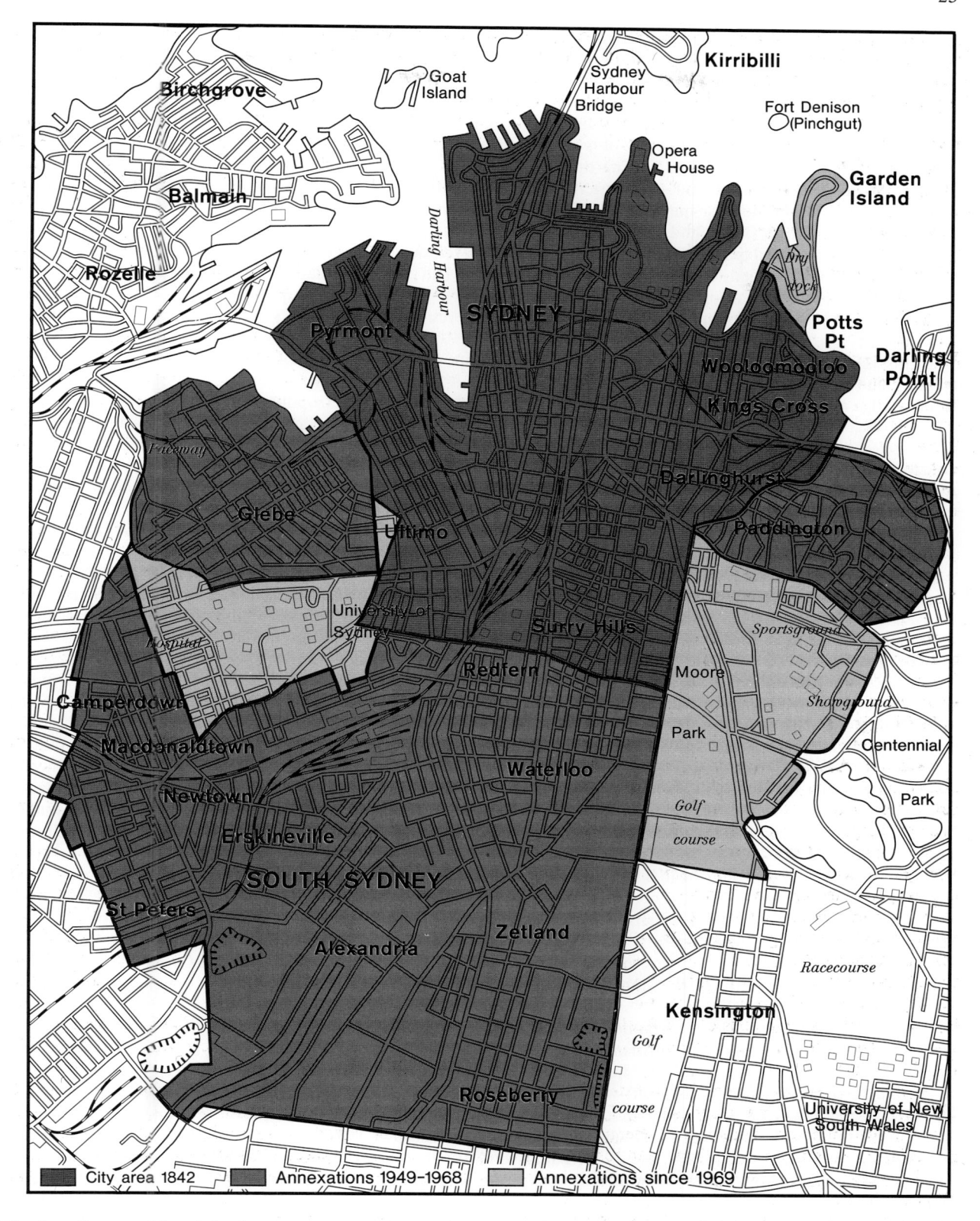

Fig. 9. Changes of Local Government boundaries of the City of Sydney, 1842–1979 (after City of Sydney strategic plan 1980, modified)

vices provided by the state on a relatively large scale may be more efficient and may guarantee a rather high degree of equalization throughout the Commonwealth, while on the other hand local governments may be much more responsive to the solution of local problems.

It has become common practice in Australia to replace local councils by *state-appointed administrators*. This is usually done on the grounds of malfunctioning, corruption or the failure to achieve a quorum for council meetings. Alternatively councils may be deprived of particular functions. For many years the Brisbane City Council, established in 1925, had been unique in bearing the responsibilities for all local activities in the metropolitan area until, in the mid-1970s, the distribution of electricity was removed from it by the Queensland Government. The metropolitan agencies established for metropolitan Sydney and metropolitan Melbourne (the Sydney Metropolitan Water, Sewerage and Drainage Board and the Melbourne and Metropolitan Board of Works) had been endowed with as much competence as a department of a state government. Melbourne lost its responsibility for a wholesale market in 1978, and it was, indeed, a momentous decision when in 1981 the Victorian Government sacked the Melbourne City Council on the grounds of its having become paralysed by two opposing groups on the issue of further strengthening the CBD versus extending shopping centres into fringe residential areas (ch. 3.1.2). The council's loss included its responsibility for strategic planning.

This is a function of key significance, particularly important in the case of the central city of a metropolis where planning concerns the CBD and where the tax revenues from it are, in the case of Melbourne, at least three times as high as the income of the municipality second in rank within the metropolitan area.

The beginnings of *town planning* in Australia can be traced back to the year 1873 when the so-called Lowlands Commission submitted a report on the location of noxious industry in Melbourne. But there were very few land-use controls in Australia prior to World War II. As Harrison (in Scott 1978, 142) put it 'there was a general reluctance to interfere with the rights and consequently the values attaching to property ownership and the procedures required to prepare and administer a statutory plan are necessarily ponderous'.

In 1943 the Federal Government raised the question of regional planning with the states, and in 1944 a Regional Boundaries Committee was established in New South Wales that came up with a proposal to divide the state into planning regions. For planning in the Sydney area the Cumberland Planning Authority was created, which in 1963 was succeeded by the New South Wales State Planning Authority. In addition to this authority the New South Wales Department of Decentralisation and Development became involved in metropolitan planning as well, resulting in the existence of two state authorities with partly overlapping functions (Woolmington in Linge & Rimmer 1971). Metropolitan planning will be dealt with in some detail in the chapters on the capital cities (chs. 3.1.1–3.1.7).

There have been some important changes in recent years in the relations between the three tiers of government in favour of local government. One of these changes was with regard to revenues. Instead of a system of money distribution aiming at equalization there was an initiative for *revenue-sharing* of the municipalities. This policy, discussed but not implemented during the Whitlam Government, was later persued by the Fraser Government so that by 1976–77 the local governments, by agreement with the states, received a share of 1.5% of personal income tax collections as a fixed share of federal revenue (McPhail in: Troy 1978). Despite such experiments federal-government expenditure remains decisive, since it is the federal government that receives more than four-fifths of all tax revenues. While in the fiscal year 1982–83 state and local tax revenues amounted to A$ 10.23 billion, Commonwealth revenues amounted to A$ 41.07 billion of which A$ 22.97 billion was derived from personal income tax. The contribution by each level of government in a particularly complicated sector of public expenditures is shown for road funding in figure 10.

Under the slogan of 'new federalism' an attempt has been made to transfer federal responsibilities back to the states and ultimately to local government. One measure characteristic of this trend was the decision by the Federal Government that grants to local governments should no longer be distributed through the Commonwealth Grants Commission but rather through the state governments; it is not clear, however, that the new system provides a more equitable basis for distribution.

Federal urban policy has undergone continual change. The establishing of a powerful Ministry of Urban and Regional Development under the Whitlam Government will be dealt with in the following chapter. With the defeat of the Labor Government in the latter half of 1975 certain measures taken by Whitlam were carried on whereas a number of programmes and institutions were abolished. As early as December 1975 the Department of Urban and Regional Development (DURD) was abolished and a new Department of Environment, Housing and Community Development (EHCD) was established, which in turn was abolished in 1978. The new Department of Housing and Construction was abolished in 1982 and its functions were dispersed among a number of existing government departments. Although another Labor Government under Bob Hawke came into power in 1983, the far reaching programmes and powerful institutions concerning urban affairs of the Whitlam Government were not revived. Urban and regional functions have remained dispersed over a number of government departments.

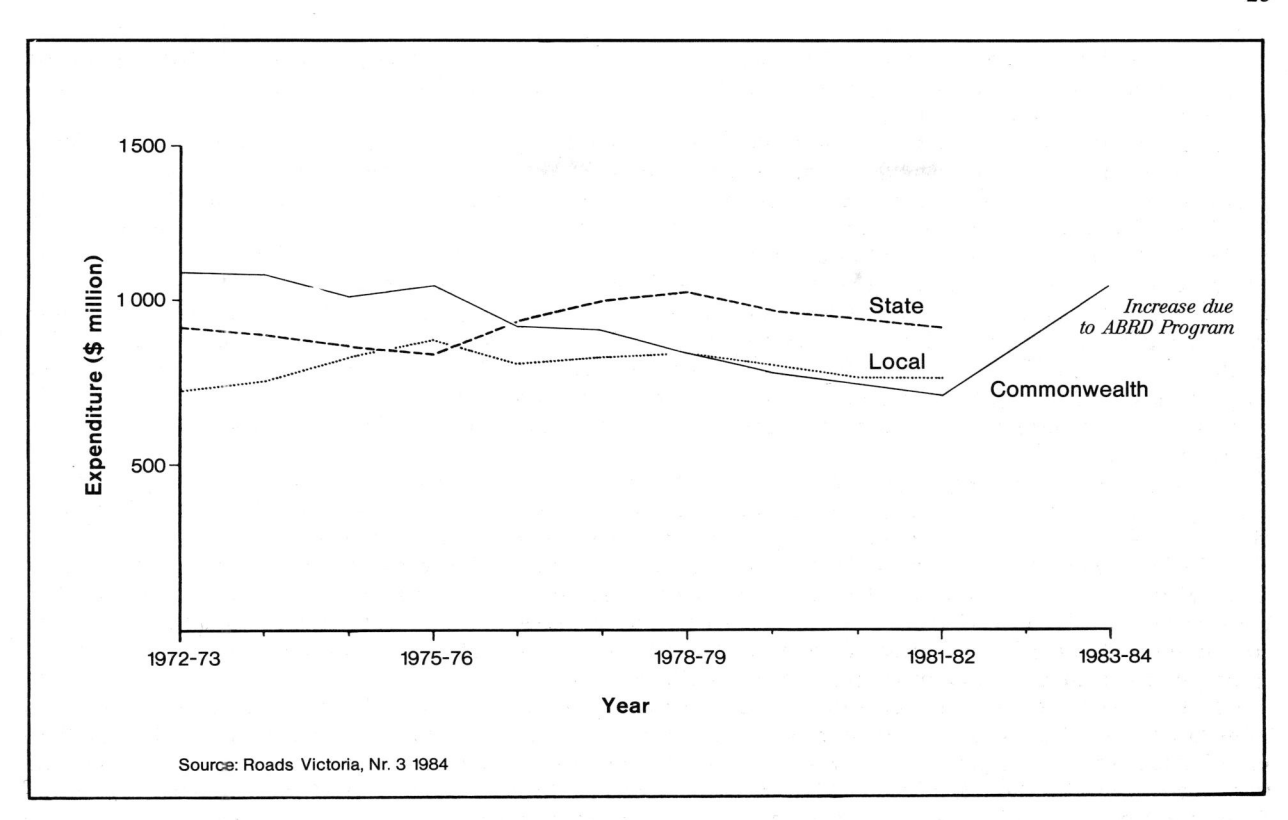

Fig. 10. Road funding in Australia

2.1.3.2 The State Housing Authorities

State intervention in the provision of housing dates back to the beginning of the twentieth century. In Queensland a so-called Workers Dwelling Board established in 1910 assisted persons on small incomes to acquire houses for themselves. In later years a State Advances Corporation was in charge of providing low-cost housing for workmen in Queensland. It was later succeeded by the Queensland Housing Commission (Cochrane 1980).

The establishment and functioning of housing authorities in the various states has very much been a matter of federal-government incentives since the early 1940s. On the one hand the Department of Postwar Reconstruction that was in operation between 1943 and 1949 gave a first impetus to urban development on the part of the Federal Government. On the other hand, the Uniform Tax Legislation Act of 1942 made it virtually impossible for the states to impose taxes, so that greater involvement on the part of the Federal Government seemed inevitable.

In 1941 Federal *rent-control legislation* was introduced. Commonwealth legislation was succeeded by state legislation in 1948. Rents had been fixed at 1939 levels, but there were no controls over house prices. In consequence of this situation 'a two-price housing market appeared, with vacant houses selling at a much higher price than those let at controlled rents' (Neutze 1978, 93). After 1950 the situation changed considerably. Many of the rented houses were converted to owner-occupation and in many cases sold to the tenants at rather favourable prices. On the other hand most new houses were built for owner-occupation from the beginning. During the post-war period home ownership reached an extremely high level, hardly matched in any country of the world (see ch. 4.1.2). There remained, however, the problem of providing a supply of adequate housing for people in the lower-income groups.

After a Housing Trust had come into existence in South Australia in 1936, Housing Commissions were established in Victoria in 1938, in New South Wales in 1942 and in Queensland in 1945, while in Tasmania the Housing Department or, as it is now called, the Department of Housing, assumed the responsibility for public housing in the state. These State Housing Authorities have been funded and operating under *Commonwealth-State Housing Agreements*. The supply of adequate housing has been subsidized by the Federal Government by means of various programmes, the most important of which have been assistance to first-home buyers under the First Home Owners Scheme, similar assistance to ex-servicemen/women under the Defense Service Homes Scheme, rebates on housing-loan interest and rates, assistance to the state and Northern Territory in the possession of subsidised public housing (rental housing and home purchase), supplementary rental assistance to low-income people, elderly persons' homes and hostels, grants to Aboriginal housing associations.

The first Commonwealth-State Housing Agreement was signed in 1945. There have been six subsequent agreements since, the latest being negotiated in 1984. The 1981 agreement was the first to specify a base level of funding, this being set at A$ 200 million per annum, with requirements for matching funds by the states. The state governments have, however, provided funds even above matching requirements.

The 1984 agreement brought six major changes as compared with the earlier agreement (Bethune 1984). Base funding was increased from A$ 200 million in 1981–82 to A$ 530 million in 1984–85 and to A$ 510 million in each of the following two years. A minimum of 75% of base funds is to be provided in the form of grants and a maximum of 25% as loans. Home purchase assistance changed to low-start deferred payment loans. Existing grants may be used to fund rent rebates. Market rents have been replaced with cost rents covering operating expenses (interest at 4.5% and depreciation). A new sub-programme provides funds to local governments and community housing associations. It will encourage alternative forms of housing management.

In addition to these organizational aspects the housing policies of the various housing authorities have not only differed but have been changing over time. Thus the Ministry of Housing for the State of Victoria has been eager to get rid of sub-standard housing. It has cleared areas of sub-standard housing and constructed *high-rise residential blocks* for great numbers of tenants, as for example in Melbourne's inner suburb of Fitzroy. The Housing Trust of South Australia puts more emphasis on *improvement* rather than on demolition. Tasmania's Department of Housing switched its emphasis from large-scale tracts to single-family homes in newly developed suburban residential areas at the metropolitan fringe to so-called *infills*, small housing projects closer to the central city where the older housing stock had become obsolete or residential suburbs had lost their character by the invasion of manufacturing and commercial businesses. These smaller projects have typically provided for marginal groups such as elderly persons, the disabled or single-parent families. In the outer suburbs the flexilot system which means varying house and lot sizes was applied in order to achieve some degree of social mixture (ch. 3.1.6; fig. 11).

For various reasons the number of households applying for public housing has been increasing considerably in recent years. According to Bethune (1984) approximately 140,000 households were on the waiting list in 1984, while in addition a large number of households in need of better and cheap housing will have failed to file applications for fear of failing to pass the selection test. The major reasons for such high demand for cheap housing are the increasing numbers of persons of the retirement age and in various beneficiary groups, the growth of numbers of non-nuclear or single-parent households, the high rents demanded in the private market in many cities and the growth of unemployment.

The contribution of the housing authorities must, however, not be overestimated. As Neutze (in: Troy 1981) pointed out 'housing in Australia is primarily provided by the market. It is regarded as a private rather than a social service". Thus the housing authorities have helped a number of people to acquire decent housing for rather low rents, but on the other hand many poor families have not received any housing assistance. Only 11% of all Australian families are housed in the public sector.

Moreover Neutze came to the surprising conclusion that by 1980 half of all publicly constructed housing had been sold to private buyers, who had thus become home owners. At the same time the majority of public tenants in the other half of the public housing stock are not to be considered poor in terms of the statistical poverty line. It follows that the majority of poor households are not tenants of the housing authorities (Neutze in: Troy 1981, Small 1979).

In the early 1970s the Federal Government, responding to rapidly increasing land prices, encouraged the establishment of *Land Commissions* in the states. Table 10 gives an impression of the movement of land prices at the time.

Table 10. Residential land prices in the capital cities, 1968–74 (in dollars for an average allotment)

Year, month	Sydney	Melbourne	Perth	Adelaide
1968	5,988	4,226	8,472	2,203
1969	6,720	4,565	9,246	2,325
1970	7,688	4,654	8,957	2,466
1971	9,233	5,592	9,605	2,387
1972 March	10,700	6,600	5,964	2,710
1972 September	12,700	7,300	7,273	2,931
1973 March	14,600	8,700	6,250	3,586
1973 September	16,400	10,300	7,907	4,435
1974 March	19,150	13,010	8,379	5,333
1974 May	20,200	12,500	n.a.	n.a.

Note: For Sydney and Melbourne twelve-month moving median prices, for Perth and Adelaide average price for year or quarter respectively, for Perth 1968–71 average for established areas.

Source: DURD: Urban land prices 1968–1974, 1974, 7, 16 and 21

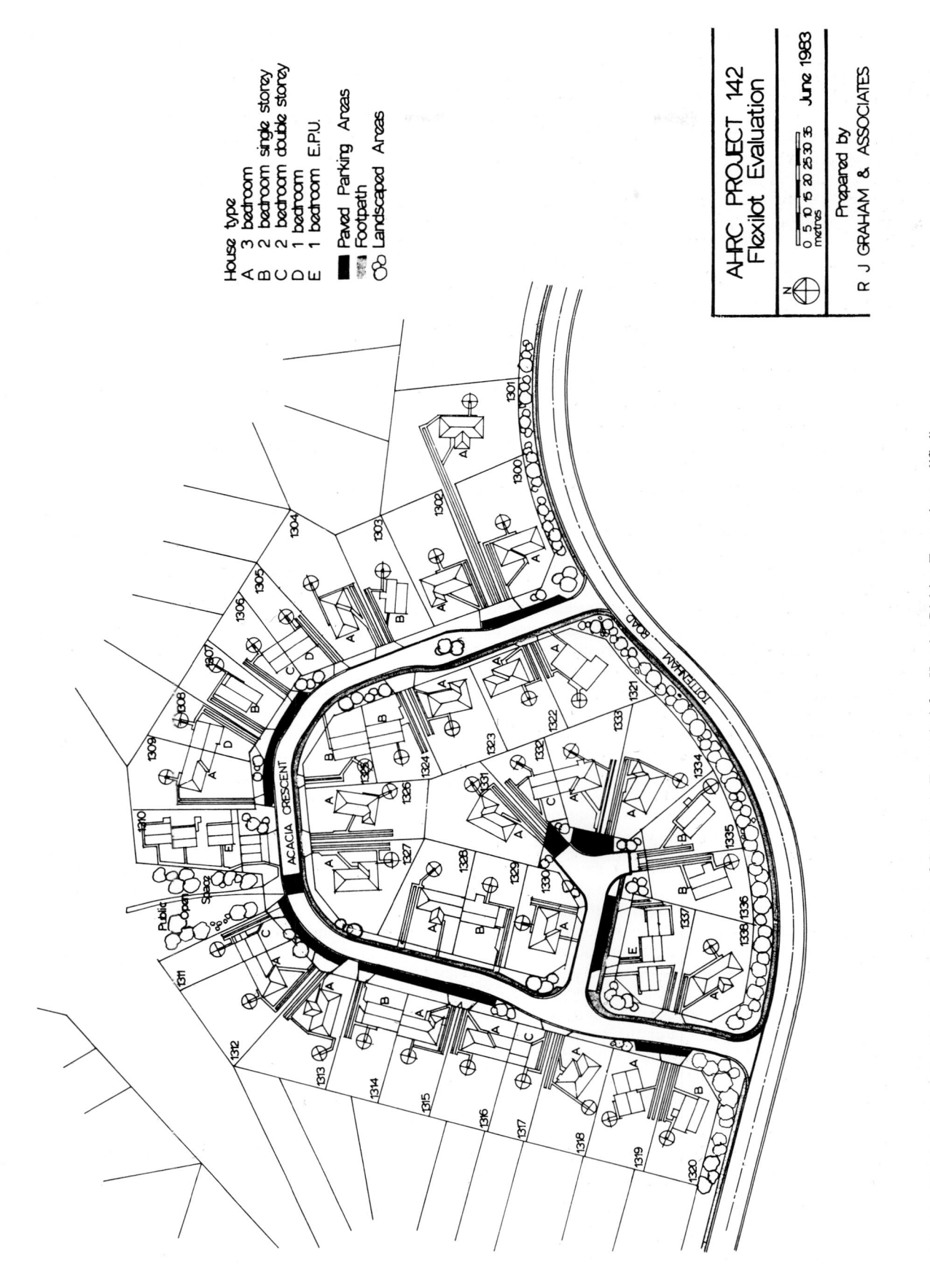

Fig. 11. Flexilot system of public housing in a section of Gagebrook, Tasmania (after Housing Division Tasmania, modified)

Fig. 12. Worrington Downs, Sydney metropolitan area, N.S.W. Commission housing under construction

During the 1970s all mainland states with the exception of Queensland established either Land Commissions or Urban Land Councils. Land Commissions, as established in New South Wales and South Australia, were endowed with statutory powers such as the capacity to purchase, to develop and to dispose of property, and they may even be given the power to override the development and planning decisions of local governments. Urban Land Councils established in Victoria and Western Australia, take the form of inter-agency committees of the various state bodies involved in urban planning. They thus have more of a co-ordinating function within the respective state governments, making recommendations and urging the competent state agencies to take actions on their behalf (Beale in: Troy 1978). To give an example, the activities of the New South Wales Land Commission within the area of the County of Cumberland are shown in table 11 (fig. 12).

2.1.3.3 Decentralization and growth-pole policy

During the early 1960s the Federal Government began to manifest an interest in decentralization. The overriding goal was to achieve a more favourable population distribution. There was the desire to counterbalance a further concentration of population in the primate cities, to strengthen the regional economy in some areas in order to promote the emergence of a number of smaller metropolitan areas below the level of the port-capitals (see ch. 2.3.2) and to prevent the further outmigration of population from small towns in rural areas.

In the early years of decentralization policy the goal was thought to be best achieved by means of the promotion of secondary industries in smaller towns and cities, a policy referred to in the literature as 'dispersed decentralization' or 'decentralized decentralization'. Because of its ineffectiveness this policy was soon abandoned in favour of what became known as 'selective decentralization' or 'centralized decentralization', with the emphasis on a *limited number of growth poles.* For this purpose a Commonwealth-States Officials Committee on Decentralization was appointed in 1965 and the number of urban places to be promoted by means of subsidies from the Federal Government was drastically reduced.

Both the governing coalition and the Labor opposition vehemently discussed urban problems during the years 1967–72. In 1967 Whitlam had become the opposition leader, and with the assistance of the shadow minister for urban affairs and environment, Uren, urged the government to resume responsibilities for the growing urban problems. Under the pressure of this strong opposition the coalition government revised its decentralization policy, establishing in 1972 an inter-departmental committee and inaugurating a 25 year programme for seven selected growth poles: Gladstone in Queensland, Albury, Bathurst and Coffs Harbour in New South Wales, Yallourn in Victoria, Murray Bridge in South Australia and Albany in Western Australia. Portland in Victoria, Tamworth in New South Wales and Townsville in Queensland had also been considered for this role (fig. 13).

Table 11. Lot production, house commencements and stock movements, County of Cumberland, 1976–80

L.G.A.	1976/77			1977/78			1978/79			1979/80		
	Lot production (a)	House commencements (b)	Net stock movement	Lot production (a)	House commencements (b)	Net stock movement	Lot production (a)	House commencements (b)	Net stock movement	Lot production (a)	House commencements (b)	Net stock movement
Baulkham Hills	553	1,136	(−) 583	717	1,139	(−) 422	1,042	1,340	(−) 298	912	1,117	(−) 205
Blacktown	504	1,617	(−)1,113	837	1,484	(−) 647	787	1,845	(−)1,058	683	1,451	(−) 768
Campbelltown	704	1,162	(−) 458	768	1,148	(−) 380	1,761	1,296	465	1,341	1,743	(−) 402
Fairfield	903	375	528	509	952	(−) 443	1,131	1,067	64	1,511	1,267	(+) 244
Hornsby	330	446	(−) 116	520	540	(−) 20	252	710	(−) 458	567	894	(−) 327
Liverpool	301	510	(−) 209	103	368	(−) 265	208	470	(−) 262	203	473	(−) 270
Penrith	944	1,568	(−) 624	762	1,292	(−) 530	1,301	1,859	(−) 558	1,468	2,073	(−) 605
Sutherland	514	647	(−) 133	721	720	1	561	910	(−) 349	598	1,068	(−) 470
Total, Release Area L.G.A.s	4,753	7,461	(−)2,708	4,937	7,643	(−)2,706	7,043	9,497	(−)2,454	7,283	10,086	(−)2,803
Balance, County of Cumberland	1,787	2,566	(−) 779	1,546	2,534	(−) 988	1,769	3,169	(−)1,400	1,822	3,045	(−)1,223
County of Cumberland	6,540	10,027	(−)3,487	6,483	10,177	(−)3,694	8,812	12,666	(−)3,854	9,105	13,131	(−)4,026

Note: (a) Lots produced, are based on: S34B Certificates issued by the Water Board; Land Commission data; Lands Department data; Lots registered in the Blue Mountains; and Lots released by Council in Wyong and Gosford. There is a slight over-estimation in the number of lots as it has not been possible to exclude commercial and rural zoned lots in some cases.

(b) House commencements derived from A.B.S.

Sources: Land Commission of New South Wales 1979 and 1980 Annual Reports.

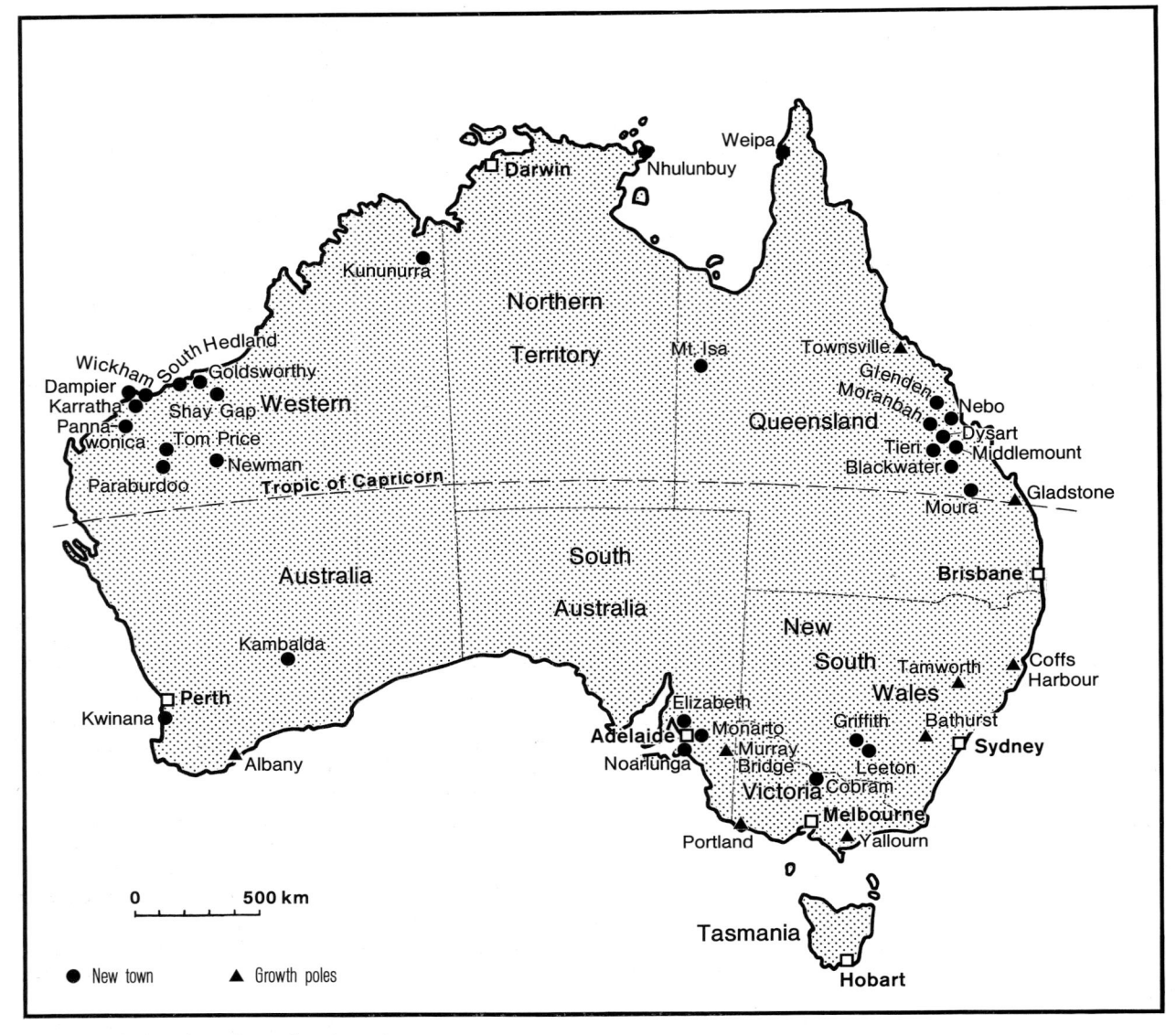

Fig. 13. The location of growth poles and new towns

The selection of the growth poles was, according to Kidd (1974), closely *related to issues of separatist movements* and political party allegiance. Aside from the historical example of the separatist movement in the Eastern Goldfields around Kalgoorlie, by means of which this region urged the colony of Western Australia to join the Federation in 1901, the regions of more continuous separatist movements have been the Riverina, New England and the Northern Rivers district in New South Wales, central and northern Queensland and western Victoria. In considering Albury, Tamworth, Coffs Harbour, Gladstone, Townsville and Portland as possible growth centres to be subsidized by the Federal Government, the major centres of the respective regions of recent separatist tendencies were thus given preference in regional growth-pole policy. In the event, however, Tamworth, Townsville and Portland were not chosen.

Thus urban and regional questions became the major issue in the 1972 elections that were won by the Labor Party. The coalition government had in 1972 established a National Urban and Regional Development Authority (NURDA), and the former commissioner of the National Capital Development Commission had been appointed its commissioner. The new 'Whitlam Government promoted an unprecendented Commonwealth involvement in urban affairs in the 1972–1975 period ...' (Parkin in: Halligan & Paris 1984, 15). Whitlam immediately established a great Ministry of Urban and Regional Development headed by Tom Uren. The Ministry's structure may be sketched as follows:

Ministry of
Urban and Regional
Development
{
DURD (Department of Urban and Regional Development)
Cities Commission, since 1975 Bureau of Cities (former NURDA)
NCDC (National Capital Development Commission)
AHC (Australian Housing Corporation, since 1975)

For further details of these agencies and their activities the reader is referred to the chapter 'A history of federal intervention' by Lloyd and Troy (in: Troy 1978) and to their book *Innovation and reaction* (1981).

The initial resistance on the part of the states against this rapidly growing Commonwealth involvement was gradually broken down by both Uren's consiliatory and constructive approach and the amount of money spent by the Federal Government. Gross outlays of the government for urban programmes increased from A$ 143,7 millions in the fiscal year 1972–73 to A$ 656,6 million in the fiscal year 1974–75. Outlays thus grew four and a half times within two years! The direct funding of growth centres changed as follows:

Table 12. Direct Commonwealth funding of selected growth centres, 1973–78 (in million dollars)

Fiscal year	Albury-Wodonga	Bathurst-Orange
1973–74	2.1	0.0
1974–75	43.3	5.0
1975–76	41.0	9.0
1976–77	24.0	3.3
1977–78	5.13	3.0

Source: Budget Papers, quoted in Christie 1979, 47

For various reasons growth-pole funding decreased to negligable amounts toward the end of the 1970s. From the very beginning there were certain difficulties inherent in the decentralization policy. As Woolmington (in: Linge & Rimmer 1971) pointed out, decentralization for the majority of people living in the big cities is a 'second-order matter' rather than a 'bread and butter issue'. It was also difficult to justify subsidies for some towns while others would not get any. It happened that a number of smaller cities, among others Wagga Wagga, submitted applications to the government for being selected as a growth pole while vividly explaining their capacities for economic and population growth. Finally, there was a division of responsibility: the initiatives for the respective programmes were more a matter of the various states whereas financial support had to come from the Commonwealth Government.

Another problem is that decentralization first of all meant decentralization of secondary industry and the creation of manufacturing jobs in smaller urban places in somewhat remote locations. But the encouragement of movement toward this goal was to a certain degree counteracted by the Federal Government's own policy of keeping wage rates and corporate taxes at more or less constant levels throughout the country (Lonsdale 1972, Linge 1967). Moreover, the state governments, although committed to official selective decentralization policy, continued to offer financial assistance to other country areas, thus pursuing both selective and dispersed decentralization simultaneously (Hanley in: Hanley & Cooper 1982, 349).

The idea was to promote growth poles in due distance from the port-capitals. Another possible measure was to establish new towns. It was also possible to contemplate a combination of the two measures, as happened later in the case of Bathurst and Orange, the two towns being considered one growth pole while the New Town of Vittoria was to be established between them.

In addition to Federal Government funding, various incentives were given by the State Governments of New South Wales and Victoria to industrial enterprises locating away from the major urban centres. Thus the Victorian Government in the early 1970s offered 100% payroll tax rebate to approved and registered firms locating more than 80 km from Melbourne, while firms locating within the 80 km ring but still outside the metropolitan area were granted a 50% rebate (Neutze 1978). Also freight concessions were granted as a subsidy to higher transport costs in places further inland. All these incentives, however, did not prove to be sufficient.

Thus *Bathurst-Orange* and Albury-Wodonga remained the two targets of decentralization policy. The New South Wales Government contributed to the development of the former by moving the New South Wales Mapping Authority there from Sydney. But despite all efforts the two towns did not hold rural and small-town populations to the extent that it had been anticipated, nor did they attract greater numbers of migrants from Sydney. As various authors have pointed out, growth would have had to be much more rapid and the provision of all kinds of services and amenities much better in order to achieve these goals (Burnley in: Burnley, Pryor & Rowland 1980). In the 1976–81 intercensal period Bathurst (1981: 19,640 residents) and Orange (27,625) were just able to hold their ranks within the urban system with very modest average annual growth rates of 1.1% and 1.0% respectively.

Albury-Wodonga at the point where the Hume Highway and the main Sydney-Melbourne railway line cross the Murray River has been a major joint Federal-State venture in selective decentralization. Within a decade approximately 8,000 work places were gained. In the intercensal period 1976–81 Albury-Wodonga (1981: 53,251 residents) ascended from rank 19 to rank 18 with an average annual growth rate of 3.4%. The Borg-Warner component plant established in Albury contributed much to this growth. The plant receives supplies from about another 20 local firms. Many of the tenants on the local housing market were recent movers from the rural hinterlands of both states, employed by Borg-Warner as assemblers, drivers or electricians whereas professionals such as draftsmen or managers came mainly from Melbourne and Sydney. Although Borg-Warner started to diversify by taking over other firms with contrasting products there has been a constant threat over their Albury plant since in 1982, when the Nissan company started to import their own gear boxes from Japan and the plant's workforce immediately dropped from about 1,300 to 800 (Adrian & Evans 1984).

Albury-Wodonga had not been the best choice for a growth pole in the beginning because five governmental bodies were involved in planning the region (the Federal Government, two State Governments, two Local Governments), the ecological stress on the Murray River was already relatively high, and there was already a housing shortage that was aggravated by the induced in-migration (Lange 1975).

Against a background of lower population growth rates, decreasing immigration and growing economic constraints decentralization in the mid-1980s is no longer an issue of importance.

2.2 Stages of urban development

2.2.1 Convict settlements along the coastlines

The Declaration of Independence of the 13 North American colonies in 1776 did not only mean that the first British Empire lost an important link in its North Atlantic sector, and that Great Britain's overseas activities were diverted to the Indian Ocean. It also meant that the United States closed her ports to British prisoners so that other outlets had to be found for the overflowing British gaols. The First Fleet that landed in Sydney Cove in 1788 was a transport of 780 prisoners with 450 sailors and soldiers as their guards.

Since the availability of convict labour was an important factor in early Australian town development, a brief overview of transportation will be provided. It is important to distinguish between *convict settlements* in a broader sense alongside their guards and free settlers where convicts were a constituent part of the population, and *penal settlements* in the narrower sense where no free settlers were allowed and only convicts and their guards were sent. Convicts in these penal settlements had usually committed crimes while already in Australia and were receiving 'secondary punishment', which meant that they were banned to very remote and isolated places. As Lewis (1973,6) put it, 'it was found necessary to establish prisons within the prison'.

During the first four decades after the landing of the First Fleet penal settlements were successively established along the coast to the north of Sydney: King's Town which later became known as Newcastle in 1804, Port Macquarie in 1822, Moreton Bay which later became known as Brisbane in 1824. To the south Hobart and Launceston were for strategic reasons established simultaneously in 1804 on the southern and northern coasts of Van Diemen's Land, in response to French activities in this part of the South Pacific, but they were destined from the beginning to be convict settlements as well. Port Arthur, Macquarie Harbour and Maria Island were established as Tasmanian penal settlements. A few years later a great number of the convicts from Norfolk Island were transferred to Tasmania.

Newcastle was eventually abandoned as a penal settlement in favour of Port Macquarie at the time when the frontier of free settlement had reached the Hunter Valley, and the escape of convicts was considered too easy. The further northward advance of the frontier of free settlement in search for coal and agricultural land led in 1830 to the end of the penal function of Port Macquarie. In Tasmania Macquarie Harbour on the west coast was a very safe place but was, at the same time so remote that communication was difficult. Governor Arthur accordingly ordered the prisoners to be relocated to the newly established Port Arthur on the southeast coast in 1830, and Macquarie Harbour was abandoned in 1834.

It is estimated that no more than 10% of all convicts ever transported to Australia saw the inside of a real penal settlement (Austral. Encycl. 3, 29).

The southernmost part of the colony of New South Wales was first settled by squatters from Van Diemen's Land in 1834. They made a treaty with the Aborigines and bought some of their land. This treaty was, however, not recognized by the New South Wales Government, and contrary to the settlers' wishes Governor Bourke in 1837 decided to establish townships on Phillip Bay and immediately sent convicts for street levelling and house construction, thus also making the Port Phillip District (Melbourne) a convict settlement.

Shortly after 1850, when the eastern colonies decided to discontinue transportation, the settlers of the Swan River Colony on the west coast that had been established in 1829 and later became known as Perth, suffered from a labour shortage. The colonists asked for convict labour, and as a result some 9,700 convicts were shipped to Fremantle between 1850 and 1868. Thus with the only exception of South Australia all the colonies had their quota of convicts.

There is a vast amount of literature on the convicts in Australia, the data presented in the following paragraphs derive in the main from Robson (1976). According to this author approximately 123,000 male convicts and 25,000 female convicts were transported to New South Wales and Van Diemen's Land, 98.2% arriving at their destination while 1.8% died during the voyage.

No more than 20,000 convicts had arrived prior to 1815. For a variety of reasons the numbers of prisoners transported to Australia then increased considerably. After the Napoleonic Wars there was no longer any threat of enemy attack on the ships during their long voyage. The substantial demobilization of the armed forces meant that criminals could no longer be sent to military service, while the post-war depression made for an increase of the number of offences. Moreover, the English dock-yards had no longer such a high demand for convict labour. At the same time, legislative changes in Great Britain made for an increase of the number of offences for which transportation was the statutory penalty. Thus after 1815 some 130,000 prisoners were transported to the eastern colonies. In Tasmania alone there were 35,500 arrivals between 1841 and 1852 as compared with 32,000 arrivals in the whole period between 1804 and 1840. Another 9,700 convicts were sent to Western Australia.

Two convicts out of every three had been tried in England, most of the rest in Ireland, very few in Scotland and in British possessions elsewhere. Approximately 50% had been sentenced to the minimum of seven years for some sort of theft or larceny. Between one half and two-thirds of them had been punished before, so that they were convicted for repeated criminal acts. Sometimes convicts were held in custody after their legal terms had expired, but on the other hand convicts could, for good behaviour, be granted so-called tickets of leave. In the late 1830s probation was normally granted after four years for seven-years prisoners, six years for fourteen-years prisoners and eight years for life prisoners (Cannon 1984). In the event of a new offence, tickets could be cancelled and the person sent to prison again.

The average of Australian convicts was 26 years so that many of them were, at the time they became emancipists, about 33 years of age or even younger. Those receiving tickets of leave could be younger still. Instead of returning to Britain, the great majority of time-expired convicts decided to stay in the new colony. This may be partly explained by the fact that approximately 75% of all prisoners were single. Many convicts also married female convicts and, after completion of their prison terms, established new households in Australia. Many convicts were from the labouring classes, their places of origin being one of the big cities such as London, Birmingham, Manchester, Liverpool or Dublin.

There were certain differences between the two colonies as to the origin of convicts. It soon became obvious that despite the fact that about one third of all convicts were Irish and Roman Catholics, the colony of Van Diemen's Land received hardly any Irish convicts. The Irish were almost exclusively sent to New South Wales. Nor was there any subsequent transfer of Irish that had arrived in New South Wales to the penal settlements of Van Diemen's Land. Only a small number of Irish was brought to the Derwent River Settlement when in 1807–08 the majority of the Norfolk Islanders were, after partial abandonment of the Norfolk Island Settlement, transferred to Van Diemen's Land. By that time, however, many of them had become emancipists: among the arrivals from Norfolk Island 132 were prisoners, 202 were settlers and other free persons and 220 were children (Walker 1973). Robson (1976, 91) has argued that 'it seems likely that the more persistent offenders were deliberately shipped to the southern colony, and, because the Irish were less likely to have been previous offenders, a policy that had determined to make Van Diemen's Land a "sink" would therefore keep them out'.

The role of the convicts in settling the continent of Australia must, however, not be overestimated. Transportation to New South Wales was discontinued in 1840, to Queensland, Victoria and Tasmania in 1853. By that time more than half of all the convicts had become ticket-of leave holders or emancipists after their term of seven years. Moreover, the colonial authorities were anxious to see that *convicts did not outnumber* the group of the sailors, soldiers and free settlers and other free persons. Only in the period prior to 1830 was there a marked majority of convicts in New South Wales, the free settlers by 1830 amounting to only 14,000 out of a total of 77,000 Europeans in the colony, or 18% of the whole. After the introduction in 1835 of the bounty system by means of which private persons were entitled to select migrants as employees and receive a government bounty for each approved person landed and also with the introduction of assisted passages, this ratio changed rapidly. During the 1830s 56% of the 116,000 arrivals were free settlers (Austral. Popul. and Immigr. Council 1977). At Sullivan's Cove (Hobart Town) early in 1804 the ratio was 3.7 : 1 but it changed quickly in favour of free people so that by mid-century the ratio was below 1 : 1. Also in Western Australia the ratio was kept below 1 : 1. By 1850, out of a total of 400,000 Europeans in Australia an estimated 15% only had arrived as convicts. This percentage decreased rapidly during the following decade, due to the influx of great numbers of free people who came in search for gold to the goldfields of Victoria, New South Wales and Queensland.

It is against this background that we have to evaluate the *availability of convict labour* for public works such as the levelling of streets, the construction of bridges and roads to neighbouring settlements, the erection of public buildings, the work in Customs Houses and other government offices, the provision of lumber and the work on government farms for the food supply of the towns. The greatest amount of convict labour was, of course, available in Sydney. Only small contingents of prisoners were sent to the penal settlements of Newcastle, Port Macquarie and Moreton Bay, and very little convict labour was assigned to work in Melbourne. As we know from documents kept in the Victorian Archives a number of soldiers were employed in the erection of public buildings in Melbourne

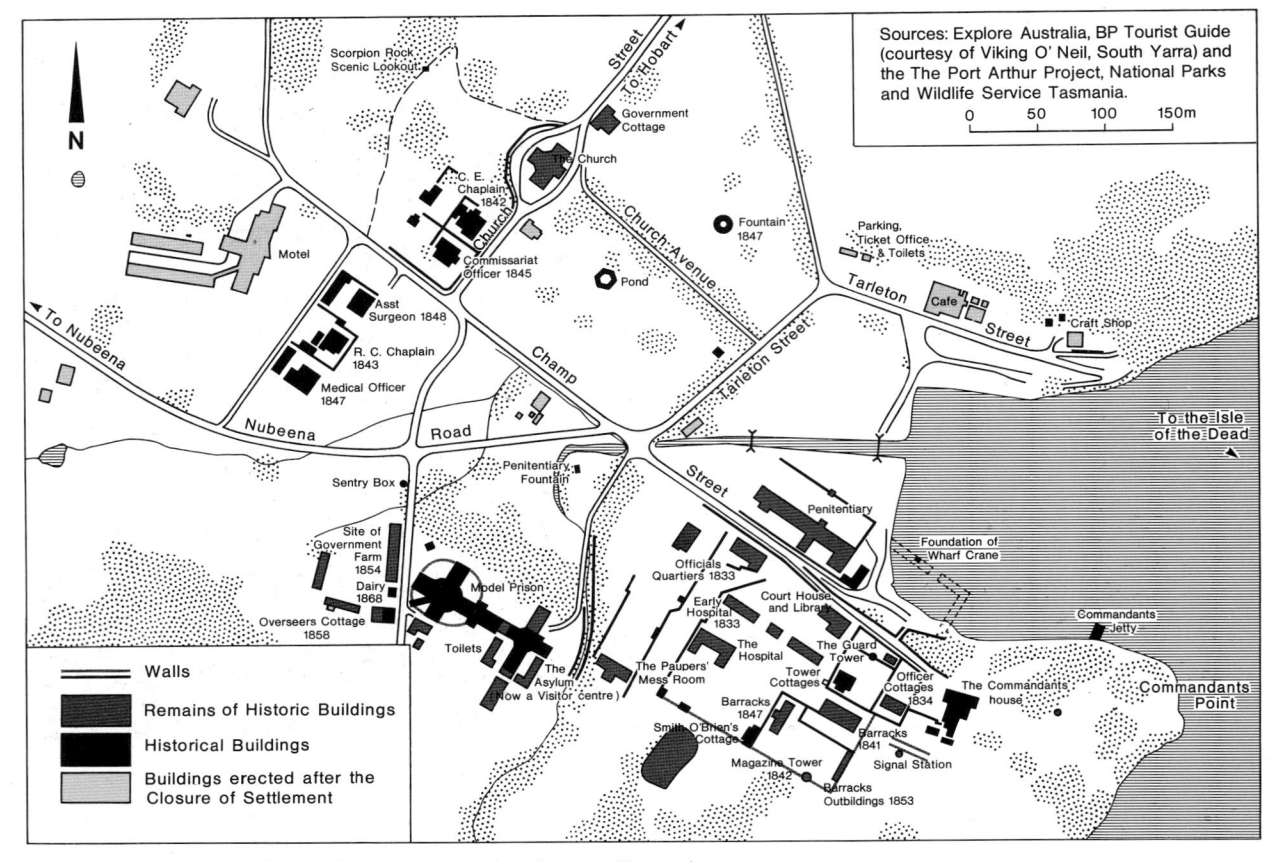

Fig. 14. Buildings in the former Port Arthur penal settlement, Tasmania

while in 1839 only 76 convicts were available for public works of any kind and no new domestic servants were assigned after 1839 (Cannon 1984).

Port Arthur, a typical penal settlement about 100 km southeast of Hobart, was made up of a huge penitentiary, a prison hospital, an asylum for the mentally ill convicts, a guard tower, the commandant's house, various officers'

Fig. 15. Port Arthur, Tasmania. Ruins of penitentiary in the conservation area of the old penal settlement

Fig. 16. Wilberforce, N.S.W. Sign identifying the town as one of the Macquarie towns

cottages and soldiers' barracks, some houses for officials, a government farm with an overseer's house, a church and a few other buildings (figs. 14, 15). All these buildings were very solidly built of local sandstone and brick. A restoration programme was started a few years ago (ch. 2.2.8).

There was even a well-known architect, Francis Greenway, among the early convicts in Sydney. Upon his arrival in Australia in 1814 he was granted a ticket of leave and two years later was appointed Government Architect and Assistant Engineer by Governor Macquarie. Among the buildings designed by Greenway are such famous buildings as St. James Church, Macquarie Lighthouse and the Government House stables in Sydney and St. Matthew's Church in Windsor (Herman 1970).

2.2.2 The Macquarie towns in New South Wales

By the year 1794 settlers from Sydney had penetrated the area on the banks of the Hawkesbury River. This first occupance had, however, been spontaneous and sporadic.

The orderly occupation and intensive use of the area was essential for two reasons. Firstly, the growing penal settlement of Sydney had an ever-growing demand for food, so that agricultural production in Sydney's hinterland had to be promoted as soon as possible. Secondly, a considerable number of convicts had been sentenced for theft for seven years and were approaching the end of their sentence, the time when they would qualify for ticket-of-leave, so that the colonial authorities were eager to get them settled down and have them farm the land in the environs. The fertile land along the Hawkesbury River was soon to become known as 'the granary of Australia' or 'the garden of Sydney'.

Soon after his arrival in the colony in 1810 Governor Lachlan Macquarie made a reconnaisance tour through the Hawkesbury Region and decided to establish *five townships* along the river. While two of them were named for localities in England, Windsor and Richmond, the remaining three townships were named for Viscount Castlereagh, William Pitt and Wm. Wilberforce, M.P. (Ellis 1958, Bowd 1979). Thus the Hawkesbury River became the second guideline for settlement of the interior and the second link for early river transportation north of the Parramatta River (fig. 16).

In the course of time Governor Macquarie's plans proved to be too ambitious. Only two of the five Macquarie towns proved to be viable and grew to urban size. Windsor as the site of the courthouse for the district and Richmond with its rail access on the line from Sydney via Parramatta opened in 1864 gained a certain position as river ports on the Hawkesbury. From 1872 until 1949 Richmond had a local-government authority of its own, the Richmond Borough Council, which was abandoned in 1949 when Richmond was incorporated into the municipality of

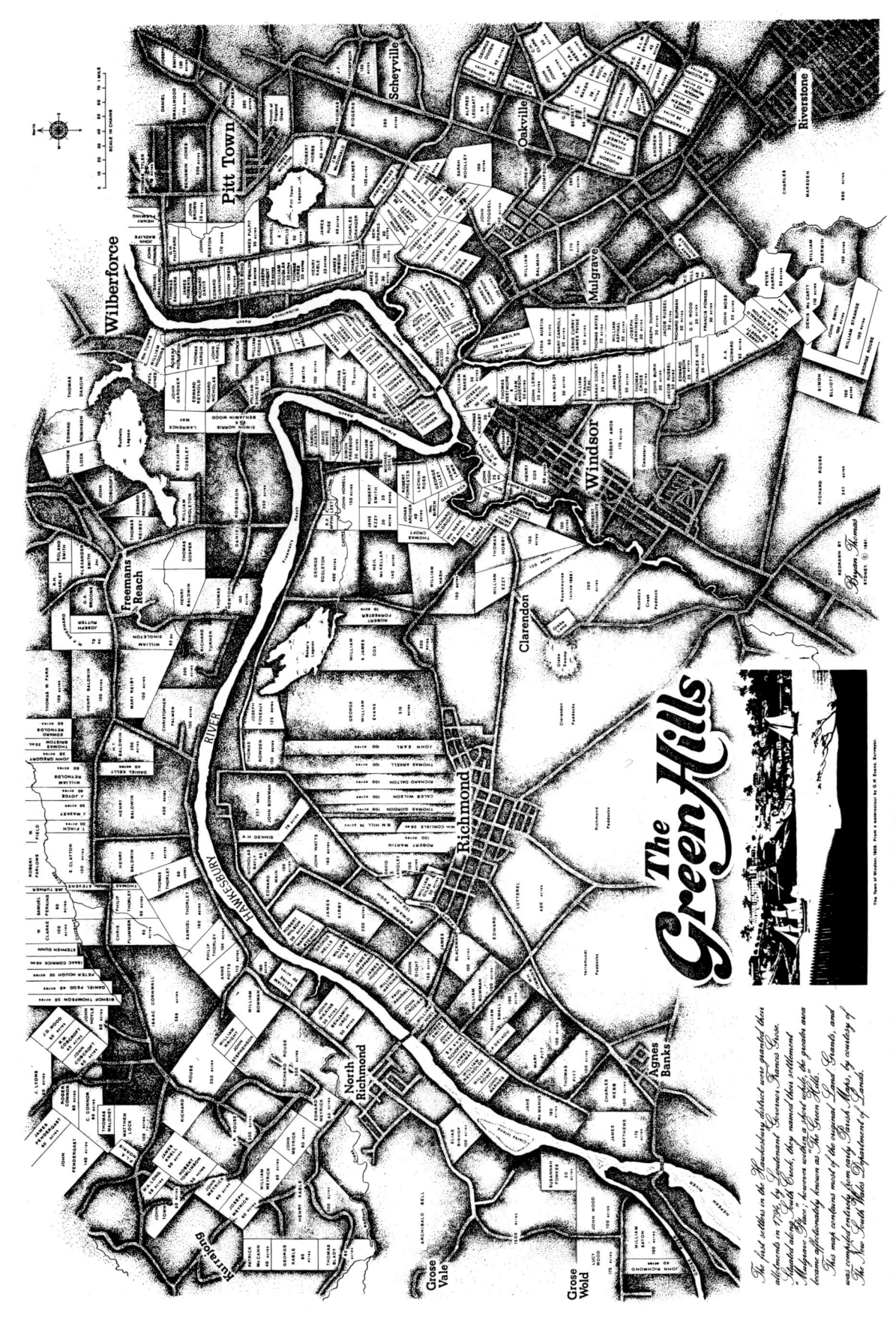

Fig. 17. The Macquarie towns in the Hawkesbury River valley, N.S.W. Castlereagh outside area shown on map.

Windsor. It is symptomatic for the automobile age that the only administrative branch remaining in town is the Motor Registry. Windsor and Richmond are the only two towns out of the five Macquarie towns to have developed a true town centre.

The three other Macquarie towns of Pitt Town, Wilberforce and Castlereagh suffered from their economic bases being too small to guarantee sustained growth. The distances between the Macquarie towns was so short that none was able to develop a hinterland large enough to support any substantial population in secondary and tertiary occupations. Moreover, Castlereagh, due to unfavourable natural conditions, lacked a link to river transport (fig. 17).

Boat building was at first prohibited in the colony in order to minimize the likelihood of escape by convicts, probably also in order to protect the monopoly of the British East India Company. Governor Macquarie, however, permitted private persons to build small trading vessels, so that the Macquarie towns in their early years were, in addition to their engagement in river traffic, occupied in boat building (Bowd 1979). To a high degree, however, economic life in these towns has always been dependent upon their agricultural environs. In this respect at least two major changes occurred during the last 100 years. Since in the early days the Hawkesbury Region was a gain-producing area, all the Macquarie towns used to be *mill towns*. In 1888 Windsor had six tanneries, and in 1892 a dairy products factory specializing in the production of butter was opened which eventually became the Hawkesbury Dairy and Ice Society.

In the three decades 1920–50 the farmers of the Hawkesbury Region promoted the growth of *vegetables and oranges*, from 1935 vegetable growing was favoured by the introduction of spray irrigation in the area. Liability to flooding was the major reason for reducing the growth of vegetables and turning to other crops. Due to the demand from American soldiers stationed on the Pacific Seabord during World War II, the growing of sweet corn was introduced to the area, leading to the establishment of a sweet-corn cannery in Windsor. In addition to sweet corn local farmers began to specialize in the growth of potatoes, cauliflower, pumpkins, cabbage and lettuce. In general terms, however, agriculture declined considerably during the 1970s. In the former LGA of Windsor the total area of rural land holdings decreased from 18,460 hectares in 1969/70 to 6,062 ha in 1977/78. On the other hand, modern *industrial estates* have been developed since 1955 in South Windsor and Mulgrave, with a variety of plants ranging from wood processing to the production of plastics and cosmetics (Windsor Munic. Council 1979).

Two major changes made for the restructuring of the Hawkesbury Region in recent years. Due to the rapid increase of private car ownership in Australia, the Hawkesbury Region became part of Sydney's metropolitan fringe. This re-evaluation of the region's location made for a rapid increase of *commuters* living in the Hawkesbury Region and working in the Sydney metropolitan area, as well as for changes of land use in favour of an increasing *recreational infrastructure* for the metropolitan population.

These changes in turn led to rapid increases of resident population and housing construction in the area. The average annual rate of population growth in the Shire of Hawkesbury was 4.91% in the intercensal period 1976–81. The population grew from 29,550 persons in 1976 to 36,756 persons in 1981 and to approximately 42,000 in 1984. It is expected to double during the last 15 years of the century. During the 1970s a total of 5,810 new dwelling units were constructed in the shire (Shire of Hawkesbury 1981).

Of course, population growth differed from place to place within the area; the development of Windsor and Richmond in particular was influenced by institutions such as the R.A.A.F. base, Australia's oldest air base dating back to the year 1916, located between the two towns, and the Hawkesbury College. Compared with the shire as a whole the very small town of Wilberforce showed a spectacular growth rate. Its intercensal population increase was from 532 to 1,117 or 109.9%. The smallest of the five towns, Pitt Town, grew from 365 to 457 persons, this being an annual growth rate of 5.04%. The in-migration is also reflected in the over-representation of the younger age groups of 0–4 years, 20–24 years and 25–39 years. This means that there has been a considerable influx of people establishing new households and raising their first children.

The recreational value of the Hawkesbury Region becomes apparent from such events as the Annual Bridge to Bridge Boat Classic between Brooklyn and Windsor held every year in May and other aquatic sports like canoeing, water skiing and raft racing as well as horseracing.

Another consequence of the change of relative location with regard to the metropolitan area is the fact that Windsor farmers started to specialize in 'ready made lawns' for Sydney suburban gardens so that, since the late 1960s, 160 hectares of farm land in the Hawkesbury Region have been converted to turf-growing (Windsor Munic. Council 1979).

By virtue of their relative antiquity, by Australian standards, the Macquarie towns enjoy a multitude of old buildings which have become the major concern of the Macquarie Towns Preservation Society. This stock of old buildings is one asset in the area's tourism potential.

Apart from the five towns of the Hawkesbury Region other towns also owing their official establishments and their original designs to Governor Lachlan Macquarie are Liverpool, now a western suburb of Sydney, Bathurst (founded in 1815 during the governor's journey to the far side of the Blue Mountains), Newcastle and Port Macquarie. Mudgee to the northwest of Sydney and Goulburn to the southwest were founded in 1821 at the very end of Macquarie's term as Governor.

2.2.3 The old mining towns and Murray River towns in the Southeast

The settling of the Southeast was very much dependent upon the discovery of gold in the early 1850s in various parts of the central and northern sectors of Victoria. There was a related increase in sheep and cattle raising farther north beyond the Murray River in southwestern New South Wales for the supply of meat to the thousands of diggers in the goldfields. Also of significance was the opening of the Murray River to steam navigation in 1853, and the construction of railway lines from Melbourne to the Murray River ports and even beyond the Murray into the colony of New South Wales.

The economic development of the region during the second half of the nineteenth century took place against the background of political tensions between the three colonies of Victoria, New South Wales and South Australia, eventually escalating to the verge of a civil war between New South Wales and Victoria over the customs issue.

Almost simultaneously in 1851, *alluvial gold* was also discovered in New South Wales. Since in the Victorian fields the richness of the deposits was greater and their accessibility easier they developed much more rapidly. Particularly significant were the Ballarat field, the Bendigo-Maldon-Castlemaine-Maryborough field (the Bendigo-Ballarat sub-province accounted for 75% of Victoria's gold production) and the northeastern field around Beechworth and Yackandanda (fig. 18).

The first diggers mainly came from nearby places, many of them from Melbourne. A second and much larger wave brought diggers from various European countries who entered via South Australia. A considerable number of Chinese also arrived (their joss house[2] in Bendigo is still in use for a small Chinese community whose graves and burial towers are found on the cemeteries of Beechworth, Bendigo and Maldon).

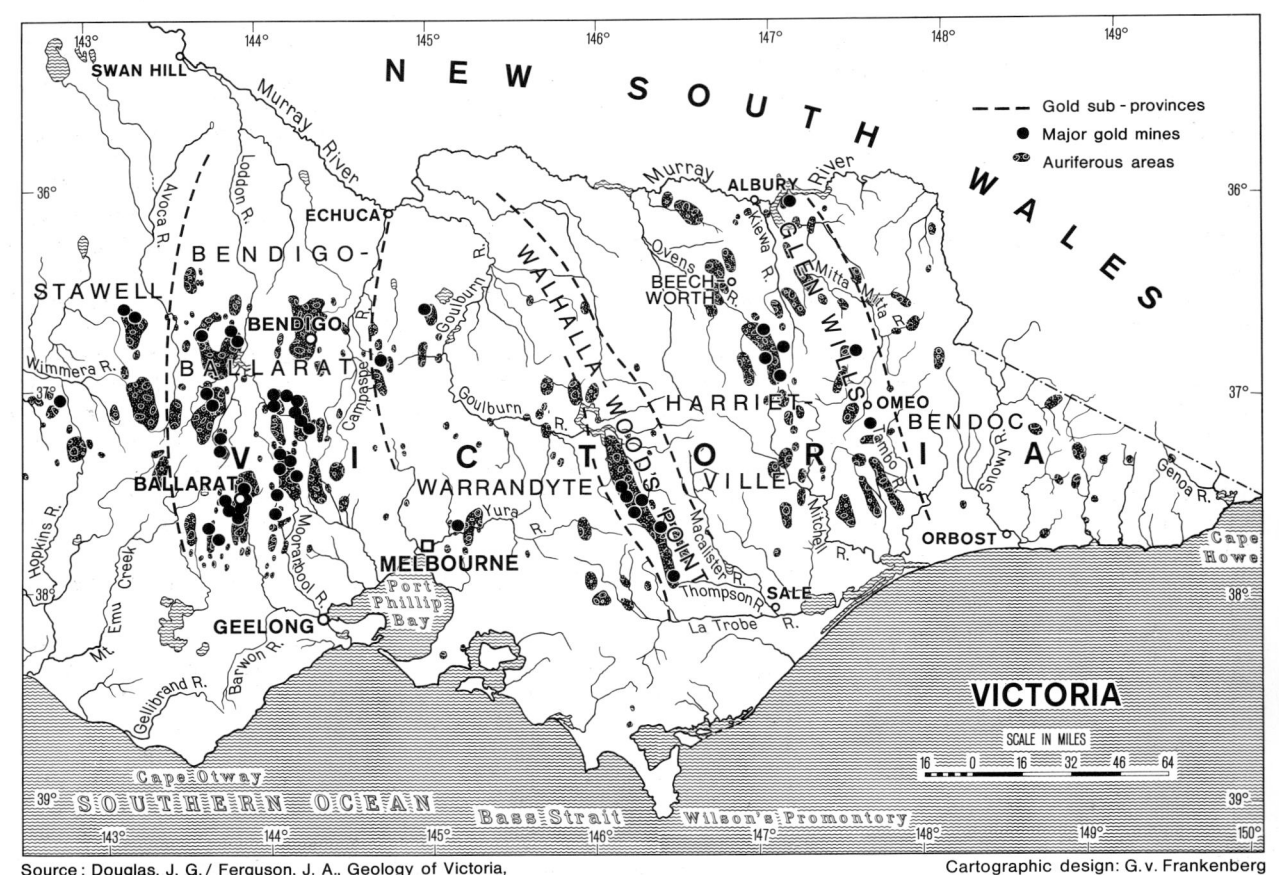

Fig. 18. The Victorian goldfields and gold mining towns

---

2 Pidgin English, from deus = god

The decade 1850–60 was the only period in Victoria's history which ended with Melbourne's share of Victoria's population being reduced to less than 25% and when 42% of the colony's population lived in the gold towns or elsewhere on the diggings. It is estimated that at the end of the year 1859 approximately 24,000 people were living in the Ballarat area, about 17,700 in the Bendigo area, 19,800 in Castlemaine, 32,900 in Maryborough, 13,000 in Ararat and 18,200 in the Ovens Valley; these figures added up to a total population of 125,000 in the goldfields.

Table 13. Population in Victorian gold mining towns

Year	Ballarat	Bendigo	Castlemaine	Maryborough	Maldon***
Dec. 1852*	5,000	23,400			
Dec. 1855*	44,998	12,303	27,173	20,800	
Dec. 1858*	37,894	11,700	28,449	23,922	
1901					3,700
1951**	42,600	32,350	6,130	6,700	
1981**	62,640	52,739	7,584	7,858	1,025

* Adult males on goldfields according to estimates of commissioners and wardens, published in G. Serle: *The golden age. A history of the colony of Victoria 1851–1861*. Carlton 1977, 388
** Dormitory population, Census figures (except Maldon)
*** Author's investigations in Maldon

The figures in table 13 are not strictly compatible but nevertheless give an approximation of the size of settlements at different times and indicate trends. Some of the gold mining towns such as Castlemaine and Maryborough had at the middle of the nineteenth century about four times as many people as a hundred years later; they are also characterized by a very modest increase of population in the last three decades. In Ballarat, however, population figures after the Second World War were equal to those of a century ago, and they have been increasing considerably since, so that the present resident population outnumbers the peak population during the gold-rush days by a fair margin. Bendigo's population in gold-rush days was only about one third of its post-war population and about one fourth of its present population.

Unter the circumstances of the 1850s it was a tremendous problem to supply 125,000 people in the goldfields. Distances of 100–250 km from Melbourne had to be overcome on the roughest of roads cut through the bush. With hardly any agricultural development in the area, it was not surprising that vast areas of range land reaching far into the southwestern sector of the colony of New South Wales were needed to raise enough sheep and cattle for the *meat supply* of the diggers. In this situation river crossings along the Murray River and its tributaries gained strategic importance.

Two of the most famous *river crossings* of those days were at Swan Hill and Echuca. Echuca's development, like that of Moama's on the opposite bank of the Murray River in New South Wales, started with the establishment of a punt-ferry by a former convict in 1853. In the same year the River Murray was opened up, as a consequence of a dramatic competition between two paddle-steamers and their daring captains, for predominance in *steam navigation* on the river. The result was that Echuca became the second port in the colony of Victoria after Melbourne and the most important river port in Australia. A further step in Echuca's development was the opening in 1864 of the *railway* from Melbourne. This made the town an important rail head for a number of years until, after 1900, the Border Railways Agreement between New South Wales and Victoria led to the extension of the railway line from Echuca northward into New South Wales as far as Balranald, using the Victorian broad gauge of 5'3". This made the town an important railway crossing on the Murray River (fig. 19).

At the end of the 1850s Echuca's population had reached the 5,000 mark, a remarkable figure for an inland town at that time. Echuca, including the tiny settlement of Moama on the north bank of the Murray, grew to a population of 9,453 residents by 1981. Swan Hill farther downstream has a population of 8,398. The complete story of Echuca-Moama has been explicitly told by Coulson in her book *Echuca-Moama. Murray River Neighbours* (1979).

What economic functions have made these interior settlements survive and some even grow after the gold mines were closed down and the river trade dwindled under the competition of rail and modern road transport? An insight into this question is provided by an examination of the former gold mining towns of Bendigo, Castlemaine, Maldon and Beechworth and the river towns of Echuca and Swan Hill. *Bendigo*, once called Victoria's 'Quarzopolis' (Cusack 1973), had a population of 52,739 in 1981 and an estimated population of 68,000 in 1985, ranking nineteenth in size among Australia's cities. It is one of the very few old mining towns to succeed in growing to a considerable size in recent years. One factor of Bendigo's continuing growth was the continuation of the earlier mining and manufacturing tradition, as represented by the Golden City Implements Foundry and the former School of Mines (now a division of the College of Advanced Education with some 2,000 students) (fig. 20).

Another favourable circumstance was Bendigo's situation in a hinterland favourable for grazing and various agricultural activities, as a result of which the city has a number of plants engaged in the processing of agricultural products, for example stock yards, food processing, egg packing, or in producing for the hinterland, such as textiles,

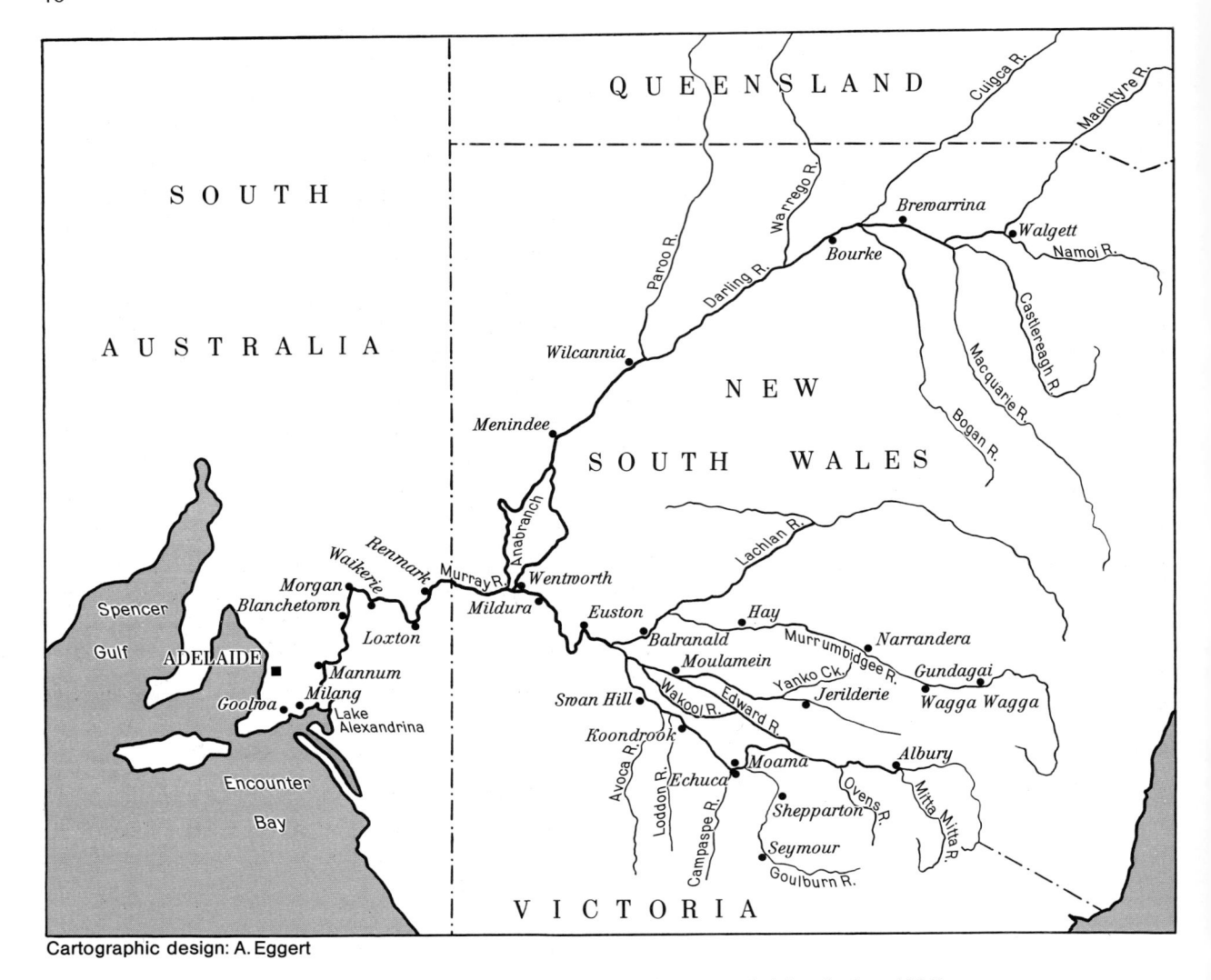

Fig. 19. Main settlements served by paddle-steamers in the Murray-Darling network (after Coulson 1981)

shoes, agricultural machinery or irrigation equipment. Bendigo functions as a regional service centre for a comparatively large hinterland including even a part of New South Wales, involving a total of purchasers probably in excess of 100,000. Bendigo's role as a transportation and communications node is shown by the existence of railway workshops employing some 500 people and by the decision of TELECOM to establish an interregional communications centre in the city.

Due to Bendigo's gaining more and more importance as the dominant centre of the northwest region of the State of Victoria the city has in recent years been able to attract manufacturing plants from Melbourne that had decided to move to some other location within the state. Such relocations have so far, however, been restricted to enterprises in heavy engineering.

Due to Bendigo's strategically favourable location away from the sea coast, yet within rather easy reach from Melbourne, Geelong and Sydney, the Commonwealth Government in 1942 decided to establish a Commonwealth Ordnance Factory in the city. Originally employing some 1,300 persons, the factory now has almost 650 employees. Approximately 40% of output is for national defense purposes and 60% for the private sector. In addition to the School of Mines and the Ordnance Factory the efforts of the State Government to develop Bendigo as the major regional centre of the northwest region are reflected in the employment of over 30% of the total workforce in government institutions.

Though Ballarat can boast approximately three times as many tourists, the Bendigo Trust as well as the Bendigo regional office of the National Trust (Victoria) have been anxious to promote tourism in the city and its environs. Tourist attractions include the city's famous architectural heritage such as the Shamrock Hotel, City Family Hotel, Post Office, Courthouse, Town Hall and School of Mines buildings and the Chinese joss house. The last gold mine,

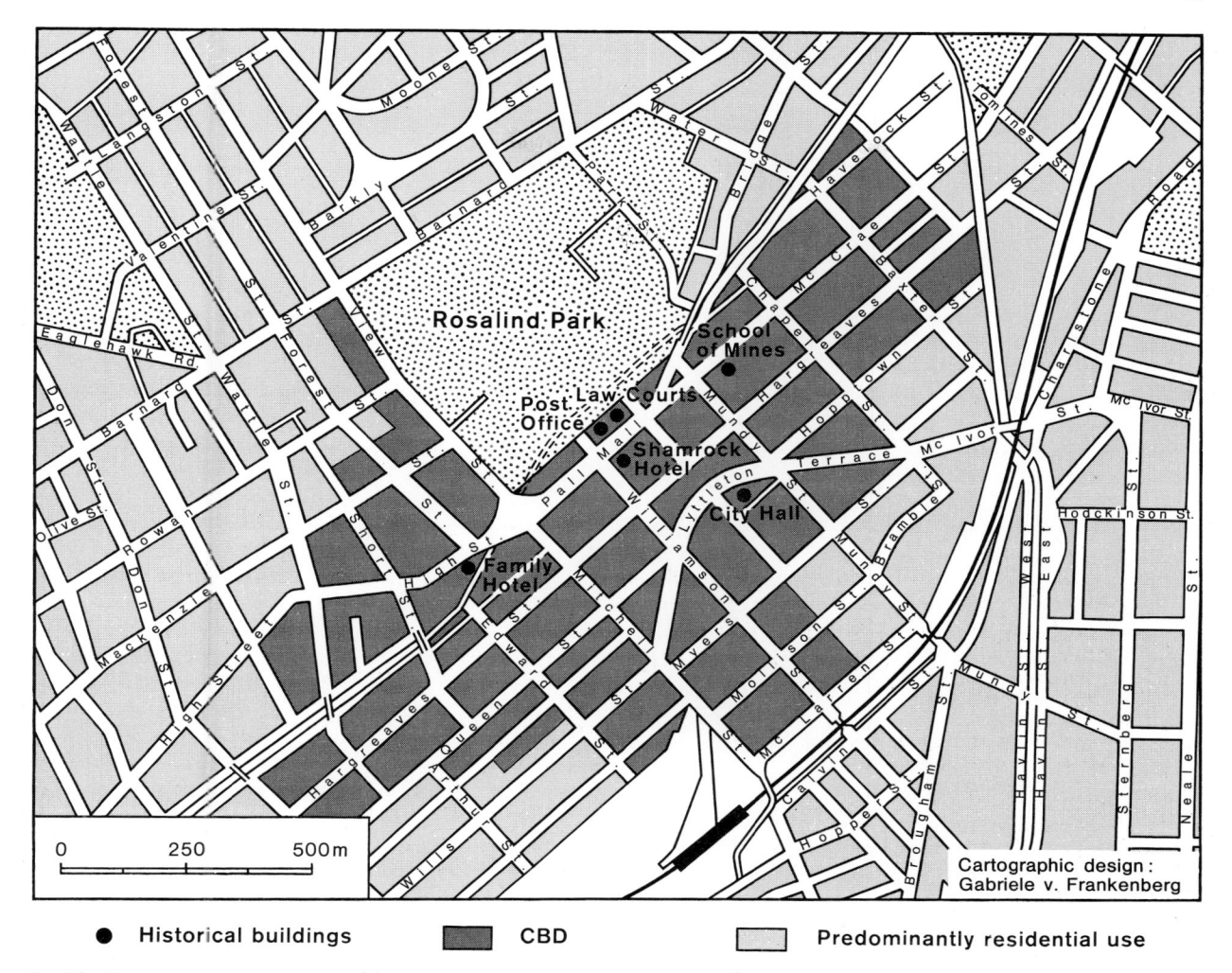

Fig. 20. Business district and historical buildings in Bendigo, Victoria (based on City Engineer's map 1980)

which closed in 1954, has been opened for tourist inspection, and may be reached by means of the 'speaking tram'. The traditional Pottery and two brick kilns and the nearby 'historical town' of Sandhurst are other attractions making for a considerable tourist potential.

In contrast to Bendigo, *Castlemaine*'s economic base is much smaller. The only economic base of any importance for the town and its 7,584 residents (1981) is whatever remains of its manufacturing activities. The once important milling industry has disappeared, as has brewing. Very much to the embarrassment of the local population the renowned Castlemaine beer is now produced at the company's headquarters in Brisbane. The importance of the present manufacturing plants is the foundry, whose products were first used in mining, somewhat later in the construction of the Melbourne-Bendigo-Echuca railway line and in more recent times in irrigation agriculture with the pumping equipment produced in town. Other important branches are the bacon packing plant and wool processing.

Maldon with its very small population of 1,025 (1981) has had to struggle even more for its survival. There are no secondary industries in Maldon, but the little town enjoys other locational advantages. It has to some extent become a dormitory town for nearby Bendigo. Maldon also proved attractive to elderly people who moved here and made the town a place of retirement. Due to this heritage from the goldrush days Maldon has also been able to attract relatively large numbers of tourists. They help to sustain a level of service provision well above needs of the small local population (see ch. 2.2.8).

Beechworth in the northeast region of the State of Victoria with a population of some 3,700 benefits from its tradition as a 'government town'. The town has a considerable number of fine office buildings solidly built of local Beechworth marble. They include the large Prison, still in use today, two houses used as Gold Warden's Offices and now taken over by the Forestry Commission, the former Sub-Treasury now used as a Police Station, the Courthouse, the Electric Telegraph Office building now used by the Lands Office and the Park Office and another three former

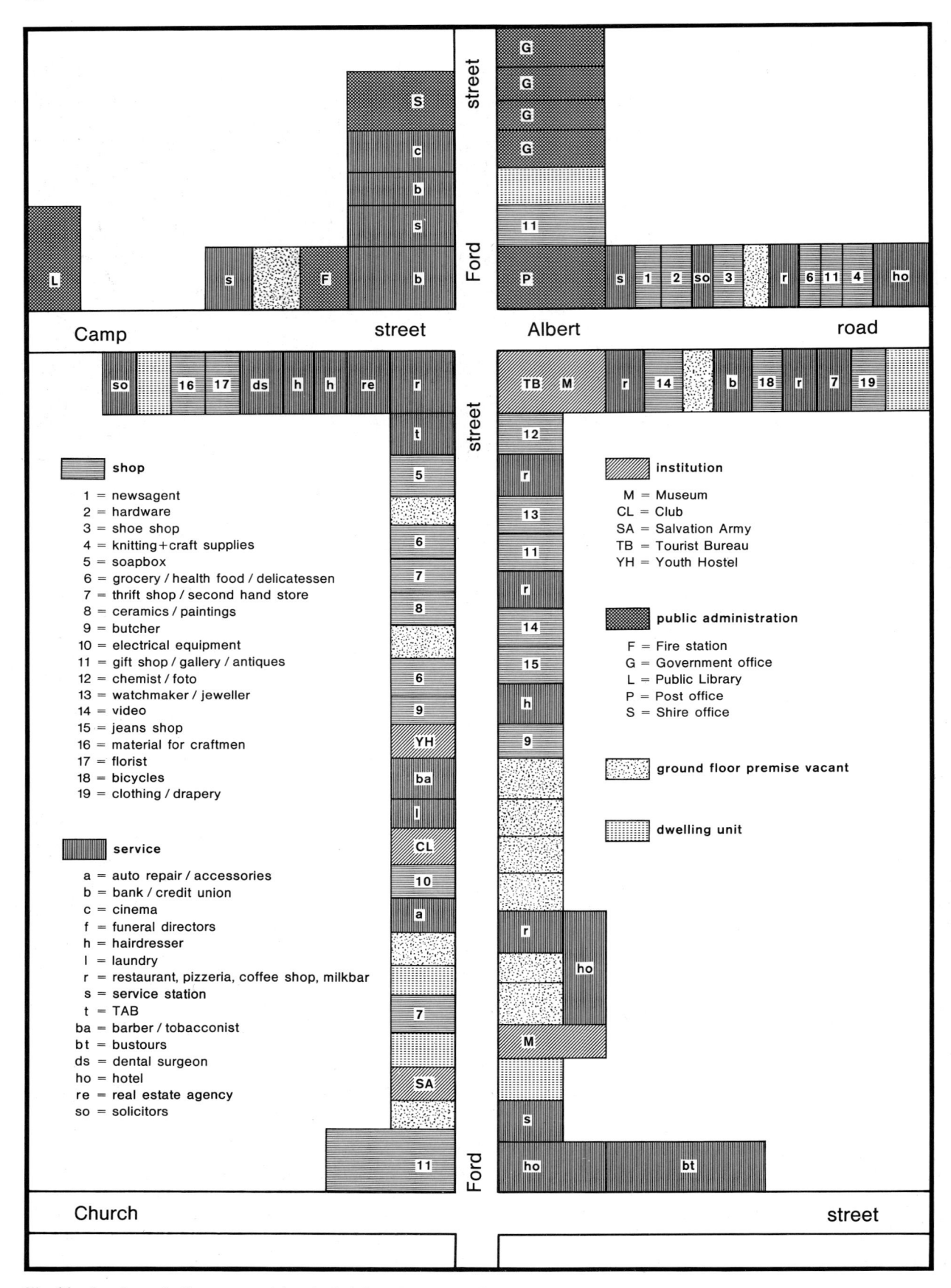

Fig. 21. Land uses in the commercial and administrative centre of Beechworth, Victoria

Fig. 22. Beechworth, Victoria. Chinese burial towers and several hundred graves of Chinese on Beechworth cemetery

Gold Offices at the main intersection now used as Post Office, Museum and Tourist Bureau and a private bank (fig. 21).

These historical buildings and their predominantly public uses point to the major sources of the town's present economic base: public administration and tourism. Beechworth owes its significance to its position as regional administrative centre for the northeastern region of Victoria. In addition to the buildings mentioned above, most of which were classified by the National Trust (ch. 2.2.8), there are such attractions as the famous cemetery with its Chinese burial towers (fig. 22), the scenic drive in Spring Creek Gorge, the recreation area of Lake Sambell that owes its existence to former gold mining activities and, within easy reach by car, the old gold mining town of Yackandanda. One may, however, have doubts whether in the long term this base will be sufficient to keep alive a community of almost 4,000 people.

In contrast to some of the mining towns the former river ports were at no time during their history, including the boom period of paddle-steamer traffic on the Murray-Darling system, larger than they are at present.

Swan Hill with its 8,398 residents (1981) relies on four sources for its economic base. The most important source is tourism. The town has nine motels (980 beds), three hotels (102 beds) and three caravan parks (400 units). The average annual occupation rate is 75%. Pioneer Settlement, a great amusement park depicting the local heritage of the goldrush days in its displays and attractions, and the river cruises on the River Murray by means of old paddle-steamers, are the two major tourist attractions. In the small CBD there are numerous restaurants, takeaways and fast-food shops. Swan Hill functions as a regional service centre for some 40,000 people with large modern supermarkets, a shopping arcade centrally located within the CBD, and a variety of specialty shops. Swan Hill also has a large district hospital. Adjacent to the CBD on its north side there is a large area reserved for light manufacturing and wholesale businesses, among others producers of trailers, of farm machinery and of cement. The processing and trade of agricultural products is geared to the hinterland's agricultural production. A shop for farm implements and an agricultural co-operative are found in the CBD (fig. 23).

Echuca (1981: 9,453) was much more important for the river trade on the Murray than was Swan Hill. Its present economic base relies on three sources. Echuca functions as a regional service centre, with a population in its catchment area more or less equal to that of Swan Hill. The main shopping area developed outside the historical core along Hare Street, whereas the central part of High Street in the old historic core retains only low-ranking functions such as car repair and accessories, second-hand shops for furniture and textiles and the like.

In Echuca much more of the old building stock has been preserved than in Swan Hill. The historical core including the port area was classified by the National Trust (Victoria) as a historic district (fig. 24). Especially after the motion picture 'All the rivers run' had been produced in Echuca the number of visitors rose from about 43,000 in 1975 to over 100,000 in 1985. There are now five antique shops and 12 gift shops partly including antiques and galleries in town. Diversified light industries concentrated on a large municipal industrial estate to the southeast of the town centre include food processing plants such as the Danish-owned Plumrose Company and the French dairy plant Yoplait, the Tisdale Winery and the municipal stock yards, a branch of Tasman Timber Products. Other plants

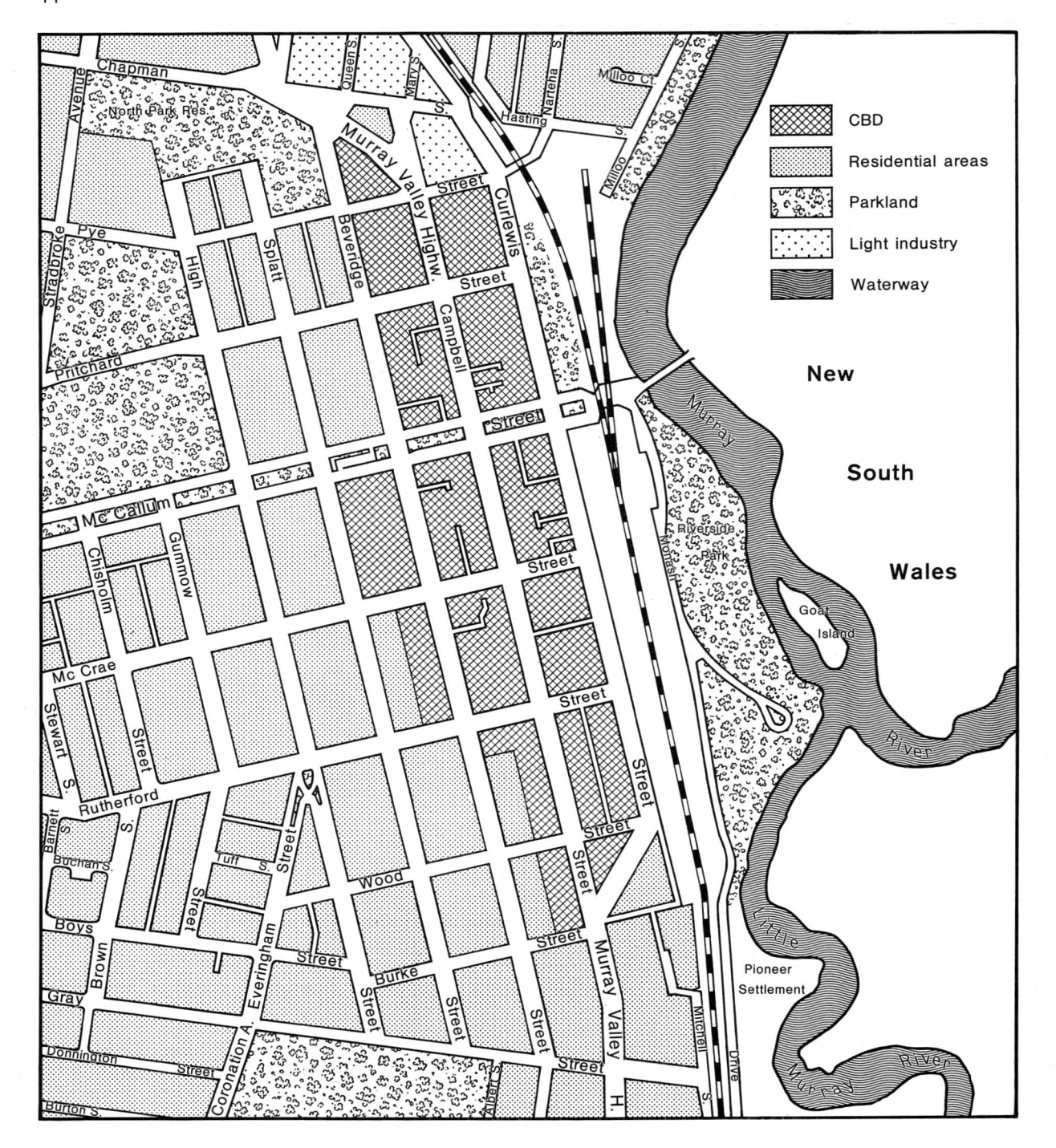

Fig. 23. Land uses in the commercial and administrative centre of Swan Hill, Victoria (Source: City of Swan Hill, Planning Scheme 1981) Catographic design: O. Hoffmann, 1986

include textiles, concrete parts, a water tank producer and a variety of smaller retailers and repair shops especially in the automobile business.

In conclusion it can be said that the success or failure in the survival of older settlements established in the nineteenth century as mining towns and river ports depended on a range of factors. Of prime significance was the degree to which manufacturing survived from the earlier mining stage. The ability of the hinterland to sustain a sizable agricultural production was also important, as was the presence of sufficient purchasing power in the region

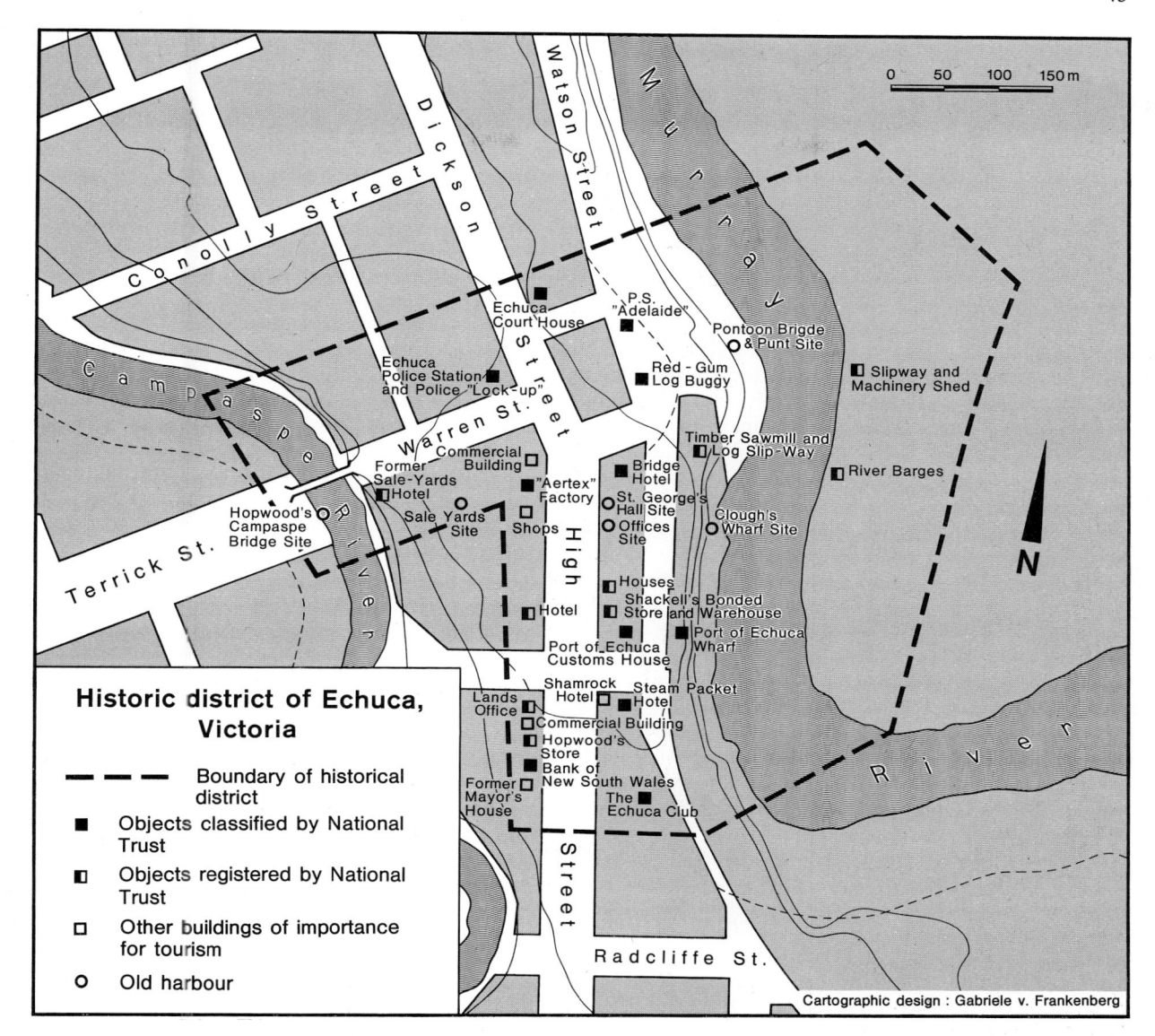

Fig. 24. Historic district of Echuca, Victoria (classified and registered buildings after National Trust of Australia, Victoria)

to secure the town's position as a service centre. A town would also benefit where rail lines were constructed so as to make it an important rail head or transportation node, or where government plans favoured the development of a regional administrative centre. Historic buildings and other attractions are also important in promoting modern tourism.

2.2.4 The parkland towns on South Australia's frontier

When by the early 1860s colonization had advanced from the Adelaide Plains to the area north of Clare and to the top of Yorke Peninsula the process suddenly came to a halt. The pastoralists who had been living in the area for over a decade were not willing to retreat before the advancing farmers' frontier but rather outbid their competitors at the land auctions. Settlers could not get enough land and existing settlers could not expand their holdings. It was this lack of land rather than the drought and wheat diseases that stopped agricultural settlement in South Australia (Williams 1974). The Scrub Lands Act of 1866 for opening up the dry sandy plain to the west and east, covered with dense mallee, was of very limited success, and the depression of the season 1867–68 induced the South Australian Government to changes in land legislation.

There were, in fact, several reasons for the government's changing land policy. It is true that rural settlement in this colony had virtually ceased. A second reason, however, was the government's desire for systematic settlement and for the provision of schools, churches and other services in the rural districts of the colony. A third factor was the growing competition of the neighbouring Wimmera district of Victoria as well as from the wheat production of the Sacramento Valley in the wake of the Californian goldrush. Last but not least the government needed money for its public works programme and did not want to leave profits of land sales to private enterprise.

It was against this background that the *Waste Lands Amendment Act* (Strangways Act) was passed in 1869 with the aim of opening up new 'agricultural areas'. The land was no longer leased to pastoralists but instead sold by the government to settlers under changed conditions. Instead of the old system of purchasing 80-acre lots for cash the new law allowed blocks of land of up to 320 acres to be bought on credit merely by making a down payment of 20%. These conditions were further eased in 1872, when the deposit required was reduced to only 10%, and at the same time the credit was extended to six years instead of four years, and the measures taken against pastoralists and land speculators became more effective (Williams 1974). This development was accompanied by the establishment of new ports along the coast and the extension of railway lines.

Much of this development took place under Governor Sir James Fergusson, 6th Baronet of Kilkerran in Scotland. His family gave the names to a number of parkland towns. For example Maitland was named for the 2nd Baronet's wife, Lady Jean Maitland, and the little port town of Edithburg was named for the governor's own wife. The western and eastern perimeter streets of Maitland were called Maitland Terrace and Kilkerran Terrace (Heinrich 1972).

According to earlier legislation dating back to the year 1836 the land was surveyed in so-called *Hundreds*, this being the second administrative level below the county in the survey hierarchy. A Hundred was supposed to be 100 square miles (259 km^2) in size, although there were deviations from the standard size up to 120 square miles (311 km^2). Williams (1974, 74) points out that the origin of the Hundred is obscure, 'but it probably lay in the promise of commonage at the rate of 2 square miles for every 80-acre section purchased'.

It was part of the land policy of the epoch that *a township be laid out within each Hundred.* There had been quite a few townships, government as well as private townships, laid out in previous periods of settlement in the colony of South Australia, but never before plans had been followed with equal rigidity. As a consequence of this practice a network of more or less evenly spaced towns arose in those parts of the colony developed after 1869. Since the rule of establishing at least one township in each Hundred became effective, two-thirds of 196 Hundreds surveyed in the period after 1869 had an average distance between pairs of local service centres of between 16 km and 20 km, while the average distance to town for most settlers of this vast area of land was between 8 km and 10 km.

Not all townships were centrally located in their respective Hundred. In some cases there was even competition between a private township and a government township established nearby. In some cases two townships were placed within one Hundred, for example a port at the coast and an interior town, two ports at different locations along the coastline, or a new railway town where the railway line had bypassed an existing township, or a township on each extremity of a Hundred. For further details the reader is referred to Meinig (1963, 166–201).

The selection of a site for the townships was not always carried out with due care. Inadequate drainage or liability to floods due to the flatness of the site or proximity to a river or a bay of Gulf St. Vincent or Spencer Gulf rendered a number of new townships more or less unsuitable for settlement. This was not the only disadvantage of many of the parkland towns.

A characteristic town plan was rather rigidly adhered to, giving the towns of this epoch a stereotype layout, creating 'little Adelaides'. Colonel Light's plan for the City of Adelaide (ch. 3.1.3) was repeated approximately 250 times from the layout of the first parkland town of Adelaide in 1836 until about 1930, when this type of town design was finally abandoned. The basic idea of the parkland town design was to create a central 'town land' urban area, surrounded by parklands that in turn were surrounded by suburban land. Each of these zones was to be surrounded by a perimeter road, while a number of other roads radiating outwards from the town-land perimeter road lead in various directions to neighbouring towns. The plan of the City of Adelaide was even copied to the degree that the various parts of the town-land perimeter road were called 'Terrace'.

Not all the townships surveyed after 1869 were endowed with parklands. Some townships had none and some others only partial parklands on one or two sides, but the great majority were endowed with full parklands, so that this type of town really deserves the name 'parkland town'. The numbers of towns in the various categories are shown in table 14 (fig. 25).

As is apparent from table 14, 249 of South Australia's 370 towns established since the foundation of Adelaide in 1836 were endowed with parklands, 211 of them had full parklands, 38 had partial parklands, 209 were surveyed after 1869.

There was, however, a wide range in the size of the parkland towns and the proportions of their three constituent parts; there was also a number of local deviations from the prototype. A number of parkland towns had a surprising-

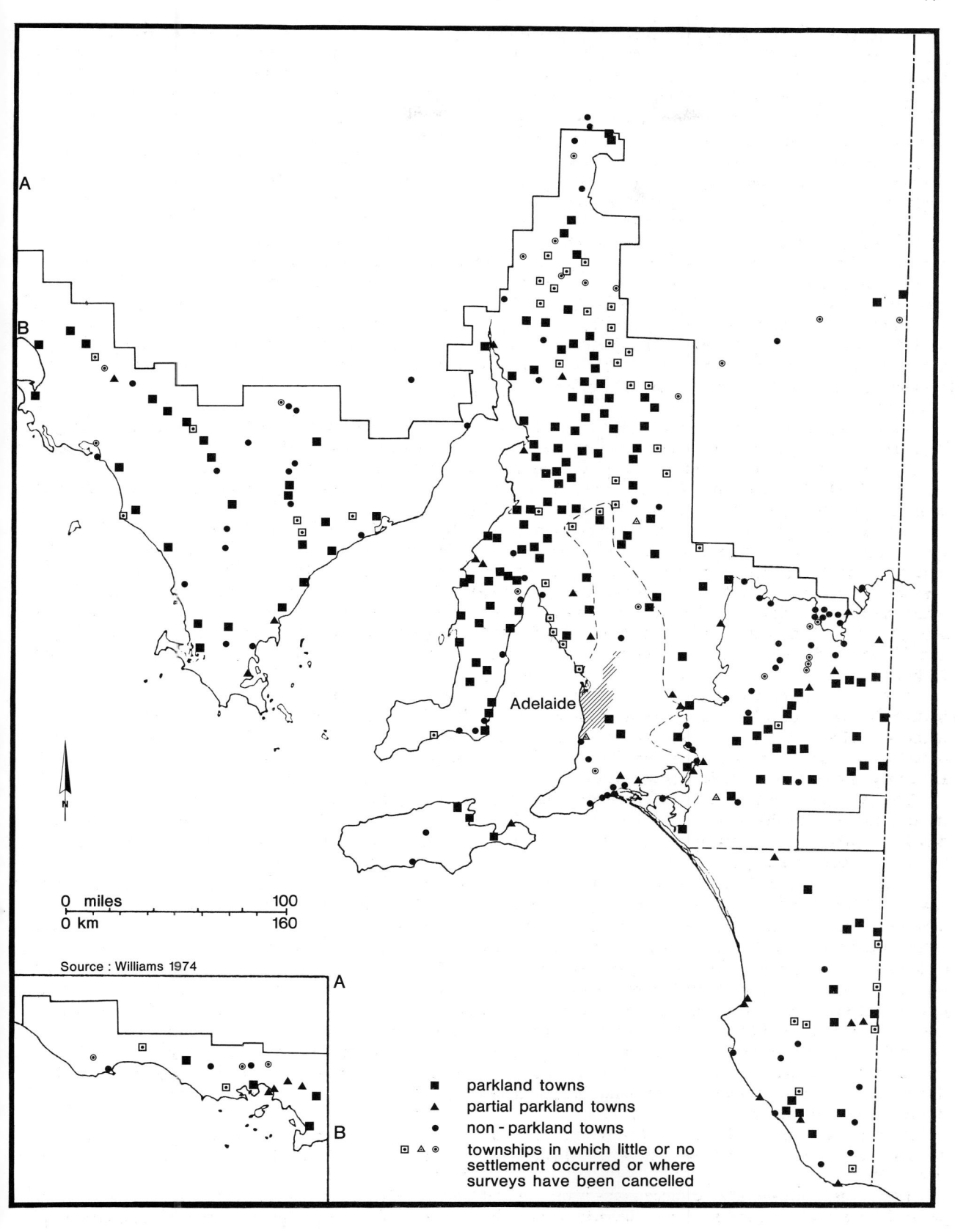

Fig. 25. The distribution of parkland, partial parkland and non-parkland towns in South Australia (after Williams 1977)

Table 14. Parklands in South Australian government townships

Date	Central region			Northern region			Southeast region			Eyre Peninsula			Murray Mallee			Out of Hundreds			Total
	NP	PP	FP	NP	PP	FP	NP	PP	FP	NP	PP	FP	NP	PP	FP	NP	PP	FP	
1836–64	7	3	4	8	5	5	4	3	2	1	1	–	–	–	–	2	–	–	45
1865–69	–	1	4	–	–	9	1	–	1	–	–	2	–	–	–	–	–	–	18
1870–79	3	–	2	5	4	66	–	3	8	–	–	6	–	–	1	2	–	1	101
after 1879	5	2	4	10	2	30	4	2	7	25	6	29	34	5	26	10	1	4	206
Total	15	6	14	23	11	110	9	8	18	26	7	37	34	5	27	14	1	5	370

NP = no parklands, PP = partial parklands, FP = full parklands
Source: Williams 1974, 362

ly large size, some of them being between 600 hectares and 800 hectares. *Maitland*, laid out in 1872 in the heart of Yorke Peninsula was 'a rather rare example of almost perfect geometric symmetry' (Meinig 1963, 175; fig. 26). Its plan made for town lands of four by four blocks totalling 101 acres, 129 acres of parkland and 580 acres of suburban land. The geometrical design was underlined by the network of ten roads radiating from the town: a diagonal from each of the four corners of the parklands, two roads in prolongation of the east-west axis, and a Y with two roads leading into northerly directions and another Y with two roads leading into southerly directions.

Carrieton with town lands of almost equal size (102 acres) had a suburban area of 2,864 acres, while Dawlish with town lands of only 71 acres had suburban lands of 882 acres. Meinig suggests that the explanation for such disproportions as well as for the enormous size of a number of townships was the government's wish to make as much money as possible from the auction of township lots (Meinig 1963).

As to the *town lands*, there is a certain range in the number of blocks. The port town of Pickering is a half-parkland town with a centre of 5 x 3 blocks (15 blocks) whereas Dawson with its 6 x 6 blocks (36 blocks) had the largest centre of all parkland towns. Deviations from the regular pattern are found, among others, in Jamestown where the town centre is cut into two parts by the Bebalie Creek, thus making for a great distortion of the street grid especially in the eastern half, and in Snowtown, where a whole row of blocks is lacking due to the railway line leading right into the centre of town. There are also variations in the division of the central blocks of the town lands.

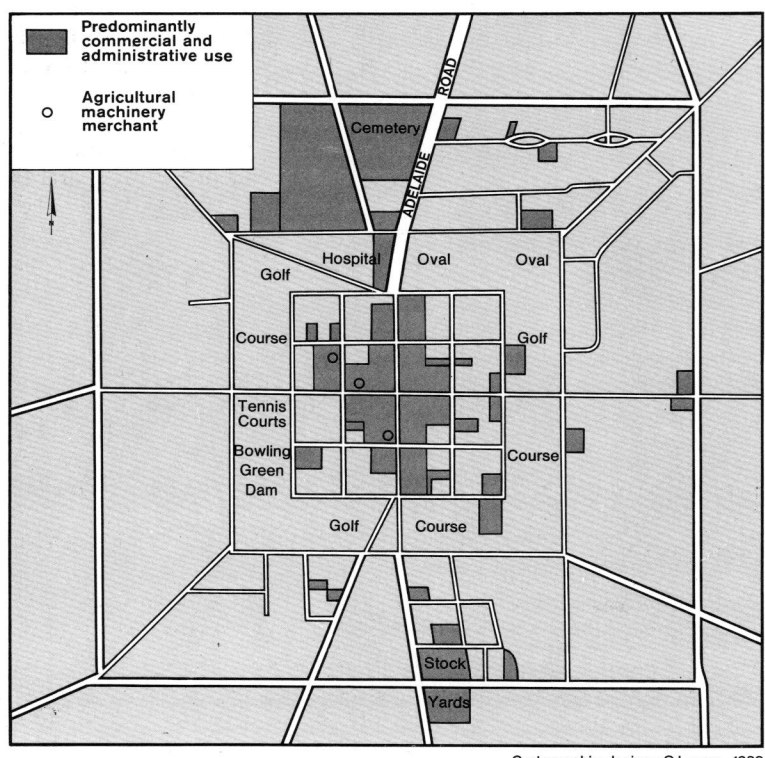

Fig. 26. Land uses in Maitland, S.A., 1985 (according to public information board)

Moonta, for example, had rectangular blocks each of which was equally divided in 2 x 7 = 14 lots. In Maitland the squares were subdivided in different ways, the blocks bordering the main street having smaller lots than those farther away from the centre. The width of streets also varies. In Maitland the streets in the town lands were laid out with a width of at least 30 m. Perhaps these streets were designed to serve a bustling business district, but in reality most of them are streets serving a residential district; service functions were restricted to a few centrally located blocks within the town lands.

This is evidence for the fact that the development of many of the parkland towns did not match up to expectations. In 1881 only Moonta had a population of 1,418 due to its function as a copper mining town. Next was Jamestown with 995 residents. The majority of the parkland towns had fewer than 300 residents. By 1882 self-government had only been granted to a small number of port towns and mining towns, one of the latter being Moonta, and to the two agricultural service centres of Jamestown and Yorketown. Obviously the carrying capacity of the country had been highly overestimated. Many of the parkland towns had been laid out on a scale appropriate to a resident population of 20,000. In a city of that size the centrally located town lands would probably have been completely used for business functions. while the residential function would have been assigned to the suburban land beyond the parklands. In reality, however, the *residential function* has become the *major land use of the town lands*.

The public and commercial uses of the town lands developed according to the varying success of each individual town. In general, these towns were endowed with a post office, a school and one or two churches. Usually they also acquired a hotel, a boarding house, a general store, a bootmaker's shop, a saddler's shop, some banking service and a so-called Institute serving the community as a library, a lecture room and a meeting hall. Some towns had a brewery, a flour mill and one or two foundries making agricultural implements.

The few present-day public and commercial functions of the parkland towns have until recently been restricted to a small part of the town centre, for instance in Maitland to the houses around the main intersection, in Moonta to the southeastern quadrant of the town lands. Retail functions are so few that none of the department store chains is represented in the business centre; many purchases by local residents are carried out through local agents of firms having their headquarters in the capital city. Some purchases will be carried out by mail order (see ch. 2.3.2). Also the service functions are so few that the post office performs a number of duties for various government agencies as well as for banking institutions. In Maitland in 1984 there were three dealers of tractors and agricultural machinery (activities normally relegated to the urban-rural fringe) within two blocks of the main intersection! There was a conspicuous number of houses for sale, evidence of further recession in the town centre.

Alienation of the parklands has been a crucial question in the development of the parkland towns. As has been pointed out, people usually felt that for the sake of convenience they should have both their businesses and their residences in the central town lands. The parklands were considered a barrier, and there was very little desire on the part of the town people to have their residences far beyond that parkland barrier in the suburban lands. On the other hand, the parklands were favourably located adjacent to the town centre, a location comparable with the valuable sites derived from land that had become available in many old European towns by dismantling their fortifications. There has understandably been a certain temptation to put these parklands to some use other than recreation.

Special legislation and the arrangement of the town corporation and of the Crown Lands Office were necessary to authorize the local administration to change the use of parts of the parklands and to erect buildings on them. This problem will be discussed in more detail in the chapter on Adelaide (ch. 3.1.3), for in the case of South Australia's capital city very extensive use has been made of the parklands, particularly on the north side of the city. In the small towns on the wheat frontier the parklands have usually been alienated on one side only and for very specific purposes. In Maitland the northern portion of the parklands was used for a hospital, a sports ground and the municipal show grounds. In Jamestown the railway station was constructed on the northern parklands, and in Snowtown the railway line cuts through their southern section. In Minlaton the northeastern part of the parklands is used as a game reserve, this use certainly coming closer to the purpose for which the parklands had originally been set aside.

Due to the reluctant growth and to recent population decreases the *suburban lands* in many parkland towns have never been used as residential areas to any extent. Even in Maitland residential quarters beyond the parklands have only been developed in the northeastern section and to a still smaller extent in the south. Thus a high percentage of suburban lands has never been claimed for the purpose for which they had been set aside. Much of this land was resurveyed at a later date and sold to farmers of the surrounding countryside, thus becoming part of the agricultural land whose owners were supposed to be served by the parkland towns.

For obvious reasons the establishment of such a great number of townships and the repetition of a rather rigid town-planning design have, to a certain degree, been a failure. Meinig in his monograph on the South Australian wheat frontier discussed the problems of the parkland towns in detail and elaborated on the consequences and critical issues of this settlement policy. Following his argument (Meinig 1963, 166–201) it may be concluded that the spacing and the size of the parkland towns were adapted to maximizing revenues accruing to the government from the auctions of township lots rather than to providing a rational system of service centres for a sparsely populated countryside with limited agricultural carrying capacity. As has been noted, many of the suburban lots remained unsold and were resurveyed into farm sections. In addition, the site selections for the parkland towns often did not take into account drainage and other problems, while the rigid layout did not take into account difficulties caused by local terrain.

In fact, the parkland town design was not really appropriate for small service centres in rural areas. '... to impress the image of Adelaide upon a hundred sites across the countryside was to clothe hamlets grotesquely in metropolitan dress ... In short, the whole township scheme, its basic elements, standardized patterns, gradations of lot size, and over-all scale was a metropolitan complex transplanted into a country setting and therefore could not possibly achieve the desired results' (Meinig 1963, 187–89). In consequence, a considerable number of these small urban places remained on a level below 1,000 residents having only very poor services, this in turn making them rather unattractive and prone to further population losses.

2.2.5 The ports of Queensland

As mentioned in chapter 2.2.1 the first white settlement in what was in 1859 to become the self-governing colony of Queensland was the penal settlement at Moreton Bay (Brisbane). It was abandoned in 1842 to become a free settlement.

In contrast to all the other colonies with the exception of Tasmania settlement in Queensland has never been highly centralized (ch. 2.3.1). Apart from the very excentric location of the capital city in the southeastern corner of the state the peculiar urban development strang out along a coast of more than 1,000 km. This is mainly due to two economic factors: the possibilities of tropical agriculture in various parts of the coastal plains and the rich and varified mineral deposits in the hinterlands of a number of smaller port towns (Hoyle & Hilling 1984, Bird 1986). Queensland's coastline is about twice as long as that of New South Wales and, in contrast to the equally long coastline of Western Australia, the coastal plain is more fertile and the interior less harsh (fig. 27).

Coal mining in Queensland began as early as 1846. Deposits were found in the immediate hinterland of Brisbane (Ipswich Basin) and in that of Bundaberg, while much larger deposits are to be found farther inland from the latitude of Brisbane (Moreton Basin) and that of Bundaberg (Surat Basin) to that of Gladstone-Rockhampton-Mackay (Bowen and Galilee Basins). These coal deposits promoted the growth of mining towns and of port towns alike.

In recent years many small steaming-coal fields have been closed whereas new large-scale projects for the mining of coking coal have led to a rapid growth of Queensland's coal production and export since the mid-1960s. Out of a total of 120.5 million tons of coal production in Australia in 1983, 66.1 million tons were produced in New South Wales and 48.6 million tons in Queensland. Total Queensland coal production which, in contrast to that of New South Wales, is mainly derived from open-cut mines, has increased rapidly, having been only 13.2 million tons in 1970 (Austr. Coal Year Book 1984–85). Due to production increases in these two states Australia had by 1984 advanced to be the world's greatest coal-exporting country.

Many other mineral deposits have been exploited in Queensland over the last 150 years. Gold was found around 1860, with mining mainly concentrated in the hinterlands of Gladstone, Mackay and Townsville. The former city became especially famous for the great gold deposits of Mount Morgan, where exploitation started in 1882. Prior to the development of mining Central Queensland, centred on Rockhampton, was economically dependent upon pastoral produce. The ports along the Queensland coast also grew through exports of minerals derived from far away in the interior. The lead and copper production of the Mount Isa mines, for example, is exported by way of Townsville, the products being hauled there over a distance of some 900 km.

The second factor promoting urban growth has been *agriculture*. The earliest use of considerable parts of the interior was *cattle grazing*. Queensland is the Australian state with the largest number of cattle; the sale of cattle for slaughtering ranks first in agricultural production ($ 768.36 million in the financial year 1978–79), followed by sugar cane cut for crushing ($ 376.98 million), and wheat ($ 248.66 million). Early export products were hides and tallow, in addition to the wool from sheep raising. The largest export meatworks today are found in the port cities of Cairns, Townsville, Mackay and Rockhampton.

The other important agricultural product has been *sugar cane*. Sugar cane was first grown in Queensland in 1862. Two years later the first commercial production of sugar and molasses took place at Ormiston near Cleveland. Sugar cane growing is very much confined to areas of high rainfall and warm temperatures as well as appropriate soil conditions, mainly provided by river alluvium. Thus the 6,105 rural holdings growing sugar cane on 237,680 hectares of land in 1978 are distributed over a considerable length of the Queensland littoral from Mossman in the north to Beenleigh in the south, with concentrations in the environs of Mossman, Cairns, Innisfail, Ingham, Ayr-Home Hill, Mackay, Bundaberg, Maryborough, Nambour and Beenleigh. The major locations of sugar refineries and sugar terminals are in the port cities of Cairns, Townsville, Mackay and Bundaberg. During the early 1980s sugar exports dropped, however, sharply due to high production costs and decreasing international competitiveness.

In the second half of the nineteenth century considerable numbers of Pacific Islanders, Italians and Chinese were employed in the cane-growing areas as cane cutters. In later years the latter moved to coastal towns such as Mackay, Townsville and Cairns, where their descendents can still be identified as an ethnic minority, in part clustered in particular residential areas (see ch. 4.2.1). The Italians, on the other hand, have to a large extent remained in Queensland's rural areas, in contrast to the position in all the other states of the Commonwealth of Australia, where a much higher percentage of the Italian migrants live in urban places. The fishing industry further adds to the im-

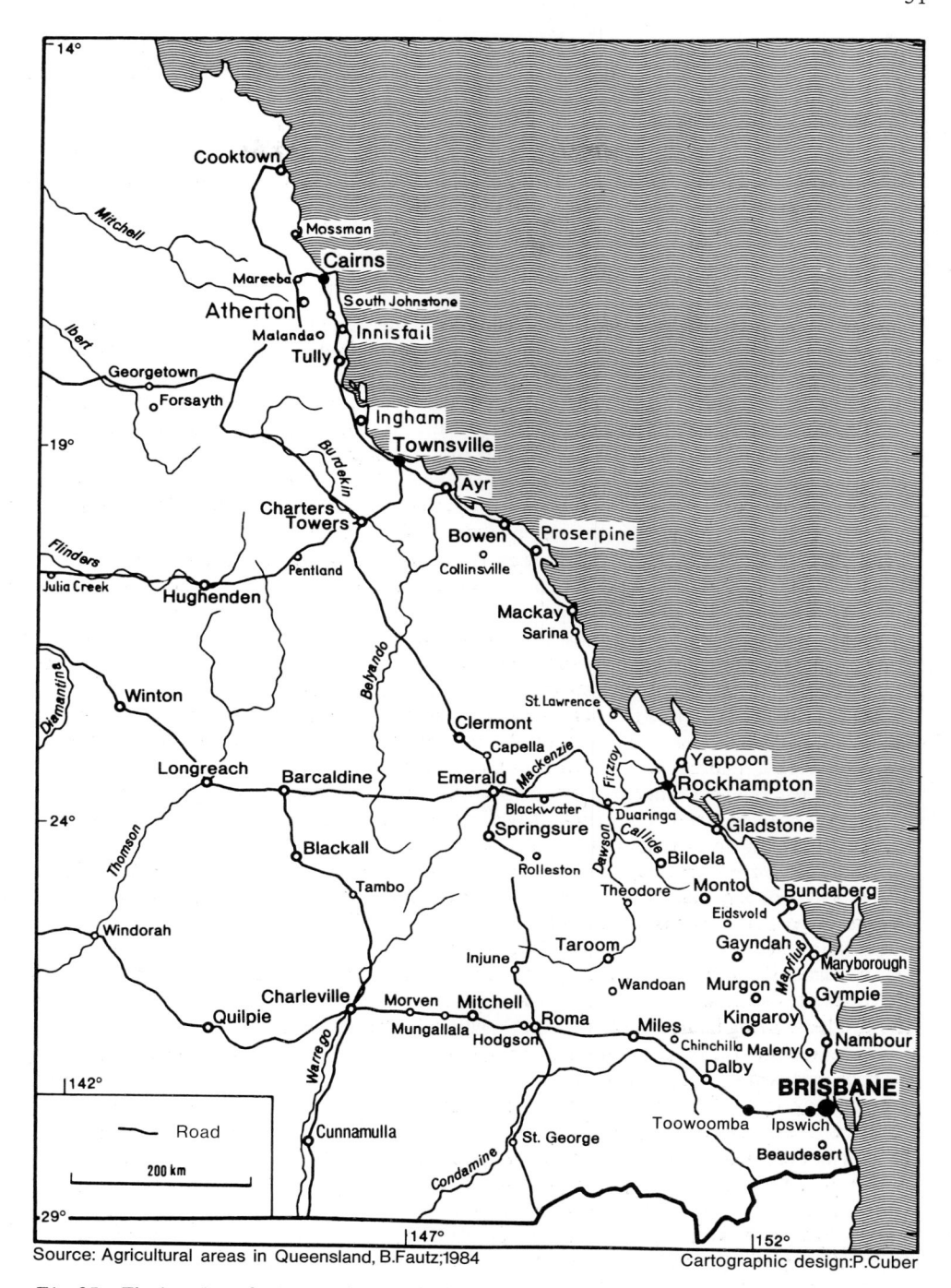

Fig. 27. The location of urban settlements in Queensland

portance of some of Queensland's ports, having contributed particularly to the growth of Cairns (marlins), Rockhampton (molluscs) and Bundaberg (molluscs).

Brisbane has never lost its predominance among Queensland's port cities. The changing fortunes of the other members of the group are well reflected in table 15 (s. page 52).

It is apparent from table 15 that Rockhampton lost its second rank to Townsville after the 1880s. Cairns and Bundaberg entered the list of the six leading ports in the period 1900–19 and Gladstone in the period 1920–39.

Since the end of World War II some of the towns have assumed still more functions so that the traditional trend of decentralization in Queensland has continued. In Gladstone the Queensland Alumina Ltd. in 1967 opened the world's largest alumina plant, processing bauxite from Weipa on the Gulf of Carpentaria. Rockhampton became the

Table 15. First six trading ports of Queensland, 1860–1939 (Totals for respective period in £ '000)

1860–1884		1900–1919		1920–1939	
Brisbane	73,543	Brisbane	216,500	Brisbane	447,900
Rockhampton	20,048	Townsville	49,900	Townsville	52,700
Townsville	10,587	Rockhampton	33,600	Rockhampton	23,000
Maryborough	9,094	Cairns	12,100	Cairns	21,100
Cooktown	5,854	Bundaberg	4,900	Gladstone	19,000
Mackay	2,049	Mackay	3,000	Mackay	12,600

Source: Lewis 1973, 272–74

administrative centre for the central Queensland coast region. Townsville was chosen the site of an electrolytic copper refinery, established in 1959, and of a nickel processing plant, cement works and workshops of the Queensland Government Railways. This development involved the creation of a whole suburb called Railway Estate, located between Ross Creek and Ross River.

Townsville with its 86,106 residents (1981) is, after Brisbane and the City of the Gold Coast (ch. 3.2), Queensland's third largest city, holding rank 12 in the rank-size order of Australian urban places. It was originally called Castleton but was in 1866 re-named after Robert Towns, owner of a company which operated several pastoral stations to the west of town. Today the city is the administrative centre of northern Queensland, with approximately 84% of all its employment in the tertiary sector. This position is underlined by the establishment of James Cook University of Northern Queensland. In the early 1980s Townsville's airport, which developed from World War II Garbutt airfield of the R.A.A.F., advanced to be the second international airport of the state of Queensland following Brisbane.

Just like Darwin after the disaster of Cyclone Tracy, Townsville is an exception to normal urban development in Australia inasmuch as it was in 1971 also struck by a tropical cyclone. The central area, between Ross Creek with its harbour facilities and Castle Hill rising behind Townsville's CBD, suffered especially severe damage. In consequence of the destructions of the 1971 cyclone considerable changes have taken place in the central area. In the course of reconstruction Flinders Street was converted to a shopping mall. At the corner of Flinders and Stokes Streets the tower of the Townsville International Hotel was erected, its nickname being the 'sugar shaker' because of its peculiar shape symbolizing the economic importance of sugar for the area and for the port. The area adjacent to Flinders Mall between Flinders and Walker Streets was reconstructed by the erection of modern office buildings on comparatively large lots; these widely spaced buildings contrast markedly with the urban texture of the undamaged part of the old city core (fig. 28).

Another peculiarity of Townsville is the nomenclature of its inner suburban areas; South Townsville is actually located on the eastern bank of Ross Creek, the West End is found on the south side of Castle Hill and North Ward is located to the west of the central city. Apparently the early settlers had similar difficulties with regard to orientation to those of Montreal, Canada.

In post-industrial society tourism has become an important factor of development for the settlements along the Queensland coast. Apart from the Gold Coast and the Sunshine Coast many of them serve as gateways to island holiday resorts based on the attractions of the Great Barrier Reef. At present more than 10% of Queensland's workforce are in tourism, the greatest number being employed in the coastal region including the islands.

2.2.6 The sawmill towns of Western Australia's southwest

The southwestern part of Western Australia, west of a line from Northam to Albany is, from the point of view of natural vegetation, one of Australia's most valuable forest regions. Most prominent are four species of *eucalyptus* each of which is dominant in one of four ecological subregions.

The Jarrah forest subregion is by far the largest, with more than 1.5 million hectares. It stretches from beyond Wanneroo in the north to Margaret River in the southwest and Albany in the southeast, and is covered with pure stands of Jarrah (*eucalyptus marginata*), with an occasional mixture of other species of minor importance. The Jarrah forest is roughly bounded by the 900 mm isohyet on the wet side and by the 600 mm isohyet on the dry side.

The Karri (*eucalyptus diversicolor*) is restricted to a comparatively small area of some 140,000 hectares receiving more than 1,100 mm of precipitation annually to the south of the Jarrah forest between Manjimup and Nannup to the northwest and Walpole and Denmark to the southeast. To the east, between the 600 mm and 300 mm isohyets, is the Wandoo Zone characterized by the shrubby type of Wandoo (*eucalyptus wandoo*). The Tuart (*eucalyptus gomphocephala*) is restricted to a narrow strip of limestone formations of the Spearwood dune system from Guilderton to just north of Busselton at Geographe Bay. This is a strip of land about 240 km long and between 10 km and 20 km wide.

With regard to European settlement of Western Australia mention must be made of the establishment of Albany

Fig. 28. Townsville, Qld. Waterfront with the modern Townsville International Hotel, the so-called 'sugar shaker'

on the south coast in 1826 by a military expedition sent from New South Wales. Albany became a whaling station which was in operation until the first decade after World War II. Perth and Fremantle were founded in 1829, and from there the first settlers soon crossed the Darling Range in search for agricultural land, founding in 1831 the town of York in the Avon Valley.

It was timber, however, that gave the Swan River Colony its first great impetus for development. The first sawmill started its operation in 1833, and ever since Jarrah and Karri have been logged and utilized by the sawmills to a great extent. In more recent years other kinds of timber have also become important, among others Red Gum or Marri (*eucalyptus calophylla*) and planted pines (*pinus radiata, p. pinaster*).

During the first decades of white settlement the region experienced a very slow growth, mainly due to the heavy manual labour involved in cutting the huge tree trunks and to the high transportation costs involved in hauling the timber to one of the port towns. In the mid-1850s some important changes took place. In 1854 the first *steam sawmill* was introduced in Wonnerup. In the same year some towns tried to prevent fire hazards by prohibiting thatched roofs. In 1855 the first important orders for timber arrived from South Australia.

It took another quarter century, however, before timber cutting and exports increased rapidly and companies were willing to invest more heavily in sawmills, railways and jetties in the port towns. The investments were first limited to the areas rather close to one of the ports so that mills were established comparatively early in such places as Lockeville, Vasse (later known as Busselton), Karridale, Jarrahdale, Collie and Denmark. The first *private railway line* was opened between Wonnerup and Vasse in 1871, and during the two decades to follow a number of short private lines were built by various timber companies. Timber exports from ports in Western Australia increased eightfold during the two decades 1879–99 from £ 65,000 to £ 553,000.

Finally the Western Australian Government felt the need to assist the settling of the region. In 1893 the *government railway Perth–Bunbury* was opened, later extended to Bridgetown and eventually to Pemberton, which was reached in 1912. Manjimup was linked to the main line by 1911. The South-Western Railway thus served the major timber areas, the Collie coal mines and the ports of Fremantle, Bunbury and Busselton. Many town sites were established along the railway lines, among others Yarloop, Mornington, Waroona, Wellington, Greenbushes. Along the South-Western Railway no less than 36 towns were established (fig. 29):

prior to 1889	Pinjarra, Bridgetown
1889–98	Mundijong, Serpentine, Ravenswood, Harvey, Wokalup, Brunswick Junction, Roelands, Boyanup, Preston, Balingup
1898–1908	Bedfordale, Byford, Waroona, Benger, Newlands, Kirup, Mullalyup, Greenbushes, Hester
1909–18	Armadale, Wungong, Keysbrook, North Dandalup, Hamel, Wagerup, Cookernup, Gwindinup, Nairnup, Palgarrup, Manjimup
1919–28	Dardanup, Jardee, Pemberton

(the constantly used suffix -up in place names is the term used by Aborigines for 'water').

It was hoped that timber cutting and land clearing would be followed by the establishment of small-scale farms,

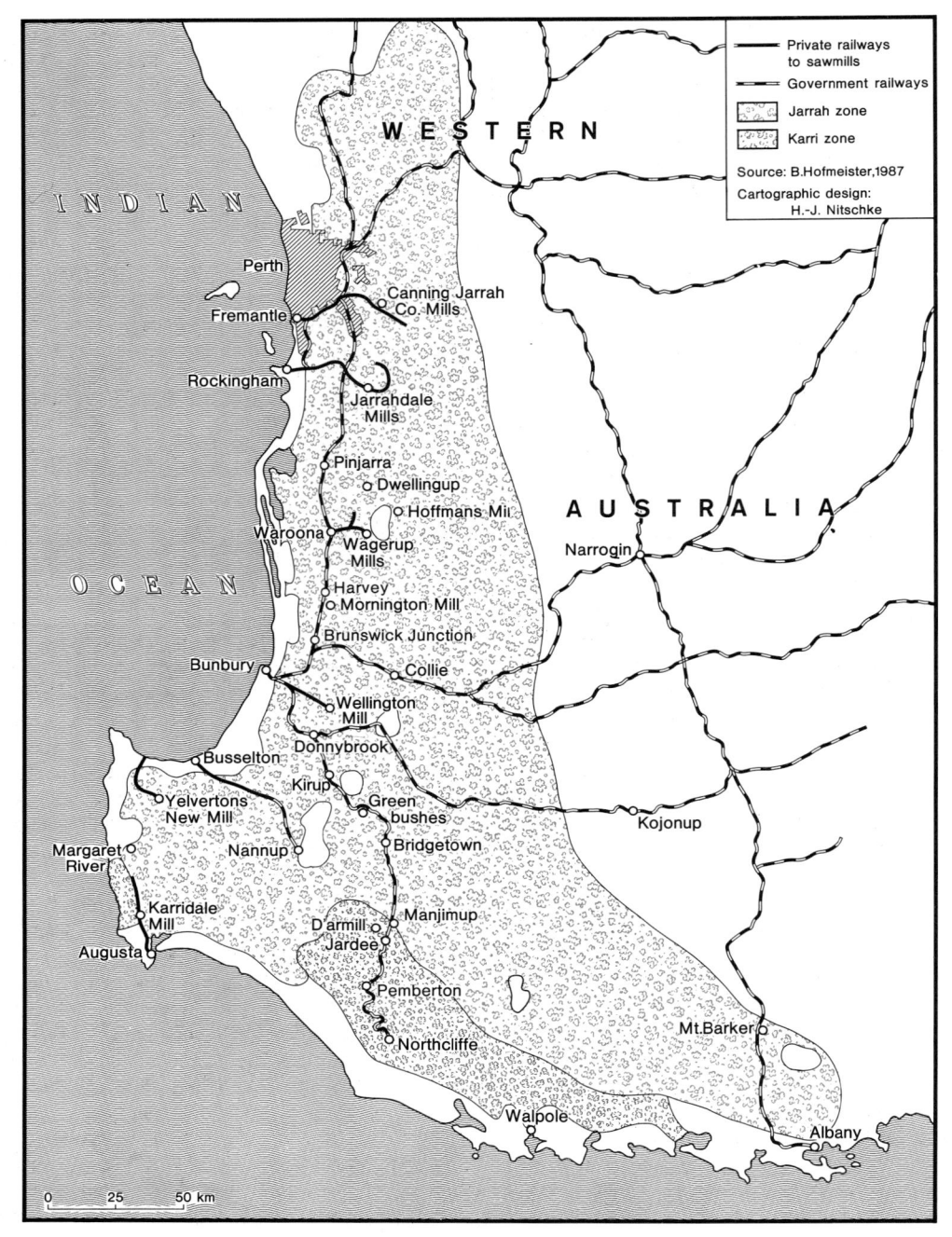

Fig. 29. Forests, railways and sawmill towns in the southwest of Western Australia

that farming would support a fairly dense agricultural population, and that this in turn would support service centres to be established *every five kilometers* along the line. This assumption proved to be completely unrealistic; of all the settlements mentioned above only Waroona, Harvey and Brunswick Junction grew to a reasonable size. Many small timber towns were just temporary creations of the timber companies and were never officially declared townships by the government.

2.2.7 Urban development since federation in 1901

At the time of federation Australia's population was just 3.757 million persons. Of these, 1.951 million or approximately 52% lived in urban places, which means that at this early date over half the Australian population was urbanized. The urban places in existence at this period included a considerable number of port cities, a few inland ports along the Murray and Darling Rivers, a number of mining towns particularly in the goldfields of Victoria and Western Australia and a few others such as Broken Hill in New South Wales or Queenstown in Tasmania. In addition there were the service centres in the pastoral and crop growing areas, such as the parkland towns in South Australia's wheat region or the sawmill towns in the southwest region of Western Australia. The degree of primacy was already remarkable with 39.8% of all Victorians living in Melbourne; the respective figures in the other states were 39.3% for Adelaide, 36.6% for Sydney and 33.1% for Perth; it was much lower in Hobart with 20.3% and in Brisbane with 18.5% (ch. 2.3.1).

During the eight decades 1901–81 Australia's total population grew fourfold to 14.923 million, a population that had become approximately 86% urban. During the same period of time the number of urban places approximately doubled. From these figures we may draw the conclusion that there must have been a conspicuous upward movement within the hierarchy of urban places. This upward movement, however, took place on different levels.

The two largest cities, Sydney and Melbourne, in 1901 just above the half-million mark, grew approximately sixfold; they have recently approached the size of three million residents each. The three capital cities of Adelaide, Brisbane and Perth, in 1901 just above the 100,000 mark, had thus entered the group of major urban areas (MUA); they have in recent years approached the size of one million residents each. Their growth was considerably faster than that of the two very large metropolises. A comparatively greater proportion of their growth was due to internal migration, whereas Sydney and Melbourne grew more through overseas immigration.

The accelerated growth of Brisbane and Perth in particular is related to a shift of importance within Australia as a whole since the 1960s to the 'underdeveloped' states of Queensland and Western Australia. This relates to Australia's 'new dependency' on minerals and mineral exports to Japan and the United States (Mullins 1980), in association with a capital inflow into these states and their capital cities mainly from foreign multinationals, and an increase of population, purchasing power and consumption.

Both the Federal Capital and the Capital of the Northern Territory experienced rapid growth rates. Canberra grew from nil to 238,377 residents (1981) with an average annual growth rate during the intercensal period 1976–81 of 2.4%. Darwin, starting with approximately 10,000 persons after the destructions of Cyclone Tracy in 1974 and the evacuation of a large portion of its population, grew from 10,000 residents in early 1975 to 56,487 residents by 1981, a rate of 7.3%.

The industrial and port cities of Geelong, Newcastle and Wollongong showed a considerable expansion. They have been termed 'semi-metropolises' by Burnley (1980), being located at distances below 150 km from their respective metropolitan markets and linked to them by rail. Newcastle, with a population of 258,956 (1981), holds rank six among Australian cities; Wollongong with 208,601 residents holds rank eight and Geelong with 125,269 residents holds rank 11.

Some regional and provincial centres enjoyed population gains due partly to internal migration from their respective capital cities. In Queensland the port cities of Townsville and Cairns and the inland service centre of Toowoomba grew at rates between 1.9% and 4.7%. In New South Wales Albury and Maitland had relatively high growth rates, in Victoria Ballarat and Bendigo. Whitelaw, Logan & McKay (1984) referred to the growth of this group of cities in the range 50,000–500,000 residents as a 'thickening of the larger towns' and found 'some infilling of this previously depleted rank'. In most recent years some resort towns added to this trend. They will be dealt with later in this chapter.

On the other hand, as was mentioned above, approximately half of all towns entered the Australian urban network in the course of the twentieth century. The question arises what the contributing factors have been. The process of opening new areas for settlement had not, as it did in the United States, come to an end by the turn of the century. One of the most conspicuous examples of the occupation of *new agricultural land* in the twentieth century was the pushing eastward of the farming frontier in the southwest of Western Australia and the opening up of the Western Australian wheat belt. This process started around 1900 and lasted till the beginning of the depression around 1930.

The construction of *new government railways* was decisive in opening the Western Australian wheat frontier. There was considerable railway construction all over Australia during the first four decades of the twentieth century, as is shown in table 16.

The peak mileage of railways in operation in Australia was reached only about 1941, whereas in Western European countries and in the United States the peak mileage was already reached at the time of World War I.

The *expansion of economic activities*, including irrigation agriculture, heavy industries and mining, also of recreational activities, contributed to the increase of the number of urban places. New towns were created such as Griffith and Leeton in the Murrumbidgee Irrigation Areas of the Riverina or Kwinana New Town near the new deep-sea harbour and industrial estate south of Perth of the same name. Other new urban developments included the mining, port and service towns of the Pilbara region (ch. 3.4.1–3.4.3). Among resort towns the most dramatic development was in the municipalities that became amalgamated in the City of the Gold Coast in southern Queensland (ch. 3.2).

Table 16. Railway mileage in operation in Australia, 1861–1981

Year	Miles of railways
1861	243
1901	13,551
1941	27,956
1951	27,602
1981	24,625

Sources: for 1861–1951 Atlas of Australian Resources, quoted in: Rimmer 1967; for 1981 Div. of Nat. Mapping: Australia, Railway Systems 1981

Some of these developments, above all the *new deep-sea harbours and coastal resort towns*, helped to thicken the already densely populated coastal regions. Much of the process was due to the rapid growth of the outer suburbs and new satellites of the metropolises. The suburbanization of population can be demonstrated by the grouping of LGAs showing either positive or negative population changes over any intercensal period. Of the 45 LGAs making up the Sydney metropolitan area, 24 experienced losses of population during the period 1971–76, the value for the City of Sydney being highest (-3.5%) followed by some of the inner suburbs such as South Sydney (-3.2%) and Leichhardt (-2.6%). The outer suburbs on the other hand experienced gains up to 8.8%, as in Campbelltown in Sydney's southwestern corridor. The boundary between the LGAs with population loss and those with population gain is located approximately 12 km from the city centre to the north, about 18 km to the west and 20 km to the southwest and south. In the smaller capital cities like Adelaide, Brisbane and Perth the boundary is found at a distance of about 8 km from the city centre.

The changes of population within the metropolitan areas were accompanied by the relocation of retail trade and employment in manufacturing. In metropolitan Melbourne, for instance, retail sales in the central city dropped in the period 1949–73 from 40% to 11% of total metropolitan sales and CBD floor space used for retail trade decreased in the period 1954–77 from 642,000 square metres to 419,000 square metres (MMBW 1980). Industrial suburbanization commenced in the interwar period 1920–45 with the outward expansion of such key industries as automobile and aircraft manufacturing to suburbs like Dandenong, Moorabbin, Oakleigh, Springvale and Sunshine. Industrial employment in the outer suburbs increased during the period 1961–76 from 157,000 or 37% of metropolitan industrial employment to 265,000 or 58% (MMBW 1981). On the other hand, offices still remained highly centralized, although some decentralization of CBD functions to inner suburban sites such as St. Kilda Road, the Royal Parade in North Parkville and Victoria Parade in East Melbourne occurred. Recent office-construction booms in the CBD and CBD expansions are clear indicators of the viability of the Australian central city. These factors will be dealt with in more detail in chapter 4.1.9.

The recent construction boom in high-rise buildings has considerably changed the urban morphology of the Australian inner city. In contrast to the United States, high-rise buildings had been almost unknown in Australia prior to World War II. It is therefore understandable that this profound change of the townscape caused considerable concern and promoted the simultaneous growth of the Australian urban conservation movement (ch. 2.2.8).

Among factors influencing the urbanization process during the 1980s have been the decrease of overseas immigration from over 100,000 to approximately 80,000 per annum, the slowing down of economic growth and in particular the decline of the manufacturing industries (absolute numbers of industrial employees decreased after the 1966 census at accelerating rates). There has also been an increasing shortage of public funds and a curtailment of government subsidies to growth centres and other urban development programmes. Of considerable importance have also been rising income levels and the rapidly growing importance of leisure in Australian society.

The major changes in the distribution of the Australian population are depicted in tables 17 and 18.

Table 17. Distribution of population in settlement categories, 1921–81

Year	Total population (millions)	Percentage population in:		
		major urban* areas	other urban areas	rural areas
1921	5.435	43.0	19.1	37.4
1933	6.629	46.9	16.9	35.9
1947	7.578	50.7	18.0	31.1
1954	8.986	53.9	24.8	21.0
1961	10.507	58.8	22.9	18.3
1971	12.728	64.5	21.1	14.4
1976	13.554	64.6	21.4	14.0
1981	14.564	63.5	22.2	14.3

* including Hobart and Canberra before they became major urban areas in 1961 and 1971 respectively.

Table 18. Growth rates and changes of employment in settlement zones, 1976–1981

Settlement zone	Percentage change by:		Employment 1976	Increase numbers	1976–81 %
	migration	natural growth			
Major urban zone	2.0	3.5	4,082,140	332,121	8.2
Closely settled coastal zone in NSW, Qld., W.A.	12.5	4.5	359,147	75,731	21.1
Closely settled coastal zone in Vic./S.A./Tas.	1.0	4.0	175,892	15,103	8.6
Moderately settled zone	–0.5	4.5	937,716	52,157	5.6
Sparsely settled zone	1.0	7.5	225,195	26,921	12.0

Source: Lamping 1986

It is against this background that we may summarize the most important of recent trends in the distribution of population and settlements in Australia:

1 For the first time since 1921 the major urban areas contained a smaller proportion of the total population at the end of an intercensal period. This proportion had decreased from 64.6% in 1976 to 63.5% in 1981.
2 The only major urban areas to grow at above the national average rate of 1.24% per annum during the period 1976–81 were the City of the Gold Coast with 9.2%, Canberra with 2.4% and Perth with 2.1%.
3 The two largest metropolises in particular showed a tapering off of their growth rates, to a mere 0.8% for both Sydney and Melbourne.
4 Hobart became the first major urban area to experience a net loss of population (-0.4%) during the period 1976–81 (if peripheral settlements as Kingston in the south and Bridgewater-Gagebrook in the north, officially located outside the metropolitan area, are excluded).
5 The proportion of population in the urban areas outside the major urban zone increased slightly from 21.1% to 21.4% during the period 1971–76 and more markedly during the period 1976–81 to 22.2%. This growth was mainly due to natural increase (four-fifths of the total growth rate) in the urban places of Victoria, South Australia and Tasmania and to the increase of employment (21.1% increase of the number of jobs) in the urban places of New South Wales, Queensland and Western Australia.
6 The proportion of the population in the rest of the country (termed 'rural areas') increased for the first time since the 1921 census from 14.0% in 1976 to 14.3% in 1981. This does not, of course, imply an increase of the agricultural population but rather the growth of small urban communities in the moderately and sparsely settled zones and urban overspill on the outer margins of the metropolitan areas.
7 The most marked population gains were experienced by the suburban zones of the metropolises, these being partly identical with modern resort towns along the sea coasts, with deep-sea harbours and with new towns established as satellites for the central cities. Population gains of this type were also to some extent associated with district centres in the suburban growth corridors along the routes of the rapid transit system promoted by political authorities, such as the Parramatta line to the west of Sydney or the Frankston and Dandenong lines to the southeast of Melbourne.

Some of the fastest growing resort towns are Budgewoi Lake (12.8%), The Entrance-Terrigal (7.5%) and Brisbane Water (6.2%) near Sydney; Cranbourne (16.4%), Melton (10.0%) and Sunbury (6.9%) near Melbourne; Beenleigh (17.2%), Maroochydoe (14.0%) and Caloundra (11.6%) near Brisbane; Crafers-Bridgewater (19.6%) near Adelaide; Wanneroo (11.2%) and Rockingham (8.2%) near Perth and Kingston (7.3%) near Hobart. Similar gains were also experienced by resort towns near Newcastle and Wollongong and elsewhere between the larger urban places.

The question has been raised whether these trends indicate a true 'turn around'. Already once before, during the intercensal period 1947–54, there had been a population increase in the urban places outside the major urban zones, only for the following census to reveal a decline. Arguments given in favour of a long-term trend refer to the movement of employment to non-metropolitan locations because of lower taxes and wage rates (employment increased by 21.1% in the urban areas outside the major urban zones of New South Wales, Queensland and Western Australia), and the growing preference of Australians for low-density living. Significant also are the lowering of the retirement age and higher retirement pension; both these factors enable elderly people to choose a residential location outside the major urban zones. The non-metropolitan areas also benefit from improved access from the major urban zones and from the outward extension of municipal services. It is, however, not unprecedented for there to be a decline of migration to the large cities during periods of economic depression. This could be taken as an argument in favour of a short-term trend and against the hypothesis of a turnaround.

2.2.8 Growing consciousness of the national heritage and the advent of urban conservation

The post-war growth of Australia's population from 7 to 15 million, the influx within three decades of some 3 million overseas immigrants of predominantly non-British origin, and the impact of the post-war building boom on Australia's cities made for changes of people's minds in search for their national identity. In a period when the 'Australian way of life' was thus challenged (White 1981) the rising 'Australian consciousness' helped to create a strong feeling for the country's tradition and the national heritage. This renaissance did not only concern products made in Australia but also Australian history and Australian thought (Nittim in: National Trust 1984).

Even the origin of white Australia in convict settlements was freed from stigma. Just like those New England families that are able to trace back their origins to the first Puritans arriving on the shores of Massachusetts, so Australians are now proud of being able to trace their origin to the 'First Fleeters', even if their forefathers were among the convicts rather than among the sailors or soldiers. As White in *Inventing Australia* (1981, 169) explained. 'The "new nationalism" was never clearly spelled out, but it related to a general pride in Australian achievement, particularly cultural achievement, and an increasing disquiet at the extent of foreign investment in Australia. From the mid-1960s, the founding of a Fellowship of First Fleeters, the expansion of the National Trust's role and the appearance of native shrubs in suburban gardens had all heralded a new confidence in being Australian'.

Mention should also be made of the Builders Labourers' Federation whose 'green bans' helped to preserve a number of buildings in the inner residential districts of Sydney and other cities. This union has not only carried on to customary battle for job security and for wage increases but has also played a part in stopping the demolition of terrace houses and other old buildings in such inner suburbs as Glebe and Wooloomooloo in Sydney, where highrise office blocks and multistorey apartment buildings had been planned (ch. 4.1.5).

During the first one and a half decades after World War II *National Trusts* were established in each of the states. New South Wales was the pacemaker with the foundation of the National Trust (New South Wales) in 1947, followed by South Australia (1955), Victoria (1956), Western Australia (1959) and Tasmania (1960).

The organization of these Trusts resembles that in Great Britain. They have been chartered as companies or associations open to interested corporate and individual members and financed by their own activities, their main sources of revenue being membership fees and donations. They receive minimal subsidies from the respective State Governments to cover their administrative expenses.

The Trusts of the various states are associated in the umbrella organization of the Australian Council of National Trusts. The total membership was approximately 80,000 by 1985.

The Trusts' main task is to initiate the protection and conservation of buildings and other objects of public interest and to make federal, state and local authorities aware of the necessity to take measures and to allocate money for such purposes. Objects worthy of protection are categorised as either 'classified' or 'registered'. A classified object is, if possible, put under immediate protection, whereas a registered object is one recommended for future protection. Usually areas of historic value will be declared 'historic districts' while individual structures within such districts may be classified in different ways.

The way in which objects have been classified by the Trusts is not unchallenged. Generally speaking, objects to be put under protection of the conservation laws are either objects of historical importance, of high architectural quality or of aesthetic quality. Since such general statements are rather vague, and the activities of the Trusts have in consequence been subjected to critical attacks, the Trusts have been eager to come to a more objective base of their classification procedures. M. Court of the National Trust (Tasmania) outlined the criteria for classification in a list of 18 points:

1. Historical importance: the site or object is associated with an important person or event;
2. Design quality: the design of the structure is of very high quality, irrespective of any particular architectural style;
3. Stylistic significance: the structure is a pure example of a particular architectural style;
4. Building evolution: additions to and changes of the original building, this being forced to adapt to changing social and economic circumstances, have been achieved successfully;
5. Unique or vernecular structures: structures being the product of a unique individual or the response to a unique problem or set of circumstances aside from formal stylistic evolution;
6. Types of building or structure: they represent a certain building type like certain generations of railway stations;
7. Beauty of materials and/or craftsmanship;
8. Ageing: the acquisition of patina, natural weathering of the material, evidence of human usage etc.;
9. Unusual or evolutionary construction techniques or materials such as primitive wattle and daub huts;
10. Architectural details such as gates, verandahs, staircases etc.;
11. Townscape importance: the object being an integral part of a historical building group irrespective of its own value;
12. Industrial archaeological importance;
13. Social significance beyond the formal architectural or townscape values;
14. Substantial quality: buildings representing a civic importance greater than current fashions such as old town halls, railway hotels etc.,

15 Authenticity and intactness: all constituent parts are still the original objects;
16 Site location: the actual location of the building on its site or its general layout has a social and visual significance in terms of site usage and street relationship etc.;
17 Local significance: objects typical for a district or region to which their occurrence is restricted;
18 Rarity.

Upon application of the above criteria the individual object is then classified according to one of the following five categories:
A Buildings having great historical significance or high architectural quality, the preservation of which is regarded as essential to the heritage of the state;
B Buildings which are highly significant, the preservation of which is strongly recommended;
C Buildings which are of considerable interest, the preservation of which should be encouraged;
D Buildings of sufficient interest to be recorded;
O Object of interest.

The Trusts' means of protecting and conserving objects are very limited. Classification and registration mean, however, that the attention of the federal, state and local authorities will be drawn to them and these bodies may be willing to contribute to their conservation. The Trusts make attempts to urge the authorities of the three tiers of government to take measures and allocate financial means toward the conservation of the object in question or to find a private customer willing to buy and restore the object. They may also promote the acquisition of the object by means of a donation or by an appeal to raise funds in order to buy and protect it.

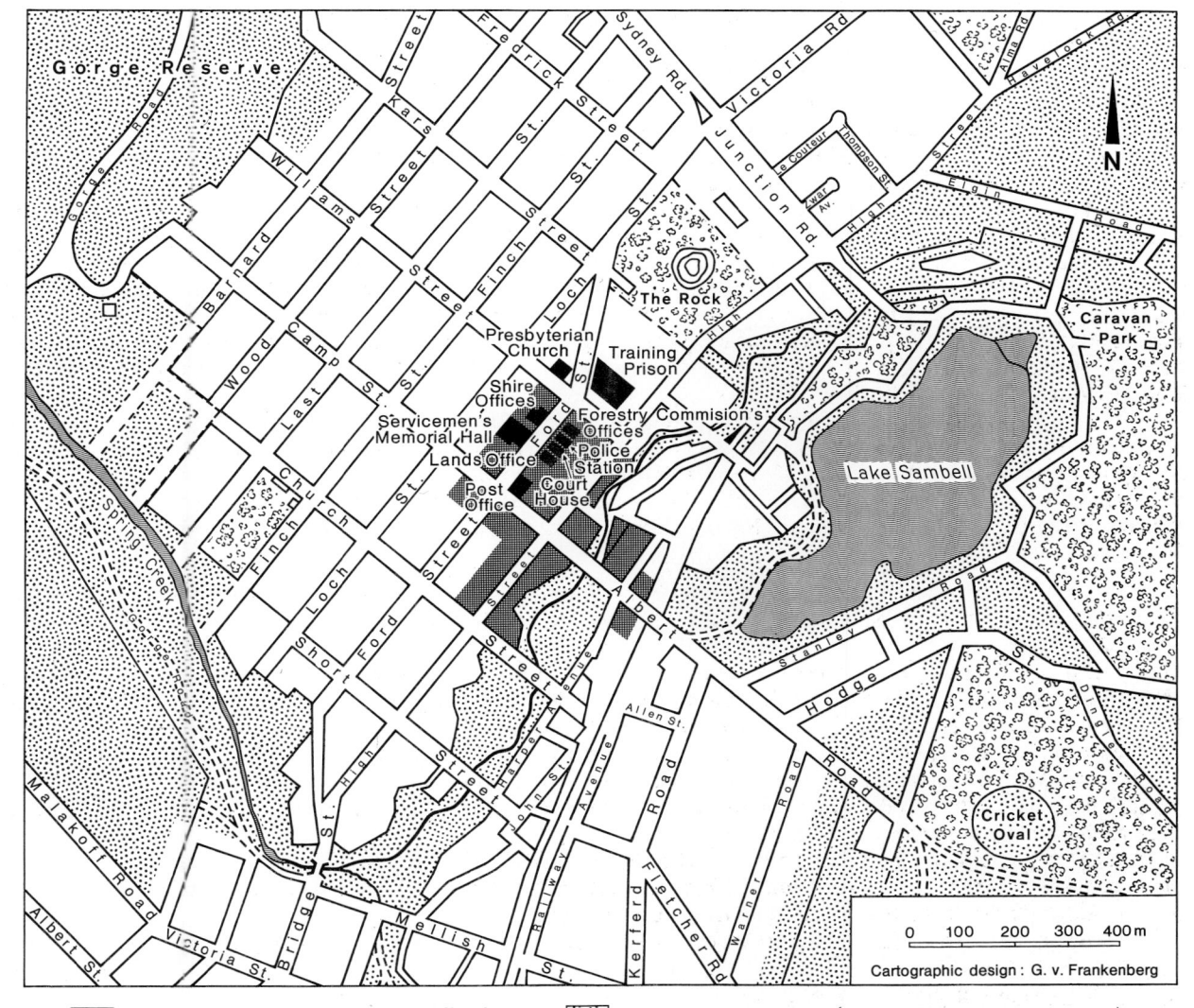

Fig. 30. Classified historical buildings in Beechworth, Victoria (based on City Engineer's map 1969)

The Trust may own an object outright, or it may have been rented by the Trust for a peppercorn rent, or may have been given to the Trust by the government to hold, with maintenance costs being borne by the government.

Although the Trusts are essential in promoting the conservation of historical objects in Australia they are by far not the only institutions to work toward this goal. In 1975 the Australian Heritage Commission Act initiated the *Australian Heritage Commission*, this being a body of consultants to the Federal Government in matters of conservation and in the administration of the National Estate. At State level the corresponding institutions are the Heritage Councils. Thus the Heritage Act of 1977 initiated the New South Wales Heritage Council as an advisory body to the New South Wales Minister for Planning and Environment.

The *Historical Societies* of the various states with their regional offices are also engaged in the conservation of their local historical heritage. Finally, there are local institutions such as the Bendigo Trust in Bendigo, Victoria, engaged in conservation and the opening as a tourist attraction of an old gold mine that is no longer in operation, thus carrying out functions complementary to those of the National Trust.

The *size of objects* put under protection varies considerably. An object under protection may be a *single building* of historic interest, such as Governor Latrobe's Cottage in Melbourne's Kings Domain, which is the oldest seat of a governor in the State of Victoria. It may comprise a row of houses or a *section of a street* (streetscape), such as the east side of Ford Street between Camp and William Streets in the old Victorian mining town of Beechworth, with the former Gold Warden's Offices, Sub-Treasury, Courthouse and Electric Telegraph Offices, all executed in fine Beechworth marble (fig. 30). It may also comprise a small number of individual buildings, each being an integral part of a group making for the atmosphere of a particular section of a town, such as the Shamrock Hotel, Courthouse and Post Office, the Town Hall and the City Family Hotel in the business district of the old mining town of Bendigo (fig. 31).

The next order of magnitude is a *historic district* like the historic core of the old Murray River port of Echuca, encompassing the wharves of the harbour and several streets, with a number of historic buildings each of which may be classified in a different category. Finally, a *historic town* or 'notable town' comprises the whole town, for ex-

Fig. 31. Bendigo, Victoria. Central district with buildings registered by the National Trust (Victoria)

"The Rocks"

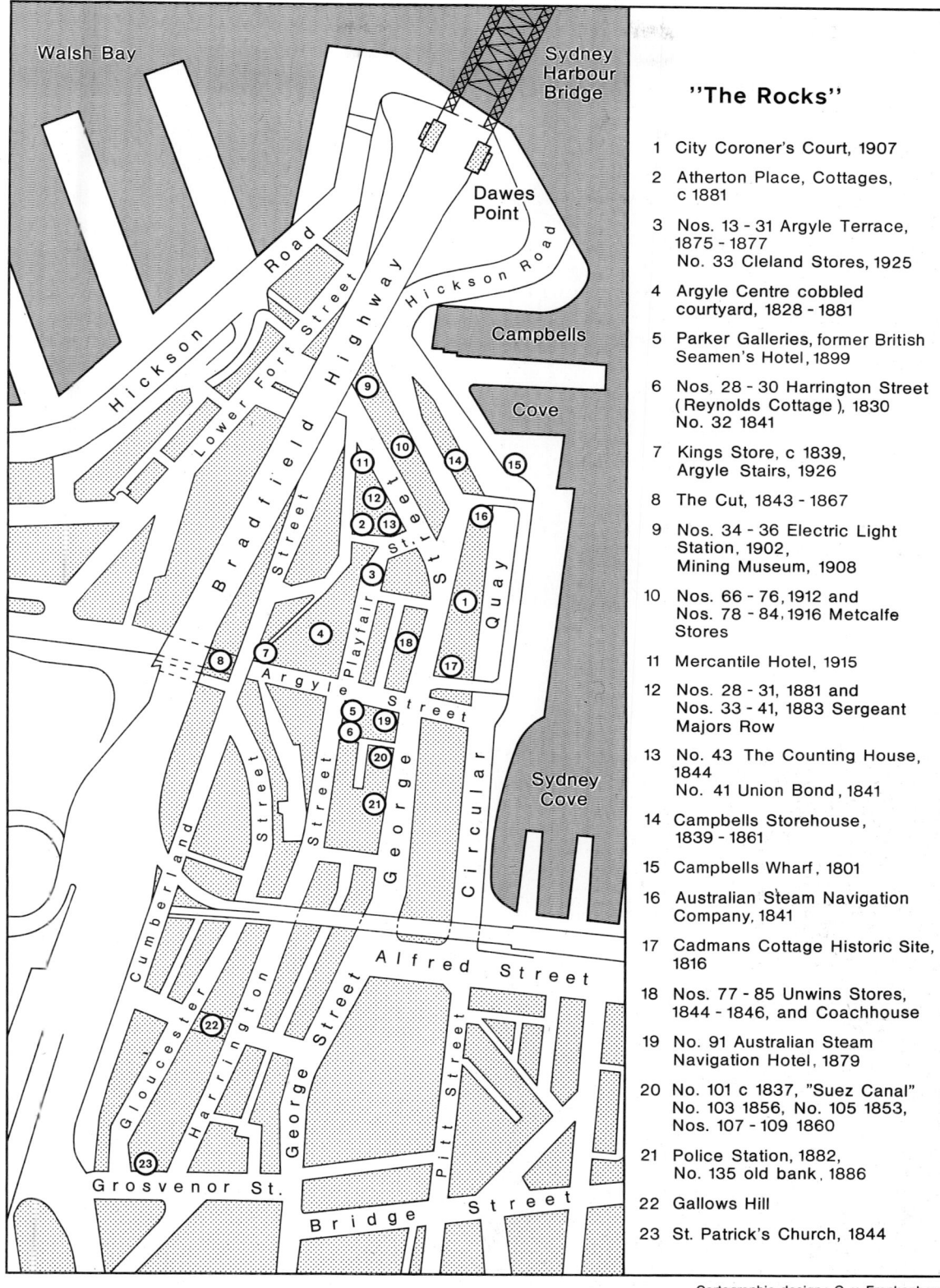

1. City Coroner's Court, 1907
2. Atherton Place, Cottages, c 1881
3. Nos. 13 - 31 Argyle Terrace, 1875 - 1877
   No. 33 Cleland Stores, 1925
4. Argyle Centre cobbled courtyard, 1828 - 1881
5. Parker Galleries, former British Seamen's Hotel, 1899
6. Nos. 28 - 30 Harrington Street (Reynolds Cottage), 1830
   No. 32 1841
7. Kings Store, c 1839, Argyle Stairs, 1926
8. The Cut, 1843 - 1867
9. Nos. 34 - 36 Electric Light Station, 1902, Mining Museum, 1908
10. Nos. 66 - 76, 1912 and Nos. 78 - 84, 1916 Metcalfe Stores
11. Mercantile Hotel, 1915
12. Nos. 28 - 31, 1881 and Nos. 33 - 41, 1883 Sergeant Majors Row
13. No. 43 The Counting House, 1844
    No. 41 Union Bond, 1841
14. Campbells Storehouse, 1839 - 1861
15. Campbells Wharf, 1801
16. Australian Steam Navigation Company, 1841
17. Cadmans Cottage Historic Site, 1816
18. Nos. 77 - 85 Unwins Stores, 1844 - 1846, and Coachhouse
19. No. 91 Australian Steam Navigation Hotel, 1879
20. No. 101 c 1837, "Suez Canal" No. 103 1856, No. 105 1853, Nos. 107 - 109 1860
21. Police Station, 1882, No. 135 old bank, 1886
22. Gallows Hill
23. St. Patrick's Church, 1844

Cartographic design: G. v. Frankenberg

Fig. 32. Historical buildings in The Rocks, Sydney (after Sydney Cove Redevelopment Authority)

Fig. 33. Sydney, N.S.W. Partial view of historic core called The Rocks with old warehouses converted to other uses

ample Maldon, which was in 1966 declared Victoria's first 'notable town'. In Tasmania which was first settled by Europeans in the early 1800s no fewer than 16 urban places were declared historic towns by the National Trust (Tasmania) (fig. 24).

Of greater interest may be the question of the selection of objects to be put under protection in Australia. With very few exceptions they date back to the first 100 years of white settlement. They include some of the *earliest penal settlements*; although frequently in ruins they bear evidence of the ample convict labour available and of the good local construction material. One of the most impressive penal settlements is Port Arthur on Tasman Peninsula, about 100 km southeast of Hobart. Here we find the remnants of the penitentiary, the hospital, an asylum for the mentally ill, the commandant's house, a church and some other buildings. In 1979 the 'Port Arthur Conservation and Development Project' was inaugurated and $ 9 million were allocated by the Federal and State Governments for restoration works to be carried out by the Tasmanian National Parks and Wildlife Service (fig. 15).

Apart from the penal settlements there were the *old seaports* and administrative centres along the coast, that had also been founded as convict settlements, but which served other functions within the newly established colony as well. The Rocks, which is the old historic core of Sydney, and thus the 'cradle of the nation' may serve as an example. The Rocks derives its unique pattern from a combination of old terrace houses and waterfront warehouses. The district's crooked streets reflect its growth on hilly terrain, also that the rules for the layout of the streets were not very carefully observed prior to Governor Macquarie's term of administration.

Since The Rocks lies in something of a cul-de-sac between the Sydney CBD and Sydney Harbour Bridge it is not surprising that it had long been prone to decay. As early as 1900 an outbreak of the plague gave rise to the demolition of several blocks of houses, and so did the construction in 1924 of the Sydney Harbour Bridge and of the Cahill Expressway in 1957. A certain number of the oldest structures had thus disappeared while others were in the process of deterioration. The New South Wales Government in 1970 established a Sydney Cove Redevelopment Authority, responsible to the Minister for Planning and Environment, which was put in charge of the future development of The Rocks. It was first intended to develop The Rocks as a CBD extension area with high-rise office buildings and some hotels and to preserve just a few historic landmarks. This policy was changed a few years later under the pressure of The Rocks' Residents' Action Group and the green bans of the Builders Labourers' Federation (Nittum 1980). A considerable number of buildings have now been restored, some new structures were designed as to fit into the historic setting of The Rocks and a number of shops and restaurants have made The Rocks a magnet for tourists and residents alike (figs. 32, 33).

The earliest and *sporadic settlements* not too far from the sea coast have the second-oldest building stock. One example is Bathurst in New South Wales, founded by Governor Macquarie in 1815 on his first tour beyond the Blue Mountains. Another is York in the Avon Valley, beyond the Darling Range in Western Australia; its pretentious buildings such as the Castle Hotel, the Post Office building and the Police Station bear witness of the ambitions of people dreaming of a great and important city. After the main railway line to the Eastern Goldfields bypassed York the town declined steadily and had to struggle for survival; its present size is about 2,000.

The next generation of settlements was made up of the *gold mining towns* of the 1850s and 1860s, and the *Murray River towns* in Victoria and New South Wales. It is this group of towns that the big money was made in the gold-rush days, reflected in opulent hotels, theatres and town halls, and where the colonial authorities demonstrated their presence through the construction of courthouses, prisons, gold offices and customs houses. The latter bear evidence of the fact that each of the colonies was a separate political entity prior to federation in 1901. Many of the buildings are excellent examples of the architecture of the Victorian epoch, while other structures such as wharves and bridges, chimneys and kilns are objects of importance for industrial archaeology. The town of Echuca has already been mentioned above as an example of the conservation of a whole historic district.

The Victorian epoch was succeeded by the revived Queen Anne style or, as it is usually called with regard to the founding of the Commonwealth in 1901, the Federation style. In Sydney the old inner suburbs of the nineteenth century are surrounded by a concentric zone, albeit a narrow one, of residential areas characterized by Federation-style houses. While some owners are eager to do maintenance work these fine houses are in danger of 'being disfigured by stripping them of their timberwork, reveneering them in texture brick, replacing their windows with aluminium, and stripping out their fine interiors' (S. Harris 1984). Although some of them have been deteriorating or have been subjected to profound modification, they have not become objects of historic conservation. On the other hand, even a recent structure as the Sydney Opera House is already under protection.

2.3 The uniqueness of the Australian urban system

2.3.1 The phenomenon of the primate city

It has been argued that the development of a primate city may be a characteristic of urbanization in the developing countries of the Third World. In this context primacy has been interpreted as 'over-urbanization' of a country the economy of which is very much primary-oriented and in which internal migration is overwhelmingly oriented toward the one huge capital city. In contrast to this argument Berry (1961) argued that a complex rank distribution reflects the complex economic patterns found in advanced economies, whereas primate dominance reflects the simplicity of economic structure characteristic of many Asiatic countries with their peasant agriculture, but also of Australia, with (at least at the time) dominant rural export industries.

Guteland (in: Australian Cities Commission 1975) made an attempt at a comparison of the ranks of Australian cities with those of other developed countries such as Austria, Finland, Norway or Switzerland. Analysing data from the 1970 and 1971 censuses he derived at the rank orders shown in table 19.

Table 19. Rank orders of cities in Australia and some European countries 1970–71 in 1,000 residents (size range in 1,000 and number of units)

Size level	Australia	Austria	Finland	Norway	Switzerland
1	2,498–2,800 (2)	1,858 (1)	800 (1)	751 (1)	719 (1)
2	701– 843 (3)	314– 356 (2)	234–239 (3)	145–228 (3)	321–381 (2)
3	159– 351 (5)	112–196 (4)	101–143 (6)	79–113 (5)	110–284 (4)
4	38– 62 (8)	30– 78 (8)	30– 88 (19)	31– 63 (11)	20– 90 (16)

Source: Australian Cities Commission 1975

From such comparisons he drew the conclusion that primacy within the Australian urban network had been highly *overestimated*, and that the rank orders of cities in Australia do not show any considerable deviation from the rank orders of cities in a number of countries with advanced economies.

What Guteland did was to look at the problem of rank orders and primate dominance from the point of view of dominance within a single national area. One may doubt, however, whether his method of comparing rank sizes within national urban networks does justice to the peculiar Australian conditions. Guteland obviously did not take into account the very size of the Commonwealth of Australia in comparison with countries such as Austria or Norway, nor did he consider the fact that each of the colonies until federation in 1901 experienced its own development from nodes separated one from another by distances up to several 1,000 km. In the present writer's opinion, both space and time within the peculiar Australian context justify an approach to the problem on the basis of *dominance within the state* rather than within the nation. As Rose pointed out as early as 1966: '... in matters of rank-size regularity or metropolitan primacy in countries of continental or sub-continental dimensions, we are dealing with two orders of reality ... If the national boundaries enclose an area small enough to be dominated by a single metropolis, primacy is high. If the included area is large enough to contain a number of such centres, the reverse will be the case' (Rose 1966, 15).

There are various measures applicable to the demonstration of primacy. One of them is the so-called primacy index, this being the quotient derived from the population figures of the largest and second largest cities of the respective territorial unit. This index is shown for the Australian state capitals in table 20.

Table 20. Primacy indices of Australian state capitals, 1981

Largest city (A)	Population in 1981	Second largest city (B)	Population in 1981	Primacy index (A : B)
Perth	809,035	Rockingham	24,932	32.5
Adelaide	882,520	Whyalla	29,962	29.5
Melbourne	2,578,527	Geelong	125,269	20.1
Sydney	2,874,415	Newcastle	258,956	11.1
Brisbane	942,636	Townsville	86,106	10.9
Darwin	56,487	Alice Springs	18,395	3.1
Hobart	128,603	Launceston	64,555	2.0

Source: Author's calculation based on ABS population data

Cloher (1979) calculated the primacy index for Melbourne at earlier dates and found it to be 5.3 by 1861 and 10.4 by 1891.

A second measure of metropolitan primacy is the percentage of population change in the states and their capital cities respectively over time. Table 21 depicts this relative growth for the time span 1911–81.

Table 21. Population changes in states and capitals, 1911–81

State	Population growth 1911–81 in state (thousands)	Population growth 1911–81 in capital (thousands)	Capital's proportion of state population growth (%)
South Australia	925.5	713.5	77.1
New South Wales	2,954.5	2,226.4	75.3
Victoria	2,678.5	1,985.5	74.1
Western Australia	1,018.0	702.0	69.0
Queensland	1,639.2	825.6	50.4
Tasmania	238.6	68.6	28.8

Source: Author's calculation based on ABS population data

A third measure which may be applied to primacy is the capital city's proportion of state population. The respective figures are given in table 22 for each state for the time span 1861–1981 (figs. 34–36).

Table 22. Percentage of populations in capital cities, 1861–1981

City	1861	1881	1901	1921	1947	1961	1981
Sydney	27.4	30.0	36.6	49.0	55.1	55.7	62.4
Melbourne	23.2	31.1	39.8	51.1	59.7	65.3	64.6
Brisbane	20.0	14.5	18.5	28.2	37.4	40.9	40.2
Adelaide	27.6	33.3	39.3	50.4	59.2	60.7	66.2
Perth	33.6	30.2	33.1	46.7	54.2	57.0	62.2
Hobart	27.8	23.3	20.3	24.9	30.1	33.1	30.0

Sources: Burnley 1980, 38 and 69; for 1981 author's calculations based on ABS population data

Two conclusions may be drawn from the data of the three preceding tables. The phenomenon of the primate city occurred at an *early stage* of urban development in Australia and has been characteristic for the role of the capital cities within the Australian urban network ever since. A high degree of metropolitan primacy has been char-

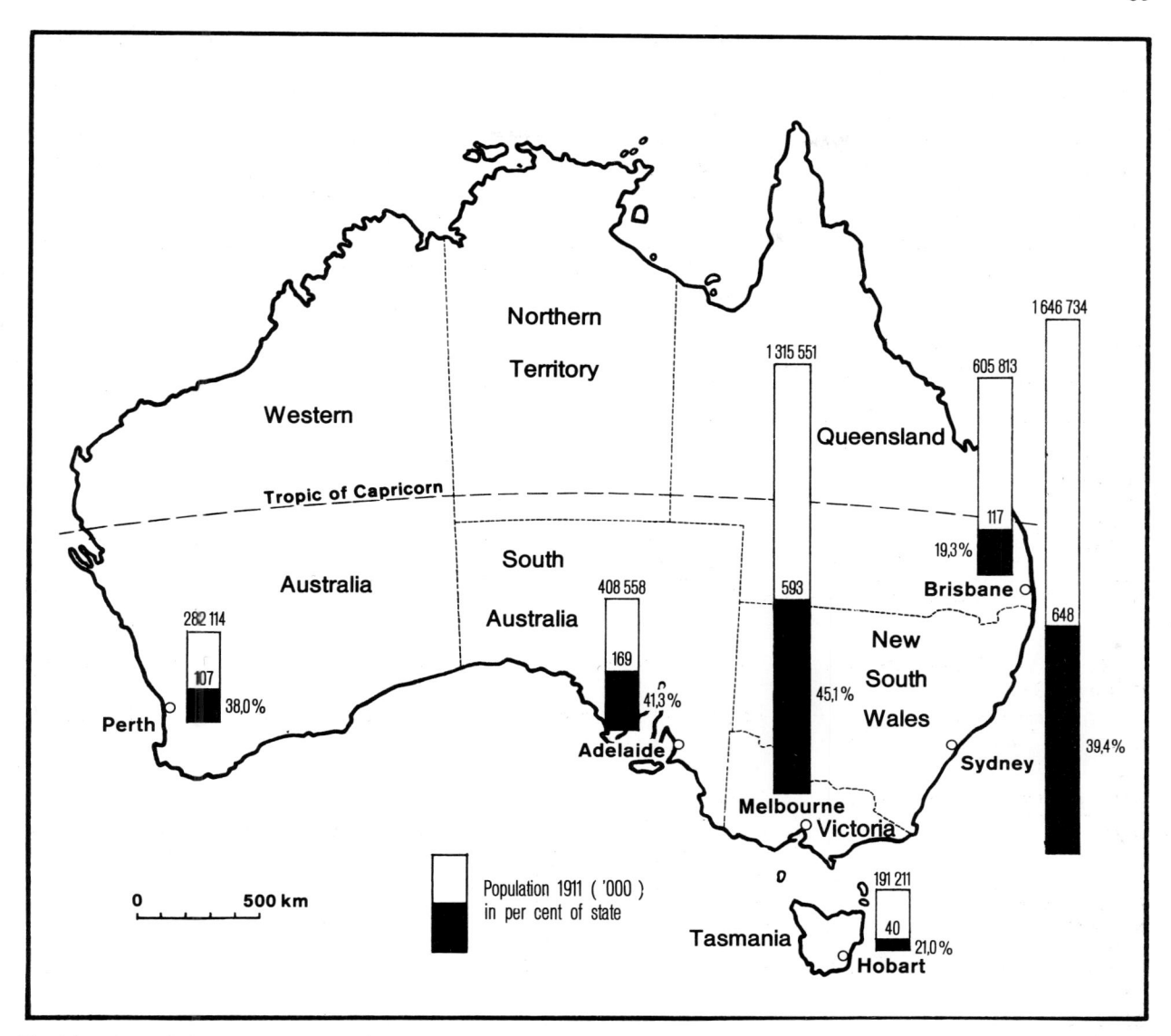

Fig. 34. The capital cities' proportion of total state population, 1911

acteristic for *four of the six states*, primate dominance being somewhat weaker in Queensland and practically absent in Tasmania for reasons that are discussed below.

In Queensland, Brisbane's location is very excentric, the capital city being located in the extreme southeastern section of a very long coastline. Due to the agricultural potential of other parts of the littoral and to mineral resources in various parts of the state, a number of other port cities have developed, each dominating a part of central or northern Queensland. In Tasmania the south and north coasts were settled simultaneously for strategic reasons. Both, Hobart and Launceston have thus struggled for territorial predominance in the island, the huge public buildings in the heart of Launceton bearing evidence of the city's ambitions to compete with Hobart for the position of state capital.

In other states the capital's dominance has never really been challenged. These colonies had, from the very beginning, but one focal point; a partial exception is Western Australia, where a settlement had been established on the south coast three years earlier than the Swan River Colony at Perth. The initial settlement of Albany suffered, however, from an extremely narrow entrance to its harbour and from its disadvantageous location on the shores of the Southern Ocean, so that at least since the expansion of the deep-sea harbour of Fremantle around the turn of the century, the town has no longer been a serious competitor of the Perth-Fremantle urban area.

The reasons for this unchallenged dominance of the Australian capital cities have been much discussed. The conclusion that may be drawn from the vast amount of literature on the issue is that multiple factors are responsible for this situation.

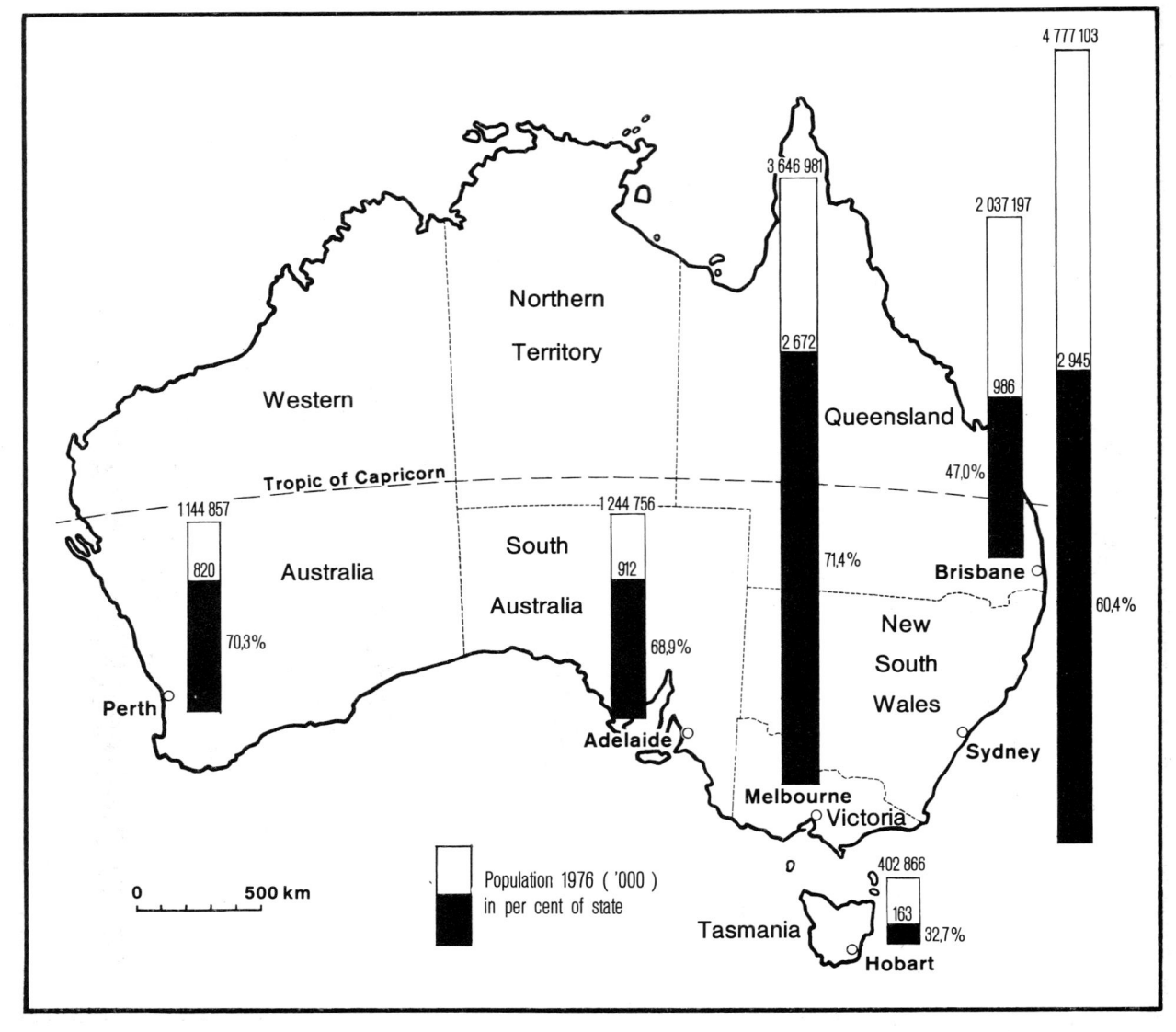

Fig. 35. The capital cities' proportion of total state population, 1976

The capital cities obviously had an *early start* as compared with other urban places. They were the oldest settlements in their respective territories, with the exception of Perth in Western Australia in respect to Albany, as mentioned above.

In contrast to the United States there was no advancing urban frontier in Australia, so that *no rivals* of the earliest coastal towns emerged as they did in the Midwest and the Far West in relation to the cities of the northeastern seaboard of the United States (Sharp 1955).

This point is related to the fact that vast parts of the Australian continental interior are scantily populated or even uninhabited. This also means that *no complete system of central places* ever developed in Australia (see ch. 2.3.2), so that many functions otherwise performed by middle-sized centres have been, for the lack of such centres within the Australian urban system, performed directly by the capital cities through vertical relationships between them and many small urban places.

The *sites* of the capital cities proved rather well chosen as far as local relief, climatic conditions, water supply and, to a certain extent, even the chances for getting food supplies from their immediate hinterlands are concerned (see ch. 3.1.7).

The coastal towns in question assumed the *administrative functions* of the respective colonies and have, since federation in 1901, served as state capitals. They became government towns through the location of all the offices of an ever increasing public administration.

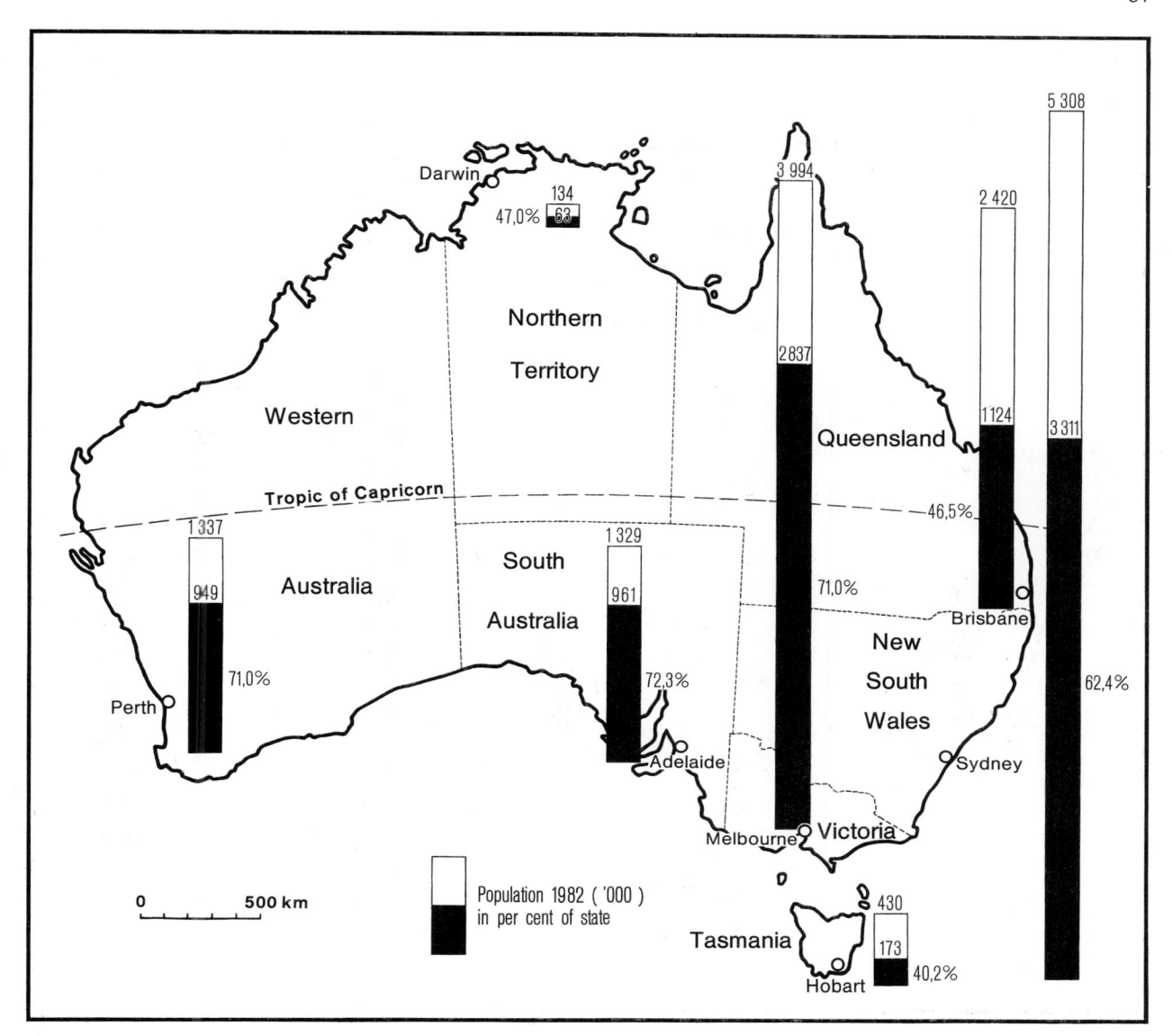

Fig. 36. The capital cities' proportion of total state population, 1982

In the Australian states there was no separation of the political capital from the major commercial port. The term 'port-capital' used in some publications suggests the *spatial coincidence* of the two decisive functions. The vital sea links to the motherland of Great Britain, 19,000 km distant, were also the seats of government and administrative power.

Sydney, Melbourne, Brisbane and Hobart are favourably located at the mouths of the Parramatta, Yarra, Brisbane and Derwent Rivers, while Adelaide and Perth were established somewhat farther inland, so that separate outports, Port Adelaide and Fremantle, had to be established simultaneously. The capital cities of Adelaide and Perth thus grew from more than one settlement nucleus (ch. 3.1.7).

Each colony developed a *railway network* of its own that, due to the different gauges applied and to the very great distances to other parts of the continent, was inevitably *focussed upon the state capital* city. The Victorian railway network, for example, is completely centred on Melbourne. To a somewhat lesser extent this holds true for Sydney, Adelaide and Perth. As already noted, in Queensland and Tasmania the situation is different.

Given the other locational advantages, *all important manufacturing industries* located in the capital cities, thus making Sydney the largest and Melbourne by a small margin the second largest industrial city of Australia. The huge industrial complex of Kwinana may be considered part of the Perth metropolitan area, just as the former industrial satellite of Elizabeth may be considered part of the Adelaide metropolitan area.

The capital cities, Sydney and Melbourne in particular, have gained the position of *managerial centres* of the Australian economy. Of the headquarters of the 100 largest Australian companies 92 are located in Sydney (68) and Melbourne (34).

The capital cities have also been the *major targets for foreign capital* flows and direct foreign investments into the Australian economy and into their own building stock. For example, between 1979 and 1981, about $ 161.8 million were invested by foreign countries into urban real estate, mainly in the capital cities (The Canberra Times, 17-11-1981).

Since the capitals are among the few large cities where numerous cultural amenities are available, it is not surprising that they have attracted *major flows of internal migration*.

The Australian economy has, to a very high extent, been dependent upon primary resources. The overspill of population from such often short-lived activities has been mainly absorbed by the few large cities. Due to rather limited employment opportunities elsewhere in the country the vast *majority of overseas immigrants* have also settled in the few large cities. They make up about 16–30% of the total population of the capital cities.

Viewed in a historical perspective, the factors mentioned above have operated at varying degrees over time. Rowland (1977) attempted to give an overview of the various concepts developed to explain primacy in Australia. According to Rowland, the first epoch may be identified as the time of development of the first major sea ports, when mainly those forces put forward in the hypotheses of Blainey and Rose were at work. Blainey in his famous 'tyranny-of-distance' concept had expressed the idea that only gold and wool were not sensitive to transportation costs, these products from relatively distant places being favourable export products promoting foreign trade from the seaports.

The second epoch, reaching from the end of the gold rushes in the eastern colonies till about 1950, was characterized by a continuous industrialization process, perhaps most effectively explained by the hypotheses put forward by Gregory and Stilwell and Galbreath. The first two authors are similar in their approaches, inasmuch as Gregory developed the concept of the 'dead heart of Australia' and Stilwell attempted to apply the centre-periphery model to Australia. Galbreath expressed the idea that the concentration of industrial activities in the hands of a small number of industrial giants operating from a few nodal points is especially characteristic of the Australian economy.

The third epoch from about mid-century to the present has been characterized by a rapid expansion of Australia's internal market, as well as export markets, a development which may be best explained by the hypothesis put forward by Woolmington. The essence of this hypothesis is, in the author's own words, that 'consumer-oriented production favors metropolitan growth' (Woolmington in: Linge & Rimmer 1971).

The Australian Federal Government has been well aware of the difficulties associated with primate dominance, and during the early 1970s, initiated a policy of decentralization (ch. 2.1.3). This, however, had scant success; the forces in favour of primacy proved to be too strong, and in a free market economy the goal of decentralization could not be achieved. It also appears that Australia, by virtue of the whole process of economic and settlement history, contradicts theories varified elsewhere in the world. According to growth-pole theory, spread effects will eventually induce economic growth in other parts of the country. But this assumption does not seem to hold true for Australia. The processes promoting dominance of the primate cities appear to have been in continuous operation for almost two centuries. It may be true that there have been signs of a certain reversal, within the last decade, of this long-lasting historical trend, but this cannot mean that primacy in Australia could possibly disappear within the foreseeable future.

2.3.2 Is there a true hierarchy of central places?

Just as the concept of primacy in Australian cities must be subjected to some modification so too must be the related question of a hierarchical pattern of urban places. Although totally rejected by some scholars, others have made attempts to apply central-place theory to the Australian urban system. The pioneering work was done by Scott and by Daly & Brown in 1964. The reader is particularly referred to the investigations of central places in various parts of New South Wales by Daly & Brown (1964), Rose (1967) and Langdale (1975), of Victoria by Fairbairn (1964), Cloher (1978, 1979) and Christie (1979), of southern Queensland by Dick (1971), of South Australia by Smailes (1969, 1975, 1977), of Western Australia by Gentilli (1979) and of Tasmania by Scott (1964). Among the general comments on the Australian urban system from the point of view of central-place theory special mention should be made of the works by Fairbairn & May (1971), Bourne (1974, 1975), Heathcote (1975), Holmes (in: Jeans 1977), Logan & May (1979), Burnley (1980), Harris & Stehbens (1982) and Whitelaw, Logan & Mackay (in: Bourne, Sinclair & Dziewonski 1984).

Christaller's central place theory has, apart from the methodology of measuring centrality, three implications. A place will, first of all, possess a relative centrality; this means a surplus product, in terms of serving more consumers than its own population. It will also be ranked in a hierarchy of central places, having a number of stages, with each succeeding stage of the hierarchy having fewer places than the one below. Finally, the area provided with goods and services by any one central place, which would ideally be circular, will through lapping with other service areas be modified to hexagonal shape.

While applying these three propositions to the Australian situation one will readily agree with the notion of *surplus product*. Even small places in the categories of a hamlet or a village are endowed with certain minor functions such as a post office and telephone exchange, which serve the neighbouring rural population. If we thus use the term central place in its broadest sense we do find central places in Australia. It is the notions of a hierarchical pattern and of a regular shape of service areas that may raise considerable doubts.

Apart from variations in the methods applied by each individual scholar (for example Scott in his investigation of Tasmanian settlements studied central functions only, without regarding market areas) the various Australian central-place studies have produced very different findings. This does not mean, however, that the results are completely incompatible. On the contrary it is only to be expected that, given the whole settlement range from the huge metropolitan areas with their suburban centres and satellite cities to the almost empty rural areas of the interior with very widely spaced service centres, we *are likely to find different settlement networks* with varying distances between each pair of urban places in any one size group in the various parts of the continent.

Hierarchical patterns of central places were recognized in some of the studies mentioned above, albeit with certain reservations. While in an advanced economy such as the Federal Republic of Germany a fully developed hierarchy of four major ranks and three intermediate ranks is found, Scott in his Tasmanian study detected six ranks of central places which he termed hamlets, villages, minor towns, towns, major towns and cities. His findings may be summarized in table 23.

Table 23. Hierarchy of central places in Tasmania

Rank	Number of settlements	Average distance (miles)	Number of functions	Typical functions
hamlet	191	3.5	up to 6	post office, hall, church, primary school
village	171	5.5	7–34	telephone exchange, service station
minor town	20	16	up to 60	doctor, trading bank
town	9	27	72–122	dentist, solicitor, furniture store, jeweller
major town	2	56	170–199	secondary school, variety store
city	2	98	over 400	department store, taxation consultant

Source: Scott 1964

Such stepped categories were also found by Daly & Brown in the Lachlan region of New South Wales, by Dick in southwestern Queensland, by Christie in the Wimmera region of Victoria and by Smailes in South Australia. Investigations made in the more densely populated southwestern part of Western Australia under the guidance of J. Gentilli came up with a stepped hierarchy of five ranks, these being called point locality, site locality, area locality, district centre and regional centre. The major criterion for determining these ranks was the person: function ratio (Gentilli 1979).

It should be noted that studies like those made by Christie and Gentilli were undertaken in parts of their respective states that did not include the state capital. In Tasmania, on the other hand, the capital city may be regarded as only a regional centre. It is, therefore, somewhat surprising to learn that there is a hierarchy of just five ranks with the much larger capital city of Adelaide included. An explanation for this seeming discrepancy may be found in the fact that in various parts of Australia certain ranks of the hierarchy are hardly represented by any settlement of the respective size. Usually the highest rank is represented by a single metropolis, that can be identified with the state capital, and the third and fourth ranks are well represented by a number of minor towns and villages respectively. There is an *obvious absence of ranks two and five* which means that there are hardly any cities in the 50,000 to 500,000 category below the metropolitan level and above the smaller towns of less than 50,000 residents.

This point has been stressed by Forward (1969) and Bourne (1974) in their comparisons of the relative locations of the major cities in Australia and Canada. These authors found a certain correlation in relative location between Perth and Vancouver, Adelaide and Winnipeg, Melbourne-Canberra-Sydney-Newcastle and Toronto-Ottawa-Montreal-Quebec, Brisbane and Halifax, Townsville and St. John's (fig. 37). But despite the pattern and size resemblances in the upper ranks, 'Canada's basic urban skeleton is supplemented by a great number of medium-sized cities' (Forward 1969, 27) whereas Australia's urban skeleton is not.

Representation in the lowest categories is also very poor. Many small settlements had either the chance to take off and enter the second lowest category or they had to bear the fate of shrinking to practical non-existence and to become ghost towns where only a handful of people may earn their living by running a little shop or takeaway for the tourists.

Thus only two or three ranks are really well represented in the Australian urban network. There is *no fully*

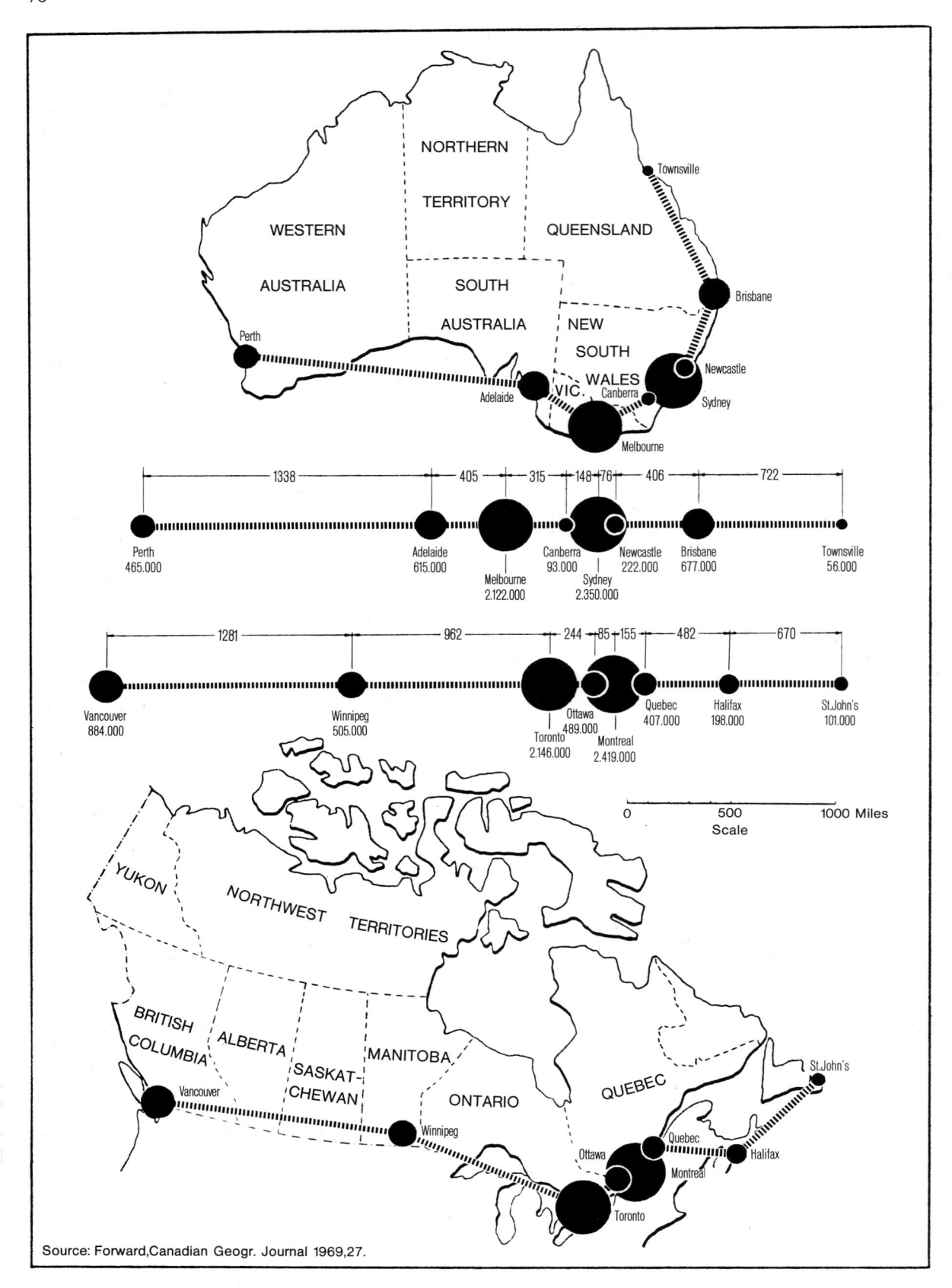

Fig. 37. Australia's and Canada's skeletal network of major cities

developed urban hierarchy as we usually find it in advanced economies. This fact has some very important implications. Rose, Smailes and Holmes pointed to the *many direct links* between centres of a lower rank and the state capital. Smailes in his study on South Australia came to the conclusion that there is not a single second-order centre below the level of Adelaide in the state. There are 11 third-order centres, and of the 72 fourth-order centres, 34 are linked directly with the capital city. Of the 435 fifth-order centres 50 are linked with the capital city and another 71 with one of the 11 third-order centres. Thus *both kinds of relations exist*, direct links to the capital as well as links with the nearest central place of the next higher rank.

It is common practice in Australia that manufacturing companies maintain country representatives acting as local ordering agents rather than establishing a network of regional offices in medium-sized centres. The clientel will file their orders with the local representative and the merchandise ordered will be delivered by truck from the metropolitan depot (Rose 1966). Analogous to this organization of retail trade there is a concentration of administrative functions. Thus in small service centres the post office functions as agent for Australian Savings Bonds, the Commonwealth Savings Bank, Defense Service Homes, Hunting Licenses, Passports, SGIC, Taxation Stamps and Telecom Australia.

The persistence of such direct metropolitan links 'has served to retard and destabilize the local urban economy' (Holmes in: Jeans 1977, 424). The small service centres appear to be *trapped in a vicious circle*. Due to local deficiencies in the supply of merchandise and services there are many direct metropolitan links, and because of the direct metropolitan links there are many local deficiencies.

In consequence of the irregularities in the ranking of central places, their functions are often *out of proportion to their population size*. As Smailes found in South Australia, 'although the typical minor town may have only 1/4 to 1/6 of the population served by the typical major town, yet it supplies, or at least offers for sale, about half of the same functions' (Smailes 1969, 40). But with just a fraction of the 'normal' population those stores and services will of necessity be of a quality inferior to that of the same establishments in a major town. The same holds true for the centres of the lowest rank. In the very small centres of the large, sparsely populated areas, 'the demand level for entry of a service is lowered, and consumers must accept smaller, less specialised, poorly stocked establishments offering less choice, as a trade-off against excessive travel to meet their needs' (Holmes in: Jeans 1977, 423).

In addition to the fact that second-order centres are completely absent in South Australia and are very few in the other states, Rose stressed the point that these *second-order centres are not regional centres in the normal sense.* Newcastle and Wollongong in New South Wales and Geelong in Victoria are modern deep-sea harbours with steel manufacturing, machine manufacturing, wool processing and export trade. Ballarat, Broken Hill and Kalgoorlie are former important mining towns. Rockingham in Western Australia is a modern resort town. With special reference to Newcastle and Wollongong Rose pointed out: '... they form no part of any normal central-place series, and their functions, which have been developed since the formation of the Commonwealth in 1901, are nation-wide rather than state-wide' (Rose 1966, 19/20).

In the chapter on primacy mention was made of the fact that the states of Queensland and Tasmania are to some extent exceptions to the general rule. In Queensland the capital city still has more than ten times the population of the second largest city, so that there is a certain degree of primate dominance in that state. On the other hand, Brisbane's location is rather excentric in relation to the state as a whole, and Queensland's proportion of urban population is lower than in other states. In Tasmania there are two major cities dominating the two more populated northern and southern coastal regions of the island state. The urban systems of Queensland and Tasmania are thus less incomplete than those of the other mainland states.

According to Smailes a certain regularity of the spacing of central places as well as the shape and size of their respective hinterlands may be found in those parts of South Australia that had, after 1869, been systematically surveyed in Hundreds (see ch. 2.2.4), and which had been settled with the intention that each Hundred be served by at least one service centre. But even under such ideal conditions there is, in practice, no very marked approximation of the theoretical regularity in the location of service centres.

In each of the wheat-growing regions of Australia peculiar patterns of service centres developed due to varying economic, political and historical factors. According to Robinson (1962a, 78): 'A *nodal* pattern characterises the Central Slopes and Plains of New South Wales, where the towns of Parkes and Dubbo occupy pivotal positions, from each of which railway lines radiate in wheel formation, with smaller towns located along the "spokes". By contrast, the largest centres of Victoria's Wimmera-Mallee division occur in the extreme south of the belt, initiating a *digital* arrangement of five parallel lines running northwards into the wheat districts. Lesser towns, located along the railway routes, are fewer and smaller than those in New South Wales. Yet another grouping is provided by the South Australian districts, where a *diffuse* pattern is built on a more intensive network of moderately-sized towns than in any of the other regions. Finally, the fourth example from Western Australia shows a distinctly *marginal* relationship between towns and service area. All the large towns remain on the extreme humid margin of the belt, actually outside the main wheat-producing zone, but economically tied to it as well as to the mixed farming region further west'.

In the less regularly settled areas the means of transportation like railways and modern highways have had a great impact on the location and spacing of settlements. Just as in parts of Canada's Prairie Provinces or in the Great

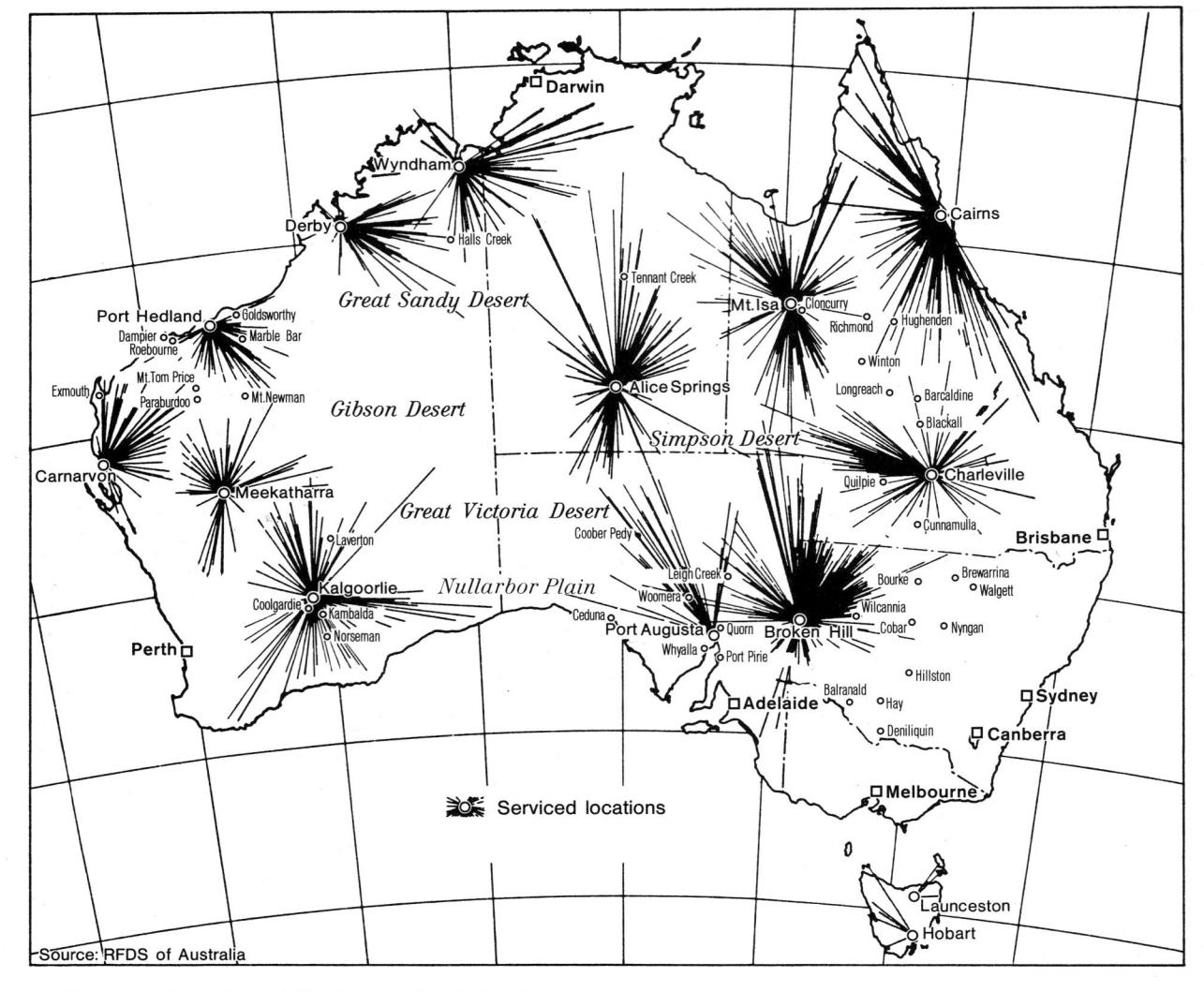

Fig. 38. Operational bases of the Royal Flying Doctor Service

Plains of the United States there is in such sparsely populated areas a *linear arrangement* of the collecting points for the agricultural products, with the huge grain elevators standing out as landmarks in the countryside.

Finally, in the almost uninhabited outback, there will be a few very widely spaced outposts originally established for the sole purpose of the maintenance of communication lines, such as Alice Springs or Tennant Creek along the Overland Telegraph or Cook on the Transcontinental Railway in the Nullarbor Desert.

A very peculiar pattern of central places has evolved in connection with the establishment of the *Royal Flying Doctor Service* operating from six bases in the east, two bases in the far north and four in the west: Broken Hill, Port Augusta, Alice Springs, Mount Isa, Charleville, Cairns, Wyndham, Derby, Port Hedland, Carnarvon, Meekatharra and Kalgoorlie (fig. 38).

It will be apparent from the preceding discussion that there is a strong tendency in Australia toward discrete state sub-systems of central places, each centered on the respective state capital (with some modification of the pattern in Queensland and Tasmania). The obvious lack of certain ranks within the urban hierarchy, and the rather high degree of irregularity in the spacing of central places and in the shape and size of their respective hinterlands, lead to the conclusion that there is in Australia no true hierarchy of central places in terms of Christaller's propositions. The question arises, however, whether other regularities may be detected in Australia's urban system or rather in the urban sub-systems (fig. 39).

Holmes claimed that there is a degree of correspondence between the Australian urban system and the *rank-size rule*. He argued that, apart from the dual status of Sydney and Melbourne as national metropolises the five largest cities more or less conform to a normal rank-size relationship 'with Perth having close to one-fifth of Sydney's population' (Holmes in: Jeans 1977, 423).

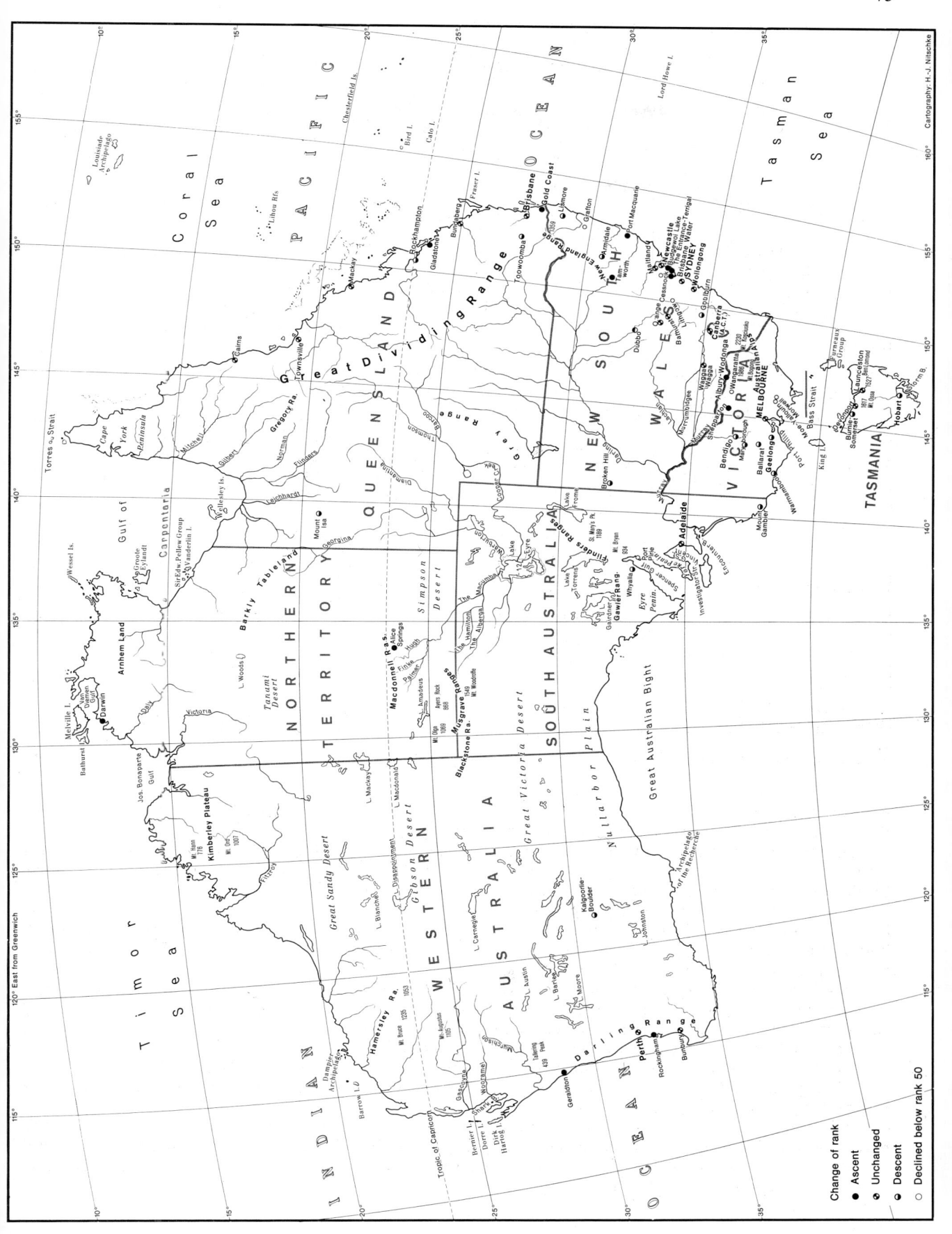

Fig. 39. Location of the 50 largest cities in 1981 and change of rank 1961–1981

The obvious divergence between rank five and rank ten in the rank-size graph is evidence for the lack of medium-sized metropolitan centres while for the ranks below ten the normal rank-size relationship is resumed, although at size levels markedly below those predicted by the rule. One may have doubts, however, about the validity of this statement as far as the first five cities are concerned; for according to the 1976 census used by Holmes Sydney with a population of 2,945 million was just about 3 1/2 times as large as Perth, with a population of 820,000. On the other hand, one may agree with Holmes's statement that the ranking of Australian urban places below rank ten displays a certain affinity with a normal rank-size relationship, albeit below the level predicted by the rule, with certain reservations.

In a more recent study Holmes (1984) by carrying out a factor analysis of inter-urban telephone traffic came to the following result: 'It confirms the exceptionally high levels of centralisation in all mainland states, with Western Australia and South Australia displaying extreme metropolitan dominance, matched by an absence of any further major high-order nodal regions. Victoria is slightly less centralised and reveals an incipient fragmentary set of higher-order regions. In New South Wales, non-metropolitan regionalisation is further developed, particularly in the northern half of the state. However, only in northeast Queensland and Tasmania is there a fully articulated set of continuous higher-order nodal regions!' (Holmes 1984, 118/119).

To sum up, there is no true hierarchy of central places in the terms of Christaller's theory in Australia. Due to the high degree of primate-city dominance at state level in at least four of the mainland states there are several sub-systems of urban places in Australia, with many direct links existing between lower-order central places and the respective metropolis. There is a conspicuous lack of second-order, medium-sized metropolises below the level of the port-capitals; those few in existence are port cities with heavy industries, former mining towns or expanding resort towns, thus not regional centres in the normal sense. In relatively more populated areas a certain correspondence with the rank-size rule may be observed for the ranks below ten, however, below the level predicted by the rule. In the less settled areas a certain linearity in the arrangement of service centres mainly along railway lines may be detected, while in the almost uninhabited areas only a few outposts in connection with communication lines are found.

2.3.3 Constant changes of rank within the urban system

A third characteristic of the Australian urban network is that since gold-rush days in Victoria in the 1850s there have been *constant and often rapid changes of rank* in terms both of population size and of functional importance. The opening up of new areas for settlement and the vigorous growth of new central places has been just as characteristic as the dwindling of the economic base of some settlements, which in consequence have shrunk or have even been completely abandoned. Such oscillations have probably occurred nowhere else in the world with the possible exception of Canada's northern frontier.

There seems, at first glance, to be a contradiction between this notion of instability in the system and the undoubted fact that the initial settlements are still the present economic focal points of the Commonwealth. There has, indeed, been hardly any change in the highest ranks of the Australian urban network, these being identical with the port-capitals of Sydney, Melbourne, Brisbane, Adelaide and Perth and the manufacturing and port city of Newcastle. Bourne (1974) certainly had these major urban areas in mind when making the statement that, in contrast to Canada, growth rates of Australian cities have been most stable. He pointed out that in Canada Quebec City was, in the 1870s, overtaken by Toronto, in later years also by Winnipeg, Ottawa, Vancouver and, still more recently, by Edmonton. St. John was overtaken by Halifax, which in turn was later bypassed by the western centres mentioned above. In Australia, on the other hand, no new generations of large cities developed, for the lack of an urban frontier advancing into the arid interior of the continent. There has not been any movement in the first six ranks of Australian cities.

There have, however, been remarkable changes below rank six, and they are still continuing. Particularly striking was the rise of Canberra from rank 11 to seven between 1961 and 1981, and in the same period there were *spectacular changes below rank 16*, such as the rise of Darwin from rank 42 to rank 17 (fig. 40). Darwin's population was reduced to less than 10,000 after the destruction caused in 1974 by Cyclone Tracy and the consequent evacuation of a large proportion of its population, but then the city experienced an unprecedented growth (see ch. 3.1.8).

After World War II the urban population outside the metropolises increased from 18.0% in 1947 to 24.8% in 1954. This seemed to be a 'real challenge to metropolitan dominance' (Whitelaw, Logan & McKay in: Bourne et al. 1984, 80), but by 1981 this non-metropolitan urban population had dropped back to 22.2%. During the 1960s a few middle-sized centres continued to gain in employment and population, thus assuming more importance with regard to their service functions, as Holmes & Pullinger (1973) could demonstrate for Tamworth, New South Wales (29,656 residents in 1981). Also Dubbo rose from rank 43 in 1961 to rank 35 in 1981 (23,986). Such towns began to provide goods and services hitherto offered only by Sydney or Newcastle: '... their devolution down the hierarchy [of the availability of such services] was in response either to an increase in demand, or to a higher degree of specialization of both demand and supply systems' (Holmes in: Jeans 1977, 423). To Holmes this seems to be the beginning of a process of towns growing functionally to the rank of major towns despite populations that were still relatively small.

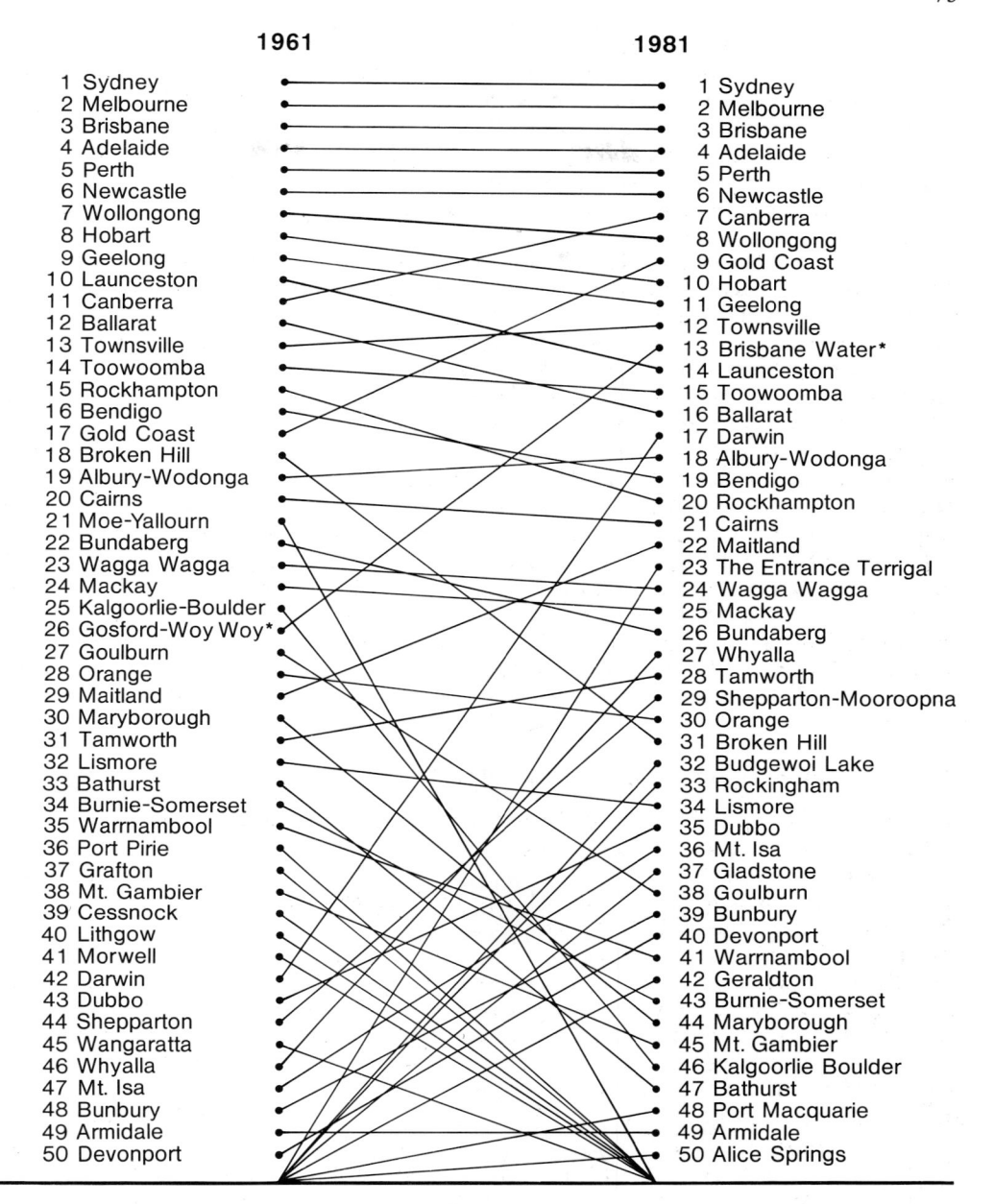

1961	1981
1 Sydney	1 Sydney
2 Melbourne	2 Melbourne
3 Brisbane	3 Brisbane
4 Adelaide	4 Adelaide
5 Perth	5 Perth
6 Newcastle	6 Newcastle
7 Wollongong	7 Canberra
8 Hobart	8 Wollongong
9 Geelong	9 Gold Coast
10 Launceston	10 Hobart
11 Canberra	11 Geelong
12 Ballarat	12 Townsville
13 Townsville	13 Brisbane Water*
14 Toowoomba	14 Launceston
15 Rockhampton	15 Toowoomba
16 Bendigo	16 Ballarat
17 Gold Coast	17 Darwin
18 Broken Hill	18 Albury-Wodonga
19 Albury-Wodonga	19 Bendigo
20 Cairns	20 Rockhampton
21 Moe-Yallourn	21 Cairns
22 Bundaberg	22 Maitland
23 Wagga Wagga	23 The Entrance Terrigal
24 Mackay	24 Wagga Wagga
25 Kalgoorlie-Boulder	25 Mackay
26 Gosford-Woy Woy*	26 Bundaberg
27 Goulburn	27 Whyalla
28 Orange	28 Tamworth
29 Maitland	29 Shepparton-Mooroopna
30 Maryborough	30 Orange
31 Tamworth	31 Broken Hill
32 Lismore	32 Budgewoi Lake
33 Bathurst	33 Rockingham
34 Burnie-Somerset	34 Lismore
35 Warrnambool	35 Dubbo
36 Port Pirie	36 Mt. Isa
37 Grafton	37 Gladstone
38 Mt. Gambier	38 Goulburn
39 Cessnock	39 Bunbury
40 Lithgow	40 Devonport
41 Morwell	41 Warrnambool
42 Darwin	42 Geraldton
43 Dubbo	43 Burnie-Somerset
44 Shepparton	44 Maryborough
45 Wangaratta	45 Mt. Gambier
46 Whyalla	46 Kalgoorlie Boulder
47 Mt. Isa	47 Bathurst
48 Bunbury	48 Port Macquarie
49 Armidale	49 Armidale
50 Devonport	50 Alice Springs

Fig. 40. Changes of rank of the 50 largest cities, 1961–1981
* Gosford-Woy Woy was renamed Brisbane Water

On the other hand, it soon became obvious that the government's policy of decentralization and the promotion of selected growth poles failed to create more large cities below the level of the state capitals (ch. 2.1.3). Of all the growth poles only Albury-Wodonga on the Murray River was able to grow to a size above the 50,000 mark (53, 251). while the second largest of the growth poles, Gladstone in southern Queensland, did not even reach half that size (22,080). Nevertheless, even without further subsidies, nine of the eleven former growth poles experienced a population increase during the intercensal period 1976–81. Six of them rose in rank: Albury-Wodonga from rank 19 to 18, Coffs Harbour from rank 66 to 61, Gladstone from rank 46 to 37, Portland from rank 96 to 95, Tamworth from rank 31 to 28 and Townsville from rank 13 to 12. Three experienced slight population increases that did not prevent them from falling in rank: Albany from rank 59 to 65, Bathurst from rank 33 to 47 and Orange from rank 28 to 30. Another two even suffered population losses: Murray Bridge fell from rank 91 to 104 and Yallourn from rank 21 in 1961 to 44 in 1976 and to 51 in 1981.

One major reason for frequent and sometimes drastic changes of rank of the smaller urban places is their reliance in their economic base on *primary resources*, vulnerable to constant fluctuation of demand. *Changing transportation patterns* have also contributed to fluctuating development. The town of Mudgee, New South Wales, may serve as an example. The advent of the railway in 1884 brought devastating competition from outside manufactured goods to the town's craftsmen; similarly improved highway conditions after 1920 forced more manufacturers to disappear from the Mudgee scene. Back in the 1850s German settlers had started wine growing and established the first wineries in the Mudgee area. Some time later the merino gained importance in the local economy, the sheep husbandry of the area being referred to as Mudgee Blood. At the same time hay in the floodplain of the Cudgegong River and the growth of lucerne known as Mudgee Lucerne became important. With the introduction of irrigation agriculture diversification took place and more emphasis was put on vegetables. Then vegetable growing almost disappeared with the great land consolidations of the 1950s and 1960s. The emphasis was now put on the raising of sheep and cattle and the growth of lucerne, corn, wheat and oats. During the late 1960s and the 1970s land divisions were carried out causing a rapid turnover of plots and the coming into existence of a number of hobby farmers or 'blockies', some of them raising riding horses (horse studs). Reflecting these agricultural changes, the processing and supply industries located in the town of Mudgee have changed over time.

In chapters 2.2.4 and 2.2.6 examples were given of regions where, through government action, too many towns were established in relation to the limited resources in terms of *agricultural productivity or timber yields*. Many parkland towns of South Australia's wheat frontier never reached the 1,000 mark or if they did eventually decreased again and fell below the 1,000 mark. On the other hand, farmers in some districts have abandoned their farm houses and moved to town, from where they practised 'town-farming', as Williams (1970) described it for the Wimmera region of Victoria. In the southwestern forest region of Western Australia some temporarily thriving saw-mill towns declined and even became ghost towns. Only in recent times has there been a change, due to the facts that forests are now being worked on the sustained yield principle. With transport methods improved, timber can also be hauled over longer distances, both of these factors making for a certain stabilization of the economic base of the surviving timber towns (Kerr 1965).

Changes related to *mining activities* were still more spectacular. Beginning with the gold-rush in Victoria, mining towns have mushroomed at various times and in various regions of Australia. The exploitation of lead, silver and zinc began at Broken Hill in 1883. Mining employment peaked at 8,700 in 1913, and population reached 35,000. From the turn of the century it was the second largest city in the state of New South Wales after Sydney. By 1976 the number of miners had declined to 4,200, and by 1981 the city's population was reduced to 26,913. Broken Hill fell from rank 18 in 1961 to rank 31 in 1981 (see ch. 3.3). Similarly Lithgow in New South Wales fell from rank 40 to rank 74, and Kalgoorlie, once the second largest urban place in Western Australia, from rank 25 to 46 (fig. 40).

The *growth of heavy industry* also brought modifications to the urban networks in some states. As early as 1871 Newcastle had become the third major port in Australia after Sydney and Melbourne, mainly due to its being linked by rail to the Maitland coalfield (ch. 3.3). The BHP steel plant also contributed to Newcastle's rising importance. Newcastle proved to be such a favourable location for steel production that the steel plant in Lithgow could no longer compete and its operators decided to relocate to Port Kembla south of Wollongong in 1928. This decision was the origin of the recent growth of these two urban places.

The Port Kembla plant got into difficulties during the depression years and was taken over by BHP in 1935. BHP then expanded further by opening a new steel plant in Whyalla. Thus both Newcastle and Whyalla as steel manufacturing cities came to rank second to the state capital in New South Wales and South Australia respectively.

Another point of interest is the *varying role of the port cities*. Rimmer (1967) made an attempt to establish a sequence of five phases of port development in Australia, leading to an increasing concentration in favour of a very small number of ports, while the majority has remained rather small and unimportant. Rimmer argues that in an early phase all ports had of necessity very restricted hinterlands, due to the difficulties of transporting goods inland. Later concentration processes worked in a selective way. One reason for changes of rank was railway construction policy. Thus the re-orientation of the Western Australian railway network on Perth after 1889 enabled Fremantle to replace Albany as the principal port of the colony, making it the major outlet for the Eastern Goldfields and an important coaling station. During the gold-rush in Victoria, Melbourne's growth slowed down considerably, while Geelong even suffered from a slow decline that was to last for almost five decades (Cloher 1979).

Then there was the rise and sometimes the subsequent stagnation or even decline of the towns that were established in newly occupied agricultural or mining districts, and industrial estates. The first *new towns* in the twentieth century were the administrative centres of the Murrumbidgee Irrigation Areas in the Riverina of New South Wales. Griffith (13, 185) has maintained its growth while Leeton (6, 498) has already started to decline. Kwinana New Town on the southern periphery of the Perth metropolitan area, is also growing (12, 355) although its older residential areas, dating back to the 1950s, have started to lose residential population. In the Pilbara region of Western Australia an earlier system of moribund mining and harbour towns has had superimposed upon it a layer of young mining towns, service centres and deep-sea harbours relating to a new cycle of ore exploration and export. For example, Port Hedland with a population of less than 1,000 in 1960 rose to rank 72 with a population of 12,948 at the 1981 census (fig. 99). The most rapid changes in terms of an upward movement occur in the group of the resort towns mentioned in chapter 2.3.2.

While towns entered the urban network after 1960, a number of other settlements decreased to less than 1,000 residents, thus officially disappearing from the list of urban places. During the intercensal period 1971–76 three urban places in Victoria (Birchip, Koroit, Rushworth), five in New South Wales (Boggabri, Hillston, Peak Hill, Smithtown, Talbuigo) and one town in Queensland (Texas), which at the 1976 census had populations ranging from 1,009 to 1,495, fell below the 1,000 mark. This is, to be sure, a matter of statistics; some service functions are still being performed in these settlements which are now officially classified as non-urban places.

2.3.4 Inter-urban relations in the Australian context

A plaque at the entrance of the Broken Hill railway station commemorates the opening in 1969 of the Australian Transcontinental Railway from Sydney to Perth, the first normal-gauge railway from coast to coast in Australia. This event took place exactly 100 years after the first Transcontinental railway line in the United States had been completed in 1869. Only seven years earlier, in 1962, the first direct rail link between the two most important cities of the continent, Sydney and Melbourne, had been opened. This was the first step toward a standardization of railway gauges in Australia. It is striking that such decisive measures directed towards the unification and integration on this vast nation continent are *very recent achievements* indeed. Due to the small number of large cities, and the long distances separating them, as well as to the long persistence of the initial occupancy in separate colonies and states, each oriented toward its own capital city, and each with its distinct railway network on its own gauge, the process of integration has been very slow. On the other hand, these recent changes are evidence of movement towards the creation of an integrated national economy and of a national urban system.

A factor of utmost importance in this process has been modern transport technology and the great increase of individual mobility, associated with a generally high standard of living and a *high rate of private car ownership*. In consequence of these changes distances in terms of travel time shrank profoundly. Around 1880 it took seven days to get from Sydney to Melbourne by road; a hundred years later it took only 14 hours, and only one hour by plane, not to speak of the almost instantaneous transfer of information by means of modern communication systems. The number of motor vehicles registered in Australia increased from 1.404 million in 1950 to 8.574 million in 1982–83, this increase making for a change of ratio of vehicles to population from 1:5.9 to 1:1.8. For the ownership of private cars (including station wagons) alone the ratio in 1982–83 was 1:2.4.

Since distances are long in Australia a particularly rapid increase of domestic flights occurred during the postwar period (table 24).

Table 24. Australian internal airlines, passenger embarkations (millions), 1950–83

Year	Embarkations (millions)	Index	Population (approximate)	Index
1950	1.5	100	8,200,000	100
1960	2.7	180	10,300,000	126
1970	5.9	393	12,800,000	156
1975	9.4	627	13,900,000	170
1980	11.7	780	14,700,000	179
1983	10.3	687	15,400,000	188

Sources: For embarkations 1950–75 Johnston, J.A. (ed.): *Society in view*, 1978, 72; for 1980 and 1983: Dept. of Sport, Recreation and Tourism: Australian tourism trends, 1985, 100.
Indices and population figures calculated by the author

The main air links are between capital cities. By the end of the 1970s there were over 300 flights per week in both directions between Sydney and Melbourne. There have been some *important additions to the network of domestic airlines* in recent years. Thus until 1978 Melbourne used to be the only mainland capital directly linked by air to Hobart, but then direct flights between Hobart and Sydney were introduced. There are still no direct flights from Hobart to either Adelaide or Perth. Formerly Adelaide was the only capital directly linked by air to Darwin, but flights are now available from Brisbane via Cairns and from Perth via Port Hedland. Flights between regional centres in different states are still infrequent; interstate connections are mainly via the state capitals.

Due to drastic rises of air fares on medium and short-haul routes in 1981 there has been a considerable decline of embarkations from the peak value of 11.7 million in 1980 to 10.3 million in 1983.

For long-distance flows of goods the development of rail and ship transport has to be considered. The development of railways and railway operations is shown in table 25.

There has been a shrinkage of the rail network from its maximum development prior to mid-century. New lines are, however, still constructed. One of the major achievements in recent years was the construction of the 'New Ghan' from Port Augusta to Alice Springs via Woomera. Its continuation from Alice Springs to Katherine, from where a line to Darwin is already in existence, is being carried out as one of the bicentennial projects.

Table 25. Length of railway tracks and railway operations, 1902–80

Year	Length of railway track open in km	Rail passenger journeys in million	Freight carried in million tons
1902	20,600	115	15.7
1950	43,500	505	41.3
1960	42,200	479	52.0
1970	40,300	450	83.7
1980	39,401		

Sources: For 1902–70 Johnston, J.A. (ed.): *Society in View*, 1978, 71; for 1980 Divis. of Nat. Mapping: Australian railway systems 1981

Interstate rail passenger activity has declined during the 1980s, whereas intra-state activity has, with the exception of Western Australia, increased. This may be due to increasing use of the private car as well as to the trend of travelling shorter distances for vacations in recent years.

Despite the general trend to a shrinkage of the rail network, the amount of freight carried annually has increased rapidly since the turn of the century. The amount of freight carried by cargo ships in cabotage between Australian ports must be added to the flows of goods by train. Of course, a great proportion of this coastal trade is in raw materials such as iron ores brought from Derby, Port Hedland and Whyalla to the steel works at Kwinana, Port Kembla and Newcastle or bauxite brought from Weipa and Gove on the Gulf of Carpentaria to the refinery in Gladstone, but it still indicates the considerable intensity of interstate economic relations. The exact proportion of interstate trade is difficult to determine for lack of adequate statistics; according to the Commonwealth of Australia's Constitution, Section 92, movements of people and goods between the states are unrestricted and hence unregistered. Various scholars have, however, made attempts to calculate interstate traffic flows.

Brown (1964) estimated interstate trade between the three southeastern states of New South Wales, Victoria and South Australia to be of the order of 1.1 billion in 1960–61 or approximately 20% of their gross domestic product (GDP). He also found that this interstate proportion had increased from 8–9% of the GDP in 1909. These figures indicate a *considerable increase of trade relations* between the southeastern states.

Relations between these southeastern states and the 'peripheral' states (Mullins 1980 speaks of the 'marginal' and even of the 'underdeveloped' states) are considerably weaker, while relations between the peripheral states are weakest of all. In a more recent investigation Holsman (1975) recognized rather strong linkages between New South Wales, Queensland and the A.C.T., and also between Victoria, South Australia and Tasmania. As to the various modes of transportation, he found New South Wales to be the centre of land links with most states, whereas the system of air-passenger flows is dominated by Victoria.

On the other hand, Mullins (1980) pointed to Australia's 'new dependency' brought about by heavy foreign investment into modern mining ventures. According to his findings there was in 1974–75 a 71% foreign ownership and an 85% foreign control of Queensland mining enterprises, as compared with 52% and 59% respectively of total Australian mining. Stilwell pointed out that the recent mineral boom in Queensland and Western Australia strengthened the links between these peripheral states and external markets in Japan, the United States, and Europe rather than tightening the links between these states and the more industrialized states of the Australian southeast (Stilwell 1979a, also Stevenson 1976). This economic development of the 1970s and 1980s is in contradiction to Geissman & Woolmington's statement that by the 1960s: 'the "colonial-style" import-export biased economy where external linkages dominate and ... the associated "captive hinterland" situation since federation slowly started to break down' (Geissman & Woolmington 1971, 70).

In addition to flows of goods Brown (1964) also studied interstate payments. He found out that by 1960–61 'payments to and from other States (together) total very considerably more than the State's domestic product', that 'every State has transactions with the rest of the Commonwealth very much larger than its overseas transactions' and that 'about one-seventh of all payments through the banking system are interstate' (Brown 1964, 370–71). The first two findings led him to the conclusion that the Australian economy is functioning as an *integrated national economy*.

Let us briefly look at a few more indicators. One of them is the changing degree of primacy. The most recent census data shows the trend depicted in table 26.

Table 26. Rates of primacy of capital cities, 1976 and 1981

City	Per cent of state population		Change (in %)
	1976	1981	
Sydney	60.4	62.4	+ 2.0
Melbourne	71.4	64.6	– 6.8
Brisbane	47.0	40.2	– 6.8
Adelaide	68.9	66.2	– 2.7
Perth	70.3	62.3	– 8.0
Hobart	32.7	30.0	– 2.7

Source: ABS census data

With the exception of Sydney there has been an appreciable *decline of the primacy rate* of the capital cities in the intercensal period 1976–81. The decline was especially marked in Perth, Melbourne and Brisbane. In Western Australia this tendency has certainly been due to the economic activities outside the capital region, mining in particular, as well as to coastal resort development. In Queensland both these factors have also played a part, with the resort development along the Gold and Sunshine Coasts, and the growth of port cities in central and northern Queensland. In Victoria vigorous decentralization and regional planning policies have caused a certain dispersion of employment opportunities and population.

A second indicator is the development of cities in the intermediate group of between 50,000 and 500,000 residents. In the intercensal period 1976–81 their number grew by only two units from 13 to 15, with another two urban places on the verge of 50,000 that will enter the group at the 1986 census. This is, indeed, a very slight increase, in itself hardly an indication of the development of a true national urban system.

The decentralizing of control centres of the economy may be used as a third indicator. As was mentioned above (ch. 2.3.1; see also ch. 3.1.7) out of the 100 greatest Australian firms in 1978, 52 had their headquarters in Sydney and 38 in Melbourne, these numbers changing to 58 and 34 respectively by 1980. Apart from the obvious shift in favour of Sydney, their combined number increased from 90 to 92, thus leaving a mere eight headquarters to the other capital cities. It is apparent that Sydney and Melbourne remained the two dominant capital cities performing nation-wide economic functions. In addition to these two economic centres Canberra performs the nation-wide political functions while the Gold Coast provides specialized holiday and resort functions for a nation-wide hinterland. Thus the core of the nation may be termed the *Melbourne-Canberra-Gold Coast-Sydney rhombus*.

A fourth indicator may be seen in the degree to which urban places are characterized by horizontal or diagonal rather than by hierarchical links. Geissman & Woolmington (1971) stressed the point that modern trade relations are dominated by large flows of goods between highly industrialized countries and also between cities. They pointed to the fact that there has in recent years been an *increasing exchange* of merchandise between the Sydney and Melbourne markets. Stewart (1977) found that since the 1960s many companies so far confined to one state found it appropriate to extend their activities beyond the boundaries of the state in which their own headquarters were located and to acquire companies in other states. For example, in the retail sector David Jones of Sydney took over department stores of other companies in Townsville, Brisbane and Cairns between 1961 and 1963. Of the 560 companies acquired by companies with their headquarters in New South Wales between August 1959 and December 1970, exactly 50% were located in other states: 137 in Victoria, 57 in Queensland, 40 in South Australia, 29 in Western Australia, 11 in Tasmania and 6 in the A.C.T. Victoria comes close to these figures whereas the figures for all other states are considerably lower.

As to interstate flows of information, Walmsley in a study of Australian mass media (1982) came to the conclusion that the Sydney newspapers under consideration had a strong home-state and eastern seaboard bias. He could show, however, that during the decade 1968–78 a trend developed toward an *increasing news coverage of the rest of Australia in the Sydney newspapers*.

In conclusion may be said that extreme natural conditions, the wide separation of the more habitable and better populated areas and the legacy of the separate historical and economic development of the various settlement nuclei during colonial times and early statehood have been to date heavy constraints upon the development of an integrated economy and a national urban system in Australia. Even recent developments such as the mining activities in Western Australia and Queensland, with their overseas export links, are apt to retard rather than to further the unification process in Australia. But in spite of the continuing high degree of primacy, including the nation-wide controls of economic functions by mainly two of the primate cities, there have since federation in 1901 been a number of trends towards the creation of a national economy and a national urban system. These include increasing interstate flows of informations, increasing transfers of interstate payments and increasing flows of interstate freight by ship, rail and truck. These linkages have been facilitated by the continuous expansion of the highway network and even the construction of new links of the railway network, and marked by a great increase of mobility of the Australian population, due to the high rate of private car ownership and the ready availability of domestic air transport.

3 Towns, cities and metropolitan areas

3.1 The capital cities

3.1.1 The metropolitan area of Sydney, New South Wales

Just as the Plymouth Plantation near Boston, founded by the Pilgrim Fathers, is considered the cradle of the United States and Capetown as South Africa's 'mother city', so the anchoring in 1788 of the 'First Fleet' under Captain (later Governor) Phillip marks Sydney Cove, at the mouth of the Parramatta River, as the beginning of white settlement in Australia. In commemoration of this event the roof of the famous Sydney Opera House, located on the waterfront, was designed to resemble a fleet of ships having set sail for a journey.

There is a saying 'Sydney or the bush'. Although it may be unjustified to contrast Australia's first-rank metropolis with the outback in the sense of 'all or nothing' the slogan suggests that Sydney has been considered the hub of the nation-continent. It is, indeed, Australia's *oldest, largest, most densely populated and most cosmopolitan* state capital. Nevertheless, the city had long been challenged by Melbourne. Victoria's capital experienced a more rapid growth in its early days due to the gold-rush for a considerable time and enjoyed the privilege of housing the Commonwealth Government. It was only in the decade after federation that, mainly in consequence of Melbourne's recession in the 1890s and its comparatively slow recovery, Sydney was able to surpass its rival in terms of resident population.

Named for Viscount Sydney, the then Secretary for the Colonies in London, Sydney Cove had been chosen as an alternative site to Botany Bay a little farther south, which had been well-known through its association with Captain Cook but which did not seem a favourable place for settlement to Captain Phillip, because of the lack of an adequate supply of fresh water.

The site at Sydney Cove proved well chosen. It provided good anchorage and is indeed one of the finest harbours in the whole of Australia. The little Tank Stream, now completely buried under concrete and asphalt, provided fresh water. Clay for making bricks was found at a nearby place called Brickfield Hill. There was, however, a certain lack of fertile soil for food production in the adjacent Cumberland Plain. Farming was started at Farm Cove, the present site of the Botanical Gardens, and further upstream at a place later called Parramatta, where we still find Experiment Farm Cottage, now in the property of the National Trust (New South Wales) (Robinson 1953, 144–160). Governor Phillip himself expressed in a letter of 1790 to W. W. Grenville that he would have preferred to establish the settlement at Rose Hill, later to become known as Parramatta, if he had had more time to carefully investigate the area (Comm. of Austr. ser. I, Vol. I, 1914, 182). Under Governor Macquarie (1810–21) an intensive search for better farmland was carried out and the Valley of the Hawkesbury River to the north of Sydney was opened up for farming (see ch. 2.2.2).

Early Sydney owes much to Macquarie's energy and imagination. The Rocks district, to the west of Sydney Cove at the foot of the present Sydney Harbour Bridge, was already in a rather desolate condition (ch. 2.2.8). One reason was the natural setting of the area. Due to the steepness of terrain, some of the streets and many house-sites had irregular patterns. The second reason was that the Governor's wishes were not always followed by the military and free settlers, so that regulations, including building regulations, were not always obeyed. Governor Phillip had given the settlement a layout with the streets running northeast-southwest taking wind directions into consideration, but neglecting the difficulties of the terrain. He had ordered the streets to be 200 feet wide and houses to be of a minimum size of 60 x 150 feet. The struggle for existence and the shortage of labour in the early years were major obstacles to regulations. Another reason may have been that only short-term leases had been granted on Crown lands so that 'generally only shoddy, makeshift buildings were erected' (Gurnani-Smith 1984, 13).

Many of these abuses were remedied within a few years. *Governor Macquarie* ordered the streets to be straightened and the houses to be brought into alignment. He allowed long-term leases, thus inducing the settlers to build more solidly and pretentiously. He appointed the former convict architect F. Greenway as Civil Architect and Assistant Engineer of the colony, and commissioned a number of public buildings including St. James' Church, the Conservatorium and the Mint (see ch. 2.2.1). He also gave orders prohibiting the further use of Tank Stream for washing clothes and of the roads as rubbish dumps (Gurnani-Smith 1984).

At the end of Governor Macquarie's term land values in Sydney were reported to be half as high as in the best situations in London! In the period 1810–21 the colony's population increased from 11,950 to 38,778; the acreage cultivated increased from 7,615 to 32, 267; the number of sheep raised in the colony increased from 25,888 to 290,158 and the revenues rose from £ 8,000 to £ 30,000 (Roberts 1968, 24–25). Sydney had thus become the administrative centre of a flourishing colony.

Difficulties of surveying the land continued, however, under Macquarie's successors. *Surveyor-General Mitchell* in 1828 wrote an instruction according to which the basic unit was supposed to be a Section of one square mile while 25 sections were to form a Parish and 64 parishes were to form a County of 1,600 square miles (Comm. of Austr. ser. I, vol. IV, 178). One year later Governor Darling published guidelines in the Sydney Gazette ordering the town's layout to be regular and uniform in half-acre plots, with the main streets 120 feet wide and the cross streets 84 feet wide, with the building-line for houses 14 feet away from the front boundary of the plot (Jeans 1972). The situation was entirely different from that of Melbourne, where the city centre developed within a frame of 32 well surveyed rectangular blocks of equal size.

The growth of the city, although after mid-century slower than that of Melbourne induced Sydney citizens in 1859 to submit a petition to the colonial government to construct a tramline. Two years later a tramline of nearly 3 km was opened by the government, then leased to private enterprise that soon began to suffer from unreasonably high costs and discontinued operations. The next step in this respect was taken in 1873. It was not before the turn of the century, however, that the great expansion of the city's tramlines occurred, with an increase from 123 km to 322 km during the period 1900–14. At the end of this period annual passenger journeys had reached almost 300 million (Wotherspoon 1983, 110–113).

The CBD developed in the area between Darling Harbour to the west and the open areas of the Royal Botanic Gardens, The Domain and Hyde Park to the east. According to the City Planning Department it is today confined within Hickson Road, Sussex, Harbour and Quay Streets to the west and Pitt Street, Wentworth Avenue, Elizabeth and Macquarie Streets to the east. It has thus an average width of 700 m and stretches north-south for 2.5 km *from Circular Quay to Railway Square* at the Central Station. These two extremities are crucial for those of Sydney's commuters not using their private cars or buses. Large numbers of commuters arrive from the Northshore by ferry at Circular Quay while many others arrive by suburban train at the Central Station (Wehling 1975). The Sydney Harbour Bridge opened in 1924 carries such a great volume of traffic that a project of a tunnel between the CBD at Macquarie Street on the south shore and Kirribilli on the north shore has recently been initiated (fig. 41).

The major concentration of office buildings is in the northern section of the CBD. Particular concentrations of public buildings are all along Macquarie Street while shipping offices are mainly found in Bridge Street. Retailing has tended to concentrate in the southern section, especially after 1906, when the railway was extended 1 km northward from its former terminal at Redfern Station to the present Central Station on Railway Square. Pitt Street in particular attracted the most fashionable shops. A *northward trend* was initiated by the opening in 1926 of the underground line to Circular Quay and in 1932 of the Sydney Harbour Bridge. Since that time many CBD functions were established on the opposite bank of the river in North Sydney, and even in places farther away from the city centre. Retail businesses also moved northward and, to a lesser extent, eastward from Brisbane Ward to Bourke Ward or else suffered from increasing competition from the modern shopping centres, leaving some buildings in the southern section unused (Wiles 1967, Edwards 1981). Government and cultural functions are concentrated on the northeast side, in part bordering the Botanical Gardens and The Domain (fig. 42).

Particular mention must be made of the small area of Chinatown, located in the southernmost blocks of Dixon and Sussex Streets in the southwestern section of the CBD. Due to widespread xenophobia, particularly on the part of the trade unions in the last century, the Chinese were restricted in area as well as in occupation. One of their occupations was market gardening, and it is in the southern parts of the two streets mentioned above that lay the origins of the huge buildings of the former vegetable and fruit market. A few hundred Chinese were also occupied as furniture-makers (ch. 4.2).

The CBD as defined by the City Council comprises part of the wholesale district that adjoins the CBD proper along York Street and then stretches around Darling Harbour, reaching as far south as Ultimo Road and west as far as Bay Street. Only about ten blocks are exclusively occupied by wholesale functions, whereas on the margins of the area there are blocks with intermingled tenements, manufacturing industries and wholesale trade (Simons 1962).

Sydney's entertainment area is located to the east of Kings Cross, a very heterogeneous area characterized by a mixture of old decaying houses and of restored and new buildings, many occupied as hotels, private pensions and tenements. Entertainment uses also occupy many high-priced and prestigious locations around Potts Point and Elizabeth Bay. In the post-war years planners envisaged an eastward expansion of the CBD into Wooloomooloo and toward Kings Cross, an area which will be treated below in greater detail. The University of Sydney is located to the southwest, between Redfern and Camperdown, while the University of New South Wales and Macquarie University are located farther out to the southeast and the north respectively.

Fig. 41. Sydney, N.S.W. View from Australia Building in the CBD over Port Jackson with Sydney Harbour Bridge and Opera House

The CBD experienced an *extraordinary building boom* during the period 1968–74 followed by a slump, the reasons and consequences being minutely described by Daly (1982). Since 1912 building regulations in Sydney had prevented the construction of buildings higher than about ten storeys. Prices had also been held in check by the Land Sales Control Act and the Landlord and Tenant Act of 1939; the former was abandoned in 1948 and the latter amended in 1958.

Substantial changes in the CBD started in 1958 with renewal projects in the northern section between Martin Place and Circular Quay, the former being transformed to a modern pedestrian mall. During the period 1967–75 new buildings were constructed offering a total of 4.85 million square metres of office and retail space (Daly 1982, 65), although data provided by the Council of the City of Sydney (1980) give considerably lower figures (ch. 3.1.7). Even though the figure given may be exaggerated, the boom was remarkable. After price controls had been eased, land prices skyrocketed, so that between 1950 and 1974 the proportion of the lot in relation to the average cumulative real-estate price increased from approximately 15% to 60%. A second factor was the rising demand for space in the CBD in the course of the overall post-war economic growth. Sydney reflecting the increasing concentration of the Australian capital market in the switching of the world market from the British pound as leading currency to the American dollar led to American, Japanese and other overseas capital being invested in increasing amounts into the Australian real estate market. Finally, the exploration of mineral resources had its impact on a financial market that began to concentrate in Sydney rather than in Melbourne. Of the hundred largest firms operating in Australia in 1980, 58 had their headquarters in Sydney as compared with 34 in Melbourne. 25 years earlier the ratio had been the other way round.

The construction boom was first reflected in the high vacancy rate of 25% in 1976, but three years later it was down to 8% (Council of the City of Sydney 1980). By 1982 almost all office space available in the new high-rise office buildings of the CBD had been occupied, while at the same time a considerable amount of office space had also been created in North Sydney, Crows Nest, Chatswood and even as far away from the CBD as Parramatta.

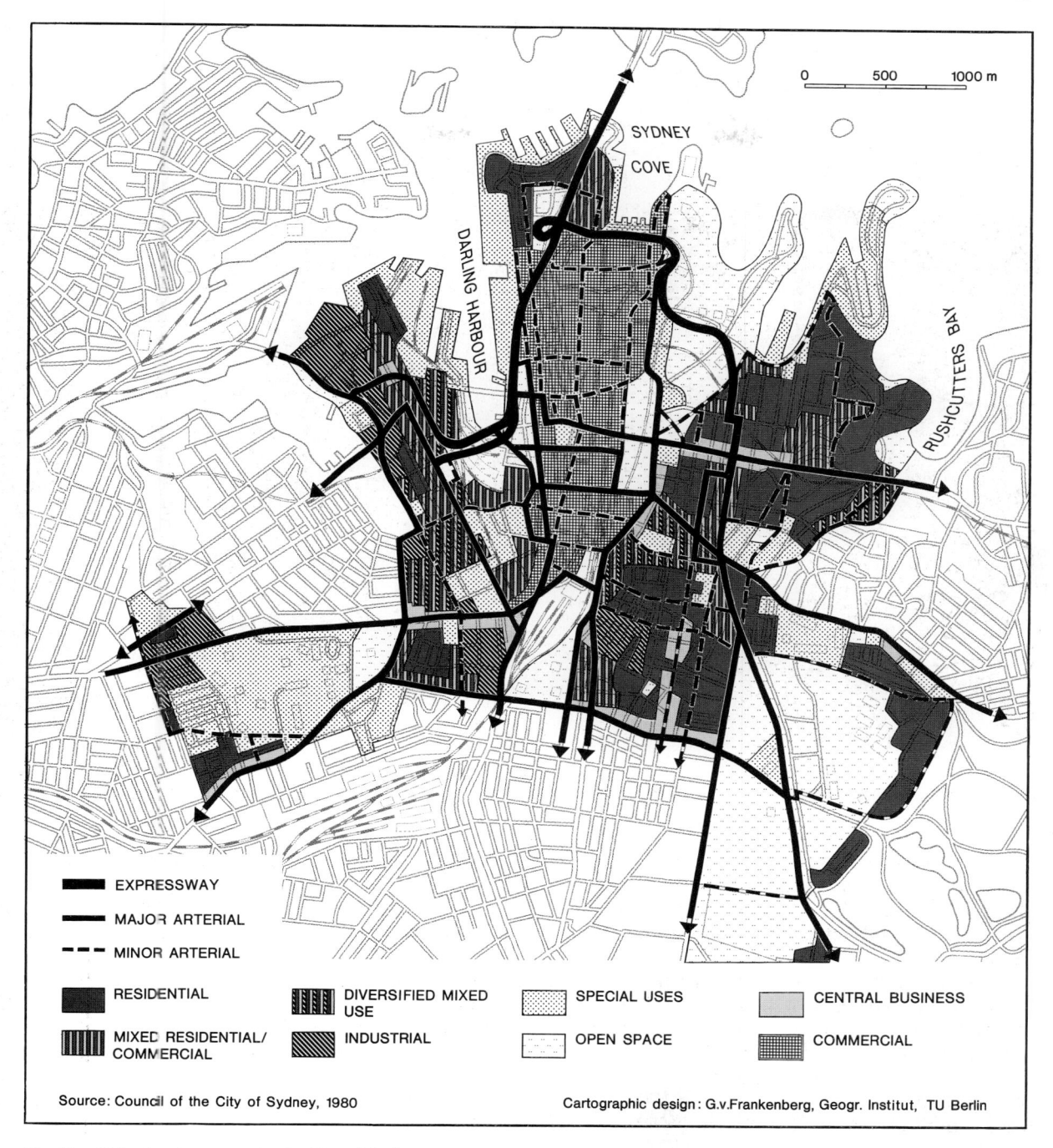

Fig. 42. Major land-use areas in the City of Sydney

Of the total employment in the CBD in 1976, 32.7% was in finance and business services, 19.1% in public administration and defense, 14.1% in wholesale and retail trade, 6.5% in manufacturing, 6.2% in entertainment and recreation, 5.7% in transport and storage, 5.6% in communication and 4.7% in community services (Council of the City of Sydney 1978).

The City of Sydney is surrounded by a ring of old, rather densely built-up, crowded suburbs such as Wooloomooloo, Darlinghurst, Redfern, Surrey Hills, Newtown, Glebe and Balmain. Their streets are narrow with numerous back alleys, and their houses are partly decayed and intermingled with factories, but there are, especially to the east, some formerly fashionable suburbs such as Paddington and Woolahra. A high percentage of houses are in *terraces* (fig. 43). They are not found to quite the same extent in Melbourne's inner suburbs, still less in the other capital

Fig. 43. Kings Cross, Sydney, N.S.W. Three-storey terrace houses

Fig. 44. Harbourfield, Sydney metropolitan area, N.S.W. Federation-style house, ca 1900

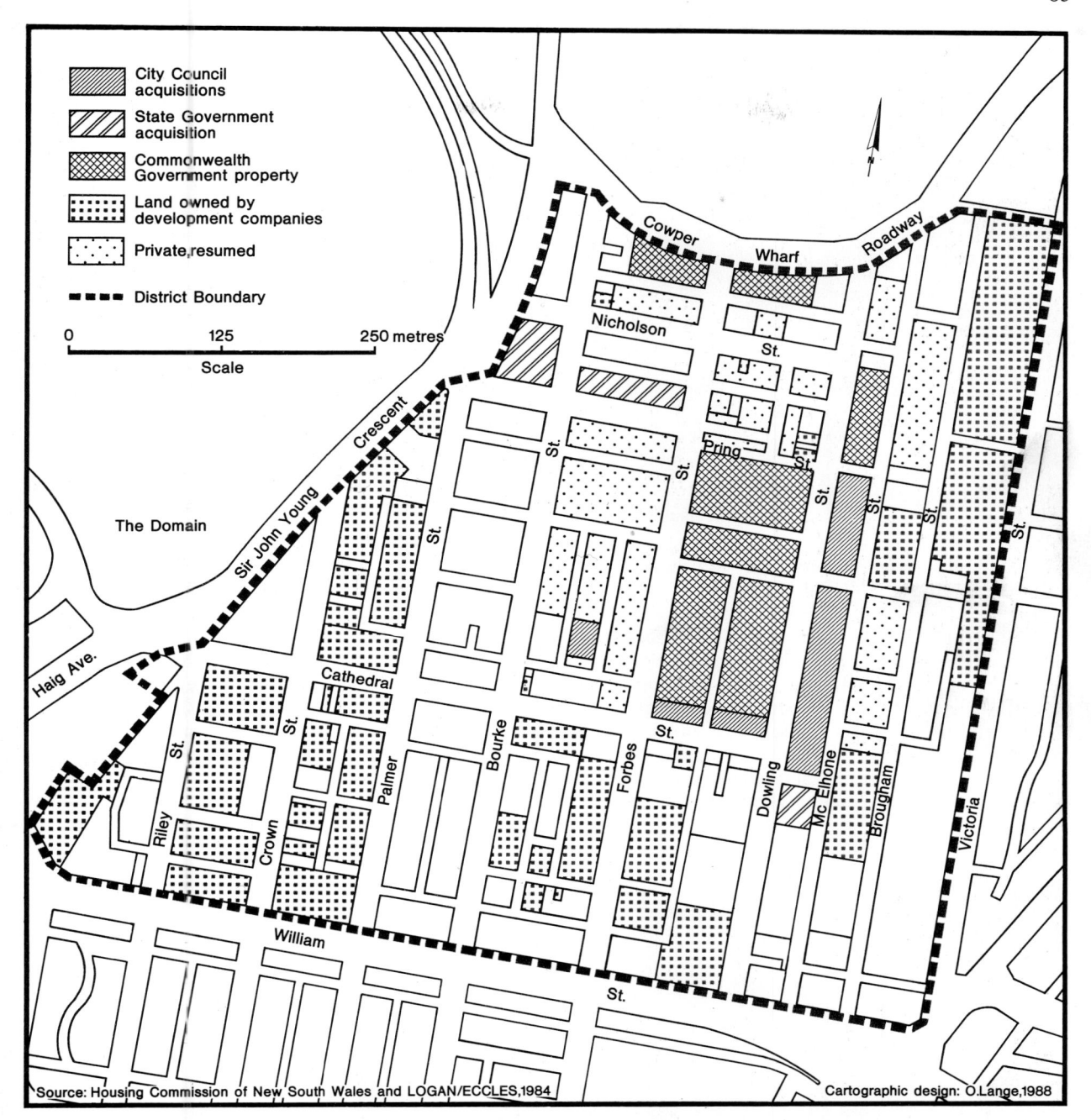

Fig. 45. The N.S.W. Housing Commission's Wooloomooloo Project (based on maps by the N.S.W. Housing Commission)

cities. This rings of inner suburbs characterized by the terrace houses extends to Kensington in the southeast, to Tempe and Sydenham to the south and Leichhardt to the west, whereas Leichhardt's neighbouring suburbs of Petersham and Haberfield are already dominated by the younger *federation-style houses*, with their red terracotta-tiled roofs, their gables with sun symbols, their leadlight and Art nouveau windows, their split columns, tiled or wooden verandah floors and winding paths through the gardens (fig. 44).

Some 5 to 6 km south of the CBD a low-lying swampy area remained for a long time unoccupied, but was eventually encroached upon by residential development. In this area of *Alexandria-Waterloo*, later amalgamated with the City of Sydney, a great industrial complex developed around the turn of the century. Since zoning regulations of 1951 restricted further industrial development in the inner suburbs and prohibited factories outside zoned industrial areas from expanding, a number of factories in this area either relocated by moving to Auburn, Bankstown and the developing southwestern industrial sector toward Campbelltown, or went out of business (Logan 1968).

Fig. 46. Wooloomooloo, Sydney, N.S.W. New residences designed as to fit in this old inner residential suburb of two-storey terrace houses

There has been much *renewal, modernization and gentrification* in some of the inner suburbs. *Wooloomooloo*, adjoining The Domain to the west and Wooloomooloo Bay to the north had been labourers' and immigrants' residential areas, linked with the docks and port-related manufacturing industries. A considerable proportion of the land was in government ownership while a great deal more had been bought by developers (fig. 45). There were plans for the construction of high-rise office buildings for an eastward expansion of the CBD. Later modifications of the original plan envisaged a dormitory town with high-rise apartment buildings.

Pressure from citizens' action groups and the green bans of the Builders Labourers' Federation (BLF) helped to make the city administration abandon these plans. The Whitlam Government contributed $ 17 million towards a

Fig. 47. Glebe, Sydney, N.S.W. Terrace houses after rehabilitation. Outhouses were preserved inspite of connecting the area to the urban sewerage system

revised development, of which $ 14 million were used to acquire an area of about 13 hectares containing some 350 dwellings. The area was then downzoned and conservation of part of the building stock was made a development guideline. New buildings were planned so as to fit in with the existing environment and consisted of a mixture of one to three-bedroom houses, in order to achieve a social mixture of the future residents. A report by the Housing Commission of New South Wales gives this description of one of the rows of new townhouses: 'It infills between Victorian terraced houses on both sides and repeats their arches, parapets and verandahs. The units are designed as generally identical plan forms with rendered brick walls on the street boundaries. Details and interest are created by adding on balcony, canopy and roof components in various ways. This allows an economical solution, providing individuality and unit identity in sympathy with the existing Wooloomooloo streetscape' (Housing Commission 1979). A primary school was built on a central site by incorporating an abandoned naval depot and a former furniture show-room (fig. 46). The procedures by which the cooperation of the architectural consultants and the Housing Commission were secured have been described by Perumal, a member of the team of consultants (1984).

Glebe to the west of the CBD had also been a labourers' residential area. In this case a greater part of the land that was to come under a renewal programme had been owned by the Anglican Church. The government bought an area of approximately 19 hectares, containing some 730 houses, and started a modernization and conservation programme. All roofs were renewed in order to preserve the houses from further decay, and a thorough survey of one residence was done in order to calculate the costs of the whole project. Although main drainage was put into the area the outside pivies were left and neatly restored to serve the residents of the houses for storing their garden utensils (fig. 47).

According to Logan & Eccles (1977, 57) 'projects worth $ 3000 million had been stopped as a result of green bans' in Sydney by mid-1973.

Other changes have taken place in the City of Sydney and the inner suburbs. Between 1947 and 1971 an estimated 5.200 dwelling units were lost to industrial uses and another 7.400 units to commercial uses in the City and parts of South Sydney and Leichhardt. Due to changes of population in some residential areas, the City's blue-collar jobs fell in the intercensal period 1971–76 from 66% to 61%. At the same time white-collar jobs rose by 7–9% in Darlinghurst, Paddington and Surrey Hills. The process of gentrification was also reflected in a decrease of the younger people below 24 years and an increase of the 25–39 years age group. In the period 1962–80 over 3.300 dwelling units in the older building stock of Kings Cross were converted to strata title or condominiums (Council of the City of Sydney 1980, 48–50).

Some of the older suburbs such as Redfern, Marrickwille, Leichhardt and Drummoyne have been areas of above-average percentage of overseas immigrants. They constitute the eastern section of an *east-west discontinous belt* from Bondi on the east side near the ocean front through the middle of the metropolitan area all the way to Parramatta and Liverpool, whereas the northern suburbs and the greater portion of the southern suburbs are dominated by Australian-born residents. This belt more or less corresponds with a *large wedge of lower socio-economic status* formed by the western suburbs, whereas the suburbs on the north shore form a very large high-status wedge and the south and east are penetrated by a number of smaller high-status wedges. An early account of social indices for Sydney's LGAs is found in Stilwell (1974, see also Badcock 1973) (fig. 48).

This general picture has then to be modified by looking at individual ethnic groups. The index of residential segregation of Sydney's population is only slightly higher for the overseas born as a whole (20.9%) than for the Australians born of Australian-born parents (19.4%). The index is 44.6% for the Italian-born immigrants, 55.1% for the Greek immigrants, 62.4% for the Lebanese who are living highly concentrated in the three areas of Redfern, Lakemba and Harris Park south of Parramatta. It is 79.0% for the Vietnamese, who were initially accommodated in hostels in Cabramatta, and have to a high degree remained close to them (Div. Nat. Mapping & ABS 1984, Burnley 1976, 1982a, 1982c).

Sydney's post-war growth was accompanied by a rapid expansion of the built-up area of the metropolis. Probably the most conspicuous feature of this growth is the continuous strip of settlement stretching westward for over 56 km from the City of Sydney to Penrith and further penetrating into the Blue Mountains along the railway line beyond Emu Flats toward Springwood. Along this route large housing schemes have been carried out in part by the Land Commission of New South Wales. One of its largest projects was the Mt. Druitt area of more than 50 hectares, with its central bus station and huge shopping centre close to the suburban railway station. Other recent developments of the Commission are at St. Clair and at Worrington Downs near Penrith (see fig. 12).

Sydney was the pacemaker of the modern suburban shopping centre in Australia. In 1957 the *first shopping centre* to be established in the country opened its gates at Top Ryde, and some 40 shopping centres have been constructed in the Sydney metropolitan area since. According to Logan (1968, 261) in Sydney 'strong competition among such large firms as David Jones, Myers, Grace Brothers and Mark Foys, has contributed to the rapid suburbanization of department stores'. This is in marked contrast with Melbourne, where the Myer Company has been dominant and has played a decisive part in the location of suburban shopping centres. In contrast with the Top Ryde Centre with its 144,000 square feet of gross floor area and its 69 stores the more recent Roselands Centre at Wiley Park has 1.134 million square feet and 98 stores. In 1981 the Macquarie Centre opened in North Ryde, with its

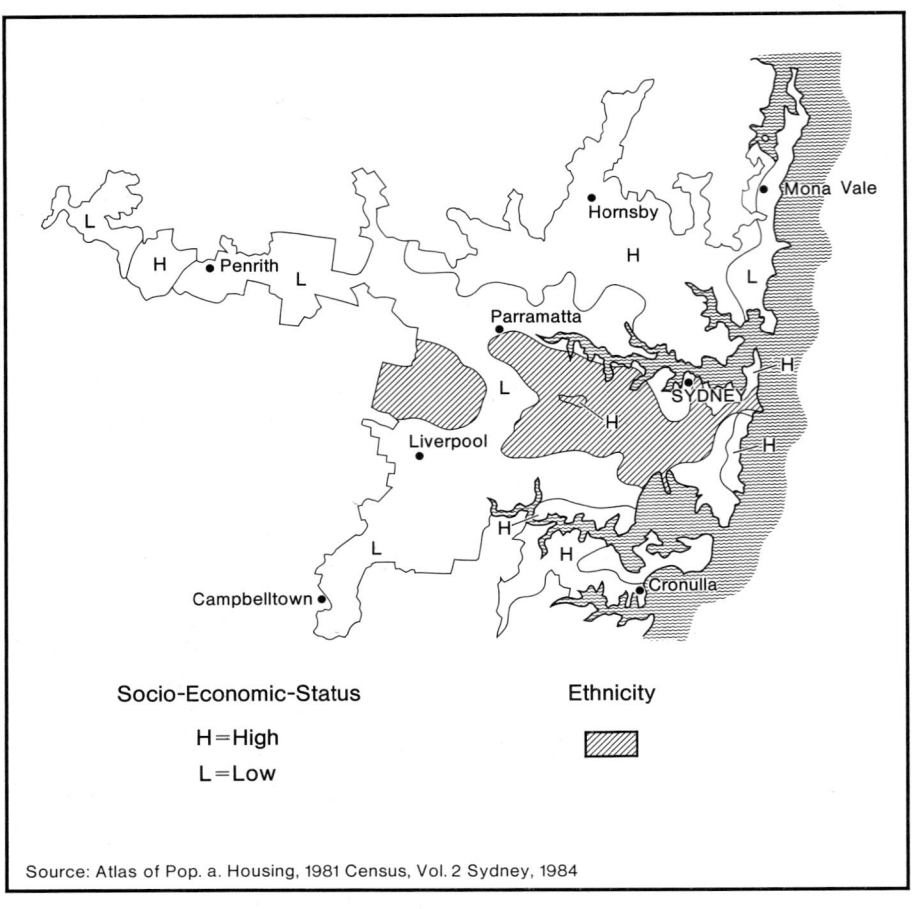

Fig. 48. Ethnicity and socio-economic status in Sydney

146 shops and services including a medical centre, a Grace Brothers department store, a Woolworths supermarket and an olympic-sized ice rink.

Sydney was also the first metropolis to have a metropolitan development plan. In 1951 the *Cumberland Plan* produced in 1948 by the Cumberland County Council was approved by the New South Wales Parliament. One of its major goals was the decentralization of industry in connection with a systematic development of the outer suburban zone and the creation of well-endowed suburban areas, these being separated from one another by sufficiently large areas of open space. The main idea behind these planning goals was the chance of good access to community services for the metropolitan population and the reduction of the daily journey to work. However, most of the outer industrial areas happened to be accessible more easily by car than by public transport, thus putting people without cars at a disadvantage. The suburban zone was preferably to be structured around *district centres*, each based on a department store. Sydney was more successful in developing new district centres in connection with rail lines and established centres of existing suburbs than were the other capital cities. For more details on this planning phase the reader is referred to Stretton (1970), Bunker (1971) and Alexander (in: Troy 1981) (fig. 49).

The plan achieved a certain degree of industrial decentralization in the Sydney metropolitan area. However, when in 1963 the State Planning Authority assumed responsibility for metropolitan planning, less emphasis was put on industrial decentralization and more on office dispersal. Despite this plan, office functions have, as mentioned above, remained highly centralized. In 1968 the *Sydney Region Outline Plan* was released, followed by the Sydney Area Transportation Study in 1974. The latter recommended considerable urban freeway construction, but in the face of local opposition and with changing policies on the part of the Whitlam Government in Canberra, not much was accomplished in this respect during the 1970s (Alexander in: Troy 1981). However, in accord with the Outline Plan, the metropolitan area mainly developed along *five corridors*. The western corridor, already mentioned above, stretches beyond Penrith along the railway line into the Blue Mountains. The northern corridor along the coast leads to Gosford and eventually to Wyong. The northwestern corridor deviates from the western corridor at Blacktown and leads to Windsor on the Hawkesbury River. The southern corridor stretches beyond Sutherland toward Wollongong and the southwestern corridor to the newly developing district centre of Campbelltown.

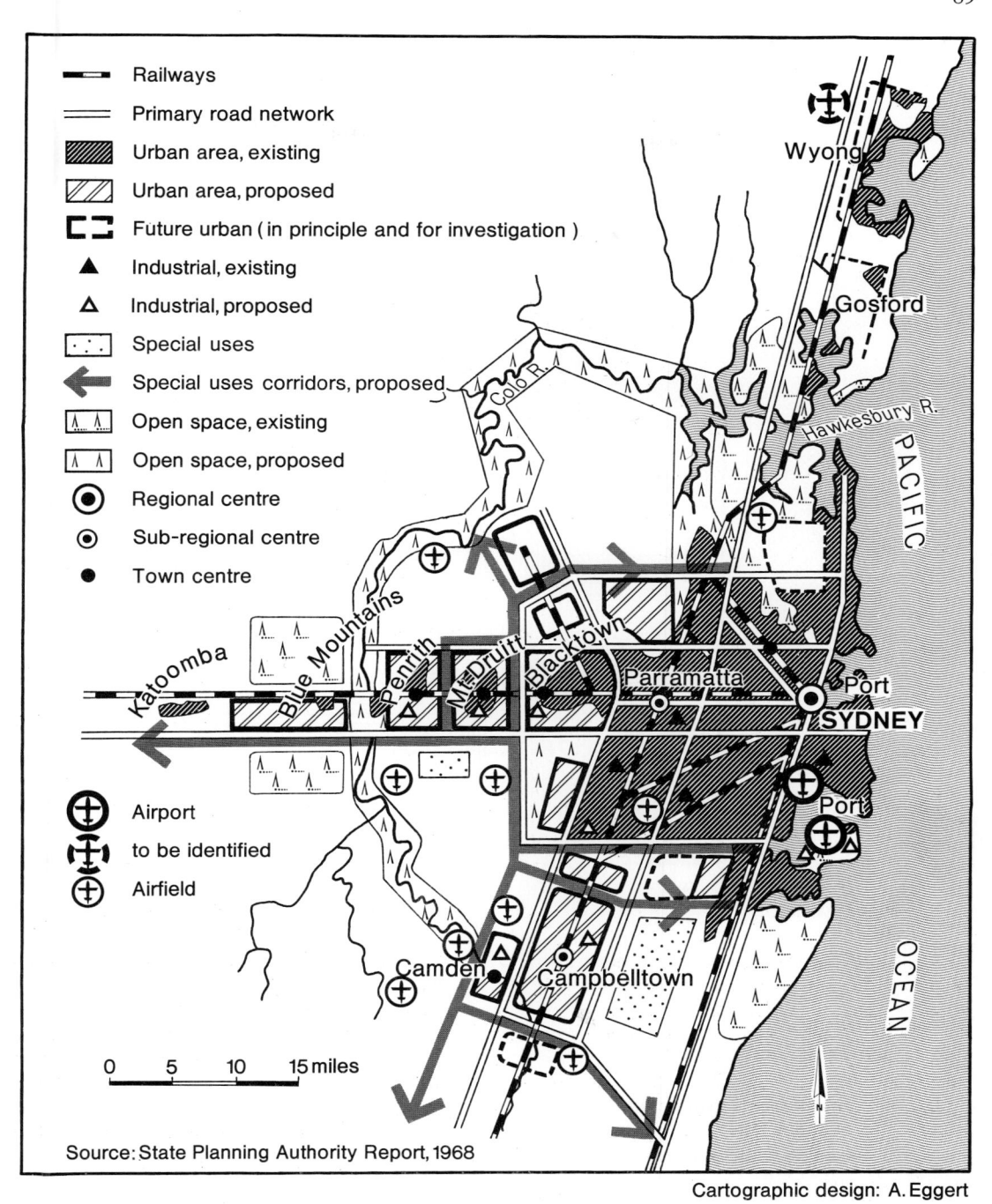

Fig. 49. The development of corridors and district centres in Sydney according to the City Region Outline Plan

In recent years the growth rates of both Sydney and Melbourne have slowed down considerably, but Sydney has been able to consolidate its leading position. As already mentioned, Sydney's share of the headquarters of the 100 largest firms in Australia was 58 in 1980, and the city also took over from Melbourne the position of Australia's leading banking centre. Sydney was also able to attract an increasing share of growth industries and services, such as data processing and transmission and the modern media of communication (fig. 50).

To sum up, Sydney is Australia's oldest and largest city. After its establishment in 1788 it was for more than half a century Australia's only colonial capital. After the gold-rush in Victoria Melbourne became a strong competitor, and Sydney only resumed first rank in population size during the first decade of the twentieth century. Sydney's harbour was the best of the colonial port-capitals, apart from Hobart's fine harbour. Sydney's street pattern was not

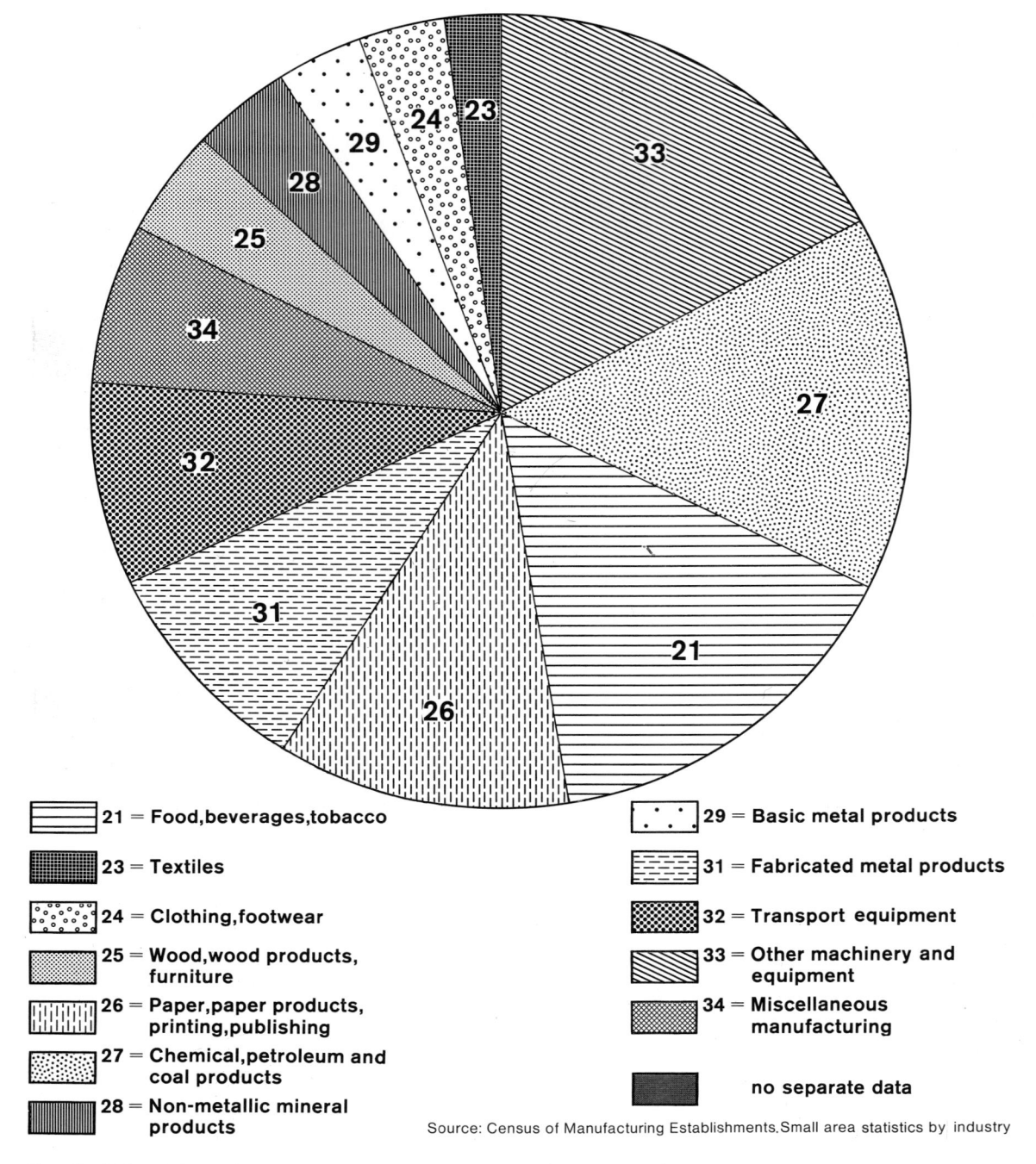

	21 = Food, beverages, tobacco		29 = Basic metal products
	23 = Textiles		31 = Fabricated metal products
	24 = Clothing, footwear		32 = Transport equipment
	25 = Wood, wood products, furniture		33 = Other machinery and equipment
	26 = Paper, paper products, printing, publishing		34 = Miscellaneous manufacturing
	27 = Chemical, petroleum and coal products		no separate data
	28 = Non-metallic mineral products		

Source: Census of Manufacturing Establishments. Small area statistics by industry

Fig. 50. Value added by industry sub-divisions in Sydney, 1982/83 (total = A$ 8.759 bill.)

as regular as that of the other capital cities and those of Adelaide and Melbourne in particular: nevertheless its historic core of The Rocks has become a major tourist attraction. The City of Sydney is surrounded by a rather solid ring of older, densely built-up, crowded suburbs, great parts of which are characterized by monotonous rows of terrace houses, which are not found in equal numbers in other Australian cities. In consequence of the nature of its housing stock Sydney has the highest residential density of all capital cities. There is an east-west discontinuous belt of low social status areas through the middle of the metropolitan area corresponding, to a certain extent, with the major concentrations of overseas immigrants. Sydney is Australia's largest industrial city in terms of value added, followed by Melbourne by a rather small margin, and there is more than double the available office space than in Melbourne. The city surpassed its rival as the seat of headquarters of the largest Australian firms, is the foremost banking place in the country and is the most important city with regard to various modern growth industries and services.

3.1.2 The metropolitan area of Melbourne, Victoria

There has always been a strong rivalry between Sydney and Melbourne. Melbourne has no doubt a number of major achievements to its credit, although Sydney's junior by 47 years, the city grew comparatively fast. Due to the goldrush and a stronger economic development in Victoria, Melbourne was throughout the second half of the nineteenth century larger than Sydney. At the time of federation both cities were at the half-million mark, with Melbourne still slightly the larger city; it was only surpassed by Sydney during the first decade of the twentieth century.

The first Parliament of the Commonwealth of Australia met in Melbourne in 1901, and the city served as the seat of the Federal Government until 1927, when Canberra was officially declared the federal capital. In fact many government agencies remained in Melbourne until their enforced relocation in 1957; a few even remain to this day.

Melbourne has the densest of the capital-centred railway networks of any Australian state. The city became a financial and commercial centre of national and international importance, with a great number of the headquarters of banks and other enterprises, mainly concentrated along Collins Street in the CBD.

Melbourne has also become a sports centre of national and international importance. It was the site of the Olympic Games of 1956, an event for which the Olympic Stadium seating over 100,000 persons was constructed. The Olympic Park, the Melbourne Cricket Ground, the National Tennis Centre and Flemington Racecourse are but some of the city's sporting facilities.

Melbourne is an important centre of tertiary education, with its 'Knowledge Precinct' housing the University of Melbourne and the Royal Institute of Technology. Apart from two other universities, Melbourne is the seat of such famous institutions as the Australian College of Surgeons and the Australian Chemical Institute.

Finally, Melbourne and Sydney are about equal in industrial production, the value-added of either city amounting to over $ 8.5 billion per annum (fig. 51).

Melbourne's birth was not without great difficulties. While officially a part of the colony of New South Wales but not in fact systematically occupied by Europeans this southeastern division of the mainland was first settled by *squatters from Van Diemen's Land* (Tasmania). A certain John Flemming had visited the south coast in 1803 and reported favourably about the banks of the Yarra Yarra, as the river used to be called by the Aborigines (reflecting their habit of doubling terms). Acting upon this news John Pascoe Faukner's Port Phillip Association in Van Diemen's Land bought the land around the present Melbourne from the Dutigalla tribe, and John Batman chose the site for settlement in 1835. This land purchase was, however, not acknowledged by the New South Wales Government, nor did the Government at first allow land sales to be held locally, insisting on land auctions being held in Sydney. It was only after a journey to the south coast that the Governor was convinced that under the existing circumstances it would have been impossible for most prospective settlers to travel to Sydney in order to participate in the auctions (Street 1937, Hopton 1941, Cannon 1984).

In 1837, two years after squatting had started, Governor Bourke travelled to the Port Phillip District, as the area was known in those early days, and ordered the surveyor Mr. Hoddle to found a settlement some 7 km upstream from the mouth of the Yarra, where sufficient fresh water was available. It was named after *Lord Melbourne*, the British Prime Minister from 1834 to 1841. Another settlement was founded simultaneously on a little peninsula beyond the mouth of the Yarra River on Hobson's Bay named *William's Town* (later: Williamstown), after King William IV. It was anticipated that this would grow to be the dominant settlement in the region, but there had been a misjudgement of the situation. Melbourne was to become the capital city of the later separate and self-governing colony of Victoria, whereas Williamstown became but one of the numerous nuclei within the present large metropolitan area of Melbourne.

In its early years the settlement had to compete with other Victorian port towns such as Geelong, Portland and Warrnambool. However, Melbourne enjoyed a more central location within the Port Phillip District, a location somewhat closer to Sydney, and had a superior harbour. Moreover, the early communications, such as the frequencies of mail route services or the telegraph and railway networks were very much in favour of Melbourne as a focal point, as Cloher (1978) has documented in a series of charts.

Between June, 1837 and April, 1839 five land sales took place during which 315 allotments were sold in Melbourne for average prices successively increasing from the first to the fifth sale from £ 36 to £ 43, £ 109, £ 125 and £ 154. Town blocks were surveyed and divided into 20 allotments of approximately half an acre (2,000 square metres) each in a way that a central alley cut each block into two halves, each having ten allotments. The six central allotments had small street frontages and ran from the street to the central alley, whereas the other four allotments were laid out as corner allotments with a longer street frontage but half the depth (Cannon 1984; see fig. 52).

Melbourne's *present CBD* is more or less congruent with the rectangle between Latrobe Street in the north and Flinders Street close to the Yarra River in the south, between Spencer Street in the west and Spring Street in the east, this rectangle amounting to 8 x 8 = 64 blocks. This city core is at present confined to the south by the railway

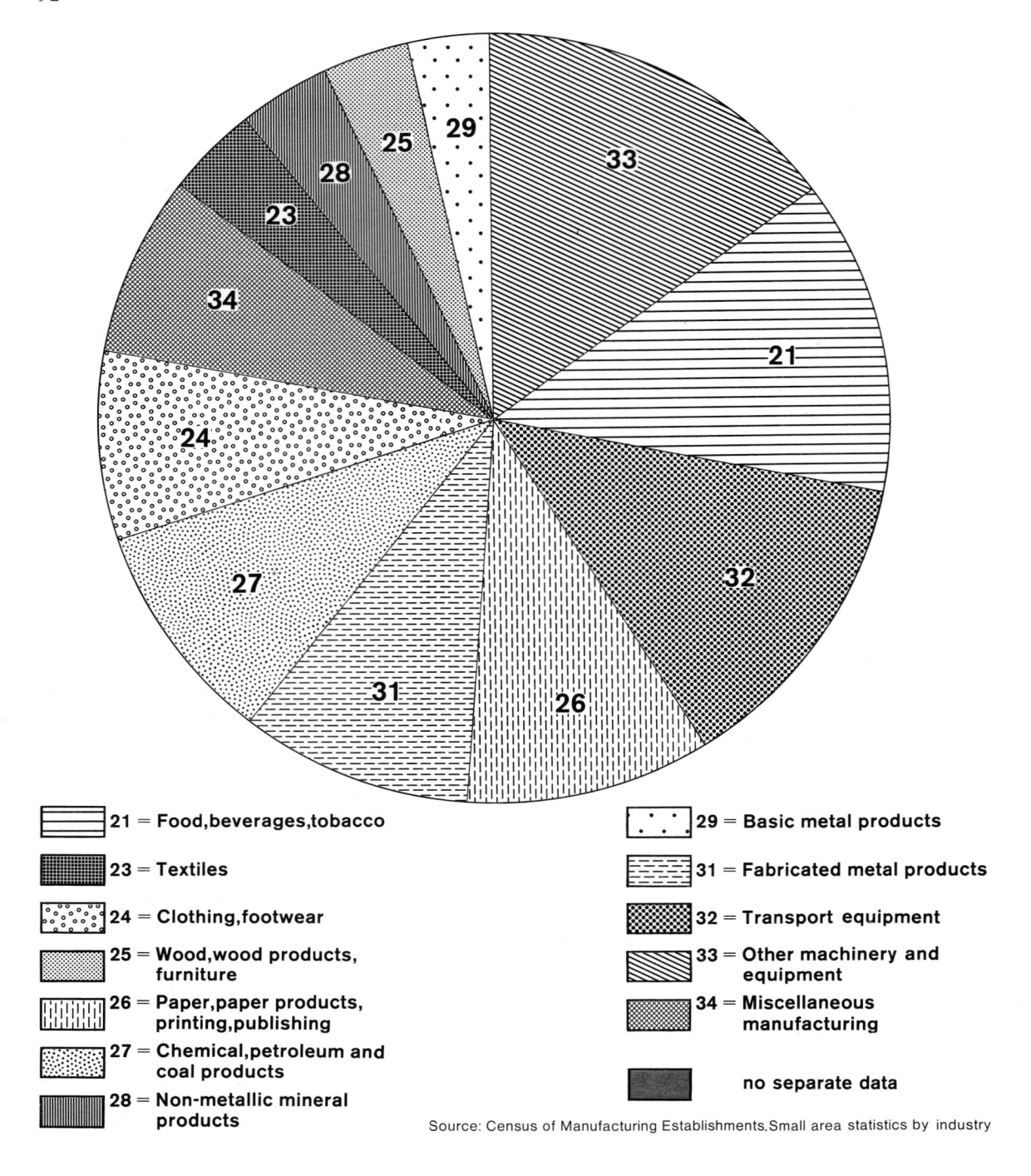

	21 = Food, beverages, tobacco			29 = Basic metal products
	23 = Textiles			31 = Fabricated metal products
	24 = Clothing, footwear			32 = Transport equipment
	25 = Wood, wood products, furniture			33 = Other machinery and equipment
	26 = Paper, paper products, printing, publishing			34 = Miscellaneous manufacturing
	27 = Chemical, petroleum and coal products			no separate data
	28 = Non-metallic mineral products			

Source: Census of Manufacturing Establishments. Small area statistics by industry

Fig. 51. Value added by industry sub-divisions in Melbourne, 1981/82 (total = A$ 8.686 bill.)

(Flinders Street Station) and the river respectively and to the west also by the railway (Spencer Street Station) and the adjoining industrial area. To the east and northeast government and other public institutions (Parliament House, Exhibition Buildings) and public parks (Treasury Gardens, Fitzroy Gardens, Carlton Gardens) adjoin the city core whereas to the north the grid more or less continues for a few more blocks, these being partly modified by the Old Melbourne Gaol and the Queen Victoria Market, that had its origin in a livestock and hay market of 1859.

The north-south *Civic Spine* along Swanston Street and St. Kilda Road from Latrobe Street in the north to St. Kilda Junction in the south has two major concentrations of public buildings: in the north around Museum

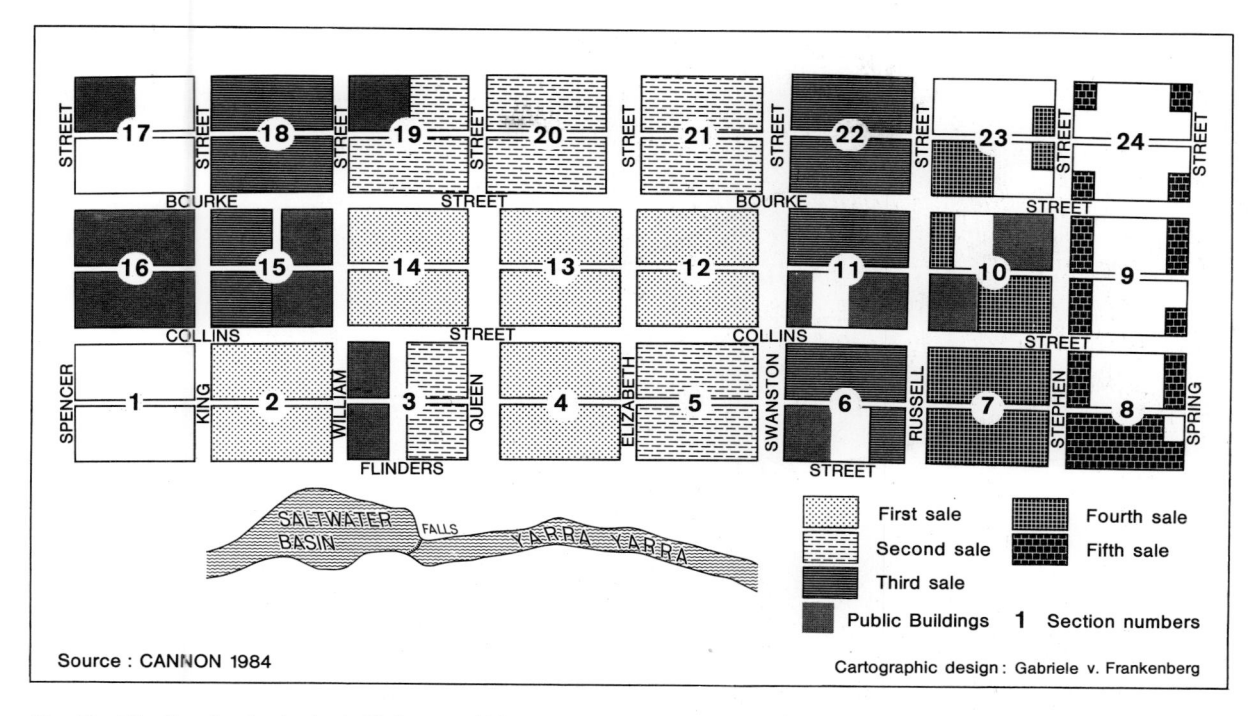

Fig. 52. The first five land sales in Melbourne 1837–39

Station we find the Museum of Victoria, the State Library and Queen Victoria Medical Centre while south of the river along St. Kilda Road on land always owned by the government Victoria's great Arts Centre was recently developed. Back in the mid-1850s there was an amphitheatre on this site, and travelling circuses set up their tents on the south bank of the Yarra River. At the turn of the century a permanent building called the Olympia had been constructed for the circus. This latter became a cinema, while nearby a horse-racing track and a roller skating rink were built. It is this traditional entertainment area that the *Victorian Arts Centre* with its Concert Hall, Art Gallery and several theatres and restaurants was completed just in time for Victoria's sesquicentenary celebrations in 1985. The 56-storey Rialto office and hotel complex (242 m high) at the corner of Collins and King Streets was not quite completed in time for the jubilee.

At the Arts Centre the Civic Spine intersects the east-west *River Corridor*, leading from the parklands to the east of the city centre, where great parts of the land are used for recreational purposes and sporting activities, through the port of Melbourne to connect with Phillip Bay. Station Pier on the bay is no longer used for maritime trade and its conversion to tourist and recreational uses has been considered (Victoria. Central Melbourne. 1984). To the east of Victoria Bridge the Jolimont railway yards provide a potential northern extension for the river corridor. To a great extent they are no longer used for railway operations and may be disposed of by other public functions.

From this discussion it becomes apparent that there is a considerable amount of *State Government and other public land*, not so much within the formal city grid of the present CBD, but adjacent to it. As well as the railway land, parts of the harbour area are considered under-used today. The Government of Victoria has come up with a number of proposals for the future uses of this land (fig. 53).

Melbourne has already sustained some growth during the gold-rush of the 1850s, but at this time the goldfields and the newly established mining towns such as Ballarat, Bendigo and a few others absorbed so many people that the city's share of Victoria's population dropped temporarily. Since the end of the 1850s the situation changed in favour of the capital city that now started to develop to a size and splendour that gained it the term *'Marvellous Melbourne'*, a slogan the visiting lecturer-journalist G.A. Sala is said to have coined or at least popularized (Serle 1980, 275). Melbourne experienced a sustained growth for the three decades 1861–91.

The 1870s was a *period of industrialization* for the city. In the inner suburbs brewing, flour-milling, clothing manufacture, the assembly of machinery and other manufacturing industries mushroomed. British entrepreneurs invested heavily in Melbourne's housing stock and Victoria's railways, these growing to a dense network totally centred on the capital. At the end of the 1880s the district of South Melbourne reached approximately 42,000 residents, followed by Prahran and Richmond while Brunswick and Footscray grew from about 6,000 to 20,000 each and suburbs such as Essendon and Hawthorn were half occupied (Serle 1980).

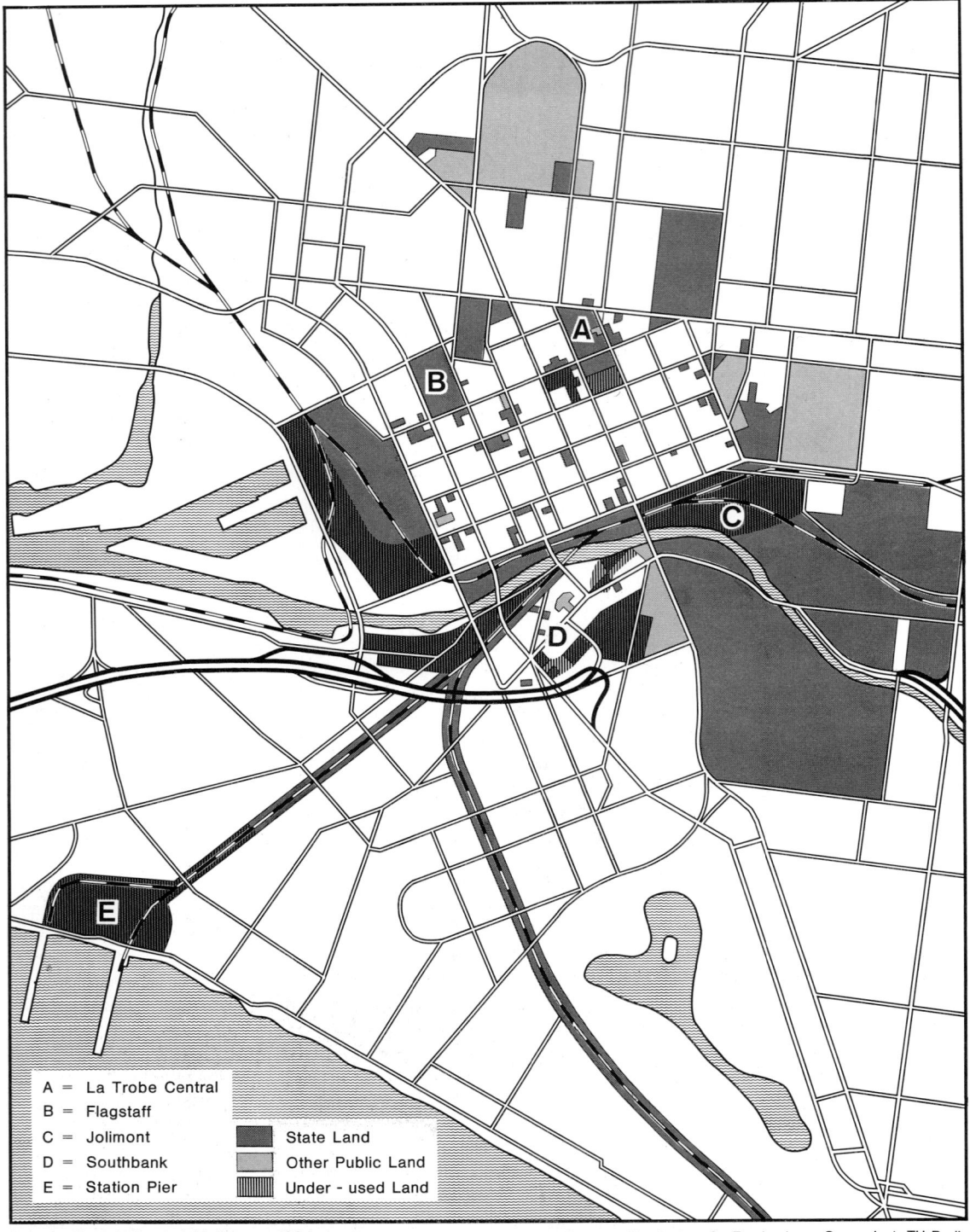

Fig. 53. State Government and other public land in central Melbourne, 1984 (after Economic Strategy for Victorian Statement no. 6, 1984, modified)

Footscray and Williamstown became known as the *'Birmingham of Victoria'*, because of their iron and metal-working factories, such as Bevan's rolling stock workshop, Robinson's wheel-making plant, Ferguson's wrought-iron, pipe-making and engineering works, the Austral Otis Elevator and Engineering Company's fitting and machine shop and many others.

Brunswick to the northeast, with its basalt deposits and claybeds along Moonee Ponds Creek, became Melbourne's most important source for building stones and bricks. The big construction boom made for the expansion of the Hoffman Brick Company and other brick works, while the Brunswick Railway opened in 1884 solved the problem of the congested road between Brunswick and Melbourne (Davison 1979b).

During the second half of the 1880s the horse-drawn trams were replaced by the *cable trams* that even today give the city much of its characteristic atmosphere. Melbourne is the only state capital to run trams, with the exception of the one line to Glenelg in Adelaide. It also boasts of a collection of fine public buildings unequalled by any other city of the former British Empire except for London. In addition to the trams and the public buildings the verandahs of the private houses also contribute to Melbourne's individual character. In the past, the grid-iron street pattern of central Melbourne, the style of architecture and the ugly telegraph poles were considered to give Melbourne an American look. The city was held to resemble New York rather than London whereas Sydney's appearance was judged to be the opposite. 'Melbourne had style, Sydney was solid; Melbourne was flashy, Sydney was slow; money was made in Melbourne, in Sydney it grew' (Serle 1980, 273). In the course of the twentieth century the two largest Australian cities developed in such a way that today the judgement would be just the other way round. Due to its temperate climate and vegetation, its building stock and its high quality of cultural and social life Melbourne has acquired a very favourable image and is now considered to be the *most 'British' city* in Australia after Hobart (fig. 54).

Fig. 54. Melbourne, Victoria. Flinders Street Station on southern margin of CBD with trams still in operation

The climax of this development was the *Centennial International Exhibition* in 1888. Since Sydney was lacking adequate buildings and no provisions had been taken in time by the New South Wales Government, the Government of Victoria took over the preparations for this event and invited all foreign governments to participate. The government initially budgeted £ 25,000 for the Exhibition, but it finally cost more than ten times that amount (Serle 1980). On the other hand, sanitary conditions in the city at this time must have been extremely poor, so that diphteria and typhoid spread over the city and caused a high mortality rate. This induced the most circulated Melbourne newspaper to refer to the city as 'Marvellous Smelbourne' (Serle 1980).

Soon after the Centennial Exhibition Melbourne began to suffer from a profound recession. Due to the falling wool and wheat prices and increasing interest rates in Britain the Victorian economy slackened and Melbourne's financial community was hit by a series of bankruptcies. 'Melbourne has perhaps been subject to more marked swings in its fortunes than any other major city in Australia' (Div. Nat. Mapp. & ABS 1984). This becomes especially evident in a comparison with Melbourne's rival Sydney, as shown in table 27.

Table 27. Population growth of Melbourne and Sydney, 1861–1933

Year	Melbourne		Sydney	
	Population in 1,000	Growth over previous census year (%)	Population in 1,000	Growth over previous census year (%)
1861	140	–	96	–
1871	207	47.9	138	43.7
1881	283	36.7	225	63.0
1891	491	73.5	383	70.2
1901	502	2.2	497	29.8
1911	589	17.3	630	26.8
1921	766	30.0	899	42.7
1933	1,053	37.5	1,315	31.6

Source: For population figures Burnley 1980, for growth rates author's calculations

It is apparent that Sydney experienced a steadier growth over the whole period, whereas Melbourne showed an extremely high growth rate of 73.5% during the 1880s followed by an extremely low rate of 2.2% during the 1890s. All the details of Melbourne's rise and fall in the last two decades of the nineteenth century have been admirably described by Davison in his historical monograph on the city (1979b).

Melbourne's more recent spacial expansion has been strongly influenced by the pattern of relief. Although there are no such distinct valley and ridge patterns as in Brisbane, Adelaide, Perth or Hobart, the Port Phillip District has some *marked contrasts of terrain.* To the north and west of the Yarra River, relatively flat basalt plains with a few deeply incised streams proved more suitable for secondary industries and labourers' quarters than for high-status residential areas, the more so as shipping facilities and railway yards developed along the lower Yarra River close to its mouth in Phillip Bay. The undulating or hilly terrain to the northeast and east was more attractive to the development of middle- and upper-class residential suburbs. To the southeast high-status residential areas developed on Tertiary sand deposits along the coast, particularly around Brighton, whereas the flatter parts were occupied by industrial suburbs such as Clayton, Dandenong, Moorabbin and Oakleigh.

An *asymmetrical settlement pattern* favouring the eastern and the southeastern sector along the shoreline of Phillip Bay in particular has long been noticed in literature. Pryor (1968) gave several reasons for this asymmetry, beginning with the fact that Port Phillip and Holson's Bays were themselves asymmetrical. The radial stream pattern in the basalt plains also acted as a repulsive force to continuous settlement, the valleys permitting the penetration of non-residential land uses towards the inner city. While the undulating topography in the east and south was more attractive to residential use, the installation of utility services was more difficult and costly in the basalt areas. The radial pattern of railways and highways has encouraged a ribbon pattern of settlement, while the lack of crossings on the lower Yarra River has impeded extension in a north-south-east-westerly direction. Metropolitan planning since 1954 has contributed to the asymmetrical pattern by the zoning for industrial uses of considerable parts of the western margins of the built-up area. The growth of both population and housing stock has clearly been much faster to the east and south than to the west and north. In the 1960s this growth reached out to approximately 19 km from the city centre to the west, 16 km to the north, 38 km to the east and 45 km to the south.

As Jones (1969) and Johnston (1969) found, the highest-status residential areas are not located in the outer zone. They are found rather in the intermediate zone on the east side, in a belt reaching from Heidelberg and Doncaster on the banks of the Upper Yarra River through Kew, Camberwell, Box Hill, Malvern to Brighton, Sandringham and Mordialloc on Port Phillip Bay, continuing down to the southern part of Frankston. Jones made the statement that in Melbourne no unambiguous gradient of socio-economic status could be detected. The fact that the highest-status population is not found in the suburbs farthest away from the city centre is underlined by the fact that much housing in areas such as the Mornington Peninsula and the Dandenong Ranges is of weatherboard rather than brick or stone, having been built to serve as summer homes for well-to-do Melbourne residents and so intended only for temporary use.

Industrial suburbanization began in the inter-war period 1920–40, with the rapid development of the manufacturing of automobiles, aircraft and agricultural machinery. This development was accompanied in the 1920s by a considerable wave of immigration from the British Isles. For the first time some of the inner suburbs experienced declining populations, for instance Fitzroy, Collingwood and Richmond. Another group of suburbs showed considerable growth, among others Footscray, Essendon, Coburg and Caulfield. Most industries accumulated in a belt south of the central city between the Yarra River and Port Phillip Bay and to the west between Altona and Sunshine. This includes the Altona Petrochemical Complex in connection with the Altona plant of Petroleum Refineries (Australia) Pty Ltd. After World War II industrialization spread more to the outer suburbs on the west side as far as Broadmeadows as well as to the east side to a belt mainly consisting of the suburbs of Moorabbin, Oakleigh, Springvale, Dandenong and Berwick.

As mentioned above Melbourne and Sydney are about equal with regard to their industrial production in terms of value added, but Melbourne has a higher proportion of its labour force in *industrial employment* (25%) than any other state capital. A little over half of the industrial labour force is employed in four categories of production: transport equipment, other machinery and equipment, food-beverages-tobacco, and clothing-footware (fig. 51). None of the leading industries belong to the so-called growth industries. Despite this, Melbourne's unemployment rate in 1983 was the lowest of all capital cities for the male workforce and the third lowest for the female workforce (Forster 1983). Maybe this low unemployment figure is a reflection of Melbourne's recent successful competition for high-technology industries and tertiary occupations.

In terms of residential location, the highest percentages of labourers, process workers and tradesmen are still to be found in a ring of inner suburbs, with Williamstown, Footscray and Sunshine in the west, Essendon, Brunswick, Coburg and Northcote in the north and Collingwood, Richmond, Prahran and St. Kilda in the east. Some of these suburbs, such as Prahran and St. Kilda, and a few others such as Albert Park and South Yarra south of the city centre, also have above-average proportions of retired people, pensioners, widowers, divorsed and other single persons (Div. Nat. Mapp. & ABS 1984).

In some of the inner suburbs, urban renewal programmes have made for a change of the old building stock. Most conspicuous among the housing schemes of the Victorian Housing Commission were the *high-rise apartment blocks in Fitzroy* built in the 1960s. For years there have been continuous renewal activities in this area, during which many of the old terrace houses and other tenements have been replaced by modern multi-storey buildings.

Most of these inner suburbs are identical with the areas of the highest proportions of overseas immigrants, but there has been a strong tendency toward an outward relocation of these groups, with the development of '*secondary concentrations*', in particular by immigrants of Greek, Italian and Yugoslav origin (McKay 1981). Outward migration mainly occurred along a western axis from Footscray to Sunshine and St. Albans, along a northern axis from Brunswick, Coburg, Northcote and Preston to Broadmeadows and Thomastown, and along a southeastern axis from St. Kilda and Caulfield to Oakleigh, Clayton, Springvale, Dandenong and Berwick. St. Kilda was formerly a preferred place of residence for people of Jewish origin (Div. Nat. Mapp. & ABS 1984) (fig. 55).

The percentage of overseas immigrants resident in Melbourne for fewer than five years was only 13.0% (1981), as compared with 18.5% of Sydney's overseas population. This rather low figure probably reflected the recent manufacturing slump. On the other hand, the proportion of all overseas born in Melbourne's total population increased during the intercensal period 1976–81 from 27.5% to 28.2%. This increase reflected the loss of Australian-born residents of Melbourne to other parts of Australia.

Metropolitan planning started in 1944, with the setting up of the Town and Country Planning Board, which has functioned in an advisory capacity to the Minister of Local Government and has proposed plans for Melbourne's growth. The more efficient planning authority has, however, been the *Melbourne and Metropolitan Board of Works* (MMBW). Since its establishment in 1891, the MMBW had been responsible for water supply and sewerage, but in 1955 it was given the power to implement a plan for the metropolitan area. The relations between the MMBW, the City Council and the Minister for Planning and Environment of the State of Victoria in recent years have been too complicated as to be treated here in any detail. For a discussion of the matter the reader is referred to Saunders (in Halligan & Paris 1984) and Stimson (1982).

As Alexander (in: Troy 1981) pointed out, the *Melbourne Metropolitan Plan* of 1954 was, in common with other plans of the 'first generation', very much concerned with industrial location. While a major objective of the plan was to limit the outward spread of settlement, it nevertheless promoted new manufacturing in the central city and inner suburbs.

The 1954 plan also provided for the promotion of five existing shopping centres as *district centres:* Box Hill, Dandenong, Footscray, Moorabbin and Preston (fig. 56). Due to various obstacles, such as fragmented land ownership, high land costs, the occurrance of congestion and the lack of parking facilities and other amenities, not all of them developed as expected. Support from the public sector was also not sufficient to attract the desired extent and range of businesses, so that some systematic development occurred only in Dandenong and Footscray. While these two

	MELBOURNE
1	MELBOURNE
2	SOUTH MELBOURNE
3	PORT MELBOURNE
4	WILLIAMSTOWN
5	FOOTSCRAY
6	ESSENDON
7	BRUNSWICK
8	NORTHCOTE
9	FITZROY
10	COLLINGWOOD
11	RICHMOND
12	PRAHRAN
13	COBURG
14	HAWTHORN

Legend:
- −10,8 to −5,1
- −3,8 to −1,8
- −1,1 to −0,2
- +0,1 to +1,1
- +1,2 to +2,1
- +2,4 to +3,2

Source: Changes of overseas immigrants as percentages of total population in Melbourne's LGAs, 1971–1976

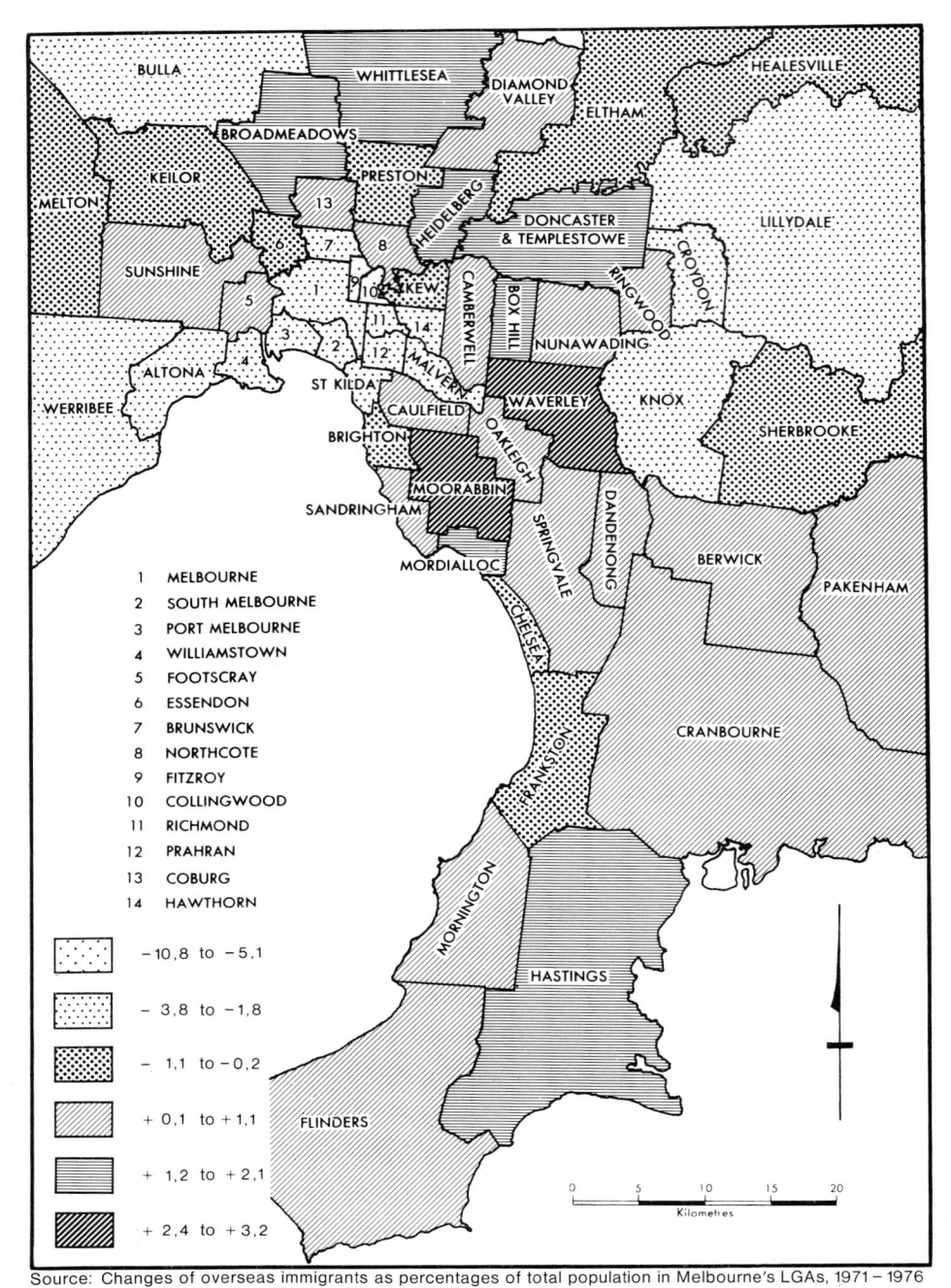

Fig. 55. Overseas immigrants in Melbourne's LGAs, changes 1971–76

centres, as well as Box Hill and Preston, were carried over into later plans for the metropolitan area, Moorabbin was altogether abandoned in favour of centres at nearby Oakleigh and Cheltenham.

The Town and Country Planning Board in 1974 advocated public land assembly for the establishment of two satellites on the west side: Melton and Sunbury. This land was to be bought at rural values and sold at urban values to prospective residents. The plan was, however, not carried out.

The requirements of a modern shopping centre of more than 30,000 square metres of retail floor area are considered to be 15 hectares. It was to meet this requirement that between 1958 and 1977 several *free-standing shopping centres* developed on open land away from suburban railway stations. With rapid suburban growth, increasing consumption and a greater use of private cars these new projects could be independent of existing centres. The *Myer department stores company* led the movement; in addition to its stores in some of the existing district centres

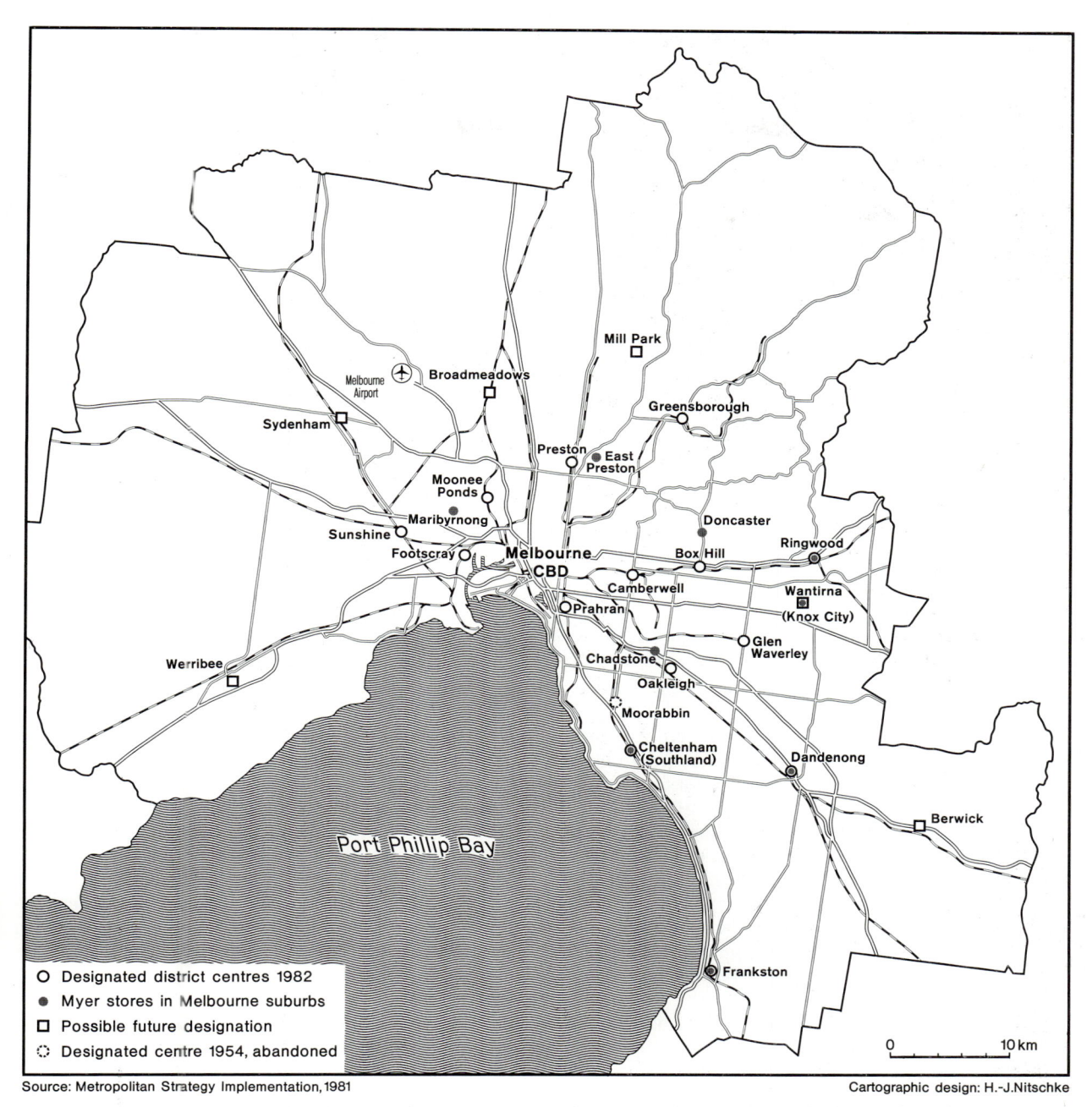

Fig. 56. The development of corridors and district centres in Melbourne

it established the Highpoint Centre at Maribyrnong, the Northland Centre at East Preston, the Doncaster Shopping Town at Doncaster, the Knox City Centre at Wantirna and the Chadstone Centre, the latter in fact the first of its kind (fig. 56).

A new metropolitan plan of 1971 was based on the assumption of rapid metropolitan growth and provided for the development of *seven radial corridors* (Gifford 1980). The Dandenong corridor was given high preference, this corridor marking the route from Melbourne to the Latrobe Valley. The growth of free-standing centres continued, however, till 1977. Usually developments required partial amendments of the plan and rezoning, a problem discussed in some detail by Logan & Ogilvy (in: Troy 1981). At about 1975 there were, in addition to the five designated district centres, six additional free-standing shopping centres at Maribyrnong, East Preston, Doncaster, Wantirna, Chadstone and Cheltenham.

Table 28. District centres and free-standing shopping centres in metropolitan Melbourne, 1954–83

Centre	Designated 1954	Free-standing 1958–77	Myer store	Designated 1983	Possible future designation
Berwick					x
Box Hill	x			x	
Broadmeadows					x
Camberwell Junction				x	
Chadstone		x	x		
Cheltenham (Southland)			x	x	
Dandenong	x		x	x	
Doncaster Shopping Town		x	x		
East Preston (Northland)		x	x		
Footscray	x			x	
Frankston			x	x	
Glen Waverly				x	
Greensborough				x	
Knox City (Wantirna)		x	x		x
Maribyrnong (Highpoint)		x	x		
Mill Park					x
Moonee Ponds				x	
Moorabbin	x				
Oakleigh				x	
Prahran				x	
Preston	x			x	
Ringwood (Eastland)			x	x	
Sunshine				x	
Sydenham					x
Werribee					x

Sources: Jones 1969; MMBW 1981, 1982; Myer store addresses; personal communication with Mr. D. Rae, Ministry for Planning and Environment Victoria of 18 March 1986

Finally, in consequence of the more recent plan of 1980 and amendment 150 on the district centre selection process (MMBW 1982), 14 district centres were selected, all of them being located in close proximity to suburban railway stations as well as major road intersections (fig. 56).

Four of them are identical with the sites of Myer department stores, whereas another five Myer stores outside the CBD are found in free-standing shopping centres (table 28). In addition to the 14 district centres another six even more peripheral locations (Berwick, Broadmeadows, Knox City, Mill Park, Sydenham, Werribee) were selected for possible future designation (fig. 56).

As well as the district-centre policy, a second planning device was provided by the concept of *preferred development areas*. These areas are found in peripheral locations within the corridors mentioned above, and were selected on the principle of efficiency in the supply of public services and utilities. Due to their location in the corridors, these areas have relatively good access to railway lines and, in some cases, to freeway entry points; they are also designed as future industrial sites.

After the Melbourne City Council had been dismissed, according to provisions of the Local Government Act of March, 1981 (Saunders in: Halligan & Paris 1984), the planning responsibilities of the MMBW for the whole metropolitan area were in 1985 transferred to the Victorian Ministry for Planning and Environment (ch. 2.1.3).

3.1.3 The metropolitan area of Adelaide, South Australia

Adelaide is Australia's fourth largest city after Sydney, Melbourne and Brisbane, with a population of 882,520 (1981). The town was founded as the last of the state capital cities in 1836 by private colonizers who, as adherents of the Wakefieldian theories (ch. 2.1.2), rejected the import of convicts. Under the influence both of the French Revolution and of the Industrial Revolution those who shared these ideals wished to create 'a new and free society' (Pike 1953). They had thus to rely on free settlers, while supporting the immigrants' fares by selling Crown lands for 12 s and later for 20 s per acre.

The town was named after King William IV' wife Adelheid, Princess of Sachsen-Meiningen (1830–37). Its site was selected by Colonel William Light, South Australia's first Surveyor-General. There was heavy opposition from the Board of Colonization Commissioners, represented in Australia by a *Resident Commissioner* (in contrast to the other colonies for which the Colonial Office was responsible) as well as from the *Governor*, a position first held by Hindmarsh. It was only after Hindmarsh's dismissal that his successor Gawler became both Governor and Resident Commissioner. The Board had recommended several other sites in Southern Eyre Peninsula, on Kangaroo Island and

Fig. 57. Adelaide, S.A. Oblique aerial photograph taken from North Adelaide looking southeast toward South Adelaide and the surrounding parklands. The Mt. Lofty Range in the background (reproduced with the permission of the Department of Lands, South Australia)

on Encounter Bay. It would have been reasonable to establish the capital city of the new colony at the mouth of Australia's largest river. But at that time the mouth of the Murray River had not yet been proved navigable, so that it seemed logical to Colonel Light that the new settlement should be located on the *eastern shores of Gulf St. Vincent*. From perspectives of the present day 'his choice of site of the east coast of Gulf St. Vincent was excellent, for it was as central a point in South Australia to the area capable of supporting intensive agricultural production and hence dense population, as any could be' (Williams in: Forster & Stimson 1977, 4). This choice of such a favourable location was, however, fortuitous, for Colonel Light could not possibly have foreseen this future adventageous location of the colony's capital.

The actual site selected was just as much disputed as the general situation. Colonel Light chose a place approximately 10 km inland, where the uplifted western edge of the Para Plateau is nearest the harbour. The site is accordingly free from inundation by the ocean, is cut through by the little Torrens River and there was plenty of fresh water available (Adelaide 1937). Although at first much criticized, Light's decision has had the very favourable result that in contrast to other Australian capital cities Adelaide's *CBD enjoys a central location* within the metropolitan area, and has been within comparatively easy reach of the bulk of its population until recent years (Williams in: Forster & Stimson 1977).

Colonel Light defended his choice of the site in a letter of 9 February 1837 to Colonial Commissioner Fisher with the words: 'The reasons that led me to fix Adelaide where it is I do not expect to be generally understood or calmly judged of at present. My enemies, however, by disputing their validity in every particular, have done me the good service of fixing the whole of the responsibility upon me. I am perfectly willing to bear it, and I leave it to posterity, and not to them, to decide whether I am entitled to praise or blame' (Light 1962).

While the sand dunes and mangrove swamps to the northwest did not appeal to Colonel Light for settlement purposes, Port Adelaide was established there as a harbour to serve the new colony. Somewhat to the south of Port Adelaide, at a place where the first colonists had landed, another settlement arose which was called Glenelg. It thus happened that in contrast to other capital cities, South Australia's capital grew from *three early settlement nuclei.*

Light's third decision was to choose the layout of the town according to the *principle of a parkland town* with the town lands in the centre, a zone of parklands surrounding the town lands, and the suburban lands beyond the ring of the parklands. This decision was to make Adelaide the only large city in Australia 'in which its implemented design clearly formalized and structured the areas to be used for specific functions — for example, business and commercial uses in South Adelaide; Park Lands for public uses; and the surrounding lands for rural and later suburban developments ...' (The Corporation 1982b, 12) (fig. 57).

The town lands were located on both banks of the Torrens River, South Adelaide on the southern bank and North Adelaide on the northern bank; both settlements are constituent parts of the present City of Adelaide. The smaller North Adelaide was originally supposed to be laid out in a way parallel to South Adelaide; however it was then 'tilted to one side to suit the contours of the country' (Adelaide 1937). Since it was located on the somewhat higher northern bank of the river it soon became the main upper-class residential quarter for physicians, lawyers and other professionals. In South Adelaide 700 acre-sections were surveyed and another 342 sections in North Adelaide, of which 42 sections were withheld for public uses, so that during the period of early settlement in all 1,000 acre-sections were offered for sale (Oldham 1945) (fig. 60).

There has been much dispute over the *origins of the town's unique layout*, with its five public squares modifying the street pattern of South Adelaide, and the surrounding parklands anticipating the greenbelt concept of later town planners. Walkley (1953) tried to refer this layout to the Roman Camp principle and argued that there was also a strong desire for shielding the town from the hot northerly winds. Parker (1937) suggested that the town was originally designed in England and that such principles of town planning had been discussed between Colonel Light and the Colonial Commissioners, whose instructions left it to him to 'make the necessary reserves for squares, public walks, and quays'. Some credit was given to the English philanthropist Granville Sharp (1735–1813) who earned praise and criticism alike for his support of American independence and advocacy of the abolition of negro slavery, notably by helping to establish Sierra Leone as a colony of freed men. In 1974 he published a book entitled 'A general plan for laying out towns and townships on the new-acquired lands in the East Indies, America, and elsewhere' . It was also assumed that earlier plans of Philadelphia (1682) and Savannah, Georgia (1733, plan by Oglethorpe) were, to a certain extent, copied in Adelaide. Others believed that the archetype was provided by European fortress cities, and in particular by Turin, where the fortifications were dismantled as early as 1801 and transformed to a greenbelt for recreational purposes (The Centenary History 1936). The parklands share with the belt of cleared fortifications the advantage of easy accessibility from both the city centre and the surrounding suburban areas. Boyd (1978, 34) wrote about Colonel Light: 'Perhaps he was also influenced by his admiration for some of the old cities of Italy, which he had travelled some time in the company of Lord Byron' and 'nobody really knows what inspired his plan since most of his personal records were destroyed by a fire caught by the thatched roof of his hut in 1839'

A particular point of interest is the *alienation of parklands* over time (Daly 1980). Of the original parklands of 920 hectares, approximately 690 hectares are still left. According to Colonel Light's plan, six roads were supposed to cut through the parklands; at present there are 36 roads, including the tracks of the tramline to Glenelg and the railway line. Since the very beginning of settlement the parklands have served a variety of purposes. The Aborigines

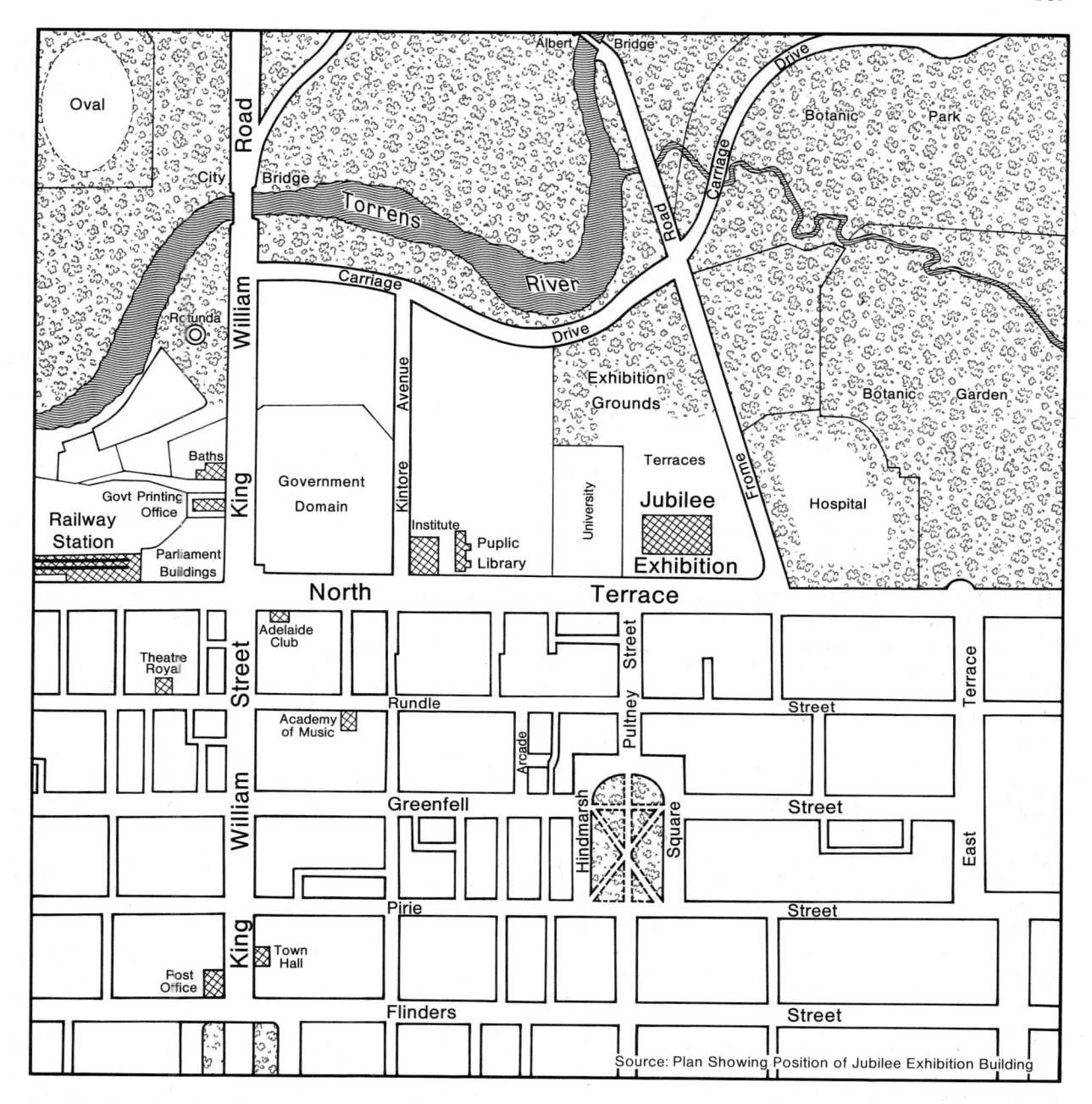

Fig. 58. The alienation of parklands in Adelaide

used them to gather wood, while clay and lime were worked for house construction. Fairs and sporting activities were also held on the parklands. In 1849 the Council of the City of Adelaide assumed the responsibilities for the parklands; special legislation authorized the use of the northern parklands for community buildings. Thus on a 'Plan showing position of Jubilee Exhibition Building' of 1888 we find, on the west side of King William Road, the Railway Station, Parliament Buildings, the Government Printing Office, Baths and Sports Oval, and on the east side government buildings on the so-called Government Domain, the Institute (ch. 2.2.4), the Public Library, the University of Adelaide, the Jubilee Exhibition Building with the Exhibition Grounds, a hospital and the Botanic Garden. In later years some more buildings were erected and some existing buildings used for other purposes. There are thus at present a museum, the Art Gallery and the buildings of the Institute of Technology and the Teachers' College. In recent years the Adelaide Festival Halls were added to this ensemble. A few public institutions are also found on the western and eastern parklands, including a cemetery, a school, the Observatory, a sports oval and a racing track (fig. 58).

In the early 1980s the *Adelaide Station Environs Redevelopment Project* (ASER) was approved by the South Australian Government, although it has been highly criticized by the public. This project encompasses the use of the air rights over most of the railway station and tracks in the parklands, including the building of a modern 23-storey hotel. The use of the parklands for an intraurban expressway has also been proposed.

In addition to the parklands proper the streets bordering the parklands are equally attractive to development. For example, Greenhill Road bordering the southern parklands has, in recent years, attracted a number of services and developers of modern multi-storey office buildings. Some parts of Greenhill Road have thus become an extension of Adelaide's CBD.

Three points must be added with regard to the alienation of parklands. Firstly, it had never been Light's intention that the parklands should remain exclusively bushland. He wanted them to remain predominantly open space, but himself suggested certain public uses. Secondly, as already mentioned, many activities were found on the parklands in Adelaide's early days. Thirdly, while most of the buildings on the parklands today are related to the cultural development of the capital city and confined to the portion of the northern parklands adjacent to North Terrace 'where they are seen as an extension of the City and its function' (The Corporation 1982a, 2), the return to public recreational use of alienated lands has always been a political issue in Adelaide's history.

According to the most recent Plan of the City of Adelaide of 1986 the so-called Park Lands District was divided into 18 parklands precincts, for each of which planning regulations were set out by the Plan Review Team. For example, the following provisions are made for the University Oval Precinct in the northern parklands.

'Precinct image
The University Oval Precinct should be maintained as an area of diverse character and usage incorporating sportsgrounds, woodland, formal gardens and lawns flanking the River Torrens.

Activities
This Precinct should provide for a range of active and passive recreational activities, particularly boating and organized sports. The introduction of tennis courts to replace those in Park 9 is appropriate.

Environment
Planting character. The University Oval Precinct should generally be characterised by informal plantings of mixed exotic and native woodland around large areas of irrigated turf and the riverbank area.

The Precinct is significant in its relationship to Government House and several listed items of heritage significance. These should be conserved and not obscured by inappropriate landscaping.
Permanent structures. New buildings should only be allowed to provide facilities for new sporting activities. Expansion of existing buildings should be restricted.
Heritage. Within the University Oval Precinct the following Items are included on the Register of City of Adelaide Heritage Items:
Albert Bridge; Frome Road
Adelaide Bridge; King William Road
University Footbridge; Across the River Torrens

Movement
Access and parking should give preference to Park Lands visitors and further expansion of car parking areas in Park 12 should be prohibited. Pedestrian access between North Terrace and the River Torrens should be improved along Kintore Avenue and through the University of Adelaide.'

Apart from the alienation of parklands there have been other changes of Colonel Light's original plan. Roadways have fragmented the parklands and city squares, while several major roads have been re-aligned. A number of secondary streets have been added to the original grid. CBD functions have migrated toward the north, for example to the present Rundell Mall and Northern Terrace, rather than around the city centre of Victoria Square, as originally planned (The Corporation 1982b).

For Adelaide's further development the city's natural setting was decisive. The northeast-southwest trending escarpment of the Mt. Lofty Range forms the eastern barrier of the *triangular Adelaide Plains*, the drier parts of which have, until recent years, been the area most favoured for settlement. In addition to the city core on the River Torrens, with its central position between the coastline and the escarpment, there were a few early nuclei of settlement on the dunes along the coast where such fashionable settlements as Glenelg developed. The Plains were then settled in successive stages along various axes, with the northwest corridor between the City of Adelaide and Port Adelaide being filled in rather early and the northeastern corridor to Tea Tree Gully along the Torrens River and the southern corridor to Noarlunga somewhat later. Due to the triangular shape of the Plains no corridor of settlement developed to the southeast.

The three corridors and a fourth corridor to the sea coast at Glenelg have been served by rapid transit lines. The railway from Adelaide to Port Adelaide was opened in 1865 and the line to Glenelg in 1873; the opening of the railway to Melbourne in 1883 made the Adelaide Hills, early summer refuges for the richer families, more accessible. In 1929 the railway line to Glenelg was converted to a tramline, still in operation. It is served by through trams with but a few intermediate stops during rush hours. It is estimated that approximately 40% of all rush-hour passengers use public transportation facilities.

During the two decades 1841–61, Adelaide grew from approximately 6,000 to 35,000 persons, 18,000 of whom were in the City of Adelaide and 17,000 in the suburbs. By 1901 total population was about 140,000 of whom 40,000 lived in the city and 100,000 in the suburbs. A certain degree of segregation, revealed by differences of house size and building materials, had already become obvious by 1861. In the *fashionable seaside suburb* of Glenelg more than 90% of all buildings were of stone or brick and only 50% had four rooms or fewer, whereas in Port Adelaide over 55% of all buildings were of wood and almost 90% had four rooms or fewer (Williams in: Forster & Stimson 1977).

By 1901 Adelaide had assumed metropolitan primacy, with more than 39% of South Australia's population, despite the fact that a number of regional port towns with feeder railway lines to their respective hinterlands had been established along the coastlines of Gulf St. Vincent and Spencer Gulf. In contrast to Queensland, however, Adelaide was able to expand its own railway network and drain the other ports of their trade; the only exception was Port Lincoln. Thus the newly emerging settlements such as Port Pirie, Port Augusta, Port Wakefield, Wallaroo were by the late 1870s tied to the *Adelaide-centred railway system*, and the southeastern ports by the end of the 1880s. 'Adelaide's biggest intercensal population increase from 51,000 to 92,000, occurred between 1871 and 1881, just when these new links were being forged' (Williams in: Forster & Stimson 1977, 12).

Adelaide experienced two phases of industrialization. The first period of growth of manufacturing was in the last three decades of the nineteenth century. It coincided with the growth of population and concentration and the expansion of the railway network mentioned above. The number of factories increased from fewer than 400 to about 850 and of manufacturing workers from 6,000 to over 17,000 by the turn of the century.

The second growth period started after World War II, with a very *active immigration and industrialization policy* on the part of the South Australian Government and a very generous housing programme by the Housing Trust of South Australia. During the two decades 1946–66 an annual average of 11,600 overseas immigrants arrived in South Australia, helping to bring Adelaide's population up from 382,000 in 1947 to 728,000 in 1966. During World War II, ammunitions and armaments factories had been established in Salisbury, Hendon and Findon 'which became the basis later of peace-time electrical and electronic industries, particularly the manufacture of refrigerators and of motor cars' (Williams in: Forster & Stimson 1977, 19). Manufacturing employment in South Australia increased by nearly 170% during the period 1939–65, the majority of the new manufacturing jobs being located in the Adelaide

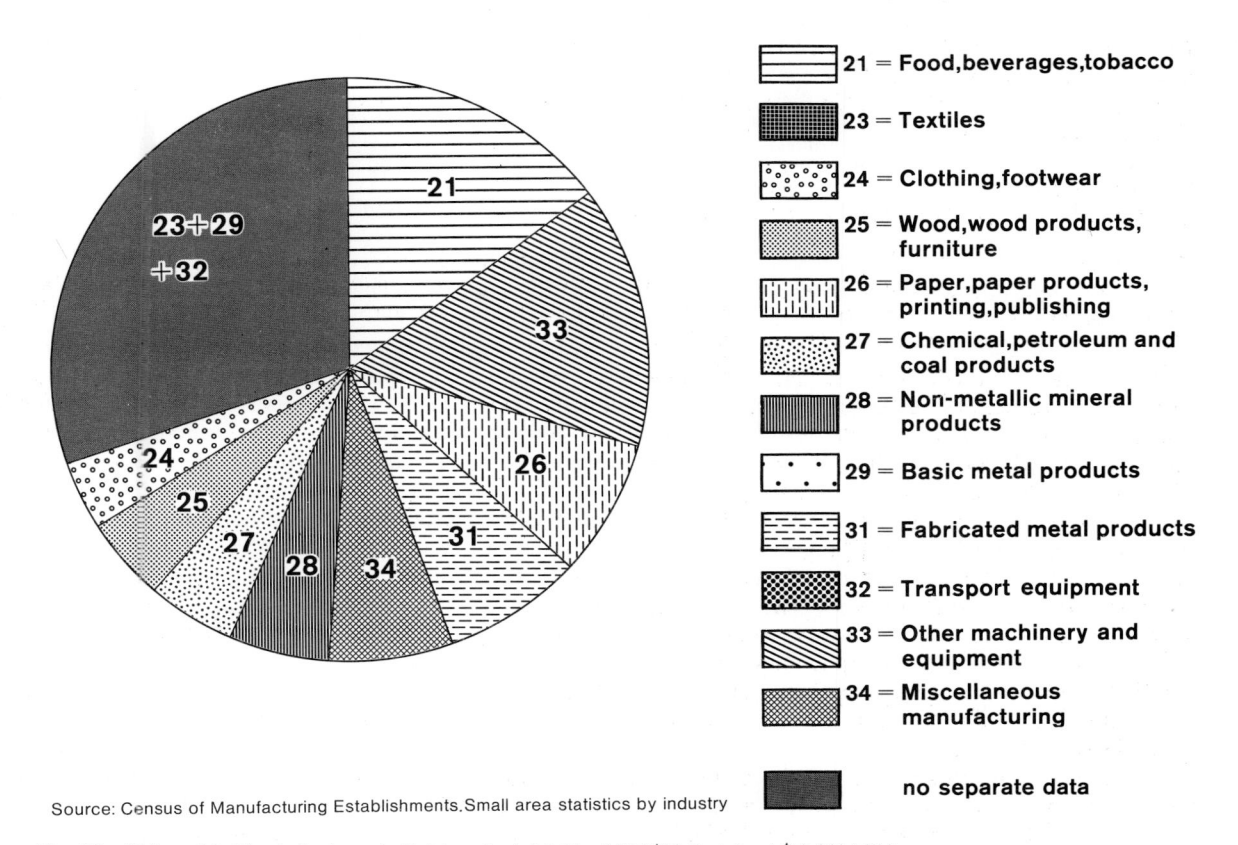

21 = Food, beverages, tobacco
23 = Textiles
24 = Clothing, footwear
25 = Wood, wood products, furniture
26 = Paper, paper products, printing, publishing
27 = Chemical, petroleum and coal products
28 = Non-metallic mineral products
29 = Basic metal products
31 = Fabricated metal products
32 = Transport equipment
33 = Other machinery and equipment
34 = Miscellaneous manufacturing
no separate data

Source: Census of Manufacturing Establishments. Small area statistics by industry

Fig. 59. Value added by industry sub-divisions in Adelaide, 1982/83 (total = A$ 2.141 bill.)

metropolitan area. The most spectacular event in this respect was the establishment of the satellite city of Elizabeth (see ch. 3.4.2). It is no wonder that by 1971, 39% of Adelaide's labour force was in blue-collar industrial occupations. The inner suburbs on the west side of the CBD such as Thebarton, Hindmarsh, Bowden and Brompton, the suburbs along the City — Port Adelaide axis of the northwest corridor, some suburbs in the northeast around Salisbury and Elizabeth and some in the southern corridor like Christies Beach have over 50% of their labour force in the group of labourers, production workers and craftsmen (fig. 59).

These suburbs also have the highest percentages of overseas immigrants, Adelaide having received the *greatest influx of immigrants* of all the capital cities except for Perth. The town of Hindmarsh, for example, has an Ethnic Cinema as well as a Women's Community Health Centre with movies and advertisements in Italian, Greek and Serbo-Croatian, and a Serbian Orthodox Church. Neighbouring Thebarton has a Greek Orthodox Church. The Vietnamese are very much concentrated in Woodville. Workers for the industries established in the satellite town of Elizabeth were recruited from the British Isles, so that the town is characterized by an extremely high percentage of immigrants from the United Kingdom and Eire. For more details on the population structure of these two inner suburbs the reader is referred to Badcock & Cloher (1981).

Adelaide is probably the capital city with the earliest and most effective influence of a state housing authority. The *South Australian Housing Trust* (SAHT) was founded in 1936, and has endeavoured to promote decentralization by the establishment of satellite towns. It was also the government's intention to keep the South Australian cost of living lower than that of Sydney or Melbourne, making South Australia more attractive to immigrants.

The SAHT was very active, and by 1970 had constructed approximately 70,000 dwellings in the Adelaide metropolitan area, most of them being houses for rent and a minor proportion for sale. There has been much construction of public housing in the northwestern and northeastern corridors between the City and Port Adelaide and Tea Tree Gully respectively while the overwhelming majority of houses in Elizabeth as well as in Christies Beach on the south side have been constructed by the Trust. The northeast corridor used to be an area of market gardening, with a conspicuous Italian minority, so that the highschool in Campbelltown was called 'Calabria Highschool'. There is a particular concentration of SAHT houses in the community of Hillcrest. About 17% of all houses in the Adelaide metropolitan area are rented from the Trust, a percentage extremely high by Australian standards. The Trust thus helped to create 'one of the world's first truly linear cities' (Williams in: Forster & Stimson 1977, 21), the distance between Elizabeth in the north and the newly developing satellite town of Noarlunga located approximately 30 kilometres to the south of the CBD being some 65 km.

The suburbs of highest socio-economic status are mainly found in the west and southwest *along the seacoast and in the hills* to the east and southeast, from Unley to Eden Hills and Blackwood, as well as in the inner-city area around North Adelaide and Walkerville. The overall distribution of the socio-economic status thus shows, to a high extent, a sectoral pattern (Div. Nat. Mapp. & ABS 1984).

By the end of World War II *Grand Junction Road* was the northern limit of the built-up area. Most of the settlement beyond this east-west thoroughfare has been developed since that time. Certain areas of unfavourable terrain closer to the metropolitan core have also been settled only in recent years. As late as 1980 the swampy areas immediately to the south of Port Adelaide were drained. Previously there had been only a few summer cottages on the adjacent dunes, but new fashionable homes were constructed on the recently reclaimed land in West Lakes and on Dolphin Island. The area a little further southeast was less in demand by private developers so that the Land Commission started housing projects in Mansfield Park. In the process of development, the last market gardening areas along the upper and lower Torrens River more or less disappeared (fig. 60).

When settlement had filled the Plains, with the few exceptions mentioned above, and when even the Mt. Lofty Ranges began to be threatened by the encroaching housing construction of post-war years, the government started to intervene. In 1955 a Town Planning Committee was appointed. The Committee's report in 1962 became the basis for the *Planning and Development Act* of 1965, which has been revised from time to time. Among other regulations, the Act made provision for the protection of the so-called *Hills Face Zone*, located in 12 local government areas, by means of the Hills Face Zone Planning Regulations of 1971. A systematic development of both the City and the vast suburban periphery led to the establishment of large modern district shopping centres in Elizabeth, West Lakes, Modbury and Marion.

The City of Adelaide Plan of 1977 put emphasis on the growth of population within the City itself. In North Adelaide this planning goal was achieved to an extent that people began to complain that the character of their neighbourhood was being changed by too much rental housing. However, the whole southern part of South Adelaide with the exception of the north-south axis of King William Street is still residential. The revised version of the plan of 1982 put more emphasis on the growth of office space. The core (C) is composed of the King William Street axis, widening in the north to comprise parts of Rundle Mall and the numerous shops and businesses run by overseas immigrants in Hindley Street. These streets are the shopping core of the CBD, whereas government and other public buildings make Victoria Place, King William Street and North Terrace the administrative centre. According to Colonel Light's intentions King William Street was supposed to develop as the main shopping street. This did, however, not happen, because King William Street as a wide north-south street has been suffering from both the northerly hot winds and the sun. Instead the much narrower and quite congested Rundle and Hindley Streets became the main

■	1880
▨	1880 - 1919
▨	1919 - 1939
▨	1939 - 1965
▧	1965 - 1978

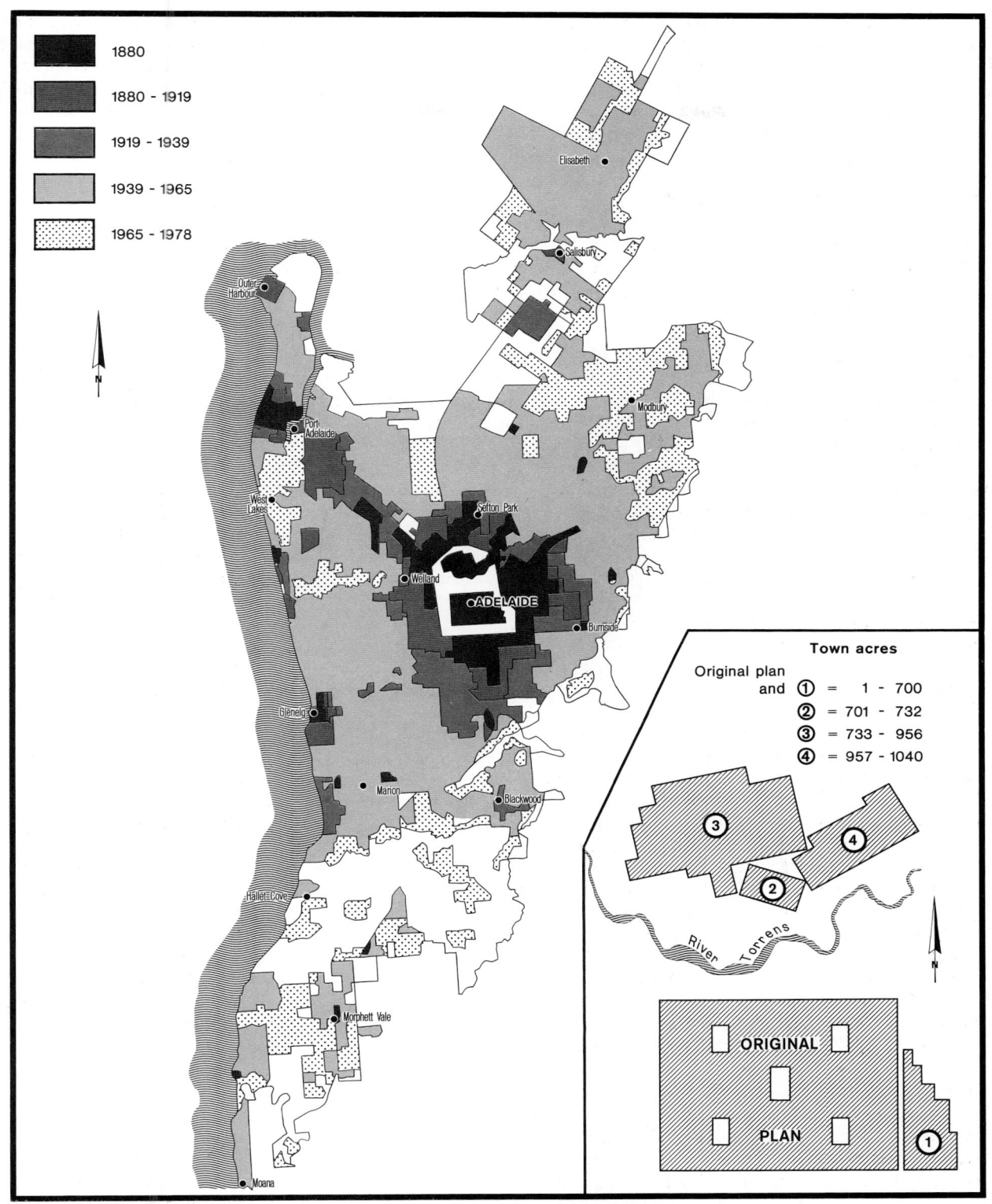

Town acres
Original plan
and ① = 1 - 700
② = 701 - 732
③ = 733 - 956
④ = 957 - 1040

Source : Atlas of Population and Housing, 1981 Census. Vol.5 Adelaide, Canberra 1984

Fig. 60. The growth of Adelaide's built-up area since 1880

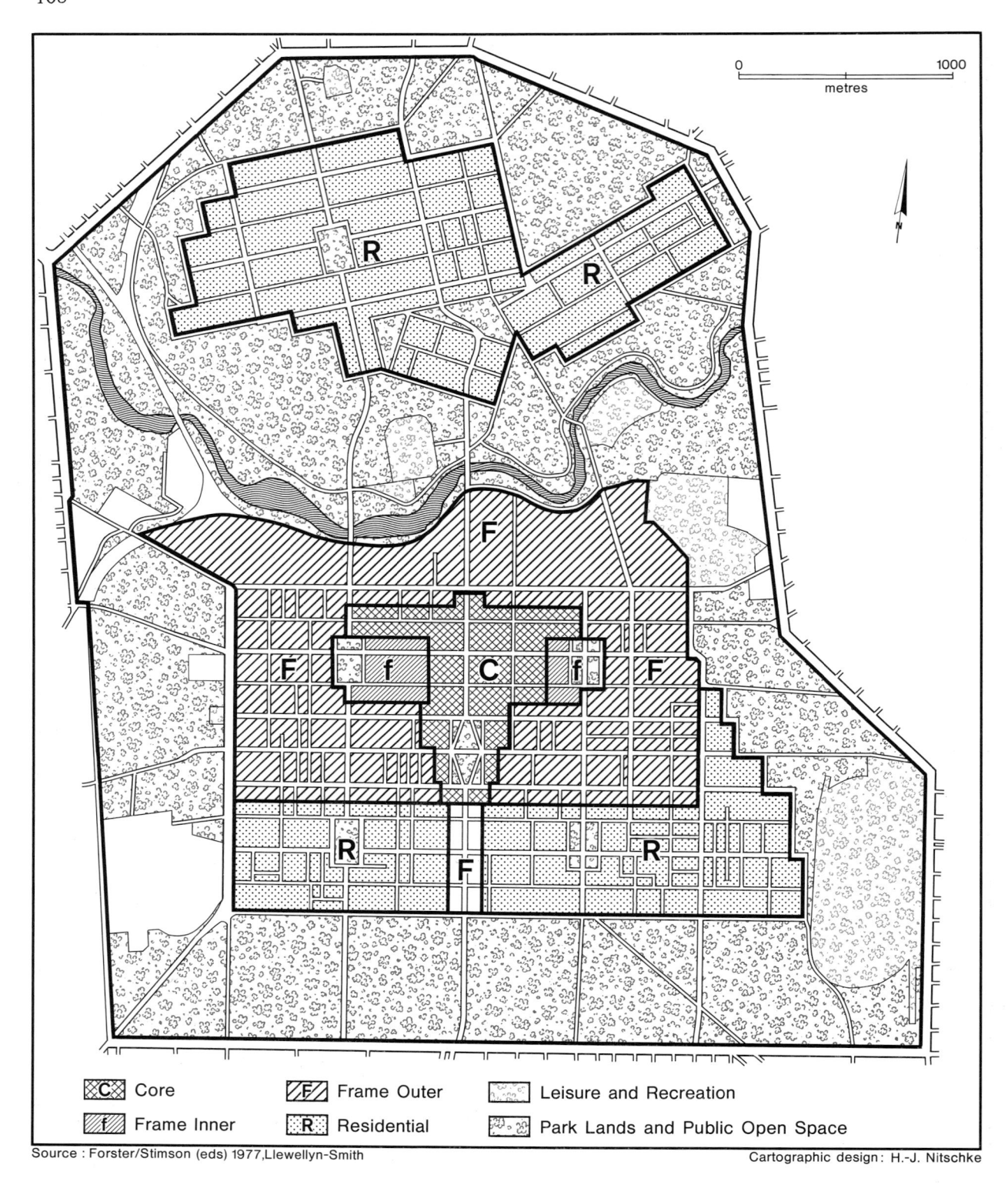

Fig. 61. Major land uses and zoning in the City of Adelaide

shopping area (Freeland 1968, 64–65). The remainder of the northern two thirds of South Adelaide is termed the Frame (F). This is a mixed area of office, commercial and even some manufacturing uses, with a potential for a still higher development of office space. The southern third is, as mentioned above, mainly residential (R), and since the building stock is the oldest in the metropolitan area there has, in recent years, been considerable urban renewal and renovation within the scope of urban conservation measures. Although there is much space for the expansion of the CBD within the town lands, a conspicuous development of office space has taken place along Greenhill Road bordering the southern parklands (fig. 61).

With a slackening of population growth to 6% during the intercensal period 1971–76 and to 2.3% during the period 1976–81, extensive plans for the development of new towns at Monarto and Noarlunga and for urban freeway construction were abandoned. The investigations for the selection of the town site for Monarto were described by Chittleborough and Wright (1974).

To sum up, the Adelaide metropolitan area grew from three settlement nuclei, South and North Adelaide, Port Adelaide and Glenelg. The city core is located approximately 10 km inland and thus has a fairly central position with regard to the entire metropolitan area. The original city was laid out according to the principles of a parkland town, thus assigning specific functions to particular parts of the town from the very beginning. Adelaide was developed by private colonizers, and has always been a settlement of free settlers. It gained primate dominance at an early date, despite a number of ports developing along the South Australian coasts. The development of the built-up area was induced by the triangular shape of the Adelaide Plains and the growth of three axes or corridors to the northwest, the northeast and the south. By the development of the satellite cities of Elizabeth in the north and Noarlunga in the south the metropolis assumed a linear pattern, the distance between these satellites being about 65 km. Postwar development and the growth of the satellite cities in particular were very much influenced by the activities of the South Australian Housing Trust. Industrial occupations are of considerable importance, and much labour has been recruited from the British Isles, particularly for the industries in Elizabeth. Apart from the strong British element in the workforce there is a significant ethnic component in the population, making Adelaide a rather cosmopolitan city.

3.1.4 The metropolitan area of Brisbane, Queensland

Queensland became separated from the mother colony of New South Wales 35 years after the penal settlement at Moreton Bay had been established, and after a number of other settlements had come into existence. In contrast to the other colonies, where the choice of the capital city was very much a matter of finding an appropriate site, in Queensland a choice had to be made between a number of existing settlements, all of them in rivalry with one another and supported by conflicting political and economic groups.

There is some confusion as to the exact date of the establishment of the Moreton Bay settlement. After John Oxley had inspected the area in 1823, the settlement was established at Redcliffe on the shores of Moreton Bay in 1824 and was then moved to a site on the banks of the Brisbane River early in 1825. This settlement may be considered to be the direct forerunner of Brisbane Town. It has also been disputed whether this place had been destined to serve as a true penal settlement. Since convicts in those years were transported in considerable numbers, and the need was felt in Sydney to establish more penal settlements, one was founded at Moreton Bay. It was, however, anticipated that it should soon be converted to a free settlement. Thus after the maximum of some 1,000 convicts had been reached in 1831, and many of them had been released after their seven years' sentences had expired, no large numbers of new convicts were sent (Steele 1975).

Colonization of the Moreton area was forbidden until in 1842 its status as penal settlement was abandoned and it was officially declared open for free settlement. No survey had been made of the settlement until this year. Brisbane, as it was then named after Governor Sir Thomas Brisbane of New South Wales (1821–25), had but little support from the countryside. 'The first Queensland squatters owed little or nothing to Brisbane and the town was not immediately used as a base for pastoral expansion as Rockhampton or Townsville would be' (Lewis 1973, 7). Many settlers preferred to rely for merchandise on Sydney suppliers rather than to patronize Brisbane merchants.

At the time of separation in 1859 Brisbane had to fight against a *number of rivals*. Claims for the position of colonial capital came, among others, from Ipswich, Maryborough, Gladstone and Rockhampton. The New South Wales Government supported Port Curtis (later Gladstone) because it believed 'that any settlement further south would win the trade of the Northern Rivers district of New South Wales' (Lewis 1973, 9). It wanted to have the division as far north as possible. Probably the strongest and longest-lasting rivalry was with Ipswich. This is why the first railway line to be constructed in Queensland in 1864 *did not start in Brisbane* but rather led from Ipswich into the interior to the west. Brisbane was not linked to this railway prior to 1876.

A final fight was with Cleveland Point on Raby Bay, which is a part of the larger Moreton Bay. This place is not located on the Brisbane River but is a little closer to the open sea. Eventually Brisbane won the fight because it had the better port conditions and political decisions had already been made in its favour; it had in 1846 been declared a Port of Entry and had in 1850 received a Customs House.

Fig. 62. Brisbane, Qld. Oblique aerial photograph of North Brisbane and South Brisbane with site of Culture Centre and Expo '88 (reproduced with the permission of Australian Aerial Mapping (Qld) Pty Ltd, Surveying and Mapping Consultants, Brisbane)

After separation political rivalries in Queensland continued between the south centred around Brisbane, the central region centred around *Rockhampton* and the north centred around *Townsville*, also those between Brisbane and *Ipswich*, but Brisbane maintained its position as the colonial capital. But it never gained a high degree of territorial primacy comparable with that of Sydney, Melbourne, Adelaide or Perth in their respective territories.

Brisbane's natural setting has had an enormous influence on its growth and inner differentiation. Brisbane was very much destined to develop along the *Brisbane and Bremer Rivers corridor*, which during the post-war period has filled in from the shores of Moreton Bay all the way to Ipswich. There was already some early development the coast especially to the east and northeast and in the foothills to the west.

In the early days of free settlement, there had been *four distinct settlement nuclei:* South Brisbane, North which in later years developed to the city's CBD), Kangaroo Point and Fortitude Valley, both of the latter being located on spurs beyond the next river meander downstream. It is the strongly meandering river that made the *construction of bridges* vital to the city's further development. Victoria Bridge leading from the city core to South Brisbane was opened in 1872 and the Indooroopilly railway bridge, that was to become extremely important for suburban rail connections to the growing suburbs, was opened in 1875 (fig. 62).

The second significant feature of Brisbane's natural setting was the juxtaposition of *numerous ridges and valleys*, these making for a peculiar sequence and kind of occupation. Apart from flood-free sites in the valley of the Brisbane River, choice locations were on the ridge tops, which offered cool breezes and good views. They also provided the routes for the early tramlines along which many businesses looked for premises. Many of the old shops created near a tram stop to serve everyday needs were later converted to antique shops or other uses. Mainly middle-class housing moved along the ridges, whereas the valleys began to be filled by low-status working class homes, so that a certain social mix developed in the various Brisbane neighbourhoods (Lawson 1973, Burnley 1980) (fig. 63).

It is on the ridges that the most pretentious 'Queenslander style homes' are found, so-called tall-stumped houses *on stilts with their walls made of weatherboard* and their roofs of corrugated iron. Their wide verandahs often became converted to 'sleepouts' in later years. This type of house construction is discussed in more detail in chapter 4.1 Due to fire restrictions in the areas of predominantly wooden structures, few terrace or row houses were erected (Burnley 1980).

In more recent times brick walls and tiled roofs became more common in Queensland, and particularly in Brisbane. However, at the 1976 census not less than 54.8% of Brisbane's houses were still predominantly built of timber, an exceptionally high percentage as compared with other large Australian cities; Melbourne ranks second with 26.9% of its houses built of timber.

Brisbane experienced four periods of growth. The first period was during the 1860s, following political separation from New South Wales. The second period was in the 1880s, the third in the 1920s and the most recent period in the post-war years until the mid-1970s. For details the reader is referred to Lawson (1973), Hogan (1982) and Holthouse (1982).

During the 1880s and early 1890s Brisbane's urban morphology changed substantially from that of a country town to that of a true capital city. Much of the old building stock in the city core was replaced by modern buildings made of brick and stone, among others the Supreme Court, Parliament House, Government House, the Treasury and the Exhibition Buildings. Lawson (1973) pointed to the fact that aside from these changes in the townscape the functional role of Brisbane as Queensland's capital was consolidated by the centralization in the city of government offices and a number of organizations such as trade unions and church administrations, as well as the business enterprises that began to realize that their presence in Brisbane was essential. The most spectacular event was the relocation in 1888 of the headquarters of the Bank of Queensland from Townsville to Brisbane.

During those two decades Brisbane experienced a remarkable growth from 31,000 residents in 1881 to 102,000 in 1891 and to 120,000 in 1901. This growth was accompanied by numerous extensions of electric tramways and rail lines and a spread of suburban areas. No wonder that as early as 1898 the desire for the formation of a 'Greater Brisbane' municipality was expressed, but the time did not seem to be ripe for such a decision. No action was taken prior to the next growth period in the 1920s.

The *City of Brisbane Act* passed in 1925 provided the basis for the formation of the Brisbane City Council (BCC), with the participation of the two cities of North Brisbane and South Brisbane, six towns, nine shires and parts of another two shires. This administrative body was endowed with wide statutory powers for the whole metropolitan area; it was only in recent years that the jurisdiction of electricity supply was withdrawn from the Council. Brisbane's successful movement towards metropolitan administration and planning makes it unique among the state capital cities. On the other hand, the zone-based organization of Queensland's electoral system has kept Brisbane's influence in the State Parliament in check, which must be considered another reason for Brisbane's not having achieved a higher degree of territorial primacy.

During the post-war period Brisbane participated in the nationwide increase of population in consequence of the baby boom, and like other great cities showed the effects of higher incomes in terms of the spread of private homes and increased car ownership. The city also gained from growth factors specific to Queensland, such as the mineral boom of the 1960s and 1970s and the increasing tourist trade.

Fig. 63. Brisbane, Qld. Partial view of northern suburbs demonstrating the ridge and valley character of terrain

Major expansions of the built-up area occurred along the Bruce and Pacific Highways. Some segments were upgraded to form the northwest-southeast *Riverside Expressway*, the concrete structure that spoils a considerable part of Brisbane's waterfront. The electrified rapid transit system underlined the spreading of settlement along major transportation routes, and a number of major housing projects were initiated. Sites offering good views over the river are favoured for *high-rise apartment blocks*, as in St. Lucia, in earlier days a sugar plantation worked by settlers from the Carribean Island of that name. The district is now the home of the University of Queensland, with its monumental main building dating back to the 1930s. The Centenary Project, on a site of over 1,400 hectares 13 km southwest of the city centre is situated between Centenary Highway and two meanders of the Brisbane River. It includes several settlement fractions such as Jindalee (started 1962), Jamboree Heights (1969), Mount Ommaney (1970), Westlake (1973), River Hills (1973) and Sumner, where an industrial estate was developed (Hajdu 1976) (fig. 64).

Large *planned shopping complexes* were opened in suburban areas. The Chermside development was one of the first of its kind in Australia; others are Booval, Carnidale, Indooroopilly, Kuraby, Michelton, Mount Gavatt and Toombul. Approximately 43% of all retail sales in the State of Queensland are done in Brisbane's CBD and the shopping complexes of the Brisbane metropolitan area mentioned above.

In the two decades prior to World War II the port of Brisbane already handled about six times as much cargo as did the next two ports of Townsville and Rockhampton together, and after the war a new modern *container port* was added. North of the river a new airport is being developed on land adjacent to the present Brisbane airport.

Only 16% of Brisbane's labour force is in manufacturing. There are hardly any branch factories of larger national corporations in the metropolitan area of Brisbane. Except for two oil refineries, most of Brisbane's manufacturing consists of the assembly of components produced elsewhere or agricultural processing, such as sugar refining, meat packing or pineapple canning (the cannery is supposedly the largest of its kind in the southern hemisphere). Nevertheless, Brisbane's share of Queensland's manufacturing in terms of value added is 48%. Major industrial complexes have developed near the airport, in the Ipswich corridor and at Acacia Ridge (fig. 65). Aside from manufac-

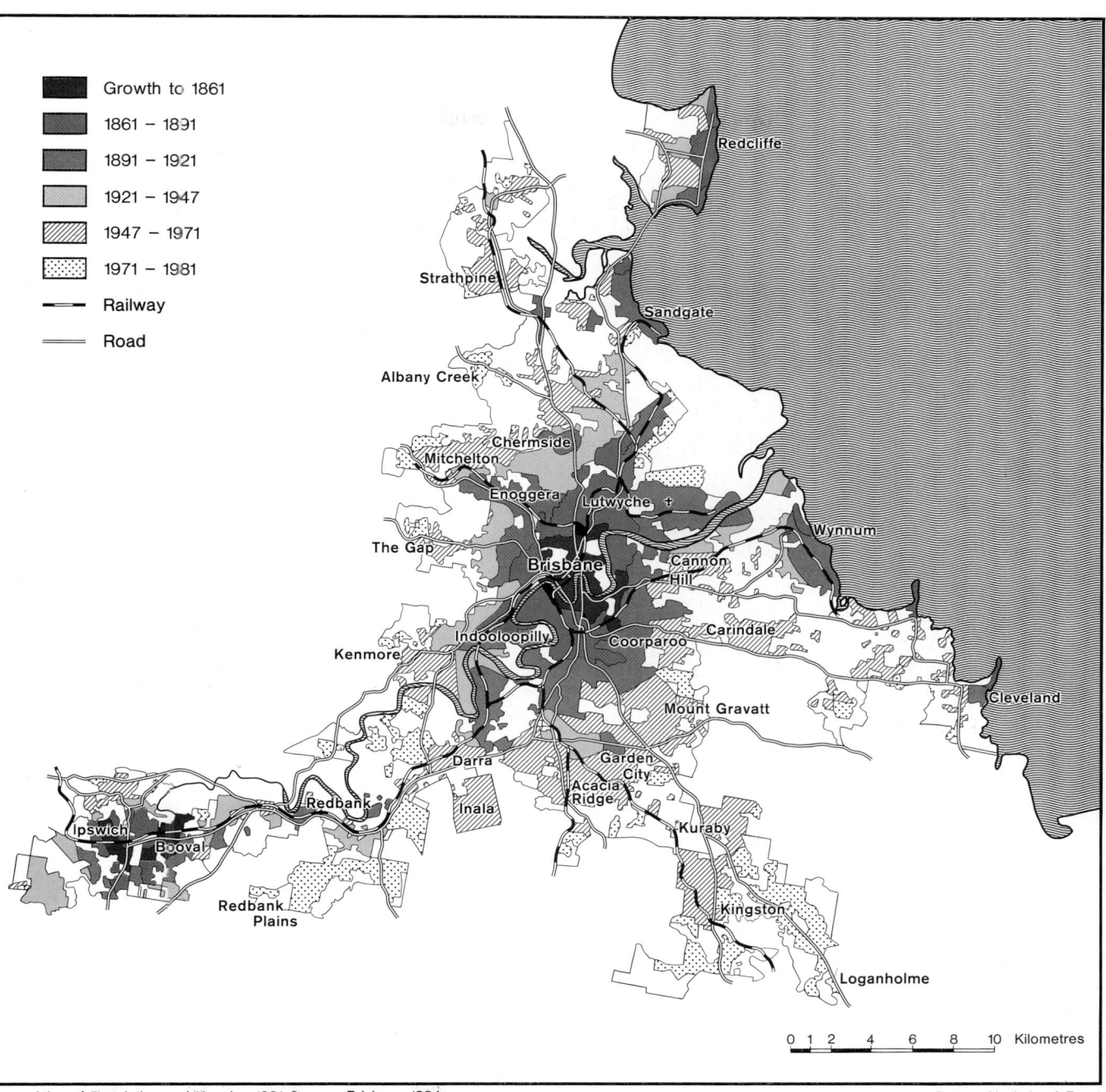

Legend:
- Growth to 1861
- 1861 – 1891
- 1891 – 1921
- 1921 – 1947
- 1947 – 1971
- 1971 – 1981
- Railway
- Road

Source: Atlas of Population and Housing 1981 Census, Brisbane 1984

Cartographic design: A. Eggert

Fig. 64. Brisbane's growth

turing, private enterprise is not well represented in Queensland's capital city; the Mt. Isa Mines Ltd. is the only major corporation to have its headquarters in Brisbane.

This rather weak development of secondary industries and other private enterprise is reflected in the comparatively *small numbers of overseas immigrants* that arrived in Australia with Queensland or Brisbane as their destination. Brisbane's 16,5% overseas-born at the 1976 census is the second lowest percentage of all the capital cities, except for Hobart, with but 12,6%. Few suburbs have over 30% overseas-born residents. Mention should, however, be made of *Fortitude Valley*, which developed as kind of a secondary CBD. In the course of time it became a somewhat rundown area, characterized by shops run by overseas immigrants, Italian and Japanese restaurants and entertainment functions. Brisbane owes its rather strong recent growth mainly to the internal migration of Australian-born people.

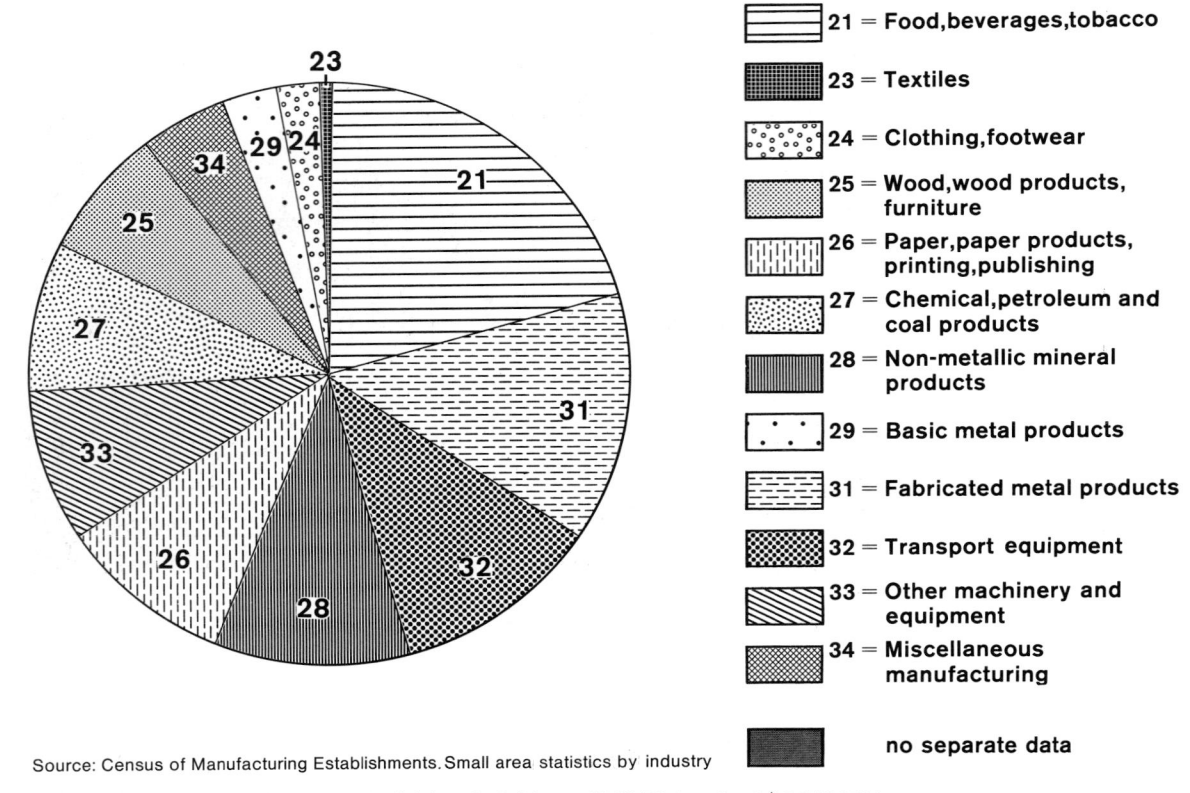

Legend:
- 21 = Food, beverages, tobacco
- 23 = Textiles
- 24 = Clothing, footwear
- 25 = Wood, wood products, furniture
- 26 = Paper, paper products, printing, publishing
- 27 = Chemical, petroleum and coal products
- 28 = Non-metallic mineral products
- 29 = Basic metal products
- 31 = Fabricated metal products
- 32 = Transport equipment
- 33 = Other machinery and equipment
- 34 = Miscellaneous manufacturing
- no separate data

Source: Census of Manufacturing Establishments. Small area statistics by industry

Fig. 65. Value added by industry sub-divisions in Brisbane, 1981/82 (total = A$ 2.093 bill.)

Since manufacturing is of minor importance for Brisbane, the city has made great endeavours to promote *tertiary functions* of various kinds. Brisbane served as host city for the Commonwealth Games in 1982. During the first half of the 1980s the large *Cultural Centre* was developed on the river bank in South Brisbane, opposite the CBD. Its component parts were opened in successive stages between 1981 and 1984: the Queensland Art Gallery in 1981, the Performing Arts Centre in 1982, the Queensland Museum in 1983 and the State Library of Queensland in 1984. The city has been preparing for being host to the World Fair Expo '88 in the jubilee year of Australia's bicentennial. The small houses of the transition zone have become heavily encroached by the advancing high-rise buildings of the CBD (fig. 66).

The 1988 Exposition has been conceived as a so-called specialized exposition with the theme 'Leisure in the Age of Technology', which appropriately reflects the characteristics and needs of the host state. A site about 40 hectares in size has been acquired for the Exposition adjacent to the Cultural Centre; the relocation of the Interstate Railway Terminal to Roma Street Station in the CBD is part of the project. Here also the so-called South Bank Centre, Brisbane's first high-technology park of approximately 32,000 square metres, is being developed (Austr. Property Rev. 1984).

In conclusion it can be said that it took 18 years from the establishment of the Moreton Bay Penal Settlement to the declaration that the district was open for colonization. Brisbane Town's aspirations to be chosen as the colonial capital of the new colony of Queensland involved it in rivalries with other port cities along the Pacific coast, notably with neighbouring Ipswich and with Cleveland Point on Raby Bay. Thus Brisbane was never able to gain a high degree of territorial primacy. In 1925, 19 local government units formed the Brisbane City Council, co-operating in respect of the metropolitan area in practically all matters of public utilities and metropolitan planning. Brisbane's suburban growth was, to a considerable extent, directed by the Brisbane and Bremer Rivers corridor or Ipswich corridor and by its terrain of ridges and valleys. The ridges were guidelines for the expansion of middle-class housing and for the early tramlines, with concentrations of shops at the tram stops. A very low percentage of Brisbane's workforce is in manufacturing, its secondary industries mainly being of the assembly and processing type, and the city attracted a comparatively low number of overseas immigrants. On the other hand, Brisbane is Queensland's outstanding port city, and in recent years developed a great Cultural Centre, was host to the Commonwealth Games in 1982 and is going to be host to Expo '88.

Fig. 66. Brisbane, Qld. Expanding CBD encroaching inner suburbs on north side

3.1.5 The metropolitan area of Perth, Western Australia

Though British settlement in the western third of the continent had begun in 1826 near Albany, formal annexation of this part of Australia by the colonial government of New South Wales took place in 1829, at the mouth of the Swan River on the coast of the Indian Ocean. Captain James Stirling, after having made a reconnaisance survey of the southwest coast in 1825, was put in charge of an expedition in 1829, in the course of which he founded the townsite of Perth. His earlier favourable report on the Swan River region was an indication of his judgement of the importance of this area within the British Empire (Cameron 1973).

Stirling chose *a site some 20 km upstream* for the administrative centre of the Swan River Colony, a site about halfway between the coast at Fremantle and the first agricultural settlement at Guildford (fig. 67). In doing so he rejected the possible sites of Buckland Hill between Rocky Bay and Leighton Beach and Mangles Bay, the present Cockburn Sound, farther south. Both of these places had been suggested by Sir George Murray, then Secretary of State for the Colonies. Presumably the main reason for Stirling's decision was his desire to have the new colony's capital protected from maritime attack. His search for an appropriate site is discussed in detail by Markey (in Gentilli 1979, 346—47). In a letter to Murray's successor Hay written in 1832 Stirling gave reasons for his choice of the site:

'On our arrival here with the expedition, the imperfect knowledge which I had of the country was of course soon extended and it was found in consequence that a town at the mouth of the estuary would be requisite for landing goods and as a Port Town, while another sufficiently high on the River to afford easy communication between the Agriculturalists on the Upper Swan and the Commercial Interests at the Port would tend much to the speedy occupation of that useful district. In selecting a site for this purpose, the present position of Perth seemed to be so decidedly preferable in building materials, streams of water and facility of communication that I was induced on these grounds to establish the Town there' (Stirling 1832).

The town was given its name in honour of the birthplace and the constituency of Sir George Murray.

The natural setting of the townsite has had a strong impact on the growth of Perth and even on present-day metropolitan planning. The site is located *in the centre of a coastal plain* of approximately 25 km in width between the Indian Ocean to the west and the Darling Range to the east. The western half of the plain consists of a series of depressions and ridges of fossilized dunes running parallel to the coastline. The lower parts of the plain were originally poorly drained and covered by a number of small lakes and swamps. During the first three decades of European settlement lakes to the north of the little town of Perth hindered development and had negative influences on the settlers' health, since they were breeding places for mosquitoes and other pests. The situation improved when drainage commenced in 1854. The low-lying swampy areas between the dune systems have to date been used for market gardening, with Italian and Yugoslav immigrants dominating this type of occupation.

Fig. 67. Perth, W.A. View of the CBD and Mitchell Freeway interchange from Kings Park Overlook

Because a bar of rock at the mouth of the Swan River prevented seagoing vessels from entering the river, from the very beginning of the Swan River Colony a port independent from the seat of administration had to be developed. During the first decades of the colony Fremantle grew almost at the same pace as Perth; the Western Australian capital thus developed from *twin foci*.

The first major line of communication was between Perth and Fremantle to the west and between Perth and Guildford to the east, resulting in a line running more or less *west-east* through the coastal plain. In contrast, all further development was mainly determined by the *north-south* extent of the coastal plain, confined between the ocean and the mountains. This tendency eventually led to the decision in 1969 by the Metropolitan Region Planning Authority to have the metropolitan area develop along north-south running corridors.

Site characteristics also led to early social segregation; three favourable residential areas proved to be attractive to people of higher incomes. These were the area overlooking Freshwater Bay and Melville Water, a coastal strip north of Fremantle encompassing such places as Cottesloe and Scarborough, and the areas on the Darling Scarp like Kalamunda and Glen Forest with their fashionable home sites set in semi-natural bushland. In the last decade South Perth, boasting of 'Perth's premier location', has experienced a great building boom.

The town site, as shown by the Arrowsmith map of 1833, was set out in three main sections focussed on a large central square running northwards from the river. The western and eastern sections were arranged on either side of the central square along the rather narrow ridge of high ground paralleling the Swan River foreshore. The third section lay along the lakes and swamps to the north of the square and the eastern section. The square was soon abandoned in favour of the uninterrupted continuation of the main streets.

Within the grid the streets enclosed blocks of between eight and ten acres, which were subdivided into lots of an average size of four-fifths of an acre or approximately 3,200 square metres each. Single detached dwellings predominated in these *large lots*; building regulations provided for all housing to be built on the centre-line of each lot with a set-back of 30 feet. While the *English country cottage* seems to have served as the prototype there were, in contrast to Sydney, only a few rows of terraces built around the turn of the century. Brick was the main material used for housing construction, since experience showed that timber would warp in the Perth climate. The western section, located close to the river approach from Fremantle and to sources of water supply, developed as the town's shopping and business district. Administrative, judicial and military functions were concentrated in the central and eastern sections of the town.

One of the major problems confronting the early administrators of the Swan River Colony was that soldiers as well as civil servants had been made large land grants for their services, so that by the late 1830s approximately 1.2 million acres had been alienated of which only 160 acres were cultivated (Roberts 1968).

Due to the lack of labour, of self-government and of effective means of communication, Perth's growth was extremely slow till mid-century; by 1850 there were fewer than 5,000 Europeans in the whole colony. During the second half of the nineteenth century considerable changes took place, but even at the turn of the century when the city had some 63,000 residents (1901) it was small enough to enable the local authorities in 1896 to declare the vast area of Kings Park a public open space.

The first change was an increase in the labour force, due to the colony's successful application to be supplied with convict labour. Just at the time when transportation was discontinued in the eastern colonies it started in Western Australia; *convicts* were brought to the colony between 1850 and 1868. The greater availability of labour stimulated construction in Perth. Streets were levelled and paved and roads and bridges were constructed. A number of substantial buildings were erected, mainly of brick or limestone, among others the Court House and Gaol in 1854, the first stage of Government House in 1859, the Old Trinity Church in 1864, the Roman Catholic Cathedral in Victoria Square in 1865 and the Perth Town Hall opened in 1871.

The second change was in the administrative status of the town. In 1856 Perth was constituted a *Cathedral City*, following the inauguration of the Bishopric of Perth. In 1858 the municipal administration of the so-called Perth Town Trust was replaced by the Perth City Council. Finally, in 1871 the City of Perth was incorporated, after reaching the 5,000 mark.

The third change was the coming of the *railway* to the colony, with Perth becoming the focal point of a growing network of railway lines. In 1881 the line between Perth and Fremantle was opened, inducing the development of Subiaco and a number of other suburbs along the line. At present Subiaco is one of those older suburbs experiencing gentrification and thus being comparable with Sydney's Paddington, Melbourne's Parkville or Hobart's Battery Point. To the east the line was first opened to Midland, then to Guildford and five years later extended to Northam and York. Midland also gained from the transfer of the railway workshops. Growth in the southeastern sector began when a passenger service was introduced on the line between Perth and Armadale.

The *City Railway Station* was located adjoining the city centre on the north side of Wellington Street, just three blocks north of St. Georges Terrace, which is the hub of the present CBD (fig. 68). This central location was only possible because the city was still very small in the 1880s, although 52 years had elapsed since its foundation. The government acquired various lots on either side of the station, the Post Office and the Central Government Building are situated immediately south of the station, while beyond the tracks to the north are such important public buildings as the State Reference Library and the Western Australian Museum. The first great department store is also located next to the station. However, the famous overland trains such as the Indian Pacific and the Prospector, operating from Perth to Sydney and Kalgoorlie respectively, arrive at and leave not at the City Station but at the East Perth Terminal.

The railway lines also gave incentives to the location of industries. A large manufacturing area developed in Leederville along the railway west of the CBD, while another manufacturing complex developed along the eastern line in Midland. It was above all the eastern suburbs between Perth and Midland that developed as low-status residential quarters.

Changes were also brought about by the first Swan River reclamation, that commenced in 1883. It added some 15 acres of land to the city area, which were reserved for recreational purposes to form the present Esplanade. During the first six decades of the twentieth century another 200 acreas were reclaimed, most of it allocated for public open space. Around the turn of the century the facilities of Fremantle were upgraded, making it a deep-water harbour and securing its dominance over Albany. The extent of the harbour works is shown on the map 'Western Australia, Fremantle Harbour Works Plan' of 1900 by the Public Works Department of Western Australia.

The fourth change was the tapping of two natural resources; the *discovery of gold* in the Eastern Goldfields and the conversion of a vast area in the southeast to the present *wheat belt*. In particular the beginning of the gold-rush in the early 1890s gave a great incentive to the growth of the Western Australian capital. During the intercensal period 1891–1901 the City of Perth's population increased from 8,447 to 27,553 residents, while the Perth MUA reached the size of 63,000. By the turn of the century Perth had clearly achieved territorial primacy, with 34.4% of Western Australia's total population.

The gold-rush brought a high demand for land and housing in Perth, so that the inner suburbs such as Subiaco, Leederville and North Perth grew rapidly. Housing estates also began to spread over the outer suburban areas, where land grants took the form of comparatively small and *long strips oriented toward the river*. Such grants were, in fact, contrary to the regulations of the Colonial Office, which required sections of a square mile each oriented on a grid of east-west and north-south running lines. The further subdivision of lots for housing construction was entirely left to

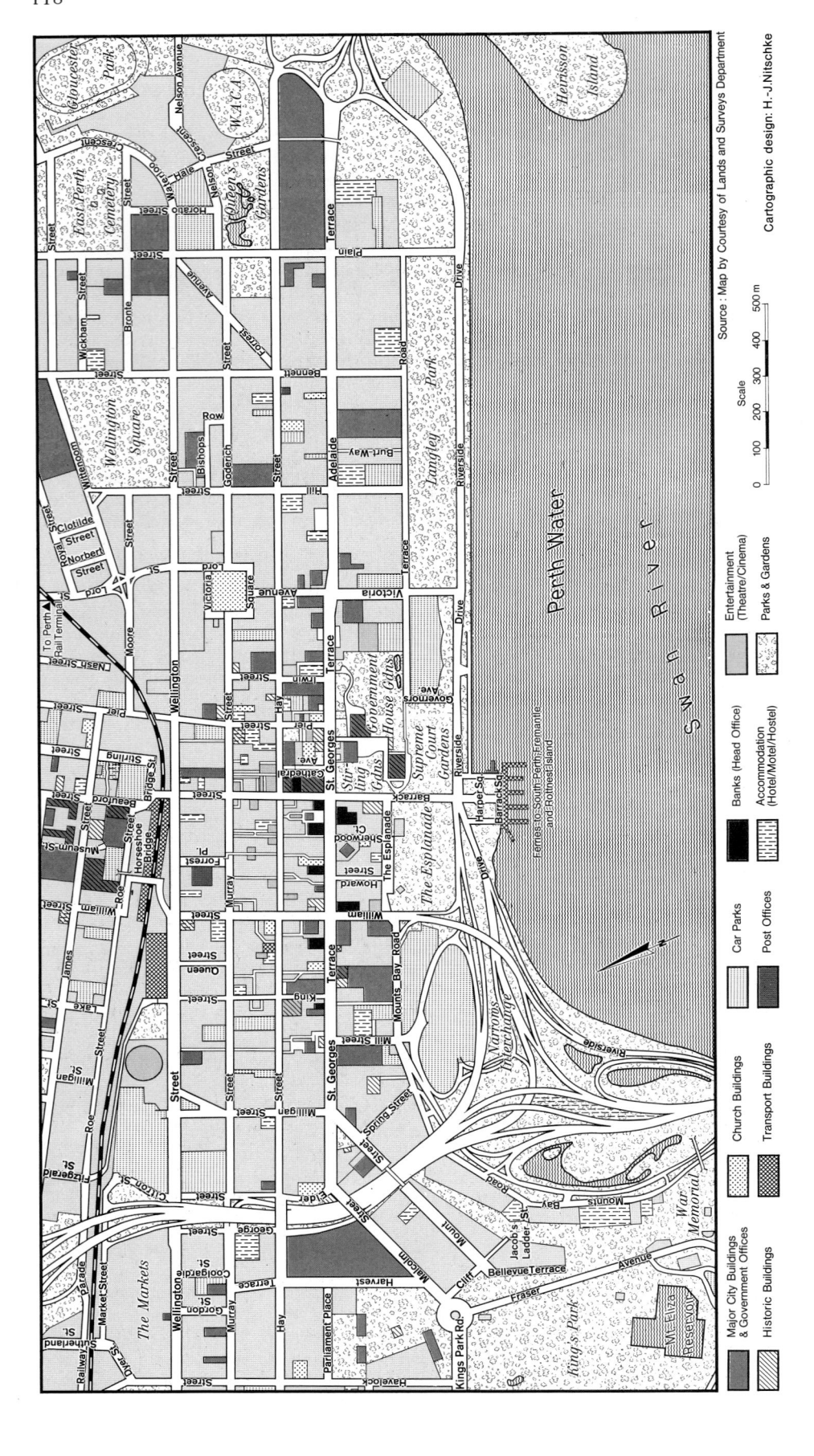

Fig. 68. Major land uses in Perth's city centre

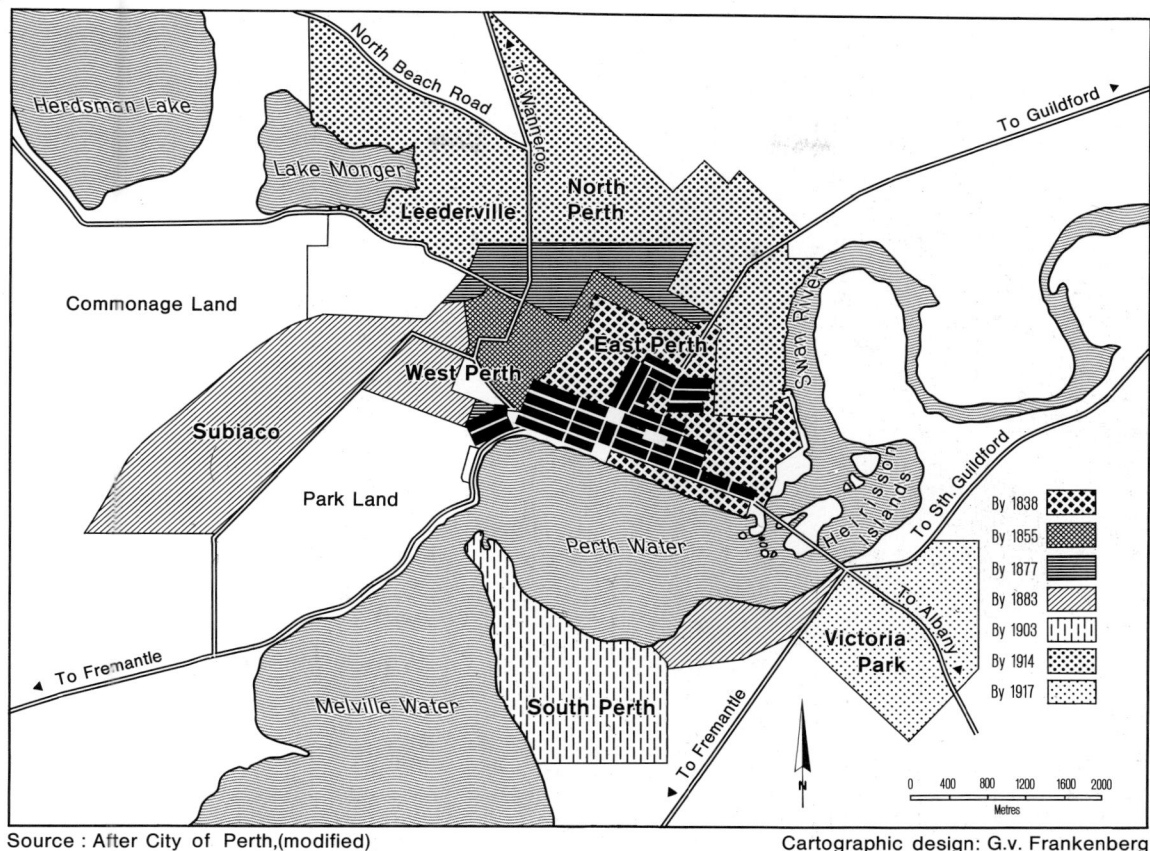

Fig. 69. Perth's growth 1838–1917

Source: After City of Perth, (modified)
Cartographic design: G.v. Frankenberg

each individual land owner; the consequent unregulated development may still be discerned in the present street pattern and in the shape of building lots.

West of the town, Crown lands were extending all the way to the sea coast. In these lands, which were called the *Perth Commonage Lands*, the City of Perth enjoyed certain rights. When in consequence of population increase the demand for land was high, the City of Perth made an attempt to use part of this land for new housing, but negotiations lasted for almost two decades. In 1902 the Government granted the City Council approximately 2,300 acres of land boardering the coast as an 'Endowment in perpetuity'. In 1917 the Council was also able to purchase the so-called Limekilns Estate, an area of approximately 1,300 acres located between the City and the Endowment Lands, so that for the first time the City of Perth gained direct access to the ocean beach. On this land two garden suburbs were developed, with ample space left as a public park and public land along the ocean frontage. At the same time the Council was able to buy land adjacent to Lake Monger, and thus get control of an area where great numbers of the famous Western Australian black swans are a major tourist attraction (fig. 69).

The population increase in consequence of the gold-rush also stimulated the establishment of secondary industries. Before the turn of the century little manufacturing was found in Perth, except for the processing of primary products, such as timber-working, clothing and leather manufacture, flour-milling and food production. During the decade 1890–1900 the number of factories located in the City of Perth trebled from 40 to 121. Most pursued the same brands of production, but others were added, for example chemical production, printing and engraving, coach building and the production of motor vehicle parts, nail-making, iron-working, galvanizing factories and the production of canvas goods (Scott in Gentilli 1979).

At about 1910 a *Greater Perth Movement* arose among a number of neighbouring municipalities, with the goal of forming a Greater Perth Council. In the following years referenda were held in those municipalities, with the result that Leederville and North Perth were amalgamated with Perth in 1914 and Victoria Park in 1916. The others refused to join the enlarged City of Perth (Webb in: Gentilli 1979). Another attempt at better administrative management of the Perth region was made just before the beginning of the Depression, when in 1928 a Town Planning Commission was appointed that submitted a report to the City Council two years later. Because of the depression years

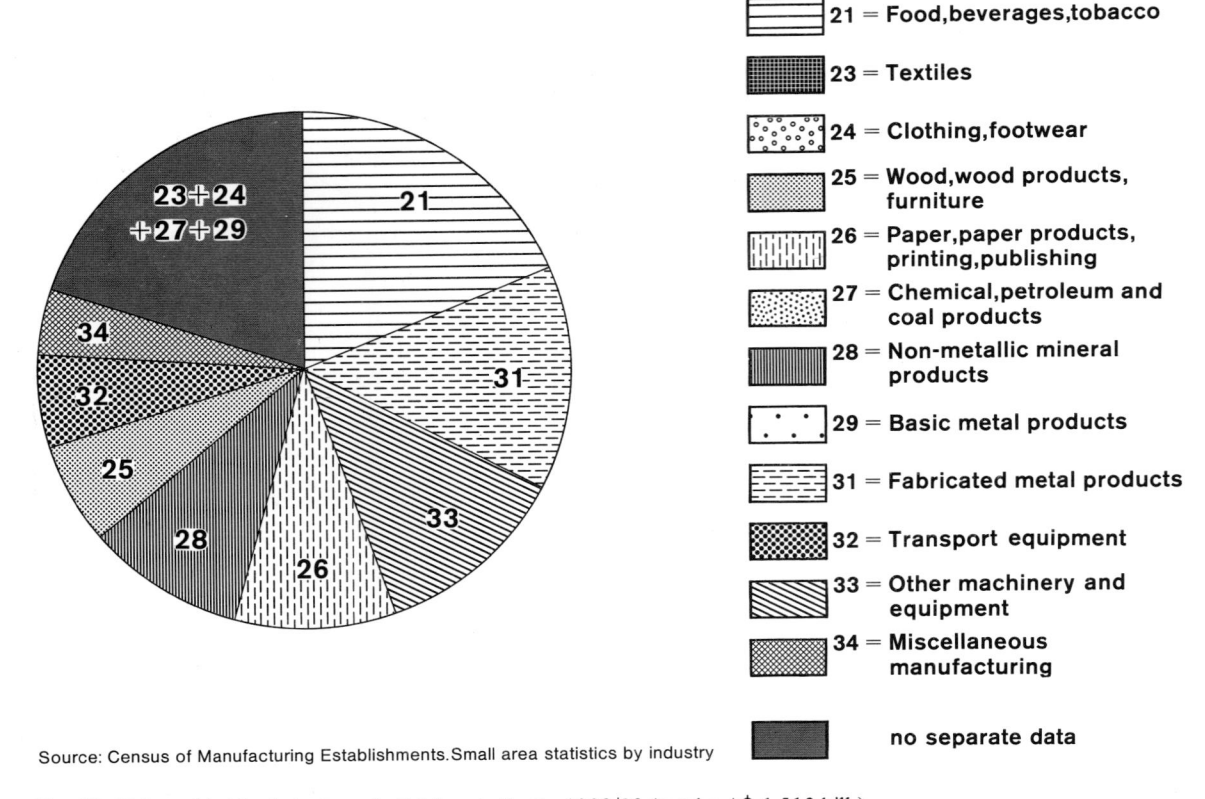

Source: Census of Manufacturing Establishments. Small area statistics by industry

Fig. 70. Value added by industry sub-divisions in Perth, 1982/83 (total = A$ 1.512 bill.)

and the outbreak of World War II most of the Commission's recommendations were not implemented; exceptions were the introduction of zoning regulations for controlling land use in the city, the appointment of a Town Planning Commissioner and the establishment of a Town Planning Authority.

War efforts after 1941 signalled the beginning of a new phase in the development of Perth's industries and in the increase of population and housing stock. On the city's eastern periphery, at *Welshpool*, a munitions works was established, that initiated the development of what was to become a great industrial area in post-war years.

After the Second World War the Western Australian Government made further efforts to promote industrialization. A major feature was its 1952 agreement with the Anglo-Iranian Oil Company to relocate their refinery from Persia to Australia. A large area adjoining Cockburn Sound was acquired that had formerly belonged to the Commonwealth Government in order to establish a modern deep-sea harbour and a huge industrial estate. This industrial area, approximately 35 km south of the Perth city centre, was developed in successive stages with the oil refinery coming first, this being followed by an integrated steel works, an aluminum smelter, a nickel refinery and a fertilizer factory. Four to five kilometres inland *Kwinana New Town* was founded to house part of the workforce of the industrial and harbour complex (see ch. 3.4.2). This large-scale development on the southern periphery of the Perth region gave rise to a comprehensive planning policy for what was to become the Perth Metropolitan Area. Despite the State Government's efforts, industrial employment in Western Australia has remained of minor importance (fig. 70). In 1980 only 12.5% of the state's total labour force was in manufacturing. Perth's share, however, was 84%!

Housing in Kwinana New Town was mainly provided by the State Housing Commission (SHC), this agency accounting for approximately 44% of all new houses in Western Australia built between the end of World War II and the year 1957. As Harman (in: Williams 1983) pointed out, the SHC since its inception in 1944 had, until 1980, built 73.8% of its housing units within the confines of the Perth metropolitan area. There were only two periods when the metropolitan area's share declined significantly: during the second half of the 1960s, when the iron ore boom diverted a large part of public funds to new settlements in the Pilbara region, such as South Hedland, Karratha or Wickham, and since the mid-1970s in connection with new bauxite and gas projects.

This development was accompanied by an increasing wave of post-war overseas immigration, of which the metropolitan area received a good share. At the 1981 census 31.2%, or close to one third, of the total population was foreign born, this being the *highest percentage* of all the capital cities. Some immigrant groups, the migrants

Fig. 71. Statistical districts of Perth with above average Italian and Greek immigrants

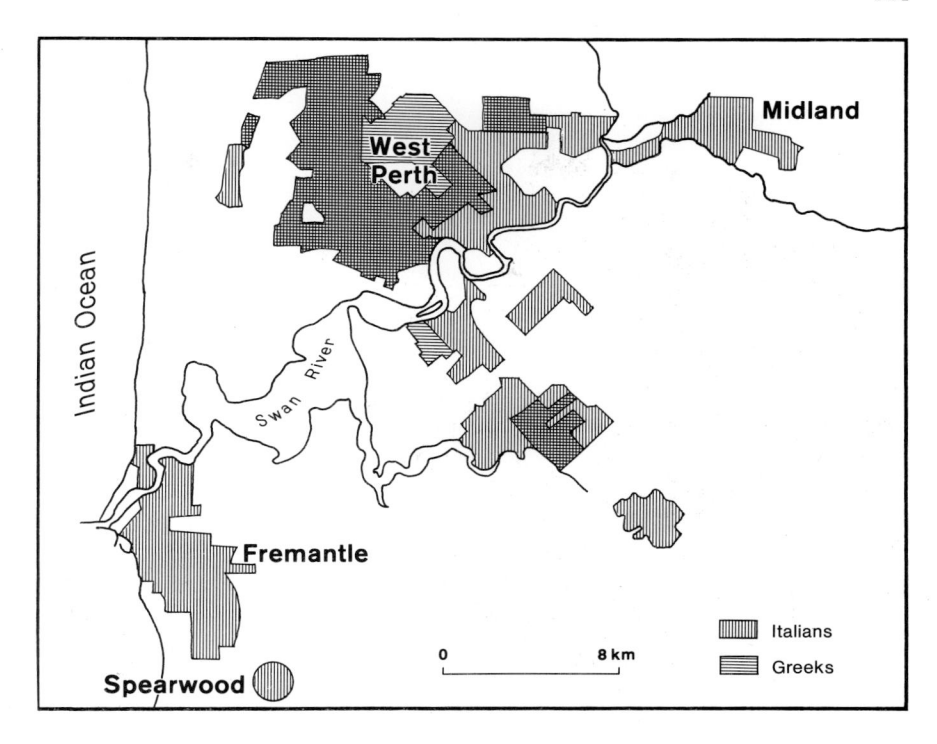

from the United Kingdom and Eire in particular, are rather widely distributed over the metropolitan area. Other groups show conspicuous local concentrations, such as the Polish manufacturing workers in Midland or the Yugoslavs in the wine-growing and market-gardening areas in the upper Swan River Valley and in Spearwood, south of Fremantle. The latter is a low-lying area between the gentle slopes of fossilized dune systems. It is characterized by lakes and swamps and a natural vegetation of paperbarks (*Melaleuca leucadendron*) and river gums (*Eucalyptus camaldulensis*). Here *market gardeners* grew grapes, olives, figs and other Mediterranean fruit and vegetables, but in recent years a growing demand for building lots has led to the conversion of some of the market gardens to home sites. Italians are also prominent among the market gardeners in Spearwood, some also being fishermen. Italians from Sicily are dominant as *fishermen* and in other maritime occupations in Fremantle (fig. 71). There is also a concentration of Italians and Greeks, and of businesses run by Italians and by few managers of other ethnic origins, along William Street on the north side of the Central Railway Station (fig. 119).

In 1962 Perth served as host to the Commonwealth Games. For this purpose an area of 78 acres in *Bold Park* was developed as the Perry Lakes Stadium complex and a suburb of garden city type constructed at City Beach to house the athletes. More than 150 houses were sold to private buyers after the event. Another big event was the America's Cup sailed from October, 1986 to February, 1987.

An unprecedented office-building boom occurred in the Perth CBD during the period 1955–75, when some 50 new high-rise office buildings of over 5,000 square metres floor space each were added to the CBD. This building boom, which continued until the early 1980s, extended well into West Perth, which today may be considered part of Perth's CBD. This development was discussed in some detail in various publications by Alexander (1974, in Gentilli 1979, 1980). Another indicator of Perth's recent growth is the *Burswood Island Resort*. This project has been carried out as an Australian-Malaysian joint venture, including a Casino that opened late in 1985, a five-star hotel, ten restaurants, an entertainment complex, a sports and exhibition centre and an 18-hole-golf course.

There were even more far-reaching plans for changing the face of inner Perth; for example, in the Perth Transportation Study the proposal was made to place the Central City Station below ground level in order to improve access from the CBD to the area north of the railway tracks. This plan was, however, abandoned at a later date.

It has been disputed whether the rapid development of iron ore mining in the Pilbara region since the mid-1960s and of other mining operations in Western Australia have had a favourable impact on the state's capital. Harman has argued that incomes per capita are relatively low in Western Australia and are hardly any higher in the metropolis than in the state generally and that Perth had in 1983 the highest male unemployment rate of all the capital cities (11.8%, followed by Adelaide with 11.6%, according to Forster 1983). In Harman's own words 'The lack of dominance appears to have come about as a result of both State policies which have directed public funds out of the metropolitan area, and the operations of mining capital which do not confirm (except in superficial ways) to the locic assumed in the centre-periphery models' (Harman in: Williams 1983, 139).

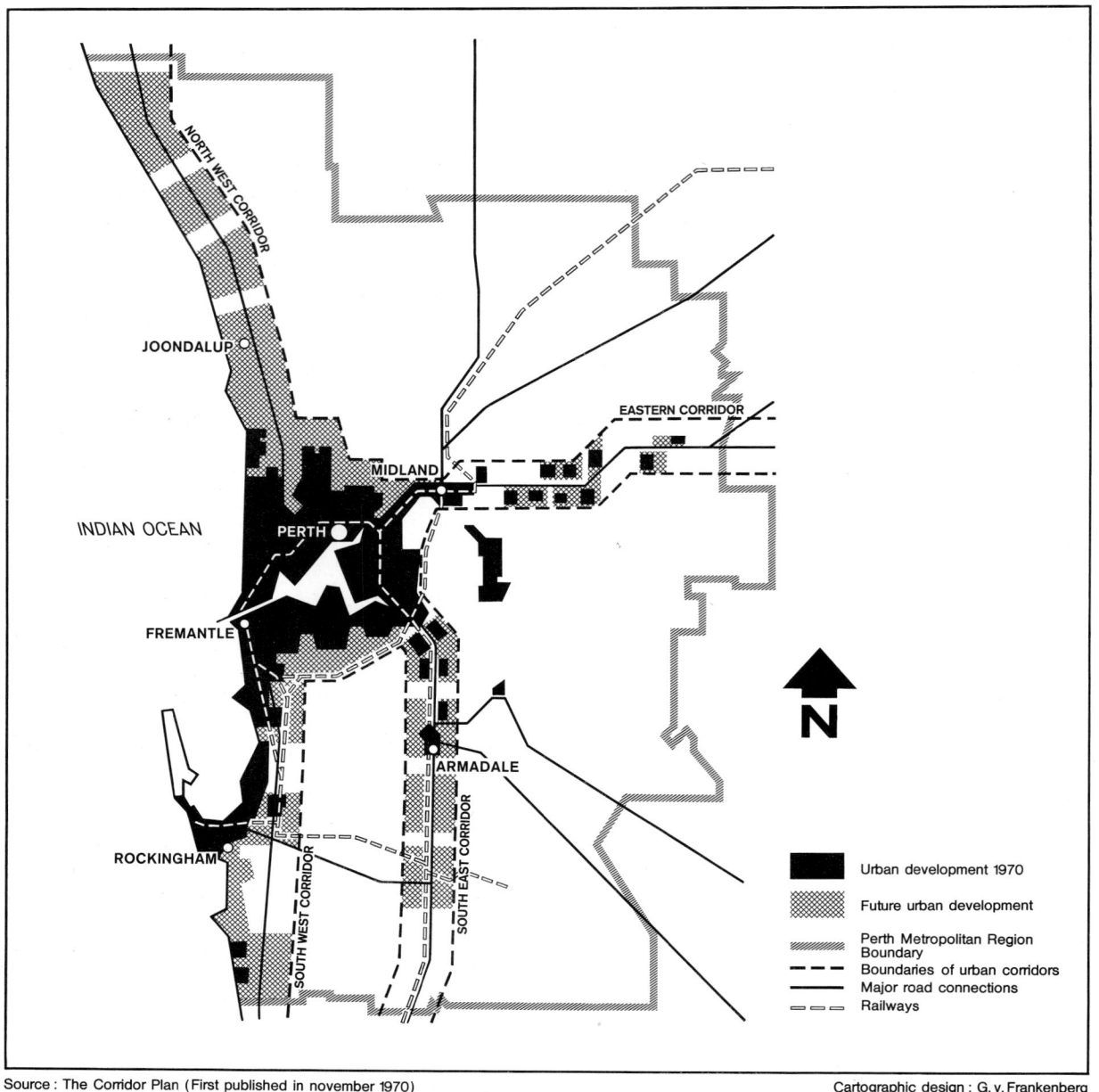

Fig. 72. The Perth Corridor Plan (after Town Planning Department, Perth)

Source: The Corridor Plan (First published in november 1970)
Cartographic design: G. v. Frankenberg

Legend:
- Urban development 1970
- Future urban development
- Perth Metropolitan Region Boundary
- Boundaries of urban corridors
- Major road connections
- Railways

As to the proportion of population living in the Perth metropolitan area, the capital has no doubt extended the territorial dominance that it had already gained by the turn of the century. At the 1976 census the primacy rate reached its maximum with 63.9% of Western Australians living in Perth; since the mid-1970s the rate has decreased slightly.

As mentioned above, metropolitan planning began with the development of the new deep-sea harbour and industrial complex of Kwinana and Kwinana New Town in the early 1950s. In 1969 the Metropolitan Region Planning Authority (MRPA) adopted the so-called *Corridor Plan*, providing for the systematic development of the metropolitan area along three corridors, to the north, the southeast and the southwest. It is the latter that causes concern because of particularly great pressures on land. It parallels the coast line from Fremantle via Kwinana to the former resort towns of Rockingham and Mandurah, and it is in danger of expanding still further south into the direction of Bunbury (Carr in: Gentilli 1979) (fig. 72).

The two major problems are the rapid growth of population, related to the new industries in Kwinana and the alumina smelters near Pinjarra and at other locations further south, this increased workforce putting more and more pressure on the land and the housing market. The increasing use of fertilizers on the relatively poor soils of the lower areas used for dairying and other agricultural production has led to the enthrophization of Peel Inlet, diminishing the recreational value of the area.

Mandurah used to be a seaside resort and a retirement town. In recent years settlement in Mandurah Shire has developed for some 28 km along the coast from Madora in the north to Parkridge in the south. Of the occupied housing units within the shire 61.1% were occupied by single-person or two-persons households. Householders of pensionable age made up 21.3% of the whole in Mandurah Shire, a figure rising to 28.6% in the Town of Mandurah (as compared with 11.5% for the Perth Statistical Division as a whole). In the shire, 39.8% of households had incomes below $ 10,000, a figure rising to 52.2% in Mandurah Town (27.1% in Perth S.D.). Residential mobility is high: only 32.1% of the shire population and 36.9% in the town were living in the same dwelling as at the previous census as compared with an average 47.5% in Perth S.D. (Caddy & Connor n.d.). The increasing influx of persons related to the new industries has begun to change the character of Mandurah confronting the MRPA with the problem of deciding whether or not to stop this development.

Rapidly increasing vehicular traffic in the metropolitan area also demanded solutions from the planners. Among the most important measures taken have been the conversion in 1971 of the section of Hay Street between Barrack and William Streets into a *pedestrian mall* and the construction of the Carillon Centre as a major shopping attraction. From 1957 onwards considerable tracts of reclaimed river foreshores were converted into off-street parking areas. The *modernization of the waterfront* included the construction of the Merlin Centre, a huge modern hotel and shopping complex and the building of *urban freeways* at a pace unknown in the other capital cities. In 1959 a reinforced concrete bridge spanning the 'Narrows' was opened and construction of the Kwinana Freeway commenced. To the northwest the Mitchell Freeway was constructed, and to the east a section of the Great Eastern Highway leading to the Perth Airport was converted to a four-lane freeway.

In conclusion it can be said that the Swan River Colony was founded some 20 km upstream while the port function was assumed by Fremantle, so that the growth of the Perth agglomeration commenced from twin foci. Perth was centrally located on a plain between the coast and the Darling Scarp, and mainly expanded in a north-south direction, according to the Corridor Plan of 1969. Perth had a slow start. Convicts were brought to the colony between 1850 and 1868, improving the labour situation, but sustained growth started only with the discovery of gold in the early 1890s and the belated appearance of the railway after 1881. The City Railway Station had a very central location, while public land and public buildings are found on either side of the tracks. On the west side the industrial area of Leederville adjoins the CBD, a situation comparable with that in many American cities. Perth developed comparatively few manufacturing industries, although the metropolitan area's share of Western Australia's industrial employment is 84%. Suburban development between the City and the ocean front was influenced by the existence and disposition of the Perth Commonage Lands. Perth received the highest percentage of post-war overseas immigrants of all the capital cities, with some conspicuous local concentrations of Italian fishermen in Fremantle and of Italian and Yugoslav market gardeners and wine growers in Spearwood and in the upper Swan River Valley. Perth experienced a great office building boom throughout the post-war period that seems, however, to counterfeit a degree of wealth not reflected by data on the population's socio-economic status. The metropolitan area experienced the construction of urban freeways at a pace unknown in other Australian capital cities.

3.1.6 The metropolitan area of Hobart, Tasmania

Hobart, named after the Secretary of State for the Colonies Lord Hobart, and picturesquely located near the mouth of the Derwent River at the foot of Mount Wellington, had its origin in a tiny settlement called Risdon Cove, on the east bank of the river, which was reached by a party from Sydney early in 1804. Dr. George Bass, when participating in Flinder's expedition from Port Jackson to Van Diemen's Land in 1798, had given a favourable description of Risdon Cove (Walker 1973, 37). Lieutenant-Governor Collins, however, upon his landing at the mouth of the Derwent in 1804, was not greatly impressed by the place, and decided that a site about eight kilometres south of Risdon Cove, on the opposite bank of the river was more appropriate. This place was called Sullivan's Cove. It enjoyed a sheltered anchorage, the chance to unload stores at any tide on Hunter's Island, and sufficient fresh water in a rivulet draining from Mt. Wellington, which in those early days was called Table Mountain (Scott 1955).

Hobart Town, as the settlement was called until 1881, has a number of advantages. It is the political and commercial centre of the State of Tasmania. Endowed with one of the finest deep-sea harbours of the entire world, it serves as the Tasmanian gateway town for traffic with mainland Australia and New Zealand. As a university city it has facilities and institutions specializing in Antarctic research. It offers attractions to international tourism, the city having both a well preserved historic building stock and a modern infrastructure, including a convention and casino complex opened in 1984 at Sandy Bay on the west bank of the Derwent River.

Despite such advantages Hobart is by far the smallest of all capital cities in Australia and the only which, in recent years, has sustained a *slight population decrease*, if we consider the statistical MUA (from which some fast growing peripheral settlements such as Kingston and Bridgewater-Gagebrook are excluded). During a whole century, between 1847 and 1947, Hobart's population grew only from 22,000 to 76,500 residents. It is also the only capital city that has failed to assume primacy within its territory (see ch. 2.3.1). There are several reasons for this situation.

For strategic reasons and to keep French ships away from coasts claimed by the British, the Governor of New South Wales in 1804 sent convicts and soldiers simultaneously to the *southern and northern shores* of the then Van Diemen's Land. Hobart in the south and Launceston in the north were thus founded at the same time, both contending for the position of capital city in Tasmania. Eventually Launceston succeeded in growing to half the size of Hobart. In addition, Burnie and Devonport developed as strong regional centres.

When transportation of convicts was discontinued in 1853, Hobart Town lost its raison d'être and thereafter grew only at a very low rate. Even a century later Hobart could, from the point of view of its building stock, still be called a *'Georgian city'*. Despite its natural advantages, the port of Hobart suffered from various set-backs over time. The end of the whaling and sealing industries, and the end of the age of sailing vessels taking advantage of the 'roaring forties', both led to a decline in port activities. In more recent years the joining of the European Common Market by the United Kingdom in 1973 caused, inter alia, the decline of fruit exports from the port of Hobart. The warehouses alongside Salamanca Place and Hunter Street, adjoining Sullivan's Cove, began to be converted to shops, restaurants and offices. The importance of the port of Hobart decreased despite subsidies from the Tasmanian Freight Equalisation Scheme[1], that had been set up by the Federal Government in order to guarantee equal tarrifs for goods produced in Tasmania and the mainland.

An event of local significance was the collapse, in 1975, of a section of the Derwent Bridge, disrupting communications between the parts of the city on either side of the river. For about four years the city centre could not easily be reached by the people living in the eastern suburbs. The equilibrium within the metropolitan area was disturbed, and the eastern suburbs gained a certain autonomy, developing the largest suburban shopping centre of the Hobart metropolitan area.

When the penal settlement of Norfolk Island was abandoned in 1807 the evacuees were brought to Hobart Town. The town's residents were supposed to accommodate the convicts until housing could be provided, and most of them were subsequently transferred to Elizabeth Town (later re-named New Norfolk), located some 30 km upstream. In 1810, Governor Macquarie, soon after taking office in Sydney, made a journey to Van Diemen's Land and laid out the grid of the town centre. The alignments and nomenclature of streets of Macquarie's plan persist with the two exceptions of Pit Street becoming Davey Street and George's Square becoming Franklin Square (Solomon 1976). Early Hobart Town was not much different from early Sydney in its uncontrolled development. Only Governor Sorell (1817–24) brought order to the settlement.

A great impetus for growth was the declaration in 1825 of Tasmania as a *separate colony*, no longer governed from New South Wales; population grew to 14,000 by 1836. Another impetus was the *founding of Melbourne* by Tasmanian settlers. 'Until the eighteen-fifties the city was the centre of civilisation for a vast, developing area of land and ocean ... The growth of Melbourne, even before the discovery of gold, put an end to this advantage, but the process of bringing Victoria itself to the take-off point of development was to the profit of Hobart Town ... The money which came into the pockets of citizens from profits being made in Victoria was used in the formation of companies, in the enlargement of existing ones, and in the transference of the residences of business people out of the main streets into villas in the fashionable areas — New Town and Battery Point, high up Davey and Macquarie Streets, and Sandy Bay' (Bolger 1968, 8–9).

Since about 1815, Hobart's harbour had been used as a base by sealers, and during the following three decades developed as one of the world's most important whaling ports. It also witnessed increasing exports of wool and timber, and large amounts of construction materials were exported to Victoria. Hobart owed much of this development to the efforts of Tasmania's Governors Sorell and Denison. In 1849 the latter wrote to Admiral Beaufort: 'There is a splendid harbour; well sheltered from every wind; plenty of water for any vessel, room enough for the whole British Navy. Even alongside of our wharves, we have from 20 to 25 feet at low water and seven or eight fathoms at 100 feet out, with good holding ground. However, no wind ever blows in the harbour to affect a vessel, or try the holding power of its anchors or cables' (Rowntree 1954, 101).

In 1857 Hobart was declared a city. In the same year its streets were lit with gas, and the city was linked by telegraph to Launceston. But these achievements occurred on the verge of a depression lasting till 1870, and another

---

1 Australian transportation policy used to favour rail transport to the general disadvantage of coastal shipping. Thus shipments between Tasmania and the mainland are automatically at a disadvantage. For many years Tasmanian consignors and consignees have therefore been subsidized by the Federal Government. In the fiscal year 1983/84, subsidy payments made under the TFES totalled $ 29.3 million. The scheme has, however, come under substantial criticism because it is clearly overcompensating for certain commodity-route combinations and undercompensating for others. For this reason the Australian Inter-State Commission was asked by the Federal Government to make investigations into the functioning of the scheme and to produce recommendations for its change. The Commission submitted its report in March 1985 (Inter-State Commission: An investigation of the Tasmanian Freight Equalisation Scheme. Vol. 1, March 1985. Parliamentary Paper No. 67/1985. Canberra 1985).

Fig. 73. Hobart, Tasmania. View from Mt. Nelson northward over Battery Point and part of the CBD with the casino-convention complex at Wrest Point in the foreground

depression occurred during the 1890s. These events made Hobart a 'sleepy town', and Tasmania for some time prior to federation was even in danger of being annexed by Victoria. Even in those days Hobart was somewhat like 'the lido, the play place of Australia' (Bolger 1968, 15). The motor cars registered in Tasmania today bear the inscription 'Holiday Isle'. Such famous *sports events* as the Royal Hobart Regatta and the Sydney-Hobart Yacht Race are associated with the Tasmanian capital.

The city centre is composed of the rather small CBD and the old harbour at Sullivan's Cove. As mentioned above, many of the old warehouses were recently converted to shops, arts and crafts galleries, restaurants and the like; Salamanca Place has become famous for its Saturday open air markets. Scott (1955) pointed to the *immaturity of Hobart's CBD* as reflected in its limited zonation and the extent of privately owned open space, even in the post-war years.

In 1984 the *Sullivan's Cove Urban Design Study* was released, proposing among other projects, a huge 18-storey international hotel complex. This project was backed by the Tasmanian Government, for the reason that the Government had been heavily involved in the recently opened convention-casino complex at Sandy Bay, and it was argued that in order to make full use of this complex a much greater capacity of international-standard hotel beds was badly needed in Hobart. The public, on the other hand, became very much concerned about this rather drastic proposal for change in the character of the harbour area. In a subsequent version of the plan, the height of the hotel was reduced to ten storeys (fig. 73).

A problem of the fringe of the CBD is the presence of *underused and vacant lots and buildings*. This is particularly obvious in North Hobart, on the northern margin of the CBD. Here, there are vacant lots abandoned by the former gas works and by the Hobart-Launceston Railways. There had also been plans for a multilane northern freeway that would have cut through North Hobart. Although this plan was abandoned some years ago, its negative consequences for the real estate market have persisted to the present day. The proposal caused irritation and made land owners move out and sell their lots, or leave them unused. Low-ranking functions like repair shops and many small

Fig. 74. Battery Point, Hobart, Tasmania. Southern inner suburb with restoration work of old building stock

commercial enterprises took advantage of the situation and migrated to this former middle-class residential area, which has become an area of mixed residential and commercial uses and interspersed vacant lots.

No wonder that North Hobart became one of the targets of the *Tasmanian Department of Housing*, whose functions are comparable with those of the Housing Commissions of other Australian states. Since 1981 the Department's policy has been more and more dominated by 'infill', trying to buy vacant lots in the inner suburbs and to construct apartment houses for marginal groups like senior citizens, disabled persons and single-parent families. As to suburban-type housing the process of 'flexi-lot subdivision' involves the creation of lots of sizes ranging from 350 square metres to 1,300 square metres, on which houses of varying sizes from one-bedroom to three-bedroom standard are constructed. Of all dwelling units constructed by the Department since 1981, this kind of housing amounts to approximately 75%. The Department of Housing has been successful inasmuch as in certain parts of North Hobart the character of a middle-class residential area has been preserved, and they even witness some up-grading.

The neighbouring suburbs of Glebe on the north side and Battery Point on the south side have become areas of recent activities by the *National Trust (Tasmania)*. Their picturesque old housing stock has to a considerable extent been preserved, although the authorities did not manage to prevent the area from being penetrated by a few high-rise apartment buildings. These suburbs have also been areas of recent *gentrification*, with many houses restored and maintained by private initiative. In Battery Point, Upper Sandy Bay and North Hobart, of which Glebe is a part, the age group between 20 and 24 years is overrepresented, because of a relatively large amount of rental housing being available for young couples with moderate income. At the same time they are the areas of high mobility, because of the high proportion of transient groups. They have the highest mobility rates in the metropolitan area, with the exception of the most recently developed outer suburbs, where people have only moved during the last few years (fig. 74).

Hobart bears evidence for the observation in respect of the other state capitals that there is hardly any coincidence between government housing and the distribution of non-British immigrant groups. Overseas immigrants, over half of whom are of *British origin*, constitute only one eighth of Hobart's total population (the lack of economic opportunities kept numbers of overseas immigrants low and make Hobart less cosmopolitan than other capitals). Immigrants are rather widely distributed over the metropolitan area, with some small local concentrations in the City of Hobart, in Upper Sandy Bay with its considerable mixture of ethnic groups, in Kingston with a certain concentration of the Dutch, and in Moonah where numerous people of Polish origin live. It has to be accepted, however, that these areas do not show any remarkable concentration of activities by the Tasmanian Department of Housing.

As to the outer suburbs, the metropolitan area of Hobart developed in a *linear pattern* for some 30 km along the Derwent River, whereas the hill slopes on either side of the Derwent Valley have, until recent years, prevented the built-up area to expand for more than two kilometres to the west or east. Only in the post-war years has a certain upslope development of housing begun to change the townscape. The axial pattern of the metropolitan area has been reinforced by the development after World War II of the Brooker Avenue and the road to Kingston, leading to the northern and southern outer suburbs respectively. The pattern has also been reinforced by the housing schemes of the Department of Housing, carried out prior to 1980. These schemes were mainly located in the northwest in Chigwell and Goodwood and in the northeast and southeast in Bridgewater, Risdon Vale, Warrane and Rokeby. Because of the concentrations of public housing these suburbs are characterized by the lowest rates of residential mobility in the metropolitan area.

In addition to this markedly linear pattern, another two elements characterize Hobart's urban structure. The first element is the location of the present *port and the adjoining industrial zone* to the north of the old city centre. This means that the northern suburbs are predominantly the residential areas of process workers, labourers and tradesmen, people of the lower income groups, with rather low educational levels. In contrast, the southwestern suburbs on *the slopes of Mt. Nelson and Mt. Wellington* (the University of Tasmania campus was in the 1970s relocated from its Domain site to the border area between the southern inner suburbs and the southwestern suburbs) are characterized by above-average percentages of people with some tertiary education, many of whom are government employees and most of whom are owners of high-standard private homes. These are the areas of the highest income levels, only Kingston has a lower percentage of people with tertiary education and more foreign-born residents.

The development of hydroelectric power in Tasmania prior to World War II stimulated *industrialization* in the island state. The electrolytic zinc works are the outstanding feature of the port zone, its products making up approximately one third of Tasmania's total exports. The Electrolytic Zinc Company of Australasia Ltd. is one of Tasmania's greatest employers, with approximately 3,300 employees in 1985 at the Risdon plant, in the Rosebery mine and on the Emu Bay Railway. Other large employers are the Australian Newsprint Mills Ltd., with its large plant at Boyer, just north of Hobart, Risby Timber, the Cadbury-Fry-Pascall Pty Ltd. at Claremont, (700 employees) producing 20,000 tons of chocolate annually, the Sheridan Silk and Textile Printers Pty Ltd., with their Derwent Park Mill employing approximately 500 persons, the Cascade Brewery Co. Ltd. employing some 600 persons and the H. Jones & Co. at Hunter Street producing jam and canned fruit and employing some 350 people. All these enterprises, however, provide only a rather modest industrial development; the major emphasis is on tertiary activities, such as research, conventions and other kinds of tourism (fig. 75).

The second structural element is the concentration of about 70% of the metropolitan area's total population on the *western bank* of the Derwent River. After the first small settlement at Risdon Cove on the east bank had lost favour and the nucleus of Hobart Town developed around Sullivan's Cove on the opposite side of the river, most further development spread along the western bank to the north and south. All connections between the river banks were by ferry until 1943, when the first floating bridge was built. The present Tasman Bridge is a very recent structure, dating back only to the year 1964. Serious problems arose in 1975, when *a section of the Tasman Bridge collapsed*. Cross-river links had to fall back on ferries and the bridge well to the north at Bridgewater. About one year after the collapse a temporary crossing of the Derwent was made possible by the opening of a Bailey Bridge a little to the north of the Tasman Bridge. It was three years before the latter could be re-opened for traffic. The many consequences of this event have been well documented by members of the Department of Geography of the University of Tasmania (Lee & Wood 1978, Lee 1980), and the following paragraphs draw on their findings.

More than 80% of eastern-shore workers held jobs on the western shore. Many commuters from the eastern suburbs who had relied on their private cars were now forced to use *ferry transport*. The percentage of eastern commuters needing less than 30 min for the journey from home to work decreased from more than 80% to some 20%. This means that the vast majority of people needed considerably more time for their journey to work, which had to be subtracted from their leisure time and other activities. In order to reduce peak-hour congestion on the ferries, *flex-time was introduced* in many enterprises and institutions.

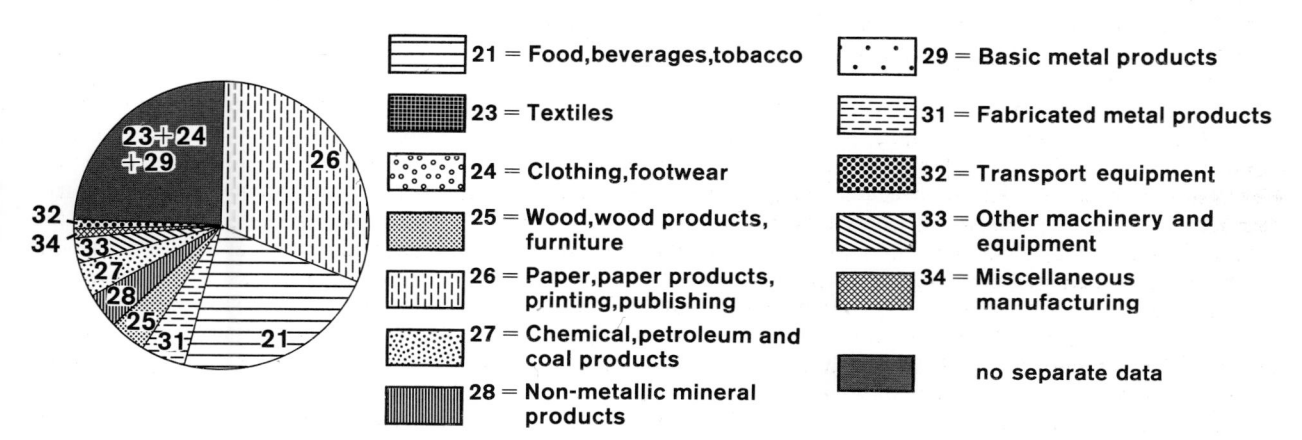

Fig. 75. Value added by industry sub-divisions in Hobart, 1982/83 (total = A$ 246 mill.)

The proportion of workers both *living and working on the eastern shore* rose between 1975 and 1978 from 18% to 25%. This reflects the opening of new shops, new offices and depots on the eastern shore, as well as job transfers from western shore to eastern shore. The reorientation of shopping patterns has been particularly conspicuous. Before the bridge collapse, 26% of households normally bought groceries on the western shore and approximately 66% relied on the western shore for banking, dental treatment, adult clothing and hardware. By mid-1978 these percentages had dropped to 10% with regard to groceries and to about 50% with regard to banking and hardware. A very important event was the opening of the *large Rosny Shopping Centre* in the eastern suburb of Rosny. The lack of a hospital on the eastern shore was felt as a major inadequacy.

The researchers of the University also found that many eastern-shore residents expressed feelings of isolation and loneliness. The usage of telephone contacts increased considerably. In the long run, a number of relations between eastern shore and western shore residents were abandoned, involving about one eighth of eastern shore households. 'Possibly of more general importance, the difficulties of cross-river travel caused many households to undertake activities on the Eastern Shore that had formerly involved a trip across the Tasman Bridge. Some of the information presented here suggests that to a considerable degree this local focussing of activity has been maintained after the restoration of the Tasman Bridge' (Lee & Wood 1978, 12).

One of the major issues arising from the discussions following the bridge collapse was the construction of a second permanent bridge; initially the Bailey Bridge was supposed to offer only temporary crossing. This leads us to the aspect of metropolitan planning, which in the Hobart region has been rather ineffective to date. In 1958 a *Southern Metropolitan Master Planning Authority* was established, this being a voluntary association without any statutory basis. Because of internal quarrels, the Hobart City Council withdrew from this organization in 1973. In 1978 a new Southern Metropolitan Planning Authority was established, but was discontinued in 1983. Since 1985 the responsibilities for metropolitan planning have been vested in the Town and Country Planning Authority of Tasmania.

While planning has been rather weak in Tasmania's capital, the extensive activities of the Tasmanian Department of Housing have had a considerable impact on the post-war development of the metropolitan area. Suburbs such as Goodwood, Rokeby, Risdon Vale and Warrane were almost completely developed by the Department (Scott 1967). The same is true of the more recent development of the large outer suburbs of Bridgewater and Gagebrook, on the far northern fringe. Mainly young families with children moved to these developments, constituting more than one third of the population since 1975. As to their socio-economic status, over 70% of all families in Gagebrook are dependent upon unemployment benefits (Div. Nat. Mapp. & ABS 1984).

To sum up, Hobart is the second oldest capital of any Australian state after Sydney, but for a number of reasons has remained the smallest of all, and has not been able to gain primacy within its territory. Owing to its old building stock and its very modest growth, urban conservation has played an important part in Hobart. The metropolitan area developed as a rather narrow linear settlement along the Derwent River, with only some recent upslope development of housing construction. The northern suburbs located close to the port and the industrial complex associated with it are mainly low-status working class residential areas, whereas the southern suburbs mainly show a high socio-economic status of their residents, many of these being in tertiary occupations. Over 70% of the total population are concentrated on the western bank of the river, and links to the eastern bank have been weak. The nature of relations between residents of the eastern and western banks was revealed by the consequences of the collapse in 1975 of the Tasman Bridge. Due to the lack of economic opportunities, only small numbers of overseas immigrants settled in Hobart; employment opportunities are mainly in tertiary occupations, such as the university or conventions and other kinds of tourism. Planning for the metropolitan area has been weak to date, whereas the activities of the Tasmanian Department of Housing as Tasmania's Housing Authority have had great impacts on the shape of the metropolitan area, even beyond the statistical limits of the Hobart MUA.

3.1.7 The state capitals: a comparative perspective

The capital cities of the Australian states or former colonies were founded within the time span of half a century, that means between 1788 and 1836, all of them thus being extremely young by international standards.

Of all the capitals, Adelaide was the only one to be established by free colonists. Sydney and Hobart started as convict settlements and Brisbane was a penal settlement for almost two decades before it was opened for free settlement. At Melbourne free settlers from Van Diemen's Land initially squatted in the area and land sales were arranged by the authorities in Sydney, but a number of convicts were subsequently introduced against the settlers' own wishes, for street levelling and house construction work. Perth started as a free colony but, in consequence of very low numbers of immigrants and a severe labour shortage, applied for convict labour at a time when transportation was discontinued in the eastern colonies. The availability of convict labour thus played a great part in the early development of the colonial capitals.

Glynn (1970) advanced the theory that to a certain extent the choice of location of the capital cities was due to the *limited knowledge* the early settlers had of the coastlines. He argued that the New South Wales capital might have been better located somewhat north of the present location of Sydney, at the mouth of the Hunter River, or somewhat farther south on Jervis Bay. Governor Phillip himself expressed the view that he would have established the first settlement further upstream at the present site of Parramatta, rather than at Sydney Cove, had he had better knowledge of the area in the beginning.

Adelaide's location was highly disputed. It would have been logical to establish the South Australian capital at the mouth of Australia's largest river, but at the time of Adelaide's foundation the navigability of the Murray River mouth had not been proved. A consequence of this decision, however, was that Adelaide received a rather central location with regard to what were to emerge as the settled parts of the state of South Australia.

From the very beginning of white settlement in Tasmania, Hobart has been in competition with Launceston, the latter city having the more favourable location on the coast in relation to the mainland. In Western Australia, Perth's position was strengthened by the eventual success of its neighbouring port of Fremantle in its competition with the somewhat older port city of Albany further south. This success was to a great extent due to the selection of Fremantle as the terminus of the railway lines to Albany and the Eastern Goldfields. Brisbane received an extremely excentric location within its territory but was, in the long run, able successfully to compete with the ports along the central and northern Queensland coasts.

It would seem that Melbourne has been the only unchallenged capital city as far as location is concerned, but even here, canal cuts and successive dredgings have had to be carried out continuously from the mid-1850s to give adequate access to the port (Rimmer 1967).

The *motives for site selection* are much disputed. Upon the arrival of the First Fleet, Captain Phillip did not find Botany Bay as desirable a place as might have been assumed from Captain Cook's descripiton, so that he ordered the fleet to move northward and finally anchored at the mouth of the Parramatta River, at a site he named Sydney Cove. It is interesting to find that with regard to modern sea-borne traffic Port Jackson at the mouth of the Parramatta River has come under heavy competition with the rapidly expanding port of Botany Bay which by 1982–83 had approached the figure for Port Jackson's overseas and coastal cargo movements by a rather small margin of 3 million tons (see table 31; Proudfoot 1982, Rimmer & Black in: Cardew, Langdale & Rich 1982). In the case of Hobart, Risdon Cove on the eastern bank of the Derwent River was felt to be not as favourable as it had been described by earlier exploring parties, so that Hobart Town was established somewhat further downstream on the opposite bank of the river at Sullivan's Cove. In the case of Brisbane, the Moreton Bay Penal Settlement had to be relocated from the bay to a site a little further inland at one of the bends of the Brisbane River, in order to escape the danger of floods. Melbourne, some miles upstream on the Yarra River, with sufficient fresh water available, proved to be a better site than Williamstown on Hobsons Bay, the latter being named after the reigning monarch in initial anticipation of a more rapid growth.

Both Adelaide and Perth were established somewhat inland on the River Torrens and the Swan River respectively so that in each case a separate outport (Port Adelaide, Fremantle) developed in a certain distance from the seat of administration, providing a second nucleus of settlement from the very beginning.

The *five major prerequisites* for a favourable site were a good anchorage, safety from flooding, the availability of sufficient fresh water, the presence of clay for making bricks, and fertile soil for farming. Good anchorage was provided by the estuaries of the Parramatta and Derwent Rivers for Sydney and Hobart, and to a lesser extent at the mouths of the Brisbane, Yarra and Swan Rivers for Brisbane, Melbourne and Fremantle (Perth). In the case of Adelaide, the separate nucleus of Port Adelaide developed to the northwest of the capital city's site, somewhat north of the outlet of the River Torrens (see Bird 1986).

The threat of flooding was a reason for the relocation of the Moreton Bay Settlement (Brisbane) to a little ridge about 17 m above the river level, and for the choice of Adelaide's site astride the River Torrens well above its mouth. The availability of fresh water played a role in the choice of Sydney Cove rather than Botany Bay and of Melbourne rather than Williamstown. The availability of clay for making bricks was reported from all the sites chosen; for example in Sydney Cove clay was found at nearby Brickfield Hill. As to fertile soils, the early settlers usually ran into trouble, food supply in the first years being a major problem. Rimmer's argument would seem, however, to be disputable: '... it was apparent that access to land for agricultural development was uppermost in the minds of the founders of the three settlements for free colonisation [Adelaide, Melbourne, Perth] rather than the quality of the port, which was capable of improvement by man-made works' (Rimmer 1967, 45).

As to the *patterns of waterfront land use*, Forward (1970) found considerable differences between Sydney, Hobart and Brisbane on the one hand and Melbourne, Adelaide and Perth on the other. The first group, being located on great estuaries, had large harbours with extensive shorelines and a variety of industrial and other uses, whereas the second group had rather small harbours with long stretches of shoreline devoted to parks, recreation and residential use, with comparatively little space left for industry, transportation and similar purposes.

From the present point of view, the choice of location and site was at least one important factor that helped the capital cities to maintain their positions as the largest and most important cities in their respective territories over a time span of 150 to 200 years. Four of them gained high degrees of primacy within their respective states, whereas Brisbane's degree of primacy in Queensland has been considerably weaker, and Hobart's rivalry with Launceston in Tasmania has inhibited any high degree of primate dominance.

The capital cities came into existence under very different circumstances; Adelaide and Brisbane can serve to illustrate the two extremes. In Adelaide the first shiploads of settlers arrived before the land had been surveyed and land sales could be started. This caused severe hardships for the settlers, such as food shortages and excessive food prices. A few years later the situation was transformed; with Colonel Light's design of the town lands, parklands and suburban lands Adelaide probably had the finest design of all the capital cities. In contrast, in Brisbane a penal settlement with levelled streets and houses built by convict labour had been in existence for eighteen years before the first free settlers arrived on the scene.

The further development of the port-capitals during the nineteenth century very much depended on the *primary resources produced in their hinterlands and shipped through their ports, to which must be added the* degree to which, since about the mid-1860s, they were able to develop *rail links* with their hinterlands. Sydney, of course, enjoyed the earliest start and the position of being the only seat of government in Australia for about six decades before Victoria, Queensland and Tasmania became self-governing colonies, separated from New South Wales. After wool had proved the most adequate staple in the Australian environment, the wool trade became a major growth factor for Sydney, Melbourne and Brisbane.

Independence from New South Wales and the gold-rush of 1851 were sources of Melbourne's early growth, although during the decade 1850–60, due to the rapid growth of the gold mining towns, the city's share of Victoria's population temporarily dropped. From the 1860s, Victoria constructed a rather dense rail network, entirely centred on the capital, that not only directed much of the state's own trade to Melbourne but also enabled the city to tap the Riverina trade and divert some of it from river transportation on the Murray and export via Adelaide. Victoria's railways and Melbourne's housing stock owed much to heavy British investments, especially during the 1880s.

Adelaide has a history of fluctuating growth. By 1880 expansion appeared to be faltering: the wheat frontier had reached its limits and the copper deposits of the Kadina-Wallaroo-Moonta triangle were exhausted. However, in the course of the nineteenth century the city was able to build rail links tapping a number of local railway lines constructed to serve individual ports along South Australia's coastline. Traffic was diverted to the port of Adelaide, and the city gained dominance over the rest of the colony.

Brisbane was not as successful in gaining prime control over its territory as Adelaide was in South Australia. It had to compete with a number of smaller ports along the Queensland coast, each serving its own hinterland as an export centre for sugar and mineral products. Hobart also suffered from the competition with Launceston and a number of other ports along the northern coast, such as Burnie and Devonport. Perth remained small throughout the nineteenth century, the gold-rush and the opening of the wheat belt in Western Australia only gaining momentum during the 1890s.

Both Sydney and Melbourne grew to half a million population by the time of federation in 1901, the former experiencing a building boom in the first half of the 1880s, the latter in the latter half of the decade. Boom conditions caused a rapid expansion of the inner suburbs, with a continuous construction of *terrace houses* beginning in the 1860s and lasting well into the 1880s. Terrace houses are a particularly conspicuous element in the morphology of Sydney, forming a rather compact ring around the city centre, whereas they are less frequent in Melbourne's older suburbs and almost lacking in the other capital cities. The economic and building boom was followed by a major recession which hit Melbourne harder and longer than Sydney. The latter had an earlier recovery from the slump and its consequences, surpassing Melbourne in terms of numbers of residents during the first decade of the twentieth century.

In Sydney and Melbourne population densities are higher than in the other capital cities, mainly because of the early development of their rather densely built-up inner suburbs. Density in terms of persons per hectare in the urban residential areas in the MUAs is highest in Sydney, with a ratio of 31.6. In Melbourne it is 25.4, not quite as high as in Sydney, due to the fact that more flat land well suited for settlement was available within a convenient radius from the city centre. In the other capital cities densities are still lower, the ratios being 21.8 for Adelaide, 21.9 for Brisbane, 21.5 for Hobart and 17.0 for Perth.

Urban densities are, to a certain extent, related to the *types of building structures* (table 29)[2]. Brisbane has the highest percentage of separate houses (86.3%) and thus the most homogeneous dwelling stock of all the capital cities. Sydney, on the other hand, has the lowest proportion of separate houses (70.0%) and the highest proportion of other types of structure, two-thirds of which are flats. Although most flats are in low-rise structures, Sydney nevertheless has the highest percentage of flats in structures above three storeys; these have mainly been built by

---

[2] According to the Indicative Council's classification the various types of dwelling stocks have been defined as follows:
    semi-detached house: one of a set of two houses (single or double storey) joined together and separated only by a wall (or floor),
    terrace or row house: one of a set of houses (single or multistorey) in a row of three or more separated only by walls extended from foundation to ceiling,
    villa unit or town house: one of a group (three or more) of single or double storey houses, separated or joined together in sets of two or more, all occupying a common block of land;
    flats or home units: includes flats in blocks, in or attached to a house.

Table 29. Occupied private dwellings: Type of structure and tenure, 1976

Type of structure	Sydney S.D. % of total	Sydney S.D. % of owners/ purchasers	Melbourne S.D. % of total	Melbourne S.D. % of owners/ purchasers	Brisbane S.D. % of total	Brisbane S.D. % of owners/ purchasers	Adelaide S.D. % of total	Adelaide S.D. % of owners/ purchasers	Perth S.D. % of total	Perth S.D. % of owners/ purchasers	Hobart S.D. % of total	Hobart S.D. % of owners/ purchasers
Separate house	70.0	79.4	76.4	83.9	86.3	79.3	77.1	85.8	80.1	80.6	85.5	77.3
Semi/terrace	6.7	48.3	5.7	48.7	2.0	24.9	9.6	15.2	7.2	35.8	4.1	28.0
Villa/town house	1.1	53.2	3.4	55.8	0.1	29.8	2.5	45.2	1.6	47.8	1.6	29.4
Flats ≤ 3 storeys	17.2	34.5	11.8	19.0	10.0	17.7	9.8	20.3	7.8	11.8	6.2	20.6
Flats > 3 storeys	3.9	40.7	1.6	10.5	0.8	44.4	0.4	20.0	2.8	15.7	1.0	36.4
Other dwellings	1.2	35.0	1.1	33.0	0.8	48.8	0.7	43.9	0.5	44.2	1.6	27.5

Note: Other dwellings include dwelling and non-dwelling combined, improvised and mobile dwellings; 'not stated' structure or occupancy were allocated proportionately between structural types and tenure types respectively.

Source: Indicative Planning Council for the Housing Industry 1980, 52, 55, 58, 61, 64, 67

private developers in favourable locations such as Elizabeth Bay or Rushcutters Bay. Melbourne is the capital city having the highest proportion of villa units and town houses, combined with the highest owner-occupancy rate. Over half of all multi-unit dwellings in Perth are flats. Brisbane has the lowest proportion of multi-unit dwellings, and Hobart the second lowest.

In the year of federation, approximately 1.3 million (36%) of a total of 3.75 million Australians were living in the six capital cities. By 1981 their proportion had grown to 8.2 million (55%) of a total of 14.9 million. These figures indicate above-average growth rates for the capital cities. In the decade 1901–11 the average annual growth rate was 2.42% for the capital cities as compared with 1.23% for the rest of Australia. Even during the depression and war years the capitals grew by 1.55% against 0.75% for the rest of the country. In the post-war period 1947–54 the respective growth rates were 3.24% and 0.97% (Merrett in: McCarty & Schedvin 1978, 174).

Of course, there were differences among the capitals, reflecting regional characteristics; for example, during the decade 1901–11, Perth enjoyed a growth rate of 11.40%, a rate almost five times as high as the average for the capital cities. There is also a considerable range with regard to primacy rates. At the 1981 census Adelaide's degree of primacy (66.2%) was highest, followed by Melbourne with 64.6%, Sydney 62.4%, Perth 62.3%, Brisbane 40.2% and Hobart 30.0%.

Looking at the major factors of capital-city growth, a conspicuous change took place after World War II with the government's *new immigration and industrialization policy*. While natural increase has always been an important factor in the growth of Australian cities, internal migration became much less important in the first half of the century: overseas immigration came to play a decisive role in post-war growth (table 30).

Table 30. Growth factors in the capital cities, 1911–47 and 1947–61 (in %)

Period	Growth factor	Sydney	Melbourne	Brisbane	Adelaide	Perth	Hobart
1911–47	natural increase	43.8	43.5	39.2	45.1	45.8	59.5
	overseas immigration	7.0	3.1	3.8	0.5	14.5	0.0
	internal migration	49.2	53.4	57.0	54.4	39.7	40.5
1947–61	natural increase	35.8	38.2	43.6	40.3	47.6	56.4
	overseas immigration	34.9	46.5	19.0	47.1	34.0	25.6
	internal migration	29.3	15.3	37.4	12.6	18.4	18.0

Source: Merrett in: McCarty & Schedvin 1978, 191 (modified)

While capital cities received the lion's share of post-war overseas immigration, there were, of course, considerable differences between them. During the period 1947–61, for example, overseas immigration contributed 47.1% to the growth of Adelaide, but only 19.1% to that of Brisbane. The percentages of Australian-born population (with both parents born in Australia) range from 41.7% in Perth to 70.1% in Hobart. Brisbane's share is 59.7%, while the three cities of Melbourne (46.9%), Sydney (48.9%) and Adelaide (49.7%) are rather similar in this respect (Div. Nat. Mapp. & ABS 1984).

Post-war immigration has been closely related to industrialization. In the nineteenth century, the colonial capitals had mainly been major ports and trade centres, in addition to functioning as seats of government. Today they play but a minor part in Australian sea-born trade (table 31, fig. 76).

At present Australia's most important ports in terms of tonnage are those handling the iron-ore export trade of the Pilbara region, such as Dampier and Port Hedland, each having over 30 million tons of cargo movements annually. They are followed by Newcastle and Gladstone, servicing steel manufacturing and aluminum production respectively.

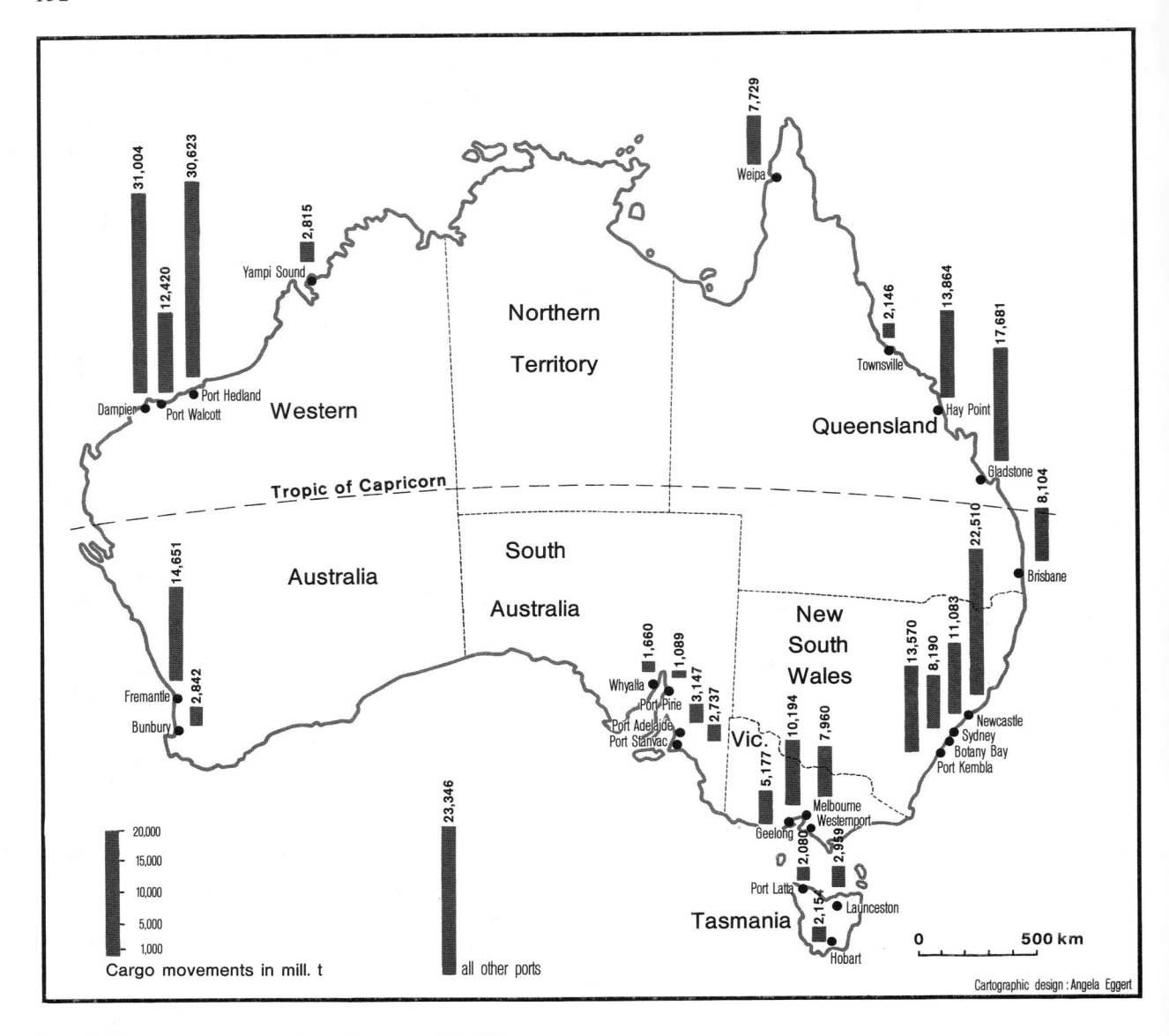

Fig. 76. Cargo movements at Australian ports, 1982/83

Of the capital cities, Perth is still comparatively important, its port of Fremantle holding rank five in the list of Australian ports. Sydney holds rank nine, although Sydney and Botany Bay taken as one port would hold rank four. Similarly, Melbourne and Westernport taken together would rank among the first four port cities of Australia. Brisbane holds only rank 12. The ports of Adelaide and Hobart are rather insignificant in the list.

The capital cities have attracted most of the industrial enterprises that have been established in Australia after World War II. In the years between 1953–54 and 1967–68 the five capital cities and the two port cities of Newcastle and Wollongong gained approximately 285,000 manufacturing employees, as compared with 39,000 manufacturing employees in the country areas of the five states (Lonsdale 1972). Logan (1966, 139) summarized the locational advantages for secondary industries in the capital cities: 'An entrepreneur faced with the problem of bringing together a variety of spatially separated production factors at a least cost position and wanting to exploit the largest market could not logically by-pass a site within a metropolitan centre unless his industry was tied to some physical resource'. The volume of manufacturing production of the capital cities with a breakdown into subdivisions according to the Australian Standard Industrial Classification is shown in table 32.

Sydney and Melbourne have become considerably more industrialized than the other capital cities. The value-added figure for their manufacturing industries is four times that of Adelaide or Brisbane and five and a half times that of Perth. Metal products and engineering are prominent, whereas in Adelaide, Brisbane and Perth the industry

Table 31. Overseas and coastal cargo movements of Australian ports, 1982–83 (in 1,000 tons)

Port	Overseas cargo loaded	Overseas cargo discharged	Coastal cargo loaded	Coastal cargo discharged	total
Sydney	5,429	2,378	219	3,057	11,083
Botany Bay	513	2,648	1,452	3,577	8,190
Newcastle	18,267	992	486	2,765	22,510
Port Kembla	6,791	415	1,755	4,609	13,570
Melbourne	2,286	2,535	1,393	1,752	7,966
Geelong	1,045	1,747	1,779	606	5,177
Westernport	1,657	63	7,742	732	10,194
Brisbane	1,965	1,323	1,195	3,621	8,104
Gladstone	12,005	435	775	4,466	17,681
Hay Point	13,864	–	–	–	13,864
Townsville	1,208	80	243	615	2,146
Weipa	2,640	86	4,992	11	7,729
Port Adelaide	768	473	336	1,570	3,147
Port Lincoln	285	109	22	117	533
Port Pirie	606	11	152	320	1,089
Port Stanvac	128	1,593	550	466	2,737
Thevenard	343	–	439	–	782
Whyalla	342	146	343	829	1,660
Fremantle	6,538	4,599	1,858	1,656	14,651
Bunbury	2,068	269	356	149	2,842
Cape Cuvier	629	–	–	–	629
Dampier	30,935	68	1	–	31,004
Geraldton	1,555	235	49	212	2,051
Port Hedland	26,089	112	4,275	147	30,623
Port Walcott	12,349	40	–	31	12,420
Yampi Sound	2,344	–	443	28	2,815
Hobart	659	160	499	836	2,154
Launceston	1,671	45	287	956	2,959
Port Latta	2,041	39	–	–	2,080
Darwin	30	385	26	168	609
Other ports					20,793

Source: Australia Yearbook 1985, 437, 441

Table 32. Manufacturing production of capital cities, 1981/82 or 1982/83 (value added in A$ 1,000 for industry subdivision according to the ASIC code)

Rank	Sydney (1982/83)		Melbourne (1981/82)		Adelaide (1982/83)		Brisbane (1981/82)		Perth (1982/83)		Hobart (1982/83)	
1	33	1,488,302	33	1,304,424	21	320,544	21	429,318	21	282,844	26	76,017
2	27	1,330,603	21	1,139,816	33	309,189	31	289,749	31	210,293	21	56,591
3	21	1,319,287	32	1,131,665	26	162,563	32	235,723	33	180,179	31	11,510
4	26	1,008,852	26	872,368	31	161,352	28	221,482	26	147,487	25	10,317
5	31	801,598	31	824,564	34	144,787	26	198,329	28	146,153	28	9,885
6	32	727,105	27	819,188	28	116,013	33	177,052	25	94,003	27	9,551
7	34	572,409	24	686,132	27	103,082	27	171,078	32	88,262	33	7,026
8	25	383,121	34	663,251	25	98,244	25	151,668	34	60,897	34	2,761
9	28	346,722	23	335,118	24	82,485	34	97,922			32	2,359
10	29	298,795	28	327,218			29	60,409				
11	24	297,501	25	297,480			24	47,208				
12	23	184,507	29	284,811			23	13,031				
total		8,758,803		8,686,035		2,141,024		2,092,969		1,511,876		246,271

Australian Standard Industrial Classification:
21 Food, beverages, tobacco
23 Textiles
24 Clothing, footwear
25 Wood, wood products, furniture
26 Paper, paper products, printing, publishing
27 Chemical, petroleum and coal products
28 Non-metallic mineral products
29 Basic metal products
31 Fabricated metal products
32 Transport equipment
33 Other machinery and equipment
34 Miscellaneous manufacturing

Source: Australian Bureau of Statistics: Census of Manufacturing Establishments; Small Area Statistics by Industry

subdivision of food, beverages and tobacco ranks first and in Hobart the subdivision of paper, paper products, printing and publishing. Brisbane is well-known for its sugar refineries, meat works, bacon curing establishments and cotton ginneries, Perth for its flour mills, butter factories and tobacco processing plants.

Merrett (in: McCarty & Schedvin 1978) points to the fact that the volume and kinds of manufacturing industries in Sydney and Melbourne are associated with some peculiar features of the two capitals. The central cities have been surrounded by a dense ring of industrial working-class suburbs, their residents lending high support to the Australian Labor Party. There is considerable female employment in Sydney's and Melbourne's manufacturing industries, and there is a remarkable Catholic influence from the many Irish in working-class politics.

Although approximately 25% of total manufacturing employment in the Newcastle-Sydney-Wollongong industrial region is still in the City of Sydney, a *strong trend toward industrial suburbanization* or decentralization could be observed in the post-war period. Some of the other suburbs, such as Dandenong in Melbourne, developed as industrial centres. New towns were also established near new great manufacturing plants, such as Elizabeth on the northern periphery of Adelaide or Kwinana New Town south of Perth (ch. 3.4.2). Despite government efforts in recent years to foster decentralization and some industrial relocation, for example from Melbourne to Victorian regional centres such as Bendigo, the capital cities have remained the dominant industrial centres of Australia.

The capital cities also remain the nation's *largest service centres*. Sydney and Melbourne have always been the two most important banking places in Australia, the latter enjoying the leadership in the nineteenth century, when great amounts of British capital flowed to Victoria, and during most of the twentieth century. Of the 100 greatest business firms operating in Australia in 1980, 58 had their headquarters in Sydney and another 34 in Melbourne. The recent development of office space in the capital cities is shown in table 33 (fig. 77).

Table 33. Office space in the capital cities, 1985–86 (in square metres)

City/Area	Total stock 31 Dec. 1984	Vacant 31 Dec. 1984	New and refurbished space to become available		Annual absorption rate
			1985	1986	
Sydney	2,400,000	110,400	128,000	90,000	105,000
North Sydney	775,000	45,700	27,000	19,000	30,000
Other North Shore	625,000	47,500	98,000	26,000	30,000
Parramatta	223,000	10,500	44,000	27,000	13,000
Metrop. Sydney	4,023,000	214,100	297,000	162,000	178,000
Melbourne	1,775,000	49,700	115,000	58,000	79,000
St. Kilda Road	206,000	1,000	43,000	12,000	20,000
Metrop. Melbourne	1,981,000	50,700	158,000	70,000	99,000
Perth	888,000	8,000	64,000	60,000	42,000
Brisbane	783,000	94,000	77,000	60,000	55,000
Adelaide	559,000	7,800	79,000	39,000	24,000

Sources: Australia Wide Property Trusts statistics in Property Review 14, 1985; for total stock in Adelaide: personal communication from Department of Environment and Planning, Adelaide, October 1984

From table 33 it is clear that metropolitan Sydney has more than twice as much office space as metropolitan Melbourne, and seven times as much as Adelaide. Secondly, office space has to date been very much centralized (Alexander 1979, 1980). The data for metropolitan Sydney seems at first glance to suggest that approximately 40% of the total available stock is outside the Central City, in places such as North Sydney and even as far away from the CBD as Parramatta, and that it is in these places that most of the new office space was offered in 1985. It has, however, to be remembered that the administrative area of the Central City is rather small, and that in contrast to U.S. cities suburban localities such as North Sydney, Crows Nest and Chatswood included as 'Other North Shore' in the table would be included within the limits of the Central City. There has been very little suburbanization of office functions in terms of new office parks. Pennant Hills, under construction in 1984 in the northwestern division of the Sydney metropolitan area, offering 26,700 square metres of office space plus an eighty-room motel with convention facilities, may be regarded Australia's first office park (Austr. Property Rev. 1984).

Why is there such a difference in modern office development between the major cities in Australia and the U.S.A.? In the United States it can be easily observed that the locations most favoured for the new establishment of offices or business parks in the metropolitan ring are close to freeway entry points, above all sites close to an intersection of a beltway and one of the radial urban freeways. Such sites guarantee easy accessibility to the CBD by car, a factor that seems to be essential to a great number of businesses moving to American suburban office parks. The lack of freeways in the Australian metropolitan areas, with the partial exception of Perth, seems to be the crucial point (ch. 4.1.9).

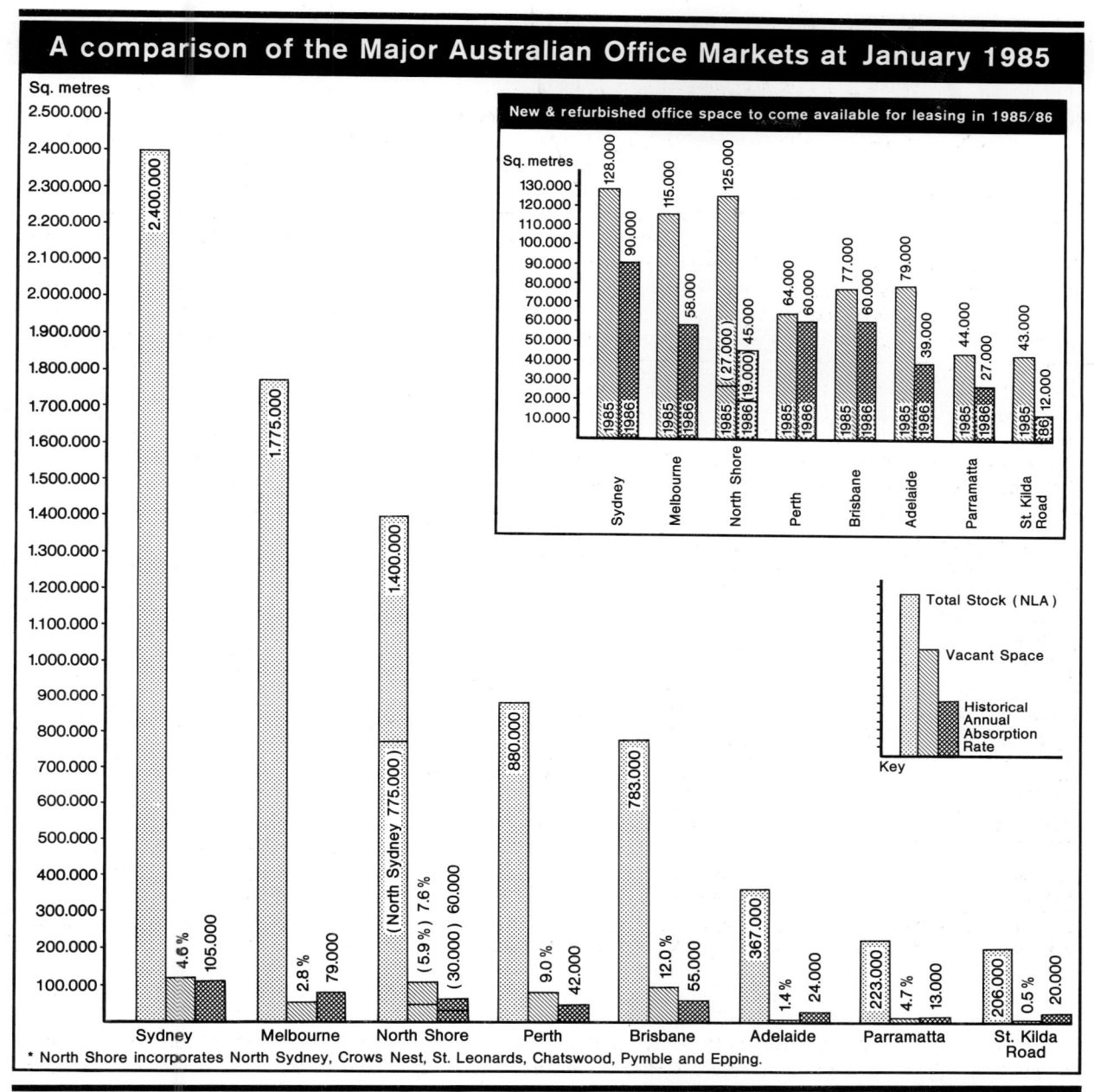

Fig. 77. Office space development in Australia's metropolitan areas 1984–86

Since 1948 all the capital cities with the exception of Brisbane have had their metropolitan planning schemes and, since 1968, even second-generation metropolitan plans. In addition the mainland capitals have also been the subject of transportation studies. Despite differing emphases and goals, some obvious similarities of proposed metropolitan development may be recognized. The major common trend is their attempt to direct further urban development to a *limited number of district centres*, as distinct structural elements of the future metropolises. In general these district centres were to be developed around shopping centres, each based on a department store, preferably located near a suburban railway station and a major intersection of two or more arterial roads. This goal has been more or less successfully persued, although in the metropolitan area of Melbourne some district centres have been initiated by the Myer department store company away from any existing nuclei and from suburban railway stations.

The second common trend, which is to an extent related to the development of the district centres, has been

Table 34. State capitals population, 1851–1981

Year	Sydney	Melbourne	Brisbane	Adelaide	Perth	Hobart
1851	54,000	29,000	3,000	18,000	–	–
1861	96,000	125,000	6,000	35,000	5,000	25,000
1871	138,000	191,000	15,000	51,000	–	26,000
1881	225,000	268,000	31,000	92,000	9,000	27,000
1891	400,000	473,000	94,000	117,000	16,000	33,000
1901	496,990	501,580	120,650	162,200	70,700	35,000
1911	656,800	600,160	143,510	199,760	111,400	40,000
1921	912,750	800,520	217,710	259,590	155,590	51,999
1931	1,200,830	995,600	283,440	310,460	215,800	60,008*
1941	1,331,290	1,114,900	344,230	350,000	234,000	76,567**
1951	1,574,880	1,330,800	453,660	447,500	322,000	95,206***
1961	2,183,388	1,911,895	621,550	587,957	420,133	110,217
1971	2,725,064	2,394,117	818,423	809,482	641,800	130,000
1981	2,874,415	2,578,527	942,636	882,520	809,033	128,603

Sources: 1851–1891 McCarty 1970; 1901–1971 Arnot 1973; 1981 Population Report 7, 1983; for Hobart 1921–1961 Solomon 1976
* 1933, ** 1947, *** 1954

the attempt to *channel urban development along a few corridors*. These are partly predestined for urban growth by the patterns of natural features (or rather natural constraints), such as mountain ranges or swamps, and partly by the existing suburban rail and road networks.

The last two decades have brought differential growth rates for the capital cities, to the effect that the two largest had the smallest growth, and the other three mainland capitals have been narrowing the size-gap with comparatively higher growth rates. Hobart's contrast with the mainland capitals in terms of population grew, the Hobart MUA with the exclusion of peripheral suburbs such as Kingston and Gagebrook even suffering from a slight population decrease in the intercensal period 1976–81. The relations of Hobart as the smallest of the capital cities to the mainland capitals were in 1947 1.0 : 3.6 : 5.0 : 5.3 : 17.5 : 22.2. The change that had occurred by 1981 is apparent from the 1981 relations that are 1.0 : 6.3 : 6.9 : 7.3 : 20.1 : 22.4. The growth of the capital cities from 1851 to 1981 is shown in table 34.

3.1.8 Darwin, capital of the Northern Territory

For a number of reasons the development and position of the capital of the Northern Territory do not allow a comparison with any of the state capitals. On the other hand, Darwin shows some parallels with the national capital.

In the nineteenth century the British were eager to get a toehold on the northern shores of Australia in order to demonstrate their claims to the whole of the continent. From the 1930s the region developed as a point of the *highest strategic importance* between the Pacific and Indian Oceans, used by both the Australian Navy and the Royal Australian Air Force (R.A.A.F.). In addition to the city's strategic importance, the strong military presence has also had a decisive impact on Darwin's urban structure. The huge airport, in combination with a R.A.A.F. air base, is probably the greatest physical constraint to rational expansion of the urban area from the old town core inland into the adjoining area to the northeast. Even in the process of reconstruction after the disaster of the 1974 cyclone nothing was changed with regard to the site of the airport. Partly related to Darwin's military importance is also the government's role in land ownership, land use control, construction of housing, employment and administration. All these factors will be treated in some detail.

While the north coast was probably the part of the continent first visited by Portuguese and Dutch explorers, as well as by fishermen from Celebes looking for trepang, it was also the part to be settled last by the British. From 1824 onward they made several attempts of colonization, all of which failed. Port Essington on Melville Island was abandoned after a very short period of settlement because of the lack of fresh water, and nearby Port Dundas because of the danger of fever in the mangrove swamps. Another unsuccessful attempt was made in 1827 with the establishment of Fort Wellington on Raffles Bay (see Bauer in: Jennings & Linge 1980, 9–27).

A new expedition was sent out in 1838 and Port Essington re-activated. In 1839 the place was visited by HMS 'Beagle', with Charles Darwin on board, the ship's name being given to Beagle Gulf. A naval officer of the 'Beagle' explored part of the coast and named the site on the inlet between Bathurst and Melville Island after the famous naturalist.

For some time the settlement at Port Darwin was also known as Palmerston, a name recently given to a newly developing satellite city in the Darwin area, but it is scarcely possible to speak of a settled place prior to the mid-1860s. The first incentive to sustained settlement was the crossing of the continent in 1862 by John McDouall Stuart, who had been commissioned by the Governor of South Australia. This colony assumed control over the

N.T. in 1864, successfully competing with New South Wales and Queensland. The actual founding of Darwin as a permanent settlement was only in 1869. Further incentives for the town's growth were the putting into operation in 1872 of the *first Overland Telegraph*, the line closely following Stuart's route of ten years earlier, and the final explorations by John Ross in 1871. Stuart had been sent on the expedition to the north coast by the South Australian Government because England had put pressure on the colonies for the extension of the overseas telegraph cable to Australia. Once the cable had already reached the Indonesian island of Java, the cities of Adelaide, Perth and Sydney were competed to be the terminal, all hoping that this would bring an increase of their business activity.

There were a great many constraints to Darwin's growth, so that even at the 1911 census the settlement had fewer than one thousand residents. Its further development was constrained by its extreme isolation and remoteness from the more densely populated regions of the continent, the distance to Sydney by air being approximately 3,300 km in the direct line, 4,500 km by road and 4,600 km by sea. A second constraint was that its tropical agricultural products were similar to those produced in the countries of Southeast Asia and so of little interest in these potential markets, which were closer to Darwin than the Australian southeast. The very slow economic development of the N.T. was a further inhibiting factor (Jaschke 1975b).

There were, on the other hand, some advantages guaranteeing Darwin's survival and its extraordinary growth in more recent years. Darwin was the only settlement of any importance along the entire north coast and the only one that could be reached from the south by an *overland route*, albeit an unsealed highway. As mentioned above, Darwin also served as the terminal of the first Overland Telegraph. Economic activities from time to time based on Darwin include some gold mining in the Pine Creek area, mainly during the 1870s, and some marine exploitation, mainly of pearl shell and shrimp, and cattle rearing, which still continues.

After nine years of negotiations between the Governments of South Australia and the Commonwealth, the latter assumed responsibility for the N.T. in 1911, installing an Administrator as its local representative in Darwin. The city's administration has always been extremely complicated, with the Federal Departments of Defense and Transport, among others, having direct responsibilities for the Commonwealth lands, the Department of Housing and Construction for public works and government housing. The latter Department also has indirect responsibilities delegated by the Federal Minister for the Northern Territory through the Northern Territory Housing Commission for low-income housing and through the Department of the Northern Territory for urban planning and land administration. Apart from these government bodies, the Corporation of the City of Darwin is responsible for minor civil functions (King 1979, 56).

After the destructions caused by Japanese air raids in 1942–43, conflicts between the Department of the Interior and the Department of Post-war Reconstruction were temporarily resolved by the establishment of an interdepartmental committee. In order to enable implementation of the committee's urban development plan, the *Darwin Lands Acquisition Act* was passed in 1945 providing for 'the compulsory acquisition of all freehold land within twelve miles of the centre of Darwin ... Darwin in 1974 had a dual system of leasehold and freehold land tenure which was unique in Australia' (King 1979, 61–62). In the 1960s and early 1970s conversion of urban leases to freehold were made possible and carried out to some extent.

On the other hand, Darwin's peculiar situation makes for an extraordinarily *high degree of rental housing* provided by the government. In addition to the Commission housing for low-income people, found in all the Australian states, in Darwin there is a considerable amount of public housing occupied by government employees during spells of military or civil service in Darwin. After a few years of service in the north many of these people move to some other place in Australia. Thus in 1971, 27.8% of all dwelling units in Darwin were government-owned as compared with the Australian average of 5.5%. Rented units comprised 61.6% of all housing, as compared with the Australian average of 27.3% (Jaschke 1975b, 42). At the same time 41% of Darwin's total workforce were employed by the Commonwealth Government, a proportion only comparable with the situation in Canberra.

As already noted, many people live and work in Darwin for a rather limited period of time. During the intercensal period 1966–71, the city experienced a population increase of 15,800 persons, but during the same period there were 26,790 newcomers. This means that in addition to the actual population increase there had been an exchange of another 10,990 persons. These are extremely high figures in relation to the city's total population of 21,671 in 1966 and 37,060 in 1971 (Jaschke 1975b, 36).

The high proportion of government employment is in turn due to the presence of military installations, scientific research institutions and administrative bodies for the N.T. Under the threat of war in the 1930s the Commonwealth Government began to develop Darwin as a military base. It set aside considerable areas as *defense reserves*, including the R.A.A.F. air base to the northeast of the original town core, which was located on the tip of a peninsula, restricted by Fannie Bay to the northwest and Frances Bay to the southeast; swampy areas further prohibited a greater expansion of the built-up area.

It thus happened that the major industrial and some commercial developments occurred *along Stuart Highway*, in a small strip squeezed in between the huge airport to the north and swamps along Frances Bay to the south. Most of the *residential suburbs spread north of the airport*, at a considerable distance from the old town core with its commercial and administrative functions. Future urban growth must mainly take place to the east of

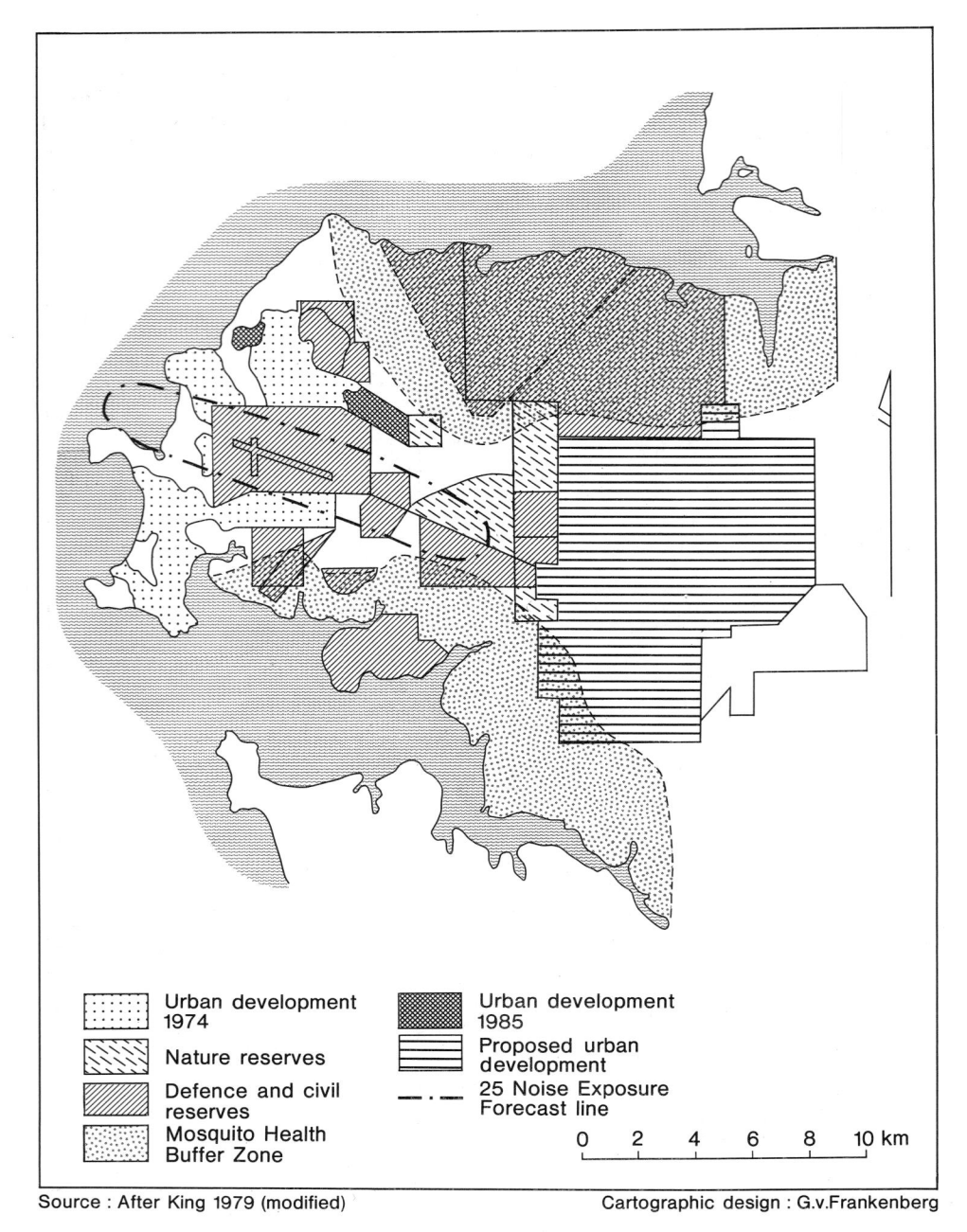

Fig. 78. Constraints on urban development in Darwin

Legend:
- Urban development 1974
- Nature reserves
- Defence and civil reserves
- Mosquito Health Buffer Zone
- Urban development 1985
- Proposed urban development
- 25 Noise Exposure Forecast line

Source: After King 1979 (modified)   Cartographic design: G.v.Frankenberg

the airport. Of the pre-cyclone population, approximately 26,000 persons lived on the north side, where only some 5,000 jobs were located, thus imposing extensive journeys to work (fig. 78). The correction of this unequal development of Darwin's urban structure ought to have been a major target for post-cyclone planning. We shall return to this aspect below.

Darwin played a pioneering part in the development of Australian civil aviation. The particular need for a means of fast long-distance travel in the vast sparsely inhabited northern part of the continent mainly comprising northern Queensland and the N.T. is recognizable even today in the name of Australia's national airline QANTAS, this being an abbreviation of 'Queensland and Northern Territory Aerial Services'. For a period of time before the jet age Darwin also served as a stop-over point for intercontinental flights. Although this function was lost through the introduction of long non-stop flights, Darwin has gained increasing importance within the Australian domestic air network (see ch. 2.3.4).

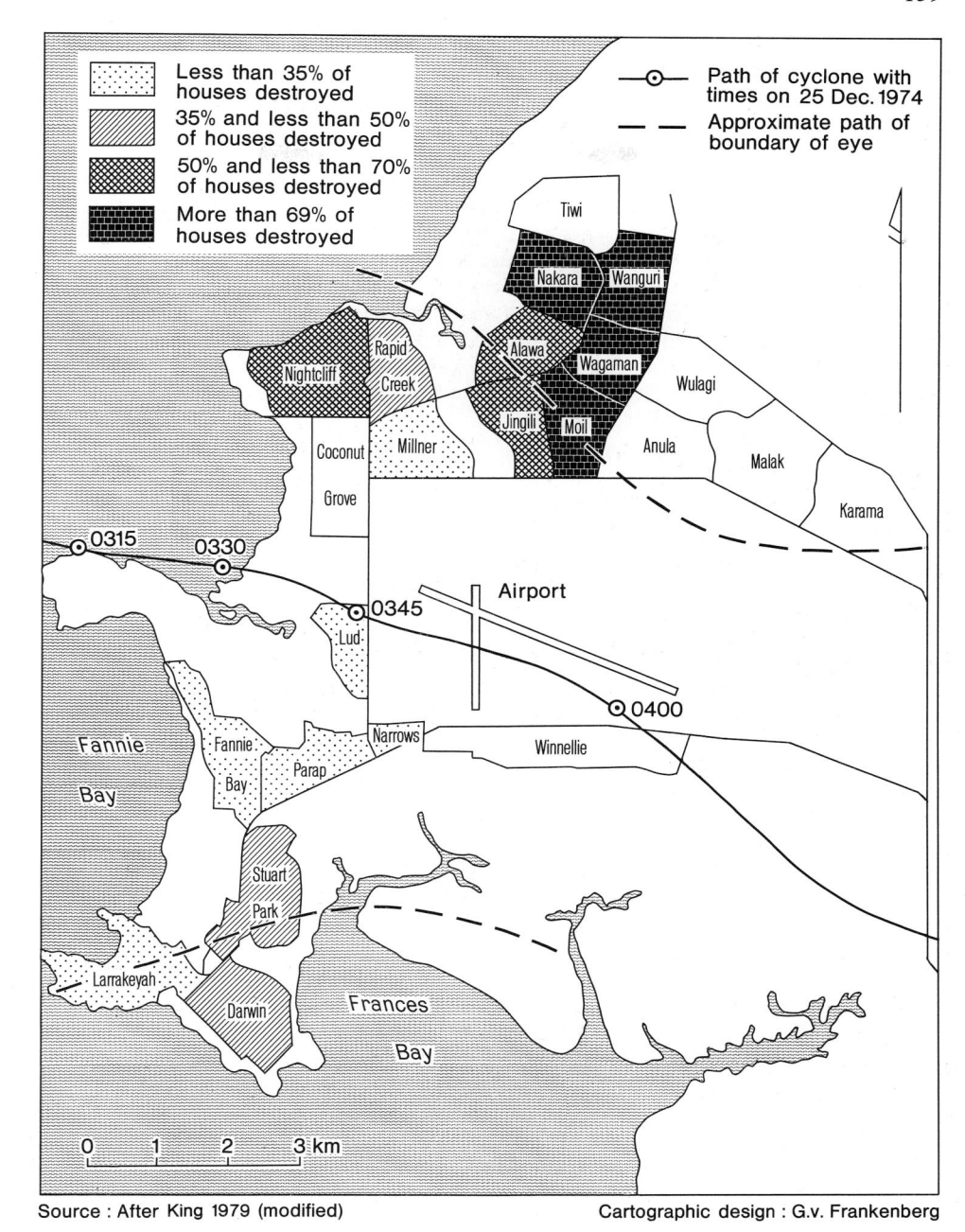

Fig. 79. Path of Cyclone Tracy and house damages in Darwin

Source: After King 1979 (modified)   Cartographic design: G.v. Frankenberg

The Darwin region has always been prone to cyclonic activities, the town suffered particularly in 1897 and in 1937. Despite the awareness of such danger, the majority of houses used to be single-family homes on concrete stilts, lightly constructed to allow optimum ventilation. Jaschke (1975b) pointed to the fact that Darwin's electricity supply always lagged behind demand, so that solidly built air-conditioned houses could hardly be constructed for residential purposes. It is this background that must be set at the disaster of *Cyclone Tracy*, in the early morning hours of Christmas Day, 1974.

The eye of the cyclone hit the continent at a peninsula north of Fannie Bay between the city centre to the south and the residential suburbs to the north, the latter being severely affected by the eye's northern boundary. In central Darwin and neighbouring areas between 35% and 50% of all houses were damaged, but in the northern suburbs much higher percentages of houses were destroyed. The destruction rates were between 50% and 69% in the suburbs of Nightcliff, Alawa and Jingili, and they were 70% or more in the suburbs of Nakara, Wanguri, Wagaman and Moil. There were 49 deaths, while hundreds of people were injured and thousands were left without a home. Most damages were due to the wind velocity and to flying debris; fortunately the cyclone coincided with neap tides, so that no damage was caused by storm surge (fig. 79). According to Jaschke (1975b, 44), 52.5% of Darwin's total building stock was completely destroyed while another 42.0% suffered from more or less severe damages.

The Government immediately declared Darwin a disaster area and initiated an *evacuation* programme. Thus of the pre-cyclone population of 46,656 persons, only 11,119 remained in January, 1975. This situation could have been the start for a completely new development at the 'Top End' as this part of the N.T. is often referred to. Jaschke (1975b, 46–48) gave strong arguments in favour of moving the Northern Territory's capital to Katherine, a town located some 340 km south of Darwin on the Stuart Highway. There was, however, no serious consideration of an alternative location of the Territory's administrative centre on the part of the Australian authorities. Nor was there any attempt at correcting the *unbalanced urban structure* of pre-cyclone Darwin mentioned above. This may have been mainly due to the fact that the R.A.A.F. did not want to have their air base relocated. The evacuated population also returned much more rapidly than had been expected.

A *Darwin Reconstruction Commission* was appointed for the reconstruction of the heavily destroyed city. The North Australia Research Unit, a branch of the Australian National University in Canberra, initiated research programmes for investigating the causes of damages by cyclones, of cyclone-proof housing construction and of surge research. It suggested that precautions should be taken in the rebuilding of Darwin so as to minimize damage if the city should be hit by another cyclone.

Although there had not been any damage caused by storm surge, an attempt was made to predict possible surge hazards. The assumption was made that extreme surges might occur, this being 6 m for Darwin, the highest value along the entire northern coastline of the continent between Brisbane in southern Queensland and Carnarvon on the Western Australian coast. A map was produced showing the possible extent of inundations for various surge heights (Pickup & Minor 1980). In Darwin all the land area below 10.8 m above sea level was declared a *surge zone*, and construction of houses prohibited. Investigations were also made into the vulnerability of various types of houses with the wind gusting at various speeds, and proposals were made for *cyclone-proof housing* construction. It was recommended that houses in areas prone to cyclone damage should be built of solid material, enabling them to withstand higher wind speeds. All windows should be protected from flying debris by *special shutters*, and a special *shelter room* provided in each house. According to Jaschke (1975b) this means additional costs of between $ 3,000 and $ 5,000 for a new single family home.

A complete remodelling of the City of Darwin proved to be impracticable for at least three reasons. One problem the authorities were confronted with immediately was the unexpectedly rapid pace at which people returned to Darwin, with a consequent demand for immediate housing provision. Within the space of a few months the population trebled, so that in mid-1975 approximately 35,000 persons were again living in the city. Further plans for major changes of the urban structure met with little response from the inhabitants, who perceived only a 'random pattern of house damage' (King 1979), and did not show much insight into the true nature of physical conditions. Finally, drastic changes in land-use patterns would have made necessary the acquisition and re-allocation of a great number of lots. The Commonwealth Government would have had to provide considerable funds for land acquisition over a short period of time. For all the details on post-cyclone planning in Darwin the reader is referred to King (1979, 98–146).

Thus Darwin's internal structure remained more or less what it had been in pre-cyclone days. The CBD was reactivated in the former city core. Manufacturing industries have again been concentrated along Stuart Highway bordering the huge airport on the south side. The major suburban residential areas are still located to the north of the airport. Some remains of the disaster are still to be observed in the city centre. The ruins of one of the churches were left untouched to stand as a memorial, and the porch of another preserved in the new church building. The remains of a bank were also built into a modern office building (fig. 80).

Darwin experienced a further rapid growth in the late 1970s (fig. 81). The granting of *self-government to the N.T.* in 1978 was an impetus for growth in the Territory in general and Darwin in particular. Plans were conceived to establish a *fully equipped university* in Darwin beyond the limited scope of the existing North Australia Research Unit. The place also gained the image of being the major port for the *growing trade with Southeast Asia*, and there has been an expansion of fishing and mining activities in the area. Also of significance was the railway project which is under way for the bicentennial. By 1981 Darwin had a population of 56,482 residents with an average annual growth rate of 7.3% during the 1976–81 intercensal period. This rate has continued in the 1980s and should bring Darwin's population to some 70,000 by the end of the decade.

The two most important problems to be solved by the planners are the provision of the necessary transportation links within the Darwin area and the development of new residential areas to house this future population. The number of major arterial roads has been too small to be of sufficient capacity for intra-urban traffic. After the new northern suburbs of Malak, Karama, Leanyer and Brinkin had reached their final stages, planners proposed the development of a new town to be called *Palmerston*, located 19 km to the east of Darwin on the Stuart Highway. The land had already been acquired by the public authorities in 1973. There were certain constraints as to the site for the

Fig. 80. Darwin, N.T. Reconstruction after disaster caused by Cyclone Tracy of CBD office building with ruin of former Commonwealth Bank building being integrated in modern structure

Fig. 81. Howard Springs, Darwin, N.T. Temporary Police Office in caravan during first phase of construction

new town. One of them was the surge zone, which is partly identical with the breeding grounds of the *Anopheles mosquito* in the north and south. Economic constraints included the desire to protect some good agricultural land and a potential gravel-working area in Darwin East from being built up (Harris & Stehbens 1981, 280–86).

A Palmerston Development Authority, consisting of representatives from the Departments of Lands, Transport and Works, Treasury and the Department of the Chief Minister was appointed in 1981 to implement the plan. The major utilities are to be developed by the Authority, whereas the reticulation works, which means the distribution to the individual users on their lots, the commercial and residential developments are to be carried out by private developers and to be approved by the Authority. Each neighbourhood is supposed to house some 5,000 residents and to be endowed with a local shopping area, while the Town Centre has an off-centre location in the northeast on Stuart Highway. In the end, Palmerston is destined to be a self-contained urban centre with a population in the range, according to various planning alternatives, between 50,000 and 90,000 residents (Palmerston Devel. Author. 1981). At this size Palmerston would not be a satellite of Darwin, but rather its *'sister city'*.

Darwin's exceptional position has been accompanied by a very peculiar population structure. The city's *ethnic and religious mixture* is comparatively high comprising, among others, Chinese, Malay, Philippine and Timor communities. By 1981 24.4% of the population were overseas-born, and another 7.1% were Aborigines. The Chinese joss house serves a community of some 5,000 persons and a mosque was opened in 1980. These minorities are widely distributed over the suburban areas; for example immigrants from Timor amount to 3.6% of the population of Stuart Park, 2.0% in Coconut Grove, 1.5% in Larakeyah, 1.4% in Alawa, 1.3% in Parap and Fanny Bay and 1.2% in Wagaman (1976). They are mixed with other ethnic groups, having similarly low concentrations.

At the 1981 census Darwin had an economically *active population of 51.4%*, a very high proportion. Of these, 41.5% were employed by the Commonwealth, Territory and Local Governments, 18.3% in public administration and defense and another 17.8% in community services, while only 9.2% (1971 13.0%) were in construction and 4.7% in manufacturing, particularly in the processing of fish and other food production. The once important meat-packing plant was closed after cattle transports were increasingly diverted to Katherine and Wyndham. A third of the employed population was unmarried. In 1981 only 25.0% of the population had lived in the same residence as five years earlier, and another 2.2% in the same LGA, while 23.1% had lived elsewhere in the N.T. in 1976. This means that half of Darwin's population had moved to the city from outside the N.T. in the intercensal period 1976–81. Only 18,562 persons were home owners or purchasers, whereas 13,858 persons were tenants of the Housing Authority and another 14,368 were other tenants (ABS 1981 Census of Pop. and Housing).

To sum up, Darwin owes much of its growth in the twentieth century to its strategic position as a naval and airforce base between two oceans. Between 1911 and 1978 the town was administered by the Federal Government, and a high percentage of the workforce consists of government employees on comparatively short-term contracts. Apart from public housing built by the Housing Commission, much of the building stock is government housing provided for the many government employees, mainly as rental units. A considerable part of the urban area is reserved for defense purposes. The huge R.A.A.F. air base and civil airport are major constraints to urban development. They have resulted in an unbalanced structure of the urban area, with the CBD in the old city core to the southwest, and the main residential suburbs to the north, with the industrial and some commercial development spreading along Stuart Highway to the south. This urban structure results in extensive journeys to work. Immigrant groups from China, Malaysia, the Philippines and Timor have added to the great ethnic mixture in the city. In December 1974, Cyclone Tracy destroyed over 50% of Darwin's housing stock and damaged much more, so that most of the present building fabric is of very recent origin. After the disaster, the city's population was down to less than 12,000, but grew within a decade to over 60,000. This rapid population influx was one of a number of factors preventing any major replanning of the post-cyclone urban structure, and leading planners to provide extensive new housing outside the former urban area, notably in the 'sister city' of Palmerston.

3.1.9 Canberra and the Australian National Territory

Canberra with 238,000 inhabitants in 1981, ranks seventh among Australia's cities, being smaller than the mainland capitals and Newcastle. It is thus Australia's largest inland city and one of the largest planned new towns in the entire world.

Just as the Americans had acted a century earlier, the Australians decided to establish a new capital city on a territory independent from any existing state, and with a distinctive design. They were eager to avoid antagonism between the established state capitals, above all Sydney and Melbourne, in competition for the position as leading political centre of the new Commonwealth of Australia. It was decided upon that the new capital should be located not less than a hundred miles from Sydney, and that the State of New South Wales would cede the land needed to create an Australian National Territory. Looking back on the decision, it has been questioned whether it was advisable to put the new nation's administrators and politicans into such an isolated place, remote from the more densely populated coastal regions of the southeast, a decision inducing Pegrum (1983) to give his book the title 'The bush capital'.

In the new federal legislature a dispute which was to last for a whole decade commenced over the site of the federal capital. At first Dalgety was nominated, a site on the Snowy River somewhat to the southwest of the present Australian Capital Territory (A.C.T.), although the place was known to have a rather harsh winter climate. Speculators had already purchased land around Dalgety, hoping to profit from rising values. In 1903 a Royal Commission investigated a number of places, of which Armidale, Orange and Lake George lay to the north of the present site, Albury, Tumut and Bombala to the southwest and south. These cities and quite a few others formed local committees to lobby for selection as federal capital.

The House of Representatives first voted for Tumut, whereas the Senate was in favour of Bombala. Disagreeing with Bombala, the House of Representatives then brought Dalgety into the discussion again. The State of New South Wales, however, refused to cede land for the National Territory at Dalgety, arguing that the locality was much too far from Sydney. Negotiations continued until 1908, in which year Dalgety and Yass-Canberra were put to the vote.

Fig. 82. Canberra, A.C.T. View from Black Mountain over Lake Burley Griffin with Captain Cook Fountain

The final vote in the House of Representatives was *39 : 31 in favour of Yass-Canberra*. Thus a site was found approximately 300 km southwest of Sydney and 650 km northeast of Melbourne. In 1911, ten years after federation, land for a National Territory was finally ceded by New South Wales. For further details of the choice of site the reader is referred to Green (1965), Pegrum (1983) and Bird (1986).

The site for the capital city had been investigated very carefully. The city was to be built in the Southern Tablelands of New South Wales, approximately 550 m above sea level. The site was generally a plain, with a few interspersed hills. It was located to the east of the *Murrumbidgee Scarp*, which here follows the western bank of the Murrumbidgee River. The land to the west of the river within the A.C.T., and extending beyond its boundaries, is thus more elevated and characterized by steeper slopes. So despite the fact that the A.C.T. is considerably larger than the District of Columbia in the United States, much of the terrain is less suitable for settlement. Considerable areas are also reserved as water catchments, as environmental protection zones, or as clearance zones of radio and space tracking stations. These restrictions have proved a limiting factor to the further southward development of Canberra's built-up area. In consequence, negotiations in the 1970s between the A.C.T. and the State of New South Wales were aiming at extending the A.C.T. to the north, beyond the present A.C.T.-New South Wales boundary line.

One of the Murrumbidgee's tributaries, the *Molonglo River*, flows westward through the plain and the present built-up area of the federal capital. Surveyor Scrivner had found this river plain the most favourable site not only with regard to the aesthetics of the landscape but also with regard to its capability of water supply for the city. The Molonglo River was dammed in 1959–64 to form Lake Burley Griffin (fig. 82).

Many suggestions were made for the name of the national capital, including Sydmeladelperbrisho, a name made up of the first syllables from each state capital! In 1913 the future capital city was named Canberra, after the Aboriginal word kamberri, meaning *'meeting place'*. Construction work was initiated according to the plan of the Chicago-based architect *Walter Burley Griffin*, selected from 137 designs submitted during an international architects' competition (Howard 1984).

Griffin was inspired by his teacher, the American architect Sullivan. Both his wife and Griffin himself had been

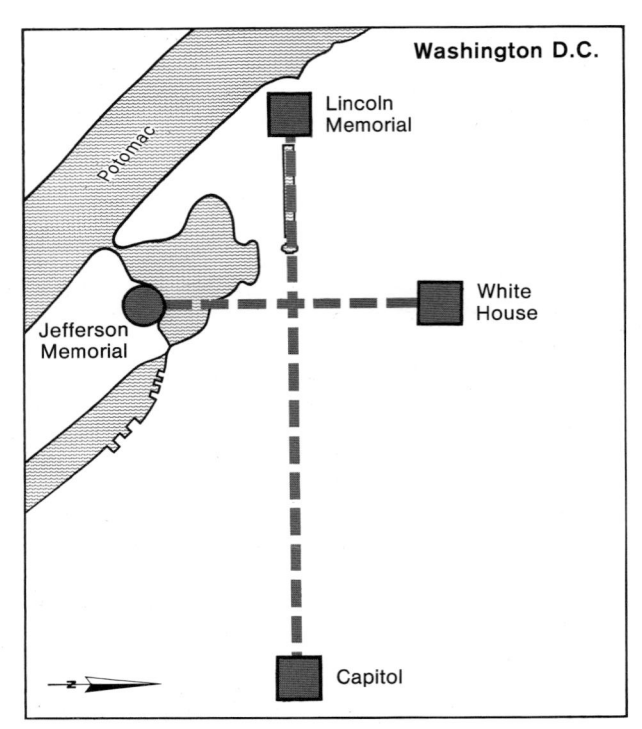

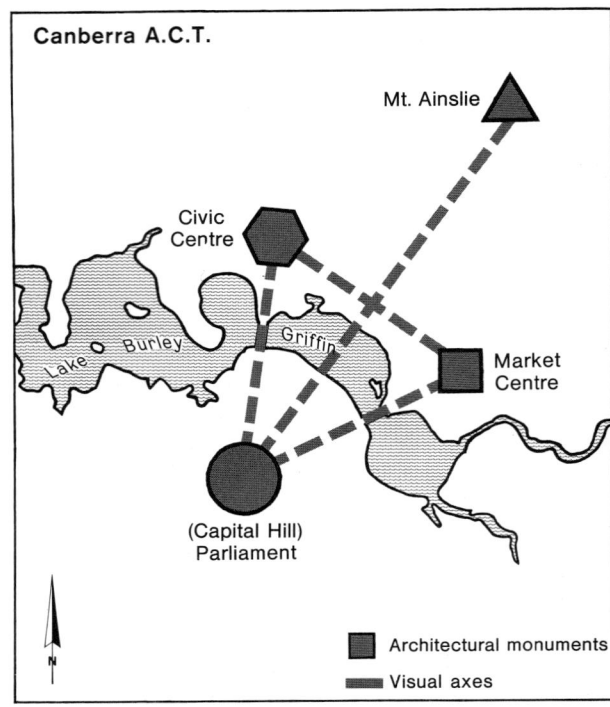

Fig. 83. The design of major axes in central Washington D.C. and in Canberra A.C.T.

working with Frank Lloyd Wright. Griffin extracted elements of his design from Wren's plan for the reconstruction of London after the Great Fire in the seventeenth century, from Haussmann's plan for the transformation of Paris in the nineteenth century, from Burnham's plan for the development of central Chicago in the early twentieth century and, above all, from L'Enfent's plan of Washington D.C. (Harrison 1979). Fischer (1986) pointed to the fact that the Indonesion temple site of Borobudur also served as a basis for the plan of Canberra.

Griffin's basic plan was an axial design, combined with circuses or hexagons at intersections (see ch. 3.4.1). One axis runs from Mt. Ainslie to Capital Hill, site of the new Parliament House; this axis corresponds with the axis from the Capitol Building to Lincoln Memorial in Washington D.C. The second axis runs from City Hill to the originally proposed Market Centre, corresponding with the axis from the White House to Jefferson Memorial.

There are, however, certain differences from L'Enfent's Washington plan. In Canberra a *third axis runs from Capital Hill to City Hill*, thus forming, together with Kings Avenue somewhat to the east of the Capital Hill-Mt. Ainslie axis, the so-called *Government Triangle* or Parliament Triangle. The three corners of the triangle were supposed to serve as the Government Centre, the Municipal Centre and the Market Centre respectively. The second difference is that *distances* in Canberra are greater, the axis Capital Hill-Mt. Ainslie being approximately 6 km in length. The third difference is the *pattern of the water bodies*, in the relative location of the Potomac River and Lake Burley Griffin respectively (Harrison 1979) (fig. 83).

Griffin's original plan was made for the city to grow to a maximum size of 75,000 people (Harrison 1968). On the north side of the river, which in this part of town was to become Lake Burley Griffin, the CBD developed at the foot of City Hill. This central district is adjoined on its western margin by the large campus of the Australian National University. Government functions were concentrated south of the river, where the provisional Parliament House is being replaced by the permanent Parliament House on top of Capital Hill, to be opened for the bicentennial. A number of important public buildings are located on the south bank of Lake Burley Griffin, including the National Library, the Supreme Court and the National Gallery. During the first four decades following federation, Australia's foreign relations were mainly transacted in London, but after 1940 more and more foreign embassies were established in Canberra, these being mainly located to the southwest and south of Capital Hill. The hill is the pivot of a number of radial streets leading into all directions, most of them bearing the names of the state capitals, including the capital city of New Zealand, which it was anticipated at the time would join the Commonwealth of Australia.

Fischer (1984) pointed out the extent to which Griffin was in the tradition of the City Beautiful movement and the Beaux-Arts background of his training, and to what extent he attempted to combine emancipist and social-reformist thoughts with the imperial tradition found in the layout of royal residences and imperial capitals. In this respect Griffin's plan is characterized by three major design elements.

In the first place, Griffin as a landscape architect was sensitive to the *natural environment* and made 'skilful use of space as a design element' (Fischer 1984, 20). While operating with axes and vistas he did not make use of the arches or obelisks that classical tradition would have employed, as in Washington D.C. Rather he used the elements of landscape, such as hills, ridges and the proposed lake for framing or terminating vistas.

A second design element was that, in supporting his 'formal Beaux-Arts composition of axes, avenues, mountains and artificial lake, Griffin defined the general outlines of a great piece of large-scale ensemble planning' (Fischer 1984, 20). An element of his original plan involved *central avenues framed by three-storey buildings*, that were never to be constructed in later years.

A third characteristic of the plan is his 'treatment of his plan as an essay in architectural symbolism' (Fischer 1984, 20); for example the ring roads around Capital Hill reflect the Commonwealth's hierarchical structure, and so do the *names* given to the ring roads and radial avenues. The two bridges, Commonwealth Bridge and King Bridge, symbolize Australia's ties with New Zealand and Great Britain respectively.

In later years Griffin's successors as Canberra's planners made re-interpretations and major changes of the original plan. Thus the market function was removed from the eastern corner of the triangle and replaced by the defense function. Instead of the Government, Municipal and Market Corners, the three corners of the triangle have thus been taken over by the CBD, the government and defense functions. The fundamental change from higher urban densities to a *predominantly suburban concept*, with single-storey houses even close to the city centre, prohibited the development of both shopping centres and ribbon developments with shopping facilities along arterial roads; there was no development of commercial strips, but only the systematic establishment of suburban Town Centres. The three-storey row houses that were destined to frame the avenues of the original plan were to a high degree replaced by single-storey buildings. 'A long-term consequence of these developments was that it not only took until the 1960s before the central triangle was completed as a configuration of avenues, but that even today the functional content of the triangle is only a fraction of that envisaged in the Griffin plan' (Fischer 1984, 37).

Griffin's plan has been called 'a successful blend of city-beautiful monumentality and garden city domesticity', while some British critics regretted 'the absence of a green belt and the rectilinear formality of the street pattern' (Freestone 1982, 32). While the garden city idea did not really gain a foothold in Australia, Canberra from its very beginning remained an exception, Canberra's recent garden suburbs or satellites being 'partly the outcome of a conscious "garden city" policy' (Freestone 1982, 44).

Canberra's growth was *extremely slow*. Until 1920 Griffin served as the Federal Capital Director. When major revisions of his original plan were proposed and problems of funding increased, Griffin resigned from his position. In 1921 a *Federal Capital Advisory Committee* was appointed. From 1925 to 1930 a *Federal Capital Commission* was in charge of planning for the capital city, while generous allocations were made by means of an independent 'Seat of Government Fund'. After the Commission had been dismissed, *several government departments* assumed the responsibility for the development of Canberra till 1955.

By 1924, 777 square kilometres of freehold land in the A.C.T. had been acquired by the Federal Government, while another 414 square kilometres of rural land still remained 'in freehold ownership without any planning or land use controls' (Harrison 1978, 112). In the city, land was granted to individuals on lease that was, with a few exceptions labelled 'residential'. However, the meaning of 'residential' was not specified, so that, for example, it was possible for anybody to build and operate a motel on such a leasehold. The question of allotment was in the responsibility of the Department of the Interior.

In 1925 the Griffin Plan was gazetted as the only official development plan for Canberra, all major changes having to be approved by Parliament. However, this decision applied only to the street pattern, whereas detailed construction principles were left to future planning decisions. Since the planners, partly under the pressure of post-war financial restrictions, have been inclined to favour a modified garden-city concept, with low-density, low-cost housing, Canberra's urban morphology diverged from Griffin's distinctly 'urban' intentions toward a more suburban appearance.

At the same time planners laid the foundation for a certain degree of *social-area segregation* within the city by allotting some areas to workmen and employees and others to higher paid groups. There are three areas in present-day Canberra still characterized by above-average percentages of 'blue-collar' workers, of households with annual incomes below $ 6,000 (1981), and of residence in flats or private-rented dwellings. These are the areas between the City and Dickson to the north, the area of Manuka-Kingston southeast of Capital Hill and, outside the A.C.T., the City of Queanbeyan.

For some time after World War II, Canberra still remained a small settlement: at the 1947 census its population amounted only to some 15,000 residents. By no means all government departments had moved from Melbourne to Canberra, and those that had moved were still in temporary accommodation. Many roads were unpaved, bridges across the Molonglo River were lacking, and the river had not yet been dammed, so that the lake did not exist. It did not seem as if Canberra would participate in the post-war economic and population growth experienced by all the state capitals. Private enterprise was very reluctant to make any investment in the 'bush capital'.

Things changed profoundly when Robert Menzies took the office as Prime Minister for the second time (1949–66). Following an inquiry into the situation of the Federal Capital a number of decisive measures were taken. In

1955 the final report of a 'Senate Select Committee Appointed to Inquire into a Report upon the Development of Canberra' was released and a *National Capital Development Commission* (NCDC) was established. It came into full operation in 1958 and has since been responsible for the planning of the Federal Capital. In matters of day-to-day administration the Department of the Interior was replaced in 1972 by the newly established Department of the Capital Territory.

In 1957 Menzies also ordered all *government departments still remaining in Melbourne to move* to Canberra. By 1975, 34,000 of a total A.C.T. workforce of 89,000 were in various Commonwealth departments, while another 19,000 were in other government institutions. This means that 53,000 persons, 60% of the total workforce, were on the government payroll.

More freehold land was also acquired by the Commonwealth Government on the basis of the Land Acquisitions Act. By 1971 an area of no less than 1,963 square kilometres, 83% of the land in the A.C.T., was owned by the Government. By 1975 only 5 square kilometres remained in freehold; for all practical purposes there is *no freehold land left* throughout the A.C.T. (NCDC 1975). Then in the course of the so-called National Works programme the NCDC carried out various projects for the development of the Federal Capital, one of the most important being the creation in 1959–64 of *Lake Burley Griffin*, a development that has undoubtedly added much to the attractiveness of the capital city.

The Commonwealth Government undertook extensive housing projects; over 50% of Canberra's households are in rented housing. However, in response to increasing demand, *private enterprise* finally began to make investments in the Federal Capital. In the mid-1960s the first department store was opened in Canberra's CBD and the first multi-storey office building was constructed.

In the two decades 1947–66 Canberra's population grew from 15,000 to 93,000 residents; in addition the numerous construction workers and other people employed in the capital city brought Queanbeyan's population up to almost 13,000 residents. At last 'Canberra was transformed from an uncertain scatter of suburbs in exile – a national embarrassment – to a city which was beginning to look like a national capital' (Harrison 1978, 109).

In consequence of this rapid development, a half-million city was envisaged for the not too distant future, so that it seemed appropriate to make greater efforts in urban planning. Two general plans and a Transportation Study for the Canberra region were launched within the short period between 1963 and 1970. Two further Transport Studies were to follow in 1970 and 1974.

In 1965 the 'Future of Canberra Plan' was released, superceded five years later by 'Tomorrow's Canberra'. The former plan propagated one of two decisive planning principles having a great impact on Canberra's present urban morphology, which was that *new towns of about 100,000 persons* each were supposed to absorb the growing population. The towns were to be built on the neighbourhood principle, with groups of three to five neighbourhoods endowed with a shopping centre and a high school. There would be an appropriate provision of town centres, and road systems would provide for internal arterial roads as well as for public-transport spine routes. Each of these suburban satellites was to be embedded in a little valley, flanked by slopes that were supposed to remain as open green space (fig. 84).

The 'Tomorrow's Canberra' drew upon the 1967 Transportation Study, which in turn drew on ideas expressed by A.M. Voorhees & Associates of Washington D.C., a firm that had worked as consultants to NCDC and had made their recommendations in their 'Canberra General Concept Plan'. In addition to the new towns concept already expressed in the 'Future of Canberra Plan' of 1965, 'Tomorrow's Canberra' introduced a second decisive planning principle, that made people lable it the 'Y-Plan'. The spatial arrangement of the future new towns was supposed to provide for *three corridors in the shape of the letter 'Y'*. One corridor was to extend southward to the margin of the more rugged countryside, unsuitable for further urban settlement. Two corridors were to run to the northwest and the northeast, eventually extending beyond the boundaries of the A.C.T., and so requiring the negotiations with the State of New South Wales mentioned above. The former radial-concentric pattern of Canberra was thus replaced by a *strongly linear pattern* (fig. 85).

These planning principles have since been followed in the development of the A.C.T. The first suburban areas to be developed were Woden and Weston Creek to the southwest of the central City, followed in 1967 by Belconnen in the northwest. In the late 1970s construction commenced in Tuggeranong, far to the south. According to estimates of 1982 there were 58,400 persons living in Central Canberra, 76,650 in Belconnen, 33,550 in Tuggeranong, 27,750 in Weston Creek and 32,450 in Woden Valley, and 240,000 in the metropolitan area as a whole.

Detailed investigations were made for the location and size of shopping centres. In consequence of such careful planning, these centres are distributed more evenly and are more suburbanized than would have been the case under normal circumstances. But even under such conditions the smaller centres began to suffer from economic difficulties. The plan to locate them near the freeways that would encircle and connect the various suburbs was abandoned in favour of shopping facilities in the *Town Centres*, because of their easier accessibility for the residents of suburbs concerned. The shopping malls of the Town Centres of Woden and Belconnen proved, however, too small to meet demand and were allowed to grow to a size exceeding that of the Canberra City Centre. Thus the concept of a perfect pyramid of shopping centres, and the plan of a radial network of urban freeways connecting all the Town Centres with one another, to the disadvantage of the existing and planned green belts, were finally abandoned (Löffler 1973, Alexander & Dawson 1979).

Fig. 84. Years of first settlement of Canberra's suburbs

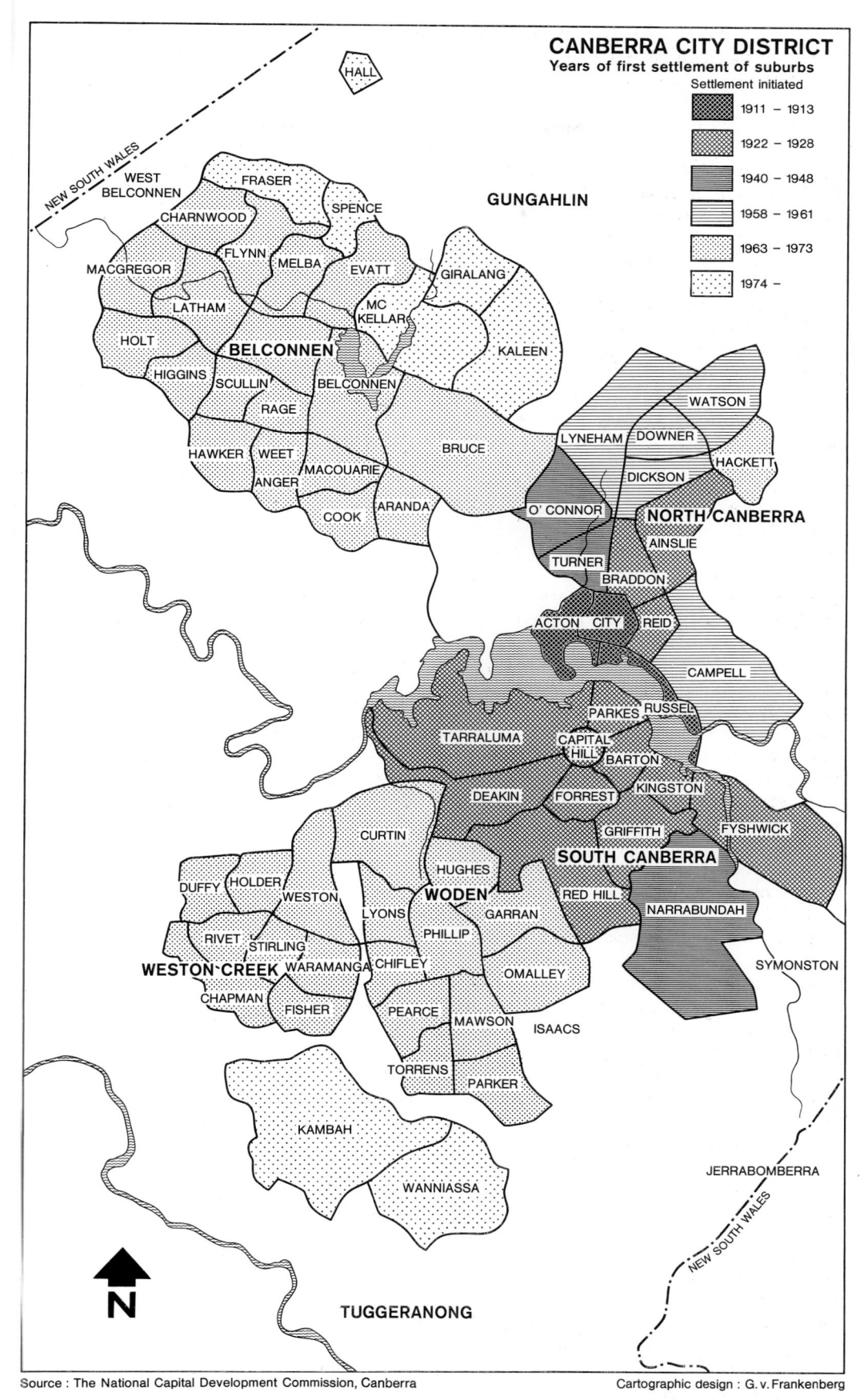

CANBERRA CITY DISTRICT
Years of first settlement of suburbs

Settlement initiated
- 1911 – 1913
- 1922 – 1928
- 1940 – 1948
- 1958 – 1961
- 1963 – 1973
- 1974 –

Source: The National Capital Development Commission, Canberra

Cartographic design: G. v. Frankenberg

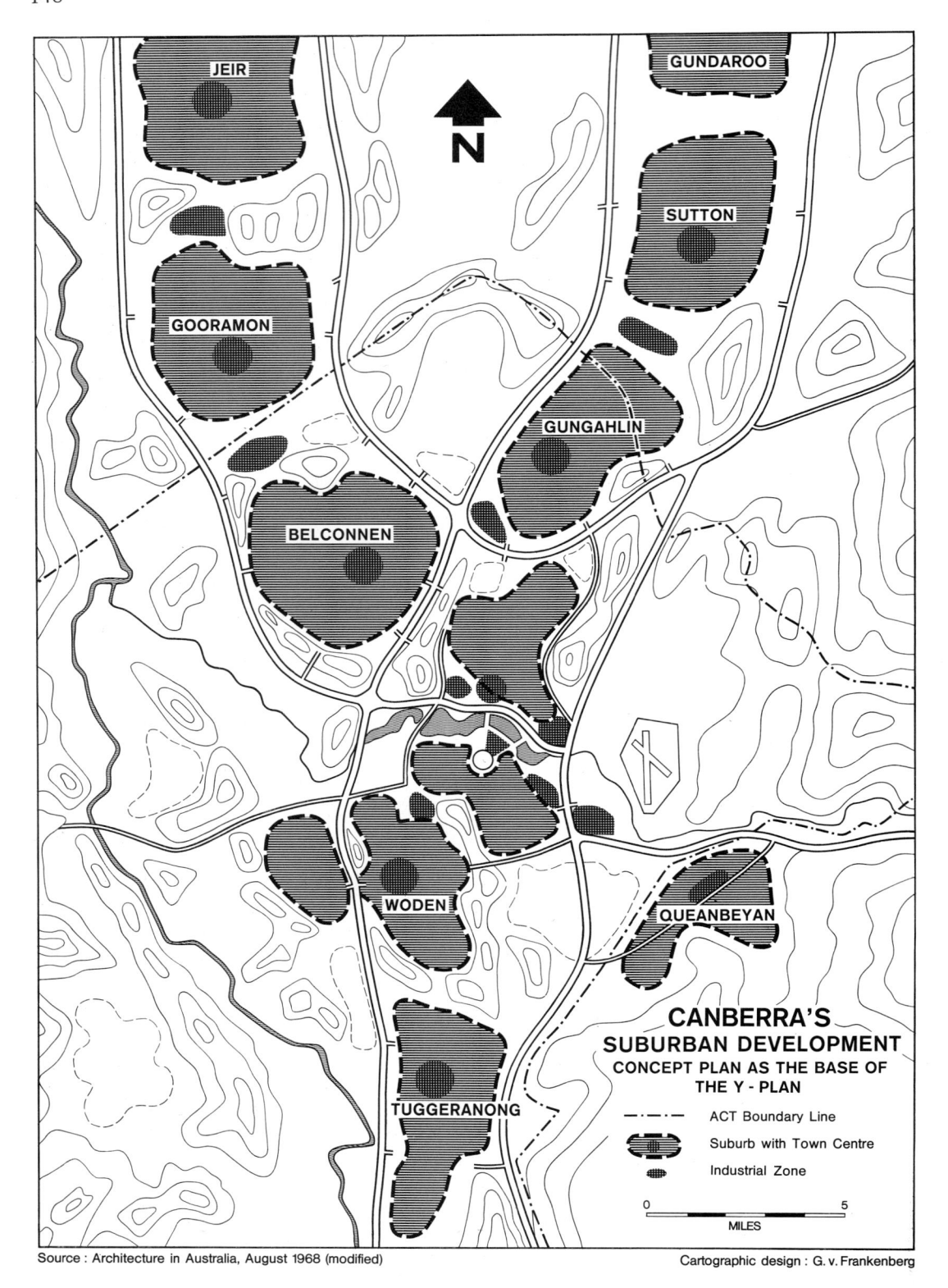

Fig. 85. Canberra's suburban development according to the Y-Plan (after Harrison 1968)

There are four small concentrations of manufacturing industries. Three of them, Fyshwick, Hume and Mitchell, are located to the east, and West Belconnen lies to the west. There are only 3,228 persons employed in manufacturing (1983) as compared with 108,900 in tertiary occupations, the greatest number of manufacturing jobs being in printing, metal processing, textiles and food processing. East of the city are also the airport and the railway station, as well as Queanbeyan's railway station, that had been opened in 1887.

At present 86% of Canberra's population live in single-family, detached houses. Fischer (1986) made the statement that this type of recent development in Canberra is adequate for younger officials' families, as well as for retired people, whereas the demands of other population groups are more or less neglected.

In the late 1970s *medium-density housing* was a big planning issue in Canberra. In this respect the NCDC was caught between the residents, usually opposed to any change of the suburban character of their residential quarters, and the retailers, looking forward to greater numbers of prospective customers in their neighbourhood. Most plans for medium-density housing were abandoned in favour of Radburn-type layouts. Thus the average residential density has hitherto been 1.7 dwellings per acre (4,000 square metres), which is very low even by Australian standards. Obviously the costs of providing services and transport for such a low-density community have not yet become inhibitive, while the costs of additional time for the residents' journeys to work and business trips are not measured in terms of public expenditure (Robinson 1973).

In general, however, there has been some reduction in the generous size of lots, and a certain equalization of housing standards. The construction of housing has been more and more handed over to private enterprise; while in 1950–51 no less than 89% of all houses completed had been government-built, this proportion had declined to 23% in 1970–71. By 1980–81, 99.7% of all houses completed were in private developments (Fischer 1984, 120). But it is still the NCDC that decides which areas are to be opened up for new housing projects and what kind of houses are going to be built, while plans and the costs of construction have to be approved by the NCDC.

Fischer (1984, 1986) pointed to the fact that hardly any other city in the world has been endowed with such idealism, financial resources, planning expertise and of power vested in the planners' hands, and that Canberra had the chance of introducing the best and most modern models and principles of urban planning from Great Britain, the United States and other countries of the western world. Moreover, in Canberra plans could be carried out on a scale only dreamt of in other cities. He comes, however, to the conclusion that the opportunities were not used, and that, with the exception of the city centre and the government district around Lake Burley Griffin, Canberra became a bungalow-suburban type of city like the rest of Australia's cities.

Pryor in his investigation of the residential population of Belconnen cast doubts on the validity of the neighbourhood planning principle employed (in: Burnley et al. 1980). He came to the conclusion that many residents made contacts in the form of social relations and membership in clubs and organizations outside their own neighbourhood and even outside their suburb. The reasons for such behaviour are that approximately half the population had lived in other parts of Canberra or in Queanbeyan before moving to Belconnen, that work-related friendship patterns made for ties to other parts of Canberra, and that a high degree of private car ownership and improved bus services were favourable for maintaining such relationships.

On the other hand, journey-to-work trips have been increased by trends in NCDC policies towards a degree of *decentralization of employment*. Office blocks were constructed in both Woden-Weston Creek and Belconnen to accommodate various government departments, this dispersion necessitating numerous interdepartmental business trips by car. In addition to the 83% of employed residents using their own car for their daily journey to work, the Australian Capital Territory Internal Omnibus Network (ACTION) transported some 23 million passengers in 1983–84.

Administratively, the A.C.T. stands out as an anomaly in Australian local government. It is interesting to note that in a 1978 *referendum* almost two-thirds of the votes cast in the Territory were against the proposed introduction of self-government. Opponents feared the inefficiency and possible corruption of a municipal government and a possible reduction in Commonwealth funding of the A.C.T. (Kanaley & Kanaley 1974, Saunders in: Williams 1984). The promoters of self-government did not give up, however. In 1981 a Committee for Self-Government was constituted and a 'Canberra Tea Party' arranged, by analogy with the Boston Tea Party of 1773. In 1982 the Commonwealth Grants Commission started its inquiry into the financial situation of the A.C.T., and in the same year a Commonwealth Government's investigation of the functions and powers of the NCDC commenced. The three major points of concern are the bureaucratic form of the NCDC, a desire for greater flexibility in political decision-making, and the call for direct representation of business interests in the planning process. Suggestions have been made in this context that 'any restructuring of the ACT planning machinery should take account of the likelihood of some form of self-government in Canberra in the near future' (Saunders in: Williams 1984, 63).

The *recession* of the late 1970s brought major changes in the urban planning of Canberra. The population of the capital at the 1981 census was some 80,000 persons below earlier estimates, and annual growth rates were down to 3%. The unemployment rate had risen from 1% in the 1960s to 5.3% (1981). This was a percentage comparable with that of Sydney or Melbourne, but had tended to escape notice because of the overall higher income level of Canberra's population. Immediate impacts on urban planning were that the large-scale developments of Tuggeranong in the south and of Gungahlin in the northeast were reduced to the completion of the neighbourhoods already commenced, and that negotiations concerning an eventual northward extension of the A.C.T. boundary into New South Wales were abandoned.

In the face of sharply declining growth rates the NCDC has since 1980 made attempts to adjust the strategic plan for Canberra and the A.C.T. to the changing circumstances. Certain basic principles of the Y-Plan have been confirmed and will be adhered to:

'The role of the City as the National Capital remains paramount. The National Capital role demands that national functions are located in a prominent position where they may operate effectively and efficiently ..

The metropolitan growth of Canberra is based on the development of separate urban districts or towns, in a linear arrangement in the form of a "Y". Each town is intended to be relatively self-contained and provide for most of the needs of its residents including employment, retail, community facilities, leisure and recreation ...

The hierarchy of centres will be maintained, with each town having a centre acting as a focal point for higher order retail functions, commercial services, offices and community facilities ...

Large volume vehicular traffic is carried on a peripheral parkway system, reducing the amount of traffic on the internal systems of the towns ...

Industrial estates will continue to be located on the edge of the urban areas in locations which conveniently serve the workforce of the towns and have good accessibility for long-distance freight movements.

The hills and ridges within and around the urban areas of Canberra will be kept largely free of urban development both to act as a backdrop and setting for the City and also to provide a means of separating and defining the towns ...' (Nat. Capital Dev. Comm. 1984, 176).

On the basis of these principles two alternatives for future development have been proposed, these two plans being labelled the 'Concentrated Plan' and the 'Dispersed Plan'. While the former plan aims at a relatively higher concentration of work places and retail activities in the Central Area (35,000 or 18.9% of total employment) and lower proportions in the satellite towns such as Tuggeranong (2,000 = 1.1%) and Gungahlin (1,800 = 1.0%), the Dispersed Plan aims at the opposite goal, which means a lower concentration in the Central Area (25,000 = 13.5%) and relatively higher proportions in Tuggeranong (18,700 = 10.1%), Gungahlin (9,000 = 4.8%) and the other satellites. Because of certain advantages such as lower costs for implementation, the Dispersed Plan is given preference to the Concentrated Plan (Nat. Capital Dev. Comm. 1984, 116–117, 167).

Apart from these trends, continuous internal migration of younger families to the new neighbourhoods of Belconnen and Tuggeranong has occurred, a movement making for increasing proportions of elderly people and lower-income groups in the central city and the older suburbs. This increasing segregation of persons is underlined by an increasingly segregated housing stock. Although in terms of social segregation Canberra no longer differs from the patterns observed in the state capitals, the distribution of ethnic minorities has always been more even over the whole area of the Canberra MUA than has been the case in the state capitals.

Owing to its peculiar employment situation, Canberra shows considerable *deviations from the Australian average* (given below in brackets) with regard to certain demographic and social data. Since Canberra's population is younger than average, it is characterized by a higher birth rate of 19.4 (15.8) per thousand and a lower death rate of 4.4 (7.6) per thousand. However, the age group above 65 years is increasing, so that during the decade 1973–83 the number of persons of pensionable age increased from 3,313 to 8,842. 48.8 (45.6) % of the residents are in active employment. Average weekly earnings in September–October 1983 amounted to $ 343.50 ($ 306.90) while the household income per head of mean population in 1982 was $ 9,010 ($ 7,486). Private-car ownership in the capital city is slightly below the Australian average, the ratio being one car to 2.2 persons (1 : 1.9) (ABS 1984).

Any description of Australia's capital would be incomplete without mentioning two specific areas. Since Canberra is an inland city, and could not possibly satisfy the demand for a port serving as base for the Australian Navy, an area of 73 square kilometres around *Jervis Bay* on the Pacific Ocean was in 1915 ceded by New South Wales to the Commonwealth as a constituent part of the A.C.T. There are large naval installations in this part of the Territory.

The second area deserving special mention is the *City of Queanbeyan*, just beyond the eastern border of the A.C.T. in New South Wales. Named for an old sqatting place, 'Quinbean' meaning 'clear water', the place became a township in 1838 and a city in 1972. Fischer (1984) called it the 'ugly face of Dorian Gray' for its major function in the twentieth century has been to keep features regarded as *undesirable* away from the A.C.T. Thus manufacturing industries that were not wanted in Canberra went to the relatively old town of Queanbeyan, which was also used to house a great portion of Canberra's construction workers and to provide building materials for the capital city. Queanbeyan provided comparatively cheap dwelling units for those who could not afford Canberra's higher priced accommodations; it also offered corner stores, gambling machines, brothels, neon signs and similar features banned from the capital city.

Queanbeyan was thus more or less dependent upon Canberra's changing attitudes toward such features, a relationship inducing King to speak of a 'Canberra-Queanbeyan symbiosis' (1954). For example, after alcohol had been permitted in Canberra in 1933, a considerable proportion of the daily commuter traffic to Queanbeyan's bars and hotels stopped, aggravating the economic consequences of the Depression in town. In 1972 poker machines were legalized in the A.C.T., so that Canberra residents no longer needed to cross the border for gambling.

On the other hand, Queanbeyan had less severe zoning regulations than in the A.C.T., lower land prices and an older housing stock. It has quite a number of buildings that are today classified by the National Trust, offering accommodations for second-hand shops, antique shops, galleries, historic restaurants and the like. 'Queanbeyan is consequently a wild patch-work of decaying 19th century houses with rusting corrugated iron roofs and weedy gardens, mixed with 20th century flats and bungalows of different styles, with garages and sheds, corner stores, supermarkets and hotels, all chaotically set between potholed roads and a dense mesh of wires and poles and signposts — all the Australian ugliness censored away from the capital and condensed within little more than three street grids' (Fischer 1984, 152).

Queanbeyan has nevertheless had its share of post-war economic and population growth: its present population exceeds the 20,000 mark.

To sum up, Australia's federal capital has been an exciting experiment in new-town planning. There have been four periods of planning in Canberra, the first from 1913 to 1920 with W.B. Griffin as the director of planning and construction, the second from 1921 to 1930 with two consecutive commissions being in charge of planning, administration and maintenance, the third from 1931 to 1958 with various Commonwealth Departments developing Canberra, and the fourth commencing in 1958 with the NCDC in charge of planning. Immediately after Griffin's resignation some major changes were made, leading to important deviations from the original plan. Decisive measures taken in the mid-1950s led to Canberra's development as a true national capital. At this period, the 'Future Canberra' plan of 1965 and 'Tomorrow's Canberra' of 1970, in conjunction with three transportation studies, established two decisive planning principles. The first was that Canberra's further growth was to be based on a number of garden suburbs, each endowed with a Town Centre and a hierarchical structure of neighbourhood groups and individual neighbourhoods, with corresponding shopping facilities. The second was the abandonment of the radial-concentric urban form in favour of a linear-type city, with the basic pattern of three corridors arranged in the form of a 'Y'; the plan of 1970 is also known as the 'Y-Plan'. All the land of the A.C.T. is now in leasehold tenure, and most of the housing stock built prior to 1960 is government housing. These factors have contributed to the rather even distribution of overseas immigrants, but could not prevent Canberra from developing some degree of social segregation. The vast majority of the workforce is in government and other service functions, manufacturing industries are very few and limited to four small industrial zones and to the neighbouring City of Queanbeyan.

3.2 The City of the Gold Coast in Queensland

The Gold Coast, as an urban development largely based on post-war resort tourism, offers a relatively new facet of Australian urbanization. The City of the Gold Coast holds rank nine in the list of Australia's urban places, with a population that increased from 74,240 persons in 1971 to 154,663 persons in 1981. During the intercensal period 1976–81, the average annual growth rate was 9.2%.

The Gold Coast stretches for approximately 45 km along the southern coast of Queensland between Paradise Point and Coolangatta/Tweed Heads at the Queensland-New South Wales border; it is part of a still longer resort strip of about 125 km that includes the Sunshine Coast north of Brisbane and the adjacent New South Wales littoral to the south.

The natural setting, as well as the built environment, show a certain *resemblance to Miami Beach* in Florida; even the place names given to some localities, such as Miami Keys, Palm Beach or Key Biscayne, suggest comparisons with its Florida counterpart. Just like in Miami Beach, *high-rise buildings* with numerous rooms and apartments offering ocean views border the ocean front, while behind the coast drainage schemes along the Nerang River have created a large number of *canal estates*, with detached houses surrounded by good-sized gardens (fig. 86).

Most of the construction activity has taken place since World War II. At the end of the nineteenth century there were two small settlements: Southport (1874) and Coolangatta (1883). In 1876 a ferry was established over the Nerang River at Elston, which in 1933 adopted the name Surfers Paradise. In 1886 a railway line was built from Beenleigh to Southport, making the place a fashionable resort. By 1933 the total population of the coastal settlements of the area was a mere 6,600 persons; most of Moreton Shire was still in forestry, dairying and sugar cane growing. In 1948, 18 townships, the most important of which were Tweed Heads, Coolangatta, Burleigh Heads, Surfers Paradise and Southport, formed the Town of South Coast. The municipality of the City of the Gold Coast was established in 1959, seven years after the large-scale sale of coastal building plots had started in the area.

Of the permanent residents of the Gold Coast in 1981, approximately 54% had migrated during the past five-year period, 49% had come from New South Wales and the A.C.T., 38% from Victoria and 36% from other places in Queensland. 14% were overseas immigrants.

Looking at the kind of people moving to and living in the City of the Gold Coast, we may be surprised to find *only 14% to be 65 years and older*. This means that only 4% more residents are in the retirement age as compared with Brisbane. This finding is in contradiction to the statement made in the literature on the Gold Coast (Hugo 1979, Burnley 1982) that there is a great deal of interstate migration of retired people into Queensland, this state being the only one to have discontinued the levying of death duties. It was not, as assumed, a great influx of interstate retired people that made for the rapid growth of the Gold Coast. Nor was there any decisive involvement of the

Fig. 86. City of the Gold Coast, Qld. Aerial view of residential development of canal estates along the Nerang River between Surfers Paradise and Broadbeach (reproduced with the permission of Australian Aerial Mapping (Qld.) Pty. Ltd., Surveying and Mapping Consultants, Brisbane)

public sector in construction; over 90% of investments into the built environment have come from the private sector. The proportion of investment has changed very much in favour of flats, mainly condominiums; investments in houses decreased from 52% to 31% during the decade 1970–71 to 1979–80.

Local authorities and the Queensland Government were of some assistance, but the major development was due to the 'innovative flair and frontier spirit of petty bourgeoisie and small capitalists' (Mullins 1984, 35). This is reflected in the data on social status: only 76% of the economically active population in 1981 were wage and salary earners, as compared with 89% in Brisbane. The *self-employed* made up 13%, and 9% were employers working alongside with their employees. Many of them came from the southern states, where they had made money in various businesses. Mullins (1984) gave some examples of such entrepreneurs. Korman, a branch of Chevron Queensland Ltd., had been in the textile business in Melbourne and invested money into the Chevron Hotel. Bruce Small Enterprises had been in bicycle manufacturing in Melbourne and invested into land and canal development in the Gold Coast. They arrived in the late 1950s, and many other small enterprises followed them.

In 1974, 1,406 hectares of canal estates had been occupied and another 1,061 hectares were approved at Southport, Surfers Paradise and West Burleigh. On the waterfront 13 high-rise apartment buildings valued at over $ 42 million were constructed in the early 1970s. In 1974 the Surfers Paradise Hotel opened in 1925 was pulled down and replaced by a $ 32 million 33-storey hotel and shopping complex. In 1977 the 36-storey Golden Gate Hotel was opened, and a 46-storey building approved 'making the summer sun disappear in parts of the beach by 3 p.m.' (Fitzgerald 1984, 474).

By 1980 the number of tourists visiting the Gold Coast annually reached the two million mark, the peak holiday population in July reaching 350 000. Approximately 50% of the tourists came from nearby Brisbane, another 45% from other parts of Australia. Only 5% were international tourists; 80% of all tourists arrived by car.

The major purpose of visiting the Gold Coast is pleasure, *hedonism* is its raison d'être. Beside the sun and the surf, there is much more to enjoy here. In Surfers Paradise the great *Paradise Centre*, with its huge amusement and restaurant areas and its giant water slide, is supplemented by a shopping mall and a great number of shopping arcades. A big $ 175 million hotel-convention complex with a casino, the fourth largest in Australia after Darwin, Alice Springs and Hobart, was opened recently. 'Condominiums (home units), canal estates (of detached houses), shops, restaurants, amusement centres, and related infrastructure, contrast sharply with the built environments of other Australian cities' (Mullins 1984, 31).

Also, a large amusement park called Dreamworld was created where visitors can enjoy, have snacks and buy souvenirs in an historical Australian environment, where they can ride the Cannonball Express or an old paddlesteamer on the Murrissippi River.

In order to give this vacation land good access a four-lane highway to Brisbane was constructed and after the railway had been dismantled in 1964, plans were made to link the Gold Coast to Brisbane by an electrified suburban railway line.

In the early post-war years much *American capital* was invested into the building stock of the Gold Coast; in the 1980s major investors have been some Arab states, HongKong and Singapore. The Foreign Investment Review Board intervened when a Singapore entrepreneur wanted to purchase the Merrimac Estate, but gave approval when an Australian company and the Singapore-based Robina Land Corporation shared investments in equal partnership.

This rapid development was not without problems, certain weaknesses of the natural environment being aggravated by human intervention. Some destruction of the sand dunes had already been reported at the end of the nineteenth century. At the end of the 1930s developers started dredging the Nerang River and pumping large quantities of sand into the mangrove areas behind the beach. About this time also sand mining for rutile and zircon commenced. The low-lying nature of the sandy terrain made parts of it prone to *flooding* and caused difficulties in the operation of public utilities, such as drainage, sewerage and water supply. In an *area prone to cyclones and high tides*, sand mining increased beach erosion; the recession of the coastline since about 1920 has been estimated at 1.2 m per annum. The rapid accumulation of dwelling units and insufficient infrastructural provision initiated water pollution.

Heavy cyclonic activities in 1967 threatened the further development of the Gold Coast. Approximately 200 businesses failed during the one year, and tourism dropped by more than 30%. In 1974 the highest tide for 35 years hit the Gold Coast and caused severe damages, parts of the Pacific Highway being washed away. Although a Queensland Beach Protection Authority had been founded in 1968, it mainly concentrated on research and advisory functions, and proved rather ineffective. Dutch engineers of Delft Hydraulics Institute were appointed consultants by the City Council, but their recommendations were only partly accepted. In the one year 1976 approximately $ 6 million were spent on antierosion schemes, mainly sand replenishment. Coastal instability has been very much worsened by the large-scale redevelopment of the estuaries and wetlands (Fitzgerald 1984, 459–69). The casino was even justified with the argument that it would pay part of the costs of beach restoration (Fitzgerald 1984, 465). The growing number of high-rise buildings was by many people considered unsuitable for this littoral environment, while on the other hand they have been defended by a movement called 'Life-style in the Vertical Environmental Organization' (LIVE).

Additional problems were caused by the high dependence of the Gold Coast on tourism, this making the area's economy prone to *changes of market conditions*. In 1981 the Gold Coast had an unemployment rate of 9%, which was almost twice the rate of Brisbane, which had a rate of 5 %. There was a recession in the early 1980s, and a slump of real estate prices to about two-thirds of the 1980 price level. In 1982 the cost of units ranged from $ 220,000 to $ 270,000; two years later the range was reduced to between $ 130,000 and $ 170,000. Quite a number of units remained unsold and 3,500 units changed hands within one year (Business Rev. Weekly, vol. 6 no. 47, Nov. 24–30, 1984). By 1985 the real-estate market of the Gold Coast had more or less recovered and a considerable quantity of Japanese and United States capital was again attracted to the City of the Gold Coast.

3.3 Seaports other than the capital cities; important inland towns

This chapter is devoted to a few very important cities within the range between 15,000 and 250,000 residents which are not discussed elsewhere in the book. It is evident that in this group of urban places quite a few are coastal settlements which, like the port-capitals, owe their existence and growth to their port facilities and to mineral resources found in their hinterlands which they export or process. Newcastle will be discussed within the context of the Newcastle-Maitland-Cessnock triangle on the lower Hunter River while Wollongong will be treated within the context of the Wollongong-Port Kembla-Shellharbour-Lake Illawara region. Both these urban areas may be considered the northern and southern parts of the large Sydney-Newcastle-Wollongong urbanized area, or Central New South Wales conurbation. The iron triangle of Whyalla-Port Augusta-Port Pirie is of similar economic importance for South Australia. Finally, Geelong in Victoria and Launceston in Tasmania will be considered.

The few large inland towns are either mining towns such as Ballarat in Victoria, Broken Hill in New South Wales, Kalgoorlie-Boulder in Western Australia and Mount Isa in Queensland, or service and communications centres such as Maitland and Wagga Wagga in New South Wales, Toowoomba in Queensland and Alice Springs in the Northern Territory.

3.3.1 Port and industrial cities

To a considerable extent the story of these urban places is the story of coal mining and steel manufacturing in Australia in general and the story of the *Broken Hill Proprietary Company* (BHP) in particular. It is this company that operates the integrated steel works in Newcastle and Port Kembla and the steel works in Whyalla, while company-owned vessels carry the ores shipped from the ports of Derby, Port Hedland and Kwinana on the coast of Western Australia, as well as the ores from Whyalla's hinterland, to Port Kembla and Newcastle.

As mentioned in chapter 2.2.1 King's Town, which later became known as **Newcastle**, was established from Sydney in 1804 as a penal settlement. The penal function was abandoned in 1823 in favour of Port Macquarie after Governor Macquarie in 1819 had ordered the Hunter Valley to be opened for settlement. Thus the frontier in early New South Wales moved rapidly northward in search of both coal and new agricultural land.

Newcastle has developed through the growing together of various separate colliery sites. The town's first major incentive for growth was its rail link with the Maitland coalfield, enabling Newcastle to function as a coaling station for an ever increasing number of coastal and overseas cargo ships. In 1889 a bridge across the Hawkesbury River was opened, diverting some of the trade of Newcastle's hinterland to Sydney, but by that time Newcastle had grown strong enough to resist this competition successfully (Rimmer 1967). Due to the former coal-mining operations within the confines of the present urban area, much land had to be kept free from housing construction because of the danger of soil subsidence. Land-use statistics reveal that approximately 50% of the urban area is open land (Lamping 1985).

The next major incentive was the opening of the steelworks in 1915. Newcastle, however, has not completely dominated its region, although its population of 258,956 (1981) by far outnumbers the other two cities in the lower Hunter Valley, **Maitland** (38,863) and **Cessnock** (16,916). There are important employment linkages among these centres as well as smaller settlements of the region; for example, some of the displaced miners of the colliery towns around Cessnock and residents from Cessnock and Maitland have become commuters to Newcastle. There is also quite a dispersal of retail trade in the region to the effect that, for instance, residents from the town of Kurri Kurri most often look for medical attention in Newcastle, for optical services in Maitland and for legal advice in Cessnock. Coalfield shoppers buy their furniture to some extent in Newcastle, but also in Maitland and in Cessnock. While this is not a strict 'dispersed city' pattern in terms of Burton's hypothesis, it is a somewhat modified version of a dispersed city with Newcastle playing the leading part and very complex employment linkages and retail connections (Daly 1968).

Maitland developed as a port town on the lower Hunter River from three distinct nuclei, the first settlement being located at the junction of the Hunter River and Wallis Creek, the second, which later became known as Morpeth, at the head of navigation for larger sailing vessels somewhat further downstream, and the third as the government town (East Maitland) between the two, situated somewhat remote from the river since the flat parts have always been prone to flooding. A severe flood in 1955 even led to serious consideration of re-siting the city. It has, for a long time, spread away from the valley floor toward the higher elevations.

Newcastle became known as a steel-producing centre and export harbour with the BHP central research laboratories, an integrated steel works including a wire mill and wire ropery, a stainless-steel and special-steel plant, and a tungsten-carbide and mining-products plant with a combined workforce in the order of 10,000 (1979) and 7,000 (1983) employees (Fagan in: Taylor 1984). It does, however, not seem quite justified to stick to Newcastle's nickname of 'Australia's industrial capital'. The industrial zone, though it is quite large, stretches along the Hunter River in the northernmost part, but rail and maritime trade have become an increasingly important element of the city's economic base. Its present economic functions are thus quite diversified, and with regard to its urban morphology the industrial zone is but a minor fraction of the total urban area, the greater part of which consists of suburban residential areas, some of which are enjoying the scenic beauty of Lake Macquarie. The major growth of the built-up area is toward the south and away from the industrial zone in the north (Golledge 1962).

South of Sydney settlement also owed its beginning to coal mining; coal was first discovered in the Illawara region in 1797. During the nineteenth century a number of small mining towns developed, for which **Wollongong** became the major administrative and service centre. Major port and industrial activities developed in nearby Port Kembla.

The original iron and steel plant was the Hoskins Works in Lithgow in the Blue Mountains to the west of Sydney; it was closed because of low profitability and competition from the BHP works in Newcastle. A new consortium of Australian and British steel interests under the name of Australian Iron and Steel Ltd. (AIS) opened a new plant in **Port Kembla** in 1928, this location enabling the steel works to make use of the better quality coaking-coal from the nearby Bulli mines as well as the iron ore from the rich Middleback Range in South Australia (Fehling 1977). Other advantages were the large space available, enabling Port Kembla to develop a huge industrial zone including the rolling mills of BHP and a great fertilizer plant, as well as its favourable location with regard to the Sydney market and overseas trade links (Britton 1962). When during the depression years AIS got in trouble, the Port Kembla works were taken over by BHP.

There had been two earlier stages in the development of Port Kembla. Before 1895 there had just been a jetty for shipping coal worked in the Illawara region by the Southern Coal Company. The first incentive to growth on the basis of secondary industry then came from the establishment in 1907 of the Electrolytic Refining and Smelting Works (ERSW), with the goal of eventually processing all the copper produced in Australia. The site was selected because of proximity to the coal needed in the smelting process, proximity to the Sydney market, the availability of cheap flat land in proximity to a place that could be easily developed into a safe deep-sea harbour, and a central position in relation to the copper mines producing at that time in New South Wales, Queensland, South Australia and Tasmania (Crago & Laundes 1931).

When during World War I a need was felt to produce a range of finished copper products, ERSW founded the Metal Manufacturers Ltd. as a subsidiary. Australian Fertilizers Pty Ltd. was another subsidiary, using surplus sulphuric acid for the production of superphosphate. Other plants include the Ulladulla Silica and Fire Bricks Company Ltd., producing fire bricks for blast furnaces, and a lime and cement works using shells from the rich deposits near Shellharbour. There was thus a sizable industrial complex in existence when the AIS plant was moved to Port Kembla.

In 1983 the Port Kembla Division of BHP employed approximately 14,440 people, about twice as many as the Newcastle Division. Employment in secondary industries in the Wollongong region, that includes Port Kembla, is much more specialized on basic metal products than the more diversified manufacturing industries of the Newcastle region. Greater Wollongong grew from some 4,000 residents in Wollongong township at the turn of the century to 208,601 residents at the 1981 census; over 30% of recent population growth resulted from overseas immigration. Most of the immigrants were housed in planned settlements around the foreshores of Lake Illawara, commuting from there to the factories at Port Kembla. Oak Flats, for example, grew from 20 houses in 1930 to over 5,000 residents in 1970. Most of these settlements, such as Thirroul, Stanwell Park or Lake Illawara, do not only function as dormitory towns for people employed in Port Kembla, but are also recreation centres for holiday makers.

With its steel works at Whyalla, BHP also obtained a foothold in the *iron triangle on Spencer Gulf* in South Australia, comprising the three port cities of Whyalla (29,962 inhabitants in 1981), Port Augusta (15,254) and Port Pirie (14,695). It is apparent from these figures that the combined population of the three port cities does not even amount to one third the size of Wollongong. Moreover, Port Augusta is the only one to show a slight increase of population in recent years, whereas the other two port cities suffered from losses in the intercensal period 1976–81. Whyalla's average annual loss was –2.1%, this population decrease being induced by an erosion of its economic base. Its BHP shipbuilding and engineering works were closed at the end of the 1970s, obviously due to growing competition from the shipbuilding yards in Japan and South Korea, and the BHP workforce dropped from 6,000 to 4,400 persons between 1981 and mid-1983 (Fagan in Taylor 1984). Nevertheless, the three port cities of the iron triangle are, according to Thomson (1955), an exception inasmuch as they became centres of secondary industries outside the metropolitan areas, and in particular outside the industrial concentration of Newcastle-Sydney-Wollongong.

Port Pirie experienced sustained growth, despite the area not being ideal for a harbour and prone to flooding and soil salinization. The initial export trade in wool was followed by the export of wheat and finally, in 1885, the export of ores to which within four years was added the processing of lead. Silver, lead and zinc from the Broken

Hill mines became the base for Port Pirie's secondary industries, to which were later added uranium ores from Radium Hill, some 300 km to the northeast. Coking-coal was imported from Port Kembla, iron and iron ore from Whyalla and zinc from Risdon in Tasmania. An extensive industrial zone developed in the northern part of town, whereas the expansion of residential areas took mainly place to the south and southwest of the city centre.

Port Augusta is located at the far end of Spencer Gulf, and has the disadvantage of a narrow approach to its harbour. In its early days, the port was completely dependent upon wool exports and thus upon the fortunes of sheep raising in its hinterland. When the latter suffered from periods of severe drought in the second half of the nineteenth century, many businesses in town went bankrupt, people left the place, and houses were left vacant and began to dilapidate. The town survived thanks to rail links with Alice Springs, Kalgoorlie and later with Port Pirie. Of particular significance was the decision to make Port Augusta the site of railway workshops, with rails imported from Newcastle and sleepers from Fremantle. Finally, the coal at Leigh Creek became Port Augusta's long-term economic base, with the successive establishment of a large power plant and a steel works.

Whyalla's harbour is an artificial creation. The city owes much of its area to land reclamation from the shallow waters of Spencer Gulf. Whyalla's steel works are based on the hematites of the Middleback Range and on coking-coal imported from New South Wales. Various processing plants have been established, producing condensors and other technical equipment. As already mentioned, shipbuilding has been discontinued.

Geelong (125,269 residents) is located some 70 km southeast of Melbourne. The town had an early start with its favourable entrepot location relative to Victoria's mining districts, but from the mid-1850s shared Melbourne's fate of an unsteady development. The town experienced a long slow decline lasting for almost the remainder of the nineteenth century. It was, however, successful in the long run as a shipping point for wool and, in more recent years, through the processing of bauxite in its large aluminium refinery. Geelong is also a centre for the processing of agricultural products and for automobile manufacturing. Because Port Phillip Bay and the Barwon River function as natural barriers the city's major growth has been to the northwest.

Geelong was named after the Aboriginal word Jillong meaning 'place of a sea bird over the white cliffs'. Had it not been for a sand bar across its natural harbour, it might have become Victoria's capital, but it has nevertheless developed to be the state's second largest city.

Launceston (64,555 residents), situated at the point where the South and North Esk Rivers join to become the Tamar River, is Tasmania's second largest city, with a commanding position on the well populated north coast of the island state. It was founded on strategic grounds at the same time as Hobart on the south coast, and has always been a rival to the latter (see chs. 2.3.1, 3.1.6). The many fine and pretentious public buildings are evidence of the city's ambitions to become Tasmania's capital. This historic building stock, together with the recently established malls in the CBD, make Launceston one of the most attractive cities in Australia. The Cliff Grounds Cataract Gorge and a number of parklands and gardens have helped Launceston in earning the name 'Garden City' of Tasmania. The valleys formed by the river system are a dicisive influence on its urban morphology.

3.3.2 Mining towns of the interior

Some of Australia's inland cities owe their existence to the exploitation of mineral resources, whether currently or in the past. Among the largest mining towns are Ballarat (62,640) in Victoria, Broken Hill (26,913) in New South Wales, Kalgoorlie-Boulder (19,848) in Western Australia and Mount Isa (23,664) in Queensland.

Ballarat was just a little rural township in Victoria's Central Highlands when in 1851 rich alluvial gold deposits were discovered. The population mushroomed to some 40,000 within two years. Ballarat has survived as the service centre of a large agricultural region, with sheep raising and vegetable growing being predominant. It has agricultural-processing industries, such as flour milling and brewing, and also some metal fabrication. Tourism has become a major source of income, the city being attractive for its galleries, antique and craft shops, museums and, above all, nearby Sovereign Hill, which is effectively an open air museum, with its reconstructed gold-mining settlement.

Broken Hill is located 1,170 km west of Sydney, to which city it was linked by rail as late as 1927. Nevertheless, it was at the turn of the century the second largest city in the State of New South Wales, with some 35,000 residents and 65 hotels. In 1883 rich deposits of lead-silver-zinc ores were discovered in the Barrier Range. Exploitation started at Silverton somewhat to the north, where population rose to 3,000 within two years. After mining was discontinued here in 1889 and moved southward to Broken Hill, Silverton became a ghost town, and is today one of the tourist attractions of the area.

The town's water supply in this arid region, with less than 250 mm of precipitation, comes from the Menindee Lakes dam some 100 km to the southeast on the Darling River and, to a smaller extent, from local storage schemes. The development of irrigation agriculture around Menindee is tending to attract some of Broken Hill's service functions to this growing town.

Due to the general unprofitability of mining activities and the termination of some of them, the number of miners employed in Broken Hill decreased from some 8,700 in 1913 to approximately 4,200 in 1976. Total population dropped from 35,000 to 26,913 (1981), and the rural population of the town's hinterland also decreased. Thus the number of potential purchases declined to the point that a number of businesses were forced to close. During the period 1953–78 retail employment in Broken Hill declined from over 1,000 to under 600. During the same period Adelaide, South Australia's capital, which is only 512 km away from Broken Hill, was able to usurp some of the retail trade of durable goods like furniture (Melamid 1980). This trend is very likely to continue, and there are hardly any expectations of the location of secondary industries or of the expansion of tertiary education beyond the existing small mining school. Tourist activity also is likely to be more easily attracted by Menindee.

Kalgoorlie is located in the heart of the Eastern Goldfields of Western Australia, where Paddy Hannan discovered gold in 1893. The miners set up tents on the far side of the so-called Golden Mile in order not to be forced to walk every day from Kalgoorlie, thus initiating the sister-town of Boulder. By 1905 population had reached its maximum of 30,000, and 93 hotels were operating in town. In this arid environment on the margin of the Great Victoria Desert almost 600 km east of Perth, water shortage was such a severe problem that water was considered more precious than gold. The problem was solved in 1903 by a 563 km pipeline from a reservoir on the Helena River south of Perth.

While some gold is still being mined at Kalgoorlie, the recent exploitation of nickel deposits at Kambalda 56 km south of Kalgoorlie, at Laverton 370 km north and at some other points provides a purchasing potential for Kalgoorlie about twice the size of the population of the city proper. Although the Australian government does not favour satellization, whereby miners' families reside in the major centre and employees are brought by air to the small mining towns for three-week periods with one week of leave between terms, 'Kalgoorlie will still benefit from supplying some services to these relatively distant settlements as in the case of Laverton' (Melamid 1980, 58). Thus prospects are somewhat brighter for Kalgoorlie than they are for Broken Hill. During the intercensal period 1976–81 Kalgoorlie had, indeed, a very slight population increase of 0.8 % per annum against a decline by -0.5 % in Broken Hill.

Mount Isa in northwestern Queensland is the youngest of the mining towns dealt with in this chapter. In 1923 a rich silver-lead deposit was discovered on the western edge of the Cloncurry Field, while some time later copper and zinc were also exploited. Finally, uranium was discovered about 50 km east of Mount Isa. Exploitation was due to export restrictions and a temporarily decreasing demand discontinued during the years 1963–76, but uranium ore is now being mined again. Ore trains from Mount Isa carry their freight to Townsville, 900 km distant, for processing and shipment. Mining operations are carried out by the Mount Isa Mining Company.

3.3.3 Inland service and communication centres

The larger inland centres to be discussed in the following section are Wagga Wagga (36,832) in New South Wales, Toowoomba (63,395) in Queensland and Alice Springs (18,395) in the Northern Territory.

After Maitland in New South Wales, that has already been dealt with in the context of the lower Hunter Valley urban region, **Wagga Wagga** is the largest inland city of New South Wales (as long as Albury is treated separately from Wodonga, the latter city being located on the opposite bank of the River Murray in Victoria). Three major factors made for a sustained growth of the city. The first is its favourable location and a sequence of developments as an important transportation node. The settlement was established at a river crossing over the Murrumbidgee. This location on the river was later improved by the rail link to Sydney, which made Wagga Wagga a stop on the line from the east coast via Narrandera to Hay. A further advantage may be seen in the fact that Wagga Wagga is located at an equal distance from the Melbourne and Sydney markets. It is located at the point where the railway connecting the two capital cities crosses the Murrumbidgee River.

A second factor is the great expansion of the city's service hinterland in the automobile era. A third factor is that preference is given by the State Government to Wagga Wagga rather than to Albury which, due to its location on the New South Wales-Victorian border, has only a partial hinterland in the territory of the State of New South Wales (Town Plann. Dept. 1983).

The first grid of streets was laid out on a meander spur, with Church Street still being centre of four churches with their respective congregation halls and denominational schools. From this point the town centre at first expanded to the southwest, but the establishment of the railway station in 1879 began to attract further development to the south, accompanied by a corresponding southward movement of the business district. Suburban development was also mainly directed toward the south, whereas the major industrial zone developed to the east. There are plans for the reclamation of the floodplain in the north and for a future integration of the somewhat isolated site of the Riverina College of Advanced Education. The city grew from some 5,100 residents at the turn of the century to over 15,000 at the end of World War II, and has more than doubled since. It has experienced an average annual growth rate of 2.3 % during the intercensal period 1976–81.

Toowoomba is the largest inland city of Queensland. It is located approximately 140 km west of Brisbane on the rim of the Great Dividing Range as a gateway to the Darling Downs, the 'Granary of Queensland', on a site the Aboriginal name of which had the meaning of 'swamp' and was adopted by the early settlers.

Toowoomba became the administrative and commercial centre of the Darling Downs, these being among the more fertile regions of Australia's interior. It developed into an important centre of secondary industries, related to the production and demands of its agricultural hinterland. There are approximately 130 manufacturing establishments in Toowoomba, including butter and cheese factories, flour-mills, the Darling Downs Co-operative Bacon Association Ltd., tanneries, clothing and shoe factories, saw-mills, engineering and railway workshops and the Toowoomba Foundry. The Wilsonton Industrial Estate has recently been developed on the east side of town near the Toowoomba Airport.

The first settlement was established in 1849, functioning as a staging-post for teamsters. The town was given a generous grid-iron layout, with wide streets and much open space in gardens and parks. Under a special street planting programme, over 3,000 street trees are planted annually. The city is famous for its many beautiful parklands and recreation areas. Aside from a Farmfest, which is a display of farm machinery, the springtime Carnival of Flowers and the Green Week, a four-day gardening education festival in April, are the major annual events. For all these activities Toowoomba became known as Queensland's 'Garden City' (Dept. of Admin. 1981). In the field of tertiary education Toowoomba received an Institute of Advanced Education and, more recently, an External Studies Centre of the Queensland University.

According to the Toowoomba City Council there was a constant increase of population until 1979. The 1981 census, however, revealed a slight annual decline of -0.2% for the intercensal period 1976–81.

Alice Springs, affectionately called 'the Alice' by many Australians, is the second largest city of the Northern Territory and in many respects a unique place. It is located to the north of Heavitree Gap, this being a gap in the Macdonnell Ranges used by the Stuart Highway to Darwin and by the usually dry bed of the Todd River (named after the then South Australian Superintendent of Telegraphs Sir Charles Todd while the settlement proper was named after the superintendent's wife Alice).

This leads directly to the settlement's raison d'être. The South Australian Government, under British pressure for an extension of the overseas telegraph cable that had reached the Indonesian island of Java, was eager to fight the competition of the other colonies and made great efforts toward surveying an overland telegraph route. After three attempts by John Macdowall Stuart during the years 1860–62, and further explorations by W.W. Mills and J. Ross in 1871, the Overland Telegraph was put into operation in 1872. Alice Springs, a few kilometres north of Heavitree Gap, was established as a repeater station (see ch. 3.1.8).

The repeater station remained the only function of the tiny settlement until well into the twentieth century. Supplies had to be brought to the completely isolated settlement by camel trains from Port Augusta, and were extremely expensive. Plans by the South Australian Government for a rail link did not materialize. After the administration of the Northern Territory had been taken over by the Commonwealth Government in 1911 it still took another 18 years before the 'Ghan', a rail line named after the Afghan camel drivers whom it replaced, reached Alice Springs in 1929. This was in turn replaced in the late 1970s by the New Ghan, with a rail bed no longer prone to flooding, while in the context of a bicentennial project the rail line is being extended to Larrimah 185 km south of Katharine, that has so far been the southern rail-head of the line from Darwin. At the time Alice Springs received its rail link to Adelaide, it had approximately 50 residents. Even by the end of World War II its population was under 1,000, so that almost its entire growth has occurred in the post-war period.

The population of Alice Springs grew to 4,668 residents by 1961, 18,395 by 1981 and an estimated 22,000 by mid-1984. The present average annual growth rate is above 6.0%. There are approximately 1,200 military personnel with their dependents and some 2,500 Aborigines in town, plus another 1,000 Aboriginal camp population in the outskirts of Alice Springs. These figures reflect the unusual growth factors at work, the most important of which are briefly mentioned below (fig. 87).

An above-average employment rate of 12% of the workforce in *construction* reflects the rapid growth of the city. Administrative functions of the *Federal Government* and, to a smaller extent, of the Government of the Northern Territory, absorb approximately 40% of the city's workforce. The presence of the Commonwealth Government is also demonstrated by the Department of Defense, upon which approximately 6% of the population depend. The city is the home to various research facilities including arid zone range-land management research by CSIRO and the N.T. Government's Arid Zone Primary Industry Research Institute (Burnley & Parkes in: Parkes, Burnley & Walker 1985). Due to the high proportion of government employees, some of whom are on limited contracts, rental housing is in great demand. Over two-thirds of all dwelling units in town are rented, 31% in the private market and 38% in the state housing market and there is an exceptionally low degree of home ownership (31% in 1976).

Alice Springs on the rail-head from Adelaide functions as a service centre for a vast, albeit very sparsely populated, region about equal in size to Great Britain. This is reflected in the fact that almost 10% of the workforce are in *transport and storage*. Alice Springs is Australia's most centrally located base for the operations of the Flying Doctor Service (fig. 38) and the School of the Air.

Approximately 7% of the workforce are in the *catering and entertainment* sector, this proportion reflecting the part the city has begun to play in the tourist business. Although the Todd River only runs after fresh floods occurring in the wet summer season, the people of Alice Springs hold an annual Henley-on-Todd Regatta, with the boats carried or moved on wheels. There are a number of natural attractions in the Macdonnell Ranges within a day tour's reach from the city. Most important, however, is the famous monolith of Ayers Rock, that was not even mentioned

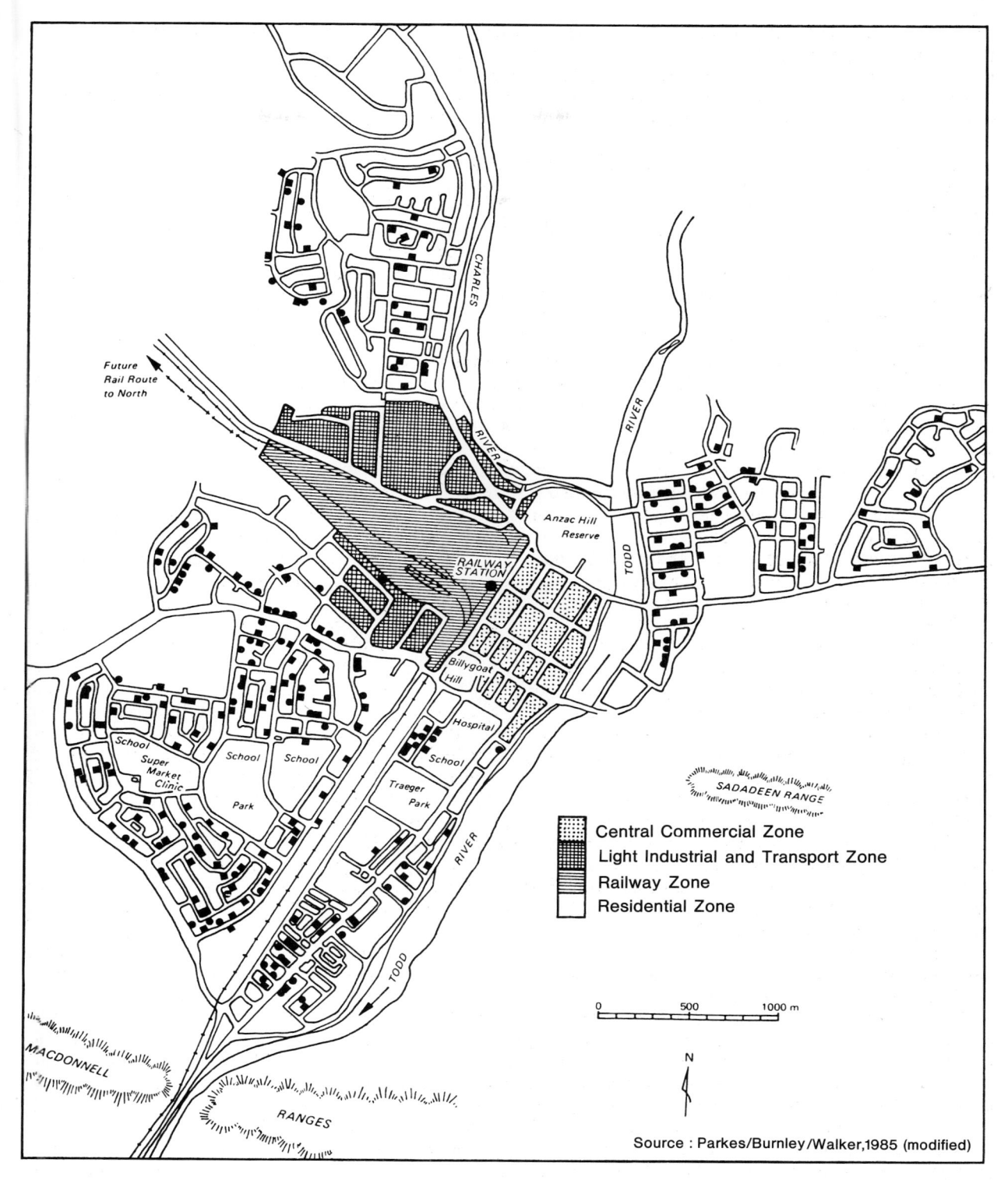

Fig. 87. Alice Springs

in the appropriate volume of the great *Handbuch der Geographischen Wissenschaft* (1930). Today Ayers Rock is, beside the Great Barrier Reef, one of Australia's greatest tourist attractions. Alice Springs serves as the gateway to 'Australia's Red Heart'. A casino was opened around 1980.

The number of Aborigines being attracted to Alice Springs from other places in Australia's north has more than doubled within one decade, and by 1978 reached approximately 3,500. This has not only induced special services and welfare activities, but has also made Alice Springs a centre of Aboriginal arts and crafts. A portion of the fringe dwellers in the squatter camps are there only temporarily; their accommodation causes serious problems. As Drakakis-Smith (1981) pointed out, the predominantly white middle-class of public servants and businessmen grown prosperous through increasing tourism has shown great concern for the city's image, and tried to bar the Aborigines from certain residential areas and types of housing. In many cases there is no other choice for them than one of the Aboriginal camping sites or the hostels run by the Aboriginal Hostels Ltd.

3.4 New towns across Australia

Throughout the twentieth century new towns have been constructed in various parts of Australia in connection with newly developed economic resources. Griffith and Leeton in the Riverina were constructed after 1913 and were supposed to serve as administrative centres for a district along the Murrumbidgee River into which irrigation agriculture had been introduced. Elizabeth to the north of Adelaide and Kwinana New Town to the south of Perth were constructed as satellite or system cities to house the workforce of huge modern industrial estates promoted by the Governments of South Australia and Western Australia in the course of their industrialization and immigration policy after World War II. Paraburdoo, Shay Gap, Newman and a few other towns were established by mining companies after 1960, when the exploitation of the rich iron ore deposits in the Pilbara region of northwestern Western Australia commenced.

The present chapter is a brief outline of the initiation of such developments, the way plans for the new towns were carried out, and how the new towns established at different times for different purposes are functioning today.

3.4.1 New towns in the Murrumbidgee Irrigation Areas

The earliest new towns established in Australia in the twentieth century were the two administrative and service centres designed for the Murrumbidgee Irrigation Areas (MIA) in southwestern New South Wales. Plans for an irrigation scheme in this region date back to 1891. By an Act of Parliament of 1906 the scheme was officially initiated which was finally to comprise some 550,000 hectares of irrigated farm land, 182,000 of which were located in the MIA proper, another 95,000 in the more recently developed Coleambally Area and approximately 270,000 of less intensively irrigated land to the west of the two original irrigation areas.

A prerequisite for the scheme was the *River Murray Waters Agreement* in 1914 between the three States of New South Wales, Victoria and South Australia and the Commonwealth Government, the latter contributing the amount of £1 million to the project. The Burrinjack Dam on the Murrumbidgee, the Blowering Dam on the Tumut, a tributary to the Murrumbidgee, and the Berembed Weir as the major water distributor were constructed. 2,350 km of irrigation channels and 1,391 km of drainage channels were also constructed, the land being surveyed and divided up into horticultural farms of 16 hectares each and mixed farms of between 180 and 200 hectares each, mainly for growing rice, winter cereals and forage crops.

All the construction work was carried out under the auspices of the predecessor to the present Water Resources Commission of New South Wales (WRC), this authority also being in charge of the construction and management of the newly established urban centres. In 1914, one year after the opening of the MIA scheme, the American architect Walter Burley Griffin, who had submitted the prize-winning design for the Australian national capital, was commissioned to design a town that was named after the then Minister for Public Works Arthur Griffith. Griffin was also responsible for the design of the second town in the district, Leeton, which is located about 70 km east of Griffith.

Before going into details of the original town plans and the degree to which they were implemented, three aspects will be briefly discussed: the question of real estate, the administrative responsibilities for the two towns and the influx of people into the district.

As with the farm lands of the environs, town lots in Griffith and Leeton were initially allocated to settlers on a *leasehold* basis. However, in 1924 provision was made by new legislation to enable the purchase of both farm land and town lots on very favourable conditions. Town lots could now be purchased for the equivalent of a 20 years' leasehold rent, to be paid in 39 semi-annual installments. In the Mirrool Area, of which Griffith is the administrative centre, land ownership developed as shown in table 35.

Table 35. Land ownership in the Mirrool Area, 1985

Type of lot	Total number	In leasehold 1985	
		number	%
Irrigation farms	1,800	156	8.7
Urban residential lots	3,000	30	1.0
Urban business lots	400	16	4.0

Source: Personal communication WRC, Griffith Office

It is apparent from the above figures that the number of lots still held in leasehold has become negligable. The reason for some lots still being held in leasehold is that some businessmen and residents prefer to make use of the favourable conditions under which leases have been given to them.

In the period ending in 1928, the predecessor to the present WRC had been in charge of the administration of the two towns and of all the services to be provided for them such as power, water supply, sewerage and road construction. Moreover, the *Commission* also promoted industrial development and operated, among others, a butter factory, a cannery and the abattoirs of Griffith. In 1928 the Wade and Willimbong (the present Leeton) Shires were established, the respective *Shire Councils* assuming most of the Local-Government functions. The butter factory, the cannery and the abattoirs were handed over to newly established co-operatives. The WRC still holds a strong position, however, for it is the Commission that is responsible for all new town extension (Planning Workshop 1976).

In addition to this peculiar administrative arrangement, another distinctive factor as compared with other country towns in New South Wales is the rather high percentage of *Italian-born residents*, particularly in Griffith. While in Leeton only 3.7% of the population are of Italian descent almost one third of Griffith's residents are of Italian origin.

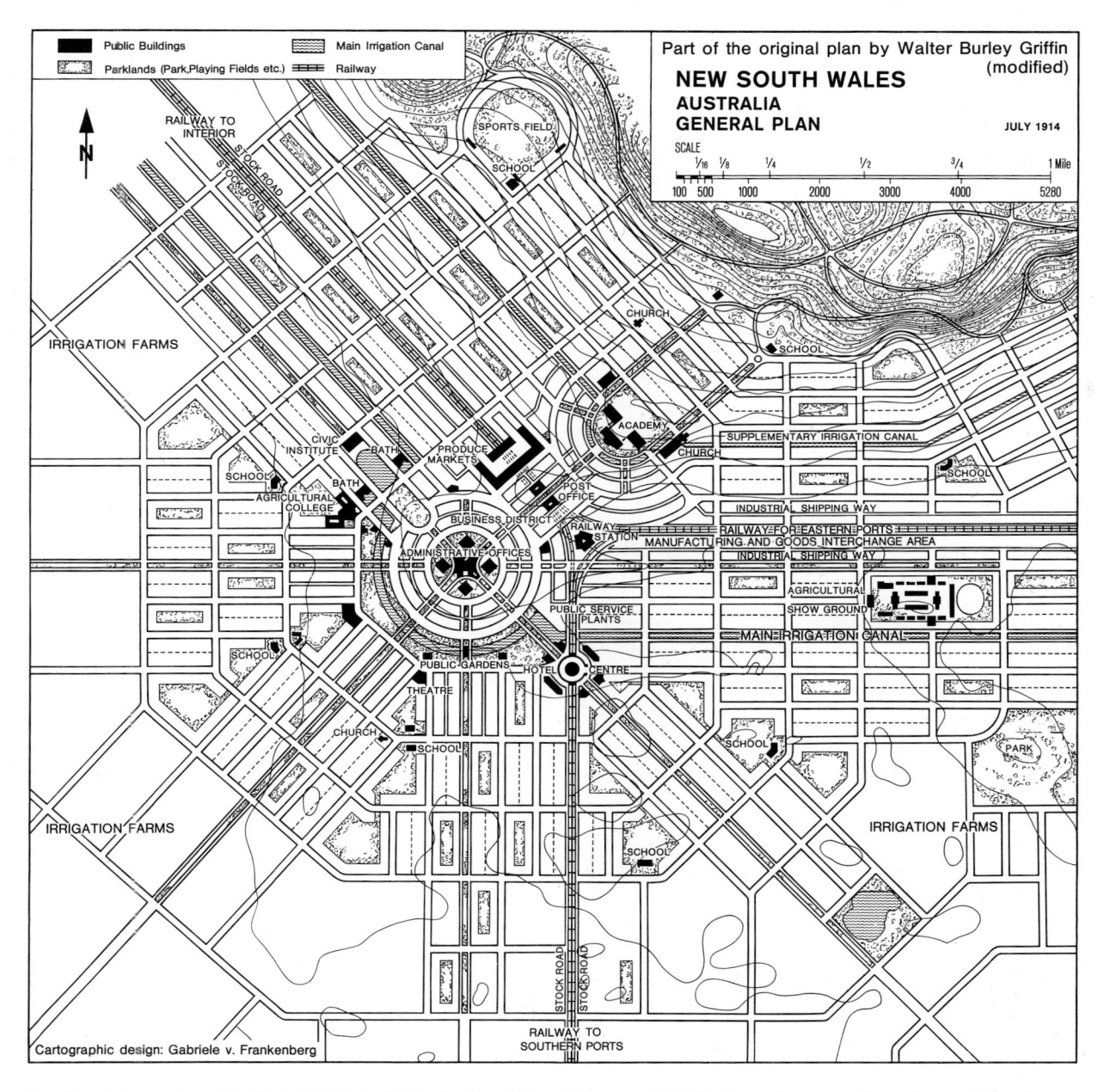

Fig. 88. Original plan of Griffith, N.S.W. by Walter Burley Griffin (Courtesy of N.S.W. Water Resources Commission, Sydney)

This is probably due to the fact that great numbers of Italian workers had been employed in the construction of the main irrigation canal and that many of them, after finishing this construction work, settled down in the area at the end of the canal. At present most of the wineries in the immediate surroundings of the town are owned by Italians, and so are many farms engaged in rice cultivation. The population was 13,185 in 1981.

The original plans of Griffith and Leeton drawn by Walter Burley Griffin reveal certain affinities with the architect's plan of Canberra, with its 'long axial vistas and streets encircling public places' (Collin C. Donges & Assoc. 1982). The *essential elements* of Griffin's plan for *Griffith* were
1   a great circle supposed to serve as the town centre, this being connected by
2   a street axis with
3   a semi-circle a little farther to the north and
4   a few more squares and circular places all of which are roundabouts within the present street system,
5   tree-lined circular streets surrounding the central circle at increasing distances.

In addition, the railway station was supposed to have a central location next to the great circle, and to function as the focal point of three lines leading east to Sydney, northwest to Hillston and south to Melbourne. The main irrigation canal was to mark the town's southern and eastern boundaries, while the railway lines and the main canal were to be bridged by a number of overpasses to easily facilitate traffic flows between the various parts of town and between the town and its surroundings (fig. 88).

In the course of time a number of deviations from Griffin's original plan have occurred. Thus the *railway station* was located approximately one kilometre farther east. The railway line to the south, supposed to give Griffith easy rail access to the seaports of the south coast and to Melbourne in particular, has never been constructed so that there is now just the one line running east-west from Sydney to Hillston. Only *some of the projected overpasses* that were supposed to bridge the tracks and canal have been constructed (fig. 89).

From all these deviations we may conclude that Griffin's geometrical town plan, mainly based on circles and semi-circles, proved to be too rigid. The deviations from his plan had, however, decisive consequences for the town's development. Above all, the location of the railway station farther to the east was a major pull factor for businesses to locate near it rather than in the area of the projected town centre around the great circle. This tendency was underlined by the fact that lots in the vicinity of the railway station were made available to settlers at a rather early stage of town development, whereas the land in the projected town centre was held back until as late as the 1950s. In consequence, Griffith's *business district developed eastward as a ribbon* along Banna Avenue, the town's major direction of further extension being to the northeast of Banna Avenue along a narrow corridor squeezed in between a natural escarpment to the northwest, which is part of a natural reserve, and irrigated horticultural land to the southeast. Further residential or business development toward the northwest is, for the time being, blocked by the airport. Negotiations regarding its relocation are pending (fig. 90).

Since most of the residential quarters had developed to the north of the railway tracks and main canal and most of the industrial enterprises had located in the southeastern section of town *considerable commuter flows* have

Fig. 89. Griffith, N.S.W. Oblique aerial photograph of central part showing the great circle and CBD development along Banna Avenue (reproduced with the permission of N.S.W. Water Resources Commission, Sydney)

Fig. 90. Griffith, N.S.W. Aerial photograph of city and irrigated fields of the environs (reproduced with the permission of N.S.W. Water Resources Commission, Sydney)

developed. These journeys to work cause difficulties because of traffic congestions due to the small number of overpasses available for intraurban traffic circulation. The railway line and main canal function as pronounced barriers.

The projected central area around the great circle and the semi-circle proved rather unattractive for higher ranking functions. With the exception of a few public institutions such as the Shire Offices only lower ranking businesses like light manufacturing, storage, repair and similar uses accumulated in this area.

The Shire Administration has been seriously concerned about these shortcomings and has, with the assistance of outside consultants, taken measures suitable to correct some of the hitherto undesirable trends of the town's development. Much attention will be given to the area originally planned as the *town centre*, which is to be revalorized. Since the business district cannot possibly be relocated, the area around the great circle is to become Griffith's administrative, cultural and educational centre. The fairly recent administration building of the Shire Offices was established on the circle. As a short-term project the construction of a live theatre and of extension buildings for the Technical College were started in the interior of the circle in 1985. The area along the main canal is to be better landscaped than in the past, in order to make the southern margin of the future town centre more attractive. More *overpasses* are to be constructed to ease commuter flows. The relocation of the airport in the northwest is under consideration.

Leeton (6,498 residents in 1981) grew to about half the size of Griffith. The original town plan drawn up by Griffin had an approximately oval shape; all subsequent residential and commercial areas are younger additions not designed by Griffin. Just as in Griffith, the original town plan proved too rigid, as shown by the fact that at one time new master plans were appearing almost every year. Changes to the plan were constantly being proposed and discussed. Some of the proposals aimed at changes of the axes within the grid and at a conversion of the rectilinear street pattern into curved and diagonal streets (fig. 91).

Apart from the problems of layout of the two towns their economic bases are somewhat different, and so are their chances for employment and growth. Griffith's population grew by 2% per annum during the intercensal period 1976–81 whereas Leeton's population declined by an annual rate of 0.7%.

Of Griffith's population 43.5% are gainfully employed. The town's major *employment* is in wholesale and retail trade (25.1%), in public administration and community services (18.6%) and in manufacturing (10.9%), the greatest employers being the Griffith Base Hospital, the Water Resources Commission, the Griffith Shire Council, primary and secondary education, the State Rail Authority and the CSIRO agricultural research facilities. The most important manufacturing plants are related to the agricultural activities in the town's hinterland, including rice milling, citrus juice extraction and poultry production. A number of plants produce agricultural equipment, including grain handling equipment and accessories, sheds, silos and diesel fuel tanks, hydraulic cylinders and other components for agricultural machinery, concrete products such as box water stops and pipe ends for the irrigation schemes.

Leeton's employment rate is 44.2%. The town's major employers are the Letona Cannery with 200 full-time and 600 part-time employees, the rice mills (390 employees), the Water Resources Commission (225), the Department of Agriculture (200), the abattoir (145), the seventy-bed district hospital (140), Leeton Steel Works, the Rice

Fig. 91. Leeton, N.S.W. Oblique aerial photograph of central part (reproduced with the permission of N.S.W. Water Resources Commission, Sydney)

Marketing Board, Leeton Citrus Juices and the Celair air-conditioning manufacturers. As can be seen from this listing, administration and community services are less important employers than in Griffith; Leeton's major industries are more strongly affiliated with agriculture and much less diversified.

In conclusion we may say that despite the rather intensively used agricultural hinterland there was a fair *chance of growth for only one service centre* in the core area of the MIA.

3.4.2 Satellite cities in connection with deep-sea harbours and heavy industries

The first new towns established in post-war Australia owe their existence to government initiatives in promoting *industrial development*, and in providing adequate housing in nearby new settlements for the workforce hired for new industrial enterprises. Two examples will be dealt with in some detail: Elizabeth 27 km north of the centre of Adelaide and Kwinana New Town 32 km to the south of the centre of Perth.

Both new towns were established during the 1950s. In the case of Elizabeth land was purchased by the Housing Trust of South Australia in 1949, and five years later housing construction commenced. In Kwinana the start was the Oil Refinery Industry Act of 1952, by which the Western Australian Government committed itself to the provision of land formerly owned by the Commonwealth Government, and for the facilities necessary for a deep-sea harbour, after the Anglo-Iranian Oil Company had made the decision to relocate from the Persian Gulf to a site on Cockburn Sound. The Government also agreed to provide 1,000 houses for the workforce of the refinery 4 km inland from its site.

Apart from the general desire to promote industry after the experiences of World War II, the establishment of new towns may be regarded a particular *manifestation of decentralization policy*. The establishment of entire new communities was supposed to channel metropolitan overspill. In this respect the two new towns are, however, somewhat different. As Forster (1977) pointed out, the town of Elizabeth was conceived as a *'system city'*, this term more or less being synonymus with satellite city. It was conceived as a self-contained city of a maximum population of 25,000, endowed with work places sufficient for its labour force. Commuting was to be kept at a minimum, and the town was supposed to be highly independent from the parent metropolis.

Perth, on the other hand, had a population of only 322,000 in 1951, and there was no real need for diverting migration from the central city to the suburban ring. Since urban planning had been non-existent in Western Australia, the industrial and housing development of Kwinana gave the incentive for a comprehensive regional planning policy in what was to become the Perth Metropolitan Area.

The site chosen for **Elizabeth** was located near the Town of Salisbury and the existing Commonwealth Weapons Research Establishment, which had been a munitions factory during the war and later began to specialize in spacecraft and rocketry. The second advantage of the site was the partially existing infrastructure, which could be used by or extended to the new community. The town site was located approximately 8 km to the east of Gulf St. Vincent and of Port Adelaide, occupying part of the foothills of the Mt. Lofty Ranges and the adjacent alluvial plain with its interspersed marshy stretches.

The town site is a rectangle approximately 10 km in length and 3 to 4 km wide, stretching in a south-southeast to north-northwest direction along the railway line and highway to Gawler. The town has been planned according to the *neighbourhood principle*, each of the ten neighbourhoods occupying between 120 and 200 hectares of land and containing some thousand homes. The layout provided a Town Centre, two industrial areas to the south and west and the reservation of almost one quarter of the total area of the town as parklands, the latter principle dating back to the layout of Adelaide and the larger number of parkland towns surveyed after 1869 in various parts of Australia (see chs. 2.2.4, 3.1.3). One third of the total area is used for residential purposes. The Housing Trust left about every tenth lot vacant, so that people interested in moving to Elizabeth were not forced to buy or rent their home from the Trust but could build a home of their own. Each neighbourhood was endowed with a little shopping centre of about 20 shops. The street pattern is heterogeneous with a certain predominance of curved roads; the Main North Road cuts the town into two halves and carries all throughtraffic between Adelaide and Gawler (fig. 92).

The overwhelming majority of houses have three bedrooms and are more or less equal in size though different in design. The architects working for the Housing Trust developed more than 50 different house styles and plans, to which the privately built homes may be added (McKnight 1965). There are several 100 appartments in two-storey and three-storey buildings as well as duplexes for rent. The Housing Trust made provisions for land-use control. Lots are sold on condition that the use be restricted to a specified purpose, and that the Trust be entitled to repurchase the lot at cost price if the owner has not commenced the approved development within a given period of time.

The large *Town Centre* of 250 acres is located between the Main North Road and the principal railway station, this being one of the five stops of the South Australian Railways line within the confines of the municipality. It was designed to serve as a major commercial, administrative, cultural and recreational centre. In addition to a greater variety of shops than is found in the neighbourhood centres, the Town Centre contains a court of branch banks, some office buildings, ecclesiastical buildings, a live theatre, a cinema, a hotel, a rollerskating rink and a swimming pool, service stations and motor garages.

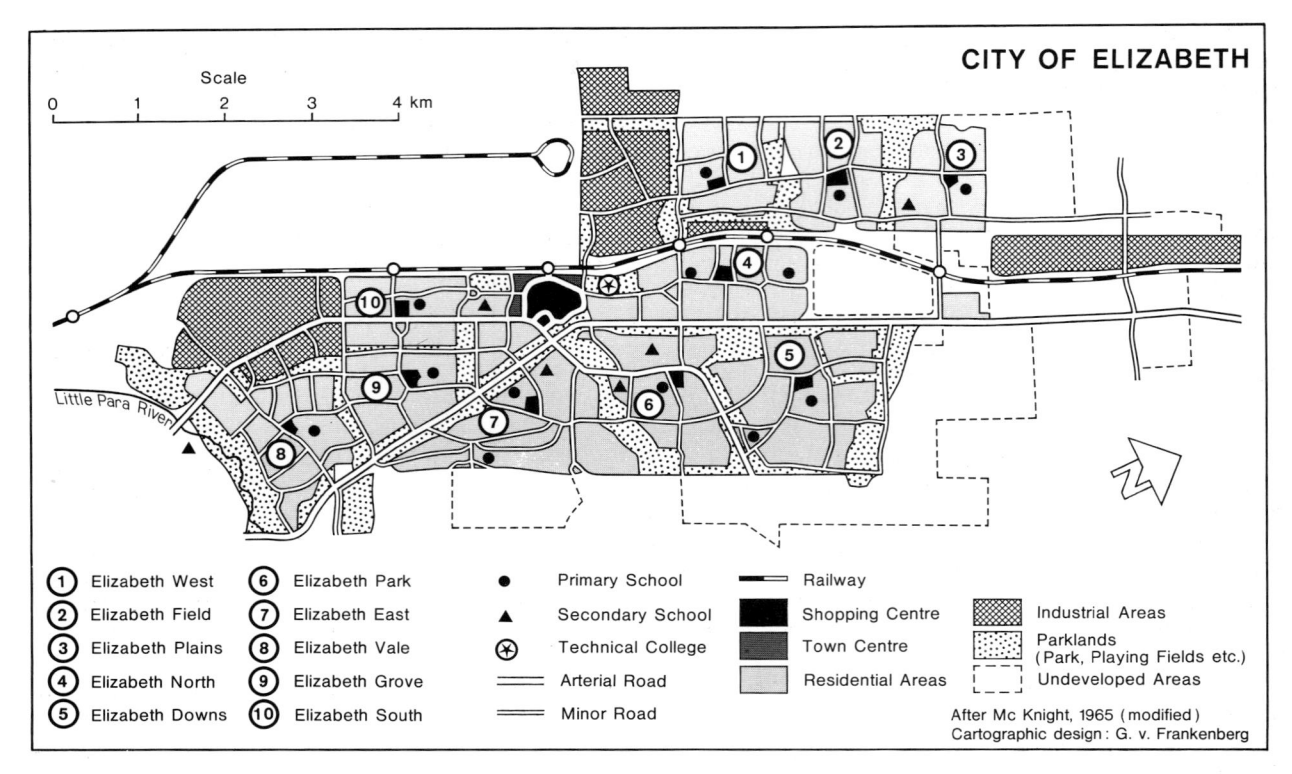

Fig. 92. Design of the new town of Elizabeth, S.A.

The two industrial areas were designed as industrial estates, with buildings provided by the Housing Trust to manufacturing enterprises for sale or lease. In the late 1970s some 20,400 people were employed in Elizabeth. The Weapons Research Establishment employed about 5,000, the newly established branch of GM Holden about 6,000, and approximately 50 firms in the two industrial estates another 5,000. Some 4,400 people were employed in the non-basic sector.

Forster in his detailed study (in: Forster & Stimson 1977) pointed to the fact that Elizabeth's *job ratio* (the number of jobs available per 100 resident workers) was 94.1, which means that there were not quite as many jobs as there were workers, but that the ratio was still very high. However, the ratio for females was only 77.0, so that it is apparent that at least a certain proportion of female workers was forced to look for job opportunities outside the new town. The vast majority of work places available in Elizabeth are *lower-paid jobs*, this being the main reason for the situation in 1976, when no less than 53% of Elizabeth's employed residents commuted to Adelaide or some other municipality within the Adelaide metropolitan area, while on the other hand 50% of Elizabeth's work places were taken by people *commuting* to Elizabeth. Thus the goal of establishing a self-contained satellite city was far from achieved.

For a period after reaching a population of 23,326 at the 1961 census, Elizabeth was the second largest city in the State of South Australia, but was soon surpassed by Whyalla (ch. 3.3). At the 1976 census the new town's population already amounted to 33,721, whereas the original plan at the time of the first land acquisition in 1949 envisaged a maximum population of 25,000. Out of the total of 33,721 residents, 15,272 or *45.3% were overseas immigrants*; 12,831 residents, 38.1% of the total population, were migrants from the United Kingdom and the Republic of Ireland, this extraordinary percentage reflecting the endeavours of the South Australian Government to favour the British Isles in the recruitment of workers for the newly established industries.

Almost half of all dwellings constructed in Elizabeth by 1961 were duplexes (41%) and apartments (5%) and a great number of dwellings were rented. These figures may be considered a symptom of a *certain degree of instability* of the resident population (McKnight 1965). It is also interesting to look at unemployment rates in this context. According to Forster (1983) Elizabeth, in common with other outer working-class suburbs in the Adelaide metropolitan area, has particularly high male unemployment. The rate rose from 5.1% to 14.8% during the intercensal period 1976–81, as compared with a rise from 3.1% to 8.3% for the City of Adelaide. It should be noted that Adelaide's rate in 1981 was the highest of all the capital cities.

Despite such shortcomings, decentralization has continued in the Adelaide metropolitan area. After Elizabeth had been firmly established, the South Australian Government in 1972 chose a site 70 km east of Adelaide near

Murray Bridge as a new growth pole. The place was considered to have a moderate climate, an adequate water supply and a good accessibility. The Mt. Lofty Ranges functioned as kind of green belt apt to prevent the merging of the built-up areas of Adelaide and the new community. On the other hand, **Monarto** would still be close enough to Adelaide to enable business enterprises to maintain close relations with the parent city.

Although finance was provided for Monarto's development the settlement never grew to even the minimum size required to be statistically considered an urban place: at the 1976 census its population was only 264. The place proved to be located too far from Adelaide to be of any use as an alternative residence or industrial satellite for the capital city. When difficulties of funding arose in the negotiations between the Government of South Australia and the Commonwealth Government, the Monarto growth-pole project was discontinued in 1976.

During the 1970s a third project was started some 60 km south of Adelaide. A terminal of the rapid transit system of the Adelaide metropolitan area was established at **Noarlunga**, and a big modern shopping centre opened next to the railway station. Although Noarlunga has also been critized for certain shortcomings (the site of the new town is some 3 km away from the coast), the Noarlunga LGA grew rapidly, population increasing during the intercensal period 1966–71 from 14,214 to 28,464, to reach 47,345 by 1976, representing an average annual growth rate of 10.7%.

The site for **Kwinana New Town**, 32 km south of the Perth city centre, was chosen in accordance with the Western Australian Government's desire to *keep great new industrial developments away* from major population concentrations. This industrial location policy would have meant that the workforce of the industrial enterprises would have been forced to endure long and time-consuming journeys to work. Housing relatively close to the new industrial site was considered essential. In order not to leave this task to private companies (it was envisaged that in addition to the Anglo-Iranian Oil Company a number of other enterprises would be involved in the new industrial development) the Government decided to establish a new town about 4 km inland from the industrial site and the adjacent deep-sea harbour of Kwinana.

The *industrial zone* was to become a large-scale development. As mentioned above it started with the Oil Refinery Industry Act of 1952, which was the basis for the Government's construction of the port facilities and of the Anglo-Iranian Oil Company's relocating its refinery from the Persian Gulf to Cockburn Sound. The second step was the establishment of the BHP steel works in 1956. Since 1951 BHP had the concession for the exploitation of the rich iron ore deposits of the islands of Cockatoo and Koolan in Yampi Sound, off the coast of the Kimberley region. Part of BHP's agreement with the Western Australian Government was a commitment to develop an integrated steel processing plant at Kwinana (Fehling 1977). Thus in 1956 a rolling mill was opened, and in 1968 the first blast-furnace for smelting iron ore brought from Koolyanobbing on the new railway line from Perth to Kalgoorlie and a pelleting plant started operations. In 1963 the Alcoa Alumina Works were established for processing local bauxite. With its capacity of over 1.25 million tons of alumina per annum, it became one of the largest of its kind in the world. The three plants employ more than 3,000 workers. In later years a fertilizer plant, a nickel refinery and a powerstation were added to the complex, and a number of small light-manufacturing enterprises moved to the area. Aside from the bulk cargo handling facilities, the Fremantle Port Authority established a huge grain terminal and storage facility at Kwinana. Thus a major portion of the area of 21.6 square kilometres zoned for industrial enterprises and port facilities has been occupied.

The site of Kwinana New Town was chosen approximately 2.5 km inland from the industrial zone. It is characterized by old dune systems situated between the coastal flats to the west and swamps and bushland to the east. There are thus natural barriers to an unlimited expansion of the community, as well as man-made ones. The coastal flats and swamps inhibit expansion, just as do the industrial land, the railway tracks, the highway to Fremantle and an area to the north that is being used for disposal of caustic waste from the alumina refinery.

Kwinana New Town was planned, as was Elizabeth, on the neighbourhood principle. The lower-lying area between the two older neighbourhoods on the west side was used for the Town Centre and main shopping area and the major access road. The older neighbourhoods are small and had reached a combined population of some 7,000 residents by 1975 whereas the more recent neighbourhoods to the east were planned for 6,500 and 10,000 residents respectively. Land has been acquired for another three neighbourhoods (fig. 93).

There are great differences in the *types of housing*. Most housing in the older neighbourhoods of Medina and Calista is of weatherboard, and of a standard design destined to be rented to manual workers, whereas in a special section brick houses of a higher standard were provided for executives and technicians. A number of three-storey blocks of flats were also constructed. In contrast to Elizabeth, the latter were not in great demand, so that the Department of Community Welfare at a very early date decided to assign vacant flats and houses to so-called problem families from all over the metropolitan area, among them some Aboriginal families. As early as 1970 these two older neighbourhoods had already experienced population losses of up to 15% of their population maximum. There was also some private construction. In the more recent neighbourhoods, developed after a decade of stagnation and after the opening of the alumina refinery and blast-furnace, houses are mainly of brick and of a somewhat higher standard. Thus out of the total building stock of Kwinana New Town only 36% of dwelling units were owned by the State Housing Commission in 1971, whereas 54% were owner-occupied (Houghton 1977). This owner-occupancy rate is much higher than that of Elizabeth.

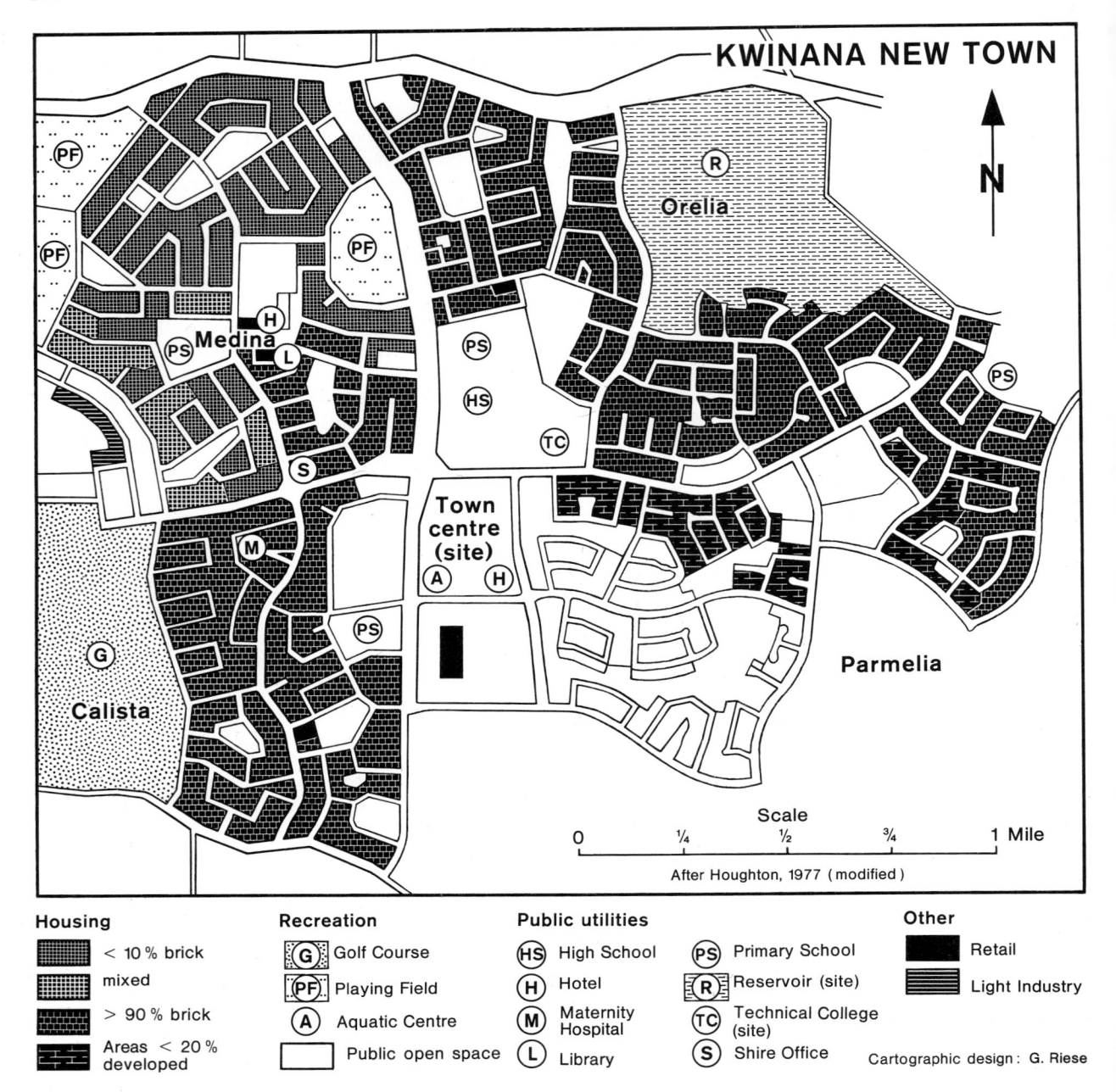

Fig. 93. Design of Kwinana New Town, W.A.

The Town Centre was planned to be much smaller than that in Elizabeth, although an ultimate population of 40,000 was envisaged. By 1975 Kwinana New Town had a senior high school, two banks, four doctors, one dentist, and two women's hair stylists, but not a single optician (there is one in Rockingham), solicitor (three in Rockingham) nor accountant (five in Rockingham). The obvious *lack of educational and entertainment facilities* and some other services, as well as the small number of tertiary employment opportunities, have been two major handicaps for Kwinana's development and the main reason for the *large amount of commuting* to work, many commuters choosing Rockingham or even Spearwood and Fremantle as their places of residence. The increased numbers of commuters to the Kwinana industries contributed to the rather rapid growth of Rockingham in the last decades.

By 1971 only 35% of male employees of the local industries lived in the New Town and another 5% elsewhere in the Shire of Kwinana, whereas 60% were commuters. Among these 23% commuted from Rockingham, 12.3% from Cockburn, 9.2% from the Fremantle area and 15.6% from various other places. A similarly high percentage of Kwinana residents commute to work places outside the New Town and industrial zone of Kwinana. Among them

10.4% commute to Cockburn, 8.7% to Rockingham, 21.0% to Fremantle and even 2.5% to the City of Perth. As we saw in the discussion of Elizabeth there is a marked shortage of jobs for women, so that only 30% of Kwinana's female work force are employed in town.

Just as in Elizabeth many *immigrants from the British Isles* have been employed in Kwinana. Out of a total population of 13,687 in 1976 7,087 or 51.8% were overseas born; 5,690 people or 41.6% had come from the United Kingdom and Eire.

As to administration, Kwinana New Town was first put under the control of a single Commissioner. In 1959 control was transferred to a newly elected Shire Council.

3.4.3 Company towns and open towns in newly developed mining areas

Other new towns have been established in conjunction with recent mining activities, the two most important examples being related to the coal mines in the Bowen Basin of southern Queensland and the iron ore mines in the Pilbara region of Western Australia. The latter will be discussed here in some detail.

Modern mining in the Pilbara commenced after the Federal Government *lifted ore export bans* in 1960. Just before the beginning of World War II, Australia's iron ore reserves within a hundred miles from the coast had been estimated to amount to 260 million tons which would, at the then annual consumption rate, have lasted for only 50 years. After a reassessment in 1959 reserves were estimated to be at least 368 million tons, which induced the Govenment to remove the bans (Heathcote 1975).

Immediately upon this decision *four mining companies* were formed with *Australian and foreign capital* to start the exploration of some of the iron-bearing ranges of the Pilbara: they were Goldsworthy Mining Ltd., Hamersley Iron Pty Ltd., Mt. Newman Mining Co. Pty Ltd. and Cliffs Robe River Iron Associates. The first company was a joint venture of the Consolidated Gold Fields Australia Ltd. of Sydney and two American companies, the Cyprus Mines Corporation of Los Angeles and the Utah Construction and Mining of San Francisco each of them holding one third of the shares. The Mt. Newman Company is owned by three Australian companies (65%), one American company (25%) and one Japanese company (10%). The Hamersley Holdings Ltd., the parent company of Hamersley Iron Ltd., is 64% Australian-owned, while 36% of the shares are held by Kaiser Steel Co. of the United States. The four partners of Cliffs Robe River Associates also represent Australian (40%), American (30%) and Japanese (30%) interests. For exploitation to start it was necessary to *secure foreign markets:* contracts were mainly signed with great Japanese firms.

The Western Australian Government and the mining companies signed *Iron Ore Agreements* in which the companies committed themselves to the construction of new communities, infrastructure and transportation facilities, while the Government offered incentives in form of tax reductions.

The details of the Government's policy with regard to the activities of the mining companies in the Pilbara region are explained by Fagan (in Linge & Rimmer 1971).

Prior to 1960 the area possessed a *very open network* consisting of a few existing gold mining towns such as Marble Bar and Nullagine, a few little old ports such as Cossack and Point Samson and the nearby administrative centre of Roebourne. Superimposed on this was another rather open network of some modern mining towns, new ports with huge iron-ore export facilities and service centres for the companies' employees. Cliffs Robe River Associates constructed the mining town of Pannawonica and linked it by rail with their export facilities at Point Lambert and the nearby company's service town of Wickham. Hamersley constructed the two mining towns of Tom Price and Paraburdoo, linked by rail with the new port of Dampier. Since Dampier on a headlands site was restricted in its growth, the Western Australian Government assisted in developing the neighbouring service centre of Karratha which was, however, an open town from the very beginning. The Mt. Newman Company founded the mining town of Newman; it was linked by rail with the port facilities at Nelson Point on partly reclaimed land in the older port town of Port Hedland. Goldsworthy founded the mining towns of Goldsworthy and Shay Gap and built a railway line to Finucane Island just opposite Port Hedland (fig. 94).

In contrast to Queensland, where the State Government extended an existing railway line to Mount Isa, the Western Australian Government did not get involved in railway construction. The companies engaged in ore exploration in the Pilbara region built their own ports, served by separate and even criss-crossing company-owned railways. The reasons for this situation are that the Government could not afford the high investment needed for all this construction work and that the companies could not agree with each other to share facilities (Aschmann 1979).

Much of the construction of the company towns took place on a trial-and-error basis. Either company staff or architects from outside were employed for the layout of the towns as well as for house design. In the latter case the drafts submitted by architects had to be approved by the company.

At least some of the company towns of the early years reflect the circumstances under which they were constructed, in a very remote area some 1,200 to 1,600 km away from Perth, a few 100 km away from the nearest larger town, in an area with rather *adverse climatic conditions* where threats of cyclones, flooding and extreme heat had to be faced. They were also constructed *within a very short period of time* and with very *little experience* to

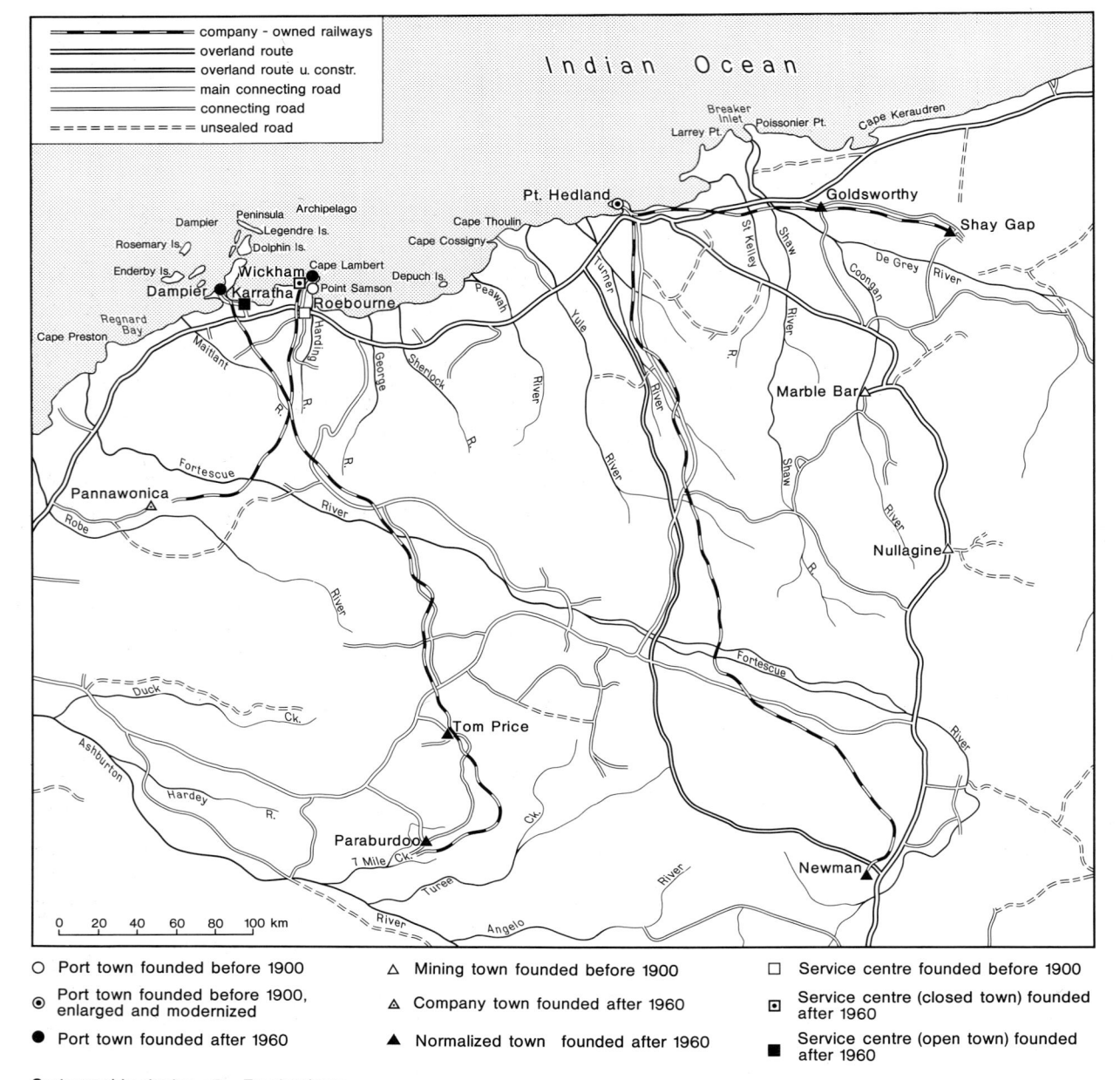

	company - owned railways
	overland route
	overland route u. constr.
	main connecting road
	connecting road
	unsealed road

○	Port town founded before 1900	△	Mining town founded before 1900	□	Service centre founded before 1900
◉	Port town founded before 1900, enlarged and modernized	△	Company town founded after 1960	▣	Service centre (closed town) founded after 1960
●	Port town founded after 1960	▲	Normalized town founded after 1960	■	Service centre (open town) founded after 1960

Cartographic design: G.v. Frankenberg

Fig. 94. Old and new ports, mining towns and service centres in the Pilbara Region of Western Australia

rely on. In some places, such as Goldsworthy the limited amount of ore resources induced the company to establish a *temporary settlement* from the beginning, which meant prefabricated houses and very few and small services and amenities. A caption of a photograph of single men's housing in Goldsworthy reads like this: 'Unshaded, unlovely and probably unloved by their occupants, these demountable units provide acceptable accommodation for men working long hours for substantial pay, especially when many of them do not intend to stay for an extended period' (Aschmann 1979, 13).

The standard layout would be a central area of two larger blocks for a shopping centre, a small library, a primary school, a few administrative functions and some sports activities. Close to this town centre would be located a large block of two-storey tenements serving as single men's quarters. This central area would be surrounded by residential areas of single-family houses of three to four bedrooms, the street pattern usually being a grid.

The town site had to be chosen very carefully. The towns were located *away from the ore body* so as not to interfere with mining activities, so as to be protected from the dust (mainly originating with the blasts in the pit)

Fig. 95. Shay Gap, W.A. Oblique aerial photograph showing the natural setting of the town (reproduced with the permission of Goldsworthy Mining Limited, Perth)

and to be conveniently provided with *fresh water*. In later years even greater efforts were made to find the most suitable town site. For Shay Gap the engineering consultants of Howroyd and Associates in Perth carried out a feasability study over a considerable period of time. In addition to the aspects mentioned above they also took into consideration *aesthetic aspects*. Shay Gap boasts of a beautiful natural setting, the town being located in a bowl encircled by a number of spectacular red ironstone pinnacles which are visible from each house (Fig. 95).

'The town is "walled off" from the inhospitable natural environment by virtue of its location amongst the range of low shade-throwing hills. These will cause an artificial summer sunset by eliminating two hours' sun from summer days. It is also anticipated that the hills will provide protection from the hot east winds and dust. Relief from any possible radiation from the hills will be afforded by the housing groups themselves which create a barrier to the immediate surroundings' (Ellson in: Austr. Nat. Comm. 1976, 269).

The companies and designers learned from experience how to improve town construction. Extensions to existing towns as well as the more recently established towns were constructed in a somewhat different manner. 'South Hedland ... represented the first radical departure in town planning, where Radburn concepts were employed in an attempt to provide a town plan suitable for the tropics and the characteristic population to be accommodated ... Shay Gap was the next major experiment in mining town planning' (Newton in: Lonsdale & Holmes 1981, 174). The grid pattern of streets was abandoned while curved streets and cul-de-sacs were applied to new residential areas. Whereas houses in the central parts of Goldsworthy or Newman had been built of weatherboard and asbestos, more recent houses were built of bricks. The windowless small shopping centre in Newman turning its ugly side and huge air-conditioners toward the outside was in 1985 replaced by a larger and modern shopping centre. The central business area of Paraburdoo was equipped with abundant parking facilities in anticipation of future growth.

Shay Gap, the Goldsworthy Company's second town, was to become a much-discussed modern experiment. All *vehicular traffic was banned* from the residential areas, these being surrounded by a perimeter road linked to car lock-ups for particular groups of houses. The buildings are clustered in *11 so-called precincts*, each of these being equipped with a distributor for water supply, power lines and other utilities, that are hidden in an underground trench system. Air-conditioning and chilled water are provided from a *central cooling station* for the entire town. The few streets needed because of this design, and the centralized cold air and chilled water supply, keep the company's maintenance costs comparatively low. Usually in this climate costs of electricity used for air conditioning are extremely high, but this electricity is free of charge for all company employees, so the advantage to the company of their central installation is obvious. Whether the banning of cars from the residences is appreciated by the people is a different story (fig. 96).

Newton pointed out that designers and architects had contrasting perceptions of the environment. For example Tomlinson claims the desert environment to be very beautiful. 'Consequently, his northern towns of Karratha, Paraburdoo and South Newman are more spread out, have a high proportion of detached houses on their own sites and include considerable uncommitted areas, uses for which are determined by residents as the town matures' (Newton in: Lonsdale & Holmes 1981, 174).

For the geographer it is particularly interesting to find out about how the problem of services to such remote

Fig. 96. Shay Gap, W.A. Houses of one precinct with surrounding hills in the background

and isolated settlements has been solved, given the present standard of living and lifestyle. Almost all supplies are brought in by truck from Perth, over a distance of about 1,500 km; only a few items come from less distant places, for instance some fruit and vegetables from Carnarvon, some fish from Onslow and Point Samson. In the early years many articles were subsidized by the companies. In more recent years subsidization is only indirect, by way of offering favourable rent conditions to shopkeepers and businessmen.

With regard to the provision of goods and services, it must first of all be realized that *not all goods are needed* in company towns. For example, there is hardly any need for furniture, since all houses are fully furnished and equipped by the company, including television sets. There is usually *one major contractor* for the basic retail outlets and services. For example, in the towns of Goldsworthy and Shay Gap the Nationwide Company runs, on behalf of the Goldsworthy Mining Company, a supermarket, a canteen or mess for single men, a travel agency, a dry cleaning shop and a few other shops.

To supplement the rather limited provision there are three complementary institutions in the mining towns. One institution is comparable with a *mail order service.* Thus Cole's of Perth distribute a weekly list of items that may be ordered from this department store chain. The items ordered are sent once a week by truck from Perth to the customers in the company towns.

Then there are the so-called *home occupations*, home industries or cottage industries. These are mainly retail, commercial or even light industrial activities carried out in some resident's living quarters, often by the miners' wives working as agents for all kinds of enterprises, such as car rental businesses, transport enterprises, insurance companies and even local newspapers and radio stations. They may have originated as hobby interests, which have at some later date expanded to a commercial activity, or as a particular person's endeavour to get hold of some good or service not available in town, which gave the incentive for providing this good or service to other residents as well, or simply as a means of additional income for the miner's family.

According to the respective surveys there were 88 home occupations in Newman in 1985 and 81 home occupations in Tom Price in 1982. Of the latter 21% were cosmetics, jewellery and clothing (sales and repair), 15% were toys, gifts, game, hobby, 12% motor vehicle sales, accessories and services, 11% food sales, 9% transport agents and operators including car rental, 7% heavy equipment sales and servicing, 4% electrical and household goods, 4% garden supplies, nurserey and florists, 2% home decorating and furnishing, and 2% accountants and income tax agents.

These home industries are naturally distributed over all the residential areas of the company towns (fig. 97). Since they provide goods and services that would otherwise be unavailable in a particular mining town they must be considered an essential part of the town's shopping system. On the other hand, they may generate excessive vehicular traffic or cause other annoyances for the neighbourhood's residents. As long as the mining companies were in charge of town administration there seem to have been no restrictions as to the establishment of home industries. As soon as some of the mining towns came under Shire administration (which will be dealt with below in greater detail), local authorities faced this problem. However, they found themselves in a difficult position while realizing that in general very little space was available in the rather small Town Centres and, given the rather high operating

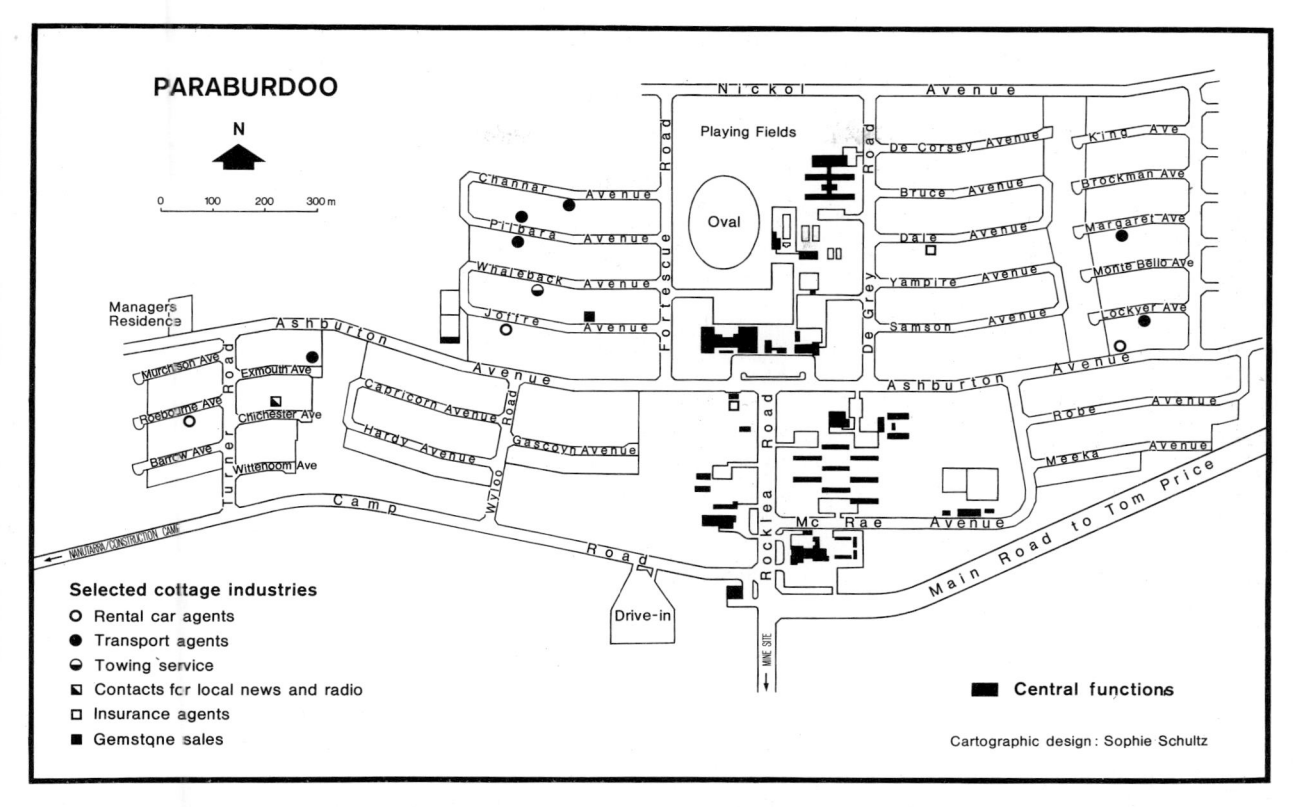

Fig. 97. Cottage industries in Paraburdoo, W.A.

costs, only about 20% of the home industries in Tom Price could have been relocated (Shire of West Pilbara: Town Planning Scheme No. 3, Tom Price).

Finally, there are certain services provided by people having their permanent residences in some other urban place and visiting the company towns *periodically*. Alternatively they may have their residences and place of business in one of the larger company towns, such as Tom Price, while offering their services at specified times in the smaller towns such as Paraburdoo. This holds true for some health services, optometrists and solicitors.

Special mention must be made of *health services* and education. The companies of course maintain ambulances and first aid stations in the mining towns. However, only the larger places such as Newman (5,466 residents in 1981), Tom Price (3,540) and Paraburdoo (2,357) have a little hospital of their own. The smaller ones such as Goldsworthy (923) and Shay Gap (853) only employ a full-time nurse and keep a couple of beds for emergencies. Patients in a serious condition are transferred immediately to the hospital in Port Hedland.

Education is a problem of particular importance, inasmuch as it has a direct bearing on labour fluctuation in the mines. As soon as a particular child reaches the highest grade offered by the local school, the family is confronted with the problem of splitting up and of sending the child to some distant boarding school, which in most cases means Perth. Rather than do this, the family may decide to leave the mines. Consequently, the better the local school system, the later the date of decision between having the child attend school at some distant place or leaving the job and the company and moving the whole family. The highest school types available in 1975 were senior high schools (grades 8 to 12) in Karratha and South Hedland, high schools (grades 8 to 10) in Mt. Newman, district high schools (grades 1 to 10) in Tom Price and Paraburdoo, and primary schools (grades 1 to 7) in Port Hedland, Wickham, Dampier, Goldsworthy, Shay Gap and Pannawonica (Fehling 1977).

The companies are very much interested in attracting families and retaining them as long as possible. Families are considered the more stable element in the workforce as compared with single men, the latter being more likely to make money in a mine for just a limited number of years and then move to some other place and maybe raise a family there.

The companies have made great efforts to retain their employees, by means of *highly subsidized housing, electricity, meals and travel*. Thus the weekly rent for a three-bedroom house was in 1985 as low as $ 26.40, the electricity for air-conditioning and chilled water being provided free of charge for the company employee. Electricity for other purposes is measured separately, with the first 1,300 units also free of charge. Single men pay a weekly amount of $ 40.— for full board, which means room and all meals included, while their weekly income is approximately

$ 600.—. Other benefits are two annual return flights to Perth for the whole family, or the equivalent in cash for a trip by car to Perth, and wages above the general level for the State of Western Australia.

For several years some companies have offered their employees the possibility of buying the house they had rented, by paying annual installments through a *home ownership scheme*. The advantage for the employee is that he would be able to acquire a house of his own that will be worth approximately $ 90,000 for annual payments amounting to just between $ 40,000 and $ 50,000 (prices as of 1985). He would thus pay only half the actual value or, allowing for the inflation rate, less than half the value of the house. The only condition is that on leaving the house must be resold to the company.

It may be surprising to learn that rather few married employees have made use of this possibility. The range is between 8.6 % in Paraburdoo (56 out of a total of 650 houses in 1985) and 24.3 % in Newman (280 out of a total of 1,140 houses). The reason for this low degree of home purchasing is that water and other maintenance costs are extremely high. Whereas the company provides water and air-conditioning free of charge, the home owner would have to pay these high costs on his own account, it is not so much the annual installments but the high maintenance costs that keep families from buying a home. Under such circumstances irrigating one's garden would become a luxury. It can be observed that in some cases home buyers have already converted their lawns to low-maintenance gardens by planting shrubs and covering the rest of the garden with woodchips.

This question of the relationship between the company and the employee leads to a very critical issue, usually referred to as 'opening up' or 'normalization' of the company town. Company towns are 'closed towns' inasmuch, as they are founded, maintained and controlled by the respective mining company. Thus *normalization* means the conveyance of the town's administrative responsibilities to some constitutional Local Authority, which is usually the nearest Shire Office. Apart from this administrative aspect, normalization also means a certain reversal of trends of the population and the housing market toward lower percentages of single men in favour of married employees, from higher to lower percentages of overseas immigrants in the workforce and from higher to lower percentages of rental housing in favour of home ownership.

Fig. 98. Newman, W.A. Aerial photograph of town and the Mt. Whaleback mine (reproduced with the permission of Mt. Newman Mining Co. Pty. Limited, Nelson Point, Port Hedland)

Fig. 99. Port Hedland's population growth, 1961–85

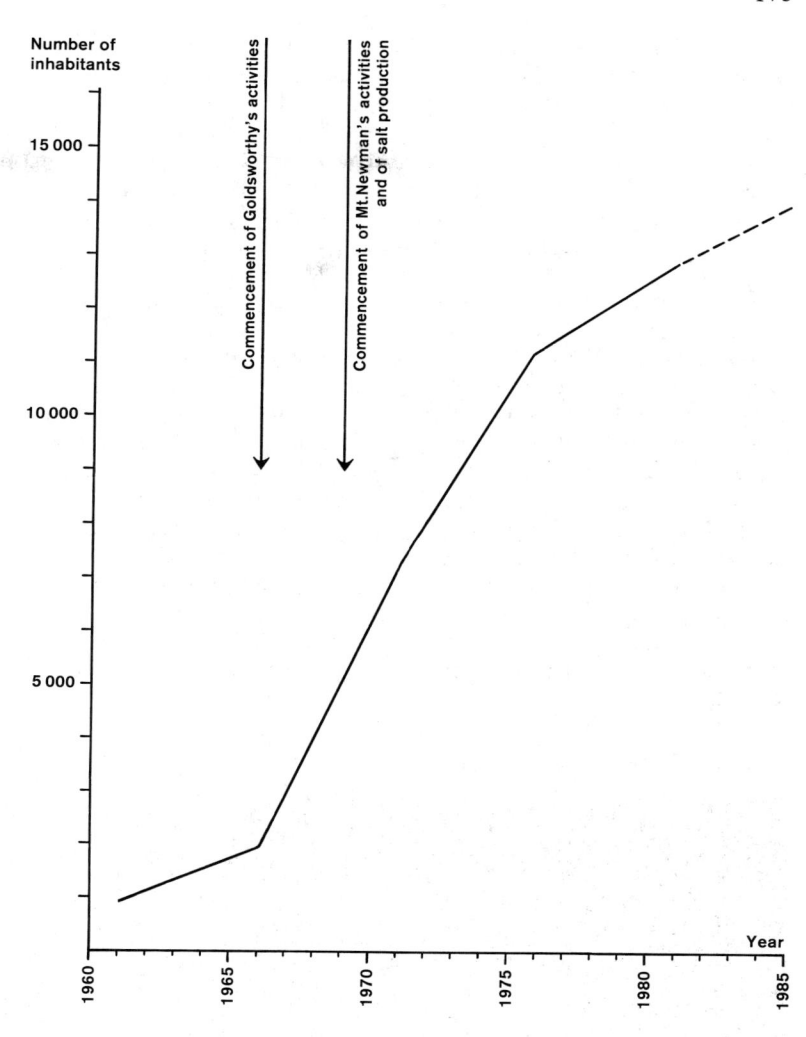

We shall first look at normalization in terms of the development from 'closed town' to 'open town'. In 1976 the Western Australian Minister for Industrial Development appointed Mr. P.L.J. Carly consultant to the Government in matters of company towns. Carly submitted the first volume of his investigation called 'Opening up. A report on considerations involved in the progressive establishment of the normal roles of local authorities, government agencies and the communities in mining towns' (hereafter referred to as the Carly Report) in 1977 (Carly 1977).

The three goals of the *Carly Report* were to point out the steps to be taken toward normalization, the assessment of the financial arrangements to achieve this goal (existing agreements between the Government and the companies had been to the effect that the former asked for less royalties and the latter took the responsibilities for constructing and maintaining the towns), and to point out the terms for future co-operation between the companies, the State Departments involved in the matter, and the Local Authorities.

The Carly Report started by setting out the advantages of 'closed towns' for the company as well as for the state. For the company the closed town means unification of control, the integration of purchasing goods and services, and control over the timing of improvement programmes. As far as the state is concerned, it would not have had the means, at least not the financial means, to provide such infrastructure to towns in such remote places.

The emphasis of the Report is, however, on the disadvantages. The Report stresses the odium that is attached to the 'Big Brother' image of the company in relation to its employees. The Report then turns to the adverse effects of the intrusion of industry on rural shires, and the rapid changes brought about for such areas by the new towns. 'Provision of capital, normally spread over, perhaps, more than 50 years in a slowly growing town is compressed into three or four years and the difficulties of this process need a little detailed attention' (Carly 1977, 7). Very high interest rates have been just one of the consequences of this development.

The Report continues with the special provisions made for the mining companies regarding valuation for rating. The Iron Ore Agreements provided valuation of all lands (with the exception of any part upon which a permanent

Fig. 100. Port Hedland, W.A. Oblique aerial photograph of 1964 showing the small port town and future site of the Mt. Newman Company's ore shipping facilities at Nelson Point (reproduced with the permission of Mt. Newman Mining Co. Pty. Limited, Nelson Point, Port Hedland)

residence would be erected) on the unimproved value, and there has been no ordinary rating of the railways, the services such as water and power supplies, and the business sites for hotels, shopping facilities and the like. 'The net result is a considerable loss of revenue or potential revenue to local authorities' (Carly 1977, 8).

In 1981 Newman, as the first of the company towns in the Pilbara region to be normalized, came under the administration of the Shire of East Pilbara, followed in 1983 by Tom Price and Paraburdoo, which have since been administered by the Shire of West Pilbara. These two shires assumed most of the administrative responsibilities for the former company towns, while the companies received franchises for continuing to provide power, water and sewerage to the communities along with the supplies for their mining operations (fig. 98).

There will be no efforts toward the normalization of 'short-lived towns and townships of insufficient size to survive other than as integrated parts of the mine facilities' (Carly 1977, 16). Small towns such as Goldsworthy and Shay Gap come under this provision. Ore resources near Goldsworthy became exhausted after 16 years of mining activities, and the Goldsworthy Company closed down the mine, leaving only the power station and railway maintenance shop in operation. Goldsworthy's population dropped from 923 (1981) to approximately 500 by 1985, a number of portable houses being transferred to the town of Shay Gap. Eventually Goldsworthy will be abandoned, whereas Shay Gap may get a chance of survival beyond the termination of hematite mining by means of operating a pilot plant for the upgrading of low-grade ores still found in abundance.

The newly established town of Karratha and the rapidly growing port town of Port Hedland have never been company towns, although the presence of the iron ore mining companies in these towns is obvious. There is a certain rivalry between the two towns, Karratha enjoying the support of the Western Australian Government, for example in the establishment of a Technical College, whereas Port Hedland is relying on the support of the Commonwealth Government. Port Hedland recently became the seat of another Technical College.

Port Hedland had been officially gazetted in 1896, but had been of only minor importance for some local imports and exports. In 1965 its population was approximately 1,200. Goldsworthy's ore shipments from Finucane

Fig. 101. Port Hedland, W.A. Oblique aerial photograph of 1980 showing the Mt. Newman Company's ore shipping facilities at Nelson Point (reproduced with the permission of Mt. Newman Mining Co. Pty. Limited, Nelson Point, Port Hedland)

Island immediately added some 2,500 persons to Port Hedland's population. After the Leslie Salt Company had commenced the operation of a solar salt industry and the Newman Mining Company had developed Point Nelson, the town's population reached 12,948 at the 1981 census and increased to approximately 15,000 by 1985 (figs. 99 to 102).

The original settlement of Port Hedland (formerly called Mangrove Harbour) was located on an island between the broad and shallow estuary of the Turner River and the Indian Ocean. There was very limited room for any extension of the built-up area. In consequence of this situation the new community of South Hedland was established approximately 14 km south of the old town. Some space between the two nuclei was developed as a light industrial area called Wedgefield. Some kilometres to the east the airport was located, with some service industries developing around it and a nearby hotel and caravan park. Across the dredged entrance to the harbour, on Finucane Island, Goldsworthy's shipping facilities and some residential quarters for their employees were developed. The present town of Port Hedland is thus spread over a vast area and is comprised of *five distinct clusters* of buildings with plenty of empty space between them, and linked with a modern network of highways (fig. 102).

South Hedland was designed around a central business area, with four cellular residential areas each surrounded by a perimeter road. All the houses and a seven-storey building of flats for single men were constructed by the Western Australian Housing Commission. Houses were then purchased from the Commission, by the Newman Company, the Goldsworthy Company, the Shire of Port Hedland and to a small extent by individuals, while a certain proportion of the houses is still owned by the Commission. From the point of view of ownership there is quite a mixture throughout the new town, although company houses are grouped together so that the individual family's neighbours are employees of the same company. The southeastern cell had not been developed by 1985, and there is still plenty of room for further extensions.

Apart from the rather long commuting distances between the various clusters, there are two points worth mentioning. Almost all important functions of the town are now concentrated in the new community of South Hedland,

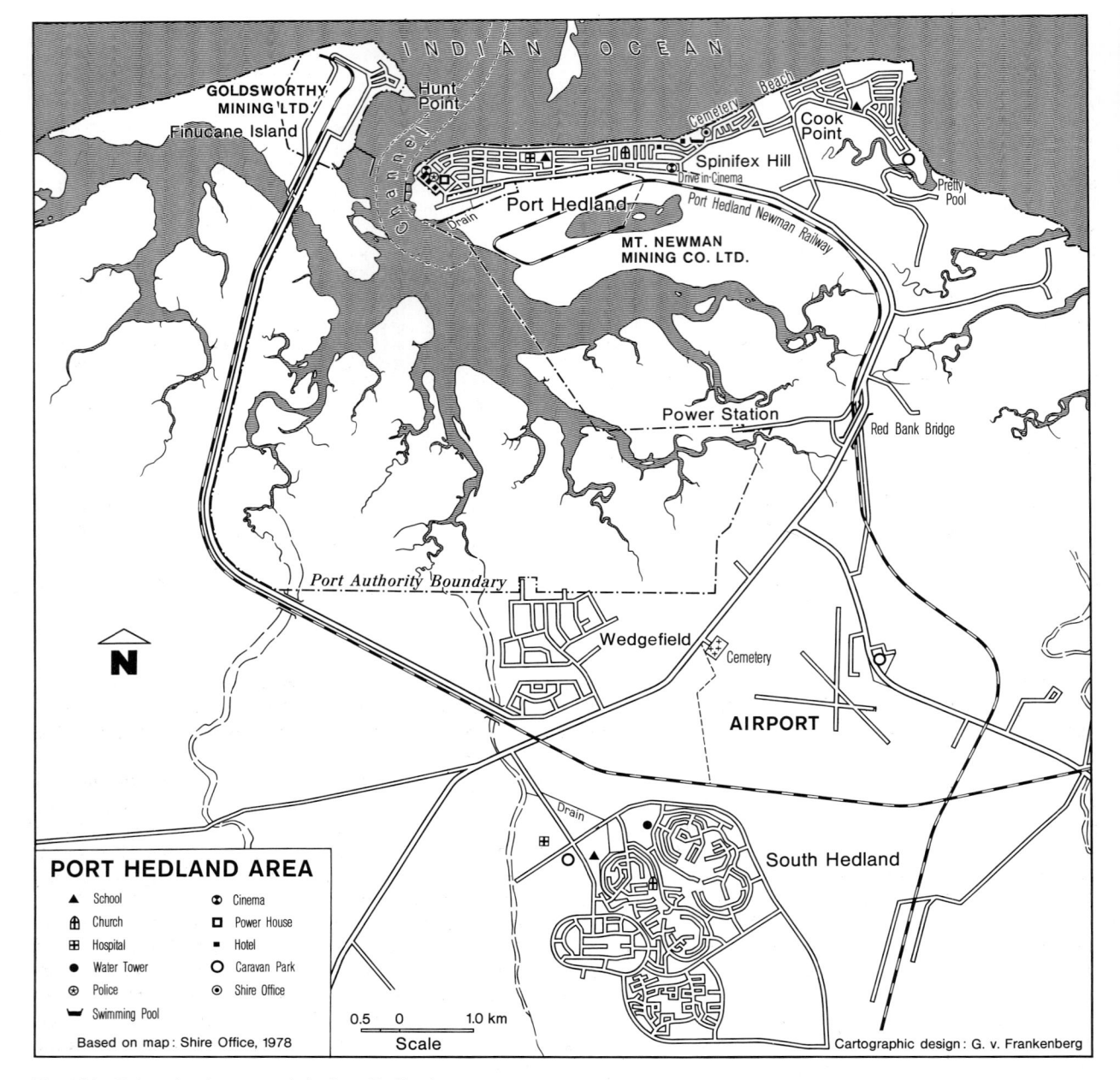

Fig. 102. Urban development of the Port Hedland area

including a large fully air-conditioned shopping centre with two department stores and a great variety of other businesses, a medical centre, a library, a T.A.B. bureau, a tavern, an aquatic centre and squash courts. Close to this centre we find the police station, various government offices and the new Technical College. It has been quite a burden on the shire budget to have certain elements of the infrastructure *duplicated* at the new centre.

While approximately 90% of the population were local people born in the area in 1965, the present population of Port Hedland is composed of some *50 nationalities.* The proportion of Muslims grew to the extent that in 1985 a mosque was inaugurated. Although not a company town in terms of its administrative status, Port Hedland housing some 1,750 employees of the Newman Company and 270 employees of the Goldsworthy Company, together with their dependants thus resembles the true company towns to a certain extent.

This consideration leads to the question whether the towns in the Pilbara region have normalized in terms of their population structures. The data for the year 1981 is presented in table 36.

Table 36. Indicators of the population of five mining towns in the Pilbara region, 1981

	Pannawonica	Tom Price	Paraburdoo	Shay Gap	Newman
Total persons 1981	1170	3540	2357	853	5466
Australian-born (%)	57.8	69.9	68.3	49.7	57.9
Overseas-born (%)	39.9	28.8	31.4	42.1	37.4
Total labour force (%)	65.0	48.4	52.9	56.7	54.5
Wage or salary earner (%)	63.1	46.4	50.8	55.5	51.8
Self employed, employer, helper (%)	0.7	0.8	1.3	0.3	0.9
Unemployed (%)	1.2	1.2	0.8	0.9	1.8
Marital status of labour force:					
Never married	43.9	30.3	35.5	40.7	34.8
Now married	47.0	62.0	58.1	50.6	55.9
Separated, divorced, widowed	9.1	7.7	6.4	8.7	9.3
Industry:					
Mining	67.6	65.0	65.6	64.8	62.4
Restaurants, hotels, clubs	1.7	5.7	8.5	1.7	6.4
Wholesale and retail trade	3.1	4.7	3.7	9.1	4.9
All other industries	27.6	24.6	22.2	24.4	26.3
Occupation:					
Miners, quarrymen	13.5	12.7	13.5	16.1	13.3
Tradesmen etc.	46.2	35.0	36.2	37.0	36.2
Transport and communication	5.6	7.9	9.4	9.8	10.7
Professional and technical jobs	6.2	11.2	11.5	5.0	10.0
All other occupations	28.5	33.2	29.4	32.1	29.8
1976 same residence	21.1	26.4	28.2	24.3	26.6
1976 other residence, same LGA	6.5	10.5	11.3	3.9	15.0

Source: ABS 1981 Census of Population and Housing

If we include the now very small town of Goldsworthy the range of population size is between 500 and 5,500. The proportion of the population in the labour force varies from 48.4% to 65.0%, these percentages being well above the national average. Unemployment rates vary between 0.8% and 1.8% and are thus distinctly below the national average.

Employment in mining varies between 62.4% and 67.6%, and is thus extraordinarily high, reflecting the fact that the mining company concerned is the only important employer. All other industries, with the exception of restaurants, hotels, wholesale and retail trade, have extremely low rates. If we consider, however, the occupational status of employees we find only between 12.7% and 16.1% to be miners and quarrymen; the majority of occupations is in the various trades, in transportation and communication as well as in the professional and technical fields.

The proportion of *overseas-born* people in the resident population of the mining towns varies between 28.8% and 42.1%[3]. The lowest percentage is found in Tom Price, a settlement that may be considered a relatively established and consolidated town, one that has become normalized in terms of political administration as well as in terms of its population structure. On the other end of the scale we find Shay Gap and Pannawonica, with relatively high proportions of overseas-born residents. They represent the less consolidated and short-lived type of company town. However, a comparison of census data reveals that during the intercensal period 1976–81 the percentage of overseas born in Paraburdoo rose from 18.5% to 31.4%. This is *in contrast* to the assumption that in the course of time the proportion of overseas-born in the population will continuously decline.

Percentages of *single men* are in the range between 30.3% and 43.9%, and are thus still very high. Again, the lowest percentage is found in Tom Price, whereas the highest percentages occur in Shay Gap and Pannawonica. The companies' policy is to encourage married employees with their families to move to the mining towns and help to stabilize the resident population. Apart from the provision of higher types of education for the miners' children the success of recruiting greater proportions of married people will at least partly depend upon the companies' ability to provide enough family housing (fig. 103).

Turnover rates are still high in the Pilbara mining towns. In the intercensal period 1976–81 only between 21.1% in Pannawonica and 28.2% in Paraburdoo stayed in the same residence and another 3.9% or 15.0% respectively in the same LGA. Again, Shay Gap and Pannawonica show the lowest figures, which means very high rates or fluctuation of their workforce. In the late 1970s some of these mining towns had annual turnover rates of their staff be-

---

[3] The evaluation of such census figures is rendered difficult since restrictions of naturalization have been eased and the Australian citizenship may be granted after just two years of residence in the country, under the condition that the applicant got a permanent job and can make credible that he is willing to take his permanent residence in Australia. Therefore short-term changes of nationality are to be encountered.

Fig. 103. Port Hedland, W.A. Cyclone-proof houses for single men employed by the Mt. Newman Company

tween 20% and 50% and of wage earners of sometimes more than 100% (Brealey & Newton in: Burnley et al. 1980, 48–66). These high turnover rates are a great burden on the companies' budget, the replacement costs for the company in 1973 ranging between $ 4,000 in Gove and $ 10,000 in Kambalda, the Pilbara mining towns ranging somewhere in between (Brealy & Newton in. Burnley et al. 1980, 60).

Turnover rates are at least partly a *psychological problem.* Much research has been done on living conditions in such remote and isolated places in a harsh natural environment. For the discussion of this aspect the reader is referred to the seminar papers of a conference held in Kambalda in 1973 'Man and the environment: New Towns in isolated settings' (Austr. Nat. Comm. for UNESCO 1976) and the United Nations University publication 'Arid zone settlement in Australia. A focus on Alice Springs' (Parkes, Burnley & Walker 1985).

In conclusion we may say that the census data analysed above reflect the situation that would be expected in rather remote and isolated, recently founded, monofunctional towns. There are certain differences between relatively older and somewhat consolidated towns and those towns that seem to be short-lived and unlikely to be normalized in administrative terms, which means opened up. It would be premature to speak of normalization in terms of population trends and structure, because proportions of single men and overseas immigrants in the workforce and fluctuation rates are still very high. Marshall (1968) recommended the development of *one large place* as the major focus of educational, medical and other services of the whole Pilbara region. But probably due to the involvement of different companies and certain critical issues in the relation between the Western Australian Government and the Commonwealth Government as to the development of the Pilbara region this proposal of Marshall's has not been materialized. The Western Australian Government made rather high financial investments into the development of the port facilities of the harbours along the Pilbara coast and of Port Hedland in particular, into the pavement of the portion of the North West Coastal Highway between Carnarvon and Port Hedland that had until the 1960s been an unsealed road, and through the W.A. Housing Commission into the housing stock of the towns of Karratha and South Hedland. These investments were made with the expectation that there would not only occur a punctual development of a few small urban places, but rather a great economic development of the whole Pilbara region with Karratha being its dominant central place. However, Karratha had just little more than 8,000 residents by 1981.

For further details on the critical issues in the Pilbara region the reader is referred to Linge (in: Jennings & Linge 1980).

4 The Australian city as a distinct cultural-genetic type

Preceding chapters have involved the discussion of the historical processes of Australian urbanization and the description of individual large cities and certain functional groups of towns characteristic of the various regions of Australia. Attention will now be turned to those traits common to the urban places of the Australian nation continent as a whole.

At first glance, the Australian city has a number of traits in common with the *North American city*. Both have a British tradition, although it must be remembered that Australia's first settlements were established at a time when parts of the North American continent had been settled for over a century and the United States had already gained independence and sovereignty. Both are characterized by the grid pattern of streets in their historic cores and by the dominance of modern high-rise commercial and office buildings in their CBDs. Cities in both countries have tens of thousands of detached and semi-detached houses in sprawling suburban residential areas, with a marked tendency to develop widespread modern suburban shopping centres and industrial estates (or industrial parks in the U.S. terminology). There are also certain similarities of lifestyle and land use, reflecting similar socio-economic characteristics in the two countries, such as high standards of living and high degrees of private car ownership and geographical mobility.

There are, however, *differences* making the Australian city a cultural-genetic type in its own right. Home ownership, for example, is much more widespread in Australia than in the United States, so that the great Australian cities in this respect resemble the metropolitan area of Los Angeles more than the cities of America's Northeastern Seaboard or Midwest. Australian cities cannot be compared with U.S. cities at all with regard to the numbers and distribution patterns of ethnic minorities, and there is certainly no equivalent of the huge 'black belts' of Chicago or New York City.

We shall therefore try and find out what elements there are that make the Australian city Australian.

4.1 Aspects of urban form and structure

4.1.1 Building materials

Brick and stone are the major building materials of houses in Australian cities, their percentages in the capital cities with the exception of Brisbane ranging between 87.4% in Adelaide and 62.0% in Sydney (table 37, fig. 104).

Table 37. Major building materials of outer walls of houses in the capital cities, 1976 (%)

Material	Sydney	Melbourne	Brisbane	Adelaide	Perth
Brick, stone	62.0	62.9	28.9	87.4	82.0
Asbest cement	18.1	2.2	8.7	3.4	9.9
Timber	13.2	26.9	54.5	1.9	4.8
Other materials	6.7	8.0	7.6	7.3	3.3

Source: ABS data, quoted in McDonald & Guilfoyle 1980

In contrast to Australia, timber has to date been the major construction material of private homes in the United States. Why are there such differences between the two countries? And why does Brisbane come closer to the situation in the United States?

The earliest settlers often applied the British *'wattle-and-daub' tradition* to the construction of their huts. 'The walls were formed by weaving branches of the *acacia* (wattle) tree into panels, then plastering over with mud. Layers of clay were often used to finish the walls' (Latta 1984, 6). For these huts they preferably used the *casuarina* which was, however, not found in the immediate vicinity of the first settlement at Sydney Cove and had to be transported

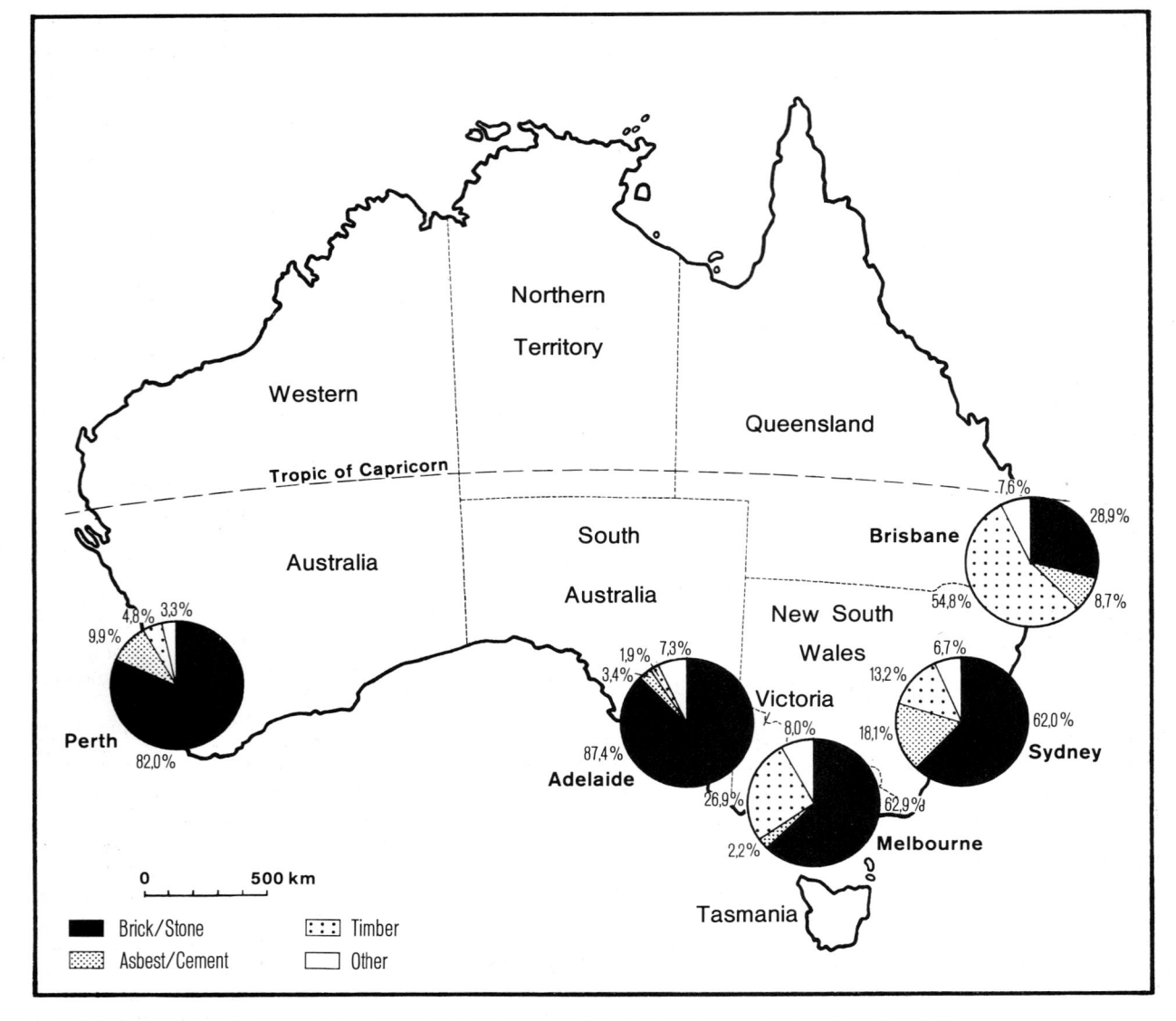

Fig. 104. Proportion of dominant building materials of outer walls of the housing stock of capital cities, 1976

over some distance. Moreover, the wattle-and-daub huts did not really withstand the weather conditions, especially the occasional heavy rainfalls in New South Wales.

Other kinds of timber were less useful for construction purposes. Many of the gum trees (*eucalyptus*) were, despite their healthy appearance, rotten inside, and the wood often split and warped. In many cases it was hard to work, the wood-working tools brought from England were easily damaged and had constantly to be repared.

Of course, there were the giant species of *eucalyptus* in Western Australia, the jarrah and karri. While the karri is prone to destruction by termites, the jarrah is very strong and resistant to them and gained the fame of being called 'Swan River mahagony'. However, it also had to be transported from the southwestern forests to the Swan River colony.

It may be assumed that one limiting factor in the extensive use of timber for house construction in Australia was the lack of a tradition of construction in wood such as had been brought to the United States by Bohemian-Moravian and Scandinavian immigrants (the log cabin). A process of innovation and diffusion, which by the addition of the British fireplace and the Dutch porch, produced the standard *American balloon frame house* that has spread by the tens of millions over the suburban areas of the American cities.

For over a century there has thus been a rather small proportion of weatherboard houses in Australia's cities. Regional differences may have been due to the availability of building materials as well as to building regulations; the more extensive use of stone and brick in South Australia as compared with the greater availability of wood in Victoria is obvious. On the other hand flooding and fire hazards made for *early changes of building regulations*. For example, although buildings in Hobart Town were supposed to be built of stone or brick, about 340 out of a total of 594 houses existing in 1823 had been built of wood. After a heavy flooding of the stream draining from Mt. Wellington in 1854, however, those regulations were more strictly observed and many wooden buildings were replaced by brick buildings (Scott 1955). A building regulation of 1855 prohibited the use of weatherboard for the construction of houses in the City of Sydney. As early as 1851, 82.9 % of all houses in Sydney and even 65.2 % of the houses in Sydney's older suburbs were built of brick (Counc. City of Sydney 1980, Scrivener 1965).

Jackson (1970) calculated that only one fifth of all rooms added during the period 1871–97 in Sydney were of weatherboard and four-fifths of brick, while outside the Sydney region a much higher proportion was of weatherboard. For Western Australia Snooks (in Stannage 1981) showed that the weatherboard proportion was 33.5 % in 1911 and remained fairly stable (1947: 34.3 %), while the percentage of rooms of private dwellings with walls made of brick, stone or concrete increased from 36.2 % to 47.9 %.

As in many suburbs of American cities, covenants have had the effect of keeping out lower income people. Such covenants set high standards as to minimum lots sizes and minimum house sizes, restricting development to single-family detached houses. Building materials other than brick and tile are excluded, in contrast to the custom in the United States, where timber has to date been extensively used as the construction material of single-family homes.

Another factor steering the use of construction materials is the attitude of *financial institutions* toward the type and material of housing. Some lenders used to prefer brick or brick-veneer construction, and refused to lend money for weatherboard houses. This attitude often had the result that better quality houses were constructed, albeit smaller and less well equipped ones (Hill 1972).

There are two exceptions to the rule. One refers to places such as Newcastle that developed out of *mining settlements*. Due to regulations of the Mines Subsidence Board, weatherboard has been the construction material most widely used in Newcastle. It is only in recent years that immigrants, Southern Europeans in particular, have tried to improve weatherboard houses by applying brick and cement during renovation work (Galvin 1974).

The greatest exception, however, is Brisbane. In Queensland the main construction material used for the outer walls of dwellings was 87.9 % timber by 1861 and was still 75.3 % by 1961. Only in recent years has brick been used more frequently in inner-city redevelopment, while new construction in outer areas has been more frequently of fibro-cement and concrete (Marsden 1966). The heavy use of timber for house construction in Brisbane is presumably due to the fact that *Queensland houses usually were built on stilts*, to provide better ventilation and protection from termites and floods; such houses were most conveniently constructed of timber. Also, the verandah encircling the Queensland house 'gradually changed from its role as an external passageway or a means of sheltering the outside walls from rain and sun, into a living area of significance ... The verandah – either netted or fenced in with wooden lattice work to provide privacy – ensured maximum ventilation' (Latta 1984, 21).

'In addition, the "downstairs" between floor and ground level provides cheap storage space, and is usually used for the household laundry, as a garage, and quite commonly, as a fernery. Such buildings must, almost of necessity, be of timber; difficulties in providing chimneys and fireplaces do not usually arise, for over much of the State winters are seldom sufficiently cold to demand internal heating' (Rose 1955, 10; also Rose 1962). In an inquiry conducted by the Queensland Bureau of Industry in the mid-1940s almost 50 reasons were given for the extensive use of stilts in Queensland housing construction. The *white ants* ranked first in the answers; since bricks and stone were not readily available the buildings were raised above ground, 'on hefty tree trunks so that the mud tunnels of the light-fearing depredators could be seen and destroyed' (Freeland 1968, 118). Climatic conditions and the provisions of *good ventilation* ranked second in the answers, while a greater number of respondents pointed to *various uses of ground level space* (Boyd 1978).

There is also a certain relation between weatherboard as the major construction material of the outer walls and local terrain. Scott (1959) in his study of building materials in the Greater Hobart area found that after timber had been extensively used for housing construction in Tasmania for over a century, weatherboard construction since the end of World War I has been very much confined to areas of steeper slopes. The reason for such local differences is that 'the price differential for weatherboard and brick is much greater than in the areas of more subdued relief' (Scott 1959, 157). This argument may well apply to Queensland and to Brisbane in particular, for the early development of Brisbane occurred along some of the many ridges on which the city was built.

In general, however, the British preferred the use of more durable construction materials for their houses. As early as July 1788 a letter sent by Governor Phillip to Lord Sydney in London contained the statement 'We now make very good bricks, and the stone is good, but do not find either limestone or chalk' (Commonw. of Austr. vol. I, 47–48). *Clay* was found near the settlement of Sydney Cove, the place still being known as Brickfield Hill. In Melbourne most of the clay for housing construction came from Moonee Ponds Creek in Brunswick, somewhat to the north of the settlement. A convict of the name of James Bloodsworth had the knowledge of brickmaking and taught his fellow convicts how to build and operate kilns (Latta 1984).

While clay was usually found in abundance and the production of bricks did not cause any problems, Governor Phillip in the early days of Sydney Cove 'could not supply the lime for mortar and the biscuit-coloured bricks had

Fig. 105. Transport of a weatherboard house on Stuart Highway

to be laid in a thick mixture of clay. The single storey, later to become a characteristic Australian building habit, was as high as such walls could stand. Even then they were liable to collapse in the face of driving rain' (Boyd 1978, 141). If we are willing to follow Boyd's argument, the *shortage of lime* was at least one major reason for the *early dominance of the single-storey house* in Australia. In later years extensive use was made of beach shells found, among other places, at Shellharbour in the Wollongong area.

Apart from bricks much *local stone* was used for house construction, as far as it was readily available in the environs of the early settlements. In New South Wales it was local sandstone, in Victoria and South Australia it was a kind of bluish-grey slate referred to as bluestone, in the latter colony also the Mt. Gambier limestone, in Melbourne's environs it was basalt, in Beechworth (Victoria) it was the local honey-coloured granite, and in Perth it was cream limestone. The local building materials were used 'to create a congenial environment, and the desire to do so was initially seen in terms of reproducing, as closely as could be achieved, a vision of Britain. This resulted in schools, gaols, hospitals and grand public buildings, designed to look as if they had been snatched intact from London. If the wide, dusty streets of the infant towns did not exactly resemble "home", the buildings certainly did' (Latta 1984, 15). Many of the historical cores of the oldest towns indeed *look very British*, and this holds true for places as far away from one another as Port Arthur in Tasmania and York in the Avon Valley of Western Australia.

As Governor Phillip had mentioned in his letter cited above the first settlers in Sydney Cove had problems with finding limestone for making mortar. 'Brick walls were layed with mud or clay to which a bonding of straw or animal hair was added' (Latta 1984, 6). This meant, however, that the walls had to be extremely thick and were still not very stable. At the beginning of the first winter Bloodsworth had erected a two-storey house of bricks for Governor Phillip, which had to be constantly repaired and reconstructed.

In contrast to the United States, mobile homes have not yet become a form of housing of any importance in Australia. While in the United States some 10.3 million people or approximately 5% of the total population were mobile home dwellers in 1976, the 1976 census for Australia, though applying a somewhat narrower definition of mobile home, stated that only 20,908 or 0.5% of all private dwellings were mobile homes (Hugo 1979). Even if we assume the high rate of four people to one mobile home, this would mean that only 0.8% of the total population could be classified as mobile home dwellers. According to an alternative source there are approximately 250,000 people living in caravans. Even this would mean only about 1.7% of Australia's total population.

Also, in contrast to the United States, prefabrication has as yet not played a major part in Australian housing construction. At the time of high demand for houses in the first post-war decade, there were 'very few private manufacturers substantial and enterprising enough for the mass-production of prefabricated houses' (Boyd 1978, 263). Moreover, prefabrication in Australia became a political issue. In 1948 there were, for example, two projects of prefabricated houses, one of which had been initiated by the Labor Government in Victoria. The Liberal Government that came into power was opposed to such projects and stopped both of them (fig. 105).

In the central cities and particularly in the CBDs other construction materials such as concrete have become more common in recent times. Thus in the central area of Perth the building stock according to main building materials is shown in table 38.

Apart from the shortage of limestone in the early years of colonization the more frequent use of brick and stone for house construction made for a *greater stability and longevity* of the housing stock in Australian cities as com-

Table 38. Major construction materials in the central area of Perth, 1980

Material	Number of buildings	Gross floor area (sq. m.)
Brick	865	947,616
Brick and concrete	534	456,176
Brick and iron or tile	71	280,246
Concrete	176	1,010,468
Masonry	56	120,035
Other	88	47,057
Total	1,790	2,861,598

Source: The Council of the City of Perth 1980, 166

pared with the wooden structures in the United States, this fact having important consequences for contemporary urban development. For example, many of the fine, solidly built Victorian terrace houses in the older established suburbs of Sydney and Melbourne are *worthwhile preserving and restoring* so that they have become objects of both official urban restoration programmes and privately financed gentrification, which will be dealt with below in greater detail.

Mention should also be made to the wide use of *galvanized iron roofs* which had a number of advantages: low cost, ease of fixing, durability, impermeability and great fire-resistance (Sumner & Oliver 1978), and of the cast-iron lacework of the many fine hotels and other old buildings (fig. 106).

4.1.2 Home ownership

The extensive use of solid construction materials had further implications. According to Jackson's estimates (1970) for the last quarter of the nineteenth century, a four-roomed brick house in New South Wales would have cost about

Fig. 106. Townsville, Qld. Hotel Buchanan, ca. 1890

three times the average annual wage, whereas a weatherboard house would have cost between about one and a half to twice the annual wage. To the higher costs of a brick house the higher price of a town lot must be added; a town lot is estimated to have cost approximately twice the price of a lot outside the Sydney region. Provided that Jackson's assumption of similar wage rates throughout the settled part of the colony is realistic, these price relations mean that the barriers to individual home ownership would have been almost four times higher in Sydney than in the rest of New South Wales.

It is against this background that we must interpret the data collected by Jackson (1970, 141) on owner-occupied and tenanted private dwelling houses in Sydney and its suburbs in 1891. In the various districts of the City of Sydney between 83% and 90% of private dwelling houses were tenanted, in the inner suburbs such as Darlington, Glebe, Newton and Paddington between 71% and 84%, in the so-called medium density areas such as Ashfield, Burwood, North Sydney and Randwick between 51% and 67%, and only in the outer areas such as Drummoyne or Hurstville were 50–64% of houses owner-occupied.

A similar investigation was undertaken by Dingle and Merrett for Melbourne. Although the level of tenancy in Melbourne was somewhat lower than in Sydney, it was still approximately 59% in the inner suburbs by 1891; in working-class suburbs such as Collingwood it would rise to 67%. An overall increase of tenancy was brought about by the depression of the late 1880s and the 1890s, bringing the proportion in the inner suburbs up to 65.3%. While in the course of the depression house prices and rents fell, many purchasers were no longer able to pay the interests

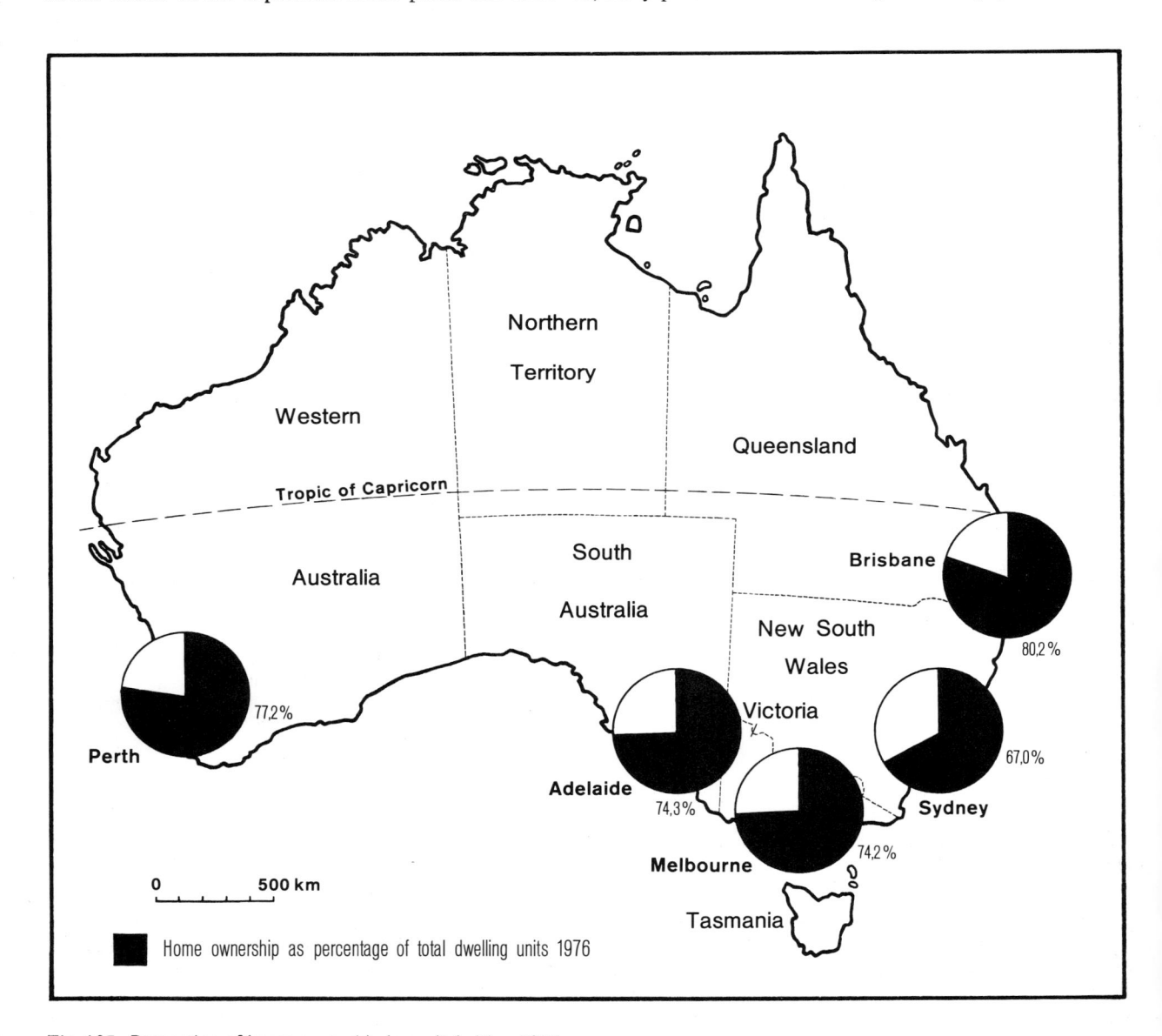

Fig. 107. Proportion of home ownership in capital cities, 1976

on their mortgages so that banks, building societies, insurance companies and trustee companies were forced to repossess much property. However, some of these also became insolvent; between 1890 and 1898 the number of Melbourne building societies dropped from 54 to 37, while the value of their properties increased from £ 359,000 to £ 1,717,000 (Dingle & Merrett 1972, 33).

After the turn of the century, most new houses were built for owner-occupancy, the percentage of owner-occupied houses rising fastest in the newly developing suburbs such as Brunswick, Malvern and Northcote. But it was *not until the 1920s that more dwellings were owner-occupied* than tenanted. The offer of more generous terms by the financial institutions made it easier for purchasers to obtain long-term, low-interest mortgages.

From the above data we may draw two conclusions. Firstly, even at the turn of the century, private home ownership was as yet comparatively low. Obviously, not very many Australians in the nineteenth century were able to afford a house of their own. At the turn of the century approximately one third of Australian households were home owners, the total population being less than four million. Today approximately two-thirds of all households are owner-occupiers, the total population being some 15 million. The enormous increase of private home ownership has thus been a development of the twentieth century.

However, there must have been an appreciable investment in real estate by wealthy people and speculators as well as by building societies and financial institutions, these *landlords building for renting* over 80% of all dwelling units in the City of Sydney and over 50% in most of the suburbs. Building societies and financial institutions were partly forced into house ownership in consequence of the depression and the inability of people to pay their interest rates to lenders. The situation does not seem to have been greatly different from that in major European cities of that era.

Secondly, the degree of owner-occupation already showed a *remarkable gradiant* prior to the turn of the century, rising from the central city towards the suburbs. Thus in the centrally located district of Chippendale (Sydney) no more than 10% of the dwelling houses were owner-occupied, while in Drummoyne the percentage rose to 64% or almost two-thirds of all dwelling houses. The spatial differences of dwelling types and the differences of home ownership over time in the metropolitan areas of the state capitals are shown in table 39 (fig. 107).

Table 39. Dwelling types in the mainland state capitals 1976 and home ownership rates, 1911–76 (%)

Zone	Characteristic		Sydney	Melbourne	Brisbane	Adelaide	Perth
Inner	Home ownership		42.7	35.3	36.6	58.5	56.6
	Separate house		28.4	24.9	52.5	66.4	70.9
	Flat/Unit		29.0	47.1	37.3	15.7	19.2
	Other		42.6	28.0	10.5	17.9	9.9
Middle	Home ownership		65.5	67.5	66.6	67.1	67.9
	Separate house		66.4	73.2	78.0	71.9	77.1
	Flat/Unit		24.6	14.1	16.9	13.1	11.9
	Other		9.0	12.7	5.1	15.0	11.0
Outer	Home ownership		74.3	80.6	76.7	77.4	75.1
	Separate house		86.6	91.5	93.7	83.6	86.8
	Flat/Unit		8.7	3.5	2.5	4.7	3.8
	Other		4.7	5.0	3.8	11.7	9.4
Total	Home ownership	1976	65.1	69.6	69.7	70.1	68.6
		1971	65.6	69.5	70.3	70.2	65.6
		1966	69.1	72.9	73.1	73.7	72.6
		1961	71.2	76.4	76.9	75.4	73.8
		1954	59.9	67.0	75.5	70.2	71.1
		1947	43.0	50.4	64.0	59.2	58.8
		1933	41	49	60	54	56
		1921	40	45	59	52	55
		1911	31	37	46	42	41
	Separate house		68.1	75.7	84.5	75.9	79.1
	Flat/Unit		20.5	13.3	10.6	10.1	10.5
	Other		11.4	11.0	4.9	14.0	10.4

Sources: ABS, quoted in Maher 1982, 65, 72, 73 and in Halligan & Paris 1984, 171 (modified)

The Australian figures are still more impressive when compared with other industrial countries (table 40).

Two conclusions may be drawn from the data in table 40. Firstly, Australia's home ownership rate is the *second highest in the world* after Iceland; it is higher than the rates for the United States and Canada, not to speak of the European industrial countries. Secondly, the degree of home ownership does not seem to be closely related to the standard of living as reflected in the per capita GNI. As to the latter, Australia only holds rank eight and Iceland rank twelve. On the other hand, there are countries like Sweden with a high standard of living and a rather low rate

Table 40. Home ownership rates (%) and rank order of per capita Gross National Income, 1971

Country	Owner-occupied dwellings	Rank order of GNI per capita
Iceland	70.8	12
Australia	68.7	8
New Zealand	68.1	14
United States	62.9	1
Canada	55.9	3
Belgium	55.9	11
Britain	50.1	16

Source: Kilmartin & Thorns 1978, 22 (modified)

of home ownership. These figures lend support to the hypothesis that the degree of home ownership is, to a considerable extent, a matter of *attitudes and living habits* and of the circumstances enabling people to realize their wishes.

As far as *British attitude* toward home ownership is concerned, there was *no real need for fortifications* and security from outside enemies. Although a number of British towns were walled in medieval times, they began rather early to spread at lower densities. Owing to climatic conditions favouring lush vegetation, the British developed a *strong preference for gardening* and a general love of country life. The aristocrat used to live in his country estate, keeping a town house in London just as a secondary residence. By means of downward cultural diffusion, the desire for living in a separate house surrounded by a good-sized garden also spread among the lower social classes (Ungerson & Karn 1980). As Hajdu commented on the meaning of 'home' to the average Australian: 'The premium placed on privacy has been at once a human need, and in its heightened form in the Australian home and suburb, a reflection of Australia's Anglo-Saxon traditions. In Australia, a home had to be one in which each family could be isolated from the other, and in turn the interior of each home had to provide privacy for the individual from the other inhabitants' (Hajdu 1979, 357). Hence the millions of detached houses and the vast suburban areas that surround the rather small central areas of the cities. There is ample evidence in the literature for the fact that the detached single family home is so much identified with the Australian way of life that the desire to acquire a home of one's own is one of the foremost expectations of many overseas immigrants in Australia (ch. 4.2.3).

Apart from the philosophy behind home ownership, there were various other reasons for Australians to acquire a home of their own. Prior to the enormous post-war building boom *prices of land and costs of construction were rather low*. Many Australians were skilled enough to do much of the construction work on a do-it-yourself basis and with the assistance of friends. There were even self-build groups, whose members formed teams of carpenters, bricklayers, plumbers and mechanics; these teams moved around from one construction site to the next, helping one another with their different skills. There was also in the past much land available that was not 'retained under community ownership'. And in most municipalities there were hardly any building regulations or restrictions to inhibit the provision of cheap and unconventional housing (Kilmartin & Thorns 1978).

Many Australians also regarded real estate as a kind of *insurance for old age*, in the absence of an effective public insurance system. A public-health insurance scheme that had been initiated by the Whitlam Government in the early 1970s was soon modified and in 1978 altogether abolished. Kemeny stressed the connection of home ownership and insurance by saying that 'Countries with high owner-occupation rates tend also to have relatively poorly developed welfare states' (Kemeny 1980, 381).

This is the point where government comes in. While the lack of public insurance had the effect of indirectly promoting private home ownership, it has for a number of reasons been directly encouraged by Australian Governments. Housing was used as an instrument of income redistribution, and home ownership was considered as contributing to *political stability*, since it was anticipated that a property-owning class would be less inclined to become involved in political unrest or upheavals. It was also regarded as a kind of supplementation for old-age pensions, enabling retired people to enjoy a shelter that had been paid for in earlier years. A sufficient supply of private urban space could also dispense the Government from the necessity to provide ample open public space (Paterson 1975, Small 1979).

Home ownership has, however, been viewed from different angles by the various *political parties*. The Australian Labor Party's membership consisted to a great extent of tenants, and the ALP used to have reservations with regard to home ownership and to be opposed 'to anyone who seemed to be exploiting rent-payers for profit' (Boyd 1978, 259). While in power, the ALP used to increase the construction of public housing and to discourage its sale, whereas the Liberal-Country Party used to reduce the public housing stock and promote the sale of government houses. The latter party has always more strongly encouraged home ownership than the ALP. The New South Wales Labor Government in power prior to World War I tried to eliminate landlords and contractors from the real estate market, and made the State Works Department become involved into construction business (Kemeny 1977, Boyd 1978).

Australian Governments, Federal and State, hardly acted as direct lenders, but rather promoted home ownership by granting various subsidies. Moreover, subsidies to builders and developers of inner city residential construction was always scarce, so that it seems justified to say that Government in this way *favoured suburbanization*. Of the total amount of loans given for the construction and purchase of houses in Australia in the fiscal year 1976–77, only 5.6% were provided by the state housing authorities while 43.0% were provided by savings banks, 27.5% by building societies and 16.4% by trading banks (Kilmartin & Thorns 1978, Beed 1981). The most important government measure was the *Home Savings Grant Scheme* of 1964, giving tax concessions on interest and bonus payments from saving accounts deemed to be for home purchase. 'The imputed rental value of owner occupation is tax exempt, while renters pay their rent out of after-tax income. This must encourage ownership rather than the alternative of renting and investing the money that would have been put in a house in other forms of investment where tax has to be paid' (Small 1979, 57).

In addition to government incentives, there have been mechanisms in the finance markets functioning in favour of owner-occupancy. Thus in times of high demand for housing, instead of raising housing-loan interest rates, these were kept low and credit rationing applied. *Loans were restricted to new houses*; they were given up to a certain limit, they were given only to borrowers who had been depositors for a certain minimum period, and the like. The policies and possibilities of mortgage-lending institutions and their impact on the housing market have been commented on in detail by Jackson (1982).

Another factor supporting home ownership is the *residential choice of overseas immigrants*. A report by the Commission of Inquiry into Poverty (1975) came to the conclusion that both the life styles of immigrants and their frequent responsibility for an extended family inevitably require a house. 'Family size often precludes the possibility of renting rooms, and a house shared even between relatives is not over-common because of culturally ingrained attitudes. Flats make it impossible for the Italian to follow his normal life style or to fulfil the responsibilities of hospitality that are traditionally placed upon him' (Comm. of Inquiry into Poverty 1975, 43). In 1971, 73% of Greek household heads were owner-buyers against 67% of all household heads in metropolitan Sydney (Burnley 1976, Williams in: Halligan & Paris 1984).

Since many immigrants are not eligible for accommodation by Government schemes, and are thus not able to accumulate the deposit necessary for purchasing a private home, these groups are often under the strain of being forced to resort to short-term and high-interest mortgages, in some cases up to three mortgages. This means that the husband is often forced to work two jobs or the wife works day-shift and the husband night-shift at the expense of their health and family life. The question of residential choice of immigrant groups will be treated in more detail in chapter 4.2.3.

Finally, in Australia the rental sector (with the exception of luxury apartments) is characterized by a number of negative features such as insecurity of tenure and low maintenance standards (Kemeny 1977).

Since the 1970s when land and house construction prices soared, strata units have become a more and more favoured kind of ownership. In some of the inner suburbs of the metropolitan areas the conversion of dwelling units in older multi-storey buildings to *strata title* have become popular. In resort towns such as Coffs Harbour a strata-unit boom has provided first and second homes for a growing clientele (Murphy 1977, 1985).

4.1.3 Property prices, public housing, residential densities

In consequence of the construction boom of the 1960s the number of dwelling units overtook the number of households. Rising land and construction costs meant, however, that the housing needs and aspirations of many Australians could not be met. It is true that since before the Second World War there had been some degree of price control through the Land Sales Control Acts (abandoned in 1948) and the Landlord and Tenant Act of 1939 as amended in 1958 (ch. 2.1.3), but these controls have not been effective in recent years. From about 1960 prices began to increase rapidly. Between 1960 and 1977 *land prices* in Sydney increased about eightfold and in Melbourne fivefold, while *house prices* increased fivefold in Sydney and fourfold in Melbourne (Kilmartin & Thorns 1978). In the short period from January 1979 to April 1980 average property prices increased from $ 46,000 to $ 61,000 in Sydney and from $ 39,500 to $ 41,000 in Melbourne.

As is apparent from the above figures, land prices rose faster than house prices, and have so become an increasing proportion of total property prices to be paid by home purchasers. Increases were considerably higher in Sydney than in Melbourne, probably because in the former city less land in flat areas is available for construction within a reasonable radius from the city centre, and a greater demand for lots and housing puts more pressure on the real-estate market. However, prices differ considerably in various sections of the metropolitan area, the land component accounting for approximately 25% in the outer suburbs and for approximately 55% in the inner suburbs (Jackson 1982).

In consequence of rising prices, home ownership is now beyond the reach of a growing proportion of the total population. Indeed, as is apparent from the figures in table 39, percentages of home ownership in all metropolitan areas reached a culmination point at the 1966 census and have slightly decreased since.

There is yet another facet to the story of home ownership and rising prices. As was mentioned above, since the turn of the century financial institutions granted more generous terms in lending money to home purchasers than they had done before. Co-operative housing societies after World War II offered *loans even up to 90%* of valuation for terms up to 30 years. Similar terms were offered by the Commonwealth Bank, while the Federal War Service Homes Division even lent 95% for 45 years (Boyd 1978). However, in the face of increasing prices, many young people had to rely on parental gifts in order to start buying a home, and a second income was often needed for a house over $ 35,000 (Jackson 1982).

In general, lending institutions were not much interested in functioning as *developers*. 'In both the U.S. and Canada financial institutions, especially life offices and trust companies have been prominent in large-scale housing development for many years' (Hill 1972, 22). In contrast, such institutions have been very little engaged in house construction in Australia. Prior to 1939 the State Bank of South Australia and the City Mutual Life at West Ryde (Sydney) in New South Wales built a limited number of houses, but they were *exceptions* to the rule. Usually banks have lent money to individuals rather than to large-scale builders, thus encouraging small detached houses and suburban growth. The importance of various lending institutions is shown in table 41.

Table 41. Sources of first mortgage, 1976 (%)

		Trading Bank	Savings Bank	Building Society	Other* Priv.	Govt.**	N.S.
Sydney	Inner	23.0	27.1	21.3	18.7	8.5	1.3
	Middle	19.2	24.3	26.0	12.9	16.9	0.8
	Outer	19.6	21.5	33.5	10.6	14.3	0.5
	Total	19.8	23.0	29.8	12.2	14.6	0.7
Melbourne	Inner	17.0	37.2	12.2	24.1	7.4	2.1
	Middle	12.8	35.9	12.5	16.5	21.1	1.0
	Outer	10.9	43.6	18.0	10.2	16.5	0.7
	Total	11.7	40.9	16.1	12.6	18.0	0.8
Brisbane	Inner	21.5	29.2	19.0	20.6	8.6	1.2
	Middle	17.1	23.9	17.9	10.0	30.7	0.6
	Outer	13.2	25.2	27.1	10.2	23.6	0.6
	Total	14.3	24.9	24.6	10.4	25.1	0.6
Adelaide	Inner	17.3	40.2	11.7	16.7	13.1	1.1
	Middle	15.5	39.8	8.6	10.5	24.8	0.8
	Outer	16.9	42.5	7.6	7.4	24.7	0.9
	Total	16.4	41.3	8.3	9.1	23.9	0.9
Perth	Inner	16.2	21.7	24.8	12.0	24.2	1.1
	Middle	14.4	20.9	30.6	8.1	25.6	0.5
	Outer	12.7	20.6	44.9	4.1	16.2	0.5
	Total	13.9	20.8	35.5	7.2	22.0	0.5

Source: ABS, 1976 Census LGA One, quoted in Maher 1982, 76
* 'Other Private' is composed of Life Assurance societies, solicitors trust funds, employers, finance companies, and other private lenders.
** Government includes state housing authority, local government body, state or Australian government department, and the defence or war service homes programmes.

Interests on loans from savings banks rose from 5% in 1955 to 13.5% in 1982. This considerable increase occurred despite the fact that the government intervenes to hold the interest on mortgages below the regular interest level (Maher 1982). Apps (1976) showed what the rise of real-estate prices and of interest on mortgages means to the home purchaser. If, due to increased house prices, a purchaser borrows $ 24,000 instead of $ 20,000 and the interest rate rises from 8% to 12% on a loan given on a 25-year term, then the monthly repayment would rise from $ 154.40 to $ 253.73 which in turn means that a 64% increase in income is required in order to achieve the same monthly repayment : income ratio. It is not surprising that by 1972 private expenditure on new buildings ranged between *25% and 30% of gross private fixed-capital expenditure*, a very high proportion by international standards (Hill 1972).

It is against this background that Australians have asked themselves 'whether we can in fact really afford to accept, as the Australian norm, ownership of the detached house on a fully serviced, quarter-acre block. The dubious nature of this traditional assumption has been obscured until recent times by the relative abundance of land, cheap petrol, high employment, continuing development, and a tolerable degree of inflation. It has also been obscured by the fact that an estimated 250,000 Australians are currently living in caravans. What has hitherto been the Australian "dream" may not really be economically sustainable as a universal entitlement' (Day in: Hanley & Cooper 1982, 320).

On the other hand, the construction of new housing has meant that some older and cheaper housing has become available for lower-income groups. In an investigation of *vacancy chains* in three Melbourne suburbs, Maher found that there had been 2.23 moves per new dwelling constructed, including the move to the new building. This means that new houses are mainly occupied by groups that had only recently left rental housing, thus releasing a vacancy only one or two steps back. He also found evidence for the fact that the majority of purchasers were recently formed households, who had been in their previous residence for only a short time and who were relatively affluent, so that they were quickly able to acquire a home of their own. Maher thus came to the conclusion that 'there may be a more direct link between new household formation, and the demand for new housing, than previously thought' (Maher 1979, 67).

The expanding ratio of households to population and the upgrading of the dwelling stock were the major reasons for the *flat boom* of the 1960s and early 1970s. Carden (in: Roe 1980) claims that in response to the preferences of many newly formed households this involved the continuation of a trend already established in the 1910s and 1920s. What Ashfield, Glebe and Petersham had experienced prior to World War II now happened in Auburn, Canterbury, Manly and Ryde.

The demand for multi-unit dwellings increased again after the late 1970s. This reflected the rise in property prices as well as changes in the age structure of the Australian population. The 20 to 30-year-old group was establishing new households and often looking for provisional accommodation, before buying a house, and similar accommodation was favoured by elderly people in the retiring age, their increasing proportion being due to a higher life expectancy. The future *demand for detached houses* is estimated to be *approximately 70%* of the total dwelling stock, while 30% will be devoted to medium or high-density forms of living (Carden in: Roe 1980).

There are, of course, regional differences in this respect. Multi-unit types of structure, such as semi-terraces, villas, town houses, or flats in low-rise or high-rise buildings account for 30.0% of all dwellings in the Sydney S.D., as compared with only 13.7% in the Brisbane S.D. Due to comparatively high prices for lots, in Sydney three-storey terrace houses were built as early as 1837. These differences have been described in some detail in chapter 3.1.7.

The *state housing authorities* have, in varying degrees, contributed to the multi-unit housing stock, their policies having a certain impact in the differences in the development of urban structure. Their activities were backed up by the development and sale of residential lots by the State Land Commissions or Councils respectively. While during the fiscal year 1974–75 the South Australia Land Commission developed 298 lots and sold 68 lots, the Commissions of South Australia and New South Wales and the Councils of Victoria and Western Australia in the following year developed and sold 4,909 and 2,375 lots respectively (Troy 1978, 145). These figures demonstrate how rapidly the activities of the Commissions and Councils expanded in the mid-1970s.

From the 1950s and through much of the 1970s the housing authorities developed mainly suburban, low-density, *detached single-family housing estates* on the metropolitan peripheries, on a large scale and at comparatively low cost (Lee 1979). Green Valley and Mt. Druitt are good examples in the Sydney metropolitan area, while Bridgewater and Gagebrook, Risdon Vale and Rokeby may serve as examples in the Hobart metropolitan area. After 1981 the Tasmanian Department of Housing put greater emphasis on *small subdivisional in-fill* in the inner suburbs. Many of these small projects were developed for use by marginal groups, such as senior citizens receiving very low rents, disabled persons and single parents. The Housing Commissions of Victoria and New South Wales were the only ones to be involved in inner-city redevelopment and the construction of *high-rise public housing*. In Melbourne the most striking example is to be found in the inner suburb of Fitzroy, with its high-rise apartment blocks reaching up to 40 storeys (ch. 4.1.4). This is why in Melbourne 40.1% of all public housing tenants in 1976 were living in the inner zone, as compared with 17.3% in Sydney (Maher 1982).

Generally speaking, the impact of government housing on urban residential densities has been very modest. On the other hand, *zoning regulations* were often to the effect that plots used for residential use got to be one sixth of an acre or even more and that such lots were prohibited in areas zoned for other purposes; hence the enormous consumption of land (Rose 1976, 205). Urban densities in terms of persons per hectare in the residential areas of MUAs range from 17.0 in Perth to 31.6 in Sydney (1981). Melbourne ranks second, with an average density of 25.4, while the other capital cities are almost equal in this respect, the indices being 21.9 in Brisbane, 21.8 in Adelaide and 21.5 in Hobart. The relation of these indices to local differences of the building stock was discussed in chapter 3.1.7. The distribution of residential densities in the metropolitan areas of the capital cities (1981) is shown in table 42.

It is apparent from the above figures that between 0.6% of the population in Sydney and 9.6% in Perth live at the lowest densities, that is below 1,000 persons per square kilometre or four persons per acre, whereas between 1.7% in Adelaide and 35.3% in Sydney live at densities above 4,000 persons/square kilometre or 16 persons/acre. Taking the population of the six capitals together, 2.9% live at the lowest densities below 4/acre, 16.1% live at densities between 4/acre and 8/acre, 35.6% live at densities between 8/acre and 12/acre, 24.6% at densities between 12/acre and 16/acre and 20.8% at the highest densities above 16/acre.

Investigations by Marsden (1966), Brine (1976), Neutze (1977), Burnley (1980) and Houghton & Johnson (1984) showed that for various reasons Australian cities do *not bear evidence for Colin Clark's rule* of a progressive decline of densities from the city centre outward in negative exponential manner. A certain approximation to the rule may be found in Sydney and Melbourne. In the former city the higher densities of above 16 persons/acre are to be found in 35% of the total residential area, mainly concentrated in the central city and the inner suburbs. These areas were mainly developed prior to 1890 with working class accommodations for rent, and in close proximity to the CBD and to the centrally located secondary industries. A high proportion of this housing consisted of rental tenements built by investors and speculators, while considerable parts were filled with terrace and row houses on small lots. Often landlords built two or more adjoining houses, sometimes *three houses on two lots*, thus cutting

Table 42. Distribution of residential densities of capital cities, 1981

Residential density per km²	Sydney		Melbourne		Brisbane		Adelaide		Perth		Hobart		Six capitals	
	Residential area* %	Persons	Population %	Residential area %	Persons	Population %	Residential area %	Persons	Population %	Residential area %	Persons	Population %	Residential area %	Persons	Population %	Residential area %	Persons	Population %	Persons	Population %
0– 1000	2.9	17,665	0.6	15.5	90,383	3.5	11.2	30,926	3.3	6.6	19,836	2.2	25.0	77,763	9.6	5.4	2,632	2.0	239,205	2.9
1000– 2000	18.8	273,265	9.5	20.2	320,966	12.5	30.9	207,573	22.0	32.0	203,037	23.0	38.1	281,501	34.8	40.4	38,407	29.9	1,324,749	16.1
2000– 3000	35.7	808,505	28.1	30.4	780,764	30.3	40.5	431,961	45.9	48.6	483,227	54.8	31.9	361,647	44.6	39.7	57,848	45.0	2,923,952	35.6
3000– 4000	24.3	760,704	26.5	22.9	799,473	31.0	14.4	209,538	22.2	12.0	161,449	18.3	3.9	60,505	7.5	13.3	26,638	20.7	2,018,307	24.6
4000– 6000	12.1	519,072	18.1	9.2	434,675	16.8														
6000–10000	4.9	331,594	11.5	1.8	152,911	5.9	3.0	61,823	6.6	0.8	14,862	1.7	1.1	28,119	3.5	1.2	3,027	2.4	1,709,721	20.8
>10000	1.3	163,638	5.7																	
Total		2,874,444			2,579,172			941,821			882,411			809,535			128,552		8,215,935	

* The proportion of the metropolitan area considered to be predominantly in residential use
Source: Div. of Nat. Mapping & ABS (eds.): Atlas of Population and Housing, 1981 Census, Vols. 2–7, 1984 and author's calculations

unit costs, a practice that would not have been open to would-be owner-occupiers (Burnley 1980, 182). The large proportion of about 55% of the total residential area with densities between 8/acre and 16/acre will be found adjacent to the city core, whereas the remaining 10% of the area with densities below 8 persons/acre will be mainly found in the peripheral suburbs.

This highly generalized picture has to be differentiated by introducing three modifying factors. Firstly, even in Sydney a number of *pockets of higher densities* are interspersed in outer residential locations such as Dee Why, Marshfield, Clyde, Cabramatta, Auburn, Liverpool, Carlton or Cronulla. Some eastern suburbs such as Waverley, that enjoy a favourable location with regard to both the beaches and the CBD and that were able to make a profit from the opening in 1979 of the eastern suburbs railway, began to be filled with modern three-storey and even high-rise apartment buildings.

Secondly, densities have been changing over time. In Sydney *densities have steadily fallen* by one half to two-thirds from a peak in 1880–1910. The fall reflected the reduction of the residential housing stock by demolitians or conversions in the most densely populated sections, the decreasing household sizes in the course of demographic transition, the aging of the population and the accelerated out-migration, especially since the end of World War II. These processes have reduced the differences between densities in the inner and outer sections of metropolitan areas (Burnley 1980).

Thirdly, differences in residential densities between the inner city and outer suburbs have always been less marked in the other capitals and in Perth in particular. In the latter city there is hardly any nineteenth century terrace housing, while redevelopment was to date much confined to parts of Subiaco and South Perth. While a general decline of densities from the inner suburbs to the metropolitan periphery may be found in Brisbane, there are some areas of higher densities in the outer parts of the metropolitan area. These can be identified with former separate settlements, such as Brighton-Sandgate, Ipswich or Redcliffe. In Adelaide, the relatively late development of the inner ring suburbs and better planning since the end of the nineteenth century produced spatial variations of density, but *no distinct outward decline*. Higher densities are found in some favourate locations such as Glenelg and in large Housing Trust areas such as Elizabeth and Enfield with their semi-detached cottages.

In general terms, with 80% of the metropolitan population living at densities below 16 persons/acre, the majority of them in detached houses, the Australian city may justifiably be termed more suburban in character than its North American counterpart. It is, therefore, not surprising that Australian town planners have been urged seriously to contemplate the provision of medium to high-density housing, at least along transport routes. This would increase population and so support a wider range of retail and other services, and also make public transportation in general and rapid transit lines in particular more attractive and economical (Jay 1978). As long as Australian central cities continue to be viable, especially with regard to their great numbers of office jobs and their present levels of retail trade, public transport is considered essential, and much more efficient than radial freeways with their negative side effects (chs. 4.1.6, 4.1.9). The Melbourne Metropolitan Plan seeks to increase densities by allowing the *dual occupancy* of a lot, under the condition that new buildings are limited to two storeys and provided that there is sufficient open space left and privacy for the residents is ensured.

4.1.4 Construction, ownership and use of buildings in the CBD

Multi-storey construction in Australian cities remained very modest until the 1950s, as compared with the United States, and is to date very much confined to the office towers in the CBD, to high-rise buildings in CBD extensions and to a few sites in residential areas particularly favourable for high-rise apartment buildings.

The first passenger lift, fixed to the top of a screw shaft and powered by a steam generator, was displayed at the Sydney International Exhibition in 1879. One year later the first lift to be put in operation was installed in a Sydney brewery building. The first truly tall building was the *Australia Building* facing Elizabeth Street in Melbourne. With its 12 storeys, it remained for about 60 years the tallest office building in the city (Latta 1984).

The CBDs of Australia's great cities did not profoundly change until the end of World War II; only then did the post-war high-rise structures make for a different townscape. Even so, their dimensions have remained modest in contrast to the development in the United States. In Chicago, for example, the 47-storey Prudential Building was the city's tallest structure during the 1950s. It was surpassed in the early 1960s by the 60-storey Marina City Towers, and this building was in turn surpassed by the 100-storey John Hancock Center in the late 1960s and by the 110-storey Sears Tower in the early 1970s. Australia's tallest building, the *Rialto* complex in Melbourne's CBD, constructed on the occasion of Victoria's sesquicentenary in 1984–85, has 56 storeys, just about half the elevation of Chicago's Sears Tower or New York's World Trade Center.

Even the great office building boom of the early 1970s did not turn the main streets of Australian CBDs into 'concrete and glass canyons'. This may at least partly be due to the early awareness of Australia's urban planners of the adverse side effects of high-rise structures. Thus in its 'Planning Policies for the Melbourne Metropolitan Region' the MMBW as early as 1971 very clearly stated that traffic congestions and pedestrian problems in the CBD could only be prevented by *restricting the number of massive high-rise structures* to be approved in the CBD and by promoting the wider distribution of new high-rise buildings over the total area of the CBD, rather than allowing them to cluster in certain limited areas within the CBD, where they could have accumulative effects (MMBW 1971). The 'Manhattan syndrome' was thus prevented from spreading over the Australian city centres.

The questions of land ownership and site development in Australian CBDs was investigated by Kilmartin & Thorns (1978). According to their findings, small owner-occupiers and builder-developers were the principal investors during the big building boom in Sydney's CBD from 1969 to 1973. They were followed by insurance companies and foreign investors. Local property-development companies were the latest to move into the CBD real-estate market. The various investors, with their respective numbers of projects and proportions of total investments in the City of Sydney are shown in table 43.

Table 43. Development applications approved by the City of Sydney, 1969–73

Initiator	Number of projects	Percentage of total number	Estimated percentage of total cost
Australian developers	28	46	44
Overseas developers	12	20	14
Insurance companies	5	8	24
Government	2	3	7
Banks	3	5	4
Others	11	18	7
Total	61	100	100

Source: Powys, quoted in Kilmartin & Thorns 1978, 52 (modified)

Table 44. Land ownership in Melbourne's CBD between Collins and Bourke Streets, 1977

Land owner	Land ownership (% of total area)	Owners Number	Percentage	Tenancy structure in % Landlords	Buildings controlled
Financial institutions	28.9	64	23.9		
Insurance companies				14.6	23.4
Banks				1.6	2.7
Other financial				11.4	12.4
Public bodies	26.1	7	2.6	1.0	2.6
Property development companies	18.8	46	17.2	22.9	30.5
Companies	8.7	43	16.1	8.3	9.7
Religious groups	8.7	8	2.9	4.2	3.9
Private individuals	3.8	83	31.1	35.9	14.6
Private trusts	0.8	4	1.5	–	–
Others	4.3	12	4.7	–	–
Total	100	267	100	99.9	99.8

Source: Kilmartin & Thorns 1978, 61, 63, 66 (modified)

Land ownership in the section of Melbourne's CBD between Collins and Bourke Streets is shown in table 44.

It is apparent that *public authorities* are important land owners in the CBD, owning approximately 26% of the total area, with the Melbourne City Council holding the greatest share, followed by the MMBW and the Victorian Government. *Financial institutions* hold the greatest area of CBD land ownership. Private individuals form the most numerous group of land owners, but they only account for 3.8% of the area. The most prominent owners are financial institutions, public bodies and property development companies.

In the Central Area of Perth, which is limited by Perth Water and the Swan River to the east and south, by the freeway in the west and by Aberdeen and Newcastle Streets in the north 39.2% of the area are owned by the State Government, 9.9% by the Local Government and 3.4% by the Commonwealth Government (Council of the City of Perth 1980). This means that altogether 52.5% of the CBD is owned by public bodies, or about twice the proportion in Melbourne's CBD. It must, however, be kept in mind that the Central Area as delimited by the Council of the City of Perth is somewhat larger in extent than the CBD proper, which makes direct comparisons with other CBDs unreliable.

The size of the CBD is dependent upon a number of factors four of which seem to be most important. One factor is the *demand for commercial uses* in the broadest sense and for office space in particular. At the end of 1984, a total of 2.4 million square metres of office space was available in the Sydney CBD, with another 1.6 million square metres outside the CBD. In the Melbourne CBD 1.8 million square metres of space was available, with another 0.2 million square metres in the rest of the metropolitan area. In contrast, the total office stock in Perth in and outside the CBD was 888,000 square metres and in Adelaide 559,000 square metres (Australia Wide Property Trusts; see ch. 3.1.7). The dominating role of Sydney and Melbourne as administrative and commercial centres is obvious, although there is also a considerable difference in rank between the two.

A second factor is the *relative location of the CBD* within the metropolitan area, to which may be added the effects of any physical constraints on outward expansion. Due to the inland location of the original settlement nuclei of Adelaide and Perth, both the Adelaide CBD and the Perth CBD are today very centrally located within their respective metropolitan area. Because the nucleus of the Moreton Bay Settlement was relocated from the coast to a bend of the Brisbane River somewhat upstream, Brisbane's CBD also enjoys a fairly central location. The CBDs of Hobart, Sydney and Melbourne are much more excentric with regard to the present extent of their metropolitan areas. Scott (1959) claimed that such excentric location of the CBD limits accessibility and thus favours suburban competition. In addition, the CBDs of Sydney and Brisbane are more or less rigidly surrounded by natural barriers,

Fig. 108. Melbourne's CBD and its extensions

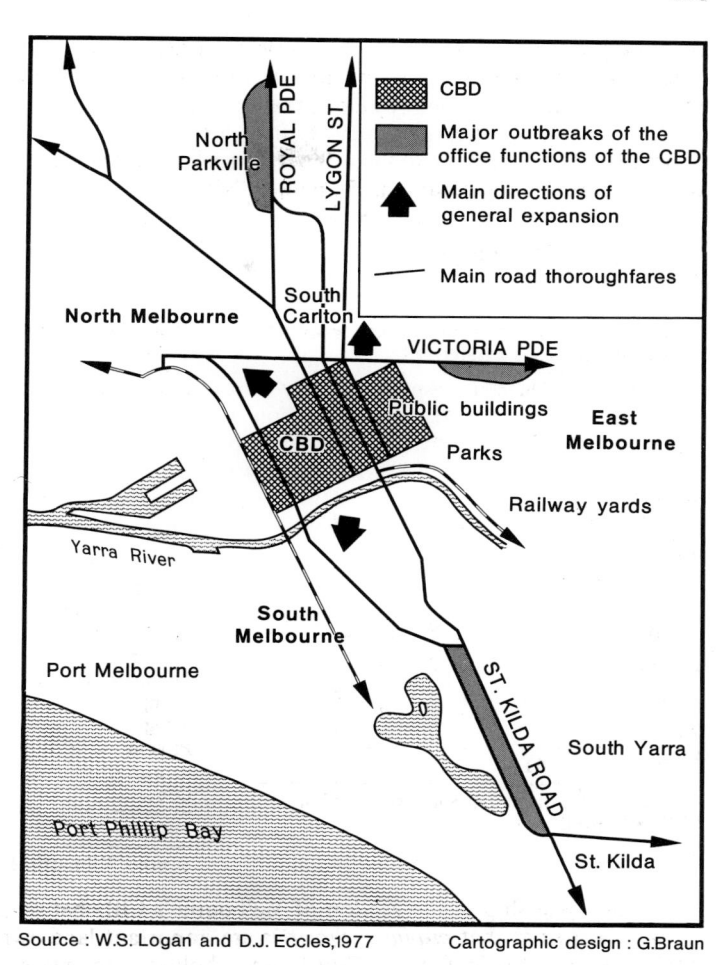

that proved obstacles to greater outward expansion. This is why Melbourne's CBD is larger in textent than Sydney's (Scott 1959).

A third factor is the tendency to *decentralize CBD activities* to favourable suburban locations. From the above figures on office space, it appears that this tendency is particularly conspicuous in Sydney. In addition to the 2.4 million square metres of office space in the City of Sydney, another 1.6 million square metres are available in North Sydney and a few other locations on the North Shore, and even as far away from the city centre as Parramatta. In Melbourne CBD extensions have to date been much more modest, with developments to the north, east and, above all, to the south along St. Kilda Road. In Adelaide the only small CBD extension is found on the south side of the parklands. In Brisbane some CBD functions concentrated to the northeast in Fortitude Valley. In Perth CBD functions extended to the west so that West Perth today may be considered part of a larger and conterminous CBD (ch. 3.1.7, fig. 108).

A fourth factor influencing the size of the CBD is *competition from district centres* in the suburbs, particularly with regard to retail sales in their modern shopping centres. These will be discussed below in more detail (chs. 4.1.7 to 4.1.9).

Scott (1959) recognized an *inner differentiation* of the Australian CBD so far as retailing is concerned, with an inner zone characterized by department, variety and women's clothing stores offering personal requisites, surrounded by an outer zone mainly offering household goods and services. In some cases the inner retail zone is divided into a larger section and a smaller section, these two being separated from one another by other CBD uses. The Sydney CBD shows a very obvious differentiation, with its retail core located adjacent to the Central Station in the southern section and an office core in the northern section, both showing a constant northward movement. While retail functions have been pushing northward, office functions have jumped across the Parramatta River to the CBD extension in North Sydney (chs. 3.1.1–3.1.7).

Special mention should be made of a few functional and locational phenomena peculiar to the Australian city. For example, the Australian chemist's shop differs from both the English chemist and the American drugstore. With regard to the former it is smaller in scale and function and, apart from the dispensing of drugs, is mainly restricted to the sale of cosmetics, toilet preparations, photographic articles, handbags, toys and costume jewelry. Unlike the American drugstore it does not provide refreshments and is usually not found at corner locations. The Australian chemist's shop is locationally associated with women's clothing stores and dispersed along pedestrian routes in the inner retail zone and, to some extent, the outer retail zone (Scott 1959).

City hotels are very often found in corner locations since they have always much relied on beer sales in their bars. 'In at least their location, therefore, hotels would seem to be the Australian equivalent to the American drug store' (Scott 1959, 311). In Hobart banks are mainly found at the corners of the main shopping streets while in the other CBDs they came to be concentrated in the inner retail zone.

Some of the more recent development has taken place in connection with the establishment of *pedestrian malls* in the city centre. This development started much later in Australia than in North America and Europe, and the malls have so far remained more modest in extent. Rundle Mall that had been built for $ 1.5 million over a length of 800 m was opened in 1976. The main reason for its creation had been the extremely dense vehicular traffic and high degree of air pollution. Approximately 300 out of a total of 1,000 shops in the Adelaide CBD are located on either side of the mall. This great concentration of shops led to the decision not to put additional stands and booths in the street, which is in contrast to most malls in European cities. Hay Street Mall in the Perth CBD was not permanently closed to vehicular traffic until 1970, and was only re-landscaped by 1975 (Monheim 1983). Other famous pedestrian areas are Bourke Street in the Melbourne CBD and Martin Place in the Sydney CBD. These and other pedestrian areas are still rather small as compared with their European and American counterparts, due to the weak municipal decision-making processes and a strong pro-car lobby (Monheim 1983). The malls in existence have remained exclusively shopping malls and have scarcely assumed any administrative, cultural or entertainment functions.

The larger malls have had a certain impact on the restructuring of their immediate environs. Shops were remodeled and modernized, and on the south side of Bourke Street in Melbourne a large commercial complex was sold and torn down to make room for a new modern shopping arcade. Sydney's CBD offers a particularly interesting case. As mentioned above there has been a long lasting tendency for office functions to move beyond the Parramatta River to the North Shore, and of retailing functions to move from the Central Station in the southern section toward the office blocks of the northern section. Thus until the 1950s, Martin Place was part of the banking and financial area of Sydney's CBD. Its conversion to a great pedestrian mall, even furnished with a small amphitheatre for musical performances, accelerated the northward movement of shops to this former area of offices[1].

4.1.5 The inner suburbs: renewal, rehabilitation and gentrification in the face of site-value taxation, resident actions and green bans

The zone adjoining the CBD is comprised of the rest of the central city and of the inner suburbs. The latter are also referred to as the older-established suburbs; they were built up and settled mainly during the nineteenth century and the first decade after federation. As mentioned in chapter 2.1.3.1 annexations were so modest and municipalities remained so small that for practical purposes and particularly for international comparisons these two areas, the central city and the inner suburbs, can be considered as identical with the 'city' whereas the outer and younger suburbs established since World War I constitute the suburban ring comparable with the metropolitan ring of U.S. cities.

This section of the metropolitan area is characterized by relatively high residential densities, which in Sydney and to a lesser extent in Melbourne are due to the large numbers of *terrace and row houses*, and in the other capital cities to the relatively high proportion of flats and dwelling units other than detached houses. The section is also characterized by some intermingling of residential areas and inner-industrial concentrations, also dating in part from the last century. It is the residential areas of this section that processes like urban renewal, residential rehabilitation and gentrification have brought about considerable changes in the post-war era.

As was found in urban studies in the United States, by Lang (1982) among others, rehabilitation and gentrification by private financial means often occurred in areas adjacent to official urban-renewal areas. There appears to be some justification in the observation that urban renewal and gentrification are, both in terms of space and time, closely related urban processes and that each dollar invested by government for urban renewal has induced several dollars of private investment for rehabilitation. In the United Kingdom this seems to be more of an exception as in the case of the London Docklands.

In the Australian situation, urban renewal has tended to occur to a lesser extent and gentrification to a greater extent than in the United States. The major reason for such difference seems to be the generally higher quality of the building stock in the inner section of Australian cities. The much greater use of solid building materials, such as brick and stone, made houses less prone to deterioration, so that *rehabilitation or restoration* appeared to be a more reasonable alternative than demolition and reconstruction. Moreover, such solidly built houses lend themselves better to being bought and modernized by private gentrifiers than highly deteriorated wooden structures.

---

1 Personal communication of Mr. J. Hajdu, Melbourne

The beginnings of government intervention in the continuous urban renewal process date back to the second half of the 1930s. The main argument for such intervention was that slum dwellers were people of inferior morals and undesirable social behaviour, so that the residential areas that spawned them should be swept away. In post-war years two different arguments were used to justify the housing authorities' engagement in urban renewal projects. One was that the deterioration and under-use of housing stock resulted in a loss in tax revenues and a waste of resources. The other was that under-use and low densities in the central city and inner suburbs were one important reason for urban sprawl, which could be curtailed by achieving higher densities in the inner city through the inclusion of multi-storey buildings in urban-renewal schemes.

Although *renewal* in Australian cities achieved nothing like the dimensions reached in many American cities, it was nevertheless carried out in some areas that were not in markedly poor condition and which might well have been saved by repair and modernization, rather than by total destruction and the substitution of completely new structures. It was also claimed that, in some cases, slum reclamation meant that the housing authority 'subsidized the private developers to whom it sold the land for redevelopment' (Kilmartin & Thorns 1978, 100). According to these authors, seven projects in Melbourne acquired by the Victorian Housing Commission between 1959 and 1967 were purchased for $ 2.86 million and sold to private developers for $ 1.26 million, or 44% of the cost of acquisition. To do justice to the housing authorities, their previous experience had exclusively been in the development of new estates on the urban periphery; urban renewal and rehabilitation of existing dwelling houses were new tasks for them. To the extent that they did not sell to private developers but rather assumed the responsibility for the renewal and rehabilitation projects themselves, they needed the co-operation of experienced architectural consultants and builders. Perumal (1984) described the situation for the projects of Waterloo and Wooloomooloo in Sydney in detail.

Two different processes helped to upgrade some areas in the central city and inner suburbs: gentrification and the conversion of multi-storey residences to strata title. The term *'gentrification'* is adopted, regardless of the fact that it has been much disputed and even rejected by some authors with the argument that it has no true relation to the word 'gentry', from which it was derived. Gentrification, in the context of urban development, means the upgrading of somewhat delapidated housing stock by private financial means of middle-class or sometimes even upper-class persons migrating into such areas. Gentrification also means the up-grading of a quarter in terms of the increasing residential representation of the professional, technical and clerical occupational groups, characterized by higher incomes and higher standards of living than the previous residents. It also means that such areas are affected by selective migration, to the effect that the former above-average proportion of elderly people and below-average proportion of school-age children is being counter-balanced by the in-migration of young adults in the 20–35-year group bringing with them above-average numbers of pre-school children.

Gentrification has occurred in a number of inner residential areas: Balmain, Darlinghurst, Edgecliff, Glebe, Paddington and Surry Hills in Sydney; Carlton, North Melbourne and East Melbourne in Melbourne; Battery Point and Glebe in Hobart, and Subiaco in Perth. The process is usually associated with increasing home-ownership and a decrease of residential densities. The proportion of residents in blue-collar jobs decreased during the intercensal period 1971–76 by seven to nine percentage points in the Sydney residential districts of Darlinghurst, Paddington and Surry Hills. A slight decrease in the proportion of overseas immigrants as compared with Australian-born residents is also ascribed to gentrification.

The areas showing incidents of gentrification are not necessarily contiguous to the CBD but, as in Sydney, may be separated from the latter by a kilometre or more of poorer housing (Burnley 1980). Moreover, gentrification is usually *restricted to rather small, patchy areas*, a fact that is hidden by the aggregate data based on LGAs usually used in urban investigations (Logan 1982). The extent of gentrification is at least partly dependent upon the quality of the building stock. Thus much of Paddington was developed by small-scale builders, who were in many cases the owner-occupiers and who ensured a good quality of construction. These circumstances made for a higher renovative potential than in areas developed by absentee landlords and speculators 'often with less quality in the construction' (Burnley 1980, 191). In a micro-level analysis of Melbourne Logan (1982) found that gentrification, as measured by a population exchange in favour of more Australian-born owner-occupiers in professional and managerial jobs, had only occurred in Darling Street (East Melbourne) and in Wilson, Garton and Drummond Streets in North Carlton, that is to say, in relatively small sections of their respective LGAs.

Similar changes of population structure, as associated with the process of gentrification, are observed as a consequence of the conversion of multi-storey residences to *strata title* (condominiums), that is to say from rental to freehold status. During the period 1962–80 over 3,300 dwelling units in the Sydney residential areas of Kings Cross, Elizabeth Bay and Darlinghurst were converted to strata title.

Both gentrification and the conversion of dwelling units to strata title resulted in a degree of displacement of lower-class residents and a decrease of low-rent housing. The latter became so scarce in some inner residential areas that Kendig (1979) came to the conclusion that Australian cities, in contrast to North American cities, have begun to suffer from a *gentrification problem* rather than from a slum problem. This statement is, however, disputed. Maher (1978) claimed that the loss of low-cost housing through demolition has been more important than the loss through gentrification.

The question of the lesser deterioration of the housing stock in the inner suburbs of Australian cities as compared with most larger U.S. cities is, however, a complex one. It cannot be answered by reference to the more solid construction materials and greater longevity of buildings, or to the internal migration of a number of middle-class people finding it worthwhile to take advantage of this situation. Other factors such as the Australian taxation system and the policy of the trades unions have substantially contributed to the conservation and rehabilitation of the building stock of the inner suburbs.

In the United States the so-called *'improved-value system' of taxation* is applied to real estate. This essentially means that the value of the house and other structures on any particular lot is assessed rather than the land. Thus when a house has been deteriorating over time the assessed value keeps decreasing all the time, until after many years the owner hardly pays any tax at all. In many cases it even happened that owners of more than one lot ceased to pay taxes so that, on the grounds of tax delinquency, the house and lot automatically fell to the municipality. Tax delinquency and high vacancy rates have become widespread in the older suburbs of U.S. cities. In some cities the problem was partially solved by 'urban homesteading' which means the transfer by the administration of such a house to a family willing to restore it for a token fee.

In contrast to the United States, the unimproved or *'site-value system' of taxation* is applied in Australia. Assessment is largely based on the value of the land, and taxes are high enough to function as an incentive to the owner for investments and improvements and for raising his own rent base. This does not only mean better maintenance of the house; this kind of taxation also encourages more intensive land development. This was one reason for the building boom of high-rise office blocks in the CBD in recent years (Ravallion 1975).

There are, however, differences from one state to the other. In Melbourne the 'net annual rate system' has been applied, which 'taxes property on the amount of rent that would be received, minus costs, were the property on the market' or, in other words, 'the bigger the building the greater would be the rates payable' (Small 1979, 55). This made for a certain reluctance on the part of investors to construct very large and very high buildings so that in Melbourne's CBD the 'Manhattan syndrome' was not experienced to the degree as it was in Sydney (ch. 4.1.4).

A characteristic Australian feature was the imposition by the Builders Labourers' Federation (BLF) of the so-called *green bans* on certain projects during the peak of the building boom in Sydney 1971–73. The background of the green ban movement is rather complicated and not easily comprehended by non-Australians. For details the reader is particularly referred to Jakubowicz (in Halligan & Paris 1984), who gives a detailed account of the situation at the turn from the 1960s to the 1970s and refers to all the forces at work that led to the emergence of the green ban movement. Reference should also be made to Daly (1982), who gave an account of the world financial market at the beginning of the building boom in Sydney and its repercussions on money flows to, and investments in, Australia in general and in Australian real estate in particular. Mundey (1981), who for a certain period of time was the president of the BLF, has described the whole situation from an insider's point of view.

Without going into all details, the four most important factors leading to the imposing by the BLF of green bans on development projects in inner Sydney shall be briefly mentioned (see also ch. 3.1.1). One factor was the formation of the *Eurodollar* market, in the wake of which more than 35 foreign banks opened up Australian branches or offices between 1969 and 1971, managing a considerable flow of money to the Australian market (Daly 1982). The indifferent results of investment in mining and manufacturing led to a diversion of major investment flows to the real-estate market. At the same time the rapid expansion of the tertiary sector of the Australian economy brought a great demand for new office buildings. The result was projects such as Wooloomooloo, where the private-owned and Commonwealth-owned working-class residences were to be replaced by high-rise office buildings to form an eastward extension of Sydney's CBD, with a certain portion of the area held back for freeway construction.

Secondly, the older *working-class residents* were thus in danger of being evicted. The protests of the residents were backed by the Australian Labor Party, particularly in ALP-controlled municipalities. Conflicts arose over gerrymandering, as successfully attempted in inner Sydney. After the Liberal Party had come to power in New South Wales in 1965, the State Government sacked the Labor-controlled Sydney City Council and changed the boundaries of the wards in a way that they would ensure a conservative majority on the reconstituted Council. For example, in Paddington the former Labor area was attached to the municipality of Woolahra to put the Labor aldermen into a minority (Jakubowicz in: Halligan & Paris 1984). Similar tensions arose in other inner suburbs of Sydney.

Thirdly, the turn from the 1960s to the 1970s was a period in which a great demand for the democratization of the decision-making process and a strong desire for more citizen participation in planning became evident. This is why the BLF was eager to get wide community support (Troy 1981, 15). *Residents' action groups* had been formed and supported the green bans in The Rocks, Wooloomooloo and elsewhere. They were backed by their umbrella organization, the Coalition of Resident Action Groups (CRAG), founded in 1971. The groups were very active, regardless of the fact that they became involved in squatting and other acts of direct confrontation by radicals participating in their campaigns. A third partner in these controversies was the Institute of Real Estate Developers (IRED), which committed itself to the support of citizens' participatory rights, to conservation and to the improvement of the environment, while trying to persuade the conflicting parties to compromise (Nittum in: Roe 1980). In some cases, for instance in The Rocks, the National Trust also intervened (ch. 2.2.8).

A fourth factor was the profound change in the nature of construction firms, of construction techniques and of the unions' response to such change. As mentioned above, this was the period when in Australia's central cities the traditional building stock began to be replaced by high-rise structures. Simultaneously the unions began to summon their members to struggle for *greater job safety and greater control* over the labour process in a changing world of production. 'Many of the industrial disputes of the green-ban period were over questions to do with working conditions, safety on the new high-rise constructions, long service leave provisions and health arrangements on-site' (Jakubowicz in: Halligan & Paris 1984, 157). This fourth factor was, apart from all the political issues mentioned earlier, the only one that could be labelled a specifically trade-union issue.

Between June 1971 and April 1973, the BLF imposed green bans on seven major development projects in the Sydney metropolitan area, on which union members would not work: Hunter's Hill, Eastlakes, The Rocks, Glebe, Waterloo, Wooloomooloo and Victoria Street in Kings Cross. By mid-1973 projects worth $ 3,000 million had been stopped (Logan & Eccles 1977). The plans for high-rises and freeways were eventually abandoned, or at least restricted and modified, being replaced by rehabilitation and, to some extent, infill renewal carried out as low-rise public housing (see chs. 3.1.1, 4.1.6).

There was also some government intervention in the projects hit by green bans. As mentioned above, the Labor Party has for a long time been inclined to take up urban issues and give financial support to urban development. Thus it must not be overlooked that the Whitlam Labor Government (1972–75) played a dicisive part in the land acquisition for rehabilitation and partial renewal in both Glebe and Wooloomooloo as stated in chapter 3.1.1.

A factor deserving more detailed elaboration is the residential choice of overseas immigrants. Since there are great differences from the patterns in U.S. cities this point will be dealt with in a separate chapter (ch. 4.2).

4.1.6 Layout: the grid, irregular street patterns, urban freeways

In the older sections of the Australian city the usual arrangement of houses was along streets cossing at right angles. There was no counterpart in Australia to the American rectangular survey system, rigorously superimposed on all the land beyond the Appalachian Mountains after 1785, and thus offering a frame for the street pattern of all settlements subsequent to that date. Nevertheless there seems to have been a consensus as to the *application of the grid* in the Colonial Office in London, and its use was required under instructions transmitted to the Governors and surveyors in the various parts of the colonies. It must also be remembered that for over 60 years New South Wales was the only colony, including both the mainland and Van Diemen's Land, so that all instructions concerning the layout of settlements came from London via Sydney.

The original grid of any settlement in Australia consisted of only a few streets. Hobart Town, for example, had seven streets: Liverpool Street, Collins Street and Macquarie Street were crossed at right angles by Argyle, Elizabeth, Murray and Harrington Streets. In later times the existing streets were elongated and some more streets paralleling the existing ones were added to the grid. In Melbourne the original 24 blocks bordered by Flinders, Little Bourke, Spencer and Spring Streets were offered in five consecutive sales between 1837 and 1839, this town core later being extended by another one and a half blocks to the north (Fig. 108).

The streets were designed to be of a *standard width*, for example in Hobart Town they were supposed to be 60 feet wide with the exception of Macquarie Street that was to be 66 feet wide. In Melbourne the streets were supposed to be 99 feet wide, and the blocks between two east-west running streets were divided by narrow *alleys*. The alleys so common in the central cities of North America are only found in a few Australian cities.

Deviations from the standard grid may range from the considerable irregularities of the street pattern in The Rocks in Sydney to the extremely geometrical design of the parkland town of Adelaide, which included five squares located at specific points of the town core. Immediately on the landing of the First Fleet in Sydney Cove, Governor Phillip had given instructions for the layout of the settlement. In the period before Governor Macquarie took office in 1810, however, these instructions were very much neglected. For one thing, the hilly topography of The Rocks did not always allow streets to be completely straight; today one element making The Rocks so attractive to tourists is the crookedness of some of its streets. Another reason lay in the tension between the military and the administration, which at times reached the verge of mutiny. Under such circumstances, regulations were not always obeyed, so that the development of Sydney prior to 1810 must have been rather chaotic (ch. 3.1.1). With regard to the streets of central Sydney being narrower than those of central Melbourne, Scott (1959, 291) commented on the high-rise structures in Sydney's CBD in the post-war period: '... there is an oppressive lack of organic relationship between street plan and building height'.

Sydney's street pattern never reached the regularity of metropolitan Melbourne's road system. The patterns of streets vary from one section of the metropolis to another. As Rose (1976, 209) put it: 'Sydney is an urban mess that has grown by piecemeal accretion rather than by enforced conformity with a compass-oriented straight jacket'. When Maitland was in the actual phase of planning and it was foreseeable that a number of towns would be created in the near future *Governor Darling* in 1829 issued a set of regulations for the guidance of the government surveyors. This ensured a uniform pattern of Australian towns with the exception of South Australia and Western Australia so that one may say that, with a few exceptions, Australian towns became 'Darling towns'.

Next to Sydney, with increasing degrees of regularity, are Brisbane and Perth. The cores of both capital cities are characterized by geometrical street patterns, though blocks differ in size in various sections of the central city. In

Hobart blocks are fairly equal in size, while in Melbourne all blocks of the original town are absolutely identical. In his study of the development of Melbourne's street pattern, Johnston (1968) pointed out that due to the lack of greater natural obstacles, the grid was widely applied, except in peripheral areas developed by the Housing Commission or private developers, and in inner residential areas of low density and high socio-economic status that have experienced more recent re-division. In the initial stage of town formation, there was only this planned town and the stock routes of the pre-urban agricultural landscape leading to it. In a second stage of development the street pattern was determined by the boundaries of agricultural lots, which were generally straight, but of differing lengths and directions; they were partly oriented on water bodies or were identical with parish boundaries.

Finally, there is Adelaide as an example of an extremely well-planned settlement. The plan of Adelaide provided a perfect grid, or rather two grids on either side of the Torrens River. It also made provisions for the functional differentiation of the settlement, dividing the original town site into three zones: the centrally located town lands, the surrounding parklands and the adjoining suburban lands. This plan was later copied by nearly 300 other settlements, making the *parkland town* a distinct regional type of urban settlement, closely identified with the colony of South Australia (chs. 2.2.4, 3.1.3).

The Adelaide plan also provided for a large square in the very centre of town and another four public squares systematically distributed over the rest of the original town. The central square was supposed to become the city centre, but this did not happen. The majority of public buildings and most of the administrative, cultural and commercial functions were attracted by the North Terrace and even by the parklands and, as far as retail trade is concerned, to the streets on the north side in close proximity to North Terrace.

There was obviously no standard as to the design of *public squares*. There are a few small public squares in The Rocks in Sydney. No true square was provided for by the original plan of Melbourne, where City Square owes its existence only to the setback of a public building. In Perth a public square provided for in the original plan was abandoned at a rather early stage of town development, so that today Victoria Square with St. Mary's Cathedral is the only square left in the Central Area. There is, however, much open space in central Perth, although this is at least partly due to the comparatively recent reclamation of land from the Perth Water. In the face of such developments, the endowment of central Adelaide with a number of fine public squares must be considered an exception.

The grid has been applied to suburban development throughout many decades. Hajdu (1979, 357) commented on this widespread use of the grid pattern: 'The attitude towards the physical environment was one of ignorance mixed with suspicion. The desirable aspect for the dwelling was frequently not considered during the planning of an estate and the siting of its houses; if it was considered at all, it showed the automatic reflex action of the Northern European to this supposedly uniformly hot continent. What has resulted from this is the hundreds of square kilometres of suburbia with rectangular street grids, filled with houses exposed to the hot westerly sun or icy southerly blasts. The more diverse street patterns which have become the norm in the last decade or so are more the reflection of the needs of traffic engineering than an increased sensitivity to the environment'.

Early deviations from the grid were provided by some *well-planned new towns* in the second decade of the twentieth century, Walter Burley Griffin's designs for the capital city of Canberra and the two administrative centres of the Murrumbidgee Irrigation Areas, Griffith and Leeton (chs. 3.1.9, 3.4.1). Particularly in Canberra and Griffith, the Chicago architect followed such famous precursors as L'Enfent, Haussman and Burnham in applying such distinct planning principles as great circles and long axes with grand vistas, but these were exceptions.

On the other hand, vistas were also an element of town planning outside the new towns. One of the most famous examples is the axis formed by Swanston Street in Melbourne's CBD and its continuation along the northern section of St. Kilda Road. While the latter eventually makes a slight turn to the right, the axis follows a footpath through the Kings Domain all the way to the Shrine of Remembrance, which is thus visible from a great distance.

But in general the grid survived until recent years. Even in the new towns of Elizabeth and Kwinana, designed and constructed during the 1950s, the basic layout is still a large block with many streets running more or less parallel. Use is made of the modern planning device of a *hierarchy of roads*, from access roads to collector roads and distributor roads and ultimately to arterial roads, with a considerable number of crescents, but, on the other hand, there is a very reluctant use of Radburn-type cul-de-sacs design. Only in the towns or subdivisions planned in the 1970s has there been a more complete deviation from the traditional grid and block pattern.

In contrast to the United States, little freeway construction has occurred to date in Australia's large cities. In 1971 all Australian MUAs had a mere 109 km of urban freeways; during the decade 1971–81 their length increased to only 177 km. Thus by 1981 only 2.5% of all urban arterial roads were freeways (Rimmer 1977, Badcock & Cloher 1981, Nat. Ass. Austral. State Road Auth. 1984) (fig. 109).

The length of urban freeways in the metropolitan areas of the capital cities are shown in table 45.

There seem to be two reasons for this *lack of urban freeways* in Australia. Prior to 1970, there were no such incentives comparable with those given in the United States by the Federal Aid Highway Act of 1962, providing 90% federal funding of urban expressways connecting with the Interstate and Defense Highway System. After 1970 the two major constraints were the general cutting of funds due to more limited financial resources and the growing opposition of citizens' actions groups to the extension of existing urban freeways.

Thus in Sydney an Anti-Expressway Campaign was started, aiming at the conservation of old buildings, the

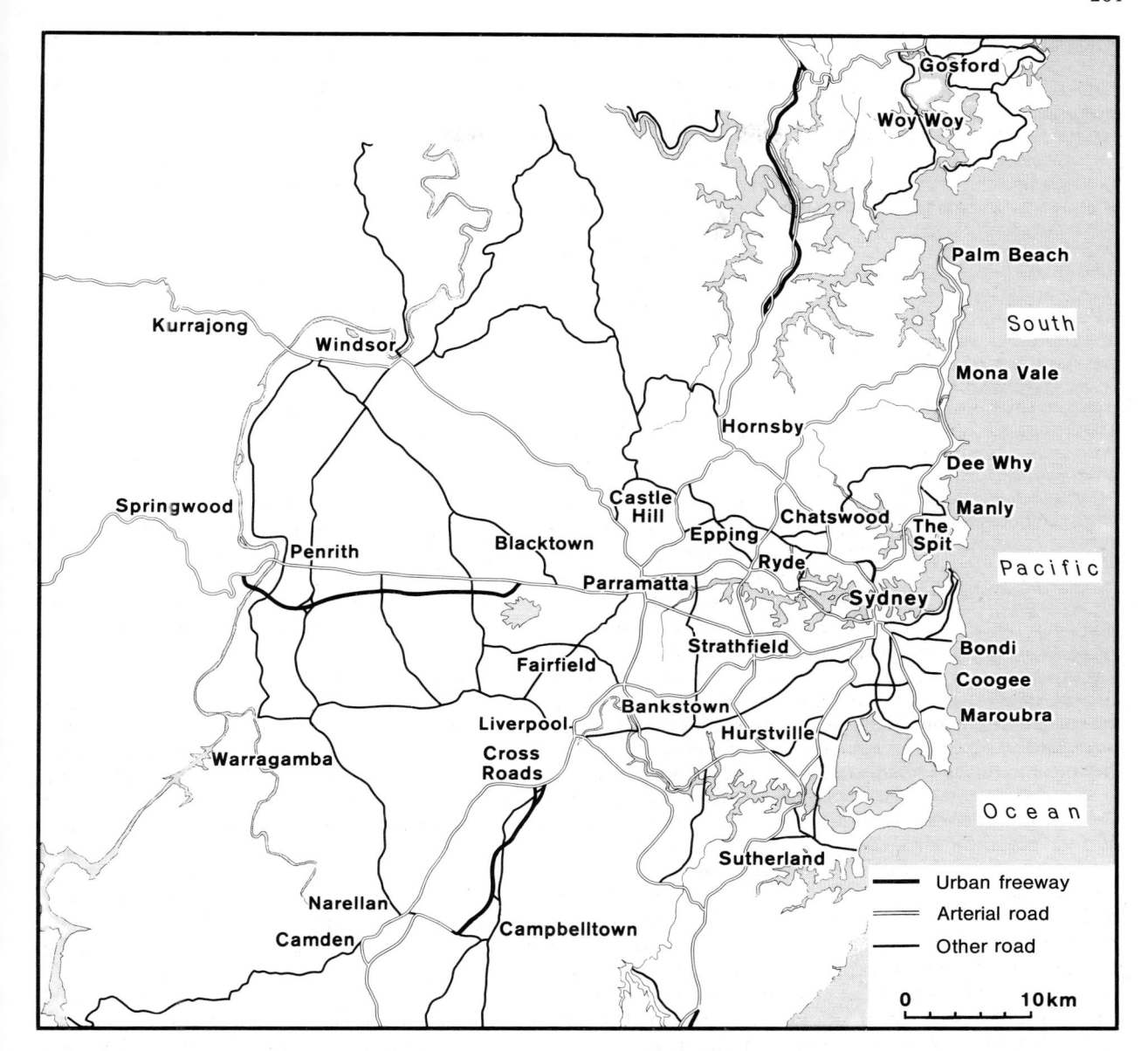

Fig. 109. The low level of urban freeway development in the Sydney metropolitan area

Table 45. Distribution of urban freeways, 1981

City	Arterial roads in km	Freeways in km	Freeways as a percentage of arterial roads
Sydney	1,484	29	2.0
Melbourne	1,788	83	4.6
Brisbane	714	17	2.4
Perth	1,062	20	2.0
Canberra	195	11	5.6
Other NSW cities		16	
Other Vic. cities		1	
Total		177	

Source: NAASRA Urban Arterial Roads Report 1984, 151, 200, 251, 340, 392

saving of low-cost housing and the improvement of public transport (Nittum in: Roe 1980). In Brisbane construction of the Southern Freeway, and the removal of residents from parts of Kangaroo Point and Buranda, was followed in 1972 by the formation of a Brisbane Freeway Protest and Compensation Committee (BFPCC). Street marches, picketing and squatting followed the announcement of the projected Northern and Central Freeways (Mullins 1979). The latter were then indefinitely postponed and no new freeways planned. In Hobart the Northern Freeway project was abandoned (ch. 3.1.6). In Melbourne an appreciable proportion of the proposed freeways were abandoned after 1974 when, during the Whitlam Labor Government, the Commonwealth Bureau of Roads recommended that a great number of intraurban freeways should not be built (Maher 1982, 103).

Perth seems to be an exception to the rule. In the early 1980s a rather comprehensive freeway construction programme was carried out in the Western Australian capital city. The question arises whether there is any connection between freeway construction in Perth and the better quality of the Perth Transportation Study as compared with the Transportation Studies of the other metropolitan areas. According to Duhs & Beggs (1977, 243) 'the Perth Study alone presents a comprehensive analysis of that range of alternative highway/public transport/land-use plans selected for consideration ...'.

Access to the suburban district centres (ch. 4.1.8) by motor vehicles is therefore in most cases by a normal arterial road or by two roads intersecting near the centre. The impact of the lack of freeway entry points on suburban development will be treated in chapter 4.1.7.

4.1.7 The suburbanization of people, jobs and retail trade

The outer suburbs are those areas predominantly built up after World War I. However, their growth during the interwar period was modest; it was very much restricted to some outer village cores and the vicinity of tramway lines and was interrupted by the Depression and World War II. Except in the 1920s, when the United States for the first time applied a quota system to immigration and greater numbers of people turned to Australia, there was no considerable influx of overseas immigrants during the period between federation and the end of World War II. Industrialization was not to the forefront, and the Australian economy was still very much based on agricultural and mineral resources.

For the reasons mentioned in chapter 2.1.2 an appreciable change occurred after the end of World War II through the Federal Government's adoption of a very active *industrialization and immigration policy.* Moreover, some State Governments were eager to promote industrial development. Between the 1947 census and 1983 Australia's population more than doubled through the addition of 7.8 million persons, approximately 3 million of whom were overseas immigrants. During the same period the proportion of home owners and home buyers increased from 53% to 68%; the ratio of private car ownership changed from 1:15.0 in 1964 (the ratio of 1:3.7 had already been reached in the U.S. by 1950) to 1:2.4 in 1983.

Apart from population increase, economic growth and the rise in the standard of living, some other factors tended to promote suburbanization. In the absence of planning restrictions during the early post-war years, cheap land was still available in large quantities, and inexpensive house construction was possible. Extensive areas were zoned for residential development on the metropolitan peripheries. When metropolitan planning was introduced in the late 1940s and early 1950s, at least some of the plans aimed at bringing together people and jobs, which means that they attempted to encourage the suburban location of manufacturing plants and other businesses. Government subsidies and the attitude of financial lending institutions favoured new houses, thus tending at the same time to favour suburbanization. Home ownership grants, subsidies for interest rates on home loans and personal income tax deductions for local rates also gave preference to new suburban homes (fig. 110).

Not only was the enormous population increase absorbed by the rapidly expanding suburban zones, but there was at the same time a net loss of population in the central cities and in some of the inner suburbs, affecting both the Australian-born population and the overseas immigrants. Recent population changes of the capital cities and their metropolitan areas are shown in table 46.

Table 46. Population change in the central cities and metropolitan areas of state capitals, 1971–76

City	Central city population		Overseas population of central city		Metropolitan population	
	1971	1976	1971	1976	1971	1976
Sydney	62,470	52,187	23,729	18,178	2,725,064	2,945,400
Melbourne	75,830	64,970	26,383	20,602	2,394,117	2,672,200
Brisbane	3,645	3,036	857	696	818,423	985,900
Adelaide	16,313	13,774	4,583	3,658	809,482	912,100
Perth	97,546	87,598	34,983	29,937	641,800	820,100
Hobart	52,426	50,384	7,998	7,825	130,000	126,600

Sources: ABS, Dept. Immgr. and Ethn. Affairs 1981

Fig. 110. Sydney, N.S.W. Aerial view of southern outer suburbs

Suburban growth was so rapid that public utilities could not always be supplied in time to new residential subdivisions. An extreme case is the Perth S.D., where even by 1976 almost 50% of private houses were *lacking sewerage* (Houghton 1979, 113), although approximately 80% of the homes concerned had been built during the 1950s and 1960s. A federal law of 1971 prohibited the construction of houses unless they were served by municipal sewerage. Most of the pre-1971 growth had taken place in areas dominated by detached houses at maximum densities of 12 persons per acre.

The growing outward movement of the resident population to the outer suburbs was accompanied by a shift of workplaces. Two trends may be observed in this respect. Firstly, the distribution of total employment in the metropolitan areas changed in favour of the outer zones. Then, at the same time, the *outward movement of blue-collar jobs was faster* than of white-collar jobs, so that the latter began more and more to concentrate in the central city while the majority of the former became available in the middle and outer suburbs. The respective changes in Sydney, Melbourne and Adelaide are shown in table 47.

Metropolitan Sydney is a good example of the reorientation of manufacturing jobs. The old and rather centrally located Alexandria-Waterloo area is more and more at a disadvantage due mainly to problems of accessibility and the lack of room for expansion. Moreover, the ability of Port Jackson to accommodate large modern vessels and to provide facilities for the expanding container trade and roll-on/roll-off traffic is limited in comparison with the capacities of Botany Bay. It is, therefore, not surprising that in 1979 the development of Botany Bay as a modern deep-sea harbour commenced. This has been an important incentive for the concentration of secondary industries in the Botany Bay area (Proudfoot 1982, Rimmer & Black in: Cardew, Langdale & Rich 1982).

While the suburbanization of blue-collar jobs was the more substantial change, there has also been an increasing shift of tertiary employment in favour of the suburban zone. Edgington in his study of the Melbourne CBD (1982) came to four interesting conclusions. Firstly, the CBD still enjoyed an increase of total employment during the 1960s, with 1971–76 the first intercensal period to show a negative balance for total CBD employment. Secondly,

Table 47. Distribution of jobs in three metropolitan areas, 1966–76 (%)

a) Total number of workplaces

Zone	Sydney 1971	1976	Melbourne 1971	1976	Adelaide 1971	1976
Inner	41.8	35.9	41.8	36.7	42.2	38.8
Middle	36.9	38.0	34.6	33.3	46.3	35.1
Outer	21.3	26.1	23.6	30.0	11.5	26.1

b) Distribution of white-collar and blue-collar jobs

Area	Professional/technical jobs 1966	1976	Craftsmen/labourers 1966	1976
Inner Sydney	9.3	13.2	39.7	27.6
Metrop. Sydney	10.1	12.7	38.8	30.6
Inner Melbourne	10.7	16.2	43.8	29.4
Metrop. Melbourne	10.3	13.0	41.0	33.8
Inner Adelaide	13.6	20.2	38.4	28.5
Metrop. Adelaide	10.9	13.8	39.1	33.7

Source: Maher 1982, 42, 53

while certain white-collar categories kept growing, *manufacturing and retail jobs* were the first to decrease; numbers in these occupations had already dropped prior to the 1966 census. These occupations continued to decrease during the intercensal period 1966–71, when *wholesale and entertainment* also encountered losses to the suburban zone for the first time. After 1971 the *construction business*, as well as *banking, finance and property*, began to show losses. There was thus a distinct sequence of job losses of the CBD to the suburbs from one intercensal period to the next. Thirdly, employment in community and business services still showed a positive balance for the CBD during the 1970s, although the rate of increase was much smaller in the CBD than it was in the suburbs, where health facilities and schools were established at rates corresponding with the growth of the suburban population. Fourthly, the only category to show increases of any extent in CBD employment in the 1970s was the *public authority and utilities* sector.

The most conspicuous change of employment and economic output occurred in *retail trade*. However, just like other developments, it occurred with a certain time lag as compared with the United States. Most retail facilities and services in the outer suburbs are found in planned shopping centres. The commercial strip so widespread along arterial roads on the peripheries of North American cities has hardly a counterpart in Australia. The reason for the *lack of commercial strips* in the Australian city is presumably the comparatively late suburban growth and the belated increase in private car ownership in an epoch when the shopping centre had already become the dominant type of supply of retail facilities and services.

There are, to be sure, *some ribbon developments* of shops and services along arterial roads. For example, in the pre-motor car era in Sydney, retailing developed along some roads leading from the CBD in various directions, such as Parramatta Road to the west through and beyong Leichhardt, or Hume Highway to the south through Newtown to Marrickville. These retailing businesses served a working-class population living in comparatively high-density areas of terraces and semi-detached houses; they depended upon the tram stops and high pedestrian flows. With the re-orientation on the motor car and the development of shopping centres, some of these shopping streets changed their character. Some shops moved up market, offering antiques, luxury cars and clothes for high-status demand; others attracted new functions, such as second-hand book stores and pet parlours. Many shops became vacant and remained unused until they were converted to other uses. Some of these shopping streets developed into community shopping centres (Burnley 1980, 149; Cardew & Simons: in Cardew, Langdale & Rich 1982, 153–54).

Such ribbon developments are referred to as shopping strips, strip (shopping) centres or string street centres in the Australian literature. Due to the old and diverse building stock, their low-rent premises offer accommodation to small businesses including second-hand and shoe-repair shops, small manufacturing businesses and offices are also found. Some of them developed to a length unfavourable for pedestrian use. They suffer from the pollution and noise of the road traffic, and pedestrian and vehicular traffic are often in conflict. Unlike the American commercial strips, that are usually found somewhat farther out and cater for the motorist with their numerous drive-in facilities, the buildings have not been sufficiently set back from the road to provide off-street parking for the present day clientele of shops and offices.

Planning authorities have become aware of the fact that these shopping strips, despite their shortcomings, are considered a welcome amenity by the population of the neighbouring residential areas. It is now accepted that they should not be sacrificed to the modern shopping centres, but that, on the contrary, their competitive position should be improved by adequate planning devices.

While in the United States the *shopping centre* dates back to the year 1925, when the Country Club Plaza in

Kansas City was opened, the first three shopping centres in Australia were the 1957 Top Ryde Centre in a Sydney suburb, the Chadstone Centre in Melbourne and the Chermside in Brisbane. During the first three decades of their development, shopping centres in the United States still showed an elongated form, somewhat in analogy to the traditional commercial strip. It was only in successive stages that they developed into the modern plaza-type shopping centre with a large central shopping core and the thousands of surrounding parking places. The vast majority of the relatively young Australian shopping centres are of the *plaza type*. In the course of time they grew larger and larger; while the Top Ryde Centre had 69 stores and a gross floor area of 144,000 square feet, the Roselands Centre of Wiley Park had 98 stores and a floor area of 1.134 million square feet. The Macquarie Centre opened in North Ryde in 1981 had 146 shops and services.

In a study covering the period 1968/69–1973/74 Alexander and Dawson (1979) showed the change of retail sales in the various parts of the metropolitan areas (table 48).

Table 48. Retail sales, changes 1968/69–1973/74 (%)

Area and time	Sydney	Melbourne	Brisbane	Adelaide	Perth
Core* 1973/74	8.4	11.4	15.0	16.8	14.8
change 1968/69–73/74	-14.3	-11.0	-15.8	- 3.0	- 9.1
Frame* 1973/74	8.4	11.4	11.5	11.0	8.8
change 1968/69–73/74	-28.4	-12.1	21.1	5.6	- 4.5
Inner suburbs 1973/74	20.2	22.3	12.8	16.6	17.4
change 1968/69–73/74	7.8	4.0	10.8	17.9	7.9
Middle and outer suburbs 1973/74	62.8	56.7	60.9	55.6	58.8
change 1968/69–73/74	40.6	31.9	58.5	37.2	56.6

* Core approximately equal to CBD, frame approximately remainder of inner city.
Source: Alexander & Dawson 1979, 79

Another trend in this period was the establishment by the prominent department store companies of new supermarket chains: Woolworth founded the Big W chain, Coles the K mart, Myer the Target chain and David Jones the Venture chain.

Recent development has led to the establishment of a *hierarchy of shopping centres*. The lowest level is represented by the neighbourhood shopping centre, consisting of a small number of shops, usually less than ten, and a rather small food mart. The next level is the community shopping centre, averaging ten to 20 shops, and having a considerably larger foot mart. The highest level is the district centre, or in the new towns, the Town Centre, endowed with one or two department stores, a huge supermarket and 50 or more other shops, a number of them highly specialized. Such centres have a number of other facilities, including a medical centre, a sports arena, a library, branch offices of various banks, a post office and a police station. The district centre usually offers the whole range of goods and services, rendering a trip to the CBD unnecessary.

Although the Edgington study (1982) showed losses in most tertiary employment categories for the CBD, *office jobs* in general remained rather highly centralized in Australian cities. This is at least partly proved by the enormous growth of office space offered in the central cities and in the CBDs in particular (chs. 3.1.7, 4.1.4), although some authors argue that the occupation of new office buildings will be at least partly due to relocations from older to modern structures and to the trend of growing per capita space in tertiary occupations (Alexander in: Cardew, Langdale & Rich 1982). Nevertheless, a certain proportion of the recent office building booms, and the eventual occupation of temporarily vacant office space, is no doubt due to the continuous concentration of certain office functions in the CBDs. Thus, apart from the outward extensions of CBD functions to such locations as North Sydney or even Parramatta, or to St. Kilda Road in Melbourne, the suburbanization of office jobs remained modest to date. The *first Australian office park* comparable with the many office parks in suburban locations of U.S. cities was *commenced in 1984* in Pennant Hills, while other office parks were proposed for Epping, Frenchs Forest and North Ryde, all of them located in the northern suburbs of Sydney. In the Melbourne metropolitan area a suburban office complex was developed in Camberwell (Austral. Property Rev. 1984).

There must be two observations on the consequences of the above-mentioned trends of suburbanization. The time and the degree of job losses were different in the various large cities. For example, while the central cities of Sydney and Melbourne experienced losses of blue-collar jobs as early as the 1960s, the City of Perth at this period was still enjoying a slight increase of such jobs (Alexander 1979a–c). Houghton (1981) therefore came to the conclusion that there is still a high proportion of blue-collar employment in the Central Area of Perth. For the inner city of Melbourne, Maher (1978) made the statement that the number of blue-collar jobs by far exceeds the number of residents in these occupations. There is thus a considerable volume of work journeys from suburban residences toward the central city. The notion of a sufficiency of inner city blue-collar jobs is supported by O'Connor's finding (1978) that in Melbourne at the beginning of the 1970s so-called *reverse commuting declined*; in other words, the surrounding areas kept employing approximately the same share of the declining inner city population, whereas U.S.

cities have experienced rising percentages of reverse commuters. On the other hand, unemployment rates among men have throughout the 1970s been higher in the inner city as compared with the suburbs, a fact that Vipond (1981) accredited in part to the decentralization of industries since this is 'putting inner city residents at a higher disadvantage'.

Regarding the relation of numbers of residents and numbers of jobs in the suburbs, the question of the *degree of self-containment* has been much disputed. While Logan in his Sydney study envisaged a 'subdivision of the metropolis into a set of largely self-contained labor sheds' (Logan 1968, 161), Houghton in an investigation of employment trends in the Perth metropolitan area came to the conclusion that during the decade 1966–76 the ratio of self-containment in the labour shed of Fremantle declined from 81.8% to 74.1%, of Nedlands from 57.9% to 48.1% and of Welshpool from 62.5% to 47.0% (Houghton 1981, 111). In other words, the volume of journeys to work to these suburban destinations increased; the numbers of jobs available in the suburban areas were larger or partly of a different quality as compared with the residential population of the respective destination zones. It was found in Sydney that the slower increase of employment opportunities as compared with the faster increase of residential population in the outer suburbs resulted in longer journeys to work and in rising unemployment (Cardew & Rich, Aplin, Burnley & Walker in: Cardew, Langdale & Rich 1982).

4.1.8 Metropolitan planning: district centres, urban corridors, industrial zones

The *concept of district centres* is commonly employed in metropolitan planning; it is closely related to the future growth of the built-up areas as well as to the development of the routes of public transport. District centres are supposed to function as 'secondary administrative, commercial, cultural and entertainment centres within the metropolitan area to serve the needs of the population of the surrounding districts' (MMBW 1981, 36). The local clustering of amenities of various kinds is their major characteristic.

This concentration is believed to guarantee the effective supply of goods and services, as well as the best use of public utilities. Among the measures to be taken to maintain the centre's compactness are the location of major shopping complexes with a minimum floor area of 4,000 square metres and of major office developments with a minimum floor area of 4,000 square metres as the centre's basic endowment. The multiple use of buildings is also encouraged, so as to achieve a considerable mixture of shops, services and other businesses. Residential land within one kilometre of public transport nodes and district centres is zoned for multi-unit housing, in order to secure a favourable number of consumers in the centre's immediate environs.

The first metropolitan plan for the Melbourne metropolitan region envisaged five district centres. With the acceleration of suburban growth, the rapid expansion in private car ownership and rise in consumer expenditure, a greater number of district centres emerged, some of them distinct from established town or village cores. This was partly in response to developments initiated by private enterprise. While the designated district centres did not develop in the way anticipated by the planning authorities, new regional shopping centres had started to grow on sites not provided for them in the plan, so that in a number of cases rezoning was necessary (Logan & Ogilvy in: Troy 1981). The development of district centres in the Melbourne metropolitan area was described in some detail in chapter 3.1.2. In Sydney the development was somewhat different from that in Melbourne. 'The sheer size of Sydney, its pattern of growth by envelopment of communities on railway routes linked to the suburban network, and lack of sites for free standing planned shopping centres has meant that established centres are commercially stronger and more numerous than in other cities' (Cardew & Simons in: Cardew, Langdale & Rich 1982, 151).

There is a certain conformity among metropolitan planning authorities in Australia as to preferable future growth of the built-up areas along a *limited number of growth corridors*. In the case of Perth this planning goal was made explicit by labelling the adopted metropolitan development plan the 'Corridor Plan'. In Canberra the latest plan is referred to as the 'Y-Plan' implicating the development of the national capital city along three corridors to the northwest, the northeast and the south. The Sydney Region Outline Plan favours five corridors for the Sydney metropolitan area. In Adelaide three major corridors are predetermined by the triangular shape of the Adelaide Plain and the early existence of Port Adelaide as a second nucleus of settlement to the northwest of the city proper. In Hobart growth is very much confined to the banks of the Derwent River so that metropolitan development is largely axial in character. In Brisbane the main area of development is the Brisbane-Ipswich corridor along the Brisbane and Bremer Rivers. It seems that in Melbourne growth is not quite as closely related to natural features, although there is one major corridor to the southeast along Phillip Bay toward the Moreton Peninsula; the other six corridors show a more transport-oriented pattern.

It is a planning goal of the respective metropolitan planning authorities that these growth corridors should '... not simply be new dormitory areas where all forms of urban development must be positively encouraged. Each corridor will need to develop its centres of specialised activity around which new communities will be established having all modern amenities and facilities such as schools, recreation, hospitals and shopping facilities, industrial and commercial employment and professional services' (MMBW 1971, 68).

The problems involved in any attempt at stopping urban sprawl become apparent from the changing policies of the MMBW for the future growth of metropolitan Melbourne. The plan of 1954 envisaged the designation of a rural zone, which was in effect to function as a green belt, in which agricultural and other non-urban uses were to be preserved. Very soon, however, urban development spread beyond the area within the 24 km radius first entrusted to the MMBW, particularly to the east and south.

The second attempt was the creation by the 1971 plan of seven corridors that were to channel urban growth into specific directions and to prevent overall sprawl. This policy was also considered unsuccessful by some scholars, inasmuch as it had certain undesired side effects upon agricultural activities. 'Within those zones land is selling at approximately twice its rural value. That in turn leads to increased liability on the part of the farmers for land tax for local-government rates. The increased land prices make it more difficult for a genuine farmer to buy in within the corridor zone, and the increased liability for rates and taxes makes it more difficult for the existing farmer to continue farming' (Gifford 1980, 12). The more recent Metropolitan Strategy Plan of 1980 made a new attempt at channeling suburban growth by the selection of designated district centres and *preferred development areas* with relation to the earlier established corridors (see ch. 3.1.2).

The relative importance of the corridors for metropolitan planning and development since about 1970 is reflected in the following data drawn from a MMBW inventory for Melbourne (MMBW 1971, 77):

Total planning area	1,942 square miles
Existing urban zones	533 square miles
Corridor zones	284 square miles
Additional urban zones	94 square miles

Viewed from this 1970 planning concept, three-fourths of future urban growth in terms of area consumption would be channeled to the corridor zones, these zones being about half the size of the already existing zones of urban uses within the metropolitan area.

With the exception of Canberra, with its suburban satellites connected by major arterial highways, the growth corridors are stretching along *suburban rapid-transit lines*. The district centres designated in the various metropolitan area plans are in turn closely related to those corridors and are almost exclusively located near stations of the rapid-transit lines.

Accessibility is an important issue in this context, since there has been, with the exception of Perth, only a very modest urban freeway construction in Australia, as mentioned in chapter 4.1.6. This lack of urban freeways means not only that vehicular traffic in the large Australian cities is threatened by congestions, but that settlement on the metropolitan fringe is not influenced (or even directed) by *freeway entry points*. In the United States the ramps of urban expressways have become preferred locations for new suburban developments, including the location of major new shopping centres, industrial parks, office parks and new residential sub-divisions (Hofmeister 1985). Duhs & Beggs (1977) gave a critical overview of the various Transportation Studies of the Australian metropolitan areas with their analyses of the demands for highways, freeways and public transport.

As early as the mid-1960s, changes of the employment structure had caused a number of journeys to work to be reversed, so as to run outwards from the central city and from some inner and middle-distance suburban areas to municipalities still farther out, such as Oakleigh, Moorabbin and Dandenong on the southeast side of the Melbourne metropolitan area (MMBW 1971, 30; see ch. 4.1.7). Such changes were due to the suburbanization of industries, initiated in the 1950s, by the establishment of large *industrial estates* or even new towns in connection with large industrial complexes.

Again, this development was somewhat later than the corresponding trends of industrialization in the United States. The Central Manufacturing District and the Clearing Industrial District in Chicago are considered the first industrial parks in the United States, both having been in existence at the turn of the century. By 1950, some 80 inudstrial parks had been established in the U.S. (Burns 1966). The planning of industrial zones in Australia followed the introduction of metropolitan planning about 1948. In the case of Perth, the sequence was even reversed, insofar as the decision to establish a new modern deep-sea harbour, with an adjoining heavy-industrial complex on the southern periphery of the metropolitan region at Kwinana gave the stimulus for the forming of a metropolitan planning authority in 1955, that was to prepare the first plan for the Perth metropolitan region.

In both Perth and Sydney the decision was made to keep heavy industries far away from the major population agglomerations, so that Kwinana and Port Kembla were developed as industrial zones in connection with modern deep-sea harbours. A similar development took place in the Melbourne metropolitan area with the location of heavy industries in Westernport, on the far side of the Mornington Peninsula. Large automobile factories were established on the peripheries of the metropolitan areas of Melbourne and Adelaide, the latter giving rise to the New Town of Elizabeth, the former to the growth of the suburb of Dandenong.

These are but a few examples for systematic post-war industrialization in Australia, the process including the selection of appropriate plant locations, the recruiting of the labour force, particularly from the British Isles, as for the automobile factories of Elizabeth and Dandenong, and the provision of housing, partly by the establishment of new towns by the responsible state housing authority.

The metropolitan plans were used to provide additional land zoned for industrial use. Thus the Melbourne

Metropolitan Plan provided reserved industrial zones in each of the seven corridors; only in the Berwick and Frankston corridors was there only restricted provision for industrial use, since it was anticipated that most industrial development in the southeastern sector of the metropolitan area would be channeled into the Westernport region on the far side of Mornington Peninsula (MMBW 1971, 81).

Alexander (in: Troy 1981) reviewed the metropolitan plans of the state capitals from the aspect of equity. He came to the conclusion that, out of the metropolitan plans of the first generation, the Cumberland Plan for Sydney was the only one to opt for considerable decentralization of industries together with other activities, thus bringing work places, people and amenities closer together. The other metropolitan plans put more emphasis on the achievement of economic efficiency in the proposed growth of the metropolitan areas.

4.1.9 Mobility and equity: The central city versus suburbia

For more than a decade urban researchers have been involved in a discussion on the changing relationship between the central city and the ring of (outer) suburbs. A certain culmination point of this discussion was the symposium held in Munich and Vienna in connection with the IGU Congress 1984 on 'The take-off of suburbia and the crisis of the central city' to which the present writer contributed a paper on the situation in Australia. The title of the symposium and the consecutive publication (Heinritz & Lichtenberger 1986) imply world-wide trends of deterioration of central cities and the simultaneous mushrooming of suburban areas, even to the extent of the development of a certain 'counter-urban' trend.

As the preceding chapters have shown, circumstances in Australia have been somewhat different. Despite the fact that the Australian population is highly suburbanized, the viability of Australia's central cities has never been really challenged. None of them has, during the post-war period, experienced a crisis comparable with that of most North American cities. This is not to say that suburbanization in Australia had no impact on the central cities, which have experienced losses of resident population, of job opportunities (particularly in blue-collar categories), of retail trade and of certain white-collar occupations. There has, however, been a number of forces and processes working *in favour of the central city:*

1. A post-war economic and construction boom introduced the high-rise structures to the Australian CBD, thus considerably changing the townscape of the central city.
2. There was a great office-building boom from about 1968 to the mid-1970s especially in Sydney. Office construction in Sydney has continued since that period at a somewhat slower pace. Perth and Brisbane, with a certain time lag, experienced parallel office-building booms. The relatively high vacancy rates in the early years of the boom have almost disappeared. In Melbourne the 56-storey Rialto complex was completed in 1985. The increase of commuting to work places in the CBD even induced public authorities in Sydney and Perth to encourage suburban office relocation.
3. Some central cities still enjoyed an increase of white-collar jobs during the 1970s, albeit a small one.
4. The decrease of the various categories of tertiary occupations was accompanied by the continuous concentration into the CBDs of white-collar employment, particularly professional, administrative, managerial, technical and clerical jobs. The one category still definitely expanding is public administration and utilities. Despite slight losses of numbers of employees, the arts and entertainment sectors are still strongly represented in the central city, as symbolized by the establishment of the great modern Arts Centres in Melbourne and Brisbane.
5. The CBDs gained attraction by the recent creation of shopping malls and arcades, accompanied by remarkable change of the building stock. Examples include Martin Place Mall in Sydney, Bourke Street Mall in Melbourne, Queen Street Mall, The Riverside Centre and the Wintergarden Centre in Brisbane, the Carillon Centre in Perth's Hay Street Mall, and the modern multifunctional Merlin Centre on Perth's waterfront.
6. Continuously expanding CBD functions have intruded into adjoining residential areas; for example during the 1970s, Inner Sydney, comprising the City of Sydney and parts of the municipalities of South Sydney and Leichhardt, lost 7,400 dwelling units to various commercial uses.
7. The rapid increase of office functions made for the areal expansion of some CBDs, such as the expansion of the Sydney CBD into North Sydney, Crows Nest and Chatswood, of the Melbourne CBD to St. Kilda Road, Victoria Parade and Royal Parade, of the Adelaide CBD to Greenhill Road south of the parklands and of the Perth CBD into West Perth, which today must be considered part of the larger CBD of Perth.
8. A number of urban conservation projects of the 1970s such as The Rocks, Glebe and Wooloomooloo in Sydney or Battery Point and Glebe in Hobart increased the attractiveness of the central cities for the resident population and the tourists alike.
9. Certain residential sections of the central cities enjoying particularly favourable locations experienced an upgrading by the conversion of parts of their multi-storey residences to condominiums. For example, during the period 1962–80, more than 3,300 dwelling units in Sydney's inner suburbs of Kings Cross, Elizabeth Bay and Darlinghurst were converted to strata title, this process making for a certain displacement of lower-class residents by middle-class home buyers.

10 A number of small residential sections within the central cities experienced up-grading by the process of gentrification, which means that usually young, middle-class people buy and remodel, mainly at their own expense, a terrace or row house. In consequence of this process certain population changes have taken place in favour of higher education levels, higher income, more white-collar occupations, higher percentages in the 25–40 age group, lower occupancy rates, lower population densities and a lower percentage of overseas immigrants.

11 According to Transportation Studies data, commuters in some large Australian cities rather heavily rely on public transport; in Sydney, for example, approximately three-quarters of the CBD office workforce get to work by means of public transport. The underground in Sydney and Melbourne, the tramlines still in operation in Melbourne, and the suburban electric rail services, seem to be much more effective in the large Australian cities than in North America, with the possible exception of the Northeastern Seaboard and Chicago. The underground rail loop in Melbourne was supposed to 'provide an incentive for distributing new buildings more evenly' over the whole area of the CBD (MMBW 1971, 71). On the other hand, the scarcity of urban freeway construction is explained in chapter 4.1.6.

A bundle of factors has thus been at work to enable the Australian central city to maintain its position as the *dominant centre of the metropolitan area*. This is in contrast to the United States, where most central cities suffered from a deep crisis; they may at best be able to assume the position of primus inter pares, on the level of a district centre or regional shopping centre. It is also apparent that for more than a decade public authorities have been anxious to take measures designed to ensure the central city's viability. Adherents to such policy even complained of the public authorities being in contradiction to their inner city planning goals by simultaneously promoting the orderly development of designated suburban district centres (Beed 1981, 260).

It was certainly to the advantage of the central city in Australia that such decisive elements of suburban development as regional shopping centres, industrial estates, suburban office parks or business parks appeared much later in Australia than in the U.S. city. The very modest rate of urban freeway construction resulted in the lack of freeway entry points, which in the U.S. cities proved to be important nuclei for further suburban development.

There was, to be sure, a *rather rapid suburban residential growth*, due to such facts as the low land and house construction prices ruling until the early 1970s, the lack of efficient planning devices to prohibit such urban sprawl, the attitude of money lending institutions and the preference of even Commonwealth-controlled banks for granting loans for new structures in suburban locations. Thus the middle-distance and outer suburbs received the lion's share of population growth, also of increases in blue-collar jobs and even in certain white-collar categories, particularly retail employment and retail sales. Even the redistribution of overseas immigrants resulted in a loss of the inner city in favour of the suburbs.

The *geographical mobility* of the Australian population is distinctly *lower* than in the United States. In the latter the annual rate is approximately 20%, which means that statistically there is a turnover of the total population within five years. In Australia the rate for the five-year period 1971–76 was 45% (Maher 1978, 1982) which means 9% per annum or a total turnover within 11.1 years. The Australian mobility rate is thus a little less than half the American rate.

According to slightly differing rates in the various metropolitan areas the turnover, in statistical terms, of the metropolitan population of Hobart will be 12.0 years, of Adelaide 11.9 years, of Sydney 11.6 years, of Melbourne 11.5 years, of Brisbane 10.6 years and of Perth 9.6 years. In addition to such interurban differences there are certain intra-urban differences, to the effect that the turnover rate tends to be higher in the inner districts than in the outer suburbs. In the period 1966–71, the theoretical turnover of the metropolitan population of the Melbourne S.D. would have been 11.2 years as compared with only 8.5 years for the City of Melbourne or 7.8 years for the inner suburb of Prahran. In some inner suburbs the rate was twice as high as in some outer suburbs.

Residential moves within the metropolitan area of Sydney were found to be rather short. From this finding Burnley (1982) concluded that there are local housing submarkets for groups at various stages of the life cycle.

In a recent study on metropolitan Perth, Jackson (1985) suggested that *home extensions* had a lowering effect on mobility, being an alternative to moving. The degree to which moving or extending are true alternatives may, however, be debatable. Jackson stated that many extenders found it cheaper to extend, although most of them had relatively small proportions of their incomes committed to mortgage repayments, and that over half of all extenders included in his sample had given moving no thought; the same held true for movers with regard to extending.

It may be concluded from the various mobility studies that lower mobility rates as compared with the United States, the trend toward relatively short moves and the relatively strong trend toward home extension are functioning to the *advantage of the central city*.

On the other hand, many recent studies on equity, well-being or welfare in the Australian city seem to reveal circumstances *disadvantageous to the central city*. Some such studies were based on data presented in the First Main Report of the Committee of Inquiry into Poverty (1975), the Henderson Report. There have been several subsequent enquiries and some individual research.

According to Walmsley (in: Hanley & Cooper 1982) *four groups of disadvantaged or problem areas* exist in Australian settlements. The first group is comprised of isolated rural areas. The second group is made up of a number of declining country towns, which have been suffering from the shrinkage of their economic base and are characterized by the continuous outmigration of their younger, skilled and more mobile residents. The third group comprises those peripheral metropolitan suburbs that suffer from the lack of adequate community services and infrastructure, due to their rapid growth and great pace of housing construction. The fourth group consists of the great number of inner metropolitan residential areas suffering from multiple disadvantages. These include the predominance of low-income occupations, with comparatively high unemployment rates. Adverse environmental conditions include high residential densities (crowding), a high proportion of multi-storey buildings and flats and poor access to general medical practitioners (GPs). The population is characterized by low educational participation rates once the period of compulsory schooling has been passed, high rates of family breakdown, personal pathologies, high proportions of single women, numerous pensioner households of one or two persons, homeless elderly males ('skid row') and residents whose language is not English.

It is not intended to discuss these aspects of multiple deprivation in any detail: they are to be found in larger cities all over the world. It is sufficient to say that Australian cities, like large cities in other countries, experienced segregation into high-status and low-status residential areas. The location of low-status areas relates partly to natural constraints such as drainage and sanitation problems and the dampness of dwellings in swampy areas, and partly to man-made pollution such as the proximity to noxious industries. Burnley (1980) pointed to the fact that in such areas developers were inclined to build cheap and uniform housing and that underprivileged groups moved into such dwellings. For further details the reader is referred to Burnley (1980, 226–94), Troy (1981) and Stimson (1982), but some aspects of particular interest are referred to below.

According to the Henderson Report the *cost of housing* is a vital factor in determining whether a person or a family are living below the acknowledged *poverty line*. In this regard there are spatial as well as age-specific differences. In small urban places and, more generally speaking, in all settlements outside the metropolitan areas, low-cost housing is usually available. This means that a higher percentage of disposable income may be used for food, clothing and other purposes, which may be sufficient to bring the respective persons above the poverty line. In the metropolitan areas, and in the middle-distance and outer suburbs in particular, expenses for accommodation are usually much higher. As far as the various disadvantaged groups are concerned, many old people own their homes so that, whatever little money they have at their disposal, this will be mainly available for things other than dwelling expenses.

According to Manning (1976), 60% of the regional variation in poverty may be explained by the distribution of disability. In very general terms, disabilities will be highest in the inner suburbs and lowest in the outer suburbs. This holds true for the respective proportions of aged persons living alone, aged couples and single women. Other deprived groups, however, show different distribution patterns. There are relatively higher proportions of single-parent families and of large families with low incomes living under conditions of poverty in the outer suburbs, whereas the group of the sick and unemployed persons is relatively highly represented in both the inner and outer suburbs, and least represented in the middle-distance suburbs.

Many enquiries have been made into the *access to educational institutions* and health services. As may be assumed, the situation is not entirely different from that in other countries of the western world. In contrast to the United States, however, residents of Australian inner cities usually need not complain of classes being too large or teachers' qualifications too low. However, inner-city school buildings are often obsolete, and lacking provision for sporting and other activities. There are no such ethnic constraints on educational attainment as in many ghetto-like inner areas of American cities; immigrant children often perform extremely well (Burnley 1980). In the special case of new towns such as the iron ore mining towns of the Pilbara region, the quality of educational provision is very important for the parents' decision of either splitting up or moving the whole family, and has thus a great impact on the fluctuation rate of company employees (ch. 3.4.3).

Health services show extremely uneven distribution patterns. There is a remarkable discrepancy between the predominantly inner-city concentration of public hospitals and the growing suburbanization of the metropolitan population. According to Donald (in: Troy 1981) the boards of established hospitals in New South Wales were determined to cling to their existing locations for reasons of prestige and parochial concern, which the New South Wales Hospitals Commission did not dare to challenge. The Commission's first regional office was established as the Western Metropolitan Health Region, this event being responsible for the fact that a considerable proportion of the public beds added to the hospitals system through the Federal Hospitals Development Program in 1974–79 were in the western and southwestern sections of the metropolitan area. The apparent undersupply of the inner western and the southern sections remained relatively untouched. Private hospitals, on the other hand, show a locational bias towards high-status areas.

The distribution of specialists and general practitioners alike is in part explained by the availability of facilities, that is by the location of public hospitals and modern suburban medical centres. The desirability of high-status areas as places of private residence as well as sources of a high-income clientele is also apparent, to a limited extent, by the demand for health services, such as the demand for consultations by people in the retiring age is of significance. The locational contradictions in health-service provision can be illustrated by reference to gynaecologists. While the demand for their services is greatest in the outer suburbs, with their high proportions of young families and a great number of wives in the child-bearing age, the majority of gynaecologists are found in the inner city, reflecting the location of maternity-hospital accommodation as well as GPs' referral habits (Donald in: Troy 1981). In 1975 there were 75 GPs to 100,000 residents in the metropolitan area of Adelaide, the range being from 18 in the northern suburb of Munno Park to 223 in the high-status eastern suburb of Burnside (Stimson 1982). In Sydney's western and southwestern suburbs the range was from 61 to 81 for 100,000 residents against 135 to 387 for 100,000 in the inner and northern suburbs. The high output of medical schools and high rate of immigration of medical doctors during the period 1974–79 tended to accentuate existing spatial disparities rather than to reduce them.

Since the mid-1970s growing *unemployment* has been a major concern of public authorities and researchers alike. While an unemployment rate of 1–2% had been normal prior to 1975, unemployment has grown since, although at varying rates. On the one hand, unemployment has been dependent on the type of occupation. Major losses of jobs occurred in the declining sectors of secondary industries. On the other hand, unemployment is related to the employee's skills, to his command of the English language if an overseas immigrant, and to his place of residence with regard to the journey to work. As O'Connor showed in a Melbourne study (1978) there is a certain dependence on good transport lines. Thus, in contrast to Port Melbourne and South Melbourne, the City of Melbourne and the inner suburbs of St. Kilda and Richmond had more than average shares of their workforce employed in the middle-distance and inner suburbs.

4.2 Overseas immigrants and their residential patterns

Badcock and Cloher (1981, 53) described the 'absence of the disincentives commonly encountered in the racially troubled and often inhospitable inner areas of U.S. cities' as one of the major characteristics of Australian cities. The contribution of overseas immigrants to Australia's population growth at various times was treated in chapter 2.1.2. The emphasis will now be put on the spatial distribution of immigrants in Australia's urban places, and on the role of ethnicity in the urban structure of the Australian city, which differs considerably from the American city in this respect.

One reason for the absence of really large ethnic residential quarters in Australian cities is the *small number of overseas immigrants* in Australia. Emigration to the United States between 1820 and 1985 was of the order of 50 million persons. In Australia there were 859,500 overseas immigrants at the time of federation; the total intake of immigrants in the period 1901–47 was 605,000 and in the period 1947–83 approximately 3.27 million so that total immigration amounts to nearly 5 million persons. This is a relation of 1:10 as compared with the United States. Only in the post-World War II era this relation changed to 1:4 when the United States' annual intake has been approximately 400,000 as compared with Australia's annual average of some 90,000 persons. In the early 1920s, 200,000 South Europeans lived in Manhattan and 50,000 in central Chicago, whereas by 1947 no more than 8,000 South Europeans lived in Sydney and 7,000 in Melbourne, about half of whom were found in the inner suburbs of Carlton, Collingwood, Fitzroy and Richmond. These are, indeed, different dimensions.

This statement also holds true for the Aboriginal population, as compared with the urban black population in the United States, although such comparison may not be quite justifiable since America's black population originated from compulsory migration. However, no more than 400,000 negroes had been transported to North America. In large U.S. cities such as New York or Chicago the number of black residents exceeds one million. The total urban proportion of Australian Aborigines is estimated to be in the order of 50,000 persons, these being distributed over the urban places of the various states as follows: 15,000 in New South Wales, 10,000 in Queensland, 9,000 in Western Australia, 5,000 in Victoria, 4,000 in the Northern Territory and 3,000 in South Australia.

The post-war increase of immigrants to Australia leads to a second consideration. The vast majority of Australian immigrants since mid-century have arrived under conditions quite different from those experienced by the great numbers of pre-war arrivals in the United States. They came at a time when they were no longer dependent on accommodation in close proximity to their work places or upon cheap public transport along tram and rail lines, when the host country was experiencing rapid economic growth, when there were good job opportunities and a high wage level. Immigrants were able to share the Australian high rates of car and home ownership and their modern means of communication.

Looking at the immigrants' distribution patterns in detail, however, it is possible to detect a bundle of factors influencing their residential choice and their varying degrees of local concentration or dispersion.

4.2.1 Initial ethnic concentrations

One factor responsible for the location of ethnic residential quarters is the existence of traditional ethnic concentrations as they came into being during the second half of the nineteenth century. The two most significant non-British groups of that time were the Chinese[2] and the Germans. The former came as diggers to the goldfields of Victoria,

---

2 In the nineteenth century Chinese were still rather easily identified. Later it has become increasingly difficult to determine who is Chinese. Statistics used to offer three figures for Chinese and other Asian groups related to their birthplace, to their nationality or to their last permanent residence. For further details in the discussion of this problem the reader is referred to 'Welfare of migrants' edited by the Commission of Inquiry into Poverty 1975, 116.

New South Wales and Queensland, some even to Tasmania, and replacing convict labour, as indentured migrants for cane cutting in Queensland. The Germans concentrated on rural areas like the Barossa Valley in South Australia or came as farm hands to the Queensland squatters, mainly to the Darling Downs where they often stayed with their employers only for the two years to which they were committed and then left for the towns such as Toowoomba to work as craftsmen or run a shop (Waterson 1968, Erdmann 1986).

A marked ethnic segregation existed in the gold mining town of Bendigo, even when it was still mainly a canvas shanty town in the early 1850s. Aside from the British there were the Irish, the Derwenters from Van Diemen's Land, the Americans from California and Nevada, the Chinese originating mainly from Canton, the Germans, French, Poles, Hungarians and others. Bendigo's heart at Long Gully became known as 'Little Cornwall', the crossing point of Bendigo and Back Creeks became 'Irishtown', and the Germans operated some of the restaurants on High Street such as the Berlin Hotel, the Club Hotel or the Hamburg Hotel (Cusack 1973).

In addition to the fact that the colonial governments soon restricted Chinese immigration (ch. 2.1.2), the majority were males and they had come 'as sojourners rather than as settlers' (Inglis 1972, 267). For both reasons their numbers dropped from a maximum of nearly 40,000 in Victoria around 1857 and 17,000 in Queensland around 1877 to 32,700 by the turn of the century and to a mere 12,000 by 1947 in the whole of Australia.

On the other hand the rate of Chinese urbanization was high. Those staying in Australia tended to leave the

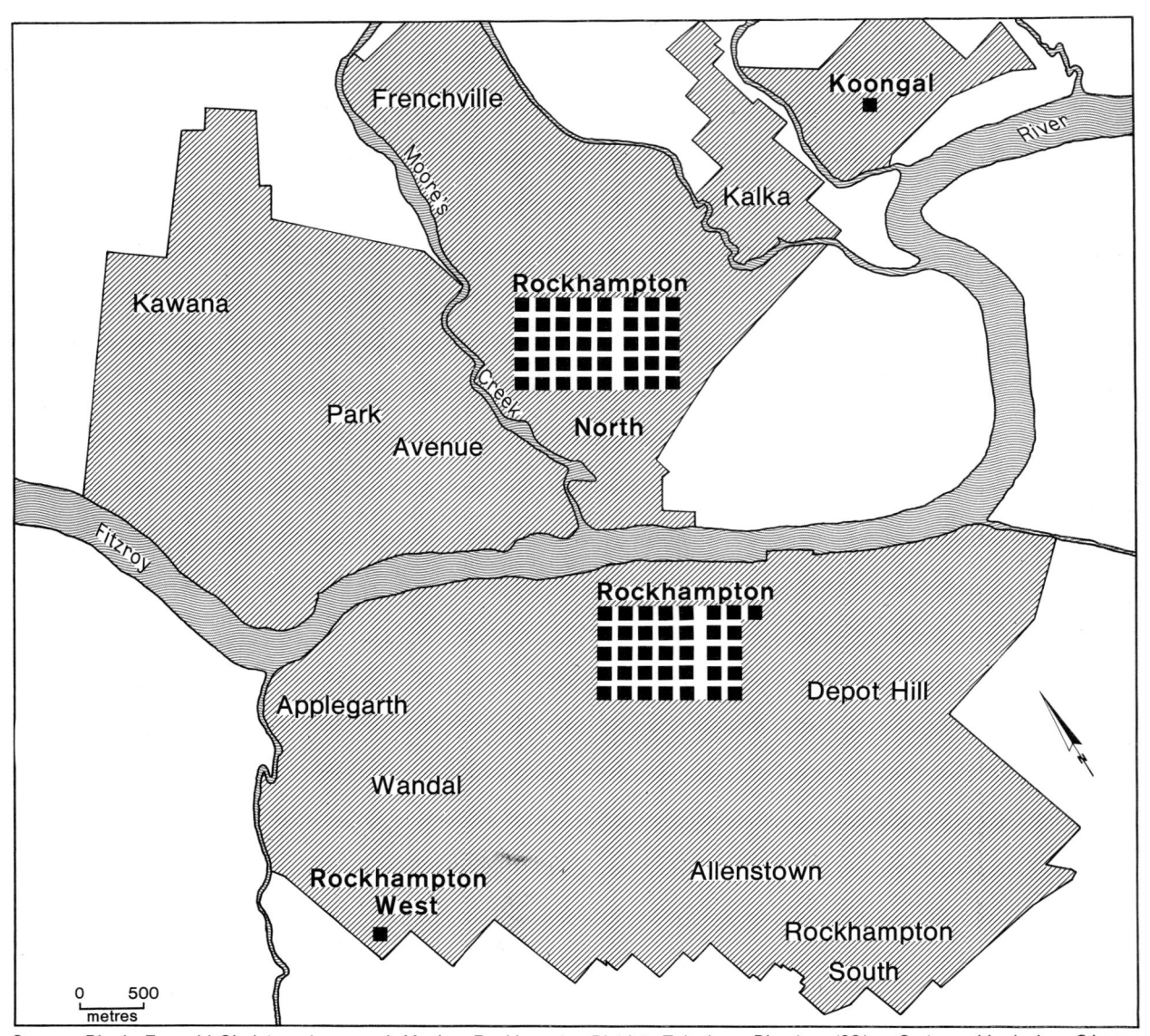

Source: Bioela Emerald Gladstone Longreach Mackay Rockhampton Districts Telephone Directory 1981   Cartographic design: O. Lange

Fig. 111. Distribution of households with Chinese surnames in Rockhampton, Qld., 1981

Fig. 112. Distribution of households with Chinese surnames in Mackay, Qld., 1981

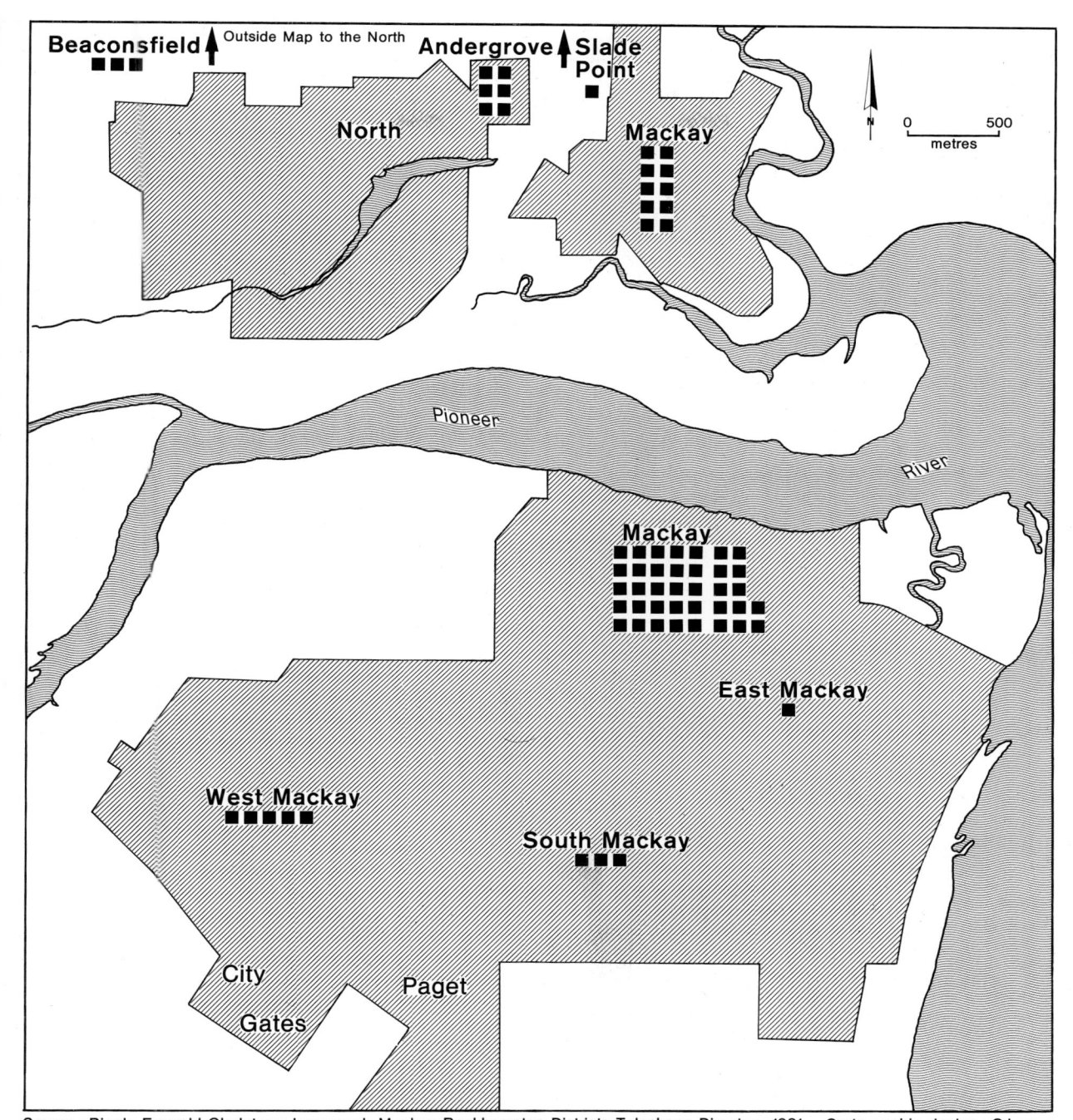

farms and mines after some time and to migrate to the cities. In general, the urbanization rate of the overseas born increased faster than the urbanization rate of the total population. Between 1861 and 1901 the proportion of non-British immigrants in New South Wales decreased from 6.8% to 2.6%, whereas their proportion of Sydney's residents rose from 2.3% to 3.2%. An alternative measure is that between 1881 and 1901 Sydney's proportion of the population of New South Wales rose from 29.4% to 36.0%, while Sydney's proportion of the overseas-born population rose from 27.4% to 43.7% (Wolforth 1974).

Queensland's *Chinese* were mainly absorbed by the coastal towns of Rockhampton, Mackay, Townsville and Cairns, but those towns have received very little recent Chinese migration. The 1976 census showed 109 migrants from China, excluding Taiwan, in Townsville, the numbers of Chinese migrants to the other three towns being below 100. This means that the many persons bearing Chinese names in these towns are the descendents of earlier migrants.

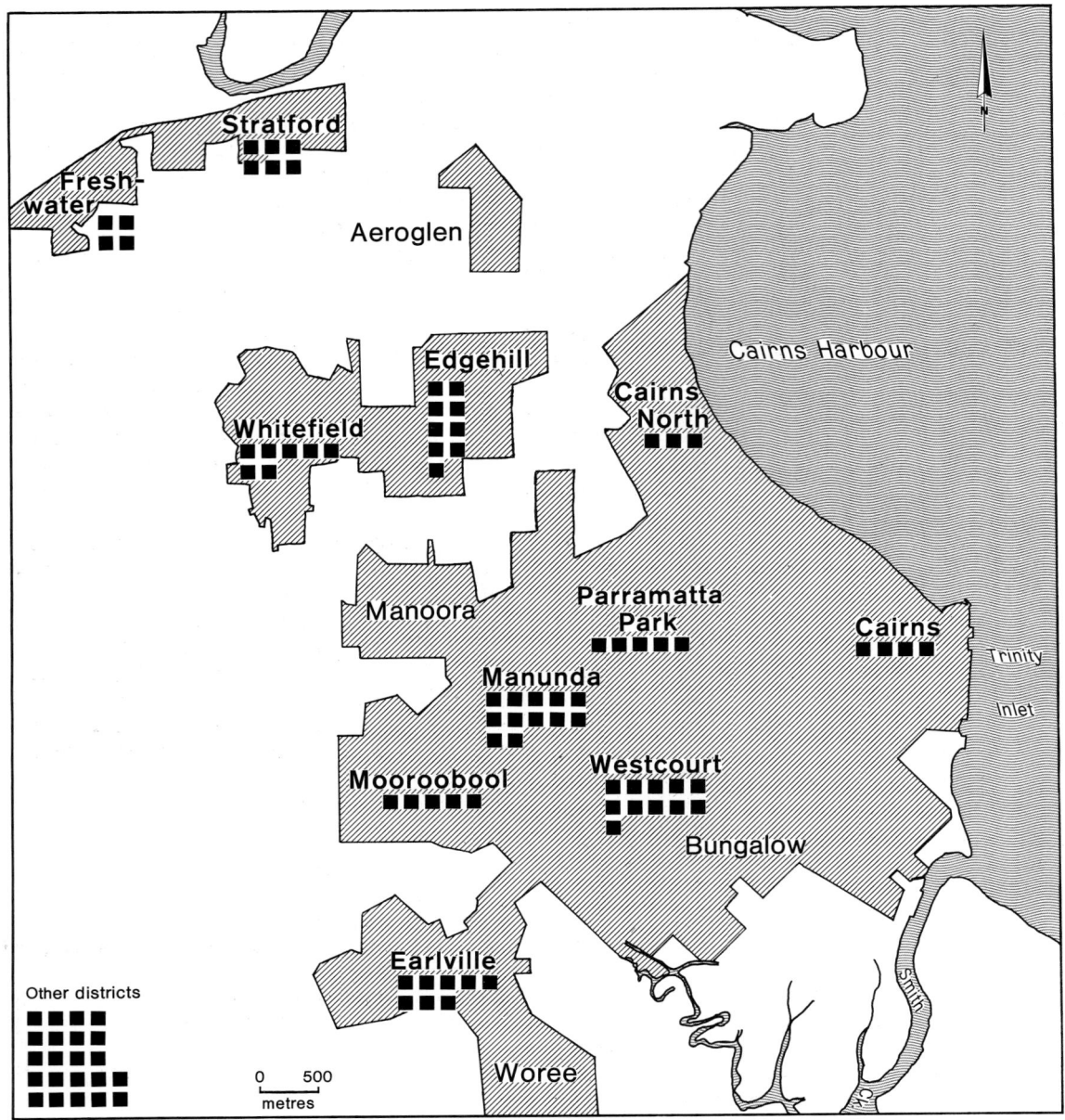

Fig. 113. Distribution of households with Chinese surnames in Cairns, Qld., 1981

An attempt was made to locate the Chinese group mainly with the aid of telephone directories. A rather marked concentration was found in *Rockhampton* (50,146 residents in 1981) where 51.3% of households with Chinese surnames live in the low-status suburb of North Rockhampton across the Fitzroy River on the north shore and another 46.2% in the City of Rockhampton, leaving a mere 2.5% for the rest of the urban area (fig. 111).

In Mackay and Cairns the households with Chinese surnames show contrasting distributions. In *Mackay* (35,356) 56.1% of these households live in the City of Mackay and another 15.2% in North Mackay while the remaining 28.7% are distributed over six suburbs (fig. 112). In *Cairns* (48,531) there is no local concentration of Chinese households at all. They are distributed over the central city and 15 suburbs, none of them showing a concentration higher than 12.5% (fig. 113).

In New South Wales the Chinese very much concentrated on *Sydney*, where they tended to form distinct clusters within the city. By 1861 no less than 61% lived in Gipps Ward in close *proximity to the wharves.* Here Sydney's first Chinatown developed along Lower George Street. Later many Chinese worked as cabinet makers in Sydney's furniture factories. Another fraction turned to market gardening; their tendency toward moving from employees to self-employed or employers was stronger than for the workforce as a whole. In the early 1900s about 35% of the Chinese workforce were in market gardening, their number making up for approximately 50% of all market gardeners in Australia (Inglis 1972). Much of the agricultural land occupied by Chinese market gardeners was at *Botany Bay*, where they formed another concentration. In the city proper they became involved in retail trade, helped by relations with their market gardener compatriots, and began to cluster close to the new *vegetable market at Belmore*, where the present Chinatown evolved in the southern sections of Dixon and Sussex Streets. Although Chinese clubs and societies are located here, Chinatown is but a small part of the Chinese community in the Sydney metropolitan area. The relations between employment and residential patterns will be treated below in more detail in chapter 4.2.4.

Some ethnic groups were much less urbanized than the Chinese prior to the great immigration wave after World War II. Thus of all the Italians living in Australia even at mid-century, no more than 38.4% were living in metropolitan areas and another 9.9% in other urban areas (Borrie 1954). The majority were still living in rural areas, for instance in the cane growing regions of Queensland. However, those who had migrated to the cities formed distinct clusters. Like the Chinese, many Italians became *market gardeners*, for example on Sydney's metropolitan fringe in Fairfield, Holroyd and Penrith or on Perth's fringe in *Spearwood*, but they also entered maritime occupations in the port cities. The *Italian fishermen's community in Fremantle* dates back to 1863, when a ship's carpenter from Livorno settled here and worked as a boat builder and part-time fisherman (Gentilli et al. 1982). Of the 246 licenced fishermen in Fremantle in 1906 more than 50% were Italians. Even in those early years they began to cluster on the south side of Fremantle, between South Terrace to the east and the ocean front to the west in the eight blocks between Bannister, Nairn, Collie, Essex, Norfolk, Suffolk, Arundel, Howard and Russell Streets (Gamba 1952, Gentilli et al. 1982).

The Italian fishermen of Fremantle are an excellent example of what has been termed *chain migration*. The term refers to continuous migration from the same region or even from the same village by people at least partly sponsored by relatives and friends that had emigrated earlier. This process does not only make for a steady growth of the respective group but is also conducive to the group's cohesion, and is thus an important stabilizing factor in the immigrants' preserving their ethnic identity. In the case of the fishermen of Fremantle, out of a total of 147 counted in 1948 77 had come from Sicily and other southern islands and another 66 from Molfetta in Apulia (Gamba 1952). The market gardeners in Spearwood, just a few kilometres from Fremantle, do not originate from the same parts of Italy, and there are hardly any relations between the two groups. Chain migration has also been typical for the Chinese and, to a somewhat lesser extent, for the Greeks, whereas it has been rather unimportant for other immigrant groups. Some examples of chain migration in Sydney are given in table 49.

Table 49. Examples of chain migration to Sydney

Group	Place of origin	Local concentration
Italians	Valtellina, Lombardy	Darlington
	Salina Island	King Street (Newton), Surry Hills
	Lipari Islands, Sicily, Vicenza, Udine	Leichhardt (between Parramatta Road, Balmain and Hill Streets)
	Reggio Calabria, Sicily	Fairfield, Holroyd, Penrith
	Lipari Islands	Clissold and Palace Streets (Sutherland), Ashfield
	Panarea (Sicily), Adrano (Catania)	Botany
	Spadafora, Comiso (Sicily)	Church and Prospect Streets (Leichhardt)
	Martone (Reggio Calabria)	Eastwood
Greeks	Castellorizo, Kythera	George Street (Redfern), King Street (Newton)
	Cephalonia, Arcadia, Ithaca, Samos, Smyrna	George Street (Redfern), King Street (Newton), Darlinghurst
	Levkas	Redfern
	Crete, Peloponnes, Macedonia	Redfern, Newton, Erskinville, Enmore (Marrickville)
	Castellorizo	Randwick, Maroubra, Coogee
Yugoslavs	Bijevcino Selo (Dalmatia)	Darlinghurst
	Podgorica (Croatia)	Cabramatta
	Smederevo (Serbia)	Harris Street (Warriewood)
	Slovenia	Marrickville
	Dalmatia	Fairfield

For detailed descriptions of chain migration to Sydney, Melbourne and Adelaide the reader is referred to Burnley (1974, 175–77; 1975, 328–30), Price (1963) and Scott (1965).

Other ethnic groups clustered to a much lesser extent. Nineteenth-century *Irish immigrants* were less urbanized, more dispersed over larger areas and more mixed in urban areas than the groups mentioned above. Many Irish settled in relatively densely populated rural areas, avoiding both the big cities and the outback. Those migrating to the cities used to live in comparatively mixed residential areas such as Bourke Ward in central Melbourne where about mid-century 'even in those seemingly Irish back alleys — Shamrock Alley and St. Patrick's Alley — one finds Irish householders alongside English and Scottish immigrants' (McConville 1979, 56). 'Australia was the region in which Irish immigrants were least marginal to the host economy, and their patterns of settlement expressed the fact. Without a powerfully entrenched native population tightly controlling the best jobs, the Australian immigrants had unusually bright chances for self-improvement and upward mobility' (Fitzpatrick 1979, 52).

Another reason for the failure of specifically Irish urban concentrations to develop was that the outward migration of higher-status residents to the suburbs began much later than in American cities. No 'Irish town' developed, because 'in the Australian ports, no middle-class area lay vacant for immigrants to seize upon. The informal yet elaborate network cast out from the Irish lodging-house, found on both sides of the Atlantic, never reappeared in Australia' (McConville 1979, 58).

To sum up, there were, by the turn of the century, initial ethnic concentrations of some of the smaller immigrant groups. The degree of concentration varied according to the country of origin and to the particular group's relation to the British-oriented host society. Also significant were the degree of urbanization of each group, the existence and extent of chain migration and cohesion within the group, types of occupation and the location of employment opportunities. The existence of such traditional clusters, however small they may have been in any particular case, is one factor determining the distribution of overseas immigrants in Australian cities after World War II.

4.2.2 Time of arrival and period of residence in Australia

As far as the post-war immigrants are concerned, income levels and choices of residence have to some extent depended upon the time of their arrival and length of stay in Australia. The time of arrival is important in relation to changing immigration policy, for instance the extent of assisted passages and the provision of accommodation by the government. Increasing white-collar employment and a slow increase of the proportion of self-employed and employers in the immigrant population tended to correlate with the length of stay in Australia (Borrie & Zubrzycki 1958).

The flow of immigrants to Australia has traditionally been dominated by the United Kingdom. Then, as mentioned in chapter 2.1.2, the Commonwealth Government between 1947 and 1953 accepted a considerable number of *displaced persons*, on humanitarian grounds. Out of a total of 612,375 immigrants during this period, 427,603 were assisted arrivals, 36.1% of whom were displaced persons, mainly from *Eastern European countries* such as Poland, Hungary, Yugoslavia and Russia, including fractions from the Ukraine and the former Baltic states. The sudden change in countries of origin is well illustrated by the data presented by Rose in his paper on European immigration (1958) in table 50.

Table 50. Immigrants by countries of origin, 1948–55 (in %)

Period	U.K.	East Europe	South Europe	Rest of Europe	Rest of World	Total
1/7/1948 – 31/12/1948	64.4	23.6	7.7	2.2	2.2	36,280
1/1/1949 – 31/12/1949	32.7	52.5	10.5	2.7	1.6	150,001
1/1/1955 – 31/12/1955	22.3	2.6	46.5	26.4	4.2	97,255

Source: Rose 1958

As is shown in table 51, most of the post-war intake of Russians, Ukrainians and Poles was in the short period ending with fiscal year 1951–52, but only a minor portion of the Yugoslavs arrived in this period (Martin 1965).

Table 51. Emigration of East Europeans to Australia, 1945–72

Years	Russians	Ukrainians	Poles	Yugoslavs
1945–48	572*	.	2,834	551
1948/49	4,311*	.	14,179	3,599
1949/50	n.a.	8,233	38,247	10,399
1950/51	n.a.	2,245	14,145	7,493
1951/52	n.a.	146	1,688	2,363
1952/53–71/72	n.a.	366	14,840	131,872
Total 1945–71/72	4,833**	10,990	85,933	156,277

* Ukrainians included, ** 1945–48/49

Source: Commission of Inquiry into Poverty 1975

The second period of post-war immigration was characterized by a larger intake of *Southern Europeans*. As was shown in table 50 these groups made up 46.5% of all arrivals in 1955, but there were changes in rank among the various Mediterranean countries during the period. In the decade 1951/52 to 1960/61, 33.1% of all arrivals were Southern Europeans, Italy alone contributing 20.6%. During the following five years (1960/61–65/66) 29.4% of all arrivals were from Southern Europe, Greece leading with 14.4%. Then during the pentade 1965/66–70/71, the Yugoslavs became the leading group. Special mention must be made of the *Maltese*. Although small in absolute numbers, Maltese immigration contributed 3.6% to Australian immigration in the period 1951/52–1961/62 and 3.8% in the period 1961/62–1965/66. Emigration from this former British possession was almost exclusively directed to Australia. During the decade 1951–61 the *Dutch* also contributed 10.5% to total immigration, many of them coming from Indonesia. Also in the early 1960s some 10,000 *Armenians* arrived from various countries which had been their last residence.

The third period since about 1970 witnessed an increasing intake from various countries of Asia. In the early 1970s, some countries of the *Middle East*, the Lebanon and Turkey in particular, as well as India, Pakistan and Sri Lanka were the most important countries of origin. From 1974 to 1979 there was a considerable change in favour of *Southeast Asia*, with countries such as Malaysia and Singapore, Thailand, Vietnam, Indonesia, Timor and the Philippines ranking high among the countries of origin. Thus out of a total of 22,577 Indians and 11,369 Sri Lankans immigrating during the period 1965/66 to 1978/79, 20,876 and 9,438 respectively came prior to 1975. On the other hand, out of a total of 10,506 Malaysians and 8,665 Filipinos immigrating during the same period, 6,980 and 6,407 respectively came after 1975 (Monk 1983). There has also been a considerable immigration from *New Zealand* and a growing influx of *South Africans*, both white and black.

Thus within little more than three decades appreciable changes as to the countries of origin of immigrant groups and considerable fluctuations in their numbers have occurred. This is very much in contrast to the more regular pattern of the United States, where large numbers of migrants from Western and Northern Europe arrived over a time span of six decades (1820–80), then large numbers of Eastern and Southern Europeans over a time span of more than four decades (1880–1925) followed by growing numbers of people from Asian and Latin American countries over a time span of three decades (1955–85). The *short-term changes* of the intake of immigrants in Australia are one factor to be considered in the context of the limited growth of ethnic concentrations in Australian cities (see also ch. 4.2.5).

The destinations within Australia of various immigrant groups differ to a certain extent. For example, Western Australia receives below-average numbers of Maltese, Cypriots and Lebanese, while other nationalities are over-represented. Apart from receiving a high proportion of immigrants from the United Kingdom, there are also above-average numbers of immigrants from some African countries such as Kenya and Malawi, these being partly people of Indian origin who had been living in Africa for some time, and from some Southeast Asian countries such as Malaysia, Singapore, Burma and from Japan (table 52).

Table 52. Origins of overseas-born population in capital cities, 1976

Region of origin	Sydney	Melbourne	Brisbane	Adelaide	Perth	Hobart
UK and Eire	34.0	30.9	53.1	53.5	56.8	52.5
Southern Europe	23.6	36.0	10.0	20.5	15.0	10.3
Asia	13.0	9.5	6.9	3.9	10.0	5.0
Other overseas	29.4	23.6	30.0	22.1	18.2	32.2

Source: ABS, quoted in Maher 1982, 39

The *urbanization rate* of the various immigrant groups differs somewhat, although relatively high for all groups. Out of a total of 2,998,769 overseas immigrants at the 1981 census, 92.4% were living in urban places. The range of variation is shown in table 53.

The table reveals the Vietnamese, Chinese, Lebanese, Turks, Cypriots and Greeks to be the *most highly urbanized groups*. With the exception of the Greeks, with their high urbanization rates in Tasmania and Western Australia, these groups are easily identified as belonging to the Southeast Asian and Middle Eastern immigrants that only arrived in the 1970s and 1980s and have thus the *shortest periods of residence* in Australia. Nearly all these recent arrivals have settled in the cities.

The figures on lowest urbanization rates are not quite so unambigous. The Dutch, Maltese and Italians mainly arrived during the 1950s and early 1960s, thus being characterized by *rather long periods of residence* in Australia. Considerable numbers of Italians are still found in the rural areas of Queensland. Immigration from the United States and Canada also decreased in recent years, so that these two groups belong to those with comparatively long periods of residence. The Turks, however, are among the more recent arrivals, and so are the immigrants from New Zealand and Oceania.

The metropolitan areas contributed much to the high urbanization rates of immigrants. The highest proportion ever reached was 31.7% in Perth at the 1971 census. The proportions of overseas immigrants of total metropolitan populations are shown in table 54.

Table 53. Urbanization rates of immigrant groups, 1981

A. Highest rates

State	First rank Group	%	Second rank Group	%	Third rank Group	%
NSW	Vietnamese	99.52	Turks	99.46	Lebanese	99.11
Victoria	Vietnamese	99.57	Lebanese	99.43	Cypriots	98.87
Qld.	Vietnamese	99.20	Lebanese	97.67	Cypriots	95.25
S.A.	Chinese	98.41	Vietnamese	97.40	Egyptians	97.35
W.A.	Vietnamese	98.85	Greeks	96.40	Lebanese	95.97
Tasmania	Vietnamese	95.77	Greeks	95.27	Lebanese	93.94

B. Lowest rates

State	Last rank Group	%	Second last rank Group	%	Third last rank Group	%
NSW	Dutch	87.87	Maltese	88.36	U.S. citizens	89.51
Victoria	Dutch	85.24	U.S. citizens	91.63	Canadians	91.73
Qld.	Maltese	71.54	Italians	76.14	U.S. citizens	77.29
S.A.	Pac. Islanders	85.94	Turks	86.77	Dutch	87.91
W.A.	New Zeal.	85.89	Dutch	87.86	Canadians	87.95
Tasmania	U.S. citizens	72.28	Canadians	73.54	Dutch	73.82

Source: ABS, calculations by the author

Table 54. Proportions of overseas-born population in metropolitan areas, 1966–81 (%)

Year		Sydney	Melbourne	Brisbane	Adelaide	Perth	Hobart
1966		22.0	25.5	15.2	26.9	26.8	12.0
1971		24.9	27.5	16.1	28.1	31.7	12.8
1976		24.4	26.8	16.6	27.6	31.6	12.7
1981	a	27.2	28.2	18.1	27.1	31.2	12.8
	b	22.3	23.6	20.9	22.3	26.2	16.2
	c	49.5	51.8	39.0	49.4	57.4	29.0

a = born overseas, b = Australian born with at least one parent born overseas, c = total.

Sources: ABS, quoted in Maher 1982, 38 and Div. Nat. Mapp. & ABS: Atlas of Population and Housing 1981, vol. Sydney, 1984

Apart from differences in urbanization rates there are differences of the respective urban fraction of each group as to their degrees of concentration or segregation within the urban areas. This is shown for four ethnic groups in Sydney and Melbourne in table 55.

Table 55. Distribution of four ethnic groups in Sydney and Melbourne, 1966 (%)

Area	Italians Sydney	Melbourne	Greeks Sydney	Melbourne	Yugoslavs Sydney	Melbourne	Dutch Sydney	Melbourne
Inner area	7.63	14.11	29.71	11.25	15.81	9.90	4.02	2.05
Inner res. suburbs	29.99	16.86	33.60	32.34	17.80	10.47	5.36	1.88
Middle-distance suburbs	33.03	43.55	30.39	43.27	33.33	45.50	27.44	22.33
Outer suburbs + rural-urban fringe	29.35	26.48	6.30	13.14	33.06	34.13	63.18	73.74

Source: Commission of Inquiry into Poverty 1975, 22, 39, 58, 98

It is apparent from the figures that the *Dutch*, with relatively long periods of residence in Australia, are widely dispersed over the metropolitan areas; they are scarcely represented in the central city and inner suburbs. Between two-thirds and three-fourths of them are living in the large ring of the outer suburbs, including the rural-urban fringe. Similarly, the *Yugoslavs* living in Australia in 1966 mainly belonged to the first wave of displaced persons, with their relatively long periods of residence. Between two-thirds and three-fourths of them are to be found in the middle-distance and outer suburbs. About two-thirds of the *Italians*, with periods of residence somewhat longer than those of the Greeks, are also to be found in the middle-distance and outer suburbs. Most of the Greeks, with their comparatively shorter periods of residence, are concentrated in the central cities and inner suburbs, with only about one third in the middle-distance suburbs and a tiny fraction in the outer suburbs.

The distribution of Ukrainians, of people from the former Baltic states and of other refugees is similar to that of the Dutch. Their choice of residence is partly related to the location of government hostels, as will be shown in chapter 4.2.3. The Poles show a degree of concentration in the inner suburbs of St. Kilda and Melbourne, due to the fact that many of them are *of Jewish descent*, and the Jews in general had a strong tendency toward congregating in particular areas, such as St. Kilda.

In the metropolitan area of Adelaide, migrants from Eastern Europe are mainly found in the City of Adelaide and in the inner suburbs of Thebarton, Hindmarsh, Bowden, Croyden Park, Unley, Parkside and Norwood, together with the suburbs of the northwestern sector between the City of Adelaide and Port Adelaide. These inner suburbs are also characterized by concentrations of Greeks, while the Italians are also found in the suburbs along the Torrens River such as Marsden, Felixstow, Klemzig, Cambelltown, Newton and Athelstone to the east and Underdale, Flinders Park and Fulham Gardens to the west, where many of them were, in former years, engaged in market gardening (Burnley 1974).

Burnley (1976) and Teo (1971) showed for the Greeks and the Chinese respectively that the period of residence also plays a part in the distribution of fractions of the same ethnic group. Burnley found that there is a strong tendency for newly arrived *Greeks* to settle with relatives or friends in the Greek residential clusters of the *inner suburbs*. Thus the index of dissimilarity in metropolitan Sydney's LGAs in 1971 was 60 for those Greeks who had been in Australia for less than five years, against 49 for those staying over five years. Teo stated that a considerably higher percentage of first-generation *Chinese* was living in the *central city and adjacent suburbs* than in the rest of the metropolitan area. It was also found that one third of Southern Europeans staying for less than six years in Melbourne lived in 'shared accommodation' with relatives of the extended family (Burnley 1974, 193).

Some groups, the Italians in particular and the Greeks to a somewhat lesser extent, have shown a strong tendency toward dispersion after a relatively short period of residence in Australia. This movement from the central city and inner suburbs to the middle-distance suburbs and, in the case of the Italians and Yugoslavs, also to the outer suburbs has been referred to as the forming of *second concentrations*. During the decade 1966–76, Italian dominance in Melbourne's inner suburbs of Brunswick and Fitzroy had dwindled, although some new concentrations in the present middle-distance suburbs of Coburg and Preston emerged. New concentrations had begun to grow through the intra-urban migration of Italian-born residents in the ring comprised by the middle-distance suburbs of Sunshine, Keilor, Broadmeadows, Doncaster-Templestone and Waverley. In 1966 rather high concentrations of Greek immigrants were found in the inner suburbs of Collingwood, Richmond, Fitzroy, Port Melbourne, Prahran and Brunswick. By 1976 Greeks in Fitzroy, Collingwood, Richmond and Prahran were less concentrated, whereas concentrations had grown in the outer suburbs of Sunshine, Keilor, Whittlesea and Waverley, but still more in Doncaster and in the southeastern middle-distance suburbs of Oakleigh and Moorabbin (McKay 1981; fig. 114; table 56).

A number of Chinese arrivals settled in some inner and middle-distance suburbs for a short period of time and then moved to high-status Northshore suburbs, to Roseville and Pymble in particular (Teo 1971).

It has also been noted that new arrivals do not always start in the same inner residential areas as earlier migrants did, but that chain migration works in such as way that new arrivals from the same region or village join their compatriots already living in the middle-distance and outer suburbs directly, without even passing through the inner residential areas (Lee 1970). *Chain migration thus contributes* to the formation and growth of *second concentrations*.

The phenomenon of second concentrations is at least partly explained by the demands for housing of the respective immigrant groups, as will be discussed below (ch. 4.2.3).

A certain *succession* of immigrant groups was observed by Burnley (1974, 1976), although this occurred to a

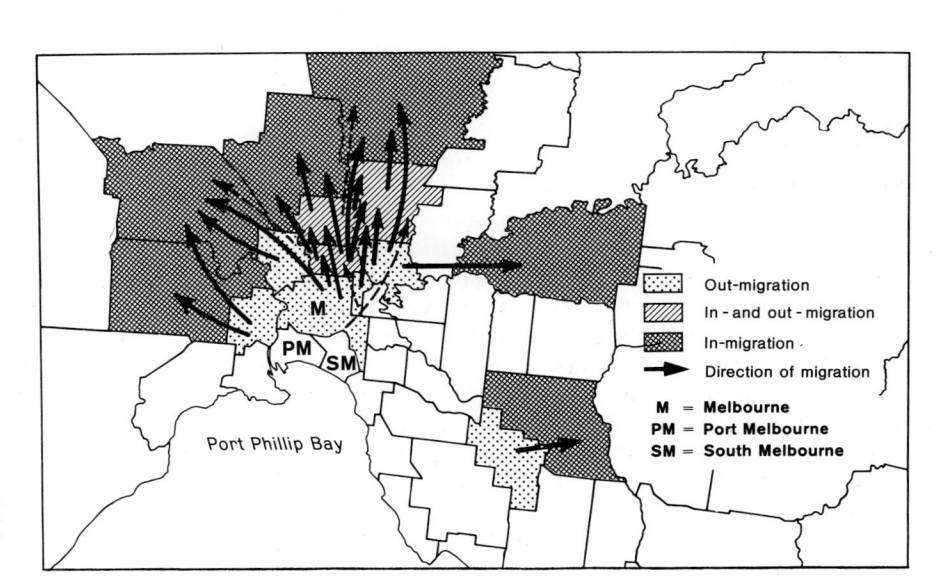

Fig. 114. Development of second concentrations of Italian immigrants in Melbourne, 1971–76 (after McKay 1981, modified)

Table 56. Index of segregation for Greeks and Italians in Melbourne, 1966–76

Name of LGA	Segregation index for Greeks		Segregation index for Italians	
	1966	1976	1966	1976
City of Melbourne	1.24	0.65	2.55	1.28
Fitzroy	5.70	2.65	4.07	2.19
Richmond	6.46	5.20	1.75	0.80
Prahran	3.61	2.71	0.37	0.24
Sunshine	0.73	0.78	0.86	1.12
Keilor	0.59	0.70	1.13	1.79
Doncaster-Templestone	0.13	0.59	0.55	0.95
Waverley	0.20	0.49	0.22	0.40
Oakleigh	0.99	2.79	1.37	1.71
Moorabbin	0.26	0.94	0.35	0.55

Source: McKay 1981, 70–71

much lesser extent than the successions reported from cities in the United States. Burnley gives the example of an area in Redfern between Cleveland, Bourke, Phillip and Botany Streets which was, prior to World War I, a residential area for people of British, German and Lebanese origins, as well as of Jewish immigrants from Russia. During the interwar period most of the British, German and Jewish residents left the area, thus making room for Greek and Italian immigrants. The latter constituted 8% of all residents in 1961, but only 2% in 1971, whereas the Greek proportion rose from 10% in 1961 to 20% in 1966. Then those Greeks who had lived in the area for several years moved out, thus in turn making room for new Greek arrivals.

Such short-term changes are evidence for an assimilation process, for which Redfern functions as a *buffer between two societies*. Carlton and Fitzroy in Melbourne perform the same function. They have sustained their character as receiving areas for successive waves of immigrants, in earlier years for waves from different countries, in more recent years for new arrivals from the same country. These immigrants spend their first years of residence in Australia in this particular area and then move to other areas within the metropolitan region (Burnley 1976).

As mentioned above, some ethnic groups and especially those with the shortest periods of residence in Australia, never settled in the central area, but were established in the outer suburbs from the very beginning. Among these recent arrivals are New Zealanders and Lebanese, Vietnamese and Chinese who are mainly English-educated and belong to the higher-income groups. The *Vietnamese* were influenced in their choice of residence by the location of Government Hostels (ch. 4.2.3).

There are also some ethnic groups with relatively long periods of residence in Australia, which showed a tendency toward settling in the middle-distance and outer suburbs from the beginning. Among them are the Dutch and Germans and, to a somewhat lesser extent, the Maltese and Poles. Though certain fractions of these groups were assisted arrivals and passed through the hostels, others did not. There is evidence that some local concentrations have attracted immigrants from various fractions of the same ethnic group, so that assisted refugees, chain migrants and 'free' settlers alike were drawn to the same locality (Burnley 1976).

There is some relation between the period of residence and the degree of intermarriage of a particular ethnic group. This problem will be discussed below (see ch. 4.2.5).

4.2.3 Demand and search for accommodation

The provision of temporary government accommodation, particularly for assisted arrivals, and the nature of the housing market have been important factors in determining the distribution of immigrant groups in the large cities.

Overseas immigrants accepted under refugee or special humanitarian programmes were eligible both for assisted passage and for government accommodation. The latter was usually in government hostels, supplemented in recent years, and to a very limited extent, by flats provided by the hostels administration. The rents were the same both for hostels and flats. In the hostels families may stay for a maximum period of one year and single persons up to six months, whereas in the flats the maximum stay is limited to six months for all persons. At least some of the hostel residents, usually the more skilled element with working wives, were able to save some money toward the deposit for a house. Others had to look for private rental accommodation.

There is evidence that many of the hostel residents looked for accommodation, whether for purchase or for rent, in the *vicinity of the respective hostel*, and preferably in the sector of the city lying between the hostel and their working place, because this is the part of the metropolitan area with which they had become familiar. This was the area in which they gained, during their stay in the hostel, the best knowledge of the housing market.

Research into the housing choices of former hostel residents in Melbourne revealed that the average distance moved was only between 7.8 km and 9.3 km for Southern Europeans and between 9.8 km and 13.3 km for British migrants, and that there was a strong *attraction toward the CBD*. Immigrants who were apparently dissatisfied with the hostel and moved after only one month, with hardly any knowledge of the city, were very much attracted by the central area and therefore moved the longest distances. Those staying longer became better acquainted with the area surrounding the hostel and developed a more selective spatial behaviour (Humphreys & Whitelaw 1979, Whitelaw & Humphreys in: Burnley, Pryor & Rowland 1980, 151–69).

The main hostels in both Sydney and Melbourne were located in the western suburbs, which means in the Sydney metropolitan area the area comprising Liverpool, Bankstown, Fairfield and Blacktown and in the Melbourne metropolitan area the suburbs of Sunshine, Broadmeadows and Altona. They were in the early 1950s the areas of rapid industrialization offering good job opportunities to many of the refugees of the Eastern European countries. At the 1954 census there were over 2,000 Poles in Bankstown and almost 2,000 Poles in Fairfield and in Blacktown, while a considerable number of Russians and Ukrainians also settled in Bankstown and Blacktown, as well as in Burwood, Concord and Ashfield (Burnley 1982, 92–93).

The location of the hostels in Liverpool and Bankstown is also responsible for a certain anomaly concerning the distribution pattern of Southern Europeans. There are distinct clusters of them in these two localities. This is in contrast to their predominant concentration in some of the inner suburbs, and it is also in contrast to the usually greater diversity of ethnic minorities in outer suburban localities (Scott 1965). In recent years the Vietnamese in particular have been influenced in their choice of residence by the location of the hostels. Out of a total of 101,171 overseas immigrants in 1982, 17,522 were accepted under special programmes, 10,789 of them under the Indo-Chinese programme (Yearb. Australia 1984, 113–15).

Apart from the government hostels the location of *rooming and boarding houses* had a certain influence on the residential choice of immigrants. When in the early 1950s labour for heavy industrial work was in high demand, considerable numbers of single males were selected for immigration intake, many of whom found their first accommodations in rooming and boarding houses that were particularly to be found in such inner-suburban areas as Darlinghurst and Wooloomooloo in Sydney or in East Melbourne (Burnley 1982). Croatians and Slovenians have been prominent among those staying for a considerable length of time in such accommodation.

The development of so-called *second concentrations* formed by Italians and to some extent by Greeks and Yugoslavs was very much due to their traditional lifestyle. Most of these immigrants came from rural areas or small towns in their countries of origin. Family size, kinship ties and the traditional responsibilities of hospitality of people from these Mediterranean countries made it inevitable for them to have a house of their own, unless they were willing to renounce much of their traditional lifestyle.

It thus often happened that in the Italian and Greek immigrant families the wife worked day-shift and the husband night-shift, or the husband had more than one job, in order to be able to save the deposit for a house and then pay the interest rates on the usually short-term, high-interest mortgages. There has also been some pooling of resources by closely related families. On the other hand, land values were still reasonable in many outer suburban areas, and in the absence of local government regulations prohibiting low-grade housing, building costs were not too high (Scott 1965). Thus many of the Italian, Greek and Yugoslav families managed to purchase a house after a relatively short period of residence in Australia, moving to one of the middle-distance suburbs or, particularly in the case of the Italians, even to the outer ones.

The Dutch are another ethnic group with a strong desire for home ownership. Many of the early arrivals of the 1950s were first accommodated in hostels, which they normally found unsatisfactory. The Netherlands Migration Service established several building societies, raising funds from the American Development Loan Fund, some insurance companies in the Netherlands and two Australian banks. By 1963 the sum of $ 14 million had been made available for loans, some of them guaranteed by the Netherlands Government (Comm. of Inquiry into Poverty 1975, 100).

4.2.4 The immigrants' skills and the labour market

In chapter 4.2.1 on initial ethnic concentrations, reference was made to Chinese clusters near the docks and vegetable market in Sydney, to the Italian fishermen in Fremantle and to the Italian market gardeners in Spearwood on the southern periphery of the Perth metropolitan area.

Post-war immigrants in Australia have carried on a number of characteristic occupations. Crissman (1967, 200) argued that migration of Chinese to cities overseas 'was in fact only a continuation in a new direction of longstanding patterns of movement within China ... The Chinese who migrated to the cities of China were ideological transients just like those who went overseas, and men from the same area tended to monopolise lines of business or particular crafts in Chinese cities as well'. In a study on Chinese households in Melbourne in 1968 Choi (1970) found 82.6% of his sample to be in *'Chinese' occupations*, such as Chinese grocers, fruit and vegetable retailers and wholesalers, cafe owners and chefs and waiters in restaurants, altogether a considerable proportion of employees and self-employed, while there were only 17.4% in *'Australian' occupations* working as professionals and, to a very small extent, as white-collar and blue-collar workers.

For the Italians Borrie found that they 'tended to follow a fairly narrow range of occupations – restaurants,

Fig. 115. Spearwood, Perth, W.A. Market gardeners of predominantly South European origin growing Mediterranean crops

fruit and vegetable growing and vending, fishing, cane cutting and farming, and to some extent mining and timber cutting' (Borrie 1954, 57, fig. 115). A higher percentage was found to be employers or self-employed than among the Greek immigrants. Borrie claims a strong correlation between this rather *narrow range of occupations and the spatial concentration* of the immigrant group. Thus it was the Italian participation in occupations such as fishing, dock work, operation of seafood restaurants, ferry boats, shop dealing in accessories for marine businesses and the like that led to 2,901 first-generation, but not yet naturalized, Italians being concentrated in Fremantle.

There is a considerable *diversification* of occupations in the *second generation and also among post-war arrivals*. Price (1968) found that prior to World War II no less than 46% of Southern Europeans in inner Sydney and Melbourne were in cafes and other catering businesses and another 20% were either working as independent skilled tradesmen such as tailors and shoemakers or employed by them. He also stated that of necessity only one son of a first-generation Italian family engaged in horticulture and vegetable growing can stay in that occupation; any other children must move to different occupations. Frequently this means a move to some other residence and some other location.

To a certain extent the immigrant's occupation and his choice of residence has been dependent upon his skills. Many post-war immigrants were hired for work in particular industries and occupations. Thus Australia recruited great numbers of blue-collar workers in the United Kingdom for the newly established automobile industries in Elizabeth on the northern periphery of the Adelaide metropolitan area (see ch. 3.4.2) and in Dandenong on the southeast side of the Melbourne metropolitan area, with much of the accommodation provided by the respective housing authorities near the industrial sites.

In the wake of the post-war migration waves, *many unskilled persons* got to Australia as well, and this is reflected in the change of occupational structure. Of the Greek-born residents living in Australia in 1947 no less than 71.6% were employed in catering, most of them working in cafes, fruit shops and fish shops. Only 7.7% were labourers and operatives. Their relatively small numbers had enabled them to find niches in the Australian economy and jobs they considered appropriate. The large numbers of newcomers in post-war years could not be absorbed by such traditional occupations, so that at the 1971 census 59.5% of Greek immigrants in Australia were employed as labourers and process workers (Bottomley 1979).

The great amount of unskilled labour in post-war Australia has made for extremely high employment turnover, in some industrial plants amounting to over 100%, which means that statistically during one year each member of the workforce changed his job at least once. From the point of view of the factory this was acceptable only because the assembly process had been simplified and mechanized to a point that new employees could be instructed within less than one hour and then be put to work (Birrell & Birrell 1981). There was a general trend for unskilled manual and service workers of all birth-place groups, but especially those populations more culturally dissimilar, to be more residentially concentrated than skilled manual workers (Burnley 1975, 17).

The proportions of skilled or unskilled migrants have changed somewhat over time, due to changing government goals and policies. Skills and occupational demand have always played a certain role in immigration policy. However, as unemployment increased, and intakes of immigrants decreased, this aspect gained importance. The so-called Numerical Multifactor Assessment System (N.U.M.A.S.) of 1979 and its modified version of 1982 put greater emphasis on this aspect.

It must not be overlooked that even prior to the recession of the 1970s, considerable numbers of *well-educated migrants* came to Australia. At the 1966 census there was a higher proportion of overseas-born males holding a degree than of Australian-born males (Birrell & Birrell 1981). Many immigrants were, however, unable to find employment in the occupations for which they had been trained, and had to accept jobs that were definitely below their level of skill. This happened first to the displaced persons accepted under a refugee scheme that involved a *two-year allocation* to employment by the State Governments. Thus the Western Australian Government was eager to place migrants in one of four industries: railways, timber milling, public works and the building and construction industry. The first three industries are mainly located in country areas. It thus happened that in 1947 the Perth metropolitan area had 59.17% of the total Western Australian workforce, but only 39.14% of male displaced persons were settled there. Due to the different nature of their employment, a higher proportion of female displaced persons was absorbed by the Perth metropolitan area.

This allocation policy had certain consequences, as Appleyard (1955) showed for the Hungarian group. By 1955 approximately two-thirds of the 1,200 Hungarians located in Western Australia were living in the metropolitan area. Of the 600 working adults, 35% were 'intellectuals' including 30 high-school teachers, 22 doctors of law, eight doctors of medicine and a number of ex-army officers, and another 30% were clerical workers with an education to about matriculation level. Almost all of them had migrated to the metropolitan area soon after or even before their two-year contracts had expired, although it had been hoped by the government that the job allocation would contribute to a certain decentralization of the state's population.

Monk (1983) investigated the search for accommodation by Indian immigrants in the Sydney metropolitan area. Only a third of recent arrivals used personal connections for their first residence, while a fifth relied completely on newspaper advertisements and estate agents. Many of the Indian immigrants are well educated and in various professional occupations, university people were often provided with at least temporary accommodation in university houses, while medical doctors had a chance to find accommodation in a hospital residence or in the house of a physician for whom they worked as a substitute. Thus some small clusters of Indians in Randwick and in the northern suburb of Ryde are related to the location of the University of New South Wales, Macquarie University and the research and medical facilities in these areas. Good job opportunities for medical doctors and engineers were also to be found in some outer industrial suburbs. In general, all these circumstances made for a rather wide dispersal of the relatively small group of Indian immigrants (see also Connell & Engels 1983).

There is some evidence that the occupational structure of immigrant groups changes rather slowly over time, which appears to cast doubt on Wolforth's (1974) argument that in cities of rapid growth and structural change, work-residence relationships will also change rather quickly, thus preventing the establishment of persistent ethnic concentrations. It seems to the author that other factors (chs. 4.2.2, 4.2.5) are more strongly working toward this end.

4.2.5 Group cohesion and in-marriage rates

As was shown in chapter 4.2.1 chain migration has often fostered group cohesion and the growth of ethnic concentration. It also made for the evolution of distinct clusters with, for example, Italians from places in North Italy having settled in different municipalities from those in which Italians from South Italy have congregated. Prior regional association has thus played a part in the development of ethnic concentrations in Australian cities. There are, however, more complicated community relations, as exemplified by the Yugoslavs, the Lebanese or the Indians.

There was no Yugoslav nation prior to the end of World War I. Thus Yugoslavs *differ by regional origin, language and religion*. Slovenes, Croatians, Serbians and Macedonians alike emigrated to Australia. The Slovenes and Croatians are predominantly Roman Catholic, Serbians are largely Orthodox while Macedonians may be Orthodox, Muslim or even Protestant. There is no exact data available as to a regional breakdown of the Yugoslav community in Australia. Out of a total of 156,277 immigrants during the period 1945–71/72, approximately 25,000 were accepted as refugees. These people mainly arrived prior to 1953 and were predominantly Slovenes, Croatians and, to some extent,

Macedonians. 104,000 came between 1965 and 1972, the majority being Macedonians and Croatians (Comm. of Inquiry into Poverty 1975). No doubt the Macedonian and Serbian Orthodox Churches and other group services and institutions that will be mentioned in more detail below (ch. 4.2.6) helped to keep ethnic identity alive.

Of a sample of Lebanese taken in Melbourne by Ata (1979), 31% were Maronites, 23% Orthodox, 23% Muslim, 14% Catholic, 6% Druze and 2% Protestant. These details are known because there is a law by which every Lebanese must be identified by his denomination in his passport (Ata 1979, 39). Burnley (1982) found that in Redfern there are Maronite and Melkite churches and an Orthodox church, in Lakemba a Maronite church and Muslim mosque, in Bankstown, Harris Park and Granville near Parramatta, Maronite and Orthodox churches. The existence of different churches and a mosque in the same residential area indicate that Lebanese of different denominations are living in reasonably *close vicinity*. Lebanese of Christian and Muslim affiliation are found in eight Sydney LGAs. While their proportions vary in six LGAs about equal numbers of either denomination are found in Auburn and Bankstown as shown in table 57 (fig. 116).

Table 57. Lebanese residents in Sydney LGAs, 1981

LGA	Christian	Muslim
Ashfield	600	150
Auburn	1,000	1,100
Bankstown	2,000	1,800
Burwood	700	160
Canterbury	4,500	2,800
Marrickville	1,700	1,000
Parramatta	3,000	500
Rockdale	400	1,100

Source: Div. Nat. Mapp. & ABS (eds.): Atlas of Population and Housing 1981, vol. 2, Sydney, 1984

On the other hand, Ata (1979) stated that the Australian Lebanese Association of Victoria, established in 1945, ran into difficulties upon the outbreak of the civil war in 1975. When in the same year a new president was elected who was affiliated with the Maronite group, other sects withdrew their support. As a consequence smaller communal societies revived, forming their own associations and extending direct help to their relatives.

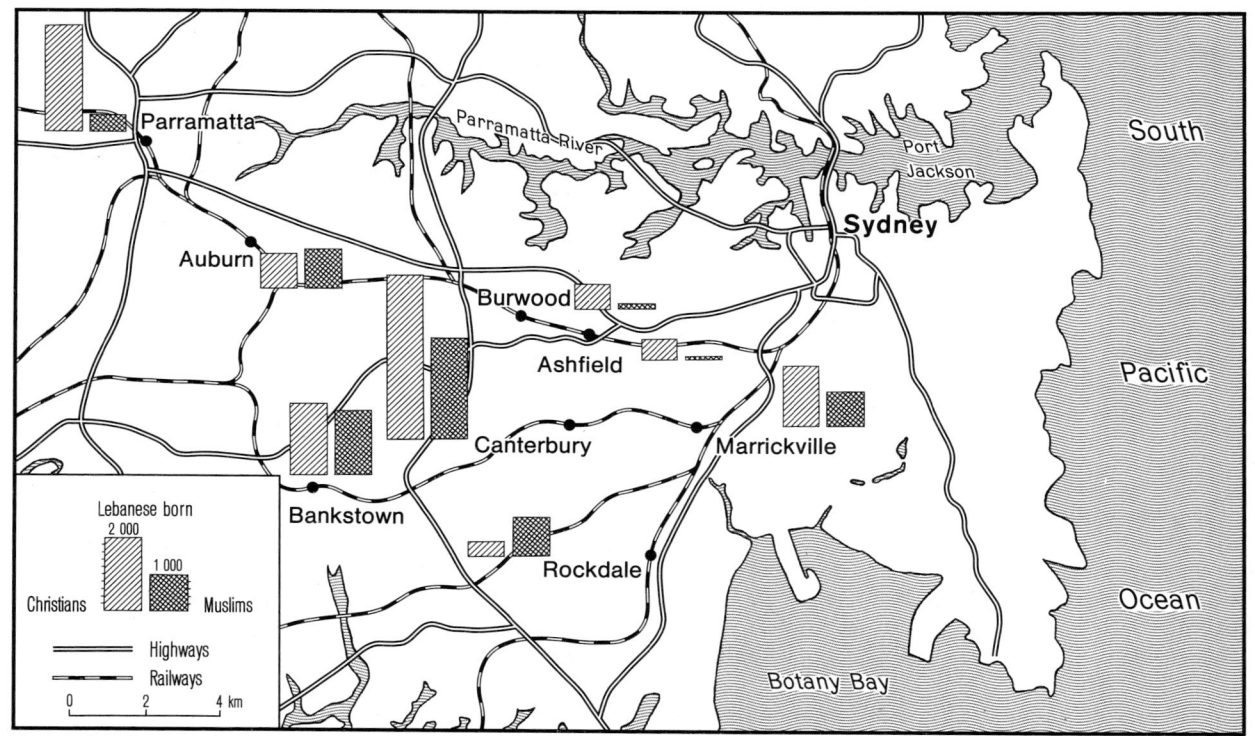

Fig. 116. Local concentrations of Lebanese Christians and Muslims in Sydney, 1981

Apart from the Indian Australian Cultural Society aiming at serving the whole Indian community in Australia, there are several organizations based on *regional or religious fractions*, such as the Bengali Society, the Hyderabad Association or the Sikh Cultural Association. Price (1975) made the statement that there is a tendency for persons to marry within their particular religious grouping. This observation applies to a higher extent to the Jewish and Orthodox denominations. Due to post-war immigration from Southern and Eastern Europe and various Asian countries the various Christian and Oriental Orthodox Churches enjoyed the greatest increase during the period 1947–71; Orthodox membership grew from 17,012 to 338,632 persons (Price 1975, 315).

There is, to the author's knowledge, as yet no investigation comparable with that by Bigelow (1976) on the marriage patterns of the Polish Americans. As Bigelow found out there was a very high in-marriage rate of first-generation Poles in the United States. Second-generation Poles showed a considerably lower in-marriage rate, but a strong tendency toward marriage within the Catholic segment of the population. Only third-generation Poles were found to marry outside the Polish or the Catholic population to any great extent.

There is, on the other hand, sufficient data on in- and out-marriage rates of the various ethnic groups in Australia. First of all, it is interesting to note that people emigrating to Australia by way of chain migration may very well be *kin*. As Bottomley (1979) pointed out, clans coming from Kythera Island were often endogamous up to three generations ago, while the tendency to marry within the island's population or even within the same municipality was still *continuing after arrival* in Australia. Similar proportions of in-group marriages were found with the Greeks from Castellorizo and Cyprus.

It has been argued that proximity of residence favours in-marriage (Timms 1969, Peach 1974). It has also been argued that high in-marriage rates favour the persistence of local concentrations of ethnic groups. Probably the two processes reinforce each other. However, intermarriage is not only a question of distance or better opportunities for getting acquainted with people from different ethnic groups; it is also a matter of *family pressures upon the individual*, as was demonstrated by Teo (1971) for the Chinese group in Sydney.

It must be taken into consideration that in-marriage rates are truly significant when applicable to ethnic groups for a time span of at least three generations. A few conclusions may, however, be drawn from in-marriage figures of one generation only which are given in table 58 for selected ethnic groups in Australia.

Table 58. In-marriage rates for selected ethnic groups, 1947–60 to 1974–80 (in %)

Ethnic group	1947–60 males	females	1974–80 males	females
Dutch	42.3	61.7	8.5	12.6
Maltese	58.2	75.8	32.2	44.7
Italians	66.2	90.4	37.1	65.6
Poles	40.1	67.2	38.0	40.2
Asians*	27.3	33.8	52.0	47.5
Lebanese	72.1	83.6	64.2	80.7
Greeks, Cypriots	84.6	89.7	64.4	82.1
English, Welsh	16.0	22.9	19.8	22.6

* excluding Indonesians, Israelis, Lebanese, Cypriots

Source: Price 1981, 40–41

It is apparent from these figures that in-marriage rates are, with the exception of the Asians (who are an extremely heterogeneous statistical group), always *higher for females* than for males; that means that brides more frequently look for a groom belonging to their own ethnic group than grooms do with regard to their brides.

Immigrants from the Mediterranean countries are characterized by relatively high in-marriage rates, which may be considered a stabilizing factor for group cohesion. There is, however, one exception to this interpretation; the Maltese are characterized by a lower in-marriage rate as compared with the Italians and Greeks, although they are more segregated than the former.

Changes of in-marriage rates over the period of one generation differ for particular ethnic groups, the rates for the Dutch, the male Italians, the female Maltese and female Poles showing considerable decreases, whereas those for the Greeks, Cypriots and Lebanese stayed very high and the rate for the male Poles remained almost stable. In-marriage rates for Asians increased, this presumably being due to the appreciable change in the countries of origin within the Asian group. A great proportion of 'Asian' arrivals before 1978 were in fact of European stock.

The overwhelming majority of English and Welsh immigrants married native Australians.

As far as statistics reveal *second-generation* intermarriage patterns, *out-marriage rates are very high* and amount to over two-thirds even for Southern European males and to over half for Southern European females. It may be assumed that this is at least partly due to an *imbalance* of the sexes in the respective immigrant group. An early case of imbalance was the domination of females in the Irish immigration around 1850, when many young unmarried girls from workhouses and orphanages were brought to Australia. The first shipload arrived in 1847, but when criticism arose because many of the girls proved unsuitable for their jobs or were disliked for their alleged lack of hygiene or low moral standards the scheme was discontinued in 1856 (Nance 1978).

In post-war times a conspicuous imbalance occurred in Italian immigration, the intake of the period 1959–1971/72 consisting of 94,593 males against 79,677 females. This resulted in many young Italian migrants taking Australian-born girls of Italian parentage, thus forcing second-generation Italian males to look for brides of Australian or other parentage. 'Heavy chain migration here retarded the assimilation of second-generation females and hastened that of second-generation males' (Price 1968, 10–11).

Apart from the high out-marriage rates in the second generation, the generally observed fall in fertility has been slower in mixed marriages than in total marriages, and *births to mixed marriages rose* during the period 1968–78 from 14.3% to 19.5% of all births (Price 1981, 36–37). From all these trends it may be concluded that there is a *rather rapid break-up of ethnic communities*, and that there will not be any continuous expansion of large ethnic concentrations (ch. 4.2.2).

Two more points related to assimilation should briefly be touched upon here. One point is the *naturalization rate* that, during the period 1945–66, was approximately 50% of all eligible Italian and Greek immigrants. At that time naturalization was granted only after a stay in Australia of five years and more. This indicates a rather strong desire on the part of the two Southern European groups for integration into the larger host society.

In addition, *return migration* rates of Southern Europeans were comparatively low, this rate being 10% of Greek arrivals and 24% of Italian arrivals for the period 1957–65 (Price 1968). These rates are considerably lower than the return migration rate of Italians from the United States. In 1967/68 the return migration rate for males temporarily rose to 33.5% for the Italians, to 30.1% for the Yugoslavs and to 18.9% for the Greeks (Birrell & Birrell 1981). Return migration rates are highest for groups such as the Dutch and Germans, this being explained by the economic growth and opportunities in their two countries of origin, at least prior to the recession of the 1970s and 1980s. Since the total numbers of Southern Europeans are much smaller in Australia than in the United States, the return migration rates are not really significant in relation to the sustained growth of the respective ethnic communities in Australia.

4.2.6 Ethnic group services

The last but not the least important factor to be considered is the number and kind of organizations and institutions serving the ethnic community in whole or in part. Many aspects could be mentioned in this context. As in chapters 4.2.1 to 4.2.5, major emphasis will be put on aspects relevant to the questions as to how far such organizations have been developed in Australia and whether they are of any importance for group cohesion and ethnic concentration. For further details the reader is referred to the report 'Welfare of migrants' issued by the Commission of Inquiry into Poverty (1975) which is a valuable source on which the author has drawn in this chapter, although the report is restricted to the consideration of only a limited number of ethnic groups and its major concern is with welfare.

The degree and nature of institutional development is very different among immigrant groups. For example, the *Greeks are highly institutionalized*. According to the above mentioned report, the Immigration Department had listed 104 Greek institutions in Melbourne and 62 in Sydney. Although there were more Italians in Sydney in 1971 (56,703) than Greeks (47,668) the number of Italian institutions in Sydney was only 20 and in Melbourne 62.

There is a *great variety of institutions* with their goals and functions partly overlapping. There are ecclesiastical parishes, religious groups, sporting clubs, social clubs and regional associations. Cultural groups include cultural clubs, teachers' associations and students' associations. There are ex-servicemen organizations, welfare organizations and the Cultural Institutes sponsored by the government of the states of origin of the immigrants. Finally there are co-ordinating bodies, federations of ethnic organizations and the like.

There has been a long dispute in Australian literature on the role of religion and the *availability of churches or services* offered by a priest of the respective denomination. While Price (1963) considers this a very important point and makes the statement that this is an incentive for immigrants from other parts of the host society to move to such places, church adherance is questioned by other authors. There are some 30 Greek Orthodox Centres in Sydney and some 25 in Melbourne. What makes things complicated, however, is that due to quarrels between the Archbishop and the Greek Community, which is the lay organization on the parish level, the Community established its own parishes, so that for instance in Melbourne the number of 17 Greek Orthodox churches rose to some 25. While the Archdiocese threatened the Community with declaring priests uncanonical, marriages illegal and children illegitimate, some people defected from both Church and Community (Bottomley 1979).

Although this seems to be a specific problem of the Greek ethnic group, other groups are having their problems as well. The *Roman Catholic Church* was opposed to separate ethnic Catholic parishes as they had been established in the United States. 'In some cases, however, Polish chapters were established as adjuncts to established parish churches' (Burnley in: Burnley et al. 1980, 125). There is a Slovenian Catholic Centre in Kew (Melbourne) containing a chapel and a hostel and other facilities that are in principle open to all Yugoslavs, but very little used by non-

Slovenians; there is a Croatian Catholic Centre and there are the Serbian and Macedonian Communities. Each of these churches serve rather small Yugoslav groups. On the other hand, they gained importance due to the fact that people desist from other ethnic institutions because of their political involvement. For example, Croatian organizations used to stress Croatia's independence from Serbian-dominated Yugoslavia while Serbian organizations are partly pro-communist and partly anti-communist. Obviously many Yugoslav immigrants do not want to get involved in such political issues concerning their country of origin. So they fall back upon the church.

Ethnic schools have often been under the guidance of the church. Much has been written about this particular aspect of ethnic life in Australia. Price (1975) pointed to the fact that antipathy on the part of Australians against education in other languages than English and the high costs of running ethnic schools led to arrangements that classes are offered after school or on weekends. This means extra time for the children, and while part of them bear this burden with patience others are opposed to it. While only a minority of children is involved in such additional education it certainly has some influence on group cohesion, and it should be kept in mind that in many cases it is in the responsibility of the respective church. In the Polish community of Melbourne the ethnic schools are run by the Polish Association, that claims 50% of Melbourne's Poles to be active members.

With regard to urban structure the point must be stressed that the rather great number of ethnic parishes and churches reflects the *wide distribution* of the respective immigrant groups over large sections of the metropolitan areas.

Another kind of voluntary organization is provided by the *brotherhoods* of the Greek ethnic community. They are based on the principle of regional origin, and may represent areas as small as a nomos or prefecture. Around 1970 84 regional brotherhoods were in existence in New South Wales. About 60 brotherhoods had been established in Sydney between 1950 and 1970. Some of the older brotherhoods that existed prior to 1950 suffered from decreasing membership, due to the fact that new Greek arrivals came from different places in Greece (Bottomley 1979). These brotherhoods must be seen in relation to the phenomenon of chain migration mentioned above.

True *welfare organizations* do not seem to be well developed among ethnic groups in Australia. Some of the institutions discussed so far fulfill welfare functions for their respective community to a limited extent. There are very few, if any, organizations whose only goal is welfare. Some Italians already involved in welfare functions in 1967 established Co-As-It as a welfare agency for Italians living in Australia and in need of assistance. The organization is supported by the Italian Govenment, which provides annual grants earmarked for welfare and for education.

The Australian-Jewish Welfare and Relief Society (AJWRS) played a great part in the resettlement of the early post-war Jewish arrivals, including their needs for accommodation. The Netherlands Migration Service, as mentioned in chapter 4.2.3, was partly funded by the Netherlands Government. It was successful in raising loan funds with banks and insurance companies and was of great assistance to Dutch immigrants in their search for accommodation.

There appears to be no Australian counterpart to the Chinese benevolent associations in the cities of the United States. According to Teo (1971) the Chinese community is, due to differences in dialect, origin, economic status and degree of assimilation, broken up into a number of sub-communities, each of them existing as a separate social entity and relying on the mutual support of their members. '... the role of Chinatown remains important only as a service centre' (Teo 1971, 592).

In Wolforth's evaluation 'the "ethnic" press, "ethnic" clubs and even "ethnic" church affiliations were not as strongly developed as in America' (Wolforth 1974, 217). The Chinatowns in Sydney and Melbourne bear evidence for this statement, although they were the original concentrations of Chinese that had moved to these cities (except for a simultaneous Chinese residential quarter near the docks in Sydney). 'The sects and societies and cafes and counting houses of Little Bourke Street are now no longer the whole but only the hub of the community' (Comm. of Inquiry into Poverty 1975, 121).

This brief overview of ethnic institutions should be supplemented by mentioning the numerous businesses run by immigrants. Local concentrations of ethnic groups in many metropolitan areas are large enough to surpass the lower threshold for small businesses. In the Italian clusters they usually comprise greengrocers, butchers, hairdressers, shoemakers, tailors, ice cream parlours and pizzerias. But there may also be travel and real estate agents run by a compatriot, and a picture theatre showing Italian movies in the original language at least twice a week. As to the patronage of such businesses, Burnley (1982) found that larger proportions of females of the respective ethnic group shopped locally, in the same street or same suburb, than Australian women of the same neighbourhood. In Leichhardt, 79% of Italian women shopped locally, about 66% in stores run by an Italian compatriot; in Redfern 60% and in Marrickville 56% of Greek women shopped locally, 40% and 48% respectively patronizing Greek stores.

4.2.7 Peculiarities of ethnic urban distribution patterns

The discussion in the previous chapters of the major factors contributing to the spatial distribution of overseas immigrants in Australian cities have given clues to the assumption that ethnic distribution patterns are quite different from the often large and ghetto-like concentrations of minority groups in the U.S. cities.

There is no municipality or Local Government Area in any Australian city where non-British ethnic concentrations would reach proportions equal to those of immigrants from the *United Kingdom and the Irish Republic*. Relatively large concentrations of immigrants from the British Isles originated from the systematic recruitment by Australian Government officials for new industrial schemes such as Elizabeth with 12,831 British or Irish (38.1%) out of a total of 33,721 migrants or Kwinana New Town with 5,690 British or Irish (41.6%) out of a total of 13,687 migrants in 1976. There are some suburbs on the metropolitan fringes of Adelaide and Perth with similarly high proportions of British and Irish immigrants, such as Munno Park (32.8%), Noarlunga (26.4%) or Tea Tree Gully (24.6%) in the Adelaide Statistical Division or Rockingham (39.8%), Armadale (28.2%) and Gosnells (27.3%) in the Perth S.D. The highest proportions reached in the two largest cities are 14.1% in Campbelltown in the Sydney S.D. and 12.5% in Dandenong in the Melbourne S.D.

The distribution patterns of immigrant groups may be viewed from two aspects, one centred on a particular immigrant group and the other on an administrative or statistical area with its ethnic concentration or ethnic mix. From the *point of view of the group* the Italians may serve as an example. In 1976, 56,703 Italians were living in the Sydney metropolitan area. They were distributed over *42 out of 45 LGAs*. In 21 or half of these LGAs over 1,000 Italians each were living, in most cases mixed with residents of different ethnic origin. In 16 LGAs they ranked first among immigrant groups while ranging between 10.5% and 1.1% of the respective LGA population. In other LGAs having some Italian population a different ethnic group was dominant; for example, New Zealanders ranked first in eleven LGAs, Greeks in six LGAs, Germans in four LGAs, Dutch in three LGAs, Yugoslavs in two LGAs, Maltese in two LGAs and Lebanese in one LGA.

The second point of view is the *area*. The highest proportion of overseas immigrants was found in the Marrickville LGA in the Sydney metropolitan area with 42.8%, followed by Brunswick in the Melbourne metropolitan area with 41.4%. There are, however, very few LGAs having in excess of 30% overseas immigrants. As a rule any Local Government Area will have two-thirds of Australian-born people. On the other hand, the 42.8% overseas-born residents of the Marrickville LGA are comprised of *30 ethnic groups* having at least 100 persons each, and some more groups with fewer than 100 persons!

The Greeks rank first in Marrickville with 12.3%. The remaining 30.5% of migrants are extremely mixed as to their countries of origin. In the Randwick LGA in the Sydney metropolitan area there are no fewer than 44 ethnic groups with over 100 persons each, and a few more with lesser numbers are represented!

All these figures suggest a *high degree of spatial dispersion* of immigrant groups, coupled with a great mixture of 'ethnics' in most parts of the metropolitan area.

The same holds true for workforce concentrations. As in the United States, ethnic minorities are not only clustered in residential areas but also at their work places in industrial areas. In contrast to the United States, where the whole workforce of a particular plant with the exception of the management has often been recruited from one particular nationality, the workforces of Australian industrial plants will be composed of different ethnic groups. Table 59 gives the composition of the blue-collar workforce of the Ford Motor Company's assembly plant at Broadmeadows in the Melbourne metropolitan area for 1972 and 1979.

Table 59. Blue-collar workers of Ford Broadmeadows Assembly Plant by birthplace (%)

Country of birth	Numbers of blue-collar workers	
	May 1972	May 1979
Australia	8.84	14.73
Greece	20.29	12.67
Italy	20.06	14.60
Turkey	14.37	14.39
Yugoslavia	13.14	12.12
Other overseas	23.30	31.49

Source: Birrell & Birrell 1981, 76 and 110 (modified)

There is a *high degree of congruence* of above-average proportions of non-British immigrants and low socio-economic status areas, particularly in Sydney and Melbourne, due to the fact that many post-war non-British arrivals were unskilled or have not always been employed according to their skills (Jupp in: Halligan & Paris 1984, Otok 1976). In Perth Houghton (1975) found a close relationship between ethnicity and average socio-economic status, rather than low socio-economic status. The distribution of all overseas-born immigrants in the various zones of the metropolitan areas at the 1976 census are shown in table 60.

Table 60. Proportions of overseas born in the various zones of metropolitan areas, 1976 (%)

Zone	Sydney	Melbourne	Brisbane	Adelaide	Perth
Inner area	33.6	35.1	24.9	26.1	34.2
Middle area	25.4	26.6	14.9	24.6	28.3
Outer area	20.4	25.2	16.4	30.9	36.5

Source: ABS, quoted in Maher 1982, 39

The 13 LGAs of the Sydney metropolitan area each with over 20% non-British immigrants form kind of a belt through the central part of the metropolitan area, from Waverley on the Pacific coast through the LGAs of Sydney/South Sydney, Botany, Leichhardt, Marrickville, Drummoyne, Ashfield, Concord, Burwood, Canterbury, Strathfield and Auburn to Fairfield on the west. Most of this belt is identical with a large area of low socio-economic status, separating the mainly high-status suburbs of the Northshore from some of the middle and high-status suburbs of the south. There are, however, some low-status areas in the southwest corridor that have very low numbers of non-British immigrants (fig. 48, fig. 116).

Out of the 56 Melbourne LGAs, 23 have over 20% of non-British immigrants. They comprise the City of Melbourne, the ring of the inner suburbs and the middle-distance suburbs to the west and north from Altona and Sunshine to Keilor, Broadmeadows and to Whittlesea. They then extend in a wedge-like pattern to the southeast, comprising the suburbs of St. Kilda, Caulfield, Oakleigh and Springvale. As mentioned in chapter 3.1.2 the western suburbs and some of the southeastern suburbs attracted most of Melbourne's secondary industries. Again, much of the area of the 23 LGAs is also in the category of low-status areas.

In Adelaide the six LGAs with over 20% non-British immigrants combine to form a belt from Gulf St. Vincent

Table 61. LGAs in Sydney, Melbourne and Adelaide with over 20% non-British immigrants, 1976

Municipality	Population	Largest ethnic groups in 1976 (Non-UK/NZ)
Melbourne		
Altona	30,272	Yugoslav 7.1, Maltese 5.9, Italian 5.8
Broadmeadows	108,744	Italian 7.4, Maltese 2.8, Yugoslav 2.0
Brunswick	46,192	Italian 15.0, Greek 9.5, Turkish 2.1
Caulfield	73,630	Polish 4.6, Greek 2.6, German 1.4
Coburg	58,379	Italian 13.6, Greek 4.2, Yugoslav 1.3
Collingwood	16,645	Greek 15.8, Yugoslav 5.1, Italian 3.5
Essendon	51,133	Italian 9.4, Greek 2.9, Yugoslav 1.3
Fitzroy	20,451	Italian 8.6, Greek 7.5, Yugoslav 6.0
Footscray	51,774	Yugoslav 11.4, Greek 5.6, Italian 5.5
Keilor	70,597	Italian 7.1, Maltese 5.2, Yugoslav 4.4
Melbourne City	64,970	Italian 5.1, Turkish 2.4, Yugoslav 2.1
Northcote	54,881	Greek 11.5, Italian 6.7, Yugoslav 2.2
Oakleigh	54,532	Greek 7.9, Italian 6.7, Yugoslav 2.2
Port Melbourne	9,356	Greek 15.2, Turkish 2.6, Italian 2.2
Prahran	48,462	Greek 7.6, Polish 1.4, German 1.2
Preston	88,384	Italian 10.2, Greek 4.2, Yugoslav 2.7
Richmond	26,179	Greek 14.6, Yugoslav 5.6, Italian 3.2
South Melbourne	21,334	Greek 9.4, Italian 1.6, Yugoslav 1.1
Springvale	72,474	Yugoslav 3.9, Italian 3.6, Greek 1.9
St. Kilda	52,154	Polish 3.7, Greek 2.4, Indian 1.4
Sunshine	76,427	Maltese 7.5, Yugoslav 5.2, Greek 2.2
Williamstown	26,348	Yugoslav 5.6, Italian 2.7, Greek 2.0
Whittlesea	30,327	Italian 10.4, Greek 7.2, Yugoslav 4.5
Sydney		
Ashfield	42,322	Italian 9.0, Greek 2.6, Yugoslav 1.9
Auburn	47,566	Yugoslav 3.9, Turkish 3.6, Lebanese 3.0
Botany	35,739	Greek 6.4, Egyptian 4.8, Yugoslav 3.3
Burwood	29,045	Italian 6.5, Lebanese 2.6, Greek 2.4
Canterbury	128,710	Greek 4.8, Lebanese 4.4, Italian 3.5
Concord	24,598	Italian 6.3, Greek 2.0, Yugoslav 1.5
Drummoyne	31,516	Italian 10.5, Greek 2.4, Egyptian 0.6
Fairfield	114,603	Italian 5.7, Yugoslav 5.0, Maltese 1.9
Leichhardt	62,550	Italian 6.3, Greek 2.4, Yugoslav 1.7
Marrickville	87,821	Greek 12.3, Yugoslav 5.7, Italian 3.4
Sydney City & South Sydney	95,615	Greek 3.3, Yugoslav 2.4, Portuguese 1.3
Strathfield	26,301	Italian 2.8, Yugoslav 1.6, Chinese 1.4
Waverley	61,693	Hungarian 2.5, Polish 1.5, Italian 1.4
Adelaide		
Campbelltown	41,252	Italian 11.0, German 1.9, Dutch 1.3
Hindmarsh	8,691	Greek 8.2, Italian 7.4, Yugoslav 4.5
Payneham	17,545	Italian 14.6, German 1.0, Greek 0.9
St. Peters	9,304	Italian 12.0, Greek 2.5
Thebarton	10,315	Greek 14.0, Italian 9.5, Yugoslav 2.2
Woodville	75,276	Italian 6.6, Yugoslav 2.1, Greek 2.1

Note: All figures are for *birthplace*. The size of the 'community' will be at least 50% higher, e.g. an Italian-born population of 20% indicates an 'Italian community' of at least 30%.

Source: Ethnic Distribution 1976, Canberra 1981, quoted in Halligan & Paris 1984, 119

to the Mt. Lofty Range, comprising the LGAs of Woodville, Hindmarsh and Thebarton on the west of the City of Adelaide and the LGAs of St. Peters, Payneham and Campbelltown to the east with a gap in between. While the western LGAs belong to the low-status corridor that stretches from the City to Port Adelaide in the northwest, of the LGAs on the east side only a part of Payneham could be labelled low status. In this part of the northeast corridor, particularly along the Torrens River, Italians had settled as market gardeners, while other minorities are represented in much smaller numbers. The LGAs in Sydney, Melbourne and Adelaide with over 20% non-British immigrants each are listed in table 61.

Various authors, in particular I.H. Burnley (1972, 1974, 1975) have attempted to produce a typology of ethnic settlements in the large Australian cities. With special reference to the metropolitan areas of Sydney and Melbourne, *Burnley* distinguished between five ecological areas as given below:

1. The central city and large sections of the older suburbs, the residential areas of which are characterized by a steeply declining Australian-born population, this population loss being partly substituted by immigrants.
2. The areas adjacent to this inner core where rather high in-migration rates of overseas born are exceeding the decrease of the Australian-born population, thus making for moderate increases of total population numbers.
3. Residential areas, in the main adjacent to the two previously mentioned areas, and developed prior to World War II, with population increases due to both internal migration and overseas immigration.
4. Newly developed industrial suburbs in peripheral locations, with a high influx of immigrants.
5. Large new suburbs in peripheral locations, with immigration contributing very little to the rapid population growth.

Galvin in her study of non-British immigrants in Newcastle (1974) came to similar results, while putting major emphasis on different degrees of dissimilation of the various immigrant groups. She distinguished between four areas:

1. Inner city suburbs with Southern European dominance where most of the Italian, Greek, Maltese and Yugoslav communities are found, many of them in areas of residential decay. Italians and Yugoslavs and, to a lesser extent, Germans customarily settle adjacent to industrial areas, while Greeks prefer locations closer to the commercial zone.
2. An intermediate zone adjacent to the previous zone but mainly of higher socio-economic status. Here immigrants of British, Irish and Jewish origin and smaller numbers of Southern European immigrants are living in larger and more substantial homes.
3. Outer suburbia and the outer industrial suburbs with considerable proportions of British and Irish, as well as German and Polish immigrants and some Southern European immigrants.
4. The rural-urban fringe with considerable proportions of Dutch immigrants, some German and British immigrants and market gardeners, mainly of Southern European origin.

A more recent attempt by *Burnley* (in: Burnley et al. 1980) was more directed toward a distinction between the *various settlement forms* which in turn may be identified with particular sections of the metropolitan areas. Burnley distinguished between five forms of ethnic settlements as follows.

1. First settlement concentrations mainly by Southern Europeans and Middle Eastern immigrant groups. They are characterized by low socio-economic status, many ethnic institutions and clubs, extended-family residence patterns, some residential overcrowding, rental accommodation rather than home ownership, shared accommodation, particularly by single persons, and high proportions of females in the labour force.
2. Second settlement concentrations. Although there is still a high proportion of manual labourers, the overall socio-economic status is somewhat higher and the other characteristics are less pronounced than in the first settlement concentrations.
3. Dispersed settlement. Socio-economic status, the degree of home ownership and the length of residence are higher than in the 'segregated' second settlement concentrations, but social isolation may cause serious problems.
4. Dispersed settlement with some socio-economic groupings, mainly by some former refugee groups. A greater tendency to casual clusters by common social status. Mainly older families with no children in their households, or families that have been reduced in size through political circumstances in their countries of origin, so that kinship has played a minor part.
5. Transition zone settlements in inner city rooming-house areas. These are not necessarily identical with larger ethnic clusters, although they may be found in locations like the proximity to the wharves and docks, where many single males are employed.

There is thus a multitude of locations and types of settlement of ethnic groups in urban Australia. From the point of view of area or space *no true ghettos with slum-like conditions* have developed as they have in many large American cities. From the point of view of time, there has been an *appreciable dynamism and degree of mobility* within the ethnic communities.

According to the present author's experience there seem to be *two types of clustering* of overseas immigrants and of businesses run by them in the inner areas of Australian cities. The first type is of the kind described by Burnley (1981) for Leichhardt (Sydney). There were a few early Italian shops such as delicatessen, fruiterers, pastry shops

Fig. 117. Italian concentration in Leichhardt, Sydney

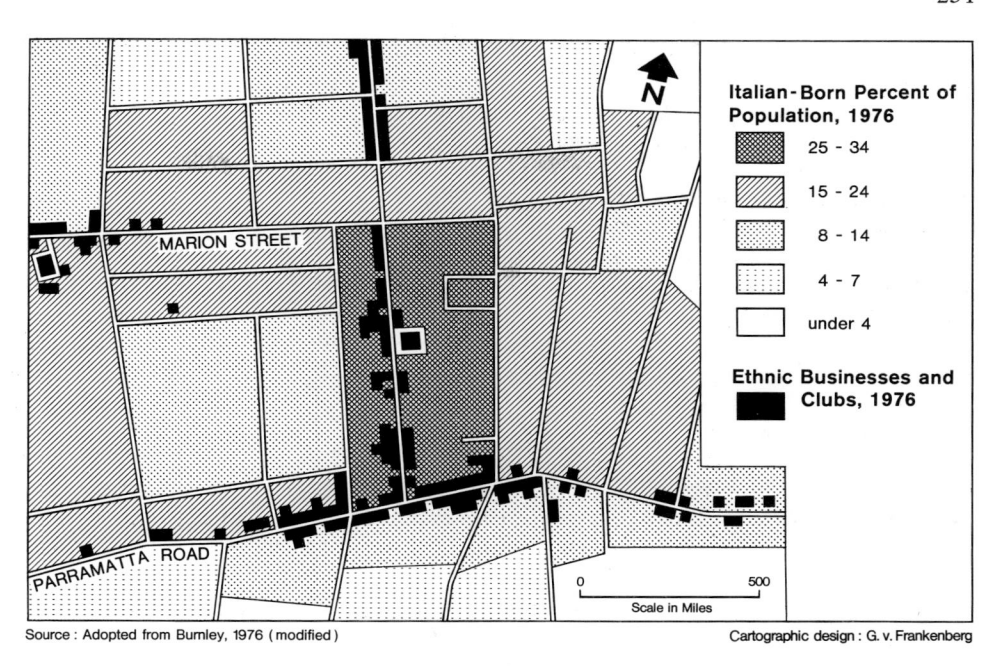

and seafood shops. By 1960 there were also found imported wine shops, fashion shops, radio shops and travel agencies. During the late 1960s and the 1970s butchers, pharmacies, bridal shops, gift shops and real estate agents were added until, by 1976, some 175 Italian businesses could be found along a two-kilometre stretch of Parramatta Road and in Norton Street. In addition some Australian stores had started to cater for an Italian clientele and to import Italian goods, while Australian banks established agencies specifically for doing business with Italian enterprises.

It is important to note, however, that the immediate environs of the intersection of Parramatta Road and Norton Street is *not by any means dominated* by Italian immigrants. Even in the two blocks on either side of Norton Street the maximum concentration is between 25% and 34% Italian born, while three blocks away from the intersection the Italian proportion of all residents drops to between 15% and 24%; beyond three blocks it is still lower (fig. 117).

Similar local clusters were described for Carlton (Melbourne) where along Lygan Street and in some neighbouring streets about 150 businesses or 38% of all commercial establishments of the area are owned by Italians, and for the shopping centre in Richmond (Melbourne), where some 75 businesses are run by Greek immigrants.

A different type of migrant presence is the existence of shopping streets with a number of *businesses run by immigrants of different origins.* Such concentrations are found in Hindley Street in the City of Adelaide and in William Street in Central Perth. Each of these occupies a very specific location that may be described as an extension of the shopping core of the CBD into an area of mixed commercial, light manufacturing and residential uses. Hindley Street is located on the northwestern margin of Adelaide's CBD between King William Street and Western Terrace and in rather close proximity to the inner suburb of Thebarton, which has 14% Greek and 9.5% Italian residents. The shopping street has a length of 1.1 km. William Street is located to the north of Perth's CBD, beyond the Central Station, but connected with the CBD by a viaduct over the railway tracks. The section of the street occupied by shops stretches for 0.9 km. Two blocks west of William Street is a residential area with some Greek population, Russell Square being the site of a Greek Orthodox church and a Hellenic Community Centre. There is also a small Italian cluster between William Street and Russell Square.

At both shopping clusters Italian managers and owners are predominant, but a number of businesses are also run by members of other ethnic groups. Out of a total of 43 businesses run by immigrants in Hindley Street 28 are Italian owned. There are seven Greek owners or managers while the remaining eight businesses are run by members of different ethnic origin (fig. 118). Out of a total of 66 businesses run by immigrants in William Street, 52 are operated by Italians. Japan, Poland and Spain are each represented by two enterprises, while Bulgaria, France, Greece, India, Lebanon, Austria, Czechoslovakia and Vietnam each have one. 21 of the businesses or almost one third are restaurants and cafes; there are six tailors (all Italians), four shops selling books, newspapers and records, four hairdressers (all Italians), four brokers, three butchers, three groceries, three travel agents and many others (fig. 119).

Brief mention should be made of Canberra and Darwin. Due to the high proportion of government employment and government housing, the distribution of ethnic migrants over the urbanized areas of the two cities continues to

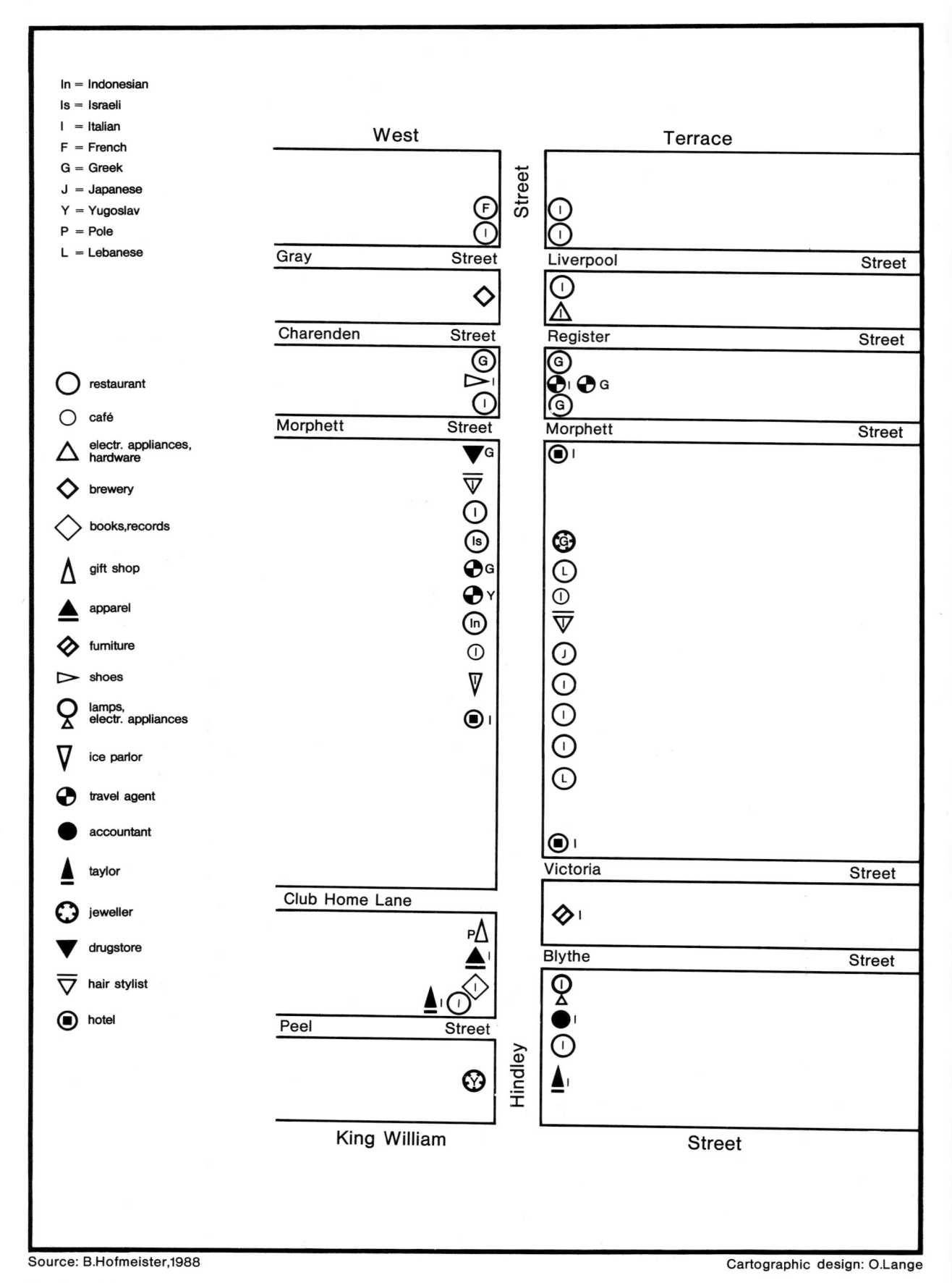

Fig. 118. Shops and services run by overseas immigrants in Hindley Street, Adelaide

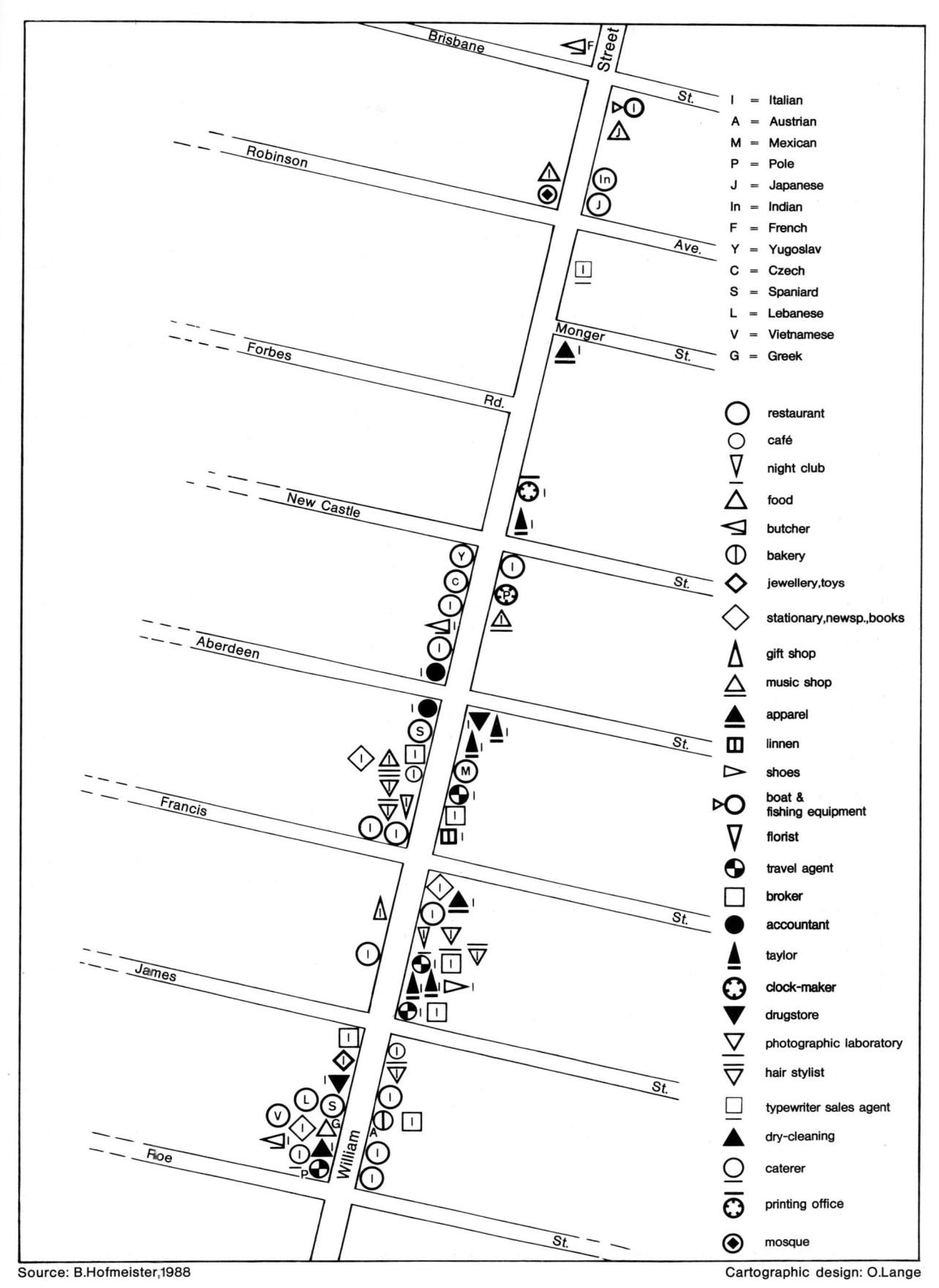

Fig. 119. Shops and services run by overseas immigrants in William Street, Perth

Source: B. Hofmeister, 1988

Cartographic design: O. Lange

I	= Italian
A	= Austrian
M	= Mexican
P	= Pole
J	= Japanese
In	= Indian
F	= French
Y	= Yugoslav
C	= Czech
S	= Spaniard
L	= Lebanese
V	= Vietnamese
G	= Greek

- restaurant
- café
- night club
- food
- butcher
- bakery
- jewellery, toys
- stationary, newsp., books
- gift shop
- music shop
- apparel
- linnen
- shoes
- boat & fishing equipment
- florist
- travel agent
- broker
- accountant
- taylor
- clock-maker
- drugstore
- photographic laboratory
- hair stylist
- typewriter sales agent
- dry-cleaning
- caterer
- printing office
- mosque

be more even than in the state capitals. In 56 out of 65 LGAs of the Canberra S.D., proportions of overseas migrants range from 13.2 to 28.6 with all but nine LGAs falling within the range 19.9–27.3. In 19 out of 22 LGAs of the Darwin S.D. proportions are between 18.3% and 28.4%, with two LGAs having lower percentages and one LGA having a higher percentage.

4.3 The structure of the Australian city

It has become a habit in modern urban research to show the culture traits specific to the urban places of a particular culture realm (as they have been elaborated for Australia in chapters 4.1 and 4.2) by means of an idealized schema or model. Such a schematic presentation of the Australian city will be presented in the present chapter.

Australian authors have made similar attempts on various occasions. In his book 'The City Centre' with special reference to Perth, *Alexander* presented a 'Conceptual model of the central area' (1974, 173–74). In this model the CBD core and the frame each characterized by a specific mixture of functions were shown. In the same year *Galvin* in her paper on overseas immigrants in Newcastle presented material related to immigrant patterns in various Australian cities by means of a schematic graph showing 'Ethnic patterns in Australian cities' (1974, 518).

Burnley in two of his recent publications made attempts toward integrated models of the metropolitan areas of Sydney and Melbourne, the earlier publication showing ethnic, status and life cycle stage patterns (1976, A155) and the more recent publication residential patterns as well as economic functions (1980, 169). The model presented in the earlier publication made a distinction between the following five zones: CBD, older inner suburbs, middle ring suburbs, outer suburbia and exurbia or rural-urban fringe. According to a grouping of LGAs by DURD in 1973 the major zones of the metropolitan areas can be delineated as follows:

Sydney:

Inner area	Leichhardt, Marrackville, Randwick, South Sydney, City of Sydney, Waverley, Woolahra.
Middle ring	Ashfield, Auburn, Bankstown, Botany, Burwood, Canterbury, Concord, Drummoyne, Hunters Hill, Hurstville, Kogarah, Lane Cove, Manly, Mosman, North Sydney, Parramatta, Rockdale, Ryde, Strathfield, Willoughby.
Outer zone	Remainder of Sydney S.D.

Melbourne:

Inner area	Collingwood, Fitzroy, City of Melbourne, Port Melbourne, Prahran, Richmond, St. Kilda, South Melbourne.
Middle ring	Box Hill, Brighton, Brunswick, Camberwell, Caulfield, Coburg, Essendon, Footscray, Hawthorn, Heidelberg, Kew, Malvern, Moorabbin, Mordialloc, Northcote, Oakleigh, Preston, Sandringham, Williamstown.
Outer zone	Remainder of Melbourne S.D.

Brisbane[3]:

Inner area	City, North City, South City.
Middle ring	Ascot, Ashgrove, Balmoral, Camp Hill, Chatsworth, East Brisbane, Ekibin, Enoggera, Fernberg, Graceville, Greenslopes, Hendra, Holland Park, Indooroopilly, Ithaca, Kalinga, Kedron, Meeandah, Morningside, Newmarket, Normanby, Nandah, St. Lucia, Tarragindi, Toowong, Windsor, Yeronga.
Outer zone	Remainder of Brisbane S.D.

Adelaide:

Inner area	City of Adelaide, Hindmarsh, Kensington/Norwood, Prospect, St. Peters, Thebarton, Unley, Walkerville.
Middle ring	Brighton, Burnside, Campbelltown, Enfield, Glenelg, Henley and Grange, Payneham, Port Adelaide, West Torrens, Woodville.
Outer zone	Remainder of Adelaide S.D.

Perth:

Inner area	Perth City.
Middle ring	Claremont, Cottesloe, Mosman Park, Nedlands, Peppermint Grove, Subiaco, Bassendean, Bayswater, Stirling, East Fremantle, Fremantle, Melville, Belmont, Canning, South Perth.
Outer zone	Remainder of Perth S.D.

---

3 Areas changed in 1974

Burnley's *second model* (1980, 169) has been more sophisticated than the former model. It is based on Burgess' concentric zone model with certain modifications as to a further distinction of some of the concentric zones. The model shows the following characteristics:

1. Burnley distinguishes between six rather than five zones by dividing Burgess' working men's zone (III) into an inner zone of working men's houses (III) and a zone of prosperous working men's houses (IV).
2. Burgess' residential zone (IV) is subdivided into the zone of better class residences that in Burnley's model becomes zone Va and into the upper middle-class zone Vb.
3. The commuter zone is further subdivided into higher-status, heterogeneous and low-status areas.
4. One modification related to an obviously wedge-like or sector development, and thus to Hoyt's sectorial model, is that the distortions caused by transport routes and contributing to the development of growth corridors are taken into account.
5. In accordance with Harris' and Ullman's multiple nuclei model, regional (shopping) centres are recognized as distinct nuclei in the outer zones, these centres having minor transition zones of their own.
6. Within the zone of transition and the inner zone of working men's houses, certain residential districts characterized by gentrification are identified as distinct small nuclei in Burnley's model.
7. Public housing estates built by the State housing authorities are identified in both the inner and outer suburbs.
8. Industrial districts often form distinct nuclei; some industrial areas are associated with seaports. Adelaide and Perth in particular were founded some distance inland, making the development of a separate harbour area inevitable.
9. Areas of ethnic concentrations are mentioned in the text, but are not shown in the idealized schema for Sydney and Melbourne (Burnley 1980, 169).

Some general findings from recent investigations into the urban structure of Australian cities have to be considered in relation to a model. Stimson (1982), basing his work on the Shevky and Bell concepts of American urbanism, found that family status tended to be represented by a concentric model and socio-economic status by a sectoral model. There is, however, no general pattern of ethnicity, which was found to be of significance only in Sydney and Melbourne, whereas it was found to be less important in Adelaide and Perth and not important at all in Brisbane and Hobart.

There are *no simple density gradients or social gradients* in Australian cities, due to a number of individual features peculiar to each city. These include varying terrain constraints, as well as human decision with regard to port locations, the location of satellite or system cities, decisions of the respective State housing authorities etc.

The overall structure of the large Australian city is, according to Logan (1968), O'Connor (1980) and Maher (1982) *multi-nodal, polynucleated or multi-nucleated*. The post-war period witnessed 'a city form characterized by continued areal specialisation and a low density spread away from the city centre' and 'a set of sub-regions consisting of linked employment areas and places of residence ...' (Logan 1968, 104). Such sub-regions were characterized by stronger internal relations than relations with other sub-regions, with both the housing and labour markets moving to a *greater degree of self-containment* over time (Maher 1982, 114–115; see ch. 4.1.7). This certainly did not occur to the degree it did in the United States, moreover such views are not disputed. For example, Houghton (1981, 107–112) presented data on the metropolitan area of Perth demonstrating a general dispersion of industrial and service functions rather than secondary concentration. The Perth data gave evidence for his statement that self-containment ratios decreased rather than increased, as had been claimed by Logan, O'Connor and Maher. However, Houghton claimed this decreasing self-containment ratio to be the norm in Australia, a statement that has not been verified. On the contrary, the Perth situation may well be an exception from the general trend toward increasing self-containment of secondary centres.

Moreover, the *time factor* has to be taken into consideration. A number of processes making for changes in the inner city such as CBD expansion and gentrification of a number of small neighbourhoods have already been mentioned. Another process to be considered is the relocation of secondary industries. For example, early manufacturing enterprises in Sydney were concentrated in the Redfern-Alexandria-Waterloo area south of the city centre. Eventually manufacturing spread further southward via Zetland and Mascot into the Botany Bay area, also westward to cheap land (and cheap labour) at Parramatta, Auburn and Bankstown.

What then are the elements of a model of the Australian city? A list of such elements is given below as a contribution to a model presented by the present writer (fig. 120).

The CBD is usually identical with the core of the original settlement and extends into some of the adjoining blocks. It is characterized by a rectangular grid pattern of streets, sometimes with additional alleys, usually adjoining a water body like a river or a bay. There are many post-war high-rise buildings, most of which are, however, lower than their North American counterparts. The CBD is often bordered by extensive public gardens and parks, containing some large public buildings. Apart from such open areas the CBD is surrounded by a:

Zone of transition, which is a very heterogeneous area of wholesaling, harbour and railway facilities and automotive-oriented activities such as parking or car sales. Separated from them by virtue of zoning laws are automobile service and repair activities. There are CBD extensions into the zone of transition at a very few particularly favour-

① CBD
② Frame (zone in transition)
③ Inner suburbs
④ Middle-distance and outer suburbs
⑤ Rural-urban fringe

A = Automotive-oriented activities
G = Gentrification
I = Industries
N = New town
P = Public housing
W = Wholesaling

- District centre
- District centre with small transition zone
- Free-standing shopping centre
- Clusters of non-British immigrants
- Immigrants in area of boarding houses
- Immigrants in hostels
- Secondary concentration of immigrants
- Market gardeners

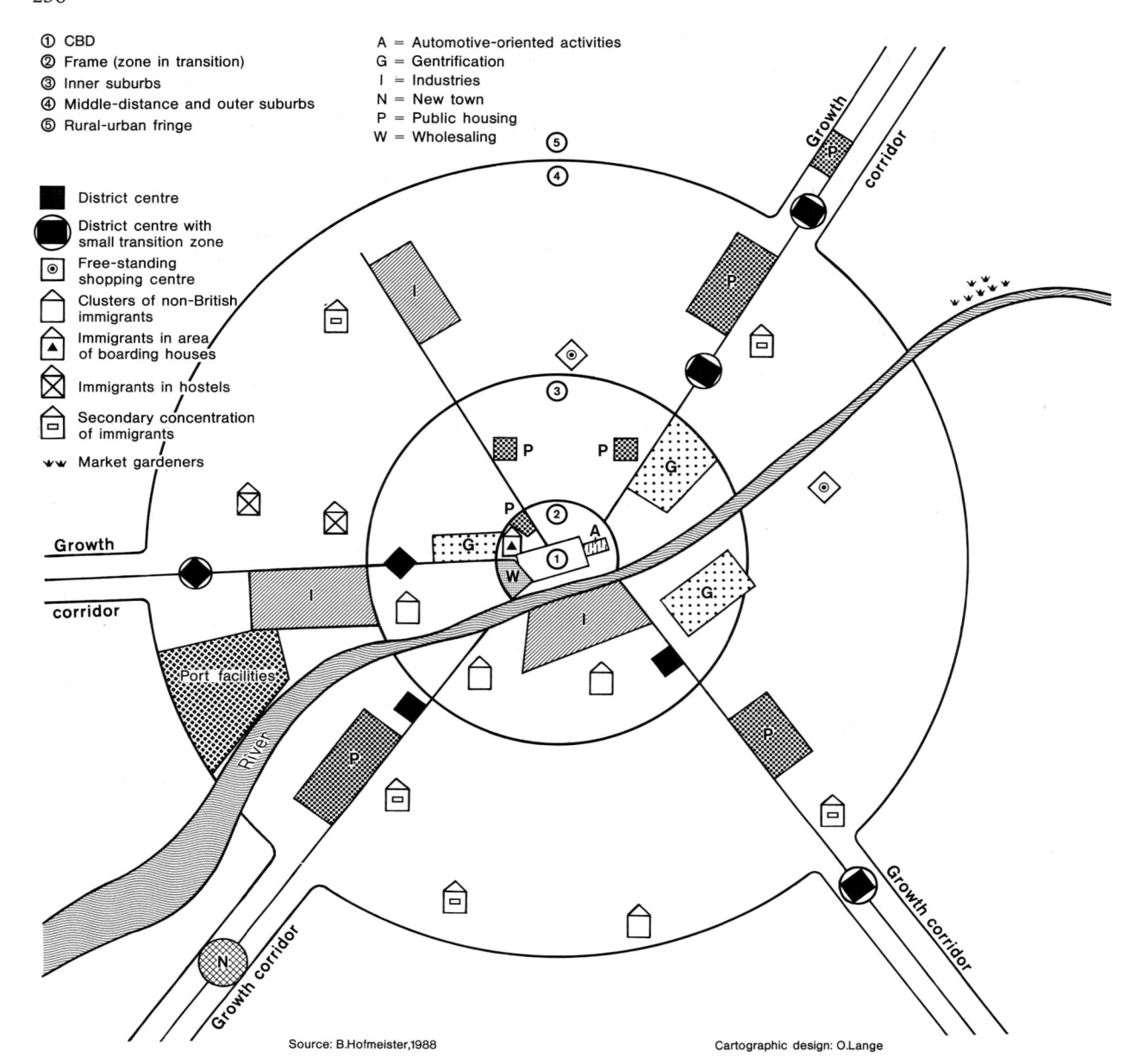

Source: B.Hofmeister, 1988   Cartographic design: O.Lange

Fig. 120. Model of the urban structure of the large Australian city

able locations. Other characteristics include transient facilities such as boarding houses and hotels, partly functioning as 'reception areas' for overseas immigrants; there is a high proportion of males and of single persons in the population. An old dwelling stock is partly replaced by nodes of high-density, multi-storey housing derived in part from the slum-clearing activities of the State housing authorities; an above-average proportion of residents live in flats, partly in rental accommodation. Interspersed light-industrial establishments are mainly in categories such as printing, food processing, engineering and wood working.

The inner or old established suburbs of the nineteenth century. Much of the housing stock, particularly in Sydney and, to a somewhat lesser extent, in Melbourne is in terraces, some of which has been refurbished by private initiative and private capital (gentrification). Residential areas are mainly low-status, with comparatively high percentages of residents belonging to various disability groups such as retired and divorced people and single-parent households, with interspersed small public housing estates and small clusters of immigrants (predominantly South European). This zone contains the older manufacturing areas in proximity to harbour and rail facilities, located partly on land formerly regarded as undesirable for residential purposes. Modern high-rise apartment buildings and multi-storey dwellings converted to strata title occupy particularly favourable locations as high-status wedges.

The middle-distance and outer suburbs of the twentieth century. Because of their prevailing low-density development in one-storey houses (bungalows) they take up a tremendous extent of the total built-up area; somewhat higher densities are provided only by older settlement nuclei along former tramlines. There are large public housing estates and small 'second concentrations' of South European immigrant groups; otherwise there are more British, New Zealand, Dutch and Vietnamese immigrants. There is a characteristically asymmetric development of high-status residential suburbs corresponding with advantages of terrain (water bodies, ranges), some of them with very low ethnicity. Couples both young and of mature age are characteristic, the former with children at school or pre-school. There are some retirement villages. The relocation of secondary industries or the establishment of large modern industrial estates with heavy industries is characteristic of less favourable suburbs; they are often surrounded by low-status residential areas. Growth corridors are mainly related to suburban rail lines and, to a much lesser extent, to the rather few urban expressways. These link officially designated district centres (regional centres) and satellite or system cities (new towns), functioning as focal points for retail trade and for medium and high-density residential developments with modest office development. These have small transition zones of their own; there are also some free-standing shopping centres.

Outer transition zone or rural-urban fringe. This zone contains remnants of the market gardening mainly carried out by South European immigrants. There may be modern deep-sea harbours and large industrial estates of heavy industries such as oil refining, steel works, nickel and aluminum refineries. New towns with above-average proportions of British immigrants are located in this zone. Some alternative lifestyle groups have also established themselves. This zone is subjected to incipient suburbanization, mainly along growth corridors.

References

Abbreviations:
AAAG	Annals of the Association of American Geographers
AEHR	Australian Economic History Review
AG	(The) Australian Geographer
AGS	Australian Geographical Studies
AIUS	Australian Institute of Urban Studies
AJES	American Journal of Economics and Sociology
AJPH	Australian Journal of Politics and History
AJS	Australian Journal of Science
AJSI	Australian Journal of Social Issues
ANZJS	Australian and New Zealand Journal of Sociology
AP	Applied Geography
AQ	The Australian Quarterly
BGS	Berliner Geographische Studien
CGJ	Canadian Geographical Journal
EDCC	Economic Development and Cultural Change
EG	Economic Geography
ER	The Economic Record
ERS	Ethnic and Racial Studies
FWSS	Frankfurter Wirtschafts- und Sozialgeographische Schriften
GA	Geografiska Annaler
GE	Geographical Education
GJ	Geographical Journal
GP	Geographia Polonica
GR	Geographical Review
HS	Historical Studies
IBGT	Institute of British Geographers Transactions
IJURR	International Journal of Urban and Regional Research
ILR	International Labour Review
IM	International Migration
IMR	International Migration Review
JAPE	Journal of Australian Political Economy
JCG	Journal of Cultural Geography
JG	Journal of Geography
JHG	Journal of Historical Geography
JHSSA	Journal of the Historical Society of South Australia
JPESA	Journal of the Proceedings of the Ecological Society of Australia
KFWS	Kölner Forschungen zur Wirtschafts- und Sozialgeographie
LE	Land Economics
MUDGPG	Monash University Dept. of Geography Publications in Geography
NARB	North Australia Research Bulletin
NZG	New Zealand Geographer
PG	Praxis Geographie
PHG	Progress in Human Geography
PHR	Pacific Historical Review
PRGSA	Proceedings of the Royal Geographical Society of Australasia
PV	Pacific Viewpoint
QGJ	Queensland Geographical Journal
RAPIJ	Royal Australian Planning Institute Journal
RS	Regional Studies
RSPSDHGP	Research School of Pacific Studies Dept. of Geography Publication
SA	Social Alternatives
SAGP	South Australian Geographical Papers
SF	Social Forces
SN	Social Networks
SSM	Social Science and Medicine
SSR	Sociology and Social Research
TESG	Tijdschrift voor Economische en Sociale Geografie
THRAPP	Tasmanian Historical Research Association Papers and Proceedings
UG	Urban Geography
URU	Urban Research Unit (Australian National University)
US	Urban Studies
USHE	University Studies in History and Economics
VHM	The Victorian Historical Magazine
WG	Western Geographer
WS	Wirtschaftsgeographische Studien
ZA	Zeitschrift für Agrargeographie
ZW	Zeitschrift für Wirtschaftsgeographie

ACHTERSTRAAT, J. (1959): De steden in Australia. – TESG, 65–70.
– (1960): De steden in Australia. – TESG, 94–106.
Adelaide – Its selection and planning. Findings of the Geographical Society. – PRGSA, South Austr. Branch, 1937, 77–81.
ADRIAN, C. (ed.) (1984): Urban service provision in Australia. – London.
ADRIAN, C. & C. EVANS (1984): Borg-Warner (Albury-Wodonga): The role of a lead firm in a regional economy. – In: TAYLOR, M. (ed.): The geography of Australian corporate power. – Sydney, 159–171.
ALEXANDER, I.C. (1974): The city centre: Patterns and problems. – Nedlands.
– (1979a): The suburbanization of retail sales. – AGS, 76–83.
– (1979b): Job location and the journey to work: three Australian cities, 1961–1971. – AGS, 155–174.
– (1979c): Office location and public policy. – London etc.
– (1979d): The central area. – In: GENTILLI, J. (ed.): Western landscapes. – Nedlands, 400–422.
– (1980a): Office dispersal in metropolitan areas. 1. A review and framework for analysis. – Geoforum, 225–247.
– (1980b): Office dispersal in metropolitan areas. 2. Case study results and conclusions. – Geoforum, 249–275.
ALEXANDER, I.C. & J.A. DAWSON (1979a): Suburbanization of retailing and employment in Australian cities. – AGS, 76–83.
– – (1979b): Employment in retailing: A case study of employment in suburban shopping centres. – Geoforum, 407–425.

ALEXANDER, J.X. & R. HATTERSLEY (1980): Australian mining, minerals and oil. – Sydney.
ALLEN, A. (1969): Frontier towns in western Queensland: Their growth and present tributary areas. – AG, 119–137.
ALSOP, D. (1982): The built environment. – In: HANLEY, W. & M. COOPER (eds.): Man and the Australian environment. – Sydney, 309–314.
ANDREWS, J. (1938): Goyder's Line: A vanished frontier. – AG, 32–36.
ANDREWS, R.L. (1979): Australia. A social and economic geography. – Sydney and Melbourne.
APLIN, G. (1979): Future urban regions and settlement hierarchies. – Proceed. Tenth N.Z. Geogr. Conference, 111–114
– (1982): Models of urban change: Sydney 1820–1870. – AGS, 144–158.
APPLEYARD, R.T. (1955): Displaced persons in Western Australia. – USHE vol. II, no. 3, 62–102.
– (1964): British emigration to Australia. – Canberra.
APPS, P. (1976): Home ownership – The Australian dream. – AQ no. 4, 54–75.
ARCHER, J. (1982): Equality and politics. – In: HANLEY, W. & M. COOPER (eds.): Man and the Australian environment. – Sydney, 302–306.
ARCHER, R.W. (1973): Site value taxation in central business district redevelopment. – Urban Land Institute, Washington, D.C.
– (1976): Planning and managing metropolitan development and land supply. – Commission for Econ. Devel. of Australia. Melbourne.
– (1977): Public land and leasehold system in Canberra, Australia: The use of leasehold land tenure base for financing the capital's development, 1958–71. AJES.
– (1979): Metropolitan planning for housing renewal and urban consolidation in Australian cities. – Proceed. Tenth N.Z. Geogr. Conference, 176–180.
ARNOT, R.H. (1973a): Population and resources: A national spatial ordering concept plan. – Town and Country Planning Board. Melbourne.
– (1973b): Regionalism and possibilities for dispersal of urban settlement in Australia. – RAPIJ, 77–85.
ASCHMANN, H.H. (1979): Amenities in the new mining towns of Northern Australia. – North Australia Research Bull. no. 5. Darwin, 1–41.
ATA, A. (1979): The Lebanese in Melbourne: Ethnicity, inter-ethnic activities and attitudes to Australia. – AQ, 37–54.
AUNGLES, S. & I. SZELENYI (1979): Structural conflicts between the state, local government and monopoly capital – The case of Whyalla in South Australia. – ANZJS, 24–35.
Australian Cities Commission & J.R. DAVIS (1975): Melbourne at the Census 1971. – Canberra.
Australian Cities Commission & G.T. McDonald (1976): Brisbane at the Census 1971. – Canberra.
Australian Coal Year Book 1984–85. – Fortitude Valley 1985.
Australian Council on Population and Ethnic Affairs (ed.) (1982): Population Report 6. Recent trends in immigration. – Canberra.
– (ed.) (1983): Population Report 7. Population change 1976–81. – Canberra.
The Australian Encyclopedia in ten volumes. – Sydney 1958
Australian Government Commission of Inquiry into Poverty (ed.) (1975): Welfare of migrants. – Canberra.
Australian Institute of Urban Studies (ed.) (1968): Bibliography of urban studies in Australia. Vol. 1 1966–68. – Canberra.
– (ed.) (1972): First report of the task force on new cities for Australia. – Canberra.
– (ed.) (1973): Managing the cities: An evaluation. – Canberra.
– (ed.) (1975): People in the cities. – Canberra.
– (ed.) (1980): Urban strategies for Australia: Managing the 80s. – Canberra.
Australian National Commission for UNESCO (ed.) (1976): Man and the environment: New towns in isolated settings. Australian UNESCO seminar, Kambalda (Western Australia), 18–23 August 1973. – Canberra.

Australian Population and Immigration Council (ed). (1976): A decade of migrant settlement. Report on the 1973 immigration survey. – Canberra.
– (ed.) (1977): Immigration policies and Australia's population. A green paper. – Canberra.
Australian Urban environmental indicators. – Canberra 1983.

BADCOCK, B.A. (1973): The residential structure of metropolitan Sydney. – AGS, 1–27.
– (1976): The spatial structure of metropolitan Sydney. – Ph. D. Thesis, Macquarie University. Sydney.
BADCOCK, B.A. & D.U. CLOHER (1981): Neighbourhood change in inner Adelaide, 1966–76 – US, 41–55.
BARDSLEY, K.L. & A.S. FRASER, R.L. HEATHCOTE (1983): The second Ash Wednesday: 16 February 1983. – AGS, 129–141.
BARLOW, M.H. (1975): Urban networks. Readings from the Australian Geographer. – Roseville East.
BARLOW, M.H. & R.G. NEWTON (1981): Patterns and processes in regional geography. Australia and New Zealand. – Sydney.
BARRETT, A.H.B. (1971): The inner suburbs: The evolution of an industrial area (Carlton Vic.). – Melbourne.
BATE, W. (1970): The urban sprinkle: Country towns and Australian regional history. – AEHR, 204–218.
– (1978): Lucky city. The first generation at Ballarat, 1851–1901. – Melbourne.
BEED, C.S. (1981): Melbourne's development and planning. – Melbourne.
BEED, T.W. (1965): The growth in suburban retailing in Sydney: A preliminary study of some factors affecting the form and function of suburban shopping centres. – Ph. D. Thesis, University of Sydney. Sydney.
BERRY, B.J.L. (1961): City size distributions and economic development. – EDCC, 573–587.
– (1975): Urban studies down under. – GR, 117–118.
BERRY, M. & L. SANDERCOCK (eds.) (1983): Urban political economy: An Australian perspective. – Sydney.
BETHUNE, G. (1978): Urban homeownership in Australia. – Ph. D. Thesis, Australian National University. – Canberra.
– (1984): The new Commonwealth-State Housing Agreement. – AIUS 17, Annual Conference 8–9 November 1984. Typescript. 12 pp.
BIGELOW, B. (1976): Changing spatial endogamy of Polish Americans. – Discuss. Pap Series Dept. of Geogr., Univ. of Syracuse no. 19. Syracuse.
BIRCH, A. & D.S. MACMILLAN (1962): The Sydney scene 1788–1960. – Melbourne.
BIRD, J. (1965): The foundation of Australian seaport capitals. – EG, 283–299.
– (1968): Seaport gateways of Australia. – Oxford.
– (1986): Gateways: Examples from Australia, with special reference to Canberra. – GJ, 56–64.
BIRRELL, J. (1964): Walter Burley Griffin. – St. Lucia.
BIRRELL, R. & T. BIRRELL (1981): An issue of people. Population and Australian society. – Australian Studies. Melbourne.
BIRRELL, R. & C. HAY (eds.) (1978): The immigration issue in Australia. – Dept. of Sociology, La Trobe University. – Melbourne.
BLACK, J. (1977): Public inconvenience: Access and travel in seven Sydney suburbs. – URU, Canberra.
BLACKSHAW, P.W. (1974): The Sydney Area Transportation Study – an economic review. – AQ 46, 1974, 56–68.
BLAINEY, G. (1966): The tyranny of distance. – Melbourne.
BOEREE, R. (1964): Land settlement on Eyre Peninsula. – Ph. D. Thesis, University of Adelaide. Adelaide.
BOLGER, P.F. (1968): The changing role of a city: Hobart. – THRAPP, 6–17.
– (1973): Hobart Town. – Canberra.
BORCHARDT, D.H. (1976): Australian bibliography. – Melbourne.

BORRIE, W.D. (1954): Italians and Germans in Australia. A study of assimilation. – Melbourne.
BORRIE, W.D. & J. ZUBRZYCKI (1958): Employment of post-war immigrants in Australia. – ILR, 239–253.
BOTTOMLEY, G. (1979): After the odyssey. A study of Greek Australians. – St. Lucia.
BOURNE, L.S. (1974): Urban systems in Australia and Canada: Comparative notes and research questions. – AGS, 152–172.
– (1975): Regulating urban systems. A comparative review of national urbanization strategies: Australia, Canada, Great Britain, Sweden. – New York.
BOURNE, L.S. & R. SINCLAIR, K. DZIEWONSKI (eds.) (1984): Urbanization and settlement systems: International perspectives. – New York.
BOWD, D.J. (1979): Macquarie country. A history of the Hawkesbury. – North Sydney.
BOWMAKER, A.E. (1968): A breef history of Leeton. – Leeton.
BOWMAN, M. (1976): Local government in the Australian states. An urban paper. – Dept. of Environment and Commun. Devel., Canberra.
– (ed.) (1981): Beyond the city. Case studies in community structure and development. – Australian Studies. Melbourne.
BOYD, R. (1961): Australia's home: Its origins, builders and occupiers. – Melbourne.
– (1978): Australia's home. Why Australians built the way they did. – Melbourne, 2nd ed.
BRADFIELD, R. (1972): Castlemaine. A golden harvest. – Kilmore.
BRAIN, J.J. & R.L. SMITH, G.P. SCHUYERS (1979): Population, immigration and the Australian economy. – London.
BREALEY, T.B. & P.W. NEWTON (1978): Living in remote communities in tropical Australia. The Hedland study. – Melbourne.
BREESE, G. (1969): Urban Australia and New Zealand. A selected bibliography to 1966. – Council of Planning Librarians Exchange Bibliography 89 and 90. Monticello.
BRENNAN, T. (1964): The pattern of urbanization in Australia. – In: ANDERSON, N. (ed.): Urbanism and urbanization. – London, 52–61.
– (1965): Urban communities. – In: DAVIES, A.F. & S. ENCEL (eds.): Australian society. A sociological introduction. – London, 296–309.
BRIGGS, A. (1963): Victorian cities. – London.
BRINE, A.E. (1976): The negative exponential model of urban population densities: Perth 1911–1971. – AGS, 49–58.
BRITTON, J.N.H. (1962): The transport functions of the port of Port Kembla. – EG, 347–358.
– (1965): Coastwise external relations of the ports of Victoria. – AG, 269–281.
BROTCHIE, J.F. (1971): Systems and urban development. – C.S.I.R.O. Melbourne.
BROWN, A.J. (1964): Australian interstate trade and payments. – ER, 363–374.
BRYSON, L. & F. THOMPSON (1972): An Australian new town: Life and leadership in a working-class suburb. – Melbourne.
BUNKER, R. (1964): Canberra's economic base. – NCDC, Canberra.
– (1971): Metropolitan form and metropolitan planning. – AG, 619–632.
– (1977): Capital cities. – In: JEANS, D.N. (ed.): Australia. A geography. – London, 386–411.
BUNKER, R.C. (1967): Metropolitan growth, function and land use in Australia. – Ph. D. Thesis, University of Sydney. Sydney.
– (1971): Town and country or city and region. – Melbourne.
BURNLEY, I.H. (1970): Immigration and metropolitan growth and change in Australia 1947–1966. – Proceed. Sixth N. Z. Geogr. Conference.
– (1971): The absorption of immigrants in Australia. – In: PRICE, C.A. (ed.): Australian immigration. A bibliography and digest, no. 2, 1970. – Canberra, A24–A45.

– (1972): European immigration settlement patterns in metropolitan Sydney, 1947–1966. – AGS, 61–78.
– (ed.) (1974): Urbanization in Australia. The post-war experience. – London.
– (1974): Urbanization and social segregation. – In: BURNLEY, I.H. (ed.): Urbanization in Australia. – London, 131–146.
– (1975a): Ethnic factors in social segregation and residential stratification in Australia's large cities. – ANZJS, 12–20.
– (1975b): Immigrant absorption in the Australian city, 1947–1971. – IMR, 319–333.
– (1976a): Social environment. A population and social geography of Australia. – Sydney.
– (1976b): Geographic-demographic perspectives on the ecology of ethnic groups in Australian cities. A review and synthesis. – In: PRICE, C.A. & J.I. MARTIN (eds.). Australian immigration. A bibliography and digest. No. 3, Part 1, 1975. – Canberra, A124–A155.
– (1976c): Southern European populations in the residential structure of Melbourne. – AGS, 116–132.
– (1976d): Greek settlement in Sydney, 1947–1971. – AG, 200–214.
– (1978): British immigration and settlement in Australian cities 1947–1971. – IMR, 341–358.
– (1980): The Australian urban system: Growth, change and differentiation. – Australian Studies. Melbourne.
– (1982a): Population, society and environment in Australia. A spatial and temporal view. – Studies in Australian Society. Melbourne.
– (1982b): Italian settlement in Sydney, 1920–78. – AGS, 177–194.
– (1982c): Lebanese migration and settlement in Sydney, Australia. – IMR, 102–132.
BURNLEY, I.H., J. PRYOR & D.T. ROWLAND (eds.) (1980): Mobility and community change in Australia. – Studies in Society and Culture. St. Lucia.
BURNS, L.S. (1966): Vorgeplante Industriekomplexe in den Vereinigten Staaten. Standortbestimmung und Erschließung von Industriegelände vol. 2. – Freudenstadt.
BURROUGHS, P. (1967): Britain and Australia, 1831–1855. A study in imperial relations and Crown Lands administration. – Oxford.
BUTLIN, N.G. (1959): Some structural features of Australian capital formation 1861 to 1938/39. – ER, 389–415.
– (1964): Investment in Australian economic development 1861–1900. – London and Cambridge.

CADDY, D.J. & M.M. CONNOR (n.d.): Shire of Mandurah social area analysis. – Mandurah (after 1981; mimeographed).
CAMERON, B. (1971): Australia's economic policies. – Melbourne.
CAMERON, J.M.R. (1973): Prelude to colonization: James Stirling's examination of Swan River, March 1827. – AG, 309–327.
CANNON, M. (ed.) (1984): Early development of Melbourne. Historical Records of Victoria. Foundation Series vol. 4. – Melbourne.
CANNON, R.W. (1972): Twenty years of Australian geography. A matrical classification, bibliography and review of the literature of Australian geography, 1950–1969. – M.S. Thesis, University of Sydney. Sydney (microfilm).
CARDEW, R. (1980): Flats in Sydney: The thirty per cent solution? – In: ROE, J. (ed.): Twentieth century Sydney. Studies in urban and social history. – Sydney, 69–88.
CARDEW, R.V. & J.V. LANGDALE, D.C. RICH (eds.) (1982): Why cities change. Urban development and economic change in Sydney. – Sydney etc.
CARLY, P.J.L. (1977): 'Opening up'. A report on considerations involved in the progressive establishment of the normal roles of local authorities, government agencies and the communities in mining towns. Vol. 1 General. – Perth ('Carly-Report').
CARROLL, B. (1972): Melbourne: An illustrated history. – Melbourne.

The Centenary History of South Australia. – Adelaide 1936.
CENTLIVRES-DEMONT, M. (ed.) (1983): Migrations en Asie. Migrants, personnes déplacées et réfugiés. Migrationen in Asien. Abwanderung, Umsiedlung und Flucht. – Ethnologia Helvetica 7. Berne.
CHITTLEBOROUGH, D.J. & M.J. WRIGHT (1974): A land study for urban site selection – Monarto, S.A. – AG, 543–550.
CHOI, C.Y. (1970): Occupational change among Chinese in Australia. – Race.
– (1975): Chinese migration and settlement in Australia. – Sydney.
CHRISTIE, D.N.M. (1979): Why country towns? Urban Australia Series Book 2. – Sydney etc.
Cities Commission (ed.) (1975): The Australian system of cities. Need for research. – Occas. Paper 3, Canberra.
CLARK, R.K. (1969): The garden city movement and Western Australia. – Architect no. 4, 25–32.
CLARKE, G. (1965): Urban Australia. – In: DAVIES, A.F. & S. ENCEL (eds.): Australian society. A sociological introduction. – London, 31–83.
CLOHER, D.U. (1976): The emergence of urban Victoria, 1834–1891. – Ph. D. Thesis, Monash University. – Melbourne
– (1978): Integration and communications technology in an emerging urban system. – EG, 1–16.
– (1979): Urban settlement process in lands of 'recent settlement' – An Australian example. – JHG, 297–314.
COCHRANE, D. (ed.) (1980): Resources atlas of Queensland. – Brisbane.
COLEMAN, P. (ed.) (1962): Australian civilization. – Melbourne.
COLLIGAN, M. (1983): Comparative views of Adelaide and Melbourne in 1838. Laissez-faire versus company organization. – In: The push from the bush. A bulletin of social history devoted to the year of grace 1838. No. 14, 65–77.
COLLINS, J. (1975): The political economy of post-war immigration. – In: WHEELWRIGHT, E.L. & K. BUCKLEY (eds.): Essays in the political economy of Australian capitalism. Vol. 1. – Sydney.
COLMAN, J. (1971): Planning and people: An introduction to urban planning in Australia. – Sydney.
Commission of Inquiry into Poverty (ed.) (1975): Welfare of migrants. – Canberra.
Commonwealth of Australia (ed.) (1914): Historical records of Australia. Series: Governors' despatches to and from England. Vol. 1 1788–1796. – Sydney.
CONNELL, J. & B.J. ENGELS (1983): Indian doctors in Australia: Costs and benefits of the brain drain. – AG, 308–318.
CONNELL, R.W. & T. IRWING (1980): Class structure in Australian history. – Melbourne.
COOPER, M.J. (1979): Urban and regional inequality in Australia: An explanation. – Proceed. Tenth N. Z. Geogr. Conference, 89–92.
– (1980): Uneven development and Australian urban form. Collected papers of the annual conference of the Institute of Australian Geographers. – Newcastle 1980, 75–82.
The Corporation of the City of Adelaide (ed.) (1982a): Final report, City of Adelaide heritage study. – Adelaide.
– (ed.) (1982b): Landscape – streetscape inventory, City of Adelaide heritage study. – Adelaide.
COULSON, H. (1981): Echuca-Moama. Murray river neighbours. – Red Cliffs, 2nd ed.
The Council of the City of Perth (ed.) (1980): City of Perth central area survey 1977. – Perth.
The Council of the City of Sydney (ed.) (1978): Central Business District Study. – Sydney.
– (ed.) (1980): 1980 City of Sydney strategic plan. – Sydney.
COURT, M. (n. d.): The scope of the national heritage and some aspects of its classification. – In: The National Trust of Australia (Tasmania) Newsletter no. 64. – Hobart.
COURTENAY, P.P. (1980): Northern Australia – Patterns and problems of tropical development in an advanced country. – Sydney.

COX, P. (1973): Historic towns of Australia. – Melbourne.
CRAGO, E.A. & A.G. LAUNDES (1931): Port Kembla and its harbour. – AG 1, part 3, 50–58.
CRISSMAN, L.W. (1967): The segmentary structure of urban overseas Chinese communities. – Man, 185–204.
CROWLEY, F.K. (1960): Australia's western third. A history of Western Australia from the first settlements to modern times. – Nedlands.
CURSON, S. & P. CURSON (1982): The Japanese in Sydney. – ERS, 478–512.
CUSACK, F. (1973): Bendigo. A history. – Melbourne.

DALY, J.W. (1980): The Adelaide parklands. A history of alienation. Thesis, Dept. of History, University of Adelaide. Adelaide.
DALY, M.T. (1964): Comparative growth of Newcastle and Wollongong. – AG, 239–40.
– (1966): The residential structure and growth of Newcastle. – Ph. D. Thesis, University of Sydney. Sydney.
– (1967): Land value determinants: Newcastle, N.S.W. – AGS, 30–39.
– (1968): The Lower Hunter Valley urban complex and the dispersed city hypothesis. – AG, 472–482.
– (1982): Sydney boom, Sydney bust. The city and its property market 1850–1981. – Sydney.
DALY, M.T. & J. BROWN (1964): Urban settlement in central western New South Wales. – Geogr. Soc. N.S.W. Res. Pap. 8. Sydney.
DAVIES, A.F. & S. ENCEL (eds.) (1970): Australian society. A sociological introduction. – Melbourne.
DAVIES, J.L. (ed.) (1965): Atlas of Tasmania. – Hobart.
DAVIS, J.R. & P. SPEARRITT (1974): Sydney at the Census, 1971. – URU, Australian National University. Canberra.
DAVISON, G.J. (1979a): The rise and fall of marvellous Melbourne. – Melbourne.
– (1979b). Australian urban history: A progress report. – In: Urban History Yearbook 1979, 100–109.
DAY, P. (1982): Urban and regional planning. – In: HANLEY, W. & M. COOPER (eds.): Man and the Australian environment. – Sydney, 315–321.
DAY, R.A. & P.J. WALSMSLEY (1981): Residential preferences in Sydney's inner suburbs: A study in diversity. – AP, 185–197.
Department of Administration of the Toowoomba City Council (ed.) (1981): Toowoomba ... Past – present – future. – Toowoomba.
Department of Housing and Construction (ed.) (1983): Residential land stock study. – Canberra.
Department of Immigration and Ethnic Affairs (ed.) (1981): Ethnic distribution 1976. Distribution of overseas-born population in Local Government Areas, Statistical Divisions and States: From census of Population and Housing 1971 and 1976. – Canberra.
Department of Industrial Development (ed.) (1981): The South-West Region – The next decade. Seminar papers, Bunbury 7–8 May 1981. – Perth.
Department of Science, Bureau of Meteorology (ed.) (1977): Report on Cyclone Tracy December 1974. – Canberra.
Department of Urban and Regional Development (ed.) (1974): Urban land prices 1968–1974. An urban paper. – Canberra.
DICK, R.S. (1972): A definition of the central place hierarchy of the Darling Downs, Queensland. – QGJ (Third Series) 1, 1972, 1–38.
DINGLE, A.E. & D.T. MERRETT (1972): Home owners and tenants in Melbourne 1891–1911. – AEHR, 21–35.
– – (1977): Landlords in suburban Melbourne, 1891–1911. – AEHR, 1–24.
Division of National Mapping & Australian Bureau of Statistics (eds.) (1979–1981): Atlas of Population and Housing, 1976 Census. Vol. 1 Perth (1979), vol. 2 Adelaide (1979), vol. 3 Brisbane and Gold Coast (1980), vol. 4 Newcastle and Wollongong (1980), vol. 5 Canberra and Hobart (1980), vol. 6 Sydney (1980), vol. 7 Melbourne and Geelong (1981). – Canberra.

Division of National Mapping & Australian Bureau of Statistics in association with the Institute of Australian Geographers (eds.) (1983–1984): Atlas of Population and Housing, 1981 Census. Vol. 1 Canberra (1983), vol. 2 Sydney (1984), vol. 3 Melbourne (1984), vol. 4 Brisbane (1984), vol. 5 Adelaide (1984), vol. 6 Perth (1984), vol. 7 Hobart (1984).

DOCHERTY, J.C. (1983): Newcastle: The making of an Australian city. – Sydney.

DONGES, C.C. & Associates (1982): Griffith town centre study. Growth strategy 1981–2000. Prepared for Griffith Shire Council.

DOUGLAS, I. (1977): Frontiers of settlement in Australia – Fifty years on. – AG, 297–305.

DOWNING, R.I. (1973): The Australian economy. – London.

DRAKAKIS-SMITH, D. (1981): Aboriginal access to housing in Alice Springs. – AG, 39–51.

DUHS, A. & J. BEGGS (1977): The urban transportation study. – In: HENSHER, D.A. (ed.): Urban transport economics. – Cambridge, 228–251.

DUNCAN, J.S. (ed.) (1982): Atlas of Victoria. – Melbourne.

EDGINGTON, D.W. (1982): Changing patterns of Central Business District office activity in Melbourne. – AG, 231–242.

EDWARDS, N. (1981): The Sydney business frontier 1856–92: A building stock approach. – AGS, 78–98.

ELAZAR, D.J. & P. MEDDING (1983): Jewish communities in frontier societies: Argentina, Australia and South Africa. – New York.

ELLIS, M.H. (1958): Lachlan Macquarie. His life, adventures and times. – Sydney etc., 3rd ed.

ERDMANN, C. (1986): Deutsche Siedlungsgebiete im südöstlichen Queensland. – BGS vol. 18, 101–123.

– (1987): Voraussetzungen für die Entstehung ethnisch geprägter Siedlungsformen in Kolonisationsräumen – am Beispiel der Deutschen in Südaustralien und Queensland. – BGS vol. 24, 39–59.

EWERS, J.K. (1971): The western gateway. A history of Fremantle. – Fremantle 2nd ed.

FAGAN, R.H. (1971): Government policy and the Australian metalliferous mining and processing industries. – In: LINGE, G.J.R. & P.J. RIMMER (eds.): Government influence and the location of economic activity. – RSPSDHGP HG 5, Canberra, 191–231.

FAIRBAIRN, K.J. (1964): Victorian towns as service centres. – Ph. D. Thesis, University of Melbourne. Melbourne.

– (1973): Melbourne: An urban profile. – Sydney.

FAIRBAIRN, K.J. & A.D. MAY (1971): Geography of central places. A review and appraisal. – Adelaide.

FAIRBAIRN, K.J. & G. ROBINSON (1967): Towns and trend surfaces in Gippsland, Victoria. – AGS, 125–134.

FALLOW, S. (1976): Decentralization. – Melbourne.

FARMER, R.S.J. (1971): The geography of migration in Tasmania, 1921–1961. – Ph. D. Thesis, University of Tasmania. Hobart.

– (1980): Migration and population change in Tasmania. – In: BURNLEY, I.H. & R.J. PRYOR, D.T. ROWLANDS (eds.): Mobility and community change in Australia. – St. Lucia, 211–231.

FEHLING, L. (1977): Die Eisenerzwirtschaft Australiens. – KFWS XXIV, Köln.

FELDTMANN, A. (1973): Swan Hill. – Adelaide etc.

FIELD, T.P. (1963): Post-war settlement in Western Australia. – Lexington.

FIRTH, H.J. & G. SAWER (eds.) (1974): The Murray Waters. Man, nature and a river system. – Sydney.

FISCHER, K.F. (1984): Canberra: Myths and models. Forces at work in the formation of the Australian capital. – Institut für Asienkunde. Hamburg.

– (1986): Canberra. Ideale Planungsbedingungen – ideale Wirklichkeit? – BGS vol. 18, 153–170.

– (1987): Paris, Los Angeles, Borobudur – Vorbilder australischer Hauptstadtplanung. – BGS vol. 24, 131–147.

FITZGERALD, R. (1982): From the dreaming to 1915: A history of Queensland. – St. Lucia.

– (1984): From 1915 to the early 1980s: A history of Queensland. – St. Lucia.

FITZPATRICK, D. (1979): Irish immigrants in Australia. Patterns of settlement and patterns of mobility. – Australia 1888, Bull. no. 2, 1979, 48–54.

FORREST, J. & R.J. JOHNSTON (1981): On the characterisation of urban sub-areas according to age structure. – UG, 31–40.

FORSTER, C.A. (1974): The journey to work and a satellite town: The cautionary example of Elizabeth. – AGS, 3–26.

– (1977): An atlas of employment in Greater Adelaide. Flinders University, Institute of Labour Studies, Working Paper 18. – Adelaide.

– (1983a): Spatial organisation and local unemployment rates in metropolitan Adelaide: Significant issue or spatial fetish? – AGS, 33–48.

– (1983b): Australian profile. Unemployment in the cities. – GE, 131–140.

FORSTER, C.A. & R.J. STIMSON (eds.) (1977): Urban South Australia: Selected readings. – Flinders University, Centre for Applied Social and Survey Research Monograph 1. Adelaide.

FOWARD, C.N. (1969): A Canadian's eye view of Australian cities. – CGJ, 26–39.

– (1970): Waterfront land use in the six Australian state capitals. – AAAG, 517–532.

FREELAND, J.M. (1968): The history of architecture in Australia. – Melbourne.

– (1972): Architecture in Australia. A history. – Harmondsworth.

FREESTONE, R. (1981): Australian geography: A guide to bibliographies and review articles. – JG, 31–34.

– (1982a): The garden city idea in Australia. – AGS, 24–48.

– (1982b): Urban Australia: Postwar to postindustrial. – Focus vol. 32, no. 4, 9–14.

GALBREATH, A. (1968): The new industrial state.

GALE, F. & J. WUNDERSITZ (1982): Adelaide Aborigines. A case study of urban life 1966–1981. – Canberra.

GALVIN, J.P. (1974): Origin and settlement of non-British migrants in Newcastle, N.S.W. – AG, 517–530.

GAMBA, C. (1952): The Italian fisherman of Fremantle. – University of Western Australia Dept. of Economics Publ. Ser. A no. 2. Nedlands.

GEISSMAN, J.R. & E.R. WOOLMINGTON (1971): A theoretical location concept for decentralization in Southeastern Australia. – NZG, 69–78.

GENTILLI, J. (1971): Perth. – Camberwell.

– (ed.) (1979): Western landscapes. – Perth.

GENTILLI, J. & D. RUMLEY (1977): Bibliography of metropolitan Perth. – Geowest 10. Nedlands.

GENTILLI, J. & C. STRANSKY, C. IRACI (1982): Italien migration to Western Australia 1829–1946. – Geowest 19. Nedlands.

GIBBINS, M.J. (1973): Housing preferences in the Brisbane area. – AIUS, Queensland Division. Brisbane.

GIBBS, R.M. (1969): A history of South Australia. – Adelaide.

GIFFORD, K.H. (1980): Planning for an Australian metropolis. – ZW, 9–13.

GIFFORD, R.M. & J.D. KALMA, A.R. ASTON, R.J. MILLINGTON (1975): Biophysical constraints in Australian food production: Implications for population policy. – Search, 212–223.

GLYNN, S. (1970): Urbanisation in Australian history, 1788–1900. – Melbourne.

GODDARD, R.F. & T.W. PLUMB (1981): Computer-assisted mapping of Australia's city dwellers. – Cartography 12, 42–47.

GOLLEDGE, R.G. (1960): Sydney's metropolitan fringe: A study in urban-rural relations. – AG, 234–255.

– (1962): Observations on the urban pattern and functional role of Newcastle, N.S.W. – TESG, 72–78.

GRAEME, H. (1983): Population change in urban and rural areas 1976–1981. – Bedford Park.
GRAHAM, R.J. Associates & T.R. LEE (1983): Flexi-lot evaluation. Evaluation of Tasmanian Housing Department's flexi-lot subdivisions. – Hobart.
GRANT, J. & G. SERLE (eds.) (1978): The Melbourne scene, 1803–1956. – Melbourne, 2nd ed.
GRAUBARD, S.R. (ed.) (1985): Australia: The Daedalus Symposium. – North Ryde.
GRAYCAR, A. (1979): Welfare politics in Australia. – Melbourne.
GREEN, F.C. (1965): The battle of the site for the federal capital. – THRAPP, 10–18.
GREENWOOD, G. (ed) (1965): Australia – A social and political history. – Sydney.
GROTZ, R. (1982): Industrialisierung und Stadtentwicklung im ländlichen Südost-Australien. – Stuttgarter Geogr. Schr. 98. Stuttgart.
– (1985): Die Industrie Australiens: Entwicklung, Probleme, Chancen. – Geogr. Rdsch., 28–35.
– (1987): Die Entwicklung des Central Business Districts von Sydney 1950–1986. – BGS vol. 24, 101–130.
GRUBB, W.M. (1976): Planning in Victoria 1910–1943. – Polis no. 2, 5–9.
GURNANI-SMITH, R. (1984): The growth of Australian cities. – The Making of Australia Series. Sydney and London.

HAJDU, J.G. (1976): Planning our communities. – Urban Australia Series Book 5. Sydney etc. 2nd ed. 1978.
– (1979): The study of the home and its micro-environment. – GE, 351–364.
HALLIGAN, J. & C. PARIS (eds.) (1984): Australian urban politics. – Australian Studies Series. Melbourne.
HANLEY, W. (1982): Decentralisation: Political football or future prospect? – In: HANLEY, W. & M. COOPER (eds.): Man and the Australian environment. – Sydney, 345–353.
HANLEY, W. & M. COOPER (eds.) (1982): Man and the Australian environment. – Sydney.
HARDMAN, P. & M. MANNING (1975): Green bans. – Australian Conservation Foundation. Sydney.
HARMAN, E. (1983): The city, state and resource development in Western Australia. – In: WILLIAMS, P. (ed.): Social process and the city. – Urban Studies Yearbook 1. Sydney etc., 114–142.
HARRIS, C.P. & P.J. CROSSMAN (1979): Growth and change in the Townsville Region 1966 to 1979. – Dept. of Economics, James Cook University of Northern Queensland. Townsville.
HARRIS, D.D. (1982): Settlement patterns and processes. – Melbourne.
HARRIS, D.D. & B. HARPER (1971): Urbs and suburbs: The city environment. – Melbourne.
HARRIS, D.D. & I.R. STEHBENS (1982): Settlement patterns and processes. – Melbourne.
HARRIS, S. (1984): The state of the art: A review of urban conservation in the 1970s. – In: The National Trust of Australia (NSW) (ed.): Urban conservation in the '80s. – Sydney, 3–9.
HARRISON, P. (1968): Approach to a metropolitan plan. – architecture in australia, 630–634.
– (1977): Major Urban Areas. Commentary to Atlas of Australian Resources, 2nd series. Dept. of National Resources, Canberra.
– (1978): Australian Capital Territory. – In: RYAN, F. (ed.): Urban management processes. – Australian National Commission for UNESCO. Canberra.
– (1979): Walter Burley Griffin and the Federal Capital design. Prepared for the National Capital Development Commission, November 1979. – Canberra.
– (1980): Government development in Canberra. – RAPIJ no. 3, 78–82.
HEATHCOTE, R.L. (1975): Australia. The world's landscapes. – London and New York.

HEFFORD, R.K. (1965): Decentralization in South Australia. – AGS, 79–96.
HEINRICH, R. (1972): Governor Furgusson's legacy. A history of the early days of the Maitland-Kilkerran districts. – Adelaide.
HEINRITZ, G. & E. LICHTENBERGER (eds.) (1986): The take-off of suburbia and the crisis of the central city. – Erdkundliches Wissen 76. Stuttgart.
HENDRY, M.J. (1979): Canberra – a city within the landscape. An evaluation of the provision of parkland and public open space. – Landscape Planning, 271–283.
HENSHER, D.A. (ed.) (1977): Urban transport economics. – Melbourne.
HERMAN, M. (1970): The early Australian architects and their work. – Sydney, 2nd ed.
HILL, M. (n. d.): Housing. – In: Finance for investment in urban development. – Urbanisation Seminar 1 and 2 December 1972, Australian National University. Canberra.
HIRST, J. & M.J. TAYLOR (1985): The internationalisation of Australian banking: Further moves by the ANZ. – AG, 291–295.
HIRST, J.B. (1973): Adelaide and the country 1870–1917: Their social and political relationship. – Melbourne.
HOFMEISTER, B. (1982): Die Stadt in Australien und USA – Ein Vergleich ihrer Strukturen. – In: Beiträge zur Stadtgeographie I. – Mitt. Geogr. Ges. Hamburg vol. 72, 3–35
– (1985a): Die strukturelle Entwicklung der australischen Stadt. – Geogr. Rdsch., 36–42.
– (1985b): Die US-amerikanischen Städte in den achtziger Jahren – Probleme und Entwicklungstendenzen. – In: Festschrift für Elisabeth Lichtenberger. – Klagenf. Geogr. Schr. 6, 53–71.
– (1986a): Denkmalschutz und Denkmalpflege in Australien. – Die Alte Stadt, 81–98.
– (1986b): What is the extent of a crisis of the central city and suburbanisation in Australia? – In: HEINRITZ, G. & E. LICHTENBERGER (eds.): The take-off of suburbia and the crisis of the central city. Erdkundliches Wissen 76, Wiesbaden, 134–141.
– (1986c): Grundzüge des australischen Städtesystems. – BGS vol. 20, 299–316.
– (1987): Neue Städte in Australien. – BGS vol. 24, 83–100.
HOGAN, J. (1982): Living history of Brisbane. – Brisbane.
HOLLAND, S. (1976): Capital versus the regions. – London.
HOLMES, J.H. (1965): The suburbanization of the Cessnock coalfield towns, 1954–1964. – AGS, 105–128.
– (1971): External commuting as a prelude to suburbanization. – AAAG, 774–790.
– (1973): Population concentration and dispersion in Australian states: A macrogeographic analysis. – AGS, 150–170.
– (1977): The urban system. – In: JEANS, D.N. (ed.): Australia. A geography. – London, 386–411.
– (1983): Telephone traffic dispersion and nodal regionalisation in the Australian states. – AGS, 231–250.
– (1984): Australian higher-order nodal regions. – AG, 104–119.
HOLMES, J.H. & B.F. PULLINGER (1973): Tamworth: An emerging regional capital? – AG, 207–225.
HOLMES, J.M. (1947): Factory orientation in metropolitan Sydney. AG, 96–113.
HOLSMAN, A.J. (1975): Interstate interaction patterns in Australia. – AGS, 46–61.
– (1977): The structure of Australian air networks. – AGS, 53–65.
– (1979): Freight flows in the Australian economy. – AGS, 131–154.
HOLTHOUSE, H. (1982): Illustrated history of Brisbane. – Sydney.
HOPTON, A.J. (1941): A pioneer of two colonies: John Pascoe Fawkner, 1792–1869. – VHM, 103–169.
HOUGHTON, D.S. (1975): City size and social differentiation. An Australian comparison. – TESG, 217–224.
– (1977): Kwinana. Year 20. – RAPIJ, 130–134.

– (1979): Perth at the 1976 Census. A social atlas. – Nedlands.
– (1981): Metropolitan growth: A spatial perspective on employment trends in the Perth metropolitan area 1966–76. – AG, 106–113.
HOUGHTON, D.S. & C.R.J. JOHNSON (1984): Population trends and urban redevelopment: Perth 1971–81. – WG, 1–9.
The Housing Commission of New South Wales (ed.) (1979): Wooloomooloo Project. The new architecture of Wooloomooloo. – Sydney.
HOWARD, A. (1984): From colonies to Commonwealth. – The Making of Australia Series. Sydney and London.
HOWE, A.L. (1978): The changing distribution of Melbourne's aged population: Patterns and implications. – AGS, 136–148.
HOYLE, B.S. & D. HILLING (eds.) (1984): Seaports and spatial change. – Chichester.
HUCK, A. (1967): The Chinese in Australia. – Melbourne.
HUGO, G. (1979): Some demographic factors influencing recent and future demand for housing in Australia. – AQ no. 4, 4–25.
– (1983): South Australia's changing population. – SAGP 1, Adelaide.
HUMPHREYS, J.S. (1973): Intra-urban migration and residential structure. – MUDGPG 6. Melbourne.
– (1975): Intra-urban migration and urban residential structure in Melbourne. – Ph. D. Thesis, Monash University. Melbourne.
– (1979): Mining communities. – Urban Australia Series Book 3. Sydney etc.
HUMPHREYS, J.S. & J.S. WHITELAW (1979): Immigrants in an unfamiliar environment: Locational decision-making under constrained circumstances. – GA 61 B, 8–18.
HUTCHINGS, A. & R. BUNKER (eds.) (1986): With conscious purpose. A history of town planning in South Australia. – Cowandilla.
HUTTON, J. (1970): Building and construction in Australia. – Melbourne.

Indicative Planning Council for the Housing Industry (1980): Report on multi-unit dwelling development in Australia. – Canberra.
INGLIS, C. (1972): Chinese in Australia. – IMR, 266–281.
– (1975): Some recent Australian writing on immigration and assimilation. – IMR, 335–344.

JACKSON, J.T. (1979): Changing patterns of post-war immigration to Western Australia. – In: JOHNSTON, R. (ed.): Immigrants in Western Australia. – Nedlands, 17–35.
– (1980): Home improvers and movers in metropolitan Perth. – Geowest 17. Nedlands.
– (1982): First-time home buyers and building societies in metropolitan Perth, 1979–80. – AGS, 231–239.
– (1985): To move or extend? A study of housing behaviour in metropolitan Perth, 1979. – AG, 207–217.
JACKSON, R.V. (1970): Owner-occupation of houses in Sydney, 1871 to 1891. – AEHR, 138–154.
– (1974): House building and the age structure of population in New South Wales, 1861–1900. – AEHR, 143–159.
– (1977): Australian economic development in the nineteenth century. – Canberra.
JACOBS & LEWIS, VINE, AITKEN Architects (1981): Ballarat. A guide to the buildings and areas 1851–1940. – Ballarat.
JARVIE, W.K. & J.G. BROWETT (1980): Recent changes in migration patterns in Australia. – AGS, 135–145.
JARVIS, N.T. (ed.) (1979): Western Australia. An atlas of human endeavour, 1829–1979. – Nedlands.
JASCHKE, D. (1975a): Darwin und seine Region – Naturraum, Wirtschaft und städtische Aufgabenstellung im tropischen Australien. – Mitt. Geogr. Ges. Hamburg 63. Hamburg, 55–113.
– (1975b): Der Wiederaufbau Darwins. – Mitt. Inst. f. Asienkunde 74. Hamburg.
– (1979): Das Australische Nordterritorium. Potential, Nutzung und Inwertsetzbarkeit seiner natürlichen Ressourcen. Mitt. Geogr. Ges. Hamburg 70. Hamburg.
JAY, C. (1978): Towards urban strategies for Australia. – AIUS Publication no. 75. Canberra.
JEANS, D.N. (1966): The breakdown of Australia's first rectangular grid survey. – AGS, 119–128.
– (1967): Territorial divisions and the locations of towns in N.S.W., 1826–1842. – AG, 231–255.
– (1972): An historical geography of New South Wales to 1901. – Sydney.
– (ed.) (1977): Australia. A geography. – London.
– (1983): Experiments of fruit and experiments of light: Human geography in Australia and New Zealand. – PHG, 313–343.
– (ed.) (1984): Australian historical landscapes. – North Sydney.
JEANS, D.N. & J.L. DAVIES (1984): Australian geography 1972–1982. – AGS, 3–35.
JEFFREY, D. (1975): Spatial imbalance in the Australian regional economic system: Structural unemployment 1955–1970. – AG, 146–154.
JEFFREY, D. & D.J. WEBB (1972): Economic fluctuations in the Australian regional system. – AGS, 141–160.
JENNINGS, J.N. & G.J.R. LINGE (eds.) (1980): Of time and place. Essays in honour of O.H.K. Spate. – Canberra.
JENSEN, R. (1974): Cities of vision. – Sydney.
JOHNSON, D.L. (1977): The architecture of Walter Burley Griffin. – Melbourne.
– (1980): Australian architecture 1901–1951: Sources of modernism. – Sydney.
JOHNSTON, J.A. (ed.) (1978): Society in view. A geographic atlas for the social sciences. – Milton etc.
JOHNSTON, R. (ed.) (1979): Immigrants in Western Australia. – Nedlands.
JOHNSTON, R.J. (1966a): Residential structure and urban morphology. – Ph. D. Thesis, Monash University. Melbourne.
– (1966b): The distribution of an intra-metropolitan central place hierarchy. – AGS, 19–33.
– (1966c): Commercial leadership in Australia. – AG, 49–52.
– (1967a): Population growth and urbanization in Australia: 1961–1966. – Geography, 199–202.
– (1967b): The Australian small town in the post-war period. – AG, 215–219.
– (1968): An outline of the development of Melbourne's street pattern. – AG, 453–465.
– (1969): Zonal and sectoral patterns in Melbourne's residential structure, 1961. – LE, 463–467.
– (1971): Urban residential patterns. – London.
– (1973): Social area change in Melbourne, 1961–1966. A sample exploration. – AGS, 79–98.
JOHNSTON, R.J. & J. FORREST (1985): Spatial-structural effects and the geography of voting in Australia, 1977. – AG, 286–290.
JOHNSTON, R.J. & C.C. KISSLING (1971): Establishment use patterns within central places. – AGS, 116–132.
JOHNSTON, R.J. & P.J. RIMMER (1967): The competitive position of a planned shopping centre. – AG, 160–168.
– – (1969): Retailing in Melbourne. – Dept. of Human Geography, Australian National University. Canberra.
JONES, D. (1976): Trinity Phoenix. A history of Cairns. – Cairns.
JONES, F.L. (1961): A social profile of Canberra. – ANZJS, 107–120.
– (1964): Italians in the Carlton area: The growth of an ethnic concentration. – AJPH, 83–95.
– (1967a): Ethnic concentration and assimilation: An Australian case study. – SF, 412–423.
– (1967b): A social ranking of Melbourne suburbs. – ANZJS, 93–110.
– (1969): Dimensions of urban social structure. The social areas of Melbourne, Australia. – Canberra.
JONES, M. (1972): Housing and poverty in Australia. – Melbourne.

JUNG, E. (1879): Australische Städte. – Mitt. d. Vereins f. Erdkunde zu Halle.
JUPP, J. (1966): Arrivals and departures. – Melbourne.
JUPP, V.J. (ed.) (1987): Encyclopedia of the Australian people. – Canberra.

KANALEY, D. & T. KANALEY (1974): The A.C.T. dilemma: Self-government and realpolitik. – AQ no. 4, 97–102.
KASPER, W. & R. BLANDY, J. FREEEBAIRN, D. HOCKING, R. O'NEILL (1980): Australia at the crossroads. – Sydney.
KELLY, M. (ed.) (1978): Nineteenth century Sydney. – Sydney.
KEMENY, J. (1977): A political sociology of home ownership in Australia. – ANZJS, 47–52.
– (1978): Australia's privatized cities: Detached house ownership and urban exploitation. – In: BURKE, T. (ed.): Housing problems and housing policy. – Centre for Urban Studies, Swinburne Coll. of. Techn., Melbourne, 39–49.
– (1980): Home ownership and privatization. – IJURR, 372–388.
– (1983): The great Australian nightmare: A critique of the home-ownership ideology. – Melbourne.
KENDIG, H. (1979): New life for old suburbs. – Sydney.
– (1981): Buying and renting: Household moves in Adelaide. – AIUS Publication 91. Canberra.
KERR, A. (1965): The south-west region of Western Australia. – Nedlands.
– (1972): Urban industrial change in Australia: 1954 to 1966. – ER, 355–367.
KIDD, G.A. (1974): New cities – An end to new states? – AQ no. 2, 57–68.
KILMARTIN, L. & D.C. THORNS (1978): Cities unlimited: The sociology of urban development in Australia and New Zealand. – Sydney etc.
KING, H.W.H. (1954a): County, shire and town in New South Wales. – AG 14–25.
– (1954b): The Canberra-Queanbeyan symbiosis: A study of urban mutualism. – GR, 101–118.
– (1956): The urban hierarchy of the southern tablelands of New South Wales. – Ph. D. Thesis, Australian National University. Canberra.
KING, S.A. (1979): More than meets the eye: Plans for land use change in Darwin after Cyclone Tracy. – NARB no. 5, Darwin, 43–159.
KIRKLAND, J.R. (1985): Settlement and resettlement of Armenian immigrants in Sydney. – AG, 195–207.
KMENTA, J. (1964): Australian postwar immigration. An economic study. – Ph. D. Thesis, Stanford University, Palo Alto (mimeographed 1985).
KOVACS, M.L. & A.J. CROPLEY (1975): Immigrants and society: Alienation and assimilation. – Sydney etc.
KUNZ, E. (1971): Refugees and Eastern Europeans in Australia. – In: PRICE, C.A. (ed.): Australian immigration: A bibliography and digest no. 2, 1970. – Canberra, A46–A61.

LAMPING, H. (1981): Entwicklungsperspektiven der Bergbaustädte im Hamersley-Gebirge Westaustraliens. – FWSS 36, 233–267.
– (1982): Australien. Grundzüge der Inwertsetzung. – PG no. 5, 5–13.
– (1985): Australien. Länderprofile. – Stuttgart.
– (1986): Neue Aspekte des Verdichtungsprozesses in Australien. – BGS vol. 18, 125–151.
– (1987): Tourismus im Spiegel der Wirtschafts- und Siedlungsentwicklung in Australien. – BGS vol. 24, 61–82.
LANCASTER-JONES, F. (1969): Dimensions of urban social structure: The social areas of Melbourne, Australia. – Canberra.
LANG, M.H. (1982): Gentrification amid urban decline. Strategies for America's older cities. – Cambridge.
LANGDALE, J.V. (1975): Nodal regional structures of New South Wales. – AGS, 123–136.
– (1976): Australian urban and regional development planning: A regional centre strategy. – AG, 264–271.
LANGE, W.L. (1975): Decentralization and Albury-Wodonga. – AQ, 50–65.
LANGFORD-SMITH, T. (1959): Landforms, land settlement and irrigation on the Murrumbidgee, N.S.W. – Ph. D. Thesis, Australian National University. Canberra.
LANSDOWN, R.B. (1971): Canberra: An example for many decentralized Australian cities. – AQ, 71–85.
LARCOMBE, F.A. (1978): The advancement of local government in New South Wales, 1906 to the present. – Sydney.
LATTA, D. (1984): Early Australian architecture. – The Making of Australia Series. Sydney and London.
LAWRENCE, G.V. & G.K. SMITH (eds.) (1975): The book of the Murray. – Adelaide.
LAWSON, R. (1973): Brisbane in the 1890s. A study of an Australian urban society. – St. Lucia.
LEE, T.R. (1970): The role of the ethnic community as a reception area for Italian immigrants in Melbourne, Australia. – IM, Vol. VIII, no. 1/2, 50–63.
– (1979a): The concentration and dispersal of immigrant groups: Policy issues and social forces. – Papers pres. to Austral. Polit. Science Assoc. Conference, Hobart August 1979 (mimeographed).
– (1979b): Urban planning for crime prevention: Some social consequences of public housing programmes. – Paper pres. to Austral. Crime Prevention Council, Tenth Nat. Conference, Hobart, Tasmania, 14 August 1979 (mimeographed).
– (1980): The resilience of social networks to changes in mobility and propinquity. – SN, 423–435.
– (1981): A social atlas of Hobart (1976). – Hobart.
LEE, T.R. & L.J. WOOD (1978): Three years of disruption: Some effects and consequences of the Tasman Bridge collapse. – Dept. of Geography, University of Tasmania, Hobart (mimeographed).
LEMON, A. & N.C. POLLOCK (eds.) (1980): Studies in overseas settlement and population. – Melbourne.
LEMPRIERE, T.J. (1954): The penal settlements of early Van Diemen's Land. – n.d.
LESTER FIRTH Associates (1983): Sullivan Cove Urban Design Study. – Hobart.
LEWIS, G. (1973): A history of the ports of Queensland. A study in economic nationalism. – St. Lucia.
LIGHT, W. (1962): Brief Journal 1839. South Australian Facsimile Editions no. 1. – Adelaide.
LIGHTON, C. (1958): Sisters of the South. – 2nd. ed. London.
LINGE, G.J.R. (1961): Canberra after fifty years. – GR, 467–486.
– (1965): Delimitation of urban boundaries. – Dept. of Geography, Australian National University. Canberra.
– (1967): Governments and the location of secondary industry in Australia. – EG, 43–63.
– (1968): Secondary industry in Australia. – In: DURY, G.H. & M.I. LOGAN (eds.): Studies in Australian geography. – London.
– (1975): Canberra: Site and city. – Canberra.
– (1979): Industrial awakening: A geography of Australian manufacturing 1788–1890. – Canberra.
– (1980): From vision to pipe dream: Yet another northern miss. – In: JENNINGS, J.N. & G.J.R. LINGE (eds.): Of time and place: Essays in honour of O.H.K. Spate. – Canberra.
LINGE, G.J.R. & P.J. RIMMER (eds.) (1971): Government influence and the location of economic activity. – Canberra.
LLOYD, C. & P.N. TROY (1981): Innovation and reaction: The life and death of the Federal Department of Urban and Regional Development. – Sydney.
LOCKWOOD, D. (1976): The front door. Darwin 1869–1969. – Adelaide etc.
LÖFFLER, E. (1973): Canberra: A city for the future? – Geoforum 13, 17–29.
– (1985): Naturräumliche Faktoren und Landnutzungspotential Australiens. – Geogr. Rundschau 1/1985, 4–11.
LOGAN, M.I. (1964a): Suburban manufacturing: A case study. – AG, 223–234.

– (1964b): Manufacturing decentralization in the Sydney metropolitan area. – EG, 151–162.
– (1965): The geography of manufacturing in an Australian city: Studies of the function and distribution of manufacturing in Sydney. – Ph. D. Thesis, University of Sydney. – Sydney.
– (1966): Capital city manufacturing in Australia. – EG, 139–151.
– (1968a): Work-residence relationships in the city. – AGS, 151–166.
– (1968b): Capital city development in Australia. – In: DURY, G.H. & M.I. LOGAN (eds.): Studies in Australian geography. – London, 245–301.
– (1976): A geographical perspective on urban and regional policies in Australia. – AGS, 3–14.
LOGAN, M.I. & L.S. BOURNE (1976): Changing urbanization. Patterns at the margin: The examples of Australia and Canada. – In: BERRY, B.J.L. (ed.): Patterns of urbanization. – Urban Affairs Annual Review 12.
LOGAN, M.I. & C.A. MAHER, J. McKAY, J.S. HUMPHREYS (1975): Urban and regional Australia. Analysis and policy issues. – Melbourne.
LOGAN, M.I. & J.S. WHITELAW, J. McKAY (1981): Urbanization: The Australian experience. – Melbourne.
LOGAN, T. (1981): Urban and regional planning in Victoria. – Melbourne.
– (1984): Local planning. Practice and potential in metropolitan Melbourne. – In: WILLIAMS, P. (ed.): Conflict and development. Urban Studies Yearbook 2. – Sydney, London, Boston, 99–118.
LOGAN, W.S. (1979): A question of size. – Urban Australia Series Book 4. Sydney etc.
– (1982): Gentrification in inner Melbourne. Problems of analysis. – AGS, 65–95.
LOGAN, W.S. & D.J. ECCLES (1977): Our older cities. Preservation, redevelopment or conservation? – Urban Australia Series Book 6. Sydney etc.
LOGAN, W.S. & A.D. MAY (1979): The Australian urban network. – Urban Australia Series Book 1. Sydney etc.
LONSDALE, R.E. (1972): Manufacturing decentralization. The discouraging record of Australia. – LE, 321–328.
LONSDALE, R.E. & J.H. HOLMES (eds.) (1981): Settlement systems in sparsely populated regions: The United States and Australia. – New York.
LYNE, J.A. (1974): Greater Melbourne. – London.

MAHER, C.A. (1976): Population change in inner Melbourne: 1961–71. – Paper, Seminar 26 November 1976 Canberra. Canberra (mimeo).
– (1978): Private housing construction and household turnover – a study of vacancy chains in Melbourne's housing market. – MUDGPG 22. Melbourne.
– (1979): The changing residential role of the inner city: The example of inner Melbourne. – AG, 112–122.
– (1980): Suburban development and household mobility in Melbourne. – In: BURNLEY, I.H. & J. PRYOR, D.T. ROWLAND (eds.). Mobility and community change in Australia. Studies in Society and Culture. – St. Lucia.
– (1982): Australian cities in transition. – Melbourne.
– (1983): Population turnover and spatial change in Melbourne, Australia. – UG, 240–257.
– (1985): Residential mobility within Australian cities: An analysis of 1976 Census data. – Australian Bureau of Statistics. Canberra.
MAHER, C.A. & J. WHITELAW (1975): Structure and change in inner Melbourne 1961–1971. – Report, Dept. of Urban and Regional Development. Dept. of Geography, Monash University. Melbourne.
MANNING, I. (1976): The geographical distribution of poverty in Australia. – AGS, 133–147.
– (1978): The journey to work. – Sydney.
MARSDEN, B.S. (1966a): Temporal aspects of urban population densities: Brisbane, 1861–1966. – AGS, 71–82.
– (1966b): A century of building materials in Queensland and Brisbane, 1861–1961. – AG, 115–131.
– (1971): Brisbane. – Longman Australian Geographies no. 31. Camberwell.
MARSDEN, B.S. & E.E. TUGBY (1981): Bibliography of Australian geography theses. Preliminary edition: 1933–1971. – Dept. of Geography, University of Queensland. Brisbane.
MARSHALL, A. (1968): Iron age in the Pilbara. – AG, 415–420.
MARTIN, J.J. (1965): Refugee settlers: A study of displaced persons in Australia. – Canberra.
– (1972): Community and identity. Refugee groups in Adelaide. – Immigrants in Australia Series. Canberra.
– (1978): The migrant presence: Australian responses 1947–1977. – Sydney.
MASSEY, J. & J. POLINESS (1983): Agricultural land use atlas, Australia 1979–80. – Dept. of Geography, University of Melbourne. Parkville.
MATHEWS, R. (ed.) (1978): Local government in transition: Responsibilities, finances, management. – Centre for Feder. Fin. Relations, Australian National University. Canberra.
MATHIESON, R.S. (1957): The validity of Reilly's Law in Australia. – AG 7, 27–32.
MAYNE, A.J.C. (1982): Fever, squalor and vice: Sanitation and social policy in Victorian Sydney. – St. Lucia.
McCARTY, J.W. (1970): Australian capital cities in the nineteenth century. – AEHR, 107–140.
– (1980): Melbourne, Ballarat, Sydney, Perth: The new city histories. – HS, 1–15.
McCARTY, J.W. & C.B. SHEDVIN (eds.) (1978): Australian capital cities. Historical essays. – Sydney.
McCASKILL, M. (ed.) (1986): Atlas of South Australia. – Adelaide.
McCONVILLE, C. (1979): Catholics and mobility in Melbourne and Sydney, 1861–1891. – Australia 1888, Bull. no. 2, 1979, 55–64.
McDONALD, G.T. & M.J. GUILFOYLE (eds.) (1981): Urban social atlas of Brisbane – 1976. – Brisbane.
McDONALD, L. (1981): Rockhampton. A history of city and district. – St. Lucia.
McILROY, W. (1937): Melbourne's land sales. – VHM.
McINTYRE, A.J. & J.J. McINTYRE (1944): Country towns of Victoria. Social survey. – Melbourne.
McKAY, J. (1981): Ethnic communities in Melbourne. An atlas of the overseas born population. – MUDGPG 26. Melbourne.
McKAY, J. & J.S. WHITELAW (1977): The role of large private and government organizations in generating flows of interregional migrants: The case of Australia. – EG, 28–44.
– – (1978): Internal migration and the Australian urban system. – Progress in Planning vol. 10 part 1. Oxford.
McKNIGHT, T. (1965): Elizabeth, South Australia. An approach to decentralization. – AGS, 39–53.
McMAHON, T.A. & C.R. WEEKS (1973): Climate and water use in Australian cities. – AGS, 99–108.
McMASTER, J.C. & G.R. WEBB (eds.) (1976): Australian urban economics. A reader. – Sydney.
McROBBIE, A. (1982): The Surfers Paradise story. – Surfers Paradise.
MEDDING, P.Y. (ed.) (1973): Jews in Australian society. – Melbourne.
MEINIG, D.W. (1963): On the margins of the good earth: The South Australian wheat frontier 1869–1884. – London.
MELAMID, A. (1980): Survival of mining cities in arid regions. – WS 7, 1980, 49–62.
Melbourne and Metropolitan Board of Works (MMBW) (1971): Planning policies for the Melbourne Metropolitan Region. – Melbourne.
– (1979a): The challenge of change. A review of Melbourne's planning options. – Melbourne.
– (1979b): Alternative strategies for metropolitan Melbourne. – Melbourne.

- (1979c): Alternative strategies for metropolitan Melbourne. Background papers. - Melbourne.
- (1980): Metropolitan strategy. - Melbourne.
- (1981): Metropolitan strategy implementation. - Melbourne.
- (1982): Amendment 150. District centre selection process. - Melbourne.
MERCER, D. & C.A. MAHER (1985): Shopping for a policy: The state and convenience store retailing in Melbourne. - In: ADRIAN, C. (ed.): Urban service provision: Institutional processes and geographic outcome. - Sydney.
MONHEIM, R. (1983): Australian pedestrian malls — Impressions from a German perspective. - Space. The Town and Country Planning Assoc. (Victoria, Australia), Febr. 1983, 15-16.
MONK, J. (1983): Asian professionals as immigrants: The Indians in Sydney. - JCG no. 4, 1-16.
MOORE, E.G. (1966): Residential mobility in an urban context. - Ph. D. Thesis, University of Queensland. St. Lucia.
MORISON, M.P. & J.G. WHITE (eds.) (1979): Western towns and buildings. - Nedlands.
MORLEY, C.D. (1967): Suburban business centres in four Australian cities. - Ph. D. Thesis, Australian National University. Canberra.
MORRIS, A. (1951): Echuca and the Murray River trade. - HS Australia and New Zealand, vol. 4, no. 16.
MORRIS, J.M. (1977): Dimensions of urban residential differentiation. - MUDGPG 15. Melbourne.
MULLINS, P. (1979a): The struggle against Brisbane's freeways: 1966-74. - IJURR, 542-552.
- (1979b): Australia's sunbelt migration: The recent growth of Brisbane and the Moreton Region. - JAPE, 17-32.
- (1980): Australian urbanization and Queensland's underdevelopment: A first empirical statement. - IJURR, 212-238.
- (1981): Theoretical perspectives of Australian urbanisation: 1. Material components in the reproduction of Australian labour power. - ANZJS, 65-76.
- (1984): Hedonism and real estate: Resort tourism and Gold Coast development. - In: WILLIAMS, P. (ed.): Conflict and development. - Urban Studies Yearbook 2. Sydney, London, Boston, 31-50.
MUNDEY, J. (1981): Green bans and beyond. - Sydney.
MURPHY, P.A. (1977): Second homes in New South Wales. - AG, 310-317.
- (1985): Development of strata units in New South Wales north coast resorts. - AG, 272-279.

NADEL, G. (1957): Australia's colonial culture: Ideas, men and institutions in mid-nineteenth century Eastern Australia. - Melbourne.
NANCE, C. (1978): The Irish in South Australia during the colony's first four decades. - JHSSA no. 5, 1978, 66-73.
National Association of Australian State Road Authorities (ed.) (1984): The NAASRA Roads Study, 1984. - Urban Arterial Roads Report. Milson's Point.
National Capital Development Commission (ed.) (1965): The future Canberra. - Sydney.
- (ed.) (1970): Tomorrow's Canberra. Planning for growth and change. - Canberra.
- (ed.) (1984): Metropolitan Canberra. Policy Plan. Development Plan. - Canberra.
National Trust of Australia (New South Wales) (ed.) (1984): Urban conservation in the 80s. - Sydney.
NEILSON, L. (1972): Business activities in three Melbourne suburbs. - URU, Australian National University. Canberra.
- (1978): New cities in Australia: The Australian government's growth center program. - In: GOLANY, G. (ed.): International urban growth policies. New-town contributions. - New York etc., 315-334.
NEUTZE, M. (1965): Economic policy and the size of cities. - Canberra.
- (1971): People and property in Randwick. - URU, Australian National University. Canberra.
- (1972): People and property in Redfern. - URU, Australian National University. Canberra.
- (1974): The case for new cities in Australia. - US, 259-275.
- (1977): Urban development in Australia. - Sydney.
- (1978): Australian urban policy. Objectives and opinions. - Sydney.
New South Wales Planning and Environment Commission (1980): Review, Sydney Region Outline Plan. - Sydney.
NEWTON, D. (1974): Coleambally: A planned town in a planned region. - B. A. Thesis, University of Sydney. Sydney.
NITTIM, Z. (1980): The coalition of resident action groups. - In: ROE, J. (ed.): Twentieth century Sydney. Studies in urban and social history. - Sydney, 231-247.
O'CONNOR, K. (1978): The journey to work of inner city residents in Melbourne 1966 and 1971. - AGS, 73-81.
- (1980): Urban spatial distributions. - SA, 48-52.
O'CONNOR, K. & C.A. MAHER (1979): Change in the spatial structure of a metropolitan region: Work-residence relationships in Melbourne, 1961-1971. - RS, 361-380.
OLDHAM, W. (1945): How Adelaide was bought and sold. - PRGSA, South Australian Branch, vol. XLV, session 1943-44, 1945, 15-23.
OSBORNE, G. & W.F. MANDLE (eds.) (1982): New history: Studying Australia today. - Sydney.
OTOK, S. (1976): A model of the socioethnic structure of Australia's metropolitan cities. - GP 33, 1976, 113-120.

Palmerston Development Authority (ed.) (1981): Palmerston Development Strategy. - Darwin.
PARKER, F.L. (1937): Annual address of the president. - PRGSA, South Australian Branch, vol. XXXVII, session 1935-36, 1937, 21-36.
PARKER, R.S. & P.N. TROY (eds.) (1972): The policy of urban growth. - Canberra.
PARKES, D. (1973): Formal factors in the social geography of an Australian industrial city. - AGS, 171-200.
- (ed.) (1984): Northern Australia. The arenas of life and ecosystems on a half of a continent. - Sydney.
PARKES, D.N. (1971): A classical social area analysis: Newcastle, N.S.W. - AG, 555-578.
- (1972): Elements of space and time for an Australian industrial city: An urban social geography. - Ph. D. Thesis, University of Newcastle. Newcastle.
PARKES, D.N. & I.H. BURNLEY, S.R. WALKER (1985): Arid zone settlement in Australia: A focus on Alice Springs. - The United Nations University. Tokyo.
PARKIN, A. (1980): The states and the cities. - AQ, 308-328.
- (1982): Governing the cities. The Australian experience in perspective. - Melbourne.
PARKIN, A. & J. SUMMERS, D. WOODWARD (eds.) (1980): Government politics and power in Australia. - Melbourne.
The Parliament of the Commonwealth of Australia (ed.) (1978): The Commonwealth Government and the urban environment. Formulation and co-ordination of policies. - Canberra.
- (1979): Planning in the A.C.T. - Procedures, processes and community involvement. - Canberra.
PATERSON, J. (1975): Home owning, home renting and home redistribution. - AQ, 28-36.
PATIENCE, A. & B. HEAD (eds.) (1979): From Whitlam to Fraser. - Melbourne.
PEACH, G.C.K. (1974): Ethnic segregation in Sydney and intermarriage patterns. - AGS, 219-229.
PEGRUM, R. (1983): The bush capital: How Australia chose Canberra as its federal city. - Sydney.
PERROTT, LYON, TIMLOCK, KESA Architects and Town Planners (1971): Port of Echuca restoration. - n. d.
PERRY, T.M. (1958): The spread of settlement in the original nineteen counties of New South Wales, 1788-1829: An historical geography. - Ph. D. Thesis, Australian National University. Canberra.
- (1966): Climate and settlement in Australia 1700-1930. - In: ANDREWS, J. (ed.): Frontiers and men. A volume in memory of Griffith Taylor (1880-1963). - Melbourne, Canberra, Sydney, 138-154.

PERUMAL, P. (1984): Planning considerations for the protection of townscape. Buildings: Residential buildings. – In: The National Trust of Australia (NSW) (ed.): Urban conservation in the '80s. – Sydney, 29–32.
PICH, G. (1975): Italian land settlement in the Murrumbidgee Irrigation Areas, 1915–1972. – Ph. D. Thesis, Australian National University. Canberra.
PICKUP, G. & J.E. MINOR (1980): Assessment of research and practice in Australian natural hazards management. – NARB 6, 1980.
PIKE, D. (1953): The utopian dreams of Adelaide's founders. – PRGSA, South Australian Branch, vol. 53, session 1951/52, 1953, 65–77.
Planning Workshop Pty LTD (ed.) (1976): Griffith town extension. – Prepared for Wade Shire Council and the Water Resources Commission. Griffith.
POPENOE, D. (1980): Urban form in advanced societies: A cross-national enquiry. – In: UNGERSON, C. & V. KARN (eds.): The consumer experience of housing. Cross-national perspectives. – Farmborough, 1–20.
POULSON, M. & P. SPEARRITT (1981): Sydney. A social and political atlas. – Sydney.
POWELL, J.M. (1968): Settlement and land appraisal in Victoria, 1834–1891. – Ph. D. Thesis, Monash University. Melbourne.
– (ed.) (1974): Urban and industrial Australia. Readings in human geography. – Melbourne.
POWELL, J.M. & M. WILLIAMS (eds.) (1975): Australian space, Australian time. – Melbourne.
POWER, J. & R. WETTENHALL, J. HALLIGAN (eds.) (1981): Local government systems of Australia. – Canberra.
POWYS, R.O. (1975): The role of the institutional investor in urban development. – Proceed. 46th ANZAAS Conference. Canberra.
PRESTON, R. (1969) (ed.): Contemporary Australia: Studies in history, politics and economics. – Durham.
PRICE, A.G. (1945): German settlers in South Australia. – Melbourne.
– (1972): Island continent: Aspects of the historical geography of Australia and its territories. – Sydney.
PRICE, C.A. (1963): Southern Europeans in Australia. – Oxford.
– (ed.) (1966): Australian immigration: A bibliography and digest, no. 1. – Canberra.
– (ed.) (1971): Australian immigration: A bibliography and digest, no. 2, 1970. – Canberra.
– (ed.) (1979): Australian immigration: A bibliography and digest, no. 4. – Canberra.
– (ed.) (1981): Australian immigration: A bibliography and digest, no. 4, Supplement. – Canberra.
– (1968): Southern Europeans in Australia: Problems of assimilation. – IMR, 3–36.
– (1975a): Australian immigration. A review of the demographic effects of post-war immigration on the Australian population. – Research Report no. 2, National Population Inquiry. Canberra.
– (1975b): Australian immigration: 1947–73. – IMR, 304–318.
– (ed.) (1975c): Greeks in Australia. – Canberra.
Price, C.A. & J.I. MARTIN (eds.) (1976): Australian immigration: A bibliography and digest, no. 3, 1975. Part 1 and part 2. – Canberra.
PRICE, C.A. & P. PYNE, E. BAKER (1981): Immigrants in the vital statistics. – In: PRICE, C.A. (ed.): Australian immigration: A bibliography and digest, no. 4 Supplement. – Canberra, 35–44.
PRIDER, R.T. (1979): Mining in Western Australia. – Nedlands.
PROUDFOOT, P.R. (1982): Development of Botany Bay as a second seaport for Sydney. – AG, 159–169.
PRYOR, R.J. (1968): The recent growth of Melbourne. – AGS, 120–139.
– (1969): Urban fringe residence in Melbourne. – AG, 148–156.
– (1976): Belconnen social survey, 1976. – Dept. of Demography, Australian National University. Canberra (mimeo).

QUINLAN, H.G. (1968): The geography of Australian internal air passenger services. – Ph. D. Thesis, Australian National University. Canberra.

RAGGATT, H.G. (1968): Mountains of ore. – Melbourne.
RAMSAY, A.N. (1957): Factors affecting the site and design of Elizabeth. – PRGSA, South Australian Branch, session 1955/56, 1957, 5–14.
RAVALLION, M. (1975): Urban problems, public policies and social structure. – AQ, 7–19.
READE, C.C. (1919): Planning and development of towns and cities in South Australia. – South Australian Parliament Paper no. 63. Adelaide.
Readings on urban growth: Selected papers from the Sydney conference of ANZAAS, 1962. – Sydney 1963.
REES, J.S. (1948): A brief history of the Adelaide parklands and a few suggestions. – Adelaide City Council. Adelaide.
REICHL, P. (1968): Ballarat. A study of a city. – Melbourne.
REINER, E. (1967): Literaturbericht über Australien und Neuseeland 1938–1963. – Geographisches Jahrbuch vol. 62. Gotha, Leipzig.
REINER, E. & E. LÖFFLER (1983): Australien. – Bern 3rd ed.
First Report of the Task Force on New Cities for Australia. – AIUS, Canberra 1972.
RICH, R. (ed.) (1982): The politics of urban public services. – Lexington.
RICHARDS, E. (1978): The highland Scots of South Australia. – JHSSA no. 4, 1978, 33–64.
RICHARDSON, A. (1974): British immigrants and Australia. – Canberra.
RICHMOND, W.H. & P.C. SHARMA (eds.) (1983): Mining and Australia. – St. Lucia.
RIMMER, P.J. (1967a): Changes in the ranking of Australian seaports, 1951–52 to 1961–62. – TESG, 33–41.
– (1967b): The search for spatial regularities in the development of Australian seaports, 1861–1961/62. – GA Ser. B 49, 42–54.
– (1967c): The Altona petro-chemical complex. – AG, 211–213.
RIVETT, K. (1976): Race, immigration and the Borrie Report. – AQ no. 3, 1976, 12–22.
ROBERTS, S.H. (1924): History of Australian land settlement, 1788–1920. – Melbourne. Reissue New York 1968.
ROBINSON, A.J. (1963): Regionalism and urbanization in Australia: A note on locational emphasis in the Australian economy. – EG, 149–155.
– (1973): A planned New Town: The Canberra experience. – LE, 361–364.
ROBINSON, K.W. (1952): Sydney, 1820–1952. A comparison in the heart of the city. – AG, 6–12.
– (1953): Population and land use in the Sydney district 1788–1820. – NZG, 144–160.
– (1962a): The political influence in Australian geography. – PV, 73–85.
– (1962b): Processes and patterns of urbanisation in Australia and New Zealand. – NZG, 32–49.
– (1963): The distinctive character of Australian urban growth. – In: Readings in urban growth. – Selected papers from the Sydney conference of ANZAAS, 1962. Sydney, 1–17.
– (1966): Australian primate cities and the problems of decentralisation. – Inst. of Austrl. Geographers, Fifth Meeting, Sydney 1966. Sydney, 1–21.
ROBINSON, R. (1966): Site and form in the valley centres of the New South Wales coast north of the Hunter. – AG, 1–16.
– (ed.) (1977): Urban Illawara. – Melbourne.
ROBSON, L.L. (1965): The convict settlers of Australia. – Carlton. Reprinted 1976.
RODDEWIG, R.J. (1978): Green bans. – Sydney.
ROE, J. (1975): Marvellous Melbourne: The emergence of an Australian city. – Sydney.
– (ed.) (1980): Twentieth century Sydney. – Studies in urban and social history. Sydney.

ROSE, A.J. (1955): The border between Queensland and New South Wales. – AG, no. 6, 3–18.
– (1958): The geographical pattern of European immigration in Australia. – GR, 512–527.
– (1962): Some boundaries and building materials in Southeastern Australia. – In: McCASKILL, M. (ed.): Land and livelihood. – Christchurch, 255–276.
– (1966): Dissent from down under: Metropolitan primacy as the normal state. – PV, 1–27.
– (1967): Patterns of cities. – Melbourne.
– (1972): Urbanization in Australia. – Paper submitted to the IGU Commission on Patterns of Urbanization. Montreal.
– (1975): Australia. – In: JONES, R. (ed.): Essays on world urbanization. – London, 93–103.
ROTHER, K. (1986): Der Beitrag südeuropäischer Einwanderer an der Gestaltung des südwestaustralischen Agrarraums. – BGS vol. 18, 93–100.
ROWLAND, D.T. (1977): Theories of urbanization in Australia. – GR, 167–176.
– (1978): Internal migration as an exchange process: A study of Victoria. – AGS, 15–28.
– (1979): Internal migration in Australia. – Census Monograph Series, Australian Bureau of Statistics. Canberra.
ROWNTREE, A. (1954): Early growth of the Port of Hobart Town. – THRAPP vol. 3, no. 6, 92–101.
ROWSE, T. (1978): Heaven and a hills hoist: Australian critics of suburbia. – Meanjin, 3–13.
RUHEN, O. (1970): Macquarie's five towns. – North Sydney.
RUTLAND, S.D. (1983): Australian government policies towards German refugee immigration, 1933–1939. – In: VOIGT, J.H. (ed.): New Beginnings. The Germans in New South Wales and Queensland. – Institut für Auslandsbeziehungen 20. Stuttgart, 114–119.
RYAN, F. (ed.) (1978): Urban management processes. – Australian National Commission for UNESCO. Canberra.
RYAN, R.J. (1969): Metropolitan growth. – In: PRESTON, R. (ed.): Contemporary Australia: Studies in history, politics and economics. – Durham.
– (1973): Urban dispersal in Australia. – AJSI, 24–30.

SANDERCOCK, L.K. (1975): Cities for sale: Property, politics and urban planning in Australia. – Carlton.
– (1979): The land racket. The real costs of property speculation. – Sydney.
SANDERCOCK, L.K. & M. BERRY (1983): Urban political economy. The Australian case. – Sydney, London, Boston.
SCHEDVIN, C.B. (ed.) (1974): Urbanization in Australia: The nineteenth century. – Sydney.
SCOTT, P. (1955): Hobart: An emergent city. – AG, 19–32.
– (1959a): Building materials in Greater Hobart. – AG, 149–163.
– (1959b): The Australian CBD. – EG, 290–314.
– (1964): Areal variations in the class-structure of the central-place hierarchy. – AGS, 73–86.
– (1965): The population structure of Australian cities. – GJ, 463–481.
– (1967): Population origins in a Hobart suburb. – AG, 197–203.
– (1968): Population and land use in Australian analysis of metropolitan dominance. – TESG, 237–244.
– (1975): Metropolitan growth and planning intervention: An Australian perspective. – PV, 216–220.
– (ed.) (1978): Australian cities and public policy. – Melbourne.
SCOTTON, R.B. & H. FERBER (eds.) (1978): Public expenditures and social policy in Australia. – Melbourne, vol. 1 1978, vol. 2 1979.
SCRIVENER, J.G. (1965): Sydney in the 1840s. A study of the social and economic patterns of suburban growth: Camperdown. – B. A. Thesis, University of Sydney. Sydney.
SEARLE, G.H. (1981): The role of the state in capitalist development: The example of non-metropolitan New South Wales. – Antipode, 27–34.
SELWOOD, J. (1979): Residential development processes in Perth. – Geowest 14. Nedlands.

SERLE, G. (1977): The golden age. A history of the colony of Victoria 1851–1861. – Carlton.
– (1980): The rush to be rich. A history of the colony of Victoria 1883–1889. – Carlton 1971, reprint.
SHARMA, P.C. (1975): Local environments in an Australian city: A geographical investigation of selected dimensions of neighbourhoods in Newcastle, N.S.W. – Ph. D. Thesis, University of Newcastle. Newcastle.
SHARP, P.F. (1955): Three frontiers: Some comparative studies of Canadian, American, and Australian settlement. – PHR, 369–377.
SHERINGTON, G. (1980): Australia's immigrants. – Sydney.
Shire of Hawkesbury (ed.) (1981): Population distribution and profile. – Windsor.
SIMONS, P.L. (1962): Sydney's wholesale district – A preliminary survey. – B. A. Thesis, University of Sydney. Sydney.
SINDEN, J.A. (ed.) (1972): The natural resources of Australia. – Sydney and London.
SMAILES, P.J. (1969): Some aspects of the South Australian urban system. – AG, 29–51.
– (1969): A metropolitan trade shadow: The case of Adelaide, South Australia. – TESG, 329–345.
– (1977): The contemporary South Australian urban system. – In: FORSTER, C.A. & R.J. STIMSON (eds.): Urban South Australia. Selected readings. – Centre for Applied Social and Survey Research Monogr. Series 1, Adelaide, 23–48.
SMAILES, P.J. & J.K. MOLYNEUX (1965): The evolution of an Australian settlement pattern in Southern New England, New South Wales. – IBGT 36, 31–54.
SMALL, A. (1979): Effects of housing policies on real income distribution. – AQ no. 2, 54–65.
SMITH, D.L. (1966): Market gardening at Adelaide's urban fringe. – EG, 19–36.
SMITH, N. & P. WILLIAMS (eds.) (1986). Gentrification of the city. – Hemel Hempstead.
SMITH, R.H.T. (1965): The functions of Australian towns. – TESG, 81–92.
SOLOMON, R.J. (1959): Broken Hill. The growth of the settlement, 1883–1958. – AG, 181–192.
– (1968): The evolution of Hobart: A study in historical geography with special reference to urban fabric and function, circa 1804–1963. – Ph. D. Thesis, University of Tasmania. Hobart.
– (1976): Urbanisation: The evolution of an Australian capital. – Sydney.
SOLOMON, R.J. & A.R. DELL (1967): The Hobart bushfires of February 1967. – AG, 306–308.
SOLOMON, R.J. & W.E. GOODHAND (1965): Past influences in present townscapes: Some Tasman examples. – NZG, 113–132.
SORENSEN, A.D. (1979): The growth of office sector employment. – In: Proceed. Tenth N. Z. Geogr. Conference Auckland January 1979, 107–111.
Southern Metropolitan Planning Authority (1979): Data Book. – Hobart.
– (1979): Trends in manufacturing industry in the metropolitan area. – Hobart.
SPATE, O.H.K. (1956): Bush and city: Some reflections on the Australian cultural landscape. – AJS, 177–184.
SPATE, O.H.K. & J.N. JENNINGS (1972): Australian geography 1951–1971. – AGS, 197–224.
SPEARRITT, P. (1976): An urban history of Sydney, 1920–1950. – Ph. D. Thesis, Australian National University. Canberra.
– (1978): Sydney since the Twenties. – Sydney.
– (1983): Australia's cities: In or out of print? – In: WILLIAMS, P. (ed.): Social process and the city. – Urban Studies Yearbook 1. Sydney, London, Boston, 209–215.
SPICER, B.M. (1973): The Melbourne CBD. – Studies in Urban Geography. Brisbane.
STANNAGE, C.T. (1979): The people of Perth. A social history of Western Australia's capital city. – Perth City Council. Perth.

State Planning Authority of New South Wales (1973): The New Cities of Campbelltown, Camden, Appin: Structure Plan. – Sydney.
STEELE, J. (1916): Early days of Windsor, New South Wales. – Sydney.
STEELE, J.G. (1975): Brisbane Town in convict days, 1824–1842. – St. Lucia.
STEINKE, J.C. (1977): Australian regional policy and regional population trends 1947–1971. – Sydney.
STEVENSON, G. (1976): Mineral resources and Australian federalism. – Canberra.
STEWART, I.C. (1977): Australian company mergers, 1960–1970. – ER, 1–29.
STILWELL, F.J.B. (1974a): Australian urban and regional development. – Sydney.
– (1974): Economic factors and the growth of cities. – In: BURNLEY, I.H. (ed.): Urbanization in Australia. – Cambridge, 17–49.
– (1979a): Australian urban and regional development in the late 1970s: An overview. – IJURR, 527–541.
– (1979b): The current economic depression and its impact on Australian cities. – AQ no. 2, 5–16.
– (1980): Economic crisis, cities and regions. An analysis of current urban and regional problems in Australia. – Oxford etc.
– (1982): Capital accumulation and regional economic performance: The Australian experience. – AGS, 131–143.
STILWELL, F.J.B. & J.M. HARDWICK (1973): Social unequality in Australian cities. – AQ, 56–68.
STILWELL, K.J. (1975): The decline of Maldon, 1891–1933: Some characteristics. – B. A. Thesis, University of Melbourne. Melbourne.
STIMSON, R.J. (1970): Patterns of European immigrant settlement in Melbourne 1947–1961. – TESG, 114–126.
– (1978): Social space, preference space and residential location behaviour: A social geography of Adelaide. – Ph. D. Thesis, Flinders University. Adelaide.
– (1981): The provision and use of general practitioner services in Adelaide, Australia: Application of tools of locational analysis and theories of provider and user spatial behaviour. – SSM vol. 15 D, 1981, 27–44.
– (1982): The Australian city: A welfare geography. – Melbourne.
STIMSON, R.J. & E.C. CLELAND (1975): A socio-economic atlas of Adelaide. – School of Social Sciences, Flinders University. Adelaide.
STIRLING, J., R.N. (n. d.): King George's Sound. Communication to R.W. Hay of 7th January, 1832. – Swan River Papers vol. 10. Perth.
STOLLER, A. (ed.) (1966): New faces: Immigration and family life in Australia. – Melbourne.
STREET, B.A. (1937): Port Phillip, 1840–1850. – VHM, 25–56.
STRETTON, A. (1976): The furious days. The relief of Darwin. – Sydney and London.
STRETTON, H. (1970): Ideas for Australian cities. – Melbourne.
SUMNER, C.R. & J. OLIVER (1978): Early North Queensland housing as response to environment. – AG, 14–21.

TAYLOR, G. (1926): The frontiers of settlement in Australia. – GR, 1–25.
TAYLOR, M.J. (ed.) (1984): The geography of Australian corporate power. – Sydney.
TAYLOR, M.J. & N.J. THRIFT (1980): Large corporations and concentrations of capital in Australia: A geographical analysis. – EG, 261–280.
– – (1981): The changing spatial concentration of large company ownership and control in Australia 1953–1978. – AG, 98–105.
– – (1981): Some geographical implications of foreign investment in the semiperiphery: The case of Australia. – TESG, 194–213.

TEO, S.E. (1971): A preliminary study of the Chinese community in Sydney. – AG, 579–592.
THOMPSON, H.M. (1981): 'Normalization': Industrial relations and community control in the Pilbara. – AQ, 301–324.
THOMSON, K.W. (1955): Das Industriedreieck des Spencergolfs als Beispiel einer Industrialisierung außerhalb der Hauptstädte. – Die Erde, 286–300.
THOMSON, N. (1979): Local government and the Grants Commissions. – AQ no. 3, 89–97.
TIBBITS, G. & B. TRETHOWAN, P. HARMER, E. VINES (1976): Beechworth – Historical reconstruction. – Research Paper, Fac. of Archit., University of Melbourne. Parkville.
TIMMS, D.W.G. (1969): The dissimilarity between overseas-born and Australian-born in Queensland: Dimensions of assimilation. – SSR, 363–374.
Town Planning Department, City of Wagga Wagga (ed.) (1983): City of Wagga Wagga. Draft local environment plan support document. – Wagga Wagga.
TROY, P.N. (1966): Urban redevelopment in Australia. – Canberra.
– (1972): Environmental quality in four Melbourne suburbs. – URU, Australian National University. Canberra.
– (1978a): A fair price. The Land Commission program 1972–1977. – Sydney.
– (ed.) (1978b): Federal power in Australia's cities. – Sydney.
– (ed.) (1981): Equity in the city. – Sydney.
TSOUNIS, M.P. (1975): Greek communities in Australia. – In: PRICE, C.A. (ed.): Greeks in Australia. – Canberra.

UNGERSON, C. & V. KARN (eds.) (1980): The consumer experience of housing. – Farnborough.
Urban Research Unit, Australian National University (ed.) (1973): Urban development in Melbourne. Aspects of the post-war experience. – AIUS, Canberra.
U'REN, N. & N. TURNBULL (1983): A history of Port Melbourne. – Port Melbourne.

Victoria. Central Melbourne: Framework for the Future. – Land use and development strategy series no. 6. Melbourne 1984.
VIPOND, J. (1981): Changes in unemployment differentials in Sydney, 1947–76. – AGS, 67–77.
VIVIANI, N. (1984): The long journey: Vietnamese migration and settlement in Australia. – Melbourne.
VOIGT, J.H. (ed.) (1983): New Beginnings. The Germans in New South Wales and Queensland. A commemorative volume. – Studies in International Cultural Relations 20. Stuttgart.
VOLGYES, I. & R.E. LONSDALE, W.P. AVERY (eds.) (1980): The process of rural transformation: Eastern Europe, Latin America and Australia. – New York.

WADE, R.C. (1964): The urban frontier. Pioneer life in early Pittsburgh, Cincinnati, Lexington, Louisville, and St. Louis. – Chicago.
WADLEY, D.A. (1982): Australian urban social atlases of the 1976 Census. A review. – AG, 182–185.
WADLEY, D.A. & E.E. TUGBY (1982): Australian theses in geography 1972–80. – Dept. of Geography, University of Queensland. St. Lucia.
WAGNER, E. (1985): Das Stadtgebiet von Carnarvon (West-australien). – ZA, 242–258.
WALKER, J.B. (1973): Early Tasmania. Papers read before the Royal Society of Tasmania during the years 1888 to 1899. – Fourth impression, Hobart.
WALKER, S.R. (1980): Changes in employment in the Australian urban system. Metropolitan dominance and the role of the tertiary sector. – Paper pres. to the Industrial Systems group, Inst. of Austr. Geographers. Sydney.
WALKLEY, G. (1953): Town and country planning in South Australia. – PRGSA, South Australian Branch, vol. 53, session 1951/52, 1953, 79–92.

- (1969): Bibliography of urban studies in Australia. – AIUS, Canberra vol. 1, 1966–68 published in 1969; vol. 9 1978.
WALMSLEY, D.J. (1974): Retail spatial structure in suburban Sydney. – AG, 401–418.
- (1980a): Social justice and Australian federalism. – Armidale.
- (1980b): Spatial bias in Australian news reporting. – AG, 342–349.
- (1982): Mass media and spatial awareness. – TESG, 32–42.
WALMSLEY, J. (1982): Welfare in Australia. – In: HANLEY, W. & M. COOPER (eds.): Man and the Australian environment. – Sydney, 209–218.
- (1982): The role of federal, state and local government. – In: HANLEY, W. & M. COOPER (eds.): Man and the Australian environment. – Sydney, 291–294.
WALSH, G.P. (1962): The English colony in New South Wales: A.D. 1803. – NZG, 149–169.
WATERSON, D.B. (1968): Squatter, selector and storekeeper. A history of the Darling Downs 1859–93. – Sydney.
WEBBER, M. & M.T. DALY (1971): Spatial and temporal variations in industrial change within cities. – AGS, 15–32.
WEHLING, H.-W. (1975): Funktionalbereiche im Großraum Sydney. – Die Erde, 90–105.
WELKE, A. & P. HARRIS (n.d.): Darwin. A map guide to the architectural heritage of the city. – Darwin.
WHITE, H.L. (ed.) (1954): Canberra. A nation's capital. – Sydney.
WHITE, R. (1981): Inventing Australia. Images and identity 1788–1980. – The Australian Experience Series. Sydney.
WHITELAW, J.S. & M.I. LOGAN, J. McKAY (1984): Australia. – In: BOURNE, L.S. & R. SINCLAIR, K. DZIEWONSKI (eds.): Urbanization and settlement systems. International perspectives. – Oxford.
WHITELOCK, D. (1977): Adelaide 1836–1976. A history of difference. – St. Lucia.
WIGMORE, L. (1963): The long view: A history of Canberra. – Melbourne.
WILD, R. (1981): Social stratification in Australia. – Sydney etc.
WILDE, P.D. (1980): Industrial structure and change in Tasmania. – Occas. Paper 7, Dept. of Geography, University of Tasmania. Hobart.
WILES, M.A. (1967): A study over time of the change in various factors in the southern frame zone of the Central City of Sydney. – M. A. Thesis, University of Sydney. Sydney.
WILLIAMS, M. (1966a): The parkland towns of Australia and New Zealand. – GR, 67–89.
- (1966b): Delimiting the spread of settlement: An examination of evidence in South Australia. – EG, 336–355.
- (ed.) (1969): South Australia from the air. – Melbourne.
- (1970a): Town-farming in the Mallee lands of South Australia and Victoria. – AGS, 173–191.
- (1970b): Places, periods and themes: A review and prospect of Australian historical geography. – AG, 403–416.
- (1974): The making of the South Australian landscape. – London and New York.
WILLIAMS, P. (ed.) (1983): Social process and the city. – Urban Studies Yearbook 1. Sydney.
- (ed.) (1984): Conflict and development. – Urban Studies Yearbook 2. Sydney.
WILMOTH, D. (1974): Communication in the urban system. – JPESA, 211–230.
WILSON, M.G.A. (1962): Some population characteristics of Australian mining settlements. – TESG, 125–132.
- (1979): Age structure change in the New South Wales urban system, 1966–1976. – Proceed. Tenth N. Z. Geogr. Conference, 116–121.
WILSON, P. (1980): Migrants, politics and the 1980s. – AQ, 75–88.
WILTON, J. & R. BOSWORTH (1984): Old worlds and new Australia. The post-war migrant experience. – Ringwood.
Windsor Municipal Council (ed.) (1979): Historic Hawkesbury. – Fourth edition, Windsor.
WINSTON, D. et al. (eds.) (1966): Australian cities – Chaos or planned growth. – Melbourne.
WINTER, M.D. (1974): Physiography of the new town of Monarto, S.A. – B. A. Thesis, University of Adelaide. Adelaide.
WOLFORTH, J. (1974): Residential concentration of Non British minorities in 19th century Sydney. – AGS, 207–218.
WONG, K.Y. (1965): The manufacturing geography of selected areas in Melbourne. – Ph. D. Thesis, University of Melbourne. Melbourne.
WOODHAMS, G.P. (1979): The Pilbara region: Analysis of a mining based urban system. – B. A. Thesis, University of Western Australia. Nedlands.
WOOLMINGTON, E.R. (1958): The distribution of immigrants in the Newcastle region of N.S.W. – AG, 85–96.
- (1965): Metropolitan gravitation in northern New South Wales. – AG, 359–376.
- (1971): Government policy and decentralisation. – In: LINGE, G.J.R. & P.J. RIMMER (eds.): Government influence and the location of economic activity. – Research School of Polit. Studies, Dept. of Human Geography Publ. HG 5. Canberra, 279–296.
WOTHERSPOON, G. (ed.) (1983): Sydney's transport. Studies in urban history. – Sydney.

ZIERER, C.M. (1942): Land use differentiation in Sydney, Australia. – AAAG, 255–308.
ZUBRZYCKI, J. (1959): Immigration. Commentary, Atlas of Australian Resources. – Canberra.
- (1960): Immigrants in Australia: A demographic survey based on the 1954 Census. – Melbourne.
- (1968): Some aspects of structural assimilation of immigrants in Australia. – IM 11, 3, 1968, 102–111.

Index of places

Adelaide 7, 8, 11, 17, 19, 46, 57, 67, 74, 77, 100–109, 129–136, 166, 167, 181, 187, 190–192, 194–196, 199, 202, 204, 206, 208, 217, 218, 228–232, 234
Albany 28, 52, 53, 65, 66, 75, 115
Albury 28, 30–32, 75, 142
Alice Springs 72, 158–160
Altona 97

Ballarat 38–41, 156
Bathurst 11, 13, 14, 28, 31, 37, 62, 75
Beechworth 38, 41–43, 60, 184
Bendigo 38–41, 60, 212
Brisbane 8, 17, 19, 32, 50, 52, 57, 65, 67, 74, 77, 79, 109–115, 129–136, 153, 181, 183, 187, 190–192, 194, 201, 202, 206, 208, 217, 218, 228, 234
Broken Hill 72, 76, 77, 156, 157
Brunswick Junction 53, 54
Bunbury 53
Bundaburg 50–52

Cairns 50–52, 72, 77, 79, 213, 214
Canberra 57, 74, 77, 79, 142–151, 200, 201, 206, 234
Carrieton 48
Castlemaine 38, 39, 41
Castlereagh 35, 37
Cessnock 154
Coffs Harbour 28, 30, 75
Cooktown 52
Cumberland County 29, 80

Dalgety 142
Darwin 74, 77, 136–142, 234
Dawlish 48
Derby 78

Echuca 39, 43, 45, 60, 62
Elizabeth 106, 165–167

Fitzroy 97
Fremantle 65, 67, 115–117, 121, 122, 129, 169, 215, 222

Geelong 76, 91, 156
Gladstone 28, 30, 50–52, 75, 78, 109, 131
Glebe 83, 86, 87, 186, 197
Gold Coast (City of the) 79, 151–154
Goldsworthy 169–171, 176

Gove 78
Griffith 76, 160–164, 200

Harvey 53, 54
Hawkesbury (Valley) 13, 35–38, 80
Hobart 7, 8, 17, 19, 32, 33, 57, 65, 67, 77, 123–136, 183, 191, 192, 194, 196, 197, 199, 202, 208, 217, 218, 228

Ipswich 109

Jamestown 48, 49

Kalgoorlie 72, 76, 157
Kambalda 157, 180
Karratha 169, 171, 173, 176, 180
Kwinana New Town 76, 78, 120, 122, 165, 167–169

Launceston 32, 65, 130, 156
Leeton 76, 160, 164, 165
Leichhardt 87, 204, 231
Lithgow 76, 155

Mackay 50, 213, 214
Maitland (N.S.W.) 76, 154
Maitland (S.A.) 46, 48, 49
Maldon 39, 41, 62
Mandurah 122, 123
Manjimup 52, 53
Maryborough (Qld.) 51, 52, 109
Maryborough (Vic.) 38, 39
Melbourne 8, 17, 19, 32, 33, 56, 57, 60, 67, 68, 74, 77, 89, 91–100, 124, 129–136, 181, 183–187, 189–197, 199, 201–206, 208, 216–221, 224, 226, 228, 229, 234
Monarto 167
Moonta 49, 130
Moreton Bay s. Brisbane
Mount Isa 50, 72, 157, 169
Mudgee 76
Murray Bridge 28, 75

Nannup 52
Newcastle 32, 76, 78, 131, 132, 154, 155, 183
Newman 169, 171–174, 176, 179
Noarlunga 104, 109, 167

Orange 31, 75, 142

Palmerston 136, 140–142
Pannawonica 169, 173, 179
Paraburdoo 169, 171, 173, 176, 179
Perth 8, 11, 17, 19, 32, 53, 57, 65–67, 74, 77, 79, 115–123, 129, 169, 181, 184, 187, 190–194, 196, 197, 201–203, 205, 206, 208, 217, 218, 228, 231, 233, 234
Pickering 48
Pitt Town 35, 37
Port Arthur 32, 34, 62, 184
Port Augusta 72, 156
Port Hedland 72, 76–78, 131, 169, 173, 175–180
Port Kembla 76, 78, 155
Portland 28, 30 91
Port Macquarie 32
Port Pirie 155, 156

Queanbeyan 150, 151

Richmond 35, 37
Rockhampton 50–52, 109, 212–214
Rockingham 122, 168, 169
Rocks, The 61, 62, 80, 90

Shay Gap 169, 171–173, 176, 179
Snowtown 48
South Hedland 173, 177
Spearwood 121, 215, 222
Surfers Paradise 151–153
Swan Hill 39, 43, 44
Sydney 8, 11, 17, 19, 21–23, 29, 35, 56, 57, 67, 68, 74, 77, 79–91, 95, 96, 129–136, 181, 183–187, 189–197, 199, 201–206, 208, 214, 215, 217, 218, 221, 226, 228, 229, 231, 234

Tamworth 28, 30, 74
Tom Price 169, 172, 173, 176, 179
Toowoomba 157
Townsville 28, 30, 50–53, 75, 79, 109, 213

Wagga Wagga 31, 157
Waroona 54
Weipa 78

Whyalla 76, 78, 155, 156
Wickham 169, 173
Wilberforce 35, 37
Williamstown 91, 97

Windsor 35, 37
Wodonga 31, 32, 75
Wollongong 132, 155
Wooloomooloo 81, 83, 85–87, 197

Yallourn 28, 75
York 62

Subject index

Aborigines 25, 32, 53, 159, 160, 167, 211
airlines, domestic 77
Arts Centre 93, 114, 208
Australian Council of National Trusts 58
Australian Heritage Commission 60

Border Railways Agreement 39
bounty system 13
brick 116, 167, 181–185
British dominance 13
Broken Hill Proprietary Ltd. (BHP) 76, 154, 155, 167
Builders Labourers' Federation (BLF) s. green bans
bushfires 7

cable tram s. tram
canal estates 151–153
car ownership 77, 202
caravan s. mobile home
Carly Report 175, 176
central places 68–74
chain migration 215, 219
Chinese 16, 38, 43, 50, 142, 211–215, 219–221, 225, 227, 229
closed town s. company town
Commonwealth-State Housing Agreements 25, 26
company town 169–180
convict settlement 13, 32–35, 109, 128
corridors 88, 99, 104, 111, 122, 136, 146, 206–208, 236
cottage industries s. home industries
Cumberland Plan 88, 208
Cultural Centre s. Arts Centre
cyclone-proof housing 140
Cyclone Tracy 139

decentralization 28, 75, 165, 166
densities (urban) 3, 149, 191, 193
Department of Urban and Regional Development (DURD) 24, 31
developer 190, 194, 198
displaced persons 18, 216, 218, 223
district centre 88, 97, 135, 206, 237

Empire Settlement Scheme 16
endogamy 225, 226
Expo '88 114

federation style 62, 85
First Fleet 13, 32, 58, 80
flexilot system 26, 27
freeways 123, 200–202, 207, 236

general practitioner (GP) 210, 211
gentrification 86, 117, 126, 185, 196, 197, 209, 236
Germans 16, 18, 76, 212
gold-rush 15, 38, 62, 93, 117, 130
government hostel 220, 221
government railways 55
Government Triangle 144
Governor 21, 100
Goyder's Line 7
Greeks 18, 19, 215, 217–222, 225–231
green bans 62, 86, 198, 199
Greenway, F. 35, 80
grid 93, 199, 200, 235
Griffin, W.B. 143–145, 160, 162, 164
growth corridors s. corridors
growth poles 28, 30, 31, 75, 167

high-rise apartment buildings 97, 112, 151, 191, 193, 236
Hills Face Zone 106
historic town 60
home extensions 209
home industries 172
home ownership 185–189, 230
home ownership scheme 174
Home Savings Grant Scheme 189
hostel s. government hostel
Hundred 46, 71

immigration 15–21, 68, 87, 97, 98, 105, 106, 113, 131, 166, 169, 179, 189, 211, 216–220, 231
Immigration Restriction Act 16
industrial estate 207
infill 26, 191
Irish 211, 212, 215, 216, 225, 226, 228, 230
Iron Ore Agreements 169, 175
Italians 18, 19, 50, 161, 215, 217–219, 221, 222, 225–231

jarrah 52, 182

karri 52, 182

Land Commission 26, 28, 29, 87, 106
Lebanese 224, 225
Local Government 21, 22, 161

Macquarie town 35–38
mall 196, 208
Maltese 18, 19, 217, 220, 225, 230
manufacturing (value added) 133
market gardener 115, 121, 215, 222, 236
Melbourne Metropolitan Plan 97
metropolitan dominance s. primacy
mobile home 184, 190
mobility 209, 230
Municipal Act 22
Murrumbidgee Irrigation Areas (MIA) 160, 200
Myer (department stores) 87, 98–100, 135

National Capital Development Commission (NCDC) 146, 149–151
National Trust 40, 43, 45, 58–62, 126
neighbourhood principle 165, 167
new federalism 24
New Ghan 158
new town 76, 160–180, 200, 237
normalization 174–176
Numerical Migration Assessment System (NUMAS) 18, 223

office park 205
office space 121, 134, 193, 194, 208
Overland Telegraph 72, 137, 158

parklands (alienation of) 49, 102–104
parkland town 45–50, 102–104, 199, 200
penal settlement 32, 62
poverty line 210
preferred development areas 100, 207
primacy 1, 62–68, 78, 79
primate city s. primacy

QANTAS 138
Queenslander (style) house 111, 183

rental housing 137, 187–189, 191, 236
residents' action group 198
revenue sharing 24
ribbon development 204

River Murray Waters Agreement 160
Royal Flying Doctor Service 72

satellite city 106, 165
second(ary) concentration 97, 219, 221, 230, 237
segregation 220
self-containment 206, 235
separatism 30
settlement zone 12, 57
shopping centre 87, 98–100, 112, 128, 170, 204, 205
shopping strip 204
social gradient 235
State Government 22
State Housing Authorities 25, 26, 87, 97, 105, 106, 120, 126, 128, 165, 166, 177, 191, 197, 235, 236
steam navigation 39, 43
strata title 189, 197, 208, 236
succession 219, 220

Sydney Cove Redevelopment Authority 62
Sydney Region Outline Plan 88
system city 106, 165

Tasman Bridge collapse 127, 128
Tasman Freight Equalisation Scheme (TFES) 124
taxation system 198
terrace house 83, 87, 116, 130, 185, 191, 196, 236
timber s. weatherboard
Town Centre 146, 164, 165, 167, 168, 172
town planning 24
tram 95, 102, 104
transcontinental railway 77
tropical division 9
turn around 57

urban frontier 3, 66
urbanization rate 1, 16, 54, 55, 217, 218

vacancy chain 190, 191

Wakefieldian principles 15, 16
Waste Lands Amendment Act 46
waterfront land use 129
Water Resources Commission (WRC) 160, 161, 164
water shortage 8
wattle-and-daube 181, 182
weatherboard 111, 167, 171, 181–184, 186
wheat-growing region 71
wool 13

Yugoslavs 18, 19, 215, 216, 218, 221, 223, 224, 226, 227, 229, 230

zoning regulations 191, 206

URBANIZATION OF THE EARTH
URBANISIERUNG DER ERDE
Edited by WOLF TIETZE · Helmstedt

So far published / Bisher erschienen:

Bd. 1: W. Manshard
Die Städte des tropischen Afrika
1977. X, 258 Seiten, 104 Abbildungen, 33 Tabellen. Gebunden DM 98,—

Bd. 2: K.-G. Schneider u. B. Wiese
Die Städte des südlichen Afrika
1983. X, 175 Seiten, 116 Abbildungen, 44 Tabellen. Gebunden DM 98,—

Bd. 3.1 und Bd. 3.2: H. Wilhelmy und A. Borsdorf
Die Städte Südamerikas
Teil 1: Wesen und Wandel. 1984. 243 S., 113 Abb., 7 Tab. DM 98,—, Teil 2: Die urbanen Zentren und ihre Regionen. 1985. 496 S., 221 Abb., 7 Tab. DM 188,—

Bd. 4: W. Rutz
Die Städte Indonesiens
1985. X, 286 Seiten, 13 Graphiken, 38 Tabellen, 6 mehrfarbige Karten im Anhang. Gebunden DM 104,—

Vol. 4 (English edition of Band 4): W. Rutz
Cities and Towns in Indonesia
1987. IV, 292 pages, 1 frontispiece in col., 13 figs., 38 tables, 6 maps in an appendix. Bound DM 130,—

Vol. 5: F.J. Costa, A.K. Dutt, L.J.C. Ma and A.G. Noble
Asian Urbanization: Problems and Processes
1988. XII, 165 pages, 53 figs., 21 tables. Bound DM 78,—

Vol. 6: B. Hofmeister
Australia and its Urban Centres
1988. XII, 254 pages, 120 figs., 61 tables.

In preparation:

A. Schinz
Cities and Towns of China

B. Hofmeister
Stadt und Kulturraum Angloamerika
1971. VIII, 341 Seiten, 102 Figuren, 36 Fotos, 21 Tabellen. 21 x 28 cm. Gebunden DM 96,—